MW00682012

Voices of the Song Lyric in China

This volume and the conference from which it resulted were sponsored by the Joint Committee on Chinese Studies, of the American Council of Learned Societies and the Social Science Research Council, with funds provided by the Andrew W. Mellon Foundation.

Voices of the Song Lyric in China

EDITED BY
Pauline Yu

UNIVERSITY OF CALIFORNIA PRESS
Berkeley   Los Angeles   Oxford

University of California Press
Berkeley and Los Angeles, California

University of California Press, Ltd.
Oxford, England

© 1994 by
The Regents of the University of California

Library of Congress Cataloging-in-Publication Data

Voices of the song lyric in China/ edited by Pauline Yu.
    p.   cm.—(Studies on China; 18)
    Includes bibliographical references and index.
    ISBN 0-520-08056-4 (alk. paper)
    1. Tz'u—History and criticism.   I. Yu, Pauline, 1949–   .
    II. Series.
    PL2336.V65   1993
    895.1'104—dc20   92-32825
                                                            CIP

Printed in the United States of America
9   8   7   6   5   4   3   2   1

The paper used in this publication meets the minimum requirements of American National Standard for Information Sciences—Permanence of Paper for Printed Library Materials, ANSI Z39.48-1984. ⊖

STUDIES ON CHINA

A series of conference volumes sponsored by the Joint Committee on Chinese Studies of the American Council of Learned Societies and the Social Science Research Council.

CONTENTS

3. FROM VOICE TO TEXT:
QUESTIONS OF GENEALOGY

INTRODUCTION

Pauline Yu

Scholars of traditional Chinese literature long approached the history of literary genres with an assumption similar to that governing the study of other historical formations in the culture: that the subjects under study experienced life cycles of birth, development, and decline analogous to those putatively experienced by the particular dynasties in which they were putatively rooted. Thus, as political regimes could be seen to rise and fall organically in smooth chronological sequence, so too could literary forms be regarded as generating their own evolutionary genealogies of descent over time. The presumption that life cycles of dynasties and literary genres followed comparable and intertwined courses provided a convenient schema for literary periodization and reinforced long-standing historicist interpretations of individual texts as well, interpretations that remained compelling well into the twentieth century.

Given this powerful paradigm of the inevitable depletion and supersession of genres dynasty after dynasty, it should perhaps come as no surprise that even in the West a major conference on the *tz'u*, or song lyric, traditionally identified with the Sung dynasty, should follow one on *shih* poetry, conventionally linked with the T'ang. Both events took place at the Breckinridge Conference Center of Bowdoin College in York, Maine, under the generous sponsorship of the Joint Committee on Chinese Studies of the American Council of Learned Societies and the Social Science Research Council, the first, Evolution of *Shih* Poetry from the Han through the T'ang, in June of 1982[1] and the second, *Tz'u* Poetry, in June of 1990.

ix

However facetious this account of the origins of the papers collected in this volume may be, such well-entrenched views did contribute, throughout much of the twentieth century, to the development of a bibliography of dissertations and monographs by Western scholars on *shih* that is longer and deeper by far than that for *tz'u*. Even more significant, however, has been the song lyric's discursive position within the traditional Chinese hierarchy of genres. Long regarded as the "other" important form of Chinese poetry, it was almost always considered in distinction from the older, more authoritative, and supposedly more serious genre of *shih*, for a complex of reasons that this conference sought to explore.

As the translation "song lyric" suggests, *tz'u* (or *ch'ü-tzu-tz'u*, "words to songs") are verses in irregular line-lengths, often stanzaic, written— or, literally, "filled in"—so that they could be sung to existing melodies. The form took shape in the T'ang and reached maturity during the Five Dynasties and Sung. Thereafter the genre underwent an eclipse until a major revival began during the early seventeenth century and continued for the next three hundred years; as is well known, the form continues to be widely composed today. Early *tz'u* were embedded in a popular tradition of songs, largely of anonymous authorship, that were performed by courtesans, professional musicians, and other private entertainers. Included among the cache of manuscripts preserved in the Tun-huang caves in northwest Kansu province and brought to light at the beginning of the twentieth century are numerous examples of *tz'u* written to set tunes on a variety of topics—ranging from the joys of love to the sorrows of war—that can be dated to early in the eighth century. Approximately two-thirds of those tune titles, moreover, appear in a catalog of musical works compiled at the imperial court during the same period, suggesting that *tz'u* were being composed and performed by entertainers at the palace as well, and indicating the wide range of audiences to which they appealed. With the onset of political instability in the middle of the eighth century, many of these court musicians dispersed, moving away from the capital and relocating to the burgeoning entertainment quarters of cities throughout the empire, where, in halls of often immense proportions, song lyrics continued to be produced and performed. Much of the further development of the genre was rooted in the interaction between courtesan-entertainers and members of the lite-

---

1. Papers from that conference were published in a volume entitled *The Vitality of the Lyric Voice*: Shih *Poetry from the Late Han to the T'ang*, ed. Shuen-fu Lin and Stephen Owen (Princeton: Princeton University Press, 1986).

rati that flourished in these urban locales during the late eighth and ninth centuries.

It was within contexts such as these that song lyric forms, once largely of unknown authorship or composed by the performers themselves, came gradually to be appropriated for use by the literati class. In many instances they were written by men using assumed female personas and then given to women singers to perform at banquets or parties, thereby often putting the woman singer in the position of expressing through the lyrics her desire for a man—and indeed, since the lyrics' writers were usually the same literary men who attended such parties, the singer might well have been compelled to speak her longing to the very person who had written the lyrics. From these beginnings, not surprisingly, issues of gender and sexual relationships acquired great importance in the genre, far more so than in any other kind of Chinese writing. Since the form often employed the conventional persona of a woman, it became strongly associated with "femininity" and presented a rich repertoire of expected response from women (expected, that is, in the imaginations of men). Moreover, one of the most famous lyricists of the Sung dynasty was a woman, and by the seventeenth century song lyrics had become especially important as vehicles for women writers, the literary genre in which they could most comfortably engage in poetic exchanges with each other or with men.

During the eleventh century the scope of the form broadened to include a male voice and many topics that had traditionally been associated with purely male experience and, indeed, that had earlier been addressed in *shih*. As the "other" genre, however, the form in which one could speak of sentiments and responses normally excluded from the more public and elevated *shih*, even this male version of the genre often sought to present what were considered to be the most delicate aspects of sensibility and the human affections. Such distinctions became more acute as the *tz'u* matured and its rigorous technical demands engendered a concern with formal perfection, leading to the development of a mode of connoisseurship quite distinct from the critique of *shih*.

Both the gender associations of the form and the connoisseurship of its stylistic refinements led to much theorizing on the distinctiveness of *tz'u* relative to its competing verse form, *shih*. To speak of it as the "other" form of Chinese poetry is to convey precisely the sense of the genre held by traditional writers and readers of the song lyric. The act of articulating or defining its alterity became therefore a central concern of *tz'u* criticism. From this process grew a large body of critical discourse, along with numerous anthologies, all of which sought to develop a canon of the genre, to valorize the form and write its history, and to enumerate the ways in which the fine points of its language corresponded perfectly to the fine points of human sentiment.

This detailed inscription, however marginal or precarious, into the literary and textual tradition succeeded, quite incidentally, in effacing almost completely the original music to which the song lyrics had been composed. Although the introduction of new songs into the repertoire was clearly instrumental in the development of new and longer song lyrics in the first half of the eleventh century, only a few decades later some critics would complain of what they perceived to be an increasing inattention to the music itself. Musical notation now survives for only seventeen lyrics, all composed by the Southern Sung poet Chiang K'uei (1155–1221) and preserved in three eighteenth-century manuscripts—whose copyists even then no longer understood the system Chiang had used, and were simply reproducing (in different versions) a manuscript dating from the mid-fourteenth century. Rather than denoting pitch values, Chiang's tablature notation appears to refer to fingerings on the Chinese flute and is of limited value in restoring the original music of a larger body of songs. Notational systems varied widely from person to person, school to school, and region to region, and Chiang K'uei was in any event probably exceptional among literati in entering—by employing a written system at all—what was more comfortably the province of trained musicians. It is largely owing to oral transmission, similarly tied to geographical location and specific figures or schools, that conventions of chanting and performance have survived to the present day.

Although some volumes of translations of *tz'u* and a scattering of books and articles, along with conventional and cursory treatments of the form in histories of Chinese literature, had appeared prior to 1974, systematic modern Western scholarship on the genre can be said to date only from the publication in that year of the late James J. Y. Liu's *Major Lyricists of the Northern Sung*, which contained texts, translations, and critical discussions of a few famous works by a few famous poets. Shortly thereafter *tz'u* studies began to flourish in a handful of North American universities, where a steady stream of theses and dissertations was produced over the next decade, covering what had come to be identified as the major figures in the genre and laying the groundwork for the study of the form in English.[2] What was essential in establishing this founda-

2. These works include: Shuen-fu Lin, *The Transformation of the Chinese Lyrical Tradition: Chiang K'uei and Southern Sung* Tz'u *Poetry* (Princeton: Princeton University Press, 1978); John Timothy Wixted, *The Song Poetry of Wei Chuang (836–910 A.D.)* (Tempe: Center for Asian Studies, Arizona State University, 1978); Kang-i Sun Chang, *The Evolution*

tion, of course, was the focus on selected individual writers or groups, and while this aggregate of monographs as a whole provides remarkably well-integrated coverage of the development and florescence of the genre from the late T'ang through the Southern Sung dynasty, it was the intention of no one author to write a comprehensive literary history of *tz'u* or to address the larger issues the form might raise.

These were some of the primary aims of the 1990 conference at Breckinridge, which sought, in addition, to expand the temporal frame of studies on *tz'u* beyond the Sung dynasty and to broaden the focus beyond critical examinations of major figures. Participants ranged from specialists in the genre or in Sung poetry more generally to individuals who had previously paid little attention to either. Although papers had been commissioned to fall into three general categories, no one anticipated that the essays would in the event prove to be engaging the same set of issues, albeit on apparently disparate topics or from quite different perspectives. Thus, the conference as a whole succeeded in articulating a common ground of discourse on the song lyric that the participants agreed could only have been realized collectively: that overlapping concerns of genre and gender have structured critical discussion of the song lyric almost from its very beginnings. These concerns have focused on the language of the form and in particular on the problem of the voice of the poem. This is a problem rooted in the song lyric's own origins in performance, especially performance of an expression of highly mediated desire, and the consequent difficulties of establishing or giving voice to an unmediated self (which had been the accepted mandate of the *shih*, or short poem).

The essays collected in this volume engage these issues from a variety of perspectives and critical approaches, ranging from close readings of song lyrics to feminist, historical, and textual studies. The "voices" of the volume's title recalls the origins of the *tz'u* as lyrics that were sung, and sung to music that, even after its disappearance, left a powerful

---

of Chinese Tz'u *Poetry: From Late T'ang to Northern Sung* (Princeton: Princeton University Press, 1980); Daniel Bryant, *Lyric Poets of the Southern T'ang: Feng Yen-ssu, 903–960, and Li Yü, 937–978* (Vancouver: University of British Columbia Press, 1982); Lois Fusek, tr., *Among the Flowers: The* Hua-chien chi (New York: Columbia University Press, 1982); Marsha L. Wagner, *The Lotus Boat: The Origins of Chinese* Tz'u *Poetry in T'ang Popular Culture* (New York: Columbia University Press, 1984); Grace S. Fong, *Wu Wenying and the Art of Southern Song* Ci *Poetry* (Princeton: Princeton University Press, 1987); and David R. McCraw, *Chinese Lyricists of the Seventeenth Century* (Honolulu: University of Hawaii Press, 1990). In addition, Stephen C. Soong has edited a volume of essays and translations titled *Song Without Music: Chinese* Tz'u *Poetry* (Hong Kong: The Chinese University Press, 1980).

legacy in terms of the shape and contexts of the genre. The word speaks as well to what became a central problem for a form that had first been written to be sung in the performance of a role: although it subsequently came to be viewed as more capable than *shih* of accurately tracing the cuts and turns of human emotion, it could never shake off doubts about the genuineness of expressed emotion that had been ineluctably implanted from the original context of entertainment. Voiced by women more often than were *shih* and plumbing depths of sentiment left unexplored by the dominant poetic genre, the song lyric was also subject to a persistent disjunction between its discursive position within the Chinese critical tradition and some other, perhaps more legitimate, place. Needless to say, the problematic nature of that situation was intimately related to the very emotions and desires to which the form was deemed capable of giving voice.

Given that questions of genre and gender and their relationship to language have shaped the critical discourse on *tz'u* for centuries, it seems only appropriate that the text that most of the essays included here begin with or return to is Li Ch'ing-chao's "Critique of the Song Lyric" ("Tz'u lun"), written early in the twelfth century. In the first chapter of this volume, "The Formation of a Distinct Generic Identity for *Tz'u*," Shuen-fu Lin opens by pointing out that this brief essay by perhaps the best-known woman song lyricist in Chinese literary history establishes the central critical statement for the genre, that it "constitutes its own household [distinct from *shih*]." Isolating the characteristics of that "household" occupied critical attention for centuries. Lin's essay is one of three that have been grouped together here in a section entitled "Defining the Song Lyric Voice: Questions of Genre"; in it he explores the formation of the genre's identity in its historical and literary contexts. Following Li Ch'ing-chao's lead, Lin examines the crucial relationship between poetry and music in general, focusing specifically on the development of what he calls the "intrinsic music" of *tz'u*—uneven line-lengths, strophic divisions, complex rhyme schemes, alternation of level and oblique tones, and intricate tonal patterns differing from those of regulated verse—that evolved in conjunction with the "extrinsic music" of banquet songs and continued to govern the aesthetics of song lyrics long after the tunes had been lost. The three most important developments in *tz'u* aesthetics, he argues, are the awareness that the genre could speak of private feelings not appropriately subsumed under the rubric of *chih*—that is, what is "intently on the mind"—which was traditionally assumed to carry moral and/or political import and whose public articulation was properly the responsibility of *shih*; the distinction between the two schools of "heroic abandon" (*hao-fang*) and "delicate restraint" (*wan-yüeh*) that expanded the thematic range of the form; and the evolution of a longer form, *man-tz'u*, that allowed for even greater emotional nuance and expressive potential. Lin discusses Li Ch'ing-chao's critical comments on her fellow song lyricists in the context of these developments and concludes by speculating on possible reasons behind the often-noted and curious omission of Chou Pang-yen from her essay: these are related, he suggests, to the fact that Chou's attention to the musical nature of the form restored what Li considered to be an essential aspect of its original identity and therefore exempted him from Li's otherwise unstinting critique of her contemporaries.

If general agreement developed that *tz'u* could express private sentiment more flexibly and "genuinely" than *shih*, what was not so clear was how "true" those private sentiments in fact were. In the second chapter in this section, "Meaning the Words: The Genuine as a Value in the Tradition of the Song Lyric," Stephen Owen argues that the origins of the song lyric in conventions of performance created a problem for literati songwriters seeking a vehicle for unmediated expression; this problem was thematized, moreover, in their very poems. In a series of close readings Owen traces the transformation of the genre from one governed by normative and typological conventions to one capable of being read, like *shih*, as the cry of a particular occasion. His discussion of Li Ch'ing-chao's famous lyric to the tune "Sheng-sheng man" provides a central example of this preoccupation with the (in)commensurability of poetic language to feeling, a problem that is made explicit and resolved in the poem itself. His concluding reading of Li Yü's famous lyric to the tune "Yü mei-jen" demonstrates how the arrangement (*taxis*) of words in *tz'u*, and in particular the framing or "quotation" of diction typical of *shih* by language from the vernacular, self-reflectively comments on the received images of the tradition and not only reanimates them, but also thereby makes that conventional language—and the lyric as the whole—resonate with an apparent truth of genuine emotion. He thereby illuminates one crucial way in which the genres of *shih* and *tz'u* are both related to and distinguished from each other.

From the perspective of the song lyric, this distinction could not but be invidious, harboring within itself a protracted discursive privileging of the earlier genre. My essay on "Song Lyrics and the Canon: A Look at Anthologies of *Tz'u*" examines the development of a response to this problem by tracing the ongoing effort to legitimize the song lyric as it took shape in the compilation of anthologies from the mid-tenth century onward. Repeated evidence of careless editing, significant lacunae in the record, and a general lack of textual integrity in the collections, as well as the polemics of marginality that color critical prefaces and commentaries attest to the questionable status of the song lyric for centuries. At the same time, however, the totalizing impulses of Chinese literary history could always recuperate the *tz'u* by locating it within a direct genealogical line of transmission from canonical poetic ancestors. In the endlessly resumed discussion about the status and definition of the genre that takes place in anthologies, I argue, there is a constant vacillation between the urge to locate *tz'u* squarely within a tradition shared with and dominated by *shih* and the wish to establish a separate space for it with its own internal demarcations.

These issues and positions—of accommodation, resistance, and appropriation—are analogous in significant ways to those that confronted women writers of *tz'u* in search of an authentic female voice and language, illustrating the significant interweaving of gender and genre theory in the history of the song lyric. The assumption that the song lyric was distinctively "feminine" in subject matter, style, language, or authorship shaped the discourse on its identity as a genre, and all of the essays in the second section in this volume, "Man's Voice/Woman's Voice: Questions of Gender," approach these issues in different ways. The first of the three, Grace S. Fong's "Engendering the Lyric: Her Image and Voice in Song," focuses on the feminine as consistently central in the aesthetics and poetics of the *tz'u* and yet paradoxically marginal, in that such constructions were largely fashioned by male poets and critics. She outlines the development of an increasingly male-dominated, "universal" poetic of the *shih* and the feminine coding of both *tz'u* as a genre and of the privileged style of "delicate restraint" within it. Such coding opened up possibilities for emotional expression foreclosed by the earlier poetic form that seemed particularly "natural" for women; at the same time, however, it undermined the legitimacy of the genre—whether employed by men or women—and also ran the risk of compromising the moral stature of real women who assumed female erotic personas. Fong traces the history of a number of searches for an authentic female voice and language among writers of song lyrics, concluding with the work of Ch'iu Chin, who rejected the image and poetics of the feminine constructed by the dominant tradition and appropriated a style previously coded as masculine as her own, with it to create the voice of a woman discontent with the shackles of both literary and social convention.

In his essay "The Poetry of Li Ch'ing-chao: A Woman Author and

Women's Authorship," John Timothy Wixted approaches this issue of a
female literary tradition in China through a focus on critical views of
one early and unquestionably prominent figure. Although there is no
evidence that Li identified with earlier or contemporary women writers
or that she served as a conscious female role model for later women
poets, she was certainly linked retrospectively to women poets before
her and became the standard by which women after her were measured.
Wixted notes that negative critical opinions of Li Ch'ing-chao's song
lyrics were usually linked to her being a woman and were paradoxically
motivated by autobiographical readings of them as if they were, in fact,
shih (the compromising situation discussed by Fong as well). By contrast, of course, any praise accorded her was not related to a specifically
female identity or language, and Wixted concludes that Li does not
occupy a position within the separate female literary tradition examined
by Fong; her status, rather, derives from being considered a "[female]
male among males," an honorary member of the poetic fraternity.

To the extent that any literary sorority did develop, it took root in the
late Ming and flourished into the Ch'ing, and particularly among the
circles studied by Kang-i Sun Chang in her chapter, "Liu Shih and Hsü
Ts'an: Feminine or Feminist?" Chang focuses on two women of markedly
different social and educational backgrounds but remarkably equal
poetic accomplishment who provided new models for women writers. As
a courtesan, Liu Shih moved freely in heavily male and literarily exalted
circles; she was instrumental to Ch'en Tzu-lung's literary innovations
but herself wrote primarily in the femininely coded style of "delicate restraint." Hsü Ts'an, by contrast, a gentry woman supplanted in her own
marriage by a concubine, transcended social restrictions on what and
how women of her station could write, and employed political language
and loyalist themes in song lyrics written in the masculinely coded style
of "heroic abandon." Although social boundaries between courtesans
and gentry women could of course be crossed through, for example,
marriage, Chang argues that two distinctive poetic styles identifiable
with the two groups did exist and that the relative timidity on the part
of courtesans in terms of style and theme resulted logically, by the eighteenth century, in their displacement from the center of the literary scene
by gentry women. Although poetry written by courtesans remained
influential as a secret model for literati women, it came to be virtually
eliminated from the literary record; gentry women, by contrast, gained
the access to circulation—for both themselves and their writings—that
had once been the privilege of the courtesans.

The third group of papers in this volume, "From Voice to Text:

Questions of Genealogy," focuses on a variety of issues having to do
with the history of the preservation, circulation, and critical reception of
tz'u. Ronald C. Egan discusses the questionable status of the genre,
already alluded to in earlier chapters, in his essay, "The Problem of the
Repute of *Tz'u* During the Northern Sung." Beneath the traditional
pairing of "T'ang *shih* and Sung *tz'u*" that would seem to imply that
each form enjoyed a stature commensurate with the other in its own
time, Egan uncovers an early disesteem and struggle for acceptance on
the part of the *tz'u* during the Northern Sung that belies accepted
literary-historical homilies and has also significantly affected the evolution of the form itself. Not only the remarkable silence on the part of
major figures of the period regarding their composition of song lyrics,
but their outright denunciations of the genre as well, provide evidence
of a profoundly ambivalent attitude that was only partially resolved, in
the case of Su Shih, by the development of stylistic and thematic innovations. Egan argues that various efforts to establish a respectable
genealogy for the genre were ultimately unconvincing and that what
legitimacy was eventually accorded it was linked most probably to the
elevation in stature of all cultural pursuits at the end of the Northern
Sung rather than to any particular revaluation of *tz'u* itself.

In his essay "Contexts of the Song Lyric in Sung Times: Communication Technology, Social Change, Morality," Stuart H. Sargent
discusses developments, particularly within the material culture of the
Southern Sung, that may have represented a partial response to the
genre's problematic status. Sargent explores the apparent contradiction
between the song lyric's ties to oral performance and its undeniably
well-developed chirographic existence. Along with another curious
development—the genre's claim to trace a morphology of feeling despite
its evident appeal to large segments of society that clearly mistrusted
such feeling—this paradox suggests an awareness of both the dangers of
the form (and its consequent disrepute) and the possibility and importance, nonetheless, of becoming detached from one's utterance. Sargent
argues that such detachment is characteristic of a literate culture and is
perhaps intensified through the proliferation of printed manuscripts,
and he discusses at great length the written record preserving *tz'u* during the Southern Sung, focusing on Chiang-nan West Circuit. Indeed,
he proposes that the rise and spread of printed texts in China coincided
precisely with the development of the song lyric, possibly encouraging,
among other things, the growing tendency toward increasingly "difficult" *tz'u* during this period; it may also have defused the moral dan-

gers of the form's emotional power, as it moved from the immediacy of performance to the remoteness of print.

Testimony to the eventual critical acceptance of the genre is provided by Yeh Chia-ying's essay on the sophisticated theory and practice of the late Ch'ing critic Wang Kuo-wei. In her essay "Wang Kuo-wei's Song Lyrics in the Light of His Own Theories," she offers a new understanding of Wang's pronouncements on what makes the song lyric distinctive by examining a selection of his own lyrics through the prism of his concept of *ching-chieh* (the poetic "setting" or "scene"). In its sense specific to the song lyric, Yeh argues, the term *ching-chieh* refers to the latent suggestive power of imagery to evoke associations beyond the ostensible topic of the poem, feelings not necessarily intended by the poet, and references that are symbolic as well as circumstantial. These possibilities can be developed within what she delineates as the three major categories of *tz'u*: those actually written as words to music; those no longer written to be sung but composed, rather, like *shih*, for the purpose of self-expression; and those approaching the elaborate expository and architectonic structures of the rhapsody (*fu*). Her close readings of four exemplary song lyrics explore the textual, contextual, and intertextual resonances of each image to illustrate the infusion of external scene with complex emotional tone and argue against previously one-sided interpretations of the works. Like Owen, Yeh suggests, through her concluding discussion of a song lyric writing of a love affair that may be real or invented, that one distinctive feature of the genre is its very self-reflectiveness.

Finally, Daniel Bryant traces the textual history of two specific collections of *tz'u* and brings his findings to bear on establishing with care the most likely version of the same song lyric discussed by Stephen Owen in his chapter, a lyric by Li Yü to the tune "Yü mei-jen." Bryant's "Messages of Uncertain Origin: The Textual Tradition of the *Nan-T'ang erh-chu tz'u*" employs computer-assisted methodology to produce a genealogy of the extant editions of this collection of song lyrics by Li Yü and his father, Li Ching. In the process, his work also affirms the authenticity of an important Sung dynasty anthology, the *Tsun-ch'ien chi*, details of whose compilation had previously been subject to considerable critical dispute, and provides the basis for a variorum edition of the collected works of the two rulers of the Southern T'ang. Bryant's painstaking detective work establishing likely archetypes, derivations, and filiations of variant readings relies in the end—somewhat to the relief of other less technologically literate conference participants—on the ability of the human brain (*jen-nao*) to make judgments between options presented by the computer (*tien-nao*). But he clearly demonstrates the importance, for any sound literary scholarship, of knowing what text one is actually working with, what questions about it can or cannot be answered, and why.

In addition to the authors who are represented in this volume, five participants at the 1990 Breckinridge conference presented papers that, regretfully, could not be included here. We are extremely grateful to Mr. Chen Bang-yan of the Shanghai Classics Publishing House, Professor Kao Yu-kung of Princeton University, Dr. Shi Yi-dui of the Institute of Literature, Chinese Academy of Social Sciences, Professor Yang Hai-ming of Suzhou University, and Dr. Yang Hsien-ch'ing (Yang Tse) of the China Daily News for their lively and insightful contributions to the discussions at all of the sessions. In particular, their chanting of song lyrics in various styles at the final session—in which other scholars also participated—provided a pleasant and salutary reminder, amid the temptations of abstract and text-oriented theorization, of the sensuous core of our subject matter. Professors David Knechtges of the University of Washington and Anthony C. Yu of the University of Chicago offered wide-ranging and valuable comments on both individual papers and the discussion as a whole, from which we all learned a great deal.

Both before and after the conference itself, many other individuals provided invaluable assistance in a number of ways. I would like to thank Stephen Owen, who was co-organizer of the conference, for his instrumental role in conceiving of and developing the plans for the meeting, which, to the deep regret of us all, he was unable to attend; his presence was sorely missed, but his thoughts and statements about the subject were in evidence throughout the proceedings and have been reflected in this introductory essay as well. I would also like to acknowledge the valuable advice and support of the other members of the planning committee, Kang-i Sun Chang, Grace Fong, Shuen-fu Lin, and Tim Wixted, who cheerfully endured a weekend of brutal heat in the summer of 1988 to draft a framework for the meeting. Edward Peng, a graduate student in Comparative Literature at the University of California, Irvine, provided crucial last-minute assistance in the preparation of the manuscript for publication, for which I am very grateful. Thanks are also due to Victor Tam and the other obliging staff members of the Humanities Computing Facility at U.C. Irvine, who resolved the countless hardware and software problems created by my attempts to coordinate and make sense of the Babel of languages and formats in which these essays arrived on my desk. The contributors to this volume benefited from the many helpful comments and suggestions offered by the two reviewers of the manuscript, although we resolutely retained the diversity of our individual voices. In addition, we are very grateful to Deborah Rudolph at the University of California Press for her extraordinarily meticulous and sensitive copyediting, and to editors Sheila Levine and Betsey Scheiner for their enthusiastic support of the volume. Finally, all of the participants at the conference owe a profound debt of gratitude to the three rapporteurs—Pauline Lin, Kathy Lowry, and Sophie Volpp—whose unstinting efforts before, during, and after the conference made possible a transmission of the record that any chronicler of the song lyric could not but contemplate with a sigh of deepest envy.

ONE

Defining the Song Lyric Voice:
Questions of Genre

The Formation of a Distinct Generic Identity for *Tz'u*

Shuen-fu Lin

Toward the end of the Northern Sung dynasty (960–1126),[1] in an essay titled "Tz'u lun," "A Critique of the Song Lyric," Li Ch'ing-chao (1084–1151?) asserted that *tz'u pieh-shih i-chia*, that "*tz'u* constitutes its own household [distinct from *shih*]."[2] This is an important claim for a self-conscious generic identity for the song lyric, one that follows a series of brief comments on the development of the form from the eighth to the late twelfth centuries and on some of the well-known poets from the Five Dynasties (907–60) through the Northern Sung. The significance of this essay cannot be underestimated, for "A Critique of the Song Lyric" is the first piece of critical discourse in the history of Chinese literature devoted especially to a discussion of the aesthetic properties of the genre as a whole.[3]

1. This important essay has always been regarded by modern scholars as a work written during the last years of the Northern Sung dynasty. In a recent article, however, Fei Ping-hsün argues that it was likely to have been written early in the Southern Sung period (1127–1279) or even late in Li Ch'ing-chao's life. "A Critique of the Song Lyric" first appeared in *T'iao-hsi yü-yin ts'ung-hua—hou-chi*, where it carried a preface dated 1167. It was not included in *T'iao-hsi yü-yin ts'ung-hua—ch'ien-chi*, which had a preface dated 1148, even though this first volume had already included some recorded statements about Li Ch'ing-chao and some comments on her song lyrics. For Fei's arguments, see his article titled "Li Ch'ing-chao 'Tz'u lun' hsin-t'an" in *Li Ch'ing-chao yen-chiu lun-wen hsüan* (Shanghai: Shang-hai ku-chi ch'u-pan-she, 1986), pp. 230–42. I don't find Fei's arguments completely convincing and will follow the majority view concerning the date of composition in this paper.

2. Huang Mo-ku, *Ch'ung-chi Li Ch'ing-chao chi* (Shantung: Ch'i Lu shu-she, 1981), p. 57. The essay can be found in pp. 56–57 of Huang's book.

3. Prior to the 'Tz'u lun,' random comments on the song lyric can be found in pref-

It might be tempting to assume that the song lyric, which had often been associated with "feminine sensibility," had to wait for a woman poet of Li Ch'ing-chao's stature to claim its generic identity. But the properties of the genre as articulated in the essay are by no means arbitrary formulations of her own particular artistic ideals. Although Li Ch'ing-chao applied a very high standard in evaluating the works of representative poets of the song lyric (and almost none of them escaped her unrelenting criticism), the general sense of its identity as a genre as set forth in her essay was in fact widely shared by poets and scholars of the second half of the eleventh and the early twelfth centuries. Despite its brevity, "A Critique of the Song Lyric" thus represents a summation of the dominant aesthetic conventions pertaining to the lyric that had been evolving since the late T'ang, in addition to serving as a response to the special developments that occurred in the poetry and poetics of the genre during the eleventh and early twelfth centuries. In what follows I will explore the formation of the song lyric's generic identity in its historical and literary contexts during this period.

CONSIDERATIONS OF GENRE

Let me first say a few words about the concept of genre as it is to be understood in this paper. Few people today, if any, would subscribe to a *prescriptive* theory of genres and urge writers and scholars to approximate some "Platonic" notion of pure forms.[4] Rather, those who still think that generic distinctions are indispensable to both writers and literary scholars generally adopt a *descriptive* theory of genres. That is, they usually derive the sense of literary kinds from existing works of literature and tend to allow the mixing of established generic norms.[5] As E. D. Hirsch, Jr., has aptly observed, the "essential elements of all

---

aces to anthologies or groups of song lyrics and in the anecdotal *shih-hua or pen-shih ch'ü.* For a general discussion of early *tz'u* criticism from the late T'ang to the end of the Northern Sung, see Wu Hsiung-ho, *T'ang Sung tz'u t'ung-lun* (Hangchow: Che-chiang ku-chi ch'u-pan-she, 1985), pp. 279–97.

4. See Allan Rodway's discussion of "two inclusive classes of kind-criticism" in his article "Generic Criticism: The Approach through Type, Mode and Kind" in *Contemporary Criticism*, ed. Malcolm Bradbury and David Palmer, Stratford-Upon-Avon Studies, no. 12 (London: Edward Arnold, 1970), p. 87. René Wellek and Austin Warren have observed that classical theory of genre is usually "prescriptive" while modern theory is by contrast "descriptive." See their *Theory of Literature*, 3d ed. (New York: Harcourt, Brace & World, 1956), pp. 233–35.

5. Allan Rodway, "Generic Criticism," p. 87.

genres are historical and culture-bound,"[6] and the evolution of genres within any given literary tradition is always a complex and dynamic process, intimately related to changing historical and cultural contexts. The creativity of individual writers also plays a significant part in the dynamic evolution of genres. But individual contributions are themselves closely related to the complex historical and cultural conditions in which the writers lived. In this discussion, therefore, genres are to be regarded not "as a hierarchy of fixed forms, each individual work belonging to one and only one such category," but "more flexibly as clusters of stylistic and thematic traits that a number of works hold more or less in common and that change irregularly over the course of time."[7]

It is true that genres were usually conceived by scholars in Sung times as a sort of "hierarchy of forms" and were used more often than not for prescriptive or evaluative, rather than purely descriptive, purposes. Nevertheless, the traits and conventions associated with genres are by no means always rigidly fixed in their formulations. The sense of a genre's identity changes over the course of time in accordance with the evolution of a whole literary culture; certain traits remain always essential to a particular genre's identity from the time of its emergence, while others lose their vitality in the genre's history and are replaced by or integrated with traits from other genres. Thus, the formation of the self-identity of the song lyric can best be approached from an evolutionary perspective. Although the song lyric never stopped evolving during the more than four centuries that elapsed from the early T'ang to the end of the Northern Sung, two periods were of particular relevance to the formation of its generic identity: the period around the year 850, when the song lyric began to evolve in the hands of literati poets into an "independent literary genre,"[8] and the late Northern Sung, when the song lyric reached a mature and sophisticated stage of development that allowed a self-conscious generic identity to appear. These two periods will serve as the foci of my attention, even though I will be discussing the evolution of the early song lyric as a whole.

6. E. D. Hirsch, Jr., *Validity in Interpretation* (New Haven: Yale University Press, 1967), p. 107.

7. One can find a brief but lucid and sensible discussion of the concept of genre in Lawrence Buell, *New England Literary Culture* (Cambridge: Cambridge University Press, 1986), pp. 16–17.

8. Kang-i Sun Chang has discussed this important development in early *tz'u* in her book *The Evolution of Chinese* Tz'u *Poetry: From the Late T'ang to the Northern Sung* (Princeton: Princeton University Press, 1980), pp. 29–32.

POETRY AND MUSIC

The term *tz'u*, or *ch'ü-tzu-tz'u* (song words) in full, designates the song form that was set to *yen-yüeh*, or "banquet music," a new kind of music that emerged in China during the late sixth century, a synthesis of music imported from Central Asia and India with native Chinese elements.[9] Li Ch'ing-chao, however, situates the form within an even larger context by opening her "Tz'u lun" with this remark: "*Yüeh-fu* and *sheng-shih* were both well known and especially in fashion during the T'ang dynasty [618–907]."[10] After making this opening statement, Li Ch'ing-chao then goes on to relate a story about a famous singer of the eighth century, Li Pa-lang, before she focuses on the song lyric itself. Li Ch'ing-chao begins her essay in this fashion clearly in order to emphasize the importance of music and performance in her discussion of the *tz'u*.

The association of the song lyric with musical settings is, of course, a significant characteristic of the genre. Yet the song lyric was obviously not the first kind of Chinese poetry to be set to music. Relying on written sources, some recent Chinese scholars of the song lyric have divided the long history of the relationship between poetry and music into three stages, beginning with the *Shih-ching*, or *Book of Songs*.[11] From ancient times to the Han dynasty, the usual practice was to adapt music to the

9. Ibid., pp. 223–40. Chou Sheng-wei, "Ts'ung shih yü yüeh ti hsiang-hu kuan-hsi k'an tz'u-t'i ti ch'i-yüan yü hsing-ch'eng," in *Tz'u-hsüeh lun-kao*, ed. Hua-tung shih-fan ta-hsüeh Chung-wen-hsi Chung-kuo ku-tien wen-hsüeh yen-chiu-shih (Shanghai: Hua-tung shih-fan ta-hsüeh ch'u-pan-she, 1986), pp. 14–15. The term *ch'ü-tzu-tz'u* was not very popular in T'ang times, however. It became widely used only after the Five Dynasties. See Jen Erh-pei's comment on this matter in his *Tun-huang ch'ü ch'u-t'an* (Shanghai: Wen-i lien-ho ch'u-pan-she, 1954), pp. 219–20.

10. Jen Pan-t'ang, *T'ang sheng-shih* (Shanghai: Shang-hai ku-chi ch'u-pan-she, 1982), 1:8. *Sheng-shih* was popular from the early T'ang through the Five Dynasties period. The tunes to which *sheng-shih* was set formed part of banquet music, but they tended to have a regular shape, providing a good setting for poems written in lines of equal length. See Jen Pan-t'ang's definition of *sheng-shih* in *T'ang sheng-shih*, p. 46. Jen Pan-t'ang indicates in his long introduction to *T'ang sheng-shih* that the manuscript of his book was first completed in Ch'eng-tu in 1958. He writes that he reread the manuscript in 1981, although he does not say whether he undertook any revision of it then. Pan-t'ang is probably a sobriquet of Jen Erh-pei (i.e., Jen Na), the author of *Tun-huang ch'ü ch'u-tan*, which was also written in the 1950s in Ch'eng-tu.

11. Although these three stages have been recognized by scholars in the past, they have not been studied in any detail until recently. See especially Liu Yao-min, *Tz'u yü yin-yüeh* (Kunming: Yün-nan jen-min ch'u-pan-she, 1982), pp. 191–218, and Shih I-tui, *Tz'u yü yin-yüeh kuan-hsi yen-chiu* (Peking: Chung-kuo she-hui k'o-hsüeh-ch'u-pan-she, 1989), pp. 131–50.

framework of verse: "first poetry, then music." The *Ch'u-tz'u*, or *Songs of the South*, as well as the *yüeh-fu* of the Han dynasty and the Six Dynasties are further examples of early poetry with musical settings. Although the custom of "adapting music to the framework of poetry" continued to exist in some fashion throughout this period, there appeared together with the rise of *yüeh-fu* poetry in the Han the practice of finding poems to set to existing music.[12] This procedure usually required the musicians to split up lines of verse, add refrains, or in some cases insert a number of nonsensical sounds to fit the text to the tune. In consequence, poetry and music were only loosely combined at best. Nonetheless, music had already begun to gain importance in its relation to poetry.

From the beginning of the eighth century, some popular songwriters began to compose words to banquet music tunes.[13] This new approach of "filling in words in accordance with the notes" (*i-sheng t'ien-tz'u*), or "first music, then poetry," allowed music to determine the shape of poems, resulting in the emergence of *tz'u* poetry with mixed line-lengths and interesting and complex tonal patterns.[14] Thus, according to this widely accepted view, the development of Chinese poetry with musical settings from the *Shih-ching* to the *tz'u* was a long process in which poetry gradually lost its predominance relative to its musical setting until finally the structure of music was recognized as dominant and poetry was forced to adapt to it. Though not completely without merit, this linear view is clearly too simplistic and reflects, no doubt, the bias of literary scholars. In the absence of archaeological evidence, it is problematic to assert that the earliest practice was indeed consistently "first poetry, then music."[15]

There is actually another view concerning the relationship between poetry and music in the Chinese tradition. Commenting on the "Ta hsü," or "Great Preface," to the Mao edition of the *Book of Songs*, K'ung

---

12. Liu Yao-min, *Tz'u yü yin-yüeh*, pp. 23–27; Shih I-tui, *Tz'u yü yin-yüeh kuan-hsi yen-chiu*, pp. 137–46.

13. Hsia Ch'eng-t'ao and Wu Hsiung-ho, *Tsen-yang tu T'ang Sung tz'u* (Hangchow: Che-chiang jen-min ch'u-pan-she, 1958), p. 2.

14. Owing to the structure of the music, a small number of *tz'u* metrical patterns with lines of equal length does exist. The phrase *i-sheng t'ien-tz'u* first appeared in the *Wen-t'i ming-pien* by Hsü Shih-tseng of the late Ming. See Lo Ken-tse and Yü Pei-shan, eds., *Wen-chang pien-t'i hsü-shuo* by Wu Na, and *Wen-t'i ming-pien hsü-shuo* by Hsü Shih-tseng (Peking: Jen-min wen-hsüeh ch'u-pan-she, 1962), p. 164. Although this statement appeared long after banquet music was lost, for the majority of *tz'u* scholars it describes concisely the lyric writers' common approach to the making of poetry and music.

15. I am grateful to Anthony Yu for raising this important point in his discussion of the relationship between poetry and music at the conference.

Ying-ta (574–648) argued that the two approaches of "making music in accordance with poetry" and "making poetry in accordance with music" had always existed, although he also believed that music had been created first in accordance with the distinctions inherent in human speech.[16] The belief that two approaches to the making of poetry and music were simultaneously practiced depending entirely on which art form was available first was held by other scholars such as Shen Yüeh (441–513) of the southern Ch'i dynasty, Yüan Chen (779–831) of the T'ang dynasty, and Huang Hsiu-fu (fl. 1001) and Kuo Mao-ch'ien (fl. 12th cent.) of the Sung dynasty.[17] On the basis of his own work on the *sheng-shih* of the T'ang dynasty, the modern scholar Jen Pan-t'ang strongly supports this view and argues that only after banquet music was lost were song lyrics ever written completely without any concern with music.[18] This theory seems more plausible than the linear view in explaining the actual practice of combining poetry with music in traditional China. However, one must not be misled by it into believing that the song lyric contributed nothing new to the history of the making of poetry and music, because the same approaches were used in all forms of poetry with musical settings from the *Book of Songs* to the song lyric of the Sung dynasty.

THE MUSICALIZATION OF POETRY

The importance of the song lyric in the long history of the relationship between Chinese poetry and music resides in the particular characteristics of the music to which the lyric was set and in the fact that it represents the culmination of generations of poets' attempts to use the distinctive features of the Chinese language to create a kind of music *in* poetry—what has been called the "musicalization" of poetry by Chinese literary historians.[19] The musicalization of poetry can be said to have begun in the fifth century, when for the first time educated Chinese became fully aware that their language possessed tonal features—that is, the tones *p'ing* (level), *shang* (rising), *ch'ü* (departing), and *ju* (entering).[20] The discovery subsequently led fifth-century poets to ex-

16. See *Mao shih chu-shu*, vol. 2 of *Shih-san-ching chu-shu* (Taipei: I-wen yin-shu-kuan, 1965), pp. 13 and 16.
17. Jen Pan-t'ang, *T'ang sheng-shih*, pp. 171, 342–44.
18. Ibid., pp. 374–79.
19. In his *Tz'u yü yin-yüeh* Liu Yao-min uses the term *shih-ko yin-yüeh-hua*, or "the musicalization of poetry," to refer to the process by which the tonal properties of the Chinese language are used to create a kind of music in poetry.
20. Ibid., pp. 100–104.

periment with employing tones for euphonic effects. Prior to this, the tones no doubt had some bearing on the rhythm of poetry (because Chinese had probably always been a tonal language), but only on an unconscious level. By contrast, the experiments of the fifth-century poets were a self-conscious attempt to create an "intrinsic music" within the written texts themselves.[21] Interestingly, this intrinsic music was first created in the form of poetry—*shih*—that lacked a corresponding musical setting, or "extrinsic music." *Shih* poetry had emerged in the first century B.C. and was in fact originally associated with folk songs, but it was not until the second century A.D. that it became popular among literati poets, who began to use it as a mode for self-expression in isolation from its original musical setting.[22] The *shih* poem is constructed almost entirely of end-stopped lines of equal length (of either five or seven characters each), which are further organized into basic units of couplets, with rhyme occurring at the end of each even-numbered line. It was within this regular and rigid form that the self-conscious poets of the fifth century tried to create a kind of music with the newly discovered tonal features of their native language.

Shen Yüeh has been traditionally credited with having defined the four tones and some of the rules of tonal euphony.[23] In the "Lu Chüeh chuan," the biography of Lu Chüeh, a contemporary and intellectual companion of Shen Yüeh, it is recorded that Shen Yüeh and others of his time "infused musical qualities into their writings and used the 'level, rising, departing, and entering' tones to regulate their resonance and euphony. . . . Within every line of five characters, all tones and final sounds differ from one another, and within every two lines, each word differs in pitch."[24] Shen Yüeh himself made a key statement about the "music" of poetry:

> One needs to make the notes alternate and the high and low sounds intermix to form a rhythm. If there is a floating sound in the front, there should be an intense sound in the rear. Within a single piece of writing, make the tones and final sounds of the words distinct; within every two lines, vary the light and heavy sounds. Only when one understands this principle can one be allowed to discuss writing.[25]

21. Ibid. The terms *nei-tsai yin-yüeh*, or "intrinsic music," and *wai-tsai yin-yüeh*, or "extrinsic music," are defined in these pages.
22. Burton Watson, *Chinese Lyricism: Shih Poetry from the Second to the Twelfth Century* (New York: Columbia University Press, 1971), p. 16.
23. Ibid.
24. Chi Yün, *Shen-shih ssu-sheng k'ao* (rpt., Changsha: Shang-wu yin-shu-kuan, 1941), pp. 154–55.
25. Ibid., p. 151.

Shen Yüeh's goal clearly was to use the four tones of the Chinese language to parallel the five notes on the pentatonic scale of ancient
Chinese music, and to use them in such a way as to create a kind of
rhythm and melody similar to that of music. By drawing an analogy
from music, Shen Yüeh thus drew attention to the aspects of variation
and modulation. But he had nothing explicit to say about harmony or
regularity of rhythm, and his arguments were limited to the individual
line and the couplet, without any concern for the overall structure of an
entire poem.

From the above quotation, we can see that Shen Yüeh spoke of the
four tones as if they possessed two sets of opposing properties. He used
the words "high" (*kao*) and "low" (*hsia*), "light" (*ch'ing*) and "heavy"
(*chung*), as well as "floating" (*fu*) and "intense" (*ch'ieh*) to describe
them. In T'ang times these pairs of opposing traits were essentially defined as the distinction between "level" (*p'ing*) and "oblique" (*tse*) tonal
qualities.[26] There are different theories regarding the exact nature of the
level/oblique distinction: it is one based on a contrast—either in dura-
tion between long and short, or in pitch between high and low, or in
contour between level and oblique—when a sound is enunciated.
Words in the level tone belong to the level category and words in the
rising, departing, and entering tones all belong to the oblique category.

Although fifth-century scholars were the first to discuss the four tones
and their bipartite division, they were by no means the first to observe
in writing the distinction between two opposing tonal categories. In a
pioneering investigation into tonal patterns in writing, Hsia Ch'eng-t'ao
argues that some observation of the distinction between two apparently
opposing categories can already be found in poetry and rhymeprose (*fu*)
composed before the fifth century.[27] He points out that in the *Book of
Songs* and the *Songs of the South*, alternation between rhyme words belonging to opposite tonal categories (as distinguished in later historical
times) often exists within a single piece; that in the rhymeprose of the
Han dynasty, the tonal properties of the words ending lines are often
found to alternate from line to line; that in some rhymeprose of the
Han, especially of the latter half of the dynasty, alternation between the

26. For a concise description of this bipartite division, see Yu-kung Kao, "The Aesthetics of Regulated Verse," in *The Vitality of the Lyric Voice: Shih Poetry from the Late Han to
the T'ang*, ed. Shuen-fu Lin and Stephen Owen (Princeton: Princeton University Press,
1987), pp. 352–53. According to Hsia Ch'eng-t'ao, Yin Fan in the eighth century was the
first person to use the terms *p'ing* and *tse* in his preface to the anthology of T'ang poetry he edited, the *Ho-yüeh ying-ling-chi*. See Hsia's article "Ssu-sheng i-shuo" in idem,
Yüeh-lun-shan tz'u-lun chi (Peking: Chung-hua shu-chü, 1979), p. 156.

27. Hsia Ch'eng-t'ao, "Ssu-sheng i-shuo," pp. 149–60.

two tonal categories is also found; and, finally, that in *shih* poetry of the second century, words in the corresponding key (i.e., the second and fourth) positions within a couplet are often found to belong to opposing tonal categories.[28] Since we no longer have the music for the works in the *Book of Songs* and the *Songs of the South*, there is no way we can determine whether, or to what extent, the tonal patterns observed there (if Hsia Ch'eng-t'ao's findings are indeed valid) were the result of setting words to music. But in light of these findings, it is at least clear that Shen Yüeh's attempt to create an intrinsic music in poetry was built upon centuries of previous experience.

The bipartite division of the four tones came into wide use by poets experimenting with the tones after the second half of the fifth century. By the seventh century, the new genre of poetry called *lü-shih*, or "regulated verse," had appeared, with its distinctive metrical structure based on the "level/oblique" tonal contrast—a major breakthrough in the musicalization of classical Chinese poetry. In regulated verse level and oblique tonal properties are organized into a rhythmic fabric. Normally, the two adjacent disyllabic metrical units within each line are opposite in level/oblique tonal distinction. Since the second syllable in each disyllabic metrical segment and the last syllable in each line are slightly stressed in reading, their tonal qualities, either level or oblique, are customarily fixed. Other unstressed places are allowed greater freedom in actual practice. This alternation between level and oblique tones in stressed positions constitutes the linear or temporal aspect of the rhythm of regulated verse. The lines in a piece of regulated verse are further organized into four interrelated couplets. The tonal properties of the corresponding lines, especially of the stressed positions, within each couplet must be opposed to one another. Both the combination of metrical units into lines and the juxtaposition of lines into couplets reflect the principle of "maximum contrast."[29] Between two adjacent couplets the same tonal properties are used in the corresponding stressed positions in the neighboring lines. The repetition of tonal qualities between adjacent couplets and the opposition of tonal qualities within each couplet create a conceptual kind of spatial layout of the rhythm of regulated verse.

The linear and spatial dimensions of rhythm discussed here constitute the intrinsic music of regulated verse, a remarkable advance from the meter of Chinese poetry prior to the late fifth century, which was

---

28. Ibid., pp. 150–51.
29. Yu-kung Kao, "The Aesthetics of Regulated Verse," p. 354.

based largely on the measure of syllables or beats.[30] This intrinsic music no doubt contributed to the beauty and dynamism of the aural aspect of regulated verse, but it also had its limitations. There were only a few metrical patterns available to poets for the expression of a wide variety of themes and feelings. Moreover, the metrical patterns tended to be extremely regular and rigid. It should be noted here that the quatrain form, *chüeh-chü*, the other form of T'ang recent-style verse (*chin-t'i shih*), which was crucial to the development of literati *tz'u* before the middle of the ninth century,[31] shared the same intrinsic music as regulated verse.

BANQUET MUSIC

The introduction of banquet music opened up significantly new possibilities for Chinese poetry. Increasingly popular in T'ang China from the eighth century onward,[32] it was viewed by scholars as *yin-sheng* (lascivious music), *Cheng Wei chih yin* ("music of Cheng and Wei," or decadent music), or *mi-mi chih yüeh* (dissolute and sensual music) that had abandoned much of the moderation contained in *ya-yüeh* and *ch'ing-yüeh*, the two previous traditional forms of Chinese music.[33] Compared with

30. The structural principles of regulated verse are discussed in some detail in my book, *The Transformation of the Chinese Lyrical Tradition: Chiang K'uei and Southern Sung* Tz'u *Poetry* (Princeton: Princeton University Press, 1978), p. 97, and in my article, "Intrinsic Music in the Medieval Chinese Lyric" in *The Lyrical Arts: A Humanities Symposium*, a special issue of *Ars Lyrica*, ed. Erling B. Holtsmark and Judith Aikin (Guilford: Lyrica Society, 1988), pp. 29–54.

31. Kang-i Sun Chang, *The Evolution of Chinese Tz'u Poetry*, pp. 25–30.

32. Kang-i Sun Chang, *The Evolution of Chinese Tz'u Poetry*, p. 26.

33. *Yin-sheng* is used by the Sung scholar Yü Wen-pao in his *Ch'ui-chien lu* to refer to *yen-yüeh* (called *i-yüeh* here). *Cheng Wei chih yin* is used by the Sung scholar Wang Ming-ch'ing in his *Hui-chu lu* to refer to the banquet music popular among the educated elite during the Southern Sung. Their remarks are quoted in Shih I-tui, *Tz'u yü yin-yüeh kuan-hsi yen-chiu*, p. 154. Li Ch'ing-chao also uses the term *Cheng Wei chih sheng*, or "the music of Cheng and Wei" (i.e., "decadent" music), to refer to banquet music in her "Tz'u lun." See Huang Mo-ku, *Ch'ung-chi Li Ch'ing-chao chi*, p. 56. Commenting on *ch'ing-yüeh*, the T'ang scholar Tu Yu says in his *T'ung-tien*: "The songs of lascivious whining from the South are already quite chaotic. Nevertheless, they still carry the lingering influence of the graceful, refined, and moderate manner of the gentleman-scholar." See the remark quoted in Shih I-tui, *Tz'u yü yin-yüeh kuan-hsi yen-chiu*, p. 155. In the *Hsü t'ung-tien*, the term *mi-mi chih yüeh* is used to refer to banquet music. See the relevant passage quoted in Liu Yao-min, *Tz'u yü yin-yüeh*, p. 270. This term probably first appeared in the "Shih-kuo" chapter of the *Han Fei-tzu* in reference to the dissolute and licentious music made by Music Master Yen for King Chou, the last ruler of the Shang dynasty. See Ch'en Ch'i-yu, ed., *Han Fei-tzu chi-shih* (Shanghai: Chung-hua shu-chü, 1958), p. 171. Both *mi-mi chih yüeh* and *Cheng Wei chih sheng* were originally terms used to condemn the "dissolute and

ya-yüeh and *ch'ing-yüeh,* banquet music possessed a larger compass of tones and tended to be more exhaustive or even to go to extremes in its expression of emotions, whether joy or sorrow.[34] Thus, as an expressive art form, banquet music was believed to be a far more lively and powerful medium than previous traditional Chinese music. Its social function, moreover, was also of relevance to its particularly expressive power. Banquet music was used primarily for entertainment at official or private banquets in the residences of aristocrats and well-to-do people, as well as in wineshops, song houses, and brothels, and the song lyrics set to these tunes were sung largely—though, until the Sung dynasty, not exclusively—by singing girls.[35] As a result, early song lyrics, especially those composed by literati, display a general tendency toward the expression of a relatively narrower world of experience and toward a more gentle, delicate, and sensual style of presentation when compared with *shih* poetry.[36]

We know that well over eight hundred banquet music tunes and more than two thousand different metrical patterns of song lyrics set to these tunes have survived from the T'ang, the Five Dynasties, and the Sung periods.[37] Compared with the quatrain and regulated verse, the song lyric offered the poet a much wider range of choices, because its tunes and metrical patterns differed from each other in atmosphere, mood, and tone, and were deemed capable of evoking different emotional responses from the listener. We can say that the tunes and metrical patterns represented different formal structures for the expression of a whole range of feelings; it was up to the poet to select the appropriate form within which to express a particular feeling. But song lyrics, especially those written by the literati poets of the late T'ang and the early Sung, were still to a large extent composed in the rhythm or intrinsic music of recent-style verse. Nonetheless, because of the presence of the

---

decadent" music produced in states whose governments were in chaos. When later scholars used these terms to refer to banquet music, it was not necessarily primarily for the purpose of condemnation.

34. See Liu Yao-min's review of comments on banquet music found in the *Wen-hsien t'ung-k'ao* and the *T'ang shu* in his *Tz'u yü yin-yüeh,* pp. 269–71.

35. Wang Cho, *Pi-chi man-chih, chüan* 1, collected in T'ang Kuei-chang, ed., *Tz'u-hua ts'ung-pien* (Taipei: Kuang-wen shu-chü, 1969), 1:27–28.

36. See the fine discussion of this point in Kao Chien-chung, "Shih-lun liang Sung wan-yüeh-tz'u ti li-shih ti-wei," in *Chung-kuo ku-tien wen-hsüeh lun-ts'ung,* vol. 4, ed. Jen-min wen-hsüeh ch'u-pan-she ku-tien wen-hsüeh pien-chi-shih (Peking: Jen-min wen-hsüeh ch'u-pan-she, 1986), pp. 125–26.

37. Hsia Ch'eng-t'ao and Wu Hsiung-ho, *Tsen-yang tu T'ang Sung tz'u,* p. 34.

extrinsic musical setting, the intrinsic music of the early song lyric already consisted of uneven line-lengths, strophic divisions, complex rhyme schemes, the alternation of level and oblique tonal properties, and intricate tonal patterns which often deviated from the standard patterns of recent-style verse.[38] This intrinsic music could reflect more precisely the atmosphere, mood, and tone of the extrinsic music—that is, the banquet music tunes—to which it was set. In the song lyric, therefore, poetry and music became truly parallel and unified arts. Without the restriction of the rigid, regular, and balanced rhythm of recent-style verse, the songwriter could express his ideas and experiences in a more complex process, in verse built up from a mixture of long and short rhythmic units with distinct curves and turns. Despite the fact that in some ways the prosody of the *tz'u* was just as restrictive as that of recent-style verse, the irregular and curving contours of this new intrinsic music could be said to resemble the spontaneous expression of powerful feelings more closely. If music is, as Susanne Langer puts it, a "morphology of feeling,"[39] the intrinsic music of the song lyric is itself a structure of feeling as well. But the musicalization of poetry did not stop at the accomplishments of the late T'ang poets.

LITERATI *TZ'U*

According to Hsia Ch'eng-t'ao's research, Wen T'ing-yün (812–72), a major poet represented in the *Hua-chien chi*, an anthology of early literati *tz'u*, was one of the very first poets to observe the distinction between level and oblique tonal categories in an attempt to bring music and poetry closer together.[40] Jen Erh-pei, however, has pointed out that earlier popular songwriters represented in the Tun-huang manuscripts had already begun to pay attention to such distinctions in *tz'u* prosody[41] and

---

38. For an analysis of this unity of intrinsic and extrinsic music in a *tz'u* by Wen T'ing-yün, see my "Intrinsic Music in the Medieval Chinese Lyric," pp. 38–42.

39. Susanne K. Langer, *Philosophy in a New Key* (New York: New American Library, 1951), p. 202.

40. Hsia Ch'eng-t'ao, "T'ang Sung tz'u tzu-sheng chih yen-pien," in idem, *T'ang Sung tz'u lun-ts'ung* (Peking: Chung-hua shu-chü, 1962), p. 53. Shih I-tui mentions that in an unpublished manuscript the contemporary scholar Sheng P'ei has presented many new findings concerning the use of the four tones in the early song lyric that correct some of Hsia Ch'eng-t'ao's observations. I hope that Sheng P'ei's manuscript, titled *Tz'u-tiao ting-lü*, will be published soon. For Shih I-tui's brief discussion of Sheng P'ei's work, see his "Chien-kuo i-lai hsin-k'an tz'u-chi hui-p'ing," *Wen-hsüeh i-ch'an* 1984, no. 3:134–35.

41. Jen Erh-pei, *Tun-huang ch'ü ch'u-t'an*, pp. 91–92, 111–12.

that some of their song lyrics could have been composed as early as the High T'ang (712–65).[42] Moreover, attention to distinctions among the four tones—rather than simply between level and oblique properties—can also be discerned occasionally in the Tun-huang song lyrics.[43] It is probably fair to say that these popular songwriters were the first to attempt to bring music and lyrics closer together and that after Wen T'ing-yün, late T'ang, Five Dynasties, and early Sung literati poets who were concerned with both poetry and music also began to pay attention to the level/oblique distinction in their song lyrics. From the late eleventh century onward, Sung poets who had dual competence in poetry and music began to observe not only the level and oblique properties, but also the distinctions among the four tones as well as the timbre of the sounds of Chinese, such as initials, finals, and allotones. I will discuss some of these developments during the Sung dynasty later in this paper.

In terms of the song lyric's intrinsic music, the mid-ninth century is significant in yet another respect. Before this time, the *tz'u* poetry written by literati "was greatly conditioned by the poetics of the *chüeh-chü* quatrain."[44] Literati poets of the early ninth century generally selected metrical patterns that were identical or very close to the patterns of the seven-character quatrain. After that date, however, literati poets began to write lyrics in accordance with a wider variety of metrical patterns, especially the two-stanza *hsiao-ling* (short song) forms of the *tsa-yen*, or "mixed meter," type. Although ninth-century poets did not adopt the longer metrical patterns available in the popular song lyric tradition, they had moved significantly away from the tradition of the highly regular recent-style verse and toward the development of unique structural principles for this new kind of poetry.

The mid-ninth century also saw the narrowing of subject matter in the song lyric of the literati tradition. The popular song lyrics preserved in the Tun-huang caves encompass a wide range of subjects. We find among them descriptions of war, conscription, frontier hardships, social injustice, the ambitions and frustrations of young students, and the quiet pleasures of the recluse, as well as Buddhist religious hymns,

---

42. Ibid., pp. 228–31.

43. Jen Pan-t'ang has observed that in all four song lyrics set to the tune "P'o chen-tzu" (which he believes to have been written in the High T'ang period) preserved in the *Yün-yao chi*, the two words that end each stanza are consistently words in "departing-level" tones. See his *T'ang sheng-shih*, p. 158.

44. Kang-i Sun Chang, *The Evolution of Chinese Tz'u Poetry*, p. 26.

physicians' mnemonic rhymes, and so forth.[45] As Wang Chung-min, a modern expert on songs from Tun-huang, notes, "Those pieces that depict boudoir sentiments and 'flowers and willows' [i.e., courtesans] do not amount to even half of the entire corpus."[46] This thematic situation contrasts sharply with that of the literati song lyrics included in the *Hua-chien chi*, which are concerned almost exclusively with the theme of love.[47]

Thematically, then, poets of the *Hua-chien chi* were "following the conventions established by the *kung-t'i-shih* or Palace Style poetry."[48] Since the pieces depicting "boudoir sentiments and 'flowers and willows'" already constitute a fairly large portion of the Tun-huang songs,[49] it can be said that the *Hua-chien chi* poets simply were drawn to the theme of love and made it their predominant subject matter.[50] But once "boudoir sentiments" (*kuei-ch'ing*) and "amorous feelings" (*yen-ch'ing*) were isolated as favorite subjects, they remained one of the most enduring elements of the "intrinsic genre," to borrow Hirsch's useful term, of the song lyric. A remark by Shen I-fu of the late Sung can be cited to support this observation: "Writing *tz'u* is different from writing *shih*. Even if the subject is flowers, one should still make use of feelings of love, or somehow involve boudoir sentiments. . . . If one only writes directly about flowers without employing any amorous or sensual words [*yen-yü*], he is not abiding by the rules of the songwriter."[51] In the hands of the literati poets of the ninth century, the song lyric was indeed transformed from its original popular song form into a medium used almost exclusively for the expression of love, displaying the common features of sensuality, narrowness, intimacy, delicacy, and ornateness (*yen, hsia, shen,*

---

45. Ibid., pp. 18–19; see also Wang Chung-min, *Tun-huang ch'ü-tzu-tz'u* (Shanghai: Shang-wu yin-shu-kuan, 1950), p. 8. For a fuller discussion of the subject matter of Tun-huang *tz'u* songs, see Lin Mei-i, "Lun Tun-huang ch'ü ti she-hui hsing" in idem, *Tz'u-hsüeh k'ao-ch'üan* (Taipei: Lien-ching ch'u-pan shih-yeh kung-ssu, 1987), pp. 45–86.

46. Wang Chung-min, *Tun-huang ch'ü-tzu-tz'u*, p. 8.

47. Kang-i Sun Chang, *The Evolution of Chinese* Tz'u *Poetry*, p. 18.

48. Ibid.

49. Although songs exploring these themes do not make up half of the corpus, they are still quite large in number when compared to songs on other themes. Yang Hai-ming has observed this in his book *T'ang Sung tz'u feng-ko lun* (Shanghai: She-hui-k'o-hsüeh-yüan ch'u-pan-she, 1986), p. 33.

50. Yü P'ing-po has made this observation in the preface to his book *T'ang Sung tz'u-hsüan*, which is collected in *Tz'u-hsüeh yen-chiu lun-wen-chi (1949–1979 nien)*, ed. Hua-tung ta-hsüeh Chung-wen-hsi ku-tien wen-hsüeh yen-chiu-shih (Shanghai: Shang-hai ku-chi ch'u-pan-she, 1982). See his comment on p. 149.

51. Shen I-fu, *Yüeh-fu chih-mi*, in T'ang Kuei-chang, *Tz'u-hua ts'ung-pien*, 1:233.

wan, mei).[52] For a long time after the mid-ninth century, even though individual poets did continue to develop their personal styles, these characteristics remained intrinsic to the genre.

Wei Chuang (836–910), for instance, usually employed the explicit mode of the first-person speaker—in the voice of either a man or a woman—in his song lyrics, in contrast to Wen T'ing-yün's preference for the implicit mode of presentation.[53] Wei effectively turned the song form into a direct, personal lyric. But his song lyrics are as narrowly restricted as those of Wen T'ing-yün to the description of the experiences of love. Feng Yen-ssu (903–60) was especially skillful in revealing delicate emotions in finely crafted images of nature. Yet the emotions revealed are also usually those of women separated from their beloved. Even in the powerful short songs from the last years of Li Yü's (937–78) life, the pain he suffered from having lost his kingdom is still expressed chiefly through the themes of separation, love, and reminiscences of his past life of indulgence. It is true that, compared with the works by other early literati poets, Li Yü's song lyrics are certainly characterized by his passionate nature and expansive, articulate energy, and they definitely influenced the *hao-fang*, or "heroic abandon," type of songs developed later in the Northern Sung, as Yeh Chia-ying has observed.[54] Li Yü's *hsiao-ling*, however, did not abandon the "obsession" with the amorous and the sensual that characterized the song lyric of the late T'ang and the Five Dynasties.

A NEW AESTHETICS OF *TZ'U*

By the beginning of the Sung dynasty, then, a distinctive *tz'u* aesthetics had already appeared, different from that of *shih* poetry in both formal and thematic aspects. The popular song lyrics from Tun-huang can still be subsumed under the broad, traditional definition of the function of poetry—*shih yen chih*, or "poetry expresses what preoccupies the mind"—but the function of the newly established literati song lyrics are perhaps better, and more narrowly, defined by the phrase *tz'u yen ch'ing*, "song lyrics express a person's innermost feelings." Traditionally, the

52. Many scholars have commented on these characteristics of early *tz'u*, but the most comprehensive review is perhaps that found in Yang Hai-ming, *T'ang Sung tz'u feng-ko-lun*, esp. pp. 12–29.

53. See Kang-i Sun Chang's discussion "The Rhetoric of *Tz'u*: Implicit Meaning versus Explicit Meaning" in her *Evolution of Chinese* Tz'u *Poetry*, pp. 35–62.

54. Yeh Chia-ying, *T'ang Sung ming-chia tz'u shang-hsi*, vol. 1, *Wen T'ing-yün, Wei Chuang, Feng Yen-ssu, Li Yü* (Taipei: Ta-an ch'u-pan-she, 1988), p. 175.

concept of *chih*—"what preoccupies the mind"—actually included *ch'ing* and referred to the entire spectrum of a person's inner life. In the context of the song lyric, however, *ch'ing* usually refers to the delicate and more subtle, complex and private aspects of a person's thoughts and feelings, of which the tender emotions associated with the experiences of love are most representative.[55] With the increasing sophistication of the song lyric form in the Northern Sung, a division of labor gradually came about. The song lyric was widely considered to be the appropriate form in which a poet's tender and subtle states of emotion and awareness could be expressed, while *shih* poetry continued to be the form employed for the expression of *chih*, or all the other aspects of a person's emotional and intellectual life.[56] This division of labor was related not only to the fundamental differences between the forms, but also to the special direction in which literati *tz'u* had been developing since the late T'ang.

Sung poets of the late tenth and early eleventh centuries, such as the *hsiao-ling* masters Chang Hsien (990–1078), Yen Shu (991–1055), Sung Ch'i (998–1061), and Ou-yang Hsiu (1007–72), essentially continued the tradition established for the song lyric by the late T'ang and Five Dynasties poets. As in the earlier periods, with some exceptions, the song lyrics of the early Sung were considered primarily as works composed for the purpose of entertaining guests at banquets, rather than as poetry written for the purpose of self-expression.[57] To be sure, these early Sung poets refined the language of the song lyric while they infused it with a certain degree of philosophical depth. Nonetheless, "boudoir sentiments" and "amorous and sensual feelings" remained the dominant subject matter of song lyrics of the *ling* type, and early Sung *tz'u* consequently continued to be characterized by softness, sensuality, and ornateness. The mutability of life and things, lovesickness, resentment against separation from one's beloved and the desire for reunion, lamentation for the passing of spring or of joyful events were common themes found in early Sung song lyrics,[58] themes that were treated in a gentle, delicate, intimate, subtle, or indirect manner.[59]

In the "hierarchy" of literary forms in Northern Sung times, *tz'u* was

55. Yang Hai-ming has discussed this in his *T'ang Sung tz'u feng-ko-lun*, pp. 37, 137.

56. Ibid., pp. 136–37.

57. Kao Chien-chung, "Shih-lun liang Sung wan-yüeh-tz'u ti li-shih ti-wei," p. 131.

58. Feng Ch'i-yung has provided an excellent discussion of the common characteristics of early Sung *tz'u* poetry in his article "Lun Pei-Sung ch'ien-ch'i liang-chung pu-t'ung ti tz'u-feng," in *Tz'u-hsüeh yen-chiu lun-wen-chi*, ed. Hua-tung ta-hsüeh Chung-wen-hsi ku-tien wen-hsüeh yen-chiu-shih (Shanghai: Shang-hai ku-chi ch'u-pan-she, 1982), esp. p. 188.

59. Ibid.

ranked lower than both *shih* and *wen* (prose). The genre was usually referred to as *hsiao-tz'u* or *hsiao ko-tz'u*, that is, with the somewhat pejorative adjective *hsiao*, "little" or "trivial," added to the appellation *tz'u*,
"song lyric."[60] Interestingly, because of this low position *tz'u* occupied
in the literary hierarchy, scholars were not always severely frowned
upon for writing sentimental and sensual song lyrics. Within certain
reasonable limits, it was acceptable for a prominent scholar-statesman
such as Yen Shu to "speak like a woman" sometimes in his *tz'u* poetry.[61]
This could not have been the case unless "femininity" and "sensuality"
were regarded, even if only unconsciously at this stage, as intrinsic
properties of the genre.[62]

LIU YUNG AND *MAN-TZ'U*

Concurrent with the evolution of this new aesthetics were two developments in early Sung *tz'u* that eventually led poets active during the late
eleventh and early twelfth centuries to an increased awareness of the
self-identity of the genre. One was the refinement of the *man-tz'u*, the
longer form of the song lyric. Although song lyrics of the *man* type had
actually appeared in the T'ang dynasty, they were largely centered in
the popular tradition and were only occasionally experimented with by
a few late T'ang and Five Dynasties literati poets.[63] This longer song
form presumably continued to exist in the popular tradition but was
largely ignored by literati poets until the eleventh century. The early
Sung *hsiao-ling* master Chang Hsien was among the first of the literati to
experiment with the longer form. His *man-tz'u* usually excelled in the
"imagistic elegance" that was typical of his *hsiao-ling* poems, but they
lacked the narrative and "sequential progression" characteristic of the
longer song lyrics composed by later poets.[64]

60. The term *hsiao-tz'u*, for instance, can be found in Ou-yang Hsiu's *Kuei-t'ien lu*,
chüan 2. Ou-yang Hsiu mentions in this book that the scholar-official Ch'ien Wei-yen
read *hsiao-tz'u* only in the privy! Ou-yang Hsiu's remark is quoted in Wu Hsiung-ho,
T'ang Sung tz'u t'ung-lun, p. 288. The term *hsiao ko-tz'u* can be found in Li Ch'ing-chao's
"Tz'u lun." See Huang Mo-ku, *Ch'ung-chi Li Ch'ing-chao chi*, p.57.

61. P'u Ch'uan-cheng referred to some *tz'u* songs by Yen Shu as "women's words"
(*fu-jen yü*). P'u's remark is recorded in Hu Tzu, *T'iao-hsi yü-yin ts'ung-hua—ch'ien-chi* (rpt.,
Taipei: Shih-chieh shu-chü, 1966) 26:176.

62. Yang Hai-ming has discussed these two intrinsic properties in his *T'ang Sung tz'u
feng-ko-lun*, p. 135. For a related discussion, see Grace Fong's chapter in this volume.

63. Kang-i Sun Chang, *The Evolution of Chinese* Tz'u *Poetry*, p. 123.

64. See Kang-i Sun Chang's discussion of Chang Hsien's *man-tz'u* in ibid., pp.
153–54.

A contemporary of Chang Hsien, Liu Yung was the first major literati poet to devote much energy to developing and refining the *man-tz'u*,
one of his many significant contributions to the development of *tz'u*
poetry. He was the only early Sung poet to have used a very large number of tunes and metrical patterns, manipulating a great variety of
forms for the expression of his feelings and experiences. In terms of intrinsic music, he was the first to observe the distinctions among all four
tones, paying special attention to the rising, departing, and entering
tones.[65] Liu Yung substantially broadened the song lyric's subject matter as well, writing about the lives of urban dwellers and prostitutes, his
own relationships with courtesans, the frustrations of the failed scholar,
and the hardships of a wandering one. Lovesickness and the pain of
separation still constituted the main themes of his song lyrics, but they
were often treated from the poet's own perspective as a man in love,
rather than from the assumed perspective of an abandoned woman
(although Liu Yung by no means relinquished this conventional
strategy entirely). Here Liu Yung continued the fine tradition of the
direct, personal song lyric established by Wei Chuang and Li Yü.

Liu Yung's most revolutionary contributions probably lay in his dar-
ing use of the colloquial, and sometimes unpolished or even "vulgar,"
expressions of the common people of the urban centers and in his development of the aesthetics of the *man* song lyric. His equal competence
in poetry and music won the praise of Li Ch'ing-chao, but his sometimes extreme use of colloquial language received harsh ridicule from
her: "The language of his *tz'u* can be as low as dust," she remarked.[66]
The use of colloquial language was, of course, not new to the song lyric,
for it was a feature of the popular lyrics from Tun-huang, and Li
Ch'ing-chao herself was in fact also fond of using colloquial expressions.
What she disliked in Liu Yung's language, therefore, was not its collo-
quialism as such, but the lack of polish and refinement present in some
aspects of his colloquial expressions. Although he wrote a fair number of
hsiao-ling, his most startling achievements are to be found in his song
lyrics in the longer *man-tz'u* form.

Liu Yung was the first *tz'u* poet to develop the technique of *p'u-hsü*, or
"extensive description and narration." This technique is what separates
his *man-tz'u* from his contemporary Chang Hsien's and from his and
other masters' *hsiao-ling*. While focusing still on lyrical expression, Liu
Yung's *man-tz'u* manifest dynamic and complex descriptive and narrative structures. Liu Yung was the first poet to use a large number of

---

65. Hsia Ch'eng-t'ao, "T'ang Sung tz'u tzu-sheng chih yen-pien," pp. 58–66.
66. Huang Mo-ku, *Ch'ung-chi Li Ch'ing-chao chi*, p. 56.

ling-chü tzu (literally, "line-leading words"), which were occasionally found in the Tun-huang lyrics.[67] Consisting of one character, or two or three, a *ling-chü tzu* could be a verb, an adverb, or an adjective appearing at the beginning of a line or group of lines. These "line-leading words" performed a special descriptive and adverbial function by unifying clusters of images, emotive expressions, and descriptive or narrative phrases into a continuous whole. They proved essential in producing a continuous, flexible, and dynamic rhythm in the *man-tz'u* and were generally used at transitional points in the song lyrics. Thus, line-leading words increased rhythmic flexibility, enhanced semantic continuity, and highlighted the distinct turns in the complex unfolding of the poet's feelings. They helped the poet portray his emotions in a manner more exhaustive than that permitted by the short and comparatively regular framework of the *ling*.[68] Through all of these techniques, therefore, Liu Yung established the distinctive aesthetics of the *man-tz'u*: the rendering of tender, complex, or powerful human feelings into a dynamic, wavelike process or rhythm. Many of his *man-tz'u* illustrate well Chiang K'uei's (ca. 1155–1221) definition of *tz'u* as "that which gives full expression to feelings in a roundabout manner" (*wei-ch'ü chin-ch'ing*).[69] One can say that the potential of the *tz'u* genre (with its intricate, irregular structure) as a lyrical form for self-expression was finally fully realized in the hands of Liu Yung.

THE CONTRIBUTION OF SU SHIH

Liu Yung's influence on the poets of the late Northern Sung was great, even if he sometimes served mainly as a popular model for poets to react against. Indeed, by the standards of the literati tradition, much of Liu Yung's colloquial language and many of his song lyrics about courtesans could be judged as "vulgar" and lowbrow. Despite the popularity of his song lyrics, therefore, Liu Yung was often a target of criticism in the late eleventh century, and Su Shih (1037–1101) the most important and vigorous critic of his popular style. Su Shih criticized Ch'in Kuan (1049–1100) for imitating Liu Yung,[70] and he prided himself on

67. For a useful discussion of Liu Yung's use of "line-leading words," see Kang-i Sun Chang, *The Evolution of Chinese* Tz'u *Poetry*, pp. 123–47.

68. For a general discussion of the function of "line-leading words," see my *Transformation of the Chinese Lyrical Tradition*, pp. 133–41.

69. Hsia Ch'eng-t'ao, ed., *Po-shih shih-tz'u chi* (Peking: Jen-min wen-hsüeh ch'u-pan-she, 1959), p. 67.

70. See *Kao-chai shih-hua*, as cited in Lung Mu-hsün, ed., *T'ang Sung ming-chia tz'u-hsüan* (rpt. Taipei: Ho-lo t'u-shu ch'u-pan-she, 1975), p. 142.

not manifesting any of the earlier poet's characteristics in his own song lyrics.[71] Su's self-conscious attempt to avoid writing in the popular style of Liu Yung enhanced awareness among his contemporaries of the nature of the song lyric and fostered the second major development in Northern Sung *tz'u*: the attempt to create a new, hard, and vigorous language for the form.

Su Shih himself had been a latecomer to this "lower" form of poetry, having begun to write song lyrics in 1072 when he was a full thirty-five years old[72] and had already established a reputation as an accomplished *shih* poet. His new interest in the song lyric was most probably connected with his acquaintance with the senior poet Chang Hsien. He wrote his first song lyric during his first year as a local official in Hangchow, where Chang Hsien spent his last years leading an extravagant life.

In an effort to elevate the *tz'u* from the popular and sometimes "vulgar" status established by Liu Yung, Su Shih frequently compared it to *yüeh-fu* and *shih*.[73] In a letter to Ch'en Chi-ch'ang, for example, he wrote, "Every line in the new song lyrics you sent me is extraordinary. They are the strong works of a *shih* poet, not just 'little songs.'"[74] In his colophon to Chang Hsien's collection of *shih* poetry, he wrote, "The brush Chang Hsien uses for writing *shih* is well seasoned and marvelous; his 'song words' represent nothing but residual skills [from his *shih* writing]."[75] And Su Shih was probably the first scholar openly to correct the traditional disparaging attitude toward the song lyric by comparing it to forms that had hitherto occupied higher positions in the hierarchy of genres.

In the actual practice of writing song lyrics, Su Shih himself was also noted for "treating *tz'u* as *shih*" (*i shih wei tz'u*),[76] a statement having several important implications. First, it most basically means that Su

71. See his "Yü Hsien-yü Tzu-chün shu," as cited in Wu Hsiung-ho, *T'ang Sung tz'u t'ung-lun*, p. 290.

72. Kang-i Sun Chang, *The Evolution of Chinese* Tz'u *Poetry*, pp. 15 and 169.

73. Wu Hsiung-ho, *T'ang Sung tz'u t'ung-lun*, p. 289.

74. "Ta Ch'en Chi-ch'ang shu," as cited in Wu Hsiung-ho, *T'ang Sung tz'u t'ung-lun*, p. 289.

75. "T'i Chang Tzu-yeh shih-chi hou," as cited in Wu Hsiung-ho, *T'ang Sung tz'u t'ung lun*, p. 289.

76. This appears in a remark on Su Shih's *tz'u* attributed to Ch'en Shih-tao and recorded in *Hou-shan shih-hua*. Lu Yu (1125–1210) of the Southern Sung doubted the authenticity of this remark. Nonetheless, Wu Hsiung-ho convincingly points out that Su Shih's younger contemporaries, such as Ch'ao Pu-chih and Chang Lei, made similar statements about Su Shih's *tz'u* poetry. See the citation of this remark and a brief discussion of related issues in Wu Hsiung-ho, *T'ang Sung tz'u t'ung-lun*, pp. 289–90.

Shih applied techniques commonly used in *shih* poetry to his song lyrics. As Kang-i Sun Chang has pointed out, "in composing his longer *man-tz'u* poems Su Shih borrowed a number of poetic devices from his own Ancient Style poetry, whereas his shorter *hsiao-ling* poems were often influenced by the poetics of Recent Style poetry."[77] Second, Su Shih made some changes in the fundamental conception of *tz'u* as a genre. He liberated *tz'u* somewhat from its previous obsession with "boudoir sentiments" and "amorous and sensual feelings" and made it almost as versatile as *shih* in depicting the whole range of experience.[78] Like Liu Yung, therefore, he can be credited with having broadened the potential subject matter for the song lyric, but Su moved in a quite different direction, steering the form closer toward the *yen-chih* tradition associated with *shih* poetry. He did not, however, completely blur the generic boundaries between *shih* and *tz'u*, for the division of labor can still be discerned in his own poetry. He seemed "to have reserved the *tz'u* form for expressing complex innermost feelings, and the *shih* for dealing with miscellaneous types of expression—for example, argumentation, social comment, and occasional writing."[79] Third, since *shih* poetry was not associated with a musical setting, Su Shih's approach in "treating *tz'u* as *shih*" often destroyed the distinctive intrinsic music that previous masters had evolved in their efforts to adapt the song words to the structure and tonality of banquet music. Although Su Shih was not entirely ignorant of music, he was not an accomplished musician like Wen T'ing-yün, Liu Yung, or Chou Pang-yen (1056–1121). He was, in fact, considered by some as being by nature too much of a free spirit ever to allow his poetic imagination to be restricted by the framework of music.[80] Moreover, Su Shih not only used strong and vigorous (instead of the conventional soft and delicate) language to write song lyrics, he also asked strong men (rather than the usual gentle singing girls) to sing them.[81] As a result, the conventional emphasis on the intrinsic femininity and delicate and gentle restraint of the song lyric was displaced, and

77. *The Evolution of Chinese* Tz'u *Poetry*, p. 170. The chapter on Su Shih, pp. 158–206, is also full of useful insights into the relationship between his *tz'u* and *shih*.

78. Shih I-tui points out that about one-third of Su Shih's 345 *tz'u* are related to singing girls and that among these songs, about forty were verifiably written expressly for these entertainers. See his article "Chien-kuo i-lai tz'u-hsüeh yen-chiu shu-p'ing" in *Chung-kuo she-hui k'o-hsüeh* 1984, no. 1:159.

79. Kang-i Sun Chang, *The Evolution of Chinese* Tz'u *Poetry*, p. 170.

80. Su Shih's younger contemporary Ch'ao Pu-chih said that Su Shih was "someone who naturally cannot be bound by tunes." See his comment in *P'ing pen-ch'ao yüeh-chang*, as cited in Wu Hsiung-ho, *T'ang Sung tz'u t'ung-lun*, p. 293.

81. Kang-i Sun Chang, *The Evolution of Chinese* Tz'u *Poetry*, p. 160.

a new style of *tz'u*, later termed the *hao-fang*, or "heroic abandon" style, was finally developed in the hands of the poet and scholar-statesman Su Shih.[82]

Before Su Shih established the *hao-fang* mode, only a handful of song lyrics by Fan Chung-yen (989–1052) and Wang An-shih (1021–86) had displayed thematic and stylistic traits differing significantly from the conventional works of the early Sung poets. Fan Chung-yen's "Yü-chia ao," recalling his own experiences of hardship on the frontier, and Wang An-shih's "Kuei-chih hsiang," his reminiscences of Nanking's past, are particularly important instances of breaking away from the "boudoir sentiments" and "amorous and sensual feelings" of the literati tradition. These two poems resemble Li Yü's works in their expansive, articulate energy; at the same time they also represent an attempt to re-turn the song lyric to the *shih yen chih* tradition that had been neglected by literati poets since Wen T'ing-yün's time. The return of the song lyric to the traditional, broader concept of *shih yen chih*, however, was not complete until Su Shih made the *tz'u* form capable of expressing almost any idea and describing almost any subject.[83]

Although Su Shih succeeded in elevating the song lyric from a lesser song form to a major poetic genre, his contemporaries were quick to observe that the original identity of *tz'u* had been lost in his works. Ch'en Shih-tao (1053–1101), for instance, is believed to have remarked, "Tzu-chan [Su Shih] treats *tz'u* as *shih*. . . . Although his works are ex-ceptionally skillful, they are not in the 'natural color' [*pen-se*, that is, orig-inal characteristics of the genre]."[84] Ch'ao Pu-chih (1053–1110), after having referred to Su Shih as someone who ignored the musical aspect of the song lyric because he would not be restrained by it, commented, "Huang Lu-chih [Huang T'ing-chien, 1045–1105] occasionally made 'little song lyrics.' Although they are lofty and marvelous, they do not contain the 'expression of a professional' [*tang hang-chia yü*]. They are

82. The distinction between the *wan-yüeh*, or "delicate restraint," and the *hao-fang*, or "heroic abandon," schools of *tz'u* poetry was made by the Ming scholar Chang Yen. Sung scholars such as Ch'ao I-tao, Chu Pien, and Shen I-fu, however, had already used the term *hao-fang* to refer to Su Shih's song lyrics. See Yang Hai-ming, *T'ang Sung tz'u feng-ko-lun*, p. 139. Here I follow Kang-i Sun Chang's translations of the two terms; see her *Evolution of Chinese Tz'u Poetry*, pp. 160 and 205.

83. Liu Hsi-tsai says, "There is no idea he [Su Shih] cannot express and no event he cannot put [into his *tz'u* poetry]" (*wu i pu-k'o-ju, wu shih pu-k'o-yen*). See his *I kai* (Shang-hai: Shang-hai ku-chi ch'u-pan-she, 1978) 4:108.

84. See the remark mentioned above that is attributed to Ch'en Shih-tao in the *Hou-shan shih-hua*, as cited in Wu Hsiung-ho, *T'ang Sung tz'u t'ung-lun*, p. 292.

shih poems that have been set to tunes for singing."[85] Within the overall context of the passage, this brief comment on Huang T'ing-chien clearly applies to Su Shih's song lyrics as well.

BOUNDARIES OF GENRE

By the late eleventh and early twelfth centuries, there was a clear consensus among the majority of literary scholars that *shih* and *tz'u* each possessed its own set of intrinsic characteristics that were to be kept distinct from each other. In point of fact, Li Chih-i, who was active at the turn of the twelfth century, came very close to defining the generic identity of *tz'u* when he said, "Choosing words well is most difficult in the *ch'ang-tuan-chü* ['long and short lines,' a common synonym for *tz'u*] because it has its own style. If one deviates even slightly from the style, awkwardness and disharmony will ensue."[86] Granted that his idea that *tz'u* "has its own style" is based chiefly on his observation concerning diction, Li Chih-i's keen sense of the form's generic identity cannot be doubted.

The increasing critical awareness of the identity of *tz'u* as a distinct genre in the minds of the literati of the late Northern Sung can be related to the remarkable achievements of Liu Yung and Su Shih. It was Liu Yung who established the *man-tz'u*, so radically different from *shih*. Despite its fundamental difference from *shih*, the *hsiao-ling* still carried traits—such as "imagistic elegance," relative balance in framework, and subtlety of expression—that could be found in the older and well-established genre. Liu Yung's *man-tz'u*, however, compelled readers and audiences to become more keenly aware of the differences between the two poetic genres, *shih* and *tz'u*. And Su Shih's method of "treating *tz'u* as *shih*" in order to realize his ideal of less inhibited but more vigorous lyrical expression challenged his contemporaries to reflect upon the distinguishing characteristics that had heretofore defined the two poetic forms, if only implicitly. By the turn of the eleventh century, the generic identity of *tz'u* had largely been formed, even though a full articulation of it was not made until a decade or two later with Li Ch'ing-chao's "Critique of the Song Lyric."

85. See the passage in *P'ing pen-ch'ao yüeh-chang*, as cited in Wu Hsiung-ho, *T'ang Sung tz'u t'ung-lun*, pp. 292–93.

86. See *Pa Wu Ssu-tao hsiao-tz'u*, as cited in Wu Hsiung-ho, *T'ang Sung tz'u t'ung-lun*, p. 294.

LI CH'ING-CHAO'S SUMMATION

In an age of cultural florescence like the late Northern Sung, important new developments could easily take shape within a few years. Thus, in addition to being a fuller treatment of the generic identity of *tz'u*, "A Critique of the Song Lyric" also presented in its conception of genre new developments not yet discussed by such scholars as Ch'en Shih-tao and Li Chih-i. While Su Shih was moving in the direction of "heroic abandon," other poets of the late Northern Sung—notably Yen Chi-tao (1141–1119?), Huang T'ing-chien, Ch'in Kuan, Ho Chu (1052–1125), and Chou Pang-yen—were trying to perfect the finer points of the art of the song lyric within the orthodox tradition of "delicate restraint." Of particular relevance was the meticulous attention Su Shih's younger contemporaries paid to the coordination of the sounds of words and the tunes of banquet music. In 1105 the Bureau of Grand Music (*ta-sheng fu*) was instituted by Emperor Hui-tsung (r. 1101–25), imperial patron of the arts, to encourage the study and cultivation of music. Such contemporary developments were paralleled by the interest of many scholars active during the last decades of the Northern Sung in refining the intrinsic music of the song lyric, a trend that is clearly reflected in "A Critique of the Song Lyric."

In discussing the aesthetics of the song lyric, Li Ch'ing-chao places foremost importance on music, arguing that it is the intrinsic music of the *tz'u* that constitutes the very identity of the genre:

> In *shih* poetry and in prose one has to observe the distinction between level and oblique tones only. In the song lyric, however, one has to distinguish the five sounds [labial, dental, glottal, apical, and nasal], the five notes [*kung* (do), *shang* (re), *chüeh* (mi), *chih* (sol), *yü* (la)], the six upper pitch-pipes, and the clear and the turbid as well as the light and the heavy [allotones induced by voiceless or voiced initials, respectively]. Moreover, in recent days, in the so-called "Sheng-sheng man," "Yü-chung hua," and "Hsi ch'ien ying," one can use rhymes not only in the level tone but also in the oblique tones. The rhyme in "Yü-lou ch'un" is originally in the level tone, but it can also be in the rising, departing, or entering tone. If one uses a rhyme in the rising tone when [a metrical pattern] originally uses a rhyme in the oblique tone, the song lyric will have harmony; but if one uses a rhyme in the entering tone, the song lyric will not bear singing.[87]

No discussion of the song lyric prior to Li Ch'ing-chao's "Critique" had paid such attention to the details of initials, rhymes, tones, and

87. Huang Mo-ku, *Ch'ung-chi Li Ch'ing-chao chi*, p. 57.

notes in music as illustrated in the passage above. Li Ch'ing-chao's terse comments on these fine points of *tz'u* prosody and music might have made immediate sense to her contemporaries, but they are opaque to the modern reader. Today, before any definite conclusions could be drawn concerning the precise relationship between words and music in the song lyric, a vast amount of research would be required both into the nature of the sounds and four tones of Late Middle Chinese as well as into the tonal patterns of *tz'u* by poets who had equal competence in music and poetry.[88] Given that little banquet music has survived, I doubt that the real situation will ever be known. In any case, for our purposes here it is important to realize that the attempt to work out a precise correspondence between words and music was a new development in the late Northern Sung and that Li Ch'ing-chao had already made use of it as a criterion in differentiating *tz'u* from *shih*.

Some of Li Ch'ing-chao's statements in the passage quoted above can still be tested in her own *tz'u* poetry. For instance, in her song lyric set to the tune "Sheng-sheng man" (which begins with the line *Hsün-hsün mi-mi*, or "Seek, seek, search, search," and is discussed by Stephen Owen at length elsewhere in this volume), she uses fifteen apical and forty-two dental sounds as well as a number of words sharing initials or finals. The result of her effort is a song lyric remarkably rich in sound effects. Although we can tell that the sound aspect of this lyric is a precise echo of its sense, we have no way of knowing exactly how the sound and rhythm of the text harmonize with the tune to which it is set, since we no longer have the music.

Li Ch'ing-chao also appears to be an extremely tough critic in her essay on the song lyric, and no poet mentioned emerges completely unscathed from her evaluations. In her view, total compliance with the structure of banquet music was an essential requirement in writing *tz'u* that would "constitute its own household" distinct from *shih*. Thus, she observes that well-known writers such as Chang Hsien and Sung Ch'i often produce marvelous expressions but that their song lyrics usually suffer from fragmentation. She further notes that the song lyrics by Yen Shu, Ou-yang Hsiu, and Su Shih (in which the intrinsic music often does not correspond to the extrinsic music) are in reality all *shih* poems with uneven lines. Similarly, the song lyrics of Wang An-shih and Tseng Kung resemble their prose works. Of the well-known Sung poets who also wrote in the song lyric form, only Liu Yung, Yen Chi-tao, Ho Chu, Ch'in Kuan, and Huang T'ing-chien are regarded as understand-

---

88. For a preliminary attempt, please see my "Intrinsic Music in the Medieval Chinese Lyric," esp. pp. 43–53.

ing the form's generic identity. Nevertheless, they all fall short in one re-spect or another as ideal practitioners of the genre. Liu Yung's language she considers "vulgar"; Yen Chi-tao suffers from a lack of *p'u-hsü*, the technique of "extensive description and narration"; Ho Chu falls short in not having a "classic weightiness" (*tien-chung*); Ch'in Kuan focuses on "emotional import" (*ch'ing-chih*) but lacks "allusive substance" (*ku-shih*); and although Huang T'ing-chien has "allusive substance," he displays many other flaws. It is obvious that Li Ch'ing-chao applies a certain sense of decorum to her evaluation of the language of these writers of the song lyric. But although the *p'u-hsü* technique was first developed by Liu Yung in the song lyric, it had been extensively used in rhymeprose for some time.[89] And the other qualities or failings she cites can be found in earlier criticism of *shih* poetry or prose.[90] It seems, therefore, that Li Ch'ing-chao might permit a certain "mixing of genres" in some areas of *tz'u* poetics as well.

Modern scholars have generally been baffled by Li Ch'ing-chao's glaring omission in her essay of any reference to Chou Pang-yen, the major Northern Sung poet and musician who synthesized virtually all previous styles of the song lyric into his own. She does mention Ch'ao Tz'u-ying, an evidently well-known songwriter and an official at the Bureau of Grand Music, of which Chou Pang-yen was once superinten-dent. Why does she discuss the works of a less accomplished writer or even of little-known figures such as Sung Hsiang (Sung Ch'i's brother), Shen T'ang, and Yüan Chiang, but not the truly major poet of the time? Perhaps Li Ch'ing-chao was not aware of Chou Pang-yen's achieve-ments when she wrote her "Critique of the Song Lyric."[91] Or perhaps the omission of Chou Pang-yen indicates that Li Ch'ing-chao found it difficult to criticize him.[92] Indeed, Chou Pang-yen's song lyrics do not

89. I am grateful to David Knechtges for pointing this out at the conference.

90. For instance, the term *ku-shih* is used by Liu Hsieh in the "T'ung-pien" chapter of *Wen-hsin tiao-lung* in a discussion of *wen*; see Chou Chen-fu, ed., *Wen-hsin tiao-lung chu-shih* (Peking: Jen-min wen-hsüeh ch'u-pan-she, 1981), p. 330. Yin Fan also uses this term in a discussion of Meng Hao-jan's poetry; see Yin Fan, *Ho-yüeh ying-ling-chi*, in Yüan Chieh et al., *T'ang-jen hsüan T'ang-shih* (Peking: Chung-hua shu-chü, 1958), p. 91. Terms such as *tien* (usually in the compound *tien-ya*), *li*, and *i* are frequently encountered in Chinese literary and art criticism.

91. Yang Hai-ming, "Li Ch'ing-chao 'Tz'u lun' pu-t'i Chou Pang-yen ti liang-chung t'an-ts'e" in his *T'ang Sung tz'u lun-kao* (Chekiang: Ku-chi ch'u-pan-she, 1988), pp. 304–10.

92. Yeh Chia-ying has expressed this opinion in a letter to Miao Yüeh. She has also suggested that Li Ch'ing-chao might not have completely agreed with Chou Pang-yen's approach to the song lyric and therefore did not praise him in her critique. See the re-

suffer from the faults Li finds in the works of Chang Hsien, Liu Yung, Yen Shu, Ho Chu, Ch'in Kuan, and Huang T'ing-chien. He further developed the technique of *p'u-hsü* innovated by Liu Yung in a refined and elegant language with "classic weightiness" and "allusive substance," although his main subjects remained "lovesickness" and "separation." Above all, his song lyrics illustrate a perfect harmony between intrinsic and extrinsic music; as a poet, he paid closer attention to all four tones than had any previous songwriter.[93]

But however sophisticated and refined, Chou Pang-yen's works represent a synthesis of the orthodox aesthetics of the genre of the song lyric as it had developed during the Northern Sung. Although Li Ch'ing-chao's omission of him from "A Critique of the Song Lyric" is a curious one, her articulation of the characteristics of the genre marks a crucial moment in its critical history, a comprehensive awareness of its identity as a distinct literary form. Only as a result of the cumulative contributions of a number of poets could she assert, therefore, that the *tz'u* now claimed a domain of its own.

---

mark as quoted in Miao's essay "Lun Li Ch'ing-chao tz'u" in Miao Yüeh and Yeh Chia-ying, *Ling-hsi tz'u-shuo* (Shanghai: Shang-hai ku-chi ch'u-pan-she, 1987), p. 339.

93. Hsia Ch'eng-t'ao, "T'ang Sung tz'u tzu-sheng chih yen-pien."

Meaning the Words:
The Genuine as a Value in the Tradition of the Song Lyric

Stephen Owen

The word "genuine" constitutes the skeleton beneath the song lyric. When the emotions are genuine and the scene is a genuine one, whatever has been written is always excellent and it's easy to consider it complete.

K'UANG CHOU-I, *HUI-FENG TZ'U-HUA* (1936)[1]

[Note: "consider it complete," t'o-kao, "to get out of draft stage," a cliché for finishing a literary work, implying a reflective process of revision. Does this mean the lyricist revises until the words "sound" genuine, or until they "are" genuine?]

ONLY A SONG

With conscious purpose the layered curtains hide our most intimate words.

重簾有意藏私語

YEN CHI-TAO, TO "CHE-KU T'IEN"[2]

The phoenix cover and the lovebird curtain are nearby
Where I would go if I could get there.
Shrimp-whisker brushes the floor and the double doors are still.
I recognize the shuffle of embroidered slippers
Invisible in the bedroom,
Her forced laugh, her voice
Light and lovely, like a woodwind.

Her makeup done,
She idly holds a lute.
Her favorite love songs—
Into every note she seems to put her fragrant heart.
Listening outside the curtain
Gets me so much heartbreak!

1. K'uang Chou-i, *Hui-feng tz'u-hua*, ed. Wang Yao-an (Peking: Jen-min wen-hsüeh ch'u-pan-she, 1982), p. 6.
2. *Ch'üan Sung tz'u*, ed. T'ang Kuei-chang (Peking: Chung-hua shu-chü, 1965), p. 227. Hereafter *CST*.

Misery such as this
Only she could share.

咫尺鳳衾鴛帳
欲去無因到
蝦鬚窣地重門悄
認繡履頻移
洞房杳杳
強笑語
逞如簧,再三輕巧

梳妝早
琵琶閒抱
愛品相思調
聲聲似把芳心告
隔簾聽
贏得斷腸多少
恁煩惱
除非共伊知道

Liu Yung, To "Listening Outside the Curtain" ("Ko lien t'ing")[3]

Moments of accidental "overhearing" were a common motif in the song lyric: sometimes overhearing words, but often overhearing song. Words overheard were clearly not directed to the accidental listener; however, the song overheard is a more interesting case, raising many questions of whom the song words are for, if anyone, and what kind of claim they make on the heart of the singer. Overhearing song, the listener may be stirred to think on his own case, or he may feel a sudden rush of sympathy for the singer, finding himself in the ancient role of *chih-yin*, "the one who knows the tone," the person who knows how the music and the song word reveal what is in the singer's heart. In poetry we can trace this motif back to "In the Northwest There Was a Building High" ("Hsi-pei yu kao-lou") from the "Nineteen Old Poems," in which a passerby overhears a woman singing a song of sorrow for a lost or absent man and feels immediate sympathy for her. In his conclusion, however, the passerby wishes that they might become a pair of birds and fly away together—hearing a song in which a woman is longing for another man, the overhearer is both touched and attracted, and inserts himself in the place of the beloved.

Liu Yung's song is a very special mode of overhearing: it is eavesdropping. And this eavesdropper is so personally implicated in what he hears that a group of questions, usually repressed, comes to the surface

3. Translation by James R. Hightower, "The Songwriter Liu Yung," pt. 1, *Harvard Journal of Asiatic Studies* 41 (1981): 375. *CST*, p. 30.

of the lyric: how true the singer's words are, what kind of truth those words claim to have, whom the words are meant for. To the singing girl's guest on the other side of the curtain, the man who is the direct recipient of the conversation and song, these words all seem as if directed to him and true—or at least he is willing to suspend disbelief and take them as true for the moment. In this case, however, the eaves-dropper knows—or thinks he knows, or wants very much to believe—that there is a difference between true words of love and a merely con-ventional performance of love's words. There is someone else sitting in the place that he wishes to be his own. His unease at being replaced, in discovering how individuals can apparently be interchanged in what is supposed to be a very particular relationship, is somehow connected to the way in which the same song can be reperformed—for different guests, by different singers, in different circumstances. From the outside the eavesdropper discovers how fine and almost invisible is the bound-ary between "meaning it" and a skillful performance of "meaning it."

The lyric begins with the site where the unseen performance will be concluded: the invisible bed, itself named by conventional synecdoche as layers of coverings—quilt and bed-curtains—both further hidden be-hind the curtains of the room outside which he listens. Such coverings are peculiar barriers, creating a maddening closeness (*chih-ch'ih*) that cannot be crossed yet permits the clear passage of sounds, sounds whose intent and truth are uncertain, open to interpretation.

He reads the event in its sounds. First, against the stillness of the room there are the sounds of things brushing the ground: the swish of the "shrimp-whisker" fringe of an inner curtain as she enters the room, then the scraping of her slippers as she comes forward to entertain the invisible guest. That intensely audible proximity paradoxically inten-sifies his sense of his distance from her: *yao-yao*, less "invisible" than "re-mote and indistinct." The next phase of her performance is pleasant banter, laughing chitchat. Here we might observe that any sounds or words from the invisible guest are silenced in the words of *this* song, for the eavesdropper makes himself the singular audience of this intimate performance, even though he is an audience displaced, receiving sounds apparently directed toward someone else. Her voice is "forced"—or so it seems to him. Is this some quality he thinks he detects in the sounds or only an assumption he wants to make? If the guest were to become aware of such "forcedness," the performance would fail by becoming patently false. Whether compulsory performance or willing perfor-mance, her words have already become a kind of music, the "woodwind" that will complement the strings of the p'i-p'a in the next stanza. It is verbal music that is *ch'ing-ch'iao*, "light and artful": a positive quality in terms of an artisan's skill, but questionable in a human who cares.

As we move into the second stanza, she becomes as if visible— probably an inference he makes, hearing the music and knowing the set phases of the performance. He has, no doubt, been there before himself, sat in the very place the guest now sits, taken all the words as genuine, which compels him to question the genuineness of what he overhears now. The phases of the "entertainment" are a set sequence: the entrance, the conversation, the song, bed—with a coda often consisting of lover's vows that this place in the heart will be occupied by no other. Liu Yung has heard such vows and believed them.

Although the phases of the love encounter differ from one culture to another, traditions of love poetry often place special emphasis on the stage just before consummation. The penultimate phase is often the displaced double of union, sexual or spiritual, and at the same time the deferment of consummation and ending. As a medieval treatise has it, *Gradus amoris sunt hii: visus et alloquium, contactus, basia, factum* ("The phases of love are these: seeing and then talking together, touching, kisses, the act"). And there is a long tradition of classical and European poems on the penultimate phase of kissing, at once the imitation, the prelude to, and explicitly the deferment of the sexual act. In the Chinese "phases of love" the penultimate stage is usually singing; and although the lyrics often remind us that the lovers go to bed after the song is done, we should remember that this bedding is part of the lyrics of a song, at once promise and deferment.[4] Through song the woman, who is supposed to be reticent and shy, is given a voice and authorized to speak what is supposed to be heart's truth (and since these women were paid singers, to hear such songs as if they were true would be reassuring). The Chinese poetic tradition was as fascinated by the expression of female desire as the Western poetic tradition has been fascinated with male desire. Once the song has permitted the woman ritually to speak the desire that is elsewhere silenced, the couple can go to bed.

On her p'i-p'a she plays "melodies of love-longing," *hsiang-ssu tiao* (love songs), which Liu Yung claims are her "favorite type," *ai-p'in*. And at this point the conventional bedroom scene of the Chinese love song begins to go astray, revealing the motives of this man standing outside the curtain, one who believes himself to be the true lover. He knows that she likes this kind of song and by such knowledge shows his own intimacy with her. Moreover, by commenting that the song she plays

---

4. Cf. Chou Pang-yen, "Ying-ch'un yüeh" (*CST*, p. 616).

belongs to her "favorite type," the eavesdropper calls into question the truth of the words she is singing to the invisible guest, their genuineness as address—perhaps she chooses a love song at this moment because she "likes" such songs in general. But he does not know *why* she likes this kind of song—whether only because it is a song, or because she enjoys the love game, or because she cares about him.

The observation that she seems to lodge her heart in every note is even more troubling and ambiguous. He seems to hear her confiding real feeling into the song she is singing, but feeling for whom—the guest who sits before her, or for him, the absent beloved who is secretly standing outside the curtain? On another level, we are not certain how to understand the "seeming": is this a function of his perception—that it seems to him that there is true feeling in the words, though of course he cannot be sure—or is the "seeming" the quality of the performance itself, an appearance of feeling when feeling is, in fact, lacking? Song, which was supposed to be the voice for the heart's truth that must otherwise be kept veiled, here becomes the source of uncertainty and pain, heard from the other side of the curtain.

At this point the speaker explicitly positions himself on the other side of the curtain, introducing himself into the scene with the situation that is also the title of the melody for which he composes the lyrics. Like so many song lyrics, this song is reflexive, concerning song and the truth of song. Both the lyricist and the invisible guest receive the "declaration," *kao*, of her song; the guest believes he understands the message and is surely filled with joy and desire; the eavesdropper and we, the audience of *his* song, receive the message but don't know what it means—we can't be certain. If there is genuine love in the words of her song, is it for him or for the guest; or is it perhaps only a song, the pleasure in the craft and the skilled performance of a feeling that is not there?

The next phase of the "performance" should be the bed; at this point song lyrics often speak of the lovers' going together inside the bed-curtains, her shyness at undressing, the bedcovers' rolling like waves. But the poet has displaced the waiting bed, unoccupied, to the beginning of his song; and in place of describing the final movement to consummation, which must cause him pain, the eavesdropper simply writes his pain: *ying-te*, this is "all he gets out of it," the experience of eavesdropping. In this phase he can no longer pretend to presence; the difference is too clear: another "gets out of it" joy and pleasure, "all he gets" is hurt.

These last lines in Liu Yung's song have their own mark of authentication, slipping into a more colloquial voice, as song lyrics often do at the end. As previously there had been a question of the woman communicating her true feelings through her song, the problem now is communicating what *he* feels. Although there was uncertainty about her song, his own song closes with the bold claim of her "knowing," *chih-tao*. Most important, he explicitly rejects the general promiscuity of song: the truth of his feeling could only be known when together with her—or expressed here negatively as a rhetorical question: "Unless together with her could it be known?"

He offers a song for a song, an attempt to sing back through the curtain and replace doubt with sure understanding and intimacy, doubt about the communication of her feelings with certainty about the communication of his own. Yet when he is "together with her," this peculiar circumstance, the occasion of doubt and pain that produces in turn the ostensibly true song, will be past.

Or perhaps there is nothing deep here, nothing that finds footing in the heart. Perhaps Liu Yung is writing only a clever variation on a common boudoir scene, something "light and clever," *ch'ing-ch'iao*, for any skilled singer to sing. Now we may recall, with some unease, that this song, whose tune is listed among the melodies of the T'ang Music Academy, the *chiao-fang*, belongs to that class of lyrics that elaborate the situation implied in the title, just as lyrics to the tune "Tsui kung-tzu" often describe a wife's reaction when her husband returns home drunk from carousing. We wanted to believe his words, we thought he "meant it"; now we doubt.

Even if this is so—and in our modern distrust, we guess it may well be—we cannot help hearing the question of the song's genuineness, even within the conventions of song. Is he merely performing or does he "mean it," and if so, how?

THE RELIABLE AND THE UNRELIABLE

When I meet her, can I interpret whether she cares or not?
相逢還解有情無

YEN CHI-TAO, TO "HUAN HSI SHA"[5]

The true word, the word meant, has great power: it brings lovers together and keeps them together across spans of time and physical distances. Other things may fade: the memory of a face. Dreams may try to span distances but cannot. In "Ts'ai-yün kuei," after describing the scene of his travels, Liu Yung moves in the second stanza to recollection

5. *CST*, p. 239.

of the beloved, as he so often does.[6] There are two powerful remainders: the lingering smell of her body and a "line" or "sentence." The one is dissipating, but the other stays clearly in mind.

> Since we parted, most painful of all,
> barely detectable in my sleeves and gown's fold,
> there is still her lingering scent.
> And I'm sure that she, on phoenix pillow, under lovebird quilts,
> cannot help brooding on it through the long nights.
> But the only thing that really pulls at my heart
> is that one line, when we were about to go our ways,
> that I cannot forget.

> 別來最苦
> 襟袖依約
> 尚有餘香
> 算得伊、鴛衾鳳枕
> 夜永爭不思量
> 牽情處
> 惟有臨歧
> 一句難忘

We do not know the content of the line, only a claim of its power. And perhaps the content of the line cannot be adequately reproduced in these lyrics he now writes, where they would become mere words of song, deprived of their connection to a person and a moment, open to repetition by anyone.

But the words of lovers may sometimes prove to be untrustworthy, as in the problematic conclusion to Liu Yung's "Ch'iu-yeh yüeh."[7] The opening stanza is a conventional situation in which the poet reencounters the beloved, but instead of their steamy and joyous reunion, something goes wrong.

> Back then we met only to part
> And I told myself there was no way ever to see her again.
> But the other day I met her unexpectedly at a party.
> While we were drinking she found a chance
> To draw her brows together and sigh,
> Rousing any number of old sorrows.
>
> Her eyes brimming with tears,
> In my ear she whispered

6. *CST*, p. 36.
7. Translation by James R. Hightower, "The Songwriter Liu Yung," pt. 2, *Harvard Journal of Asiatic Studies* 42 (1982): 18. *CST*, p. 23.

A thousand secret reproaches:
"Too bad you had things in your heart
There was no way to see."
I would like to believe she is telling the truth
And has no other ties.
Maybe I'd better just curb my fancy
And go on with her forever.

當初聚散
便喚作、無由再逢伊面
近日來、不期而會重歡宴
向尊前、閒暇裏
斂著眉兒長歎
惹起舊愁無限

盈盈淚眼
漫向我耳邊
作萬般幽怨
奈你自家心下
有事難見
待信真箇
恁別無縈絆
不免收心
共伊長遠

If the speaker is uncertain what is in the other's heart, the song's readers or audience are equally uncertain who is speaking and what is being said. Hightower's decision in handling the conclusion here is only one among several possibilities. For example, we might easily extend the woman's speech two more lines, so that instead of having the man doubt her sincerity in turn, we finally have only her distrust of him, at which he is so ashamed that he decides to stay true to her.

"I'm certain that in your heart
things were concealed.
I would like to believe what you say is true,
and that you were not involved with anyone else."
At this I can't help reining in my fancies
and going on with her forever.

Another, no less plausible interpretation would have the entire end in the voice of the male speaker, distrusting her, yet deciding he can't help returning to her in the end.

I'm certain that in your heart
there are certain things concealed.

I'd like to believe she is telling the truth
and that she's not involved with anyone else.
Yet I can't help stopping these fancies
and going on with her forever.

Someone distrusts the words of someone else; each reader or member of
the audience may tell the story according to his or her own anticipa-
tions. Although the decision is less urgent for us, we stand in the position of Liu Yung outside the curtain, hearing the repeatable words of
the song and not knowing to whom they are directed.

We might want to believe the lyricist when he tells of his pain at
hearing his beloved entertain another man; but he may be only invent-
ing a situation to elaborate the title of an old melody. In his lyrics he
wonders if the beloved "means the words" in the song *she* sings. But the
singer may be no more than a bird that repeats the same syllables with
meaningless and mindless skill. In the famous Tun-huang version of
"Ch'üeh t'a chih" ("Tieh lien hua") the exasperated woman locks away
the magpie that keeps bringing the good news of her husband's return,
words without any truth to back up their repeated syllables: "You bring
good news, but when has it ever had any basis?" *sung-hsi ho-ts'eng yu
p'ing-chü.* As the magpie later complains, the words were only to cheer
her up, pure rhetoric—perhaps like the singer's profession of love in the
song. And at last the magpie wishes for the husband's return so that the
message of its words will be substantiated and it will be set free.

The love song is both the stylized imitation of love and at the same
time the words in which a truth of love can be spoken. The singer is
both a professional, paid to enact passion, and a human being, to whom
love, longing, and loss can actually happen. We would be overly credu-
lous to believe every statement of love-longing is indeed love; we would
be foolishly cynical to believe that every statement of love-longing is
purely professional or part of a hollow game. And we can't tell the difference. We may, as readers eight centuries later, say it doesn't matter;
but it did seem to matter to the lyricists whose songs we now can only
read, who were ever looking for evidence that the singer really meant it.
We can say, with more acumen, that the fantasy and role-playing of
these love games easily blurred into genuine feeling; but the participants
themselves were concerned with an unambiguous experience of genuineness. Because overt statements and gestures were always potentially un-
reliable, they looked closely for the accidental slip, or some gesture or
expression coming from the woman when she thought she was unobserved, free of the pressure of performance. If voyeurism is an impor-

tant motif in the song lyric, it comes from an intense concern with the genuine; and that concern in turn follows from a suspicion of mere artfulness, of being manipulated.[8] The lyricists knew that the singer's skill could instigate unskillful passion in the listener:

> Before the song comes to its most tender moment,
>   her brows take on a seductive expression;
> as the drinking companions grow tipsy,
>   their eyes become still wilder.

歌逢嬝處眉先嫵
酒伴酣時眼更狂

Ho Chu, to "Che-ku t'ien"[9]

She is not speaking what is in her heart: she is performing a text; she knows the words that are coming and strikes a pose for their appearance.

Yet there might be a moment, barely noticed or dimly seen, when role and true feeling come apart, as in the following lyrics to "Ts'ai sang-tzu" by Yen Chi-tao:[10]

> I saw her then, under the moon,
>   in the western mansion,
> trying to smooth over her tear-streaked powder unobserved;
> and when the song was over, she knit her brows again;
> I regret I could not see her perfectly,
>   across the smoke rising from the censer.
>
> Since we parted, the strands of willows
>   dangling beyond the mansion
> have how many times changed their spring green?
> Yet I, weary traveler in the red dust,
> will always recall that woman in the mansion,
>   her powder streaked with tears.

西樓月下當時見
淚粉偷勻
歌罷還顰
恨隔爐煙看未真

別來樓外垂楊縷
幾換青春
倦客紅塵
長記樓中粉淚人

8. For a discussion of voyeurism in poetry, see Paul Rouzer, "Watching the Voyeurs: Palace Poetry and *Yuefu*," *Chinese Literature: Essays, Articles, Reviews* 11 (1989): 13–34.
9. *CST*, p. 516.
10. *CST*, p. 251.

The curtains that hid the singing beloved from Liu Yung here in Yen Chi-tao's lyrics become a partially transparent veil of smoke. He thinks that he has seen her trying to wipe away the tracks of tears unobserved and frowning once she relaxes the professional pose assumed in song (those brows having been trained to assume a seductive frown when she reaches the most tender moment in the song). But *k'an wei chen*, he can't see clearly enough, can't tell for sure (the *chen* here being the term of the "genuine"). These gestures and expressions on her face are marks of hidden distress, a code of loss and love-longing, but for him or for someone else?—we cannot be sure, and perhaps even he could not be. It almost doesn't matter: the particular object of love here seems less important than the moment when genuine response appeared, an uncertain vision that is fixed in memory and celebrated in this song. Such a moment, like the reliable words of Liu Yung's beloved in the earlier lyric, is something that survives time's passage, that stands in contrast to the world of public life in the red dust.

Tears or the inexplicable frown were among the oldest tropes of genuine feeling rising to a concealing surface, as in Ho Ning's famous "Ts'ai sang-tzu," where after a lovely young girl has been described,[11]

> For no reason she knits her brows,
> making her mother suspicious that she has springtime longings.

無事顰眉
春思翻教阿母疑

Or in Ho Chu's "Su chung-ch'ing":[12]

> Facing the wind again, she sings of the circular fan,
> her true feeling fixed on which man?
> Lightly she jokes,
> then barely frowns:
> you can tell it's love.

臨風再歌團扇
深意屬何人
輕調笑
淺凝顰
認情親

Song lyric teaches a close attention to the most subtle expressions— "barely frowns"—for it is in such ripples in the surface of public

---

11. Lin Ta-ch'un, ed., *T'ang Wu-tai tz'u* (1933; rev. ed., Shanghai: Wen-hsüeh ku-chi k'an-hsing-she, 1956), p. 102. Hereafter *TWTT*.
12. *CST*, pp. 530–31.

appearance that reliable marks of true feeling are to be found. And yet once these become motifs in song, these too can be feigned.

One of the most striking examples of the inexplicable frown is in Chou Pang-yen's "Wang Chiang-nan":[13]

> At the party with singers
> the most wonderful things are those glances of love.
> Jeweled coiffures glitter, from which jade swallows hang aslant;
> embroidered shawls, soft and glossy, gauzes steeped in perfume.
> There should always be plenty of what people like.
>
> For no reason at all
> how come she furrows her brows?
> Lightly made-up, as if seen in a painting.
> Yet her brilliant conversation is better than hearing her sing,
> not to mention the swaying dance.

> 歌席上
> 無賴是橫波
> 寶髻玲瓏欹玉燕
> 繡巾柔膩掩香羅
> 人好自宜多
>
> 無箇事
> 因甚斂雙蛾
> 淺淡梳妝疑見畫
> 惺鬆言語勝聞歌
> 何況會婆娑

The opening stanza of the lyric is the opulent naming of paraphernalia that is typical of one type of party song, concluding with a wonderfully crass statement of indulgence—the more of what people (sc., men) like, the better. Into such unreflective pleasures intrudes the frown "for no reason at all." Other lyricists may be quick to interpret the frown's meaning, a certain index of love; but Chou Pang-yen offers it to us as a question: "How come?" And in leaving the frown as a question, he raises a larger question of interiority. The frown is the mark of interiority—silent expression, as words are voiced expression. But there are two kinds of words: those produced from oneself and the formalized words of a song. Chou first gives us the "pretty as a picture" cliché to objectify the frowning singer, but then be qualifies this "speaking picture" with one of the more unexpected statements in the tradition of party song: her conversation is superior to her song, even though song is the phase that will lead to bed (or the bushes). The frown undercuts the

13. *CST*, p. 615.

momentum of the party song; the appearance of the genuine complicates the love game.

REPETITION

Attention to the presence of genuine feeling and the marks by which it could supposedly be recognized sustained many conventional motifs in the thematic repertoire of song lyric. The inherent contradiction here should be obvious. Insofar as figures of genuineness became categorical terms in a stylized language of feeling, they could be used—as the terms in any language can be used—to lie. Through such thematization of the genuine, we can see the pervasiveness and depth of the concern; but the genuine itself can never adequately appear in its thematization, which is open to repetition and "use."

The genuineness of repeatable words is inherently suspect. And yet the song lyric was a form in which repetition in performance was essential. Here we must distinguish two versions of repetition: there is one in which the repeated words belong to the singer's present; and there is another in which repetition recalls words said at a given moment in the past, in which the singer is enacting words recognized as belonging to another person and another time.

This appears figured in one of the strangest passages in all of Liu Yung's song lyrics, in which two voices are superimposed, each repeating the same words. One of those voices is repeating words that matter, that are recognized as belonging to another person and to time past; the other voice is a mockery of performance, the merely skillful repetition of sounds that have no footing in the heart:

> She leans on the railing beside the pool, sad, no companion.
> What's to do about these living alone feelings?
> Together with the parrot in the golden cage
> She says over the things her lover said.[14]

> 池上凭闌愁無侶
> 奈些箇、單棲情緒
> 却傍金籠共鸚鵡
> 念粉郎言語

---

14. "Kan ts'ao tzu" (*CST*, pp. 14–15). Translation by James R. Hightower, "The Songwriter Liu Yung," pt. 2, p. 10. The rare use of *nien*, "to recite," is interesting here in that it has another usage in *tz'u*, in the prose *nien-yü* or "recited preface," that may precede the performance of a *lien-chang* (*tz'u* sequence). Here the performer speaks the words of the author, words explicitly the author's own. In contrast to the lyrics themselves, where the speaker is often indeterminate, in the *nien-yü* the singer "performs" someone else's words, as the woman does above when she "recites" what the beloved said.

The human version of the parrot's repetition, speaking in an eternal present, is, of course, more complicated. The repeatable party song often takes precisely this aspect of its performance as a theme, speaking for complete absorption in the present moment, forgetting past and future; such songs appeal to the human yearning to become animal and to take the animal's anonymous pleasures, to be free of memory. Yet their absorption in the moment is something desired, articulated against the human truth of memory and anticipation.

As an example, we may quote the famous version of "Huan hsi sha" by Yen Shu.[15] This represents a normative language in song, to be sung by any singer to any guest at any party; its version of "the moment" is any moment and every moment. The singer may "mean the words" or she may be only skillfully repeating the words; but the words belong to no fixed moment in human history when they were or were not genuine:

> Only a moment, this season's splendor,
> this body, a bounded thing;
> to part now as if it didn't matter
> easily breaks the heart;
> so don't be hasty, refusing
> the party's wine, the banquet's song.

> Mountains and rivers fill our eyes, but care
> is wasted on things too far;
> besides which, this grief at spring passing,
> at wind and the rain bringing down flowers;
> it is better by far to take as your love
> the person before your eyes.

> 一向年光有限身
> 等閒離別易銷魂
> 酒筵歌席莫辭頻

> 滿目山河空念遠
> 落花風雨更傷春
> 不如憐取眼前人

As the performer who sings such a song can be endlessly replaced, so too can the body, the anonymous "person before the eyes."

Most of Ou-yang Hsiu's song lyrics are similar to Yen Shu's in this respect, including a party song to "Yü-lou ch'un" beginning "North and south of West Lake, a vast sweep of misty waves."[16] However, when Su Shih hears Ou-yang Hsiu's ("the Drunken Old Man's") lyrics being performed a generation later, we note that a significant change has

15. *CST*, p.90.
16. *CST*, p. 133.

taken place. When the lovely woman stands before Su Shih and sings
the pleasures of the party, instead of taking delight in "the person before
his eyes," Su Shih responds quite differently:[17]

> In lingering frost I've lost sight
> of the sweep of the long River Huai;
> I hear only the trickling current
> of the clear Ying.
> The lovely woman still sings
> the songs of the Drunken Old Man;
> but forty-three years have gone by
> like a sudden sheet of lightning.

霜餘已失長淮闊
空聽潺潺清潁咽
佳人猶唱醉翁詞
四十三年如電抹

Ou-yang Hsiu's song lyric no longer inhabits an eternal present; hearing it recalls its maker and a particular time in the past.

We might consider the analogy between the two modes of understanding song above and the versions of song in Liu Yung's "Listening
Outside the Curtain." As Liu Yung listened to the beloved, he won-
dered if and how the beloved "meant the words"; he recognized those
lyrics she sang only as a category, "her favorite type" (*ai-p'in*), "love
songs" (*hsiang-ssu tiao*). In the second version, the question is whether
Liu Yung "means the words" of his own song lyric, a question that can
be answered only by understanding the words of the song in terms of
the circumstances of its composition (this question of meaning the
words in regard to the circumstances of composition *can* be posed here,
as it cannot be posed in Yen Shu's "Huan hsi sha"). This is a reading of
the song lyric on the model of *shih*. Whether the singer ("the person before your eyes") does or does not invest genuine feeling in the repeated
words must remain forever suspect; the most immediate and familiar
model for genuine words was one of words bound to a particular moment in the past, words that always recalled the circumstances of their
origin.[18]

Between Li Yü at the very beginning of the Northern Sung, and the

17. *CST*, p. 283. The first stanza of a "Mu-lan hua ling," the same tune pattern as
Ou-yang Hsiu's "Yü-lou ch'un," and matching his rhymes.

18. We might note how important this act of displacement into the past became in
the thematics of later love songs. Later, and often even in Liu Yung, genuine romance
was rarely the problematic, perhaps dubious "person before your eyes," but more often a
love recollected and its sites revisited.

time of Su Shih, the song lyric underwent a transformation from a normative and typological song form to a highly circumstantial form, sometimes truly occasional and sometimes not.[19] I would suggest that the problem of genuineness was an important factor in this transformation.[20]

To remark on the interest in genuineness and its consequences for both reading and composition, is in no way to suggest that such lyrics actually *are* genuine, either in the sense that the author "means the words," or in the sense that they are necessarily occasional or grow out of real life experience. In "Listening Outside the Curtain" Liu Yung may simply have been elaborating an incident suggested in an old tune title; however, as he persuasively dramatizes his own "genuine" concern for the genuineness of the beloved's song words, he drives the reading of song lyric toward being more like that of *shih*. Later, when the singer performs this lyric by Liu Yung, the words will be understood as representing Liu Yung's sentiments, and no longer those of the singer. This has two important consequences. First, it contributes to the formation of the legend of the great lover Liu San-pien (Liu Yung) as a biographical frame for reading the lyrics. Second, the reperformance of such lyrics contributes to a dramatized Liu San-pien, who eventually became a popular figure in Chinese theater.

THE CATEGORICAL AND THE PARTICULAR

Insofar as meaning the words (or the appearance thereof) became a value in song lyric, those texts that somehow managed to embody "genuineness" within the words themselves would be particularly valued. Here we should stress the lyric's difference from *shih*. *Shih* could

19. This transformation has been amply documented by many historians of *tz'u*, such as Kang-i Sun Chang in *The Evolution of Chinese Tz'u Poetry: From Late T'ang to Northern Sung* (Princeton: Princeton University Press, 1980). The normative and typological tends to be associated with *hsiao-ling*, while the circumstantial tends to be found in *man-tz'u*; however, this formal division is not at all a strict one: Li Yü writes circumstantial *hsiao-ling*, while Liu Yung writes typological *man-tz'u*. I use the term "circumstantial" as referring to a category broader than the "occasional," which it includes. Thus, we might consider many of Chou Pang-yen's lyrics as circumstantial, but not truly occasional; that is, although we may doubt that such lyrics were composed for a particular experiential occasion, they create a strong sense of a particular, non-repeatable moment.

20. It is significant that Yen Chi-tao, the last master of the Northern Sung typological party song, was also the lyricist for whom the question of genuineness posed the largest problem. In his song lyrics he raises the possibility of the beloved's lack of true feeling and potential falseness with remarkable frequency.

make the *assumption* of genuineness (which is not to say that all *shih* are genuine or aim for that value). In contrast, genuineness was a *problem* in the song lyric.

In addition to a circumstantiality that increasingly bound (or seemed to bind) the words of the song lyric to some moment in the past, the song lyric sought other ways to embody the particularity of feeling and experience. The desire to write genuine feeling into language, in the text rather than in the performance, inevitably encountered a basic limitation of language. Words like "love," "longing," and "sadness" are general categories and only crude ways of articulating particular and constantly changing states of feeling. Using categorical language, the song lyric sought ways to speak of states of feeling more particular, more immediate, and more variable than language readily permitted.

As we might expect, both the particularity of feeling and the inadequacy of categorical language came themselves to appear as themes within the song lyric. Older statements of the inadequacy of language, such as the anecdote of Wheelwright P'ien in the *Chuang-tzu* or T'ao Ch'ien's famous fifth poem of "Drinking Wine," tended to declare the absolute ineffability of "what" was known. In contrast, the lyricists usually accepted the essential validity of categorical language and faulted only language's capacity to convey adequately the precise quality of feeling. Comments on the particularity of feeling occur frequently in the song lyric tradition, as in the famous passage from Li Yü's (attrib.) "Wu yeh t'i" (or "Hsiang-chien huan"); first he gives the category ("the sorrow of being apart"), then declares its singularity:[21]

> Cut but not severed,
> put in order, but then a tangle again—
> that's the sorrow of being apart.
> It is a flavor all of its own kind in the heart.
> 剪不斷
> 理還亂
> 是離愁
> 別是一般滋味在心頭

Or when Liu Yung speaks of a sensation of being ill at ease after sex, he says: "It's a disturbing quality of feeling all of its own kind."[22] And Li Ch'ing-chao, perhaps echoing Li Yü, describes an elusive apathy in spring's bad weather: "It's a flavor of tedium all of its own kind."[23]

21. *TWTT*, p. 231.
22. "Yü-ch'ih pei" (*CST*, p. 21).
23. "Nien-nu chiao" (*CST*, p. 931).

In the passages from Liu Yung's song lyrics quoted earlier, the lover does not give the precise words the beloved said; he or she can only declare that there are words remembered and repeated. In the same way, the lyricist cannot "name" the distinction of the feeling; he can only gesture toward it, often using the phrase *pieh-shih*, "all of its own kind."[24] It is significant that Li Ch'ing-chao picks up that phrase pattern, indexing singularity, when making the first statement of *tz'u*'s own singularity as a genre in the "Tz'u lun." "*Tz'u*," she says, "is something all of its own kind." She is not able to define the particular quality of the genre with precision; rather, she can only point to its distinctness.

Perhaps the finest, and certainly the most famous, statement of the

24. One of the most telling occurrences of the gesture toward the singularity of feeling, the particular as opposed to the categorical, appears in a rather different context, articulating genuine love and the singularity of the object of affection, against the categorical and unspecific. In Liu Yung's "Jui che-ku" (*CST*, p. 49), after a stanza describing the beauty and popularity of a singing girl, the second stanza turns to describe her performance:

Her stance, absolutely still,
　　covered in folds of rose hue.
Then note upon note from the ivory castanets,
the pain in her longing scarcely to be borne.
And when the sounds are clear and piercing,
they drown out the soft and low pipes and strings.
From time to time she looks around
　　and knits black brows in such a way
that she helplessly enthralls the hearts of gentlemen.
Yet they should trust
that as her feelings emerge
　　and her thoughts are lodged in the song,
there is someone else altogether to understand the song.

凝態掩霞襟
動象板聲聲
怨思難任
嘹亮處
迴壓絃管低沉
時凭迴眸斂黛
空役五陵心
須信道
緣情寄意
別有知音

The "someone else altogether to understand the song," *pieh yu chih-yin*, separates the true lover and true beloved from the audience. The public song seems to call to all, but it is intended for only one: the particular is lodged in the categorical. The beloved is the only one who can understand. The term of distinction, *pieh*, unites the singular person loved and the singularity of the feeling.

problem of categorical language and the particularity of emotion is to be found in Li Ch'ing-chao's "Sheng-sheng man":[25]

Searching and searching, seeking and seeking,
so chill, so clear,
dreary, and dismal, and forlorn.
That time of year when it's suddenly warm, then cold again,
now it's hardest of all to relax.
Two or three cups of weak wine—
how can they resist the sharpness of the wind that comes with evening?
The wild geese pass—
that's what hurts most—
and yet they're old acquaintances.

Chrysanthemum petals fill the ground in piles,
looking wasted, damaged—
as they are now, who could bring herself to pluck them?
Keeping by the window,
how can I wait alone until the blackness comes?
The wu-t'ung tree, and on top of that the fine rain,
until dusk,
drop after drop.
In a situation like this
how can that one word "sorrow" grasp it?

25. *CST*, p. 932. One should mention here the equally famous, later, and much darker lyric on the relation between language and emotion, Hsin Ch'i-chi's "Ch'ou nu-erh" (*CST*, p. 1920), also commenting on sorrow's "flavor":

When I was young, I knew nothing of sorrow's flavor.
I loved to climb high in a tower,
I loved to climb high in a tower,
and writing new songs, to force myself to speak of sorrow.

But now I know sorrow's flavor all too well.
I'm ready to speak of it, then stop,
I'm ready to speak of it, then stop,
and say instead "Cool weather—a nice autumn."

少年不識愁滋味
愛上層樓
愛上層樓
為賦新詞彊說愁

而今識盡愁滋味
欲說還休
欲說還休
却道天涼好箇秋

This calls into question the genuineness of the poetic word, its capacity to express genuine feeling, except when feeling is obliquely inferred. It does, however, presume the ability to speak truly about the ability to speak truly.

尋尋覓覓
冷冷清清
悽悽慘慘戚戚
乍暖還寒時候
最難將息
三盃兩盞淡酒
怎敵他、晚來風急
雁過也
正傷心
却是舊時相識

滿地黃花堆積
憔悴損
如今有誰堪摘
守著窗兒
獨自怎生得黑
梧桐更兼細雨
到黃昏
點點滴滴
這次第
怎一箇愁字了得

To see how song lyric claims for itself the capacity to immediately convey genuine feeling, we should begin with the vernacular question at the end, which appears at first glance to be a simple critique of language's capacity to represent feeling. The precise phrasing, however, redeems the closing lines from being merely a restatement of the commonplace critiques of language. The first and most obvious element is the specific reference to the single categorical word: *i-ko ch'ou tzu*. Not only is the problem explicitly located in the single word, the term used is *tzu*, "the written word."[26] Yet this reference to *tzu*, the written word, is made within a sentence whose syntax and diction mark it strongly as colloquial; and even though the text as we have it is written, not performed, it presents itself to us not so much as "the written language," but as using the written language to represent speech.

The second important element in this passage is the term used to indicate what the written word cannot do: *liao-te*, "fully get it," with a strong sense of finishing or completion.[27] The single word (*i-ko [ch'ou] tzu*) is not essentially wrong, only radically incomplete; and thus her rhetorical question is filiated to a long tradition of statements on lan-

26. This is not to suggest that Li Ch'ing-chao is thinking of "writing" per se here. Rather, when she wants to isolate a single term from the more or less natural phrasings of speech (*yü-tz'u*), this is the only term she has recourse to.

27. For parallel usages see Lung Ch'ien-an, *Sung Yüan yü-yen tz'u-tien* (Shanghai: Shang-hai tz'u-shu ch'u-pan-she, 1985), p. 39.

guage's quantitative inadequacy (e.g., the *Hsi-tz'u chuan*'s *"yen pu chin i"*). *Liao-te* is the militantly vernacular phrase (*yü-tz'u*) replacing the more classical word (*tzu*) *chin*, "to exhaust," conventionally used negatively in statements of poetic value: that a poem should "contain inexhaustible meaning in reserve," *han pu-chin chih i*.

"Meaning" (*i*), of course, is not the issue here, not what she hopes to convey, but rather "this situation," *che tz'u-ti*. *Che tz'u-ti* is gestural, ostensive, referring to something present and particular, unlike the more abstract "meaning" (you might even say: *tsen i-ko "i" tzu liao-te*). "Situation," *tz'u-ti*, encompasses both the inner state and its external determinations, without raising the issue of the conventional dichotomy in poetics between "scene" (*ching*) and "feeling" (*ch'ing*).

We now come to that venerable question in the philosophy of language, which is how it is possible to speak the "what" of "what language cannot convey." With the colloquially ostensive "this," *che*, she gestures toward it; but by this point in the song lyric the object of her gesture is no mere blank space. We cannot tell whether the "situation" to which she gestures is the full sequence of experiences given earlier in the lyric or the precise moment that is their outcome. But a tacit claim is made through the gesture that we should recognize "this situation"— that the lyric has already adequately given us the object of the ostensive "this." "*Tz'u* is something all of its own kind," says Li Ch'ing-chao, implicitly articulating the genre against *shih*, which, though still recited, had already become very much "written poetry." Song lyric should enable the reader or listener to "fully get it" through language, if not in any particular word. *Shih* may *chin i*, "exhaust the meaning"; song lyric turns the phrase into the vernacular with significant substitutions: *[chiang] tz'u-ti liao-te*, "fully get the situation."

From the time of Chang Tuan-i's *Kuei-erh chi* of the 1240s, traditional critics recognized that Li Ch'ing-chao's "Sheng-sheng man" was an exceptional song lyric, and I do not believe it is rash to assume that Li Ch'ing-chao recognized in writing it that it was a great lyric. Rather than despairing of language's power to convey the immediacy of feeling, the closing passage may be taken as an oblique expression of her pride of accomplishment (the reader shakes his or her head and says: "Yes, how can a word express *this*?"). Here, then, is a rare case in which the theme of the problem of expressing genuine feeling in words is conjoined to what tacitly claims to be a successful example of genuine feeling embodied in words. At this point our discussion moves from the relatively simple task of describing the question and showing that it was an explicit concern in song lyric to the far more elusive problem of how song lyric "does it," how it actually gives the sense of genuine feeling in words—not only in categorical words, but in some of the most hackneyed images and motifs of the *tz'u* tradition.[28]

The remarkable series of doublets (*tieh-tzu*) that opens the lyric has always caught the attention of critics. Since such accumulation of doublets was generally avoided, we may wonder what made them so effective in this case.[29] In addition to describing qualities (often implicitly unifying external and interior conditions), such doublets may also suggest intensification and continuous action.

We may note that although every pair in the first three lines is formally a doublet, each line represents a rather different kind of doublet; by placing them together, Li Ch'ing-chao uses their formal identity to make them work in similar ways. *Hsün-hsün* and *mi-mi* are doubled verbs, each not surprising in itself, but neither commonly doubled and unusual in being put together. When we find paired doublets, it is usually with bound mood terms, such as we have in the third line (where, again violating convention, we have a series of three, rather than a pair of doublets).[30] Verbal doublets, such as *hsün-hsün* and *mi-mi*, tend to suggest continuous and intensified action; however, by pairing these verbal doublets in the manner of mood doublets and by placing them in a matrix of mood doublets, the "action," intense and continuing, tends to take on the quality of a mood or a state of mind.

The next pair of doublets, *leng-leng* and *ch'ing-ch'ing*, are physical sensations of qualities in the external world, but also carrying strong

28. Although the close stylistic analysis that follows tries to show how *tz'u* "does it," the present author is painfully aware of the incongruity between his topic (conveying immediate and genuine emotion) and the inevitable heavy-handedness of stylistic analysis, more appropriate in the classroom than in writing. Therefore, any reader who wishes at this point to skip ahead to the next section is forgiven beforehand.

29. Rather than being categorical names for conditions (such as "sorrow"), such doublets give a more differentiated sense of a condition's quality: "how" it is. About such doublets as they were used in the *Shih-ching*, Liu Hsieh said in the "Wu-se" chapter of *Wen-hsin tiao-lung: i-yen ch'iung li . . . liang-tzu ch'iung hsing,* "One phrase gave the fullness of the principle [of the thing] . . . two characters gave the fullness of its form." (Note how the question of adequate presentation returns here, though using *ch'iung*, rather than the roughly synonymous and more commonplace *chin.*) The Southern Dynasties poet Chiang Yen could write a poetic exposition on "Grief" ("Hen fu"), giving many examples; likewise, one could look up the categorical emotions in an encyclopedia, which would provide a storehouse of precedent cases. However, the doublets, such as *ch'i-ch'i* or *ts'an-ts'an,* are not such categories: one cannot write a poetic exposition on one of them as a "topic," nor can they constitute headings in an encyclopedia.

30. By "bound term" I mean two-syllable words whose individual syllables are normally, though by no means always, compounded.

mood associations. Like the verbal doublets in the first line, each of these is normally a single syllable (or compounded with another word). Making these syllables into doublets suggests intensification of the sensation (hence the translation "so"). Each doublet in the third line, *ch'i-ch'i ts'an-ts'an ch'i-ch'i* (in the Sung the first and third were phonologically distinct), primarily describes a quality of feeling, though often with ties to external circumstance. These are bound terms, and as mentioned above, it is common to find them in pairs, but not in groups of three.

Each line of doublets is, in some way, twisted away from habitual usage; and by placing them in a common matrix, they are made to be "of the same kind." What would normally be distinguished as action, physical sensation, and mood here blur together. Thus, the initial "action" is joined to sensation and mood and becomes itself an interior state; on the other hand, the terms of mood are linked to physical sensation and the (mental) restlessness of the opening line. The matrix works to break down conventional distinctions between the exterior (*wai*) and interior (*nei*).

Most important is the initial *hsün-hsün mi-mi*, "searching and searching, seeking and seeking." Of all actions, these verbs of seeking require an object in order to be complete. Seeking, to be itself, must seek *something*. Without an object, it becomes more of a condition than an act. Moreover, made into doublets, the verbs connote intensified and continuous seeking, lacking an "end" in several senses. Moving to the second and third lines, the seeking is left incomplete, without an object; and the strong associations of isolation and the absence of another in the second and third lines echo that sense of incompleteness. Thus, emotion here is given the form of intensely purposive movement, but only the pure form, lacking objectified purpose.

> That time of year when it's suddenly warm, then cold again,
> now it's hardest of all to relax.

Weather and human emotion are often associated (in Western literature as in traditional China, where both are qualities of *ch'i*). From the intense steadiness of the opening, where the chill was an ongoing condition, there is all at once a volatility.[31] The mode of the opening was con-

---

31. This association between the quickly changing temperatures of seasonal junctures and wavering mood was already established in the tradition of the song lyric, the most famous example being in Chang Hsien's lyrics to "Ch'ing-men yin" (*CST*, p. 83), whose firgt stanza reads:

tinuation of the same; all at once we enter "suddenness" and alternation of opposites (warmth and chill). From a language of vague poetic mood, we suddenly enter a discursive language: placing, explaining, commenting. In contrast to the opening, where interior and exterior conditions were undifferentiated, here external changes are observed, changes of the weather that also anticipate changes of sensation and feeling: as in the conjunction of the second and third lines, physical sensation blurs into state of mind. Emotion (the Greek *pathos*, "what is endured," *kan*) is involuntary, being the object of forces over which one has no control. The voice, restless but unable to attach her restlessness to any object, tells us explicitly that she cannot settle down, cannot "get hold of herself," cannot relax.

The opening was pure condition; these lines introduce a self-consciousness in which she is aware of the weather as something external, its variability due to the changes in the season. She can conceive of the possibility of relaxing, even though it is beyond her powers. In contrast to the opening lines, here she attempts to "define" her position, to explain her restlessness in terms of this particular moment of the year; now relaxing is "hardest of all," a comparative difficulty. Insofar as song lyric can embody feeling in language, it does so through *movements*—not in statements per se, but in the way one statement "sounds" in relation to other statements. The movement here from the immediacy of the first three lines to the "explanation" offerred in these two lines is the dominant "move" of this lyric: using words to try "fully" to grasp a condition that is both changing and beyond one's control.

"Suddenly warm, then cold again": she stresses the unexpected suddenness of the changes (even while restricting them to this particular time of the year). This is neither a steady "in-between" condition nor a set of predictable alternations, but sudden and unexpected change, all the more forceful because she anticipates the possibility of sudden

---

Suddenly warm, and then a light chill,
wind and rain settle down with evening.
Stillness on the porch by the yard,
    the Ch'ing-ming festival draws near.
Feeling the effects of the wine among the last of the flowers,
once again, the same indisposition as last year.

乍暖還輕冷
風雨晚來方定
庭軒寂寞近清明
殘花中酒
又是去年病

change without knowing when it will occur.[32] No wonder it is hard to
"relax," *chiang-hsi*, combining rest, relief from pressure, and taking care
of oneself.

As she futilely tries to get the situation under control in words ("It's
that time of year, you know"), she also tries to control it by action—not
the sudden spells of welcome warmth recalling departing summer, but
the chill that always returns with the evening wind in autumn. She
takes wine against it, wine that might promise both warmth and relaxa-
tion; but it is inadequate in quantity and strength. We should take careful note of how she phrases the failed intention of the act: *tsen ti*. She
wants to "oppose" or "counterbalance" those external forces that can
work upon her, that affect her mood through physical sensation. But
this gesture of opposition also fails, either in fact or in anticipation (if
we read the lyric as the course of a day, with evening falling later).

> The wild geese pass—
> that's what hurts most—
> and yet they're old acquaintances.

"The wild geese pass," *yen kuo yeh*: the beauty of the line depends on
the *yeh*. It isolates the fact, separates the statement from the flow of discourse. It is given to us as a neutral observation (another consequence
of the quality of *yeh*, as opposed to more emotional particles), something
safely external. But immediately this mere fact impinges on her mood.
Suppose we combined the first two lines into a *shih* line: *yen kuo cheng
shang hsin*, "The passing of the wild geese hurts most" (or "is what hurts
right now"). That would be a simple statement of feeling. But *yen kuo
yeh / cheng shang hsin* first delivers something ostensibly as a neutral fact,
then seems to "discover" a consequence of the fact, a relation to it. The
cheng ("most of all" or "at this moment") attempts to localize response,
to give the real source of the mood by focusing response on the preceding scene. But that too fails adequately to explain why she feels as she
does. *Ch'üeh-shih chiu-shih hsiang-shih*, "and yet they're old acquaintances." She generalizes, compares past and present, contrasts how she
ought to feel (welcoming old acquaintances) with how she does feel
(*cheng shang hsin*). She takes an old cliché of song (the wild geese appearing as old acquaintances) and uses it against the feeling, but it rings
hollow. We don't believe it is a valid consolation; she doesn't believe it
is a consolation. The poetic cliché is as thin and weak as the wine. Its

---

32. "Anxiety," as Freud defines it against "fear" and "fright" in *Beyond the Pleasure
Principle*, depends on knowing that you may well encounter something without knowing
exactly when.

value in the song is not "what" it says but its function as gesture, as a
futile attempt to interpret the emotional force of the fact.

> Chrysanthemum petals fill the ground in piles,
> looking wasted, damaged—
> as they are now, who could bring herself to pluck them?

The first stanza was too full of motions and countermotions to bear a
strong stanzaic shift (*huan-t'ou*). The fallen flowers are, of course, the
counterpart of the aging woman. And the realization that no one will
pluck them brings in the absent figure of the man or friend, someone
who might pluck blossoms—even these last blossoms of the year—but
only at their proper time.[33] Inevitably in the background of such a scene
we find T'ao Ch'ien, who did pick the chrysanthemums in their season,
who watched the birds fly off to South Mountain (their passage did not
"hurt"), and from such a scene attained an aloof pleasure, rising above
the shifting "flavors" of depression that beset Li Ch'ing-chao. And we
may recall also that in the same poem, the fifth "Drinking Wine," T'ao
concluded with the difficulty of finding the right words for what was in
his mind.

"As they are now, who could bring herself to pluck them?" She sees
herself in her figurative double, and in being herself unwilling to pluck
the tattered blossoms, she recognizes her helplessness, being the object
of outer forces—the weather, the passage of time that wastes persons
and flowers, and even in the most hopeful situation, dependency on
someone to pick and appreciate. Li Ch'ing-chao is not passive, but she
is impotent: she is the object of outer forces, scenes, actions. She opposes them by constructs of words and deeds, but she is always defeated,
always overcome. Although tempting, the question of the author's
gender is not, I think, of paramount importance here; such helplessness,
the condition of emotion (*ch'ing*), is equally a convention in the lyrics of
many male poets—though one might argue it is an essentially feminized
stance.

> Keeping by the window,
> how can I wait alone until the blackness comes?

---

33. One may note the relation between this passage and the earlier attempt to unify
the exterior and interior qualities. Here as she looks out into the exterior scene, she finds
the figure of the bedraggled flowers as the self's double; and as she has no inclination to
lay claim to the blossoms, so she herself is unclaimed (the refusal to pluck balancing the
seeking of the opening). There is an interesting relation between poetic modes of isolation
and the solipsistic project of unifying interior experience (*ch'ing*) and the external world
encountered (*ching*).

The wu-t'ung tree, and on top of that the fine rain,
until dusk,
drop after drop.

Although her mood may be restless and uneasy, her body is fixed to one
spot, gazing out the window that gives her one scene after another that
reminds her of autumn. The *shou-che*, "keeping to," is as if willful, drawn
to this frame of disturbing visions. Then, instead of another depressing
item in the visual iconography of autumnal melancholy, the next thing
that is to appear is night's blackness, an absence of vision. In such darkness, for all its ominousness, she might have been able to escape from
those visual impressions that impinge on her mood and cause pain. But
even though the visual world might be muted, there is an equally
oppressive aural world, sounds traditionally associated with melancholy
and loss.

The song lyric aims for a "way of speaking" that sounds genuine, and
often it depends for its effects on particles. The eventual darkening of
the scene is the external fact. The vernacular *tsen sheng te*, "how can I
wait," places her in an intense relation to the fact. More subtle, but no
less important, is the *keng-chien*, "on top of that." She might simply have
said *wu-t'ung yü*, "rain on the wu-t'ung tree"; but *keng-chien* "adds" the
elements, as if they were not a unified scene but some itemization of the
causes of her painful impressions, like the "drip-drip drop-drop," *tien-
tien ti-ti*, each single one drawing attention to itself and adding to the
store of pain.[34]

Li Ch'ing-chao, intensely aware of the tradition of the song lyric, is
here troping on the second stanza of the sixth of Wen T'ing-yün's
"Keng-lou-tzu" lyrics:[35]

On the wu-t'ung tree
rain of the third watch
has no concern how feelings at being apart are at their most painful.
on every single leaf
sound after sound
drips on the empty stairs until daylight.

34. Compare Li Yü's "Wu yeh t'i" (*TWTT*, p. 221):
Last night's wind, together with the rain,
on the curtains the soughing sounds of autumn.
昨夜風兼雨
簾幃颯颯秋聲

35. *TWTT*, p. 62. The admiration for this passage in the twelfth century is suggested
by the fact that it was singled out for praise in the *T'iao-hsi yü-yin ts'ung-hua—hou chi*, *chüan*
17 (dated 1167), one of the few comments on Wen's song lyrics in the Sung.

梧桐樹
三更雨
不道離情正苦
一葉葉
一聲聲
空階滴到明

From the indeterminate "seeking" of the opening, to "keeping to" her
window, to the rains lasting until dusk, the lyric reinforces the idea of
"continuing," bound in uncertain anticipation of some hidden end. Outside is a drama of autumn, which she somehow feels compelled to watch
and listen to until the true darkness of night, with the dripping rain
serving, like the water clock, as the monotonous marker of time. At last
she brings in her act of interpretation, the failure of naming, gesturing
to "this situation," which can be crudely classified as "sorrow" or
"melancholy," but whose particularity belies the "single word." The
name should "complete," should fully account for the phenomenon; yet
here the name is held up for comparison with the "situation," which
throughout embodies incompleteness, continuing, uncertainty, seeking
in vain some end that will make it a whole and thus to be understood
and named.

In the song lyric the conventional name always sits uneasily and im-
perfectly on experience that can only be lived through, or it has more
detail and nuance than the appropriate categorical word. At last the
categorical word may come to be used ironically, implying its own
failure to account for the complexity of "this situation."

> Every phase of the heart, every yearning:
> there is no adequate way to tell them all—
> it's just "love-longing."
>
> 心心念念
> 說盡無憑
> 只是相思
>
>   Yen Shu, to "Su chung-ch'ing"[36]

TAXIS AND QUOTATION

The song lyric sought the means to embody and convey apparently
genuine and particular phases of feeling in categorical words.[37] It was

---

36. *CST*, p. 97.

37. Literary genres are inevitably the recipients of historically diverse interests, and it
is wrongheaded to try to characterize them by any single question. Often genres take
shape around sets of antithetical values; and it is through such contradictory pairings,

early discovered that this could be accomplished, not by the words
themselves, but by the relations implied between phrases, lines, and
stanzas.[38] The words themselves belong to a common normative language, but the quality of movement from one normative verbal segment
to another may imply an interior motion of mind or feeling, a motion
that can seem immediate and private. This is to suggest that the verbal
embodiment of subjectivity was achieved not "in" words but "in between" words (and since the smaller groupings of words were often conventional, primarily between phrases and lines). The relations between
these verbal segments are the empty spaces, which make the workings
of the song lyric so elusive to describe.[39]

In a large sense this is a question of *taxis* ("arrangement," the se-
quencing of words and periods); however, I would like to distinguish
the general question of *taxis* from a more particular case, which I will
call, for want of a better term, "quotation." By "quotation" I mean an
interplay between segments recognized as "classical" or "poetic" (in the
sense of *shih*) and more discursive, often vernacular elements. In
"quotation" the received poetic language loses its exclusive authority:
by being embedded in a longer discursive unity, it is as if placed inside
quotation marks.

The *taxis* of T'ang *shih* was based on a tradition of rhetorical exposition that had roots in a shared assumption about the order of the world,
both the order of the physical world and the normative order of experience. Such assumptions supported the role of *shih* as a social and secular
rite, particularized by the moment, place, and person; all that was particular found a reassuring place in normative pattern.[40] There was room

---

rather than by any single quality, that the genre takes on a distinct identity in relation to
other genres. In song lyric the concern with embodying genuine feeling was bound to an
antithetical interest in obvious artificiality, figuration, and overt marks of conscious
craftsmanship. Careful craftsman and helpless victim of passion are frequently conjoined;
it is less a contradiction to be reconciled than an antithesis whose poles lend energy to
the genre.

38. Sometimes this occurs in the relation between individual words; however, in *tz'u*
the primary semantic unity is more often the compound or phrase than the individual
word. In this *tz'u* approached, in its own way, the polysyllabic and phrase-oriented vernacular.

39. "Empty," *hsü*, was the attributive of feeling (*ch'ing*), and linguistically was associated with the subjective quality of a statement, most commonly (though not always)
achieved in the "particle," or "empty word," *hsü-tzu*.

40. To give just one example of normative *taxis* in *shih*, *shih* generally made an
assumption of temporal linearity: first things come first, second things second, and so on.
Unmarked flashbacks are rare. However, in *tz'u*, governed by the time of subjective con-

within the form for non-normative sequences of lines and subjective associations, but these usually had to be reconciled with a normative structure of exposition.[41] In much of the best eighth-century poetry everything private and subjective was reconciled with normative order.

This gross generalization is in no way meant as an adequate description of, all poetry in the T'ang. During the ninth century that older structure of exposition broke down; middle and late T'ang poetry differ from High T'ang poetry far more in *taxis* even than in diction. However, such a generalization can serve as the starting point from which to consider large shifts in literary history and generic economies. From the mid-T'ang moving into Sung there was a strong interest in making *shih* into a medium that could persuasively embody the particularity of a mind's movements and of experience (subjectivity). One solution was the "rambling" *shih*, in which the elements and their sequence were not bound together by any recognizable structure other than the accidents of experience and the quirky associations of mind.[42] Another example was the witty poem, in which a clever interpretation, articulated against the normative and commonplace response, was the signature of the singularity of *this* poet's mind. In different ways both of these tendencies in mid-T'ang and Sung *shih* were shared by the song lyric.

Tz'u's formal asymmetries made possible certain moves, however, of which the more linear *shih*, with its internally complete couplet, was incapable. *Tz'u* could isolate a phrase, add a single long line as if an afterthought; it could formally enact a sudden shift, an odd association, a flashback, an image left hanging. *Shih* tended to balance and complete utterances. *Tz'u* tended to shifts that left things incomplete, to asymmetries, to elements standing alone.[43] It would be impossible in *shih* to put together the sequence of phrases that appears in the following characteristic example of a *tz'u* passage, which concludes Wang Yü-ch'eng's "Tien chiang ch'un":[44]

---

sciousness, rather than the time of external world, unmarked flashbacks are not at all uncommon.

41. It is significant that the T'ang poet with the most idiosyncratic sense of *taxis* was also the poet with the strongest influence on the *tz'u* tradition and the poet whose collection was designated not simply as poetry, but as "song and poetry" (*ko-shih*): this was Li Ho.

42. There are interesting analogies here to Surrealist literary theory, and the conviction that subjectivity can appear only in the complete abrogation of normative order.

43. An exception in *shih* might be the closing image, a device adopted extensively by *tz'u*. Yet this is usually less an asymmetry than a framed figure for contemplation, a summation.

44. *CST*, p. 2.

All that has happened in my life—
at this moment staring fixedly.
Who understands my state of mind here on the stairs?

平生事
此時凝睇
誰會憑闌意

We know that there is a relation between "all that has happened" in
the speaker's life and his fixed gaze, but *tz'u* allows the components
simply to be thrown together in ways that are impossible in *shih* (even
when the two hemistiches of a line of a regulated couplet are thrown
together in such an indeterminate relation, as occurs sometimes in the
poetry of Tu Fu, Tu Mu, and Li Shang-yin, the indeterminacy tends to
be counterbalanced by the second, often parallel line). Such rapid
alternations and open juxtapositions are common in *tz'u*. They imply
subjectivity because they cannot be unified as a sequence on the level of
rhetoric or a simple proposition; they point to a subject who makes the
connection for his own unstated reasons. They are a signature of what is
private and interior. And it is significant that Wang Yü-ch'eng makes
an explicit claim of just such inaccessible interiority in the final line.

The abrupt shift or indeterminate paratactic juxtaposition is only one
way in which *taxis* is used to point to a subjective unity behind the
words. The rich possibilities of non-normative *taxis*, invited by a given
melody pattern and the ways in which lines are grouped by a rhyme
unit, often require that we posit a unified movement of mind to hold the
disparate elements together. To return to a passage quoted earlier, a
(very weak) *shih* poet might write: *li-ch'ou chien pu tuan*, "The sorrow of
being apart can be cut but not severed." That is a simple claim or proposition. The question is how such a propositional line differs from:

Cut but not severed,
put in order, but then a tangle again—
that's the sorrow of being apart.
It is a flavor all of its own kind in the heart.

剪不斷
理還亂
是離愁
別是一般滋味在心頭

In the first two lines here the topic, the "sorrow of being apart," is
withheld.[45] Heard or read, these two predicates are apprehended as re-

45. The analogous syntactic form in *shih* offers a striking contrast, as in the line from
Tu Fu's "Pei Ch'ing-pan": "The green is the smoke of beacon fires, the white is bones."

ferring to a topic in the speaker's mind, a topic of which the auditor or reader has not been informed; that is, the speaker takes for granted something only he can know. This is a signature of interior monologue rather than address to others: the two predicates are given *as if* they are what comes to mind, what is important. Then when he provides the topic of the predicates in the third line, he does so not for the explanatory necessity of address characteristic of *shih*, but as a subjective claim, that in fact these two predicates explain the essence or the entirety of "the sorrow of being apart." Our hypothetical *shih* line, "The sorrow of being apart can be cut but not severed," offers a predicate that is only one aspect of the topic (presumably many more things could be predicated on "the sorrow of being apart"). This version offers a more extreme claim: "Cut it, but it's not severed; try to put it in order, but it becomes a mess again—*that's* the sorrow of being apart." The precise quality of the *taxis* here is open to other interpretations, but each interpretation must be more gestural and dramatic than our hypothetical *shih* line. Any particular decision on how the lines sound is less significant than the fact that some interpretation of the tone of the lines is demanded by the *taxis* of the *tz'u*, as it would not be by our weak *shih* line. Whether read as a surprising discovery, a hyperbolic definition, or an exclamation of exasperation, all are truly "voiced" versions, whose voicing is articulated against the unvoiced proposition: "The sorrow of being apart can be cut but not severed."[46]

The final line adds another qualification, in which the experience of this emotion is objectified for evaluation.[47] Here the vernacular plainness and unsurprising quality of the observation is played off against the importance and weight given to final lines. The poet's voice speaks as if curiously distant from an emotion that he has just informed us is over-

---

Ch'iu Chao-ao, ed., *Tu-shih hsiang-chu* (Peking: Chung-hua shu-chü, 1979), p. 316. In this case the displacement of the topic to a position after the qualification suggests the order of empirical experience: first one sees the colors, then identifies what they are. This is the way in which problematic syntactic sequence was explained in *Ch'un-ch'iu* commentary. Writing inscribes the external empirical order that governs perception.

46. By "voiced" here I mean something like what a good actor must do with a speech in poetic drama. The passage may offer a rich variety of possibilities in assigning stresses, pauses, ironic intonations—and anyone who has seen many performances of a well-known play knows how deeply such decisions can change the character and the effect of a particular speech. Some versions of dramatic "interpretation" are more effective and credible than others; but all are superior to an unvoiced poetic drone in reading the lines.

47. The reader should not overlook the close similarity of this final "move" to the conclusions of Li Ch'ing-chao's "Sheng-sheng man" and Wang Yü-ch'eng's "Tien chiang ch'un."

whelming. The emotion has become a "flavor," implying both immediacy but at the same time reflective distance—it is an agony to be savored
and judged. What is most important is that the categorical emotion,
"the sorrow of being apart," is *not* itself the subjective condition, the
state of mind, embodied in the lyric; rather, the subjective condition is
in the poet's self-consciousness and changing relation to the categorical
emotion, the way he thinks about it or feels about it. The categorical
emotion is only the object on which the speaker broods, precariously
balanced between torment and reflective distance.

Song lyric works with clichés, normative responses, and commonplace categories of feeling, such as "the sorrow of being apart." However, the real interest of the genre lies in representing particular experience, often involving a reflective relation to the normative category of
feeling. Precisely through the objectification of one's own state of mind a
changing relation is possible; for example, not simply "being in love"
but exasperation at finding oneself helplessly in love. The song lyric's
continual reflection on the categories of feeling is not a dispassionate
distance, but the means by which the interiority and shifts of feeling can
be represented. The mere fact that the sorrow of being apart "is a flavor
all of its own kind in the heart" is uninteresting in its own right; what
animates it is the tone in which we imagine the statement is made and,
inferred from that, the way the speaker feels about the categorical fact.

The second means of embodying the particularity of feeling in categorical words is "quotation." Although we use the term in reference to
a way of speaking rather than as actual citation of a text, it sometimes is
citation, quoting a passage from earlier poetry or a commonplace. As
with categorical statements of feeling, the nature of such "poetic" elements is qualified by the way in which they are embedded in more
discursive language, often including particles (*hsü-tz'u*) or vernacular
elements.[48]

Let us consider a very ordinary, conventionally "poetic" line of
seven-character regulated verse: *i-chiang ch'un-shui hsiang tung liu*, "A
riverful of spring water flowing to the east." If this line had been set in
the right context, an early T'ang or High T'ang poet could have made it
a convincing closing for a poem, a universal truth of Nature that would
in some way serve as the displaced embodiment of the poet's response.
By the ninth and especially by the tenth century, such a closing line

---

48. Northern Sung *shih* eventually evolved its own means of animating earlier poetic
discourse by "quotation," most notably in the poetry of Huang T'ing-chien. The possibility that Huang's *shih* style was based on an aesthetic device primarily characteristic of
song lyric awaits further examination.

would have become painfully banal, a device that had become all too familiar. But what happens if we qualify the line with a short phrase, not only set apart from the familiar rhythms of the seven-character line, but also markedly different in diction? *Ch'ia-ssu i-chiang ch'un-shui hsiang tung liu*, "It's just like a riverful of spring water flowing to the east." The poetic line has been "framed," put into the quotation marks of a speculative simile (we can exaggerate the effect in English by using an extra set of quotation marks: "It's just like 'a riverful of spring water flowing to the east'"). The conventionally "poetic" image loses its autonomy in the longer line, its status as simple natural fact. The first, seven-character line version had presented "what is"; the longer, qualified version reduces natural fact to only an image occurring in the poet's mind. The poet might have drawn this speculative simile from experience or poetry—we cannot know. We know only that it comes to mind at this moment as an appropriate "image." "Just like," *ch'ia-ssu*, he says, admitting there are degrees of appropriate comparison, and that in his purely subjective opinion, this "image" is the most apt.[49] This "empty" (*hsü*) frame contextualizes the image, and in doing so, marks the difference between a poetic, permanent, and natural fact, and the circumstantial application of that fact in a private, subjective comparison. The beauty of the line is in its tone, humanizing the conventional image and making it immediate—"It's just like . . ."

This line of subjective comparison comes as a response to a question posed by the speaker himself. First we might consider how the lines would sound if the answer had been left unqualified by the circumstantial frame phrase:

I ask you, how much sorrow can there be?—
a riverful of spring water flowing to the east.

問君能有幾多愁
一江春水向東流

English translators are often wise to join such questions and answers with a dash after the question mark, to indicate a discontinuity of level between the question and the answer. The autonomy of the "poetic" image, set against the more discursive question, gives the second line a

---

49. There is an interesting question regarding exactly what the "line" of Li Yü's famous *tz'u* is: whether it is the text as we have it with the *ch'ia-ssu*, or the seven-character line "quoted" in the text. In the *Hsüeh-lang-chai jih-chi* (*T'iao-hsi yü-yin ts'ung-hua—hou-chi*, *chüan* 59), Huang T'ing-chien is supposed to have quoted it as the seven-character line, rather than the full nine characters of the text. Such reference to lines of *tz'u* by their "poetic" segments is not uncommon in the Sung.

peculiar authority, an answer that seems to occur in nature rather than in the human mind. Human questions seem to be answered by the world before your eyes or by a silence that lets the questioner know the answer is beyond words. This abrupt shift from question to image had been a favorite device of T'ang poetry.[50]

If we were to leave our "riverful of spring water flowing to the east" unqualified, we would have precisely such a poetic form. When the response is "framed," the human, with human uncertainty, poses the question, and then offers a merely human answer, a subjective opinion, a comparison. Nature as an external presence has been written out of the poem; it survives only as a possibility in mind, a "poetic image."

There are permanent things, things that are real and belong to the world but that are strangely foreign to mind. They survive in mind as "poetic images." The fact that such natural things are somehow no longer immediate is understandable if the person happens to have been removed from or to have lost such permanent presences—for example, a ruler deposed and taken away from his palaces and that Yangtze riverful of spring water. For such a person the world's permanent poetic "things" survive only as remembered images, to be "quoted" by mind:

Carved balustrades and stairs of jade—
    I'm sure they are still there.
雕闌玉砌應猶在

In this case the order of poetic image and subjective qualification is reversed: first the things are given—two parallel compounds—then the

---

50. To cite just two famous examples there is the famous ending of Wang Wei's "Ch'ou Chang shao-fu":

You ask of the rule behind success and failure—
a fisherman's song penetrates deep over the shore.
君問窮通理
漁歌入浦深

Perhaps the most famous example is Li Po's version of the answer of silence. As usual, Li Po cannot leave the truth implicit in the answer of silence unspoken, and while refusing even an image to his questioners, provides one for us, in "Shan-chung wen-ta":

You ask me why it is that I lodge in green hills.
I smile but do not answer; mind at peace with itself.
Peach blossoms and flowing waters go off out of sight;
there is another world, that is not of mortal men.
問余何事棲碧山
笑而不答心自閒
桃花流水窅然去
別有天地非人間

supposition—*ying yu tsai*, "I'm sure they are still there"—qualifying the image as does the comment *ch'ia-ssu*, "just like."[51] In the line that follows, this poetic element embedded in a supposition is further framed by another thought, marking itself as a movement of mind in response to the supposition:

It's only the color of a young man's face that changes.

只是朱顏改

The beauty of this song does not lie in its hackneyed images, but in the relation created between the framing phrases and the embedded images. *Chih-shih*, "It's *only* the color of a young man's face that changes"—but it's not true: all things change and have changed, even lovely palaces in Chin-ling, as a ruler who once had his capital in that city of ruins must have known all too well. *Chih-shih*, "It's only that . . ." is an untruth that becomes a subjective truth, a mark of feeling rather than an opinion; and we read the words as such.

The formal sequence of these two lines is a poetic image that is qualified by a subjective frame and finally moves to purely private and interior response.[52] The initial image is permanent, parallel, and "poetic"; then comes the first frame comment, the supposition that joins the speaker to the "poetic"; finally there is the second qualification, which is purely subjective truth.

51. The variant *i-jan* may be preferred by some. This will produce a loose heptasyllabic song line, also common in *tz'u* (the reading *ying yu* would be uncommon in T'ang *ko-hsing* or *sheng-shih*). My concern here is not which is the correct reading but that the version *ying yu tsai* occurs. For an extensive discussion of the variants, see Daniel Bryant's essay in this volume.

52. This structure of a "poetic" segment framed by a subjective qualification, followed by a line in some way marked as distinct from *shih* diction is quite common in *tz'u*. One example can be found in the opening of Liu Yung's famous "Pa-sheng Kan-chou" (*CST*, p. 43):

I face the pounding of the evening rain
    falling through the sky over the river,
in one time it washes clear autumn.

對蕭蕭暮雨灑江天
一番洗清秋

The perfect seven-character line is qualified by the verb *tui*, "I face," making the scene that is the object of perception also a "poetic" scene and line of poetry. In this case, the subsequent line is not a subjective comment, but a line marked as *tz'u* style both by its phrasing and diction and by the kind of figuration ("washes clear autumn") more characteristic of *tz'u* than *shih*. The "artfulness" of figuration locates the line in the lyricist's mind rather than in nature: as with vernacular framing phrases, nature is given to us in an explicitly mediated way.

To offer another example of such a sequence (in a *tz'u* we might strengthen this pattern by placing two examples of the pattern in the same position in two different stanzas), we could think of something permanent, a common poetic image, a parallel pair of compounds such as:

Spring flowers, autumn moonlight—
春花秋月

Like the "carved balustrades and stairs of jade," these are not what is before a person's eyes—in this case, because no one can see "spring flowers" and "autumn moonlight" at the same time. Like the preceding palace scene, these occur in mind, words drawn from older poetry. Then, duplicating the formal structure of the lines above, we would add the first framing qualification—here not a supposition but a rhetorical question that sets the "poetic" images in the context of the speaker's cares:

when will they end?
何時了

Like *ying yu tsai,* "I'm sure they are still there," this qualification establishes a relation to the poetic image and specifically addresses the question of permanence, the limits of subjective knowledge, permanence as inference. Finally there is the second frame comment that marks off the purely subjective truth, knowledge as idea:

How much of what is past can we know?
往事知多少

or:

I wonder how much has gone by?

There is an obliquity between this and the preceding line (what does "knowing what happened" have to do with the question of the eternity of "spring flowers" and "autumn moonlight"?). We can explain the relation between this and the preceding line in many ways, but that relation is not immediate; it requires explanation. As we suggested earlier, such obliquity is the signal of a private movement of mind.

Such purely subjective comments are, in traditional linguistic categories, "empty," *hsü*—and they need constantly to be reattached to something physical and tangible. If the poetic truth of the permanence of spring flowers and autumn moonlight is realized subjectively in the rhetorical question "when will they end?" then that subjective comment requires a supplement, a grounding in some particular event of cyclical repetition—say, the return of spring's east wind that will once again bring back spring flowers:

> In the small building last night,
>   spring wind once again.
> 小樓昨夜又東風

Important here is the *yu*, "once again," the marker of repetition that explains *why* the preceding lines came to mind. Equally important is "last night," *tso-yeh*, locating the recurrent cycle as a particular event known from the perspective of an individual's place in time. The particular event is understood in its repetition and sameness with the past; from the perspective of today it is ranked with other past occurrences of the same (the spring wind arrived last night as it arrives every year). And since one repetition (the return of spring) can be captured by the retrospective mind, perhaps others can also be recaptured, images that go with the autumn moonlight and thus complete the opening opposition between "spring flowers" and "autumn moonlight." Let us round this out as a poetic couplet:

> In the small building last night, spring wind once again.
> To my homeland I turn my head in the bright moonlight.
> 小樓昨夜又東風
> 故國回首月明中

One return and recurrence, that of the spring wind, leads to another, the possibility of return home, and the gesture, the turning of the head, that embodies desire. But if the desire is too strong, the impossibility of fulfillment makes it painful, and the gesture is repressed. Instead of actually (figuratively) "turning his head" to look back to his homeland, the gesture is only "quoted" in poetic words:

> In the small building last night, spring wind once again.
> To my homeland I *dare not* turn my head in the bright moonlight.
> 小樓昨夜又東風
> 故國不堪回首月明中

The "dare not," *pu k'an*, stands out as the intruded qualification that transforms the poetic gesture into the *thought* of a poetic gesture, a subjective relation to a poetic gesture.

Let me now draw the *disjecta membra* of Li Yü's famous song lyric, "Yü mei-jen," together:[53]

53. *TWTT*, p. 221.

Spring flowers, autumn moonlight—when will they end?
How much of what is past can we know?
In the small building last night,
spring wind once again.
To my homeland I dare not turn my head
in the bright moonlight.

Carved balustrades and stairs of jade—
I'm sure they are still there,
it's only the color of a young man's face that changes.
I ask you, how much sorrow can there be?—
it's just like a riverful of spring water flowing to the east.

春花秋月何時了
往事知多少
少樓昨夜又東風
故國不堪回首月明中

雕闌玉砌應猶在
只是朱顏改
問君能有幾多愁
恰似一江春水向東流

The question is why is this a beautiful piece of poetry (though its
beauties may be utterly invisible in the translation above). By the standards of *shih* it should be neither beautiful nor even very interesting:
everything about it is worn and hackneyed. The answer to the question
of why it is beautiful should tell us something not only about the aesthetics of this song, but also about the aesthetics of song lyric in general.

As was the case with Liu Yung, the persuasive dramatization of
genuine feeling tends to bind the song lyric to a moment in time; it contributes to the formation of a character, real or legendary, who could
have written it. Liu Yung was only the second character created by
good song lyrics; the first was Li Yü. One easy answer to this question
of why the song is beautiful has to do with the tradition of anecdotal
framing, the tradition of reading this song in the context of Li Yü's life.
The art form in this case is not the song by itself, but rather the song in
the context of an assumed story—irrespective of whether that story is
historically true or not. That story is the supplement that the song
seems to require, readers and exegetes finding the circumstances that
can restore fullness to the words.

It is true that the beauty of Li Yü's song cannot be entirely separated
from the later frame of story that has grown up around it, the exiled and
captive ruler longing for his former kingdom. But the primary source of
the song's appeal is within the song itself. It lies precisely in the way in

which a voice quotes and comments on the received images of poetry, changing them in the process and making them animate again.

Whether this song actually represents genuine feeling and "meaning the words" is beyond my knowledge and the knowledge of anyone else. Even Li Yü himself, were the question posed, would no longer be able to answer it perfectly. In one scenario the lyric just came out that way— the poet, a captive in Pien-ching, was overwhelmed by remembrance of his lost southern kingdom, which survived in memory as poetic images. In this scenario the form of the song lyric and the force of feeling in his situation came together to produce a lyric with a genuineness of voice almost impossible in *shih*. In another scenario (uncomfortable precisely because of the fact that genuineness was both a value and a problem) we can imagine Li Yü, under house arrest in Pien-ching, as the master craftsman, essentially happy and well fed—though a bit nostalgic. He works over the words again and again until at last it "sounds genuine." For "the word 'genuine' constitutes the skeleton beneath the song lyric. When the emotions are genuine and the scene is a genuine one, whatever has been written is always excellent and it's easy to consider it complete [*t'o-kao*: to complete one's revisions]."

Song Lyrics and the Canon:
A Look at Anthologies of *Tz'u*

Pauline Yu

Writing tz'u *is difficult; selecting* tz'u *is even more difficult.*[1]

POETRY ANTHOLOGIES AND CANON-FORMATION

The intimate connection between anthologies of poetry and the shaping of Chinese literary history and theory is well known; it is one that may follow naturally from the fact that the earliest specimens of the genre appear in a text whose provenance in a sage's act of selection represents one of the first assertions to be made about it. The various accretions of prefatory material to the *Shih-ching* (Book of Songs), moreover, established other precedents for later collections—and critical discourse as well—by virtue of their interest in the origins, lineage, and contexts of literary works. Following upon this canonical forebear, these collections engaged issues that proved central to the Chinese poetic tradition, including questions concerning the definition and nature of literature, its relationship to history, theories of periodization and genre, and modes of interpretation and evaluation.[2] And indeed, as this list may suggest, anthologies served, both overtly and covertly, as important loci for attempts at defining the secular poetic canon itself.[3]

---

1. Ch'en T'ing-cho (1853–92), *Pai-yü-chai tz'u-hua*, in Ch'ü Hsing-kuo, ed., *Pai-yü-chai tz'u-hua tsu-pen chiao-chu*, 2 vols. (Tsinan: Ch'i Lu shu-she, 1983), 1:761 (hereafter cited as *Tsu-pen chiao-chu*). In the *Tz'u-hua ts'ung-pien*, ed. and printed by T'ang Kuei-chang (24 volumes in four boxes, preface dated 1934; hereafter cited as *Tz'u-hua ts'ung-pien*), this statement can be found in vol. 22, 8.8a.

2. For a discussion of these questions, see Pauline Yu, "Poems in Their Place: Collections and Canons in Early Chinese Literature," *Harvard Journal of Asiatic Studies* 50 (1990): 163–96.

3. Although he is drawing on a number of forebears, Kao Ping (1350–1423) offers the most cogent example of this process in his *T'ang-shih p'in-hui*.

The role played by anthologies in the process of canon-formation has not gone unnoticed by a variety of critics. In her preface to an anthology of English and American women poets, for example, Louise Bernikow observes that "what is commonly called literary history is actually a record of choices. Which authors have survived their time and which have not depends on who noticed them and chose to record the notice. Which works have become part of the 'canon' of literature, read, thought about, discussed, and which have disappeared depends, in the same way, on the process of selection and the power to select along the way."[4] Although Bernikow is specifically concerned with the gendered nature of literary-historical empowerment in England and America, her argument for the social and historical construction of value by means of editorial selection offers insights into Chinese literary history as well. In the case of the short lyric poem or *shih*, the primary questions center on the inclusion or exclusion of individual poets, as they do for Bernikow, with choices being made among writers working within, generally speaking, a common social and linguistic milieu and, perhaps more important, employing a genre blessed with an unimpeachable genealogy. This being so, given the variety of disagreements that ensue nonetheless regarding the critical issues mentioned above, it should come as no surprise that the same lack of consensus holds, *a fortiori*, for anthologies of the song lyric, or *tz'u*. This is a discourse, moreover, that must concern itself above all with the question of its own legitimacy. As a genre whose own status within the tradition was ineluctably compromised by the questionable nature of its origins, a genre that for centuries did not even possess a fixed name, the song lyric found itself continually in the position of having to justify itself vis-à-vis that tradition. We can find traces of this gesture in the collections that have written—and rewritten—the history of the form for us, which has been colored from the beginning by the polemics of marginality.

One clear index of the marginal status of the song lyric is the slender and evidently ravaged nature of the body of texts that has survived. It is well known that literati of the late T'ang and Sung dynasties did not choose to include their *tz'u* in the collections of their own works that many of them were beginning to assemble themselves; contemporary accounts of their writings often do not bother to mention that they worked within the genre.[5] Individual collections of *tz'u* that were com-

4. Cited by Elaine Showalter in her review article, "Literary Criticism," *Signs* 1 (1975): 438.

5. Ch'i Huai-mei gives three examples of literati whose catalogs of works given in the

piled, such as the *Chin-ch'üan chi* ascribed to Wen T'ing-yün (812–70), were both few and aleatory. As Lung Mu-hsün observed some time ago, the relatively small number of individual *tz'u* collections from the T'ang through the Chin dynasties that are known to have existed—only a few hundred in all—suggests the low esteem of a genre that the literati evidently took great pleasure in but did not deem worth their time and effort to collect.[6] Needless to say, the survival rate has been unimpressive.[7] And poets whose primary activity consisted of working within the genre of *tz'u* have been treated rather capriciously by some literary historians. Biographical information on them, for example, is more often than not both scant and riddled with error. Not only were they likely, over time, to be provided with wrong birthplaces or wrong dates, but they were sometimes even placed within wrong dynasties.[8]

The same holds true for the anthologies of *tz'u* that are known to have been compiled, even during the genre's period of greatest florescence. Although the count varies slightly from source to source, there appear to be only nine anthologies that have survived from the T'ang and Sung dynasties, with an additional thirteen whose existence has been recorded but that have long since disappeared.[9] The losses are difficult to imagine, as is the treatment accorded to the survivors. What is even more remarkable is the fact that only two of these anthologies— the *Hua-chien chi* and the *Ts'ao-t'ang shih-yü*—appear to have been widely known to readers of the Yüan and Ming dynasties. All of them were subjected to violations of their textual integrity, ranging from revisions, additions, and deletions of individual poems to division into varying numbers of fascicles, reorganization according to entirely different systems of categorization, and reappearance of identical titles for utterly different volumes. And in many cases, with a few notable exceptions, the very notion of textual integrity is arguable, given the lack of any dis-

dynastic histories do not identify them as also having written *tz'u*. See "*Hua-chien chi* chih yen-chiu" in *Tai-wan sheng-li Shih-fan ta-hsüeh kuo-wen yen-chiu-so chi-k'an* 4 (1960): 516.

6. In his "Hsüan tz'u piao-chun lun," *Tz'u-hsüeh chi-k'an* 1, no. 2 (August 1933): 1.

7. Exhaustive research documenting the traces of individual collections from the T'ang through the Chin dynasty has been conducted by Jao Tsung-i in his *Tz'u-chi k'ao*, vol. 1 (Hong Kong: Hsiang-kang ta-hsüeh ch'u-pan-she, 1963).

8. As noted by T'ang Kuei-chang and Chin Ch'i-hua in "Li-tai tz'u-hsüeh yen-chiu shu-lüeh," *Tz'u-hsüeh* 1 (1981): 8.

9. This is the count given by She Chih in "Li-tai tz'u-hsüan-chi hsü-lu," pt. 2, *Tz'u-hsüeh* 2 (1982): 234. His list begins with the *Yün-yao chi* and goes on to include the following: *Hua-chien chi, Tsun-ch'ien chi, Yüeh-fu ya-tz'u, Mei yüan, Ts'ao-t'ang shih-yü, Hua-an tz'u-hsüan, Yang-ch'un pai-hsüeh chi*, and *Chüeh-miao hao-tz'u*.

cernible order to or rationale for inclusion of the contents. Editorial claims regarding the desultory manner of compilation are familiar from the *shih* anthological tradition but more often than not belie a careful and systematic, if unarticulated, program; in the case of *tz'u* collections, however, there may be good reason to believe them.

Small wonder, then, that the now-familiar slogan (motivated by assumptions of the cyclicality of both dynasties and genres) juxtaposing T'ang *shih* and Sung *tz'u* requires some qualification. Already discredited as faulty periodization by those who have unearthed the roots of the song lyric in the T'ang and examined the richness of its reflorescence in the Ch'ing, it is equally susceptible to the critique that the nice balance of the juxtaposition belies a true incommensurability in status between the two elements. At the same time, however, the assumption regarding the evolution of genres underlying this mode of periodization resurfaces continually as one of the most persuasive arguments for validation of the *tz'u*. In what follows I will examine the discourse of legitimation as it takes shape in the prefaces to the major anthologies of T'ang and Sung song lyrics that have come down to us as well as in other textual material surrounding them. I should clarify from the outset that my discussion will focus more on the theoretical and rhetorical concerns of the various editors, articulated both explicitly and implicitly in their collections, than on the questions of what texts were available to them and how that affected the representation of works in their anthologies. Consideration of the relationship between the accessibility of sources and the actual practice of selection is clearly necessary but must await another study.

THE LEGITIMIZING EFFORT OF THE *HUA-CHIEN CHI*

Ou-yang Chiung (896–971) provides us with the first critical statement on the *tz'u* in his preface (dated 940) to the *Hua-chien chi* edited by Chao Ch'ung-tso. Although this volume was not the first collection of song lyrics to be compiled, it was long assumed to be,[10] and as the first statement on *tz'u* by and for members of the literati class it was clearly instrumental in establishing precedents for subsequent discourse on the genre. In both language and allusions, the ornate parallel prose of the text evokes the preface to Hsü Ling's (507–83) *Yü-t'ai hsin-yung* by stressing the virtues of embellishment and craft in a milieu of languorous ex-

---

10. The *Ssu-k'u ch'üan-shu tsung-mu t'i-y'ao*, 5 vols. (rpt., Taipei: Shang-wu yin-shu-kuan, 1976), for example, identifies it as the oldest anthology of *tz'u* (5:4457).

travagance. After opening, for example, with the declaration that "engraved jade and carved jasper mimic [nature's] transforming craft with a different art; cut flowers and scissored leaves steal spring's allure and vie in freshness,"[11] it situates itself within a line of love poetry that extends from the legendary encounters between King Mu and the Queen Mother of the West, through the *yüeh-fu* tradition, to the song lyrics of Li Po and insists that the poets of the present day need not feel ashamed before these predecessors.

This link to *yüeh-fu* is stressed throughout the later literature on *tz'u*; it is a logical one, given the shared connections of the two forms with musical performance. Moreover, just as *yüeh-fu* had been institutionalized in both governmental structures and literary practice (having become literati practice), so might the *tz'u*, too, hope for some similar sort of legitimation. Ou-yang Chiung does not allude to the putative origins among the people common to both forms; all of his forebears belong rather to elite circles, even though, ironically enough, the title of the song supposedly sung by the Queen Mother of the West to King Mu, "Pai-yün yao," was given to the collection of anonymous popular *tz'u* whose very style and sources Ou-yang Chiung wishes to distance himself from, the *Yün-yao chi*. Having sketched the opulent setting of the poetry of the Ch'i and Liang dynasties to which the *tz'u* in the *Hua-chien chi* bear such strong resemblances, he hastens to distinguish the latter from the eventual contamination from the pleasure quarters suffered by the former: "When the palace-style [poetry] of the southern states was riffled with the songs of the northern wards, not only was the language uncultured, but while elegant, it was without substance." To this phenomenon, recalled at the end of the preface as the "ditties of the lotus boat," he opposes the contents of the *Hua-chien chi*, explicitly labeled as the "song lyrics of poets" (*shih-k'o ch'ü-tzu-tz'u*).

That these are song lyrics of "poets," rather than of "beauties from the southern states" (*nan-kuo ch'an-chüan*), reveals Ou-yang Chiung's well-known desire to elevate the social status of the *tz'u*. One might also note that the poems themselves are organized by their authors, who are arranged—in good canonical fashion—in chronological order of birthdate, a principle that of course implicitly identifies a writer as belonging to a class for whom one would trouble to ascertain such dates. As if to

11. From Hua Chung-yen, ed., *Hua-chien chi chu* (Honan: Chung-chou shu-hua-she, 1983), p. 1. Lois Fusek's translation of the preface is complete and annotated, if somewhat loose, in *Among the Flowers: The* Hua-chien chi (New York: Columbia University Press, 1982), pp. 33–36.

emphasize further the social distinction between these "poets" and other likely composers of *tz'u* (for example, women, monks, and similar social marginalia), they are referred to by official title or, in the absence of a respectable position, as "scholars in retirement" (*ch'u-shih*).

Leading off the collection both in position and, with sixty-six lyrics, in number of poems (and literally referred to later as its "cap") is Wen T'ing-yün. As Wu Hsiung-ho points out, during the Five Dynasties the peripheral state of Shu appears to have offered writers of *tz'u* a relatively more peaceful setting for their pursuits than would have been possible in the capital on the war-ravaged central plain, a presumption suggested by the unearthing of a variety of musical instruments from the grave of Wang Chien, who established the Western Shu dynasty in Ch'eng-tu (907–25).[12] It should come as no surprise, then, that almost all of the eighteen poets included were natives of or officials in Shu, the most notable exception being Wen T'ing-yün. Wen is also the only poet mentioned by name in the preface, and his anomalously prominent position suggests that Chao Ch'ung-tso was conducting an effort toward valorization on several fronts: valorization of his region's songs, which are being situated in a line going directly to the center of the empire and an era preceding the political disintegration of the T'ang; of the genre itself, being plied with evident accomplishment by a true *shih-k'o*, a member of the educated elite, no matter how unsuccessful and profligate he may have been; and of Wen's refined and pedigreed style, which, though by no means the only one included in the anthology, clearly dominates the collection.[13] Thus, despite the lack of any articulated intent to promulgate a particular school, we can see here the desire to recuperate the *tz'u* as "literature"; even if situated at best on the fringes, it could certainly partake of the compromised respectability of the *Yü-t'ai hsin-yung*. At the same time, because of this emphasis on sanctioned authorship, its thematic scope was significantly circumscribed in comparison with the broad range of topics addressed in songs of more popular origin—for example, the texts discovered in the Tun-huang

12. In *T'ang Sung tz'u t'ung-lun* (Hangchow: Che-chiang ku-chi ch'u-pan-she, 1985), p. 175.

13. Thus, for instance, although the *tz'u* by Huang-fu Sung (mid-9th cent.) selected by Chao Ch'ung-tso for the *Hua-chien chi* clearly echo Wen's style, Marsha Wagner provides examples of a quite different sort, also composed by Huang-fu, in *The Lotus Boat: The Origins of Chinese* Tz'u *Poetry in T'ang Popular Culture* (New York: Columbia University Press, 1984), pp. 146–47. Her book argues persuasively for the mutual infiltration of elite and popular influences in the development of *tz'u*, but I am focusing rather on the motivations behind the literati discourse on separation.

caves.[14] The range of tunes employed is also different from that associated with entertainment originating from and intended for a broader
social spectrum; the popular tunes whose titles are included in Ts'ui
Ling-ch'in's mid-eighth-century *Chiao-fang chi*, for instance, generally
correspond with the tunes to which lyrics are composed in the oldest
known anthology, the *Yün-yao chi*, compiled before 922 and preserved
at Tun-huang.[15] It may well be that such sacrifices were deemed essential toward defining the new genre as an activity appropriate to members of the literati class.

Additional conclusions follow from considering the *Hua-chien chi*
within the context of other collections. One is the evident murkiness of
the line between *shih* and *tz'u* that is suggested by the fact that many of
the lyrics included in the anthology also appear in T'ang collections of
shih.[16] Another is the curious system by which its contents are arranged;
though ordered chronologically by author, the five hundred poems are
simply divided into ten fascicles of fifty songs each, which in several instances necessitates breaking up the corpus of selections from an individual poet. Later commentators' displeasure with this system has been
virtually unanimous, but the very fact that it appears to be so utterly
mechanical suggests the lack of any further programmatic drive moti-
vating the collection. Thus, although the anthology might have hoped
to establish the writing of *tz'u* as an acceptable literati activity, it did
not aspire to claim for it the canonical functions of *shih*. As Wu Hsiung-
ho points out, what is therefore notable about the *Hua-chien chi* lies as
much in what it does not say as in what it does. Accordingly, for example, although known for his views on the moral obligations of the *shih*
poet, Ou-yang Chiung breathes no word of them in his preface here,
and Niu Hsi-chi (fl. 930), who rails against "lascivious" writing (*wen*)
elsewhere, is nonetheless represented by eleven lascivious song lyrics in
this collection.[17]

Implicit in these two examples is perhaps one of the major obstacles
that confronted any attempt to establish the *tz'u* within the canon: the
fundamentally binary nature of Chinese discourse in general and of
literary discourse in particular. It is well known that discussions of liter-

14. This point is well made by Yang Hai-ming, who notes that the later distinction
suggested by Li Ch'ing-chao (*tz'u pieh shih i-chia*, "*tz'u* constitutes its own household [dis-
tinct from *shih*]") is in fact one that pertains specifically to the *shih* and *tz'u* of the literati
alone. See his *T'ang Sung tz'u lun-kao* (Hangchow: Che-chiang ku-chi ch'u-pan-she, 1988),
p. 52.
15. Ch'i Huai-mei, "*Hua-chien chi* chih yen-chiu," p. 515.
16. As noted in the *Ssu-k'u ch'üan-shu tsung-mu t'i-yao*, 5:4457.
17. Wu Hsiung-ho, *T'ang Sung tz'u t'ung-lun*, p. 284.

ary function and style developed and explored the distinction between *wen* and *pi*, patterned and plain writing, respectively, during the Six Dynasties, to be replaced by a pairing of *shih* and *wen*, poetry and prose, in the T'ang. To *shih*, as the classics put it, was accorded the function of "expressing what was intently on one's mind" (*yen chih*), the direct manifestation of genuine emotion that could provide access to the fundamental character and political disposition of the poet. And *wen*—as scholars from Han Yü to Niu Hsi-chi had already claimed, and Sung neo-Confusions would argue further—was to serve as an instrument of pedagogical transformation, a vehicle for the Tao. This schema, with its emphasis on personal expression and moral purpose, left little space for the song lyric, which, given its nature as something in the voice of, and often voiced by someone other than, the poet, was of necessity distanced from an original *chih* and might at best, as Wu Hsiung-ho points out,[18] claim a share of what Lu Chi in his "Wen fu" had ascribed to the *shih*, the ability to "trace sentiments with exquisite ornateness" (*yüan ch'ing erh ch'i-mi*). As has been the case with marginalized genres and figures elsewhere, a freedom is hereby made possible, but a vulnerability to frustration and attack as well.

This is nowhere so clear as in colophons to various editions of the *Hua-chien chi*. At the end of the Shao-hsing period edition of 1148, for example, Ch'ao Ch'ien-chih remarks that these are "all long-and-short verses of talented scholars from the end of the T'ang. The sentiments are sincere and the melodies transcendent, the thoughts profound and the language delicate. Although the writing is ornate and of no salutary [benefit] to the world, it can nonetheless be called skillful."[19] What he grants with one hand he then just as quickly snatches away with the other. Less equivocal and more controversial are two colophons by Lu Yu (1125–1210) that appear in Mao Chin's (1599–1659) reprinting of his family's Sung dynasty edition of the text. The first observes that the collection "consists entirely of writings of people from the T'ang and Five Dynasties. During precisely this period, when the world was in great peril and the people were struggling ceaselessly to stay alive, scholar-officials degenerated to this point. This is worth sighing over!"[20] The second offers a somewhat more extensive account of the decline of poetry over the course of the T'ang and likens the introduction of writing songs for the purpose of entertainment to the attitude of reckless

18. Ibid.

19. Included in Li I-mang, ed., *Hua-chien chi chiao*, 2d ed. (Hong Kong: Shang-wu yin-shu-kuan, 1973), p. 221.

20. Ibid., p. 232.

abandon characteristic of the Six Dynasties, an attitude that Lu Yu feels permeates the *Hua-chien chi*. Thus, song lyrics represent an inferior genre following only upon the degeneration of the *shih*, and he finds it difficult to understand how individuals can apply their talents to it: "Brush and ink flow with equal speed, so to be able [to write] one and not the other can never be fathomed by reason."[21]

Lu Yu's incredulity notwithstanding, poets did write song lyrics, himself included. What his comments share with the praises of Ou-yang Chiung is a tension generated by an impulse toward what Michel Foucault terms a "total history," described as follows:

> The project of a total history is one that seeks to reconstitute the overall form of a civilization, the principle—material or spiritual—of a society, the significance common to all the phenomena of a period, the law that accounts for their cohesion—what is called metaphorically the "face" of a period. Such a project is linked to two or three hypotheses; it is supposed that between all the events of a well-defined spatio-temporal area, between all the phenomena of which traces have been found, it must be possible to establish a system of homogeneous relations: a network of causality that makes it possible to derive each of them, relations of analogy that show how they symbolize one another, or how they all express one and the same central core; it is also supposed that one and the same form of historicity operates upon economic structures, social institutions and customs, the inertia of mental attitudes, technological practice, political behaviour, and subjects them all to the same type of transformation; lastly, it is supposed that history itself may be articulated into great units —stages or phases—which contain within themselves their own principle of cohesion.

To this Foucault opposes the notion of a "general history" that allows one to conceive of discontinuity and rupture, that "speaks of series, divi-

---

21. Ibid., p. 233. Interestingly enough, the *Ssu-k'u ch'üan-shu tsung-mu t'i-yao* takes issue with both of these statements. To the first it counters that Lu Yu "has not yet reflected upon the basic reasons behind the imperiled state of the world." And in reference to the second it observes that Lu Yu "does not know that literary genres and styles may be high or low and human learning and vigor may be strong or weak. When one's learning and vigor are incommensurate with genre and style, then there won't be enough to carry it off. If learning and vigor are commensurate with genre and style, then there will be more than enough to carry it off. Regulated verse descended from ancient verse; thus, during the middle and late T'ang much ancient verse was not skillful, and of regulated verse there were at times some fine compositions. Song lyrics in turn descended from regulated verse; thus, during the Five Dynasties poets' *shih* did not match those of the T'ang, and *tz'u* alone flourished. This is like being able to lift seventy catties: lift a hundred catties and you'll fall down; lift fifty catties and you can move around as you please. Why is it that this cannot be fathomed by reason?" (5:4457–58).

sions, limits, differences of level, shifts, chronological specificities, particular forms of rehandling, possible types of relations."[22] Foucault's
version of a "total history" aptly characterizes the typically historicist
assumptions of Chinese literary history (and hermeneutical practice as
well) that motivate the tracing of generic development. In this view
change comes not as discontinuity or rupture but as mutation or transformation (*pien*) from within, with value connotations—if articulated at
all—of decline rather than progress. Thus, a new form like the song
lyric possesses an immediate genealogy that is also immediately problematic: on the one hand, the identifiable lineage can ratify the genre by
situating it within a network of relations and evolutionary forebears and
yet, on the other, it can undermine it as a sheer symptom of decay.
Typically, therefore, the introduction to the section on *tz'u* in the *Ssu-k'u
ch'üan-shu tsung-mu t'i-yao* begins by discussing the unsavory origins and
ignoble backgrounds of the first practitioners of the genre but then, because it does not question the notion of the evolution of genres through
a succession of transformations (*pien*), it cannot deny that the heritage
of the song lyric goes back to the *Shih-ching*. It is, however, but the
"aftertone of the *yüeh-fu* and the last outflow of the poets of the 'Airs.'"[23]
Moreover, as we have already seen, any attempt to valorize the form
must be conducted on preexisting terms, those of the canon. In the case
of the *tz'u*, of course, those terms are set by the discourse on *shih*, and
one of the major issues with which critics and anthologists therefore
grapple is how—or indeed whether—to work within them.

SOUTHERN SUNG REVALUATIONS AND
A NEW ORTHODOXY DEFINED

Whether one traces any surviving anthologies to the Northern Sung depends on how one dates the *Tsun-ch'ien chi*; it is an argument that has
been waged for centuries and about which I offer no new information.
This collection of 260 lyrics by thirty-six poets is referred to as a collection from the T'ang in the same breath as is the *Hua-chien chi* by Chang
Yen (1248–1320?) in his *Tz'u-yüan*.[24] The authors included date from
the T'ang and Five Dynasties period and include emperors and high
ministers from T'ang Ming-huang onward, arranged, appropriately,

22. From *The Archeology of Knowledge and the Discourse on Language*, trans. A. M. Sheridan Smith (New York: Pantheon, 1972), pp. 9–10.
23. 5:4418.
24. In the opening of the second fascicle of the work, included in *Tz'u-hua ts'ung-pien*
2.1a.

largely in descending order of status. Its compiler had clearly seen the *Hua-chien chi* and essentially followed the earlier collection's sequence of poets; duplications, supplementations, and revisions (often erroneous) are all clearly evident, accumulated through at least three layers of editorial accretion. Some Sung dynasty sources assumed it was a T'ang collection; Ku Wu-fang's preface to the edition he printed in 1582, on the other hand, suggests that he was responsible for its compilation, and Mao Chin believed that Ku had indeed selected the poems.[25] Internal evidence, however, seems to indicate that it was compiled during the first half of the eleventh century.[26] In any event, the *Tsun-ch'ien chi*—like other collections (no longer extant) that were compiled in the wake of the *Hua-chien chi* and given similar titles referring to banquet contexts— does not appear to have aspired to do more than serve as a convenient songbook. Moreover, its hitherto disputed textual history renders it of little value for the purposes of this discussion.

Whatever the *Hua-chien chi*'s success in establishing the writing of *tz'u* as an acceptable literati activity, Northern Sung poets regarded it essentially as a pastime for or about entertainment, and not as a serious form comparable to *shih* or *wen*.[27] This is true despite the fact that the history of literary criticism tells us that many Sung dynasty *shih-hua* have *tz'u-hua* embedded within them, and that what could be regarded as the first critical work on *tz'u*, the *Pen-shih ch'ü* of Yang Hui (1017–88), dated to 1071, was written close in time to Ou-yang Hsiu's (1007–72) *Liu-i shih-hua*, one of the first examples of its genre.[28] Certainly the dearth of

25. She Chih, "Li-tai tz'u-hsüan-chi hsü-lu," pt. 1, *Tz'u-hsüeh* 1 (1981): 282–83, and the *Ssu-k'u ch'üan-shu tsung-mu t'i-yao*, 5:4458. See Daniel Bryant's essay in this volume for an extensive discussion of the anthology's authenticity.

26. The *Tsun-ch'ien chi* includes a poem attributed to Li Yü to the tune of "Tieh lien hua" that three Sung sources identify rather as having been composed by Li Kuan, who lived during Jen-tsung's reign (1023–64). At the other end, there is a colophon to the *Yang-ch'un chi* by Ts'ui Kung-tu that can be dated to the Yüan-feng period of Shen-tsung's reign (1068–78). I am relying on Hsia Ch'eng-t'ao's argument that the collection was compiled in the T'ang (based on Sung statements to this effect in the *Li-tai shih-yü tz'u-hua*, the *Hua-an tz'u-hsüan*, and Chang Yen's *Tz'u-yüan*), his consequent chiding of the *Ssu-k'u* editors' unwillingness to trust the sources enough to date it definitively, and his subsequent recanting of his position after having been persuaded by Wang Chung-wen that it should indeed be dated to the Northern Sung. See his "*Ssu-k'u ch'üan-shu* tz'u-chi t'i-yao chiao-i," in idem, *T'ang Sung tz'u lun-ts'ung* (Hong Kong: Chung-hua shu-chü, 1973), pp. 263–65.

27. Yang Hai-ming cites examples of this attitude in his *T'ang Sung tz'u lun-kao*, p. 58.

28. As noted by Wu Hsiung-ho, *T'ang Sung tz'u t'ung-lun*, pp. 285–86. Only fragments of the *Pen-shih ch'ü*, which is mentioned in Hu Tzu's (fl. 1147–67) *T'iao-hsi yü-yin ts'ung-hua*, have survived, having been pieced together by Chao Wan-li; She Chih speculates

anthologies from the Northern Sung should not be blamed solely on the ravages of time; it attests as well to a persistent ambivalence, one that is examined by Ronald Egan elsewhere in this volume. It remained for poets in the Southern Sung to make the case for a different attitude to the genre.

These strategies can be seen in the surviving anthologies from that period and take different but related forms. One involves the concerted effort to situate the song lyric within a tradition that could be called *ya* ("elegant" or "refined," but with distinct classical and canonical overtones as well) and subsequently to identify this quality as in fact the "orthodoxy" (*cheng*) of *tz'u*. This strategy not only aims to valorize the song lyric vis-à-vis the dominant *shih* form, but, even more important, to establish a distinctive and central tradition within the genre of *tz'u* itself. Another focuses on the individual authorship of *tz'u*, to shift attention from the conventional and socially conditioned circumstances of its composition and function to its potential as a vehicle for personal expression. These efforts coalesce—during the Southern Sung itself but even more so during the Ch'ing—in the drive to establish schools (*p'ai*) with a model master at the head of each (much as Wen T'ing-yün could be identified as the head of the *Hua-chien chi* tradition). And what they share is the fact that whether the terms with which they are working are borrowed from prior discourse on *shih* or represent new coinage of the realm of *tz'u*, they are removed, significantly, from the former's grounding in history and moral intent, facilitating a consequent obsession with questions of language, form, and style.[29] To what extent these concerns may have undermined the effort toward legitimation that was, in any event, being conducted on alien turf remains to be seen.

Early efforts in this direction are transparent from the record, for among the handful of Southern Sung anthologies whose existence has been noted, two contain the word *ya* in their titles. Both were evidently compiled shortly after the move south, a transition that no doubt further stimulated the search for legitimacy. One, entitled the *Fu-ya ko-tz'u*, was edited by someone who refers to himself simply as the "Retired Scholar of T'ung-yang" (T'ung-yang chü-shih) and has not yet been

---

that it had probably disappeared by the end of the Yüan dynasty ("Li-tai tz'u-hsüan-chi," pt. 2, p. 235).

29. These strategies can be seen as ways of formulating three of the four aims Lung Mu-hsün isolates as characteristic of anthologies: to be used for singing (*pien-ko*), to transmit the person (*ch'uan-jen*), to establish a tradition (*k'ai-tsung*), and to dignify a form (*tsun-t'i*); "Hsüan-tz'u piao-chun lun," p. 27. These three aims represent, of course, strictly literary—and literati—concerns.

identified. The preface is dated 1142 and has been preserved, but the collection itself, which included over 4,300 song lyrics in fifty fascicles from the T'ang through the Northern Sung, has been lost. Its size would seem to have precluded any really rigorous selectivity, but the preface indicates that its primary concern was rather with establishing a creditable genealogy for the genre.[30] And, indeed, the "return to elegance" announced by the title attests to an awareness that some canonical center to the culture had been lost but, more important, proclaims that it has successfully been recuperated. Another collection, the *Yüeh-fu ya-tz'u* compiled by Tseng Tsao (preface dated 1146), is clearly attempting to link the song lyric with a genre that had already acquired the mantle of respectability. It singles out *ya-cheng* as its standard for selection and voices its determination to exclude works that are erotic or jocular and thus leaves out, for example, song lyrics by Liu Yung. Notable, however, is the distinct lack of any discernible "elegance" or "correctness" to its haphazard method of arranging its contents, which consist of song lyrics by thirty-four identified poets of the Sung and over one hundred anonymous pieces. It is not mentioned in any texts from the Yüan or Ming.[31]

Yet a third and slightly earlier collection employs a somewhat different strategy toward similar ends. Titled *Plum Garden (Mei yüan)*, it was compiled, according to its preface, by Huang Ta-yü (cognomen Tsai-wan) in 1128, although the edition now extant includes lyrics of later date as well. Like the *Hua-chien chi*, it contains five hundred works (of poets from the T'ang through Sung dynasties) arranged in ten fascicles, all of which treat the same subject: the compilation of the collection, Huang tells us, had been inspired by a plum tree planted outside his study. Although this topical focus might suggest simply an interest on his part in producing a volume appropriate to a specific social context, it is important to note as well the particular quality of elegance that the plum blossom represents. As the *Ssu-k'u* editors observe, the collection contributes to the burgeoning effort during the Sung to single this flower out,[32] and in such a way, we might add, that allowed it to become an emblem for the virtues of the scholar. The *Mei yüan* thus simultaneously emphasizes an elegance of style and suggests an interest in attesting to an elegance of the song lyricist's character as well.[33]

30. See Wu Hsiung-ho, *T'ang Sung tz'u t'ung-lun*, pp. 303–5.
31. She Chih, "Li-tai tz'u-hsüan-chi," pt. 1, p. 283.
32. 5:4458–59. See also Maggie Bickford's study, *Bones of Jade, Soul of Ice: The Flowering Plum in Chinese Art* (New Haven: Yale University Art Gallery, 1985).
33. For further information on this volume, see She Chih, "Li-tai tz'u-hsüan-chi," pt.

A century later, we find renewed interest in placing the song lyric within the *shih* tradition of individual expression, an interest opposed to the anonymity of the lyrics in the *Yün-yao chi* and already evident in the arrangement of the *Hua-chien chi*—and the *Tsun-ch'ien chi* as well—by author. Essential to the effort to legitimize the genre, however, was the status of its representatives. As mentioned earlier, the strict chronology of the *Hua-chien chi* marks it as a collection that includes only the members of society for whom dates—and thus social position—could be ascertained. One Southern Sung anthology that shares this concern is Huang Sheng's *Hua-an tz'u-hsüan*, which combines two separate collections of ten fascicles each, the *T'ang Sung chu-hsien chüeh-miao tz'u-hsüan* and the *Chung-hsing i-lai chüeh-miao tz'u-hsüan*. There are two short prefaces dated 1249, one by Huang Sheng and the other by Hu Te-fang, and the statements by both of them are highly reminiscent of those made in prefaces to T'ang anthologies of *shih*. Hu's opens by emphasizing the rigorousness with which the editor selected the *tz'u* in the collection from a pool of extremely high quality:

> Ancient *yüeh-fu* are no longer composed, and long-and-short verses [*tz'u*] have emerged in their wake. The venerable officials and superior scholars of our dynasty take pleasure in letters, and many have also turned to these [*tz'u*]. They are scattered among various collections, however, and are not easy to examine as a whole. In this anthology Yü-lin [Huang Sheng] has been generous in scope and frugal in selection, sending out marvelous tones from a multitude of musical harmonies and bringing forth perfect gems from the midst of a myriad of treasures all on display. Thus, whoever obtains this volume will be able to see in their entirety the wonders of *tz'u* poets. His [Huang Sheng's] accomplishments are prodigious indeed![34]

Huang Sheng's own preface self-consciously situates what he is doing within the brief history of the genre:

> Long-and-short verses began in the T'ang and flourished in the Sung. T'ang *tz'u* are all included in the *Hua-chien chi*, and Sung *tz'u* for the most part can be seen in what Tseng Tuan-po [Tseng Tsao] edited. And the *Fu-ya* collection selects from both T'ang and Sung; it goes up to the end of

---

1, p. 285, who notes that despite the unremarkable and—not surprisingly—repetitive quality of many of the lyrics in the collection, it is extremely useful as a source for works, or versions of them, that do not appear in any other anthology of song lyrics. I should like to thank Professor Yang Hai-ming for stressing the importance of the *Mei yüan* in his comments during the discussion of my conference paper.

34. Huang Sheng, *Hua-an tz'u-hsüan* (rpt., Hong Kong: Chung-hua shu-chü, 1973), p. 4.

Hsüan-ho [1126], with more than 4,300 poems in all. Ah, how complete it is! Now, in addition, since the revival of the dynasty writers have emerged one after the other all the way up to the present day. Every individual has *tz'u*, and each *tz'u* has different forms. Those who know this but haven't yet seen them, or who have seen some but not all, are countless. In my leisure time I have collected from among several hundred poets and am calling this *Selections of Surpassingly Fine Song Lyrics*.[35]

And he goes on to catalog the variety of styles that he is seeking to represent.

Critics generally agree on the judgment Huang Sheng's title passes on his own powers of discernment (although what might strike the contemporary reader as a balance of representation has also been criticized by some as a lack of discrimination). Notable as well is the attention he devotes to establishing proper social and literary-historical credentials for his poets (and his volumes) by arranging them in chronological order; supplying information as to cognomens, sobriquets, and offices held, titles of individual collections, and relevant background details to the poems; and offering his own critical evaluations as well as those of contemporary readers. Such meticulous editorial concern is particularly noteworthy in view of the fact that no contemporary anthologies of *shih* provide such an impressive critical apparatus (although collections of individual poets certainly do). It is more extensive for the Southern Sung anthology than for the earlier one, and his standards for inclusion have become more socially stringent as well, for, unlike the earlier volume, it contains no song lyrics by monks or women.

Lung Mu-hsün observes that the *Hua-an tz'u-hsüan* is clearly directed toward "transmitting the author," as indeed this careful attention to biography would suggest. He notes further that this concern leads Huang at times to make questionable judgments about the authenticity of individual lyrics, guided as he was by his own notions of an author's personal style.[36] Given this penchant for a directly personal mode of expression, as opposed to one focused on the skillful performance of a role, it should come as no surprise that the poets who are best represented in the anthology as a whole are Su Shih and Hsin Ch'i-chi, with thirty-one and forty-two lyrics, respectively. Yang Hai-ming also notes that fondness for Hsin Ch'i-chi's patriotic *tz'u* in particular is reflected in the selection of lyrics on similar topics by other authors as well.[37] This interest in the potential for the song lyric to serve as a means of personal

35. Ibid., p. 158.
36. Lung Mu-hsün, "Hsüan-tz'u piao-chun lun," p. 13.
37. Yang Hai-ming, *T'ang Sung tz'u lun-kao*, p. 291.

and specifically political expression suggests the powerful temptation to appropriate for the *tz'u* elements of the critical tradition that had grown up around the *shih*. Huang Sheng's exploration of these possibilities still takes place, however, within the context of an interest in style more elusively and aesthetically conceived. And it was, in any event, not a particularly influential nor widely appreciated direction; if Huang wished seriously to promulgate a particular mode of composition, he was neither polemical enough in his comments nor one-sided enough in his selection to succeed. Despite the recognized quality of the selection, no Sung edition of the *Hua-an tz'u-hsüan* survives, the earliest extant version dating from 1574.[38]

Chou Mi's (1232–98) *Chüeh-miao hao-tz'u* shares with Huang Sheng's collection(s) a disappearance from the literary record that is even more curious and, most obviously, a remarkably similar title. Indeed, one of the main reasons for putting Huang's collections of *Surpassingly Fine Song Lyrics* from two dynastic periods together and renaming the volume was to distinguish it from Chou's *Surpassingly Fine Excellent Song Lyrics* (among whose nearly four hundred *tz'u* by 132 poets he includes his own, perhaps a bit immodestly, in greatest number; most poets are represented by only a handful of works apiece). From the very beginning, critical esteem for this anthology has been as impressive as the precariousness of its transmission. Chang Yen in his *Tz'u-yüan*, for example, writes that

In recent times the achievements of *tz'u* poets have been numerous. For example, the *Yang-ch'un pai-hsüeh chi*[39] and the *Chüeh-miao tz'u-hsüan* [by Huang Sheng] can indeed be looked at, but what [their editors] have selected is neither quintessential nor unified. How can they compare with the quintessential purity of what Chou Ts'ao-ch'uang has selected in the *Chüeh-miao hao-tz'u*? It is regrettable that its printing blocks have not been preserved; I'm afraid some meddler has also hidden away the printed editions.[40]

38. This edition is rarely seen. See She Chih, "Li-tai tz'u-hsüan-chi," pt. 2, p. 229.

39. An anthology in eight fascicles edited by Chao Wen-li that includes song lyrics in what would later be characterized as the *wan-yüeh* style, arranged not by author but apparently by tune (but unsystematically at that). Its title alludes to the two songs mentioned by Sung Yü in "Tui Ch'u-wang wen" whose difficulties elude the talents of most musicians (*Wen-hsüan*, ch. 45; noted by Lois Fusek, *Among the Flowers*, p. 33 n. 5). Chao places his volume explicitly in the tradition of the *Ts'ao-t'ang shih-yü*, claiming to be including the song lyrics omitted by the earlier collection; the two anthologies were aiming primarily to serve as songbooks, and they share a reputation for a certain editorial laxity. For a brief discussion, see She Chih, "Li-tai tz'u-hsüan-chi," pt. 2, pp. 230–31.

40. Ch. 2; in T'ang Kuei-chang, *Tz'u-hua ts'ung-pien*, 2:9a.

And this was written at most only two decades after the compilation of the anthology.[41] Rediscovered during the Ch'ing, the *Chüeh-miao hao-tz'u* then acquired a useful set of annotations with literary, biographical, and historical information—some of it, typically, arrived at inductively from reading the lyrics themselves—from the hands of Cha Wei-jen and Li O (1692–1752) in 1749. In his colophon to the text Li O makes comments similar to those of Chang Yen: "Sung anthologies of Sung *tz'u*, like Tseng Tuan-po's *Yüeh-fu ya-tz'u* and Huang Shu-yang's [Huang Sheng's] *Hua-an tz'u-hsüan*, yield [to the *Chüeh-miao hao-tz'u*] in terms of quintessential purity. It sets the standards for *tz'u* poets."[42] This opinion is echoed by the *Ssu-k'u* editors, who add: "Collections of song lyrics by Sung poets have also for the most part not been passed down to the present day. And even the names and surnames of the writers were not known to the world in their entirety. These scattered pearls and chips of jade have all been preserved thanks to this [the *Chüeh-miao hao-tz'u*]. Among anthologies of song lyrics, it is by far the best edition."[43]

Although the Ch'ing edition of the *Chüeh-miao hao-tz'u* we have today treats the song lyrics included with a literary-historical eye trained on the reading of *shih*, these critics also recognize that Chou Mi's primary concern lay rather with defining and promoting a distinctive style of *tz'u* that could, in effect, be considered canonical. Although no preface by him has come down with the collection, this program was evident to later readers in the poets and song lyrics represented in the volume. Cen-

41. There is a preface to the *Tz'u-yüan* by Ch'ien Liang-yu that is dated 1317, and some scholars have therefore assumed that the work was completed within two or three years of that date. Wu Hsiung-ho, however, has argued on the basis of both internal and external references that it was written between 1297 and 1307. He also notes that the latest poem in the *Chüeh-miao hao tz'u* can be dated to 1295 and that the collection itself was thus probably compiled shortly thereafter, since Chou Mi died in 1298. See his *T'ang Sung tz'u t'ung-lun*, pp. 315–16, 344–45.

42. Included, with other prefatory material, in Chou Mi, *Chüeh-miao hao-tz'u chien* (Shanghai: Shang-hai ku-chi ch'u-pan-she, 1983), p. [xvix].

43. *Ssu-k'u ch'üan-shu tsung-mu t'i-yao*, 5:4460. Anthologies like the *Yang-ch'un pai-hsüeh chi* mentioned above were notorious for the inconsistency and carelessness with which they treated names of *tz'u* poets included, thus providing small confirmation for Kao Shih-ch'i's opinion, evidently based on Chou Mi's accomplishments, regarding the relative ease of collecting poets of one's own time: "I have discussed how when anthologies examine the past from the present they suffer from being too far away. This is what the *Ku-liang* [*chuan*] calls listening to a distant tone and hearing what is fast and not hearing what is slow. When compared with how contemporaries can research and learn extensively, consider and examine carefully, eliminating infelicities and correcting what is farfetched, later generations have it ten times more difficult." From his preface to the *Chüeh-miao hao-tz'u*, included in *Chüeh-miao hao-tz'u chien*, p. [xvi].

tral to it were the terms being explored by many Southern Sung writers, as noted above, of *ya* and *cheng*, with their associations with notions of elegance, classicism, correctness, and orthodoxy.[44] Chang Yen, for example, opens the second section of his *Tz'u-yüan* with the statement that ancient forms of music all "come from *ya-cheng*," and states somewhat later that "in song lyrics one desires elegance and correctness."[45] In marked contrast to Huang Sheng, who had considered lyrics of what were later to be characterized as the *hao-fang* and *wan-yüeh* styles to be "surpassingly fine" in equal measure, for Chang Yen and Chou Mi only the latter meet the criteria of classical elegance and orthodox correctness. Thus, Chang writes that "among the writings of Hsin Chia-hsüan [Hsin Ch'i-chi] and Liu Kai-chih [Liu Kuo, 1154–1206], the song lyrics with heroic [*hao*] spirit are not *elegant* song lyrics."[46] And as if in agreement with this opinion, Chou Mi includes only three of Hsin's lyrics in his anthology, none of which is written in the patriotic, "heroic" mode with which the latter is associated, but rather in the *wan-yüeh* style that was becoming marked as the essence of the genre.[47]

CONFLICTING POSITIONS

It would be convenient to be able to say that the effort to gain acceptance for the song lyric into the Chinese literary canon was immediately successful and confirmed by the textual record. Unfortunately, however, the evidence indicates that although it was clearly common practice by the end of the Sung for literati to compose song lyrics, the collections that proved most popular in succeeding dynasties were not those that

44. For a succinct account of the differing but related poetics within which this concept developed, see Grace Fong, *Wu Wenying and the Art of Southern Song Ci Poetry* (Princeton: Princeton University Press, 1987), esp. pp. 44–56.

Since the notion of *cheng* was traditionally paired with that of *pien* in critical discourse going back to the "Great Preface," it should come as no surprise that one persistent tangent pursued by *tz'u* critics was the determination of the moments in which the history of poetry, or that of the song lyric, witnessed transformations as well. They commonly defined the *tz'u* itself as a transformation of the regulated verse or of the *chüeh-chü* and also located various subsequent "mutations" within the genre itself. These included, for example, those identified as having occurred after Wen T'ing-yün, after Su Shih, after the Northern Sung, and after the Southern Sung.

45. *Tz'u-hua ts'ung-pien*, 2:1a and 9b.

46. Ibid., 2:10a. Emphasis mine. The distinction between the *hao-fang* and *wan-yüeh* styles was made by the Ming dynasty Chang Yen in his *Shih-yü t'u-p'u* of 1594–95, in which he states in the introduction that in general the latter is the orthodox style for *tz'u*. As noted by Wu Hsiung-ho, *T'ang Sung tz'u t'ung-lun*, pp. 157–58.

47. As noted by Yang Hai-ming, *T'ang Sung tz'u lun-kao*, p. 291.

promulgated the most literary, elegant, or classical vision of *tz'u*. As mentioned above, the only two anthologies that seem to have circulated at all during the Yüan and Ming dynasties, each in multiple editions, were the *Hua-chien chi* and the *Ts'ao-t'ang shih-yü*,[48] with the others literally disappearing from sight. Nor does the handful of collections produced during this period deviate noticeably from the model set by the latter. The principles of selection are similarly unclear,[49] and so are the methods of organizing the lyrics, although they tend to be arranged either by topic or by tune length. In the case of the *Tz'u-lin wan-hsüan* of Yang Shen (1488–1559), for example, the *tz'u* selected vary widely in quality and appear in no discernible order, with songs by the same author scattered widely throughout the volume. There is no system to the nomenclature, with individuals referred to variously by given name, cognomen, or sobriquet, and there are frequent errors in attribution of authorship.[50]

48. The full title of this volume as it appears on the earliest extant edition, dating from 1392, is *Tseng-hsiu chien-chu miao-hsüan ch'ün-ying ts'ao-t'ang shih-yü*. Broad in coverage and of unknown editorial hand, this Sung collection has been criticized roundly for the lack of rigor in its selection. It is notable both for its arrangement by topic, which suggests close ties to an entertainment context and function as a source for songs appropriate to a particular situation, and for the remarkable disregard for this aspect of textual integrity over time. On the first point, Yang Hai-ming cites the Ch'ing scholar Sung Hsiang-feng's (1776–1860) observation that the versions of many lyrics as they appear in the anthology often differ from those in the poets' individual collections, disclosing revisions that were evidently made to render them more suitable for singing (*T'ang Sung tz'u lun-kao*, pp. 289–90). And as for the second, one Ming edition of 1538 tinkered with the text by reducing the number of topics, placing the songs in a different order, and revising many of the annotations. Another volume, edited in 1550 by Ku Ts'ung-ching and titled *Lei-pien ts'ao-t'ang shih-yü* (which enjoyed the widest circulation but was itself subject to further emendations), completely rearranged the songs from categorization by topic into categorization by tune pattern and length, reflecting, among other things, a loss of almost all of the actual music by the Ming and the consequent need to have the songs' prosodic forms presented in a more marked fashion. As the *Ssu-k'u* editors point out, the versions of the songs in this edition were used as bases for character counts of tunes in later prosodic registers of *tz'u* (*Ssu-k'u ch'üan-shu tsung-mu t'i-yao*, 5:4459). For further information on the *Ts'ao-t'ang shih-yü*, see She Chih, "Li-tai tz'u-hsüan-chi," pt. 2, pp. 226–27.

49. One notable exception, however, is the *Ming-hung yü-yin* compiled during the Yüan by P'eng Chih-chung (Hsien-yu-shan tao-shih), an anthology of "Taoist" *tz'u* written by thirty-six poets from the T'ang dynasty on. Many of the song lyrics included have to do with meditation, fasting, and alchemy, and a fair number of the tunes employed appear to be sui generis, having been devised for a particular occasion or topic. See Chao Tsun-yüeh, "Tz'u-chi t'i-yao," pt. 4, in *Tz'u-hsüeh chi-k'an* 3, no. 1 (March 1936): 41–44.

50. She Chih, "Li-tai tz'u-hsüan-chi hsü-lu," pt. 3, *Tz'u-hsüeh* 3 (1985): 276. The *Ssu-k'u ch'üan-shu tsung-mu t'i-yao* (5:4480) also takes issue with both the claims and the quality

Yang Hai-ming observes that this phenomenon reveals what kind of *tz'u*—those with no loftier aspirations than to suit an entertainment context—were valued throughout this period.[51] There seems obviously, at the same time, to have been a remarkable fall-off in the composition and preservation of all types of *tz'u* in general; the introduction to a seventeenth-century collection of *tz'u* by women, for example, laments the loss of what it estimates to have been half of all song lyrics ever written and bewails the difficulty ("ten times greater") of collecting *tz'u* when compared to *shih*, for which individual collections are both of higher quality and more accessible.[52] The familiar theory of the evolution of genres would account for the virtual disappearance of the song lyric by pointing to the supersession of *ch'ü*, but that, of course, tells us very little.

What does seem clear, first, is that the movement whose development we have been tracing is one whose outlines are visible probably only in hindsight. We have in truth but scattered bits of evidence: two anthologies with the word *ya* in their titles; later critics' approbation and discussion of a collection about whose aims its own editor, Chou Mi, was silent; and a few isolated critical statements, however articulate. Second, the discourse on *tz'u* seems as yet unable to resolve its potentially contradictory aims, either of accommodating itself to the legitimating terms established by the *shih* tradition or of insisting on its own distinctiveness as a genre, heralded by Li Ch'ing-chao's oft-cited statement in her "Tz'u-lun" that the song lyric was of a different species altogether—an attitude evident in Chang Yen's *Tz'u-yüan* as well. The accommodation was as yet halfhearted, for the attractions of a space and mode within which to speak those things that could not be spoken in *shih* were powerful ones, yet the insistence on absolute differentiation ran the risk of utterly marginalizing that mode. Third, the lack of a systematic attempt at this point to canonize either the genre itself or its

---

of Yang Shen's collection, criticizing the credibility of his assertion in the preface that he had gone through the collections of five hundred T'ang and Sung *tz'u* poets; the fact that the anthology turns out to include poets from the Chin, Yüan, and Ming dynasties as well resolves this problem of numbers but then opens the way for another critique regarding the lack of correlation between the preface and the contents of the volume. The editors also object to what they consider to be the crudeness of Yang's comments on the lyrics themselves.

51. Yang Hai-ming, *T'ang Sung tz'u lun-kao*, p. 289.

52. As cited by She Chih, "Li-tai tz'u-hsüan-chi hsü-lu," pt. 4, *Tz'u-hsüeh* 4 (1986): 246–47. The volume is the *Lin-hsia tz'u-hsüan*, edited by Chou Ming; three prefaces to the collection are dated 1671.

specific practitioners should hardly surprise us, given the fact that that process was just seriously getting under way for *shih*. Yen Yü's *Ts'ang-lang shih-hua*, which ground the historical, theoretical, and critical lenses within which T'ang poetry was to be examined, was itself but a product of the Southern Sung, and Kao Ping's *T'ang shih p'in-hui*, the first anthology to develop Yen Yü's model at length, did not appear until the beginning of the fifteenth century. Indeed, one might partially attribute the lack of attention paid to *tz'u* during the Yüan and Ming dynasties to the obsession with both defining the canon of *shih* and, implicitly, defending the latter's traditionally venerated position against the increasingly powerful encroachments of the claims of *wen*, or prose, as the truly serious vehicle of expression (demonstrated quite graphically, for example, in the elimination of a test of *shih* composition from the civil service examination until the middle of the eighteenth century). As suggested earlier, the tendency for discussions to set their terms in binary relationships—in this case, *shih* and *wen*—left little space for *tz'u*, the tertiary other. Thus, even in the Ch'ing dynasty we find an anthologist resorting to an involved argument that first creates a legitimate space for *tz'u* but then consigns it to the margins of respectability.

This text, Fu Hsieh-t'ung's *Tz'u-kou ch'u-p'ien*, which exists only in manuscript, displays the potentially contradictory attitudes just outlined. In the middle of his preface, for example, Fu presents a history of the song lyric from the *Hua-chien chi* that catalogs the variety of styles developing throughout the Sung and asserts, in a gesture designed to accommodate difference, that "[Huang] Hua-an's *Chüeh-miao tz'u-hsüan* both continues the *Hua-chien chi* and also paves the way for the *Ts'ao-t'ang*. Now alluring thoughts and intricately beautiful language are stimulated and proceed in many ways," and just as the ancients regaled themselves on delicacies of many different sorts—leeks, mullet, broth, and wine, all served at the same meal—so can *tz'u* "be joined together with *shih* and *wen* to please all tastes." He then reviews poetic forms of the past, from the *Shih-ching* through the *yüeh-fu* of the Han and up to the T'ang *chüeh-chü*, defining each as the song lyric of its respective era. In doing so, he provides the *tz'u* with nearly hegemonic validity.

Fu makes clear that his primary interest is in the music of *tz'u*, whose vanishing he can only lament. "Therefore," he continues, "since what is included in this cannot seek to accord with the ancients by means of their music, it must use the syntax and diction of contemporary *tz'u* to accord with the syntax and diction of ancient *tz'u*. As for the melodies and pitches, they will await someone who knows the tones." In his "General Principles" for the anthology, however, Fu invokes this concern with rhyme and pronunciation to downplay what might have been the literary aspirations of the collection. He offers it as the reason behind his relatively casual manner of compilation, which, he claims, simply sets the song lyrics down as he read them, in no particular order and without regard for, or indication of, an author's official status or biography. And he concludes with a remarkably straightforward assessment of the prevailing disesteem for the genre—"*tz'u* is certainly the Lesser Path [*hsiao tao*]"—and explains: "Writers of *shih* and *wen* for the most part regard filling in song lyrics as an inferior form, and students of the classics also see it as an activity that is not pressing. Therefore, while those who have found it interesting to dip their writing brushes in it are numerous, specialists in this path are few."[53]

CANONS AND CANONICITY IN THE CH'ING

Given the lack of a canonical definition of the origin and function of *tz'u* analogous to that possessed by *shih* (however restrictive the latter may have proved for both practice and interpretation), it is small wonder that so much critical energy came to be expended on providing some self-definition for the song lyric. Nor, furthermore, that the urgency—if not insecurity—endemic to its situation ran the risk of ossifying those definitions into rigid, exclusionary "schools" for whom only certain individuals could serve as exemplary models or "patriarchs." Nor, finally, that this discussion developed into a preoccupation with aspects of prosody, language, and style that marked a domain to which the other genres did not care to lay first claim.[54]

53. Included in Chao Tsun-yüeh, "Tz'u-chi t'i-yao," pt. 3, *Tz'u-hsüeh chi-k'an* 2, no. 3 (April 1935): 83, 88–90. Li O, who together with Cha Wei-jen had provided annotations to Chou Mi's *Chüeh-miao hao-tz'u*, comes to a similar conclusion in his preface to the *Ch'ün-ya tz'u-chi*. He argues there that because the song lyric is intrinsically a low form, if it does not possess elegance as its woof (*wei*), it will lose its correctness (*cheng*). As cited by Lung Mu-hsün, "Hsüan-tz'u piao-chun lun," p. 20.

54. It should go without saying that this emphasis on the stylistic distinctiveness of *tz'u* was shared by all critics, whatever their aspirations for the position of the genre. One Ch'ing anthology, for example, that explicitly places itself in the tradition of the *Ts'ao-t'ang shih-yü*—against which scholars promoting a more elegant notion of the form railed bitterly—provides one of the most succinct statements to this effect. This is the *Ts'ao-t'ang ssu-hsiang* in four fascicles, edited during the K'ang-hsi period by Ku Ts'ai. The title of the volume, of course, acknowledges its model, as does its specification of a certain number of topics and organization into *chüan* by length of tune (with *hsiao-ling* defined as consisting of any lyric up to 59 words, *chung-tiao* as 60 to 92 words, and *ch'ang-tiao* as anything longer; Ku observes that Chu I-tsun criticized these limits, but Ku defends himself by saying that "since these names exist, it can be done"). At the same time, however, the

Wu Hsiung-ho, in discussing the aftermath of the Ming dynasty Chang Yen's distinction between *wan-yüeh* and *hao-fang*, argues that it was made both with a very personal sense of style in mind—as opposed to a more generalizable doctrine—and also on the basis of a limited acquaintance with *tz'u* poets of the Sung, and that it was only later that critics like Wang Shih-chen (1634–1711) transformed features originally intended merely to characterize particular individuals into schools with identifiable "patriarchs."[55] Even more central to this new discourse on the song lyric was Wang's contemporary Chu I-tsun (1629–1709), who has traditionally been credited with the resurgence of *tz'u* to the critical and literary-historical arena after several centuries of relative slumber.[56]

---

introductory principles to the collection offer interesting refinements on some of the standard war-horses of the critical tradition. On the theory of the evolution of genres, for example, Ku writes that "when *shih* died out and then *tz'u* were composed, it was not that *shih* died out, but that the means of singing *shih* died out. And when *tz'u* died out and Northern and Southern *ch'ü* were composed, it was not that *tz'u* died out, but that the means of singing *tz'u* died out." He also presents a rhetorically effective argument for the specificity of the song lyric as a genre:

> If one can use T'ang *shih* to write *tz'u*, then one's *tz'u* will be excellent; however, *tz'u* are definitely not *shih*. If one can use Sung *tz'u* to write *ch'ü*, then one's *ch'ü* will be excellent; however, *tz'u* are definitely not *ch'ü*. For *tz'u* has a form and structure peculiar to *tz'u*, and a music and sentiment peculiar to *tz'u*. If it resembles *shih* then it will be too literary, and if it resembles *ch'ü* then it will be too unpolished, and both of these are defects. As a comparison, if one uses the *Shih*[-*chi*], the *Han* [*shu*], and the Eight Great Masters to write *pa-ku-wen*, it will certainly be excellent, but will *pa-ku-wen* thereupon become *ku-wen*?

Included in Chao Tsun-yüeh, "Tz'u-chi t'i-yao," pt. 1, *Tz'u-hsüeh chi-k'an* 1, no. 1 (April 1933): 96, 95.

55. In his *Hua-ts'ao meng-shih*, for example, Wang Shih-chen identifies his fellow natives of Chi-nan, Li Ch'ing-chao and Hsin Ch'i-chi, as the exemplars of the two styles, respectively. Wu's discussion also touches on the various ways in which other critics disagreed with or modified the distinction (*T'ang Sung tz'u t'ung-lun*, pp. 158–64).

As Wu points out earlier, the notion of "school" goes back to Lü Pen-chung's (1136 *chin-shih*) grouping of twenty-five poets into the Chiang-hsi *shih-p'ai* with Huang T'ing-chien as its patriarch, based on similar practices already common in Ch'an hagiography (p. 152). A version of this can be seen in Wang Cho's linking of *tz'u* poets with either Su Shih or Liu Yung in Wang's *Pi-chi man-chih* (ca. 1145–49) (ch. 2, included in *Tz'u-hua ts'ung-pien*, 1.1b; also noted by Wu Hsiung-ho, *T'ang Sung tz'u t'ung-lun*, p. 155). But the precedent for establishing genealogies is, of course, of much older vintage, having been set early in the sixth century by Chung Jung in his *Shih-p'in*, which identified poets being ranked as belonging to the tradition of either the *Shih-ching* or the *Ch'u-tz'u*.

56. Impressive evidence to this effect strikes the eye immediately when one opens T'ang Kuei-chang's *Tz'u-hua ts'ung-pien*. Of the eighty-five *tz'u-hua* included, eleven date from the Sung, two from the Yüan, four from the Ming, and all of the rest from the Ch'ing.

The reasons behind this renaissance, and Chu's particular contributions toward it, are too numerous and complex to be examined here.[57] Among others, one might cite the widespread fascination during the early Ch'ing with antiquity in general and the Sung dynasty in particular; the regional interest of Chu, a native of western Chekiang, in the many Southern Sung poets from that same geographical area;[58] his discovery and reprinting of Chou Mi's *Chüeh-miao hao-tz'u*; and the contemporary preoccupation, profoundly conservative at its core, with collecting, defining, and mastering the entire literary tradition. This effort shapes his *Tz'u-tsung*, compiled by 1678.

It is well known that Chu compiled this anthology in twenty-six fascicles (with four more added by Wang Sen [1653–1726]) of song lyrics from the T'ang through the Yüan dynasties on the basis of a limited number of individual collections, and even fewer anthologies, that were circulating at the time. His introduction comments on the losses that he knows to have occurred (to which later scholars have added), lists the volumes he has been able to peruse, and catalogs the various options other editors have employed in recording the name, title, place of birth, and so on, of the poets included. Also well known is Chu's desire to revise significantly the image of the *tz'u* prevalent at the beginning of the Ch'ing, requiring a small, profound, and oft-cited revision of literary history: "People now say that one must praise the *tz'u* of the Northern Sung; however, only in the Southern Sung did *tz'u* reach the ultimate craft, and only at the end of the Sung did it reach the ultimate transformation. Chiang Yao-chang [Chiang K'uei] is the most outstanding [poet of the genre]. What a pity it is that of Pai-shih's [Chiang K'uei's] *yüeh-fu* in five fascicles today only twenty-odd pieces have survived."[59]

Wang Sen's preface to the *Tz'u-tsung* articulates the theoretical program of the anthology at somewhat greater length. He begins by offering a famous attack on the view of literary history that had characterized the song lyric as the "remnant" of the *shih*, an attitude encapsulated in the very title of the much-reviled *Ts'ao-t'ang shih-yü*. Long-and-short verses, he opens, have been around as long as *shih*, so the *tz'u* can boast a lineage as venerable as that of its better-placed cousin. Moreover, the

<hr>

57. Madeline Chu touches on some of these issues in her article "Interplay between Tradition and Innovation: The Seventeenth-Century Tz'u Revival," in *Chinese Literature: Essays, Articles, Reviews* 9 (1987): 71–88.

58. Chu articulates this interest clearly in his preface to *Meng Yen-lin tz'u*, as cited by Lung Mu-hsün, "Hsüan-tz'u piao-chun lun," pp. 18–19.

59. Chu I-tsun, *Tz'u-tsung* (1691; rpt., n.p.: Chung-hua shu-chü, 1973) 1.5b.

familiar evolution from ancient verse to *yüeh-fu* to regulated verse to *tz'u*, he declares, has produced forms that are like horses with "separate bits but galloping side-by-side, not one in front and the other behind. To say that *shih* degenerated to become *tz'u* or to consider *tz'u* as the remnant of *shih* is not an argument that penetrates the whole."[60] After touching on the vibrant but qualitatively mixed early history of the genre, he identifies his patriarch: "Chiang K'uei of Hsiang-yang emerged, with lapidary verses and refined words that return to purity and elegance. Thereupon Shih Ta-tsu and Kao Kuan-kuo flanked him on either side. Chang Chi and Wu Wen-ying took him as master first, and Chao I-fu, Chiang Chieh, Chou Mi, Ch'en Yün-heng, Wang I-sun, Chang Yen, and Chang Chu studied him afterward."[61] Whatever disagreements one might have with the hierarchy Wang provides here—and they have been numerous—the point remains that he is singling out *tz'u* poets from the Southern Sung who embody in different ways ideals of elegance and refinement that he and Chu are seeking to establish as the preeminent style for the genre.[62] Their instrument will be this anthology, which he hopes "may eliminate at once the vulgarity of the *Ts'ao-t'ang*; those who write to music will then know the orthodox tradition [*tsung*]."[63]

The language Wang employs here and the critical order of evaluation he presents are reminiscent not only of descriptions of the Kiangsi poetry group,[64] but of Kao Ping's categorization of the T'ang poets as well, which in turn was heavily influenced by Yen Yü's example. And the selection of song lyrics for the volume itself, however hampered by the limited number of sources and deficient in text-critical oversight,[65] also reflects the priorities that the two compilers established. Whereas some poets only have one song lyric each included, those from the

---

60. Chu I-tsun, *Tz'u-tsung* 1.2a–2b.

61. Ibid. 1.3a–3b.

62. Chiang K'uei was a particularly appealing model because, as Lin Shuen-fu puts it, his life was one "almost entirely devoted to the cultivation of art." See *The Transformation of the Chinese Lyrical Tradition: Chiang K'uei and Southern Sung Tz'u Poetry* (Princeton: Princeton University Press, 1978), p. 58.

63. Chu I-tsun, *Tz'u-tsung* 1.5a–5b.

64. As noted by Lung Mu-hsün, "Hsüan-tz'u piao-chun lun," p. 17.

65. Ting Shao-i, who compiled a *Ch'ing tz'u-tsung pu* in 1894 (rpt., Peking: Chunghua shu-chü, 1986), says that he has corrected many—but not all—of the errors in the *Tz'u-tsung*, which he attributes both to the unavailability of good editions of Sung and Yüan *tz'u* and to Chu's failure to compare versions from one edition to the next. In his *T'ing-ch'iu-sheng-kuan tz'u-hua*, as cited by She Chih, "Li-tai tz'u-hsüan-chi hsü-lu," pt. 5, *Tz'u-hsüeh* 5 (1986): 257.

Southern Sung mentioned in the introduction and preface are heavily represented in the anthology; the thirty-two *tz'u* of Chiang K'uei, for example, probably constituted a significant proportion of the total number of works by the poet that Chu had seen, and the lesser members of the group are present in similar depth. The collection's insistence on the stylistic distinctiveness of the song lyric as a genre confirms what John Guillory, drawing on Bakhtin, has argued to be fundamental to the process of canon-formation, the marking of a language that can be defined as the specifically "literary" coin of a hermetic, privileged community and the final expunging of the popular or "vulgar" traces of the form.[66]

Arguments waged, however, concerning the precise nature of that language. However unsuccessful Chu I-tsun may ultimately have been in eliminating "heterodox"—whether "vulgar" or "heroic"—styles of *tz'u* and controlling the quality of lyrics written according to "orthodox" models, his influence on the subsequent history of the genre is undeniable. Although critical opinion agrees that followers of the Che school eventually declined into a vacuous or, worse, "lascivious," preciosity, Chu's framing of the discourse was adopted by later scholars who were adamantly opposed to his aims. The very fact that critical discussion coalesced into schools with distinct programs may reflect to a certain extent the power of Chu's example. Moreover, many of his key assumptions remained intact, albeit developed in very different ways. Thus, scholars associated with the Ch'ang-chou school that flourished a century later might have rejected his notion of what was orthodox but not the presumption that *some* orthodox or canonical style existed and should be promulgated. Chou Chi (1781–1839) in his *Tz'u-pien*, for example, clearly identifies a tradition beginning with Wen T'ing-yün that he considers *cheng* and one starting with Li Yü that is *pien*, and he meticulously lists the poets that fall under either category. Other critics, following a model developed earlier for discussing and classifying painters, which itself was borrowing a precedent established in Ch'an Buddhism, divided *tz'u* poets into a Northern and a Southern tradition (*tsung*) and, much as had been the case in the visual arts, found the latter decidedly superior.[67]

The Ch'ang-chou critics differed significantly from the earlier Che school, however, in the manner by which they sought to establish the canon of the song lyric. Rather than insisting on the peculiar distinctiveness of *tz'u*, scholars like Chang Hui-yen (1761–1833) and Chou Chi

66. See his "Canonical and Non-canonical: A Critique of the Current Debate," *ELH* 54 (1987): 483–527.
67. As noted by Wu Hsiung-ho, *T'ang Sung tz'u t'ung-lun*, p. 163.

sought to rehabilitate the genre by appropriating for it the hermeneutics that had developed in connection with the *Shih-ching*, thereby accommodating it to the established *shih* tradition. Thus, the inscription of the male gaze and the ascription of male desire to the languishing woman in lyrics by poets like Wen T'ing-yün could be re-viewed as the figuration of political concern about the state of the empire and the frustration of a loyal official at his inability to do anything about it. The details of this program have been discussed at length by Chia-ying Yeh Chao[68] and need not be recapitulated here. Suffice it to say at this point that although Chang Hui-yen has been faulted both for his outrageously improbable allegorical interpretations and for assuming that a valid comparison could be made between the song lyric and the *Book of Songs* at all, the former had already been accepted practice for several centuries and the latter could be supported, as we have seen, by several textual precedents within the literature on *tz'u* as well.

LATER REDEFINITIONS

Other *tz'u* scholars in the nineteenth century followed Chang's and Chou's leads in different ways. The rich literature on and of the song lyric in the nineteenth century attests to the transforming influence of the Ch'ang-chou school, and I shall mention only two examples. The first is a general discussion introducing an unpublished anthology in eight fascicles, the *Tz'u-kuei* (dated 1863), compiled by Yang Hsi-min, who makes a number of points that suggest his decision to situate the song lyric unambiguously within the *shih* historical and critical tradition. First, he interprets the *shih-yü* epithet in such a way as to insist on the connection, rather than the differentiation, between the two forms: "Long-and-short verses are remnants of *shih*. This being so, *shih* then is the source and *tz'u* the tributary. If the source is not distant, how can the tributary be long?" And he goes on to stress the fact that *tz'u* poets like Wen T'ing-yün, Wei Chuang, Yen Shu, Yen Chi-tao, Ch'in Kuan, and Ho Chu could all write *shih* poetry as well; that Su Shih and Huang T'ing-chien were especially renowned for the latter; and that *tz'u* poets whose other writings are not worth reading are "like tributaries without the source." Second, he de-emphasizes the distinguishing feature of the song lyric, its musical performance, by arguing that "even though the ancient poems all were written to music, later poems without music are

---

68. In "The Ch'ang-chou School of *Tz'u* Criticism," in *Chinese Approaches to Literature from Confucius to Liang Ch'i-ch'ao*, ed. Adele Austin Rickett (Princeton: Princeton University Press, 1978), pp. 151–88.

numerous and are not therefore prevented from being good poems. But a tone and rhythm that come naturally cannot be lost. With *tz'u* the situation is the same. If you can sing, you will certainly be good; but if you cannot sing, are you therefore not a *tz'u* poet?" He then observes that few people can understand the musical notation Chiang K'uei provided for his song lyrics.

Yang Hsi-min also argues that critical concepts apply with equal validity to the two genres. For example, he writes that "some people think that in *tz'u* one esteems having the meaning within and the words on the surface [*i nei yen wai*], but those who understand this are few. They fail to realize that having meaning within words is true of all writing of subtlety, and not just the song lyric." The most compelling incorporation of the *shih* tradition can be seen in a statement that appears more than once in his discussion, a statement to the effect that "in studying *tz'u* one should begin with *yüeh-fu* of the Han, Wei, and Six Dynasties, and then take Wen [T'ing-yün], Wei [Chuang], the two Yens, Ch'in [Kuan], and Ho [Chu] as the canonical orthodox tradition [*cheng tsung*]."[69] Chao Tsun-yüeh notes that this is modeled on Kao Ping's discussion of T'ang poetry, but the precedent in fact goes back to Yen Yü, who was particularly concerned with the question of systematic study of past models.[70]

As the admiring reference above to Su Shih and Huang T'ing-chien should suggest, Yang Hsi-min's tastes run precisely to the Northern Sung *tz'u* poets whose standing Chu I-tsun and his school had been anx-

69. Chao Tsun-yüeh, "Tz'u-chi t'i-yao," pt. 2, *Tz'u-hsüeh chi-k'an* 1, no. 2 (August 1933): 83–84.

70. Yen Yü's prescription, of course, appears in different forms and is considerably longer. One version recommends the following:

> First, one must thoroughly recite the *Ch'u-tz'u* and sing them morning and night so as to make them his basis. When he recites the "Nineteen Old Poems," the "Yüeh-fu in Four Sections," the five-syllabic poetry of Li Ling and Su Wu and of the Han and the Wei, he must do them all thoroughly. Afterward, he will take up the collected poetry of Li [Po] and Tu [Fu] and read them [the poems] in dovetail fashion as people of today study the classics. Next, he will take up comprehensively the famous masters of the High T'ang. Having allowed all this to ferment in his bosom for a long time, he will be enlightened spontaneously [*tzu-jan wu-ju*]. Although he might not attain the ultimate of study, still he will not go off the correct road.

From *Ts'ang-lang shih-hua chiao-shih*, ed. Kuo Shao-yü (Peking: Jen-min wen-hsüeh ch'u-pan-she, 1962), p. 1. Trans. (with slight revisions) Richard John Lynn, "Orthodoxy and Enlightenment: Wang Shih-chen's Theory of Poetry and Its Antecedents," in *The Unfolding of Neo-Confucianism*, ed. W. T. de Bary, Studies in Oriental Culture, no. 10 (New York: Columbia University Press, 1975), p. 220.

ious to diminish. Ironically enough, Yang employs the same verb *hsi*, "wash away," "eliminate," that Wang Sen had used in speaking of the *Tz'u-tsung's* accomplishment vis-à-vis the *Ts'ao-t'ang shih-yü*, to describe the contribution made by major Northern Sung poets: "Ou[-yang Hsiu], Su [Shih] and Huang [T'ing-chien] are unrestrained and unconventional, genial and liberal, heroic and strange. They eliminated at once the practice of writing about latticework and gauze; this is how the orthodox was transformed and became [a new] orthodoxy." He also takes Tsou Hsü-shih (Tsou Chih-mo, 1658 *chin-shih*) to task for criticizing Northern Sung poets' failure to write long *tz'u* in great numbers. This reflects a poor understanding of literary history, Yang argues, for all forms of a genre are not always simultaneously to a poet's hand at any given moment in time. To say that Su and Huang could not write long *tz'u* makes little sense if Liu Yung was the first to develop the form. Like Chu and other early Ch'ing critics, Yang concludes, Tsou is too one-sided: "When shopping for food, he only knows how to buy what is inexpensive; he has never heard the subtleties of *tz'u*."[71]

An earlier passage of the text articulates in a different manner Yang's rejection of the narrow, doctrinaire exclusivity that he finds characteristic of critics at the beginning of the dynasty:

> Now writing has its roots in inborn emotions and is assisted by learning; when both are present, then as soon as one sets the brush down to send forth words, the workings of heaven will start of themselves. Nothing has been determined with regard to long composition or short piece, nor between the "clear and empty" [*ch'ing-k'ung*] and the "solid and substantial" [*chih-shih*] styles. The *Shih*[-*chi*] is not the same as the "[Li-]sao"; the "Sao" is not the same as the *Chuang-tzu*; the *Kung*[-*yang*] and *Ku*[-*liang*] are not the same as the *Tso*[-*chuan*] and the *Kuo*[-*yü*]—how can one therefore settle on one explanation?[72]

Although considerably more eclectic and flexible in his judgments, Yang Hsi-min has clearly been influenced by the views of Chang Hui-yen; he nonetheless feels that the latter's school has still not paid suf-

71. In Chao Tsun-yüeh, "Tz'u-chi t'i-yao," pt. 2, p. 85. Tsou Chih-mo's position is also presented by Grace Fong in her *Wu Wenying and the Art of Southern Song Ci Poetry*, p. 164. One might, of course, take Yang to task in turn for assuming that genres have life histories of their own that evolve independently of human agency, but given the established discourse, it would have been difficult for him to think otherwise.

72. Chao Tsun-yüeh, "Tz'u-chi t'i-yao," pt. 2, p. 84. *Ch'ing-k'ung* and *chih-shih* were terms first used by Chang Yen in his *Tz'u-yüan* to establish the superiority of Chiang K'uei as the exemplar of the former style. Along with the Ming dynasty Chang Yen's distinction between *wan-yüeh* and *hao-fang*, they stand at the center of the critical terminology developed to refer specifically to the song lyric.

ficient attention to a significant dimension of *tz'u* history. Thus, on the one hand he notes that in selecting songs for his anthology he has looked for those with *pi-hsing*, "comparison and evocative images," in other words, metaphorical imagery that would lend itself to the interpretive operations favored by the followers of Chang Hui-yen's method. He also credits Chang for having liberated scholars of *tz'u* from the fetters of Chu's *Tz'u-tsung* by "going against the current" to bring Wen T'ing-yün to prominence, thereby "opening up a new realm" in which *tz'u* incorporates *pi-hsing*. On the other hand, however, he then chooses to focus his critical attention on a group of poets different from that favored by the earlier critic: "But the path of [Ou-yang] Liu-i, [Su Tung-]p'o, and [Huang Shan-]ku has not yet been traversed by many wooden clogs. For an era to have brave heroes, it must not shrink from asking where the ford is."[73] And there is no question that this relatively broad-minded attitude has indeed been evident throughout his entire discussion.[74]

Finally, we can see a balance between the positions of Chu I-tsun and Chang Hui-yen explored quite literally in the writings of the late Ch'ing critic Ch'en T'ing-cho. Ch'en is best known as a proponent of the theories associated with the Ch'ang-chou school, which he discussed in his *Pai-yü-chai tz'u-hua* of 1892 and illustrated in his anthology *Tz'u-tse*. Less than twenty years earlier, however, in 1874, Ch'en had edited a collection entitled *Yün-shao chi* and explained the principles behind it, which at that time were wholeheartedly those of Chu I-tsun, in a work called the *Tz'u-t'an ts'ung-hua*. A recent reprinting of the *Pai-yü-chai tz'u-hua* provides extensive documentation on these two efforts, so I shall not discuss them in detail here. The two pairs of texts do, however, not only articulate quite clearly the general principles of both the Chu and the Chang schools, but also present us with positions that are somewhat more supple than those of either faction.

The *Yün-shao chi*, which exists only in draft form, includes 3,434 songs by over 1,100 poets from the T'ang through the Ch'ing dynasties. Interestingly enough, given Ch'en's repeated insistence in the *Tz'u-t'an ts'ung-hua* on the distinctiveness of *tz'u*, the anthology is modeled on Shen Te-ch'ien's (1673–1769) *Ku-shih yüan* in being organized chronologically by dynasty and, within each section, by the social status

73. Ibid. The last allusion, of course, is to *Lun-yü* 18/6.
74. As has been noted by others, the more supple and balanced rethinking of Chang Hui-yen's ideas had already been evident in the critical work of Chou Chi. See Chia-ying Yeh Chao, "The Ch'ang-chou School," pp. 176–83, and Grace Fong, *Wu Wen-ying and the Art of Southern Song Ci Poetry*, pp. 167–73.

of each author.[75] (Women come at the end, preceding only a fascicle of "miscellaneous forms" [*tsa-t'i*] that includes some lusty "mountain songs" [*shan-ko*] that Ch'en evidently could not bear to leave out.) The preface to the collection borrows shamelessly from Chu I-tsun's introduction to his anthology,[76] although it does admit that its model is the *Tz'u-tsung*. There is the same recounting of the evolution of *tz'u*, an argument similar to Wang Sen's against the notion of *tz'u* as the remnant of *shih* ("*tz'u* is that by which one remedies the deficiencies of *shih*; it is not the remnant of *shih*"),[77] and the declaration that he "considers *ya-cheng* to be the orthodox tradition."[78] Song lyrics from the Southern Sung are represented in greatest number within the collection; Ch'en's *Tz'u-tan ts'ung-hua* in fact announces that he regards the Southern Sung as the "orthodox tradition,"[79] and there are references throughout to the importance of prosodic rules and to his esteem for the *wan-yüeh* and marginalization of the *hao-fang* styles, all of which stems from Li Ch'ing-chao's critical dictum regarding the distinctiveness of *tz'u* and the theories of Chang Yen and Chu I-tsun. At the same time, however, Ch'en cannot resist confessing to a fondness for the songs of Wen T'ing-yün, whom Chu had not valorized but whose style Ch'en feels many critics of his time have failed to understand, and for the song lyrics of the Northern Sung. The Che school, of course, had given pride of place to the Southern Sung, but Ch'en writes that he personally prefers the loftiness and naturalness of the earlier *tz'u*, which are, admittedly, more "vulgar" and "impure" than those of the following era. If one thinks of the former as analogous to the "Airs" and the latter as the "Elegances," he argues, then there is room for both.[80]

Less than two decades later Ch'en T'ing-cho declared that Chang Hui-yen's *Tz'u-hsüan* was ten times finer than Chu I-tsun's *Tz'u-tsung*.[81]

---

75. *Tsu-pen chiao-chu*, 2:855. This system had an earlier precedent within the *tz'u* anthological tradition, for the *Chung-hsiang chi*, a collection of song lyrics by women compiled by Ch'ien Yüeh in the last decades of the seventeenth century, arranged its over four hundred works by author in descending order of social status, from wives of high officials to singing girls. As noted by She Chih, "Li-tai tz'u-hsüan-chi," pt. 4, pp. 249–50. The same ordering principle can be found, of course, in certain anthologies of *shih*.

76. This is graphically presented in a chart in the recent reprinting; see *Tsu-pen chiao-chu*, 2:894 n. 10.

77. Ibid., p. 805.

78. Ibid., p. 806.

79. Ibid., p. 846.

80. Ibid., p. 816.

81. Ibid., 1:11 (*Tz'u-hua ts'ung-pien*, vol. 1/2a), and 2:533 (*Tz'u-hua tsung-pien*, vol. 5/11b). Ch'ü Hsing-kuo discusses the reasons behind Ch'en's change of views—key among

The influence of the Ch'ang-chou school is evident throughout this work in its insistence on treating *tz'u* and *shih* in the same critical terms. Both genres, for example, share a list of traits to be avoided:

> No matter whether one is composing *shih* or composing *tz'u*, one cannot have the style of a rotten Confucian, nor the style of a common person, nor the style of a talented scholar. Though people realize that the rotten Confucian and the common styles are impermissible, they don't realize that the talented scholar's style is also impermissible. . . . As soon as people see the rotten Confucian and the common person's styles, they detest them; but when it comes to the talented scholar's style, there's no one who sees it who doesn't take pleasure in it. Thus, the defect therein is even more profound.[82]

In addition to linking *shih* and *tz'u* here from a negative perspective, Ch'en T'ing-cho also insists on their relationship and comparability for other purposes as well. More than once in the *Pai-yü-chai tz'u-hua*, therefore, Ch'en remarks on the analogies between their stages of evolution: "If we compare *tz'u* to *shih*, the T'ang is like the Han and Wei; the Five Dynasties is like the Western and Eastern Chin and Six Dynasties; the Northern and Southern Sung are like the T'ang; the Yüan and Ming are like the Northern and Southern Sung; and Ch'ing *tz'u* are like Ch'ing *shih*."[83] As the two can be periodized, so can they be collected in similar manners. The *Pai-yü-chai tz'u-hua* includes the general preface to Ch'en's *Tz'u-tse* that describes the selection and organization of its 2,600 songs into four categories: "great elegances" (*ta-ya*), "heroic songs" (*fang-ko*), "calmed emotions" (*hsien-ch'ing*), and "distinctive modes" (*pieh-tiao*), with the first group defined as the orthodox and the other three as its subordinates.[84] Not only are the titles of the groups drawn largely from specific texts in the *shih* tradition, but the arrangement and the discussion that frames it echo those found in Po Chü-i's famous letter to Yüan Chen concerning his collected poems.[85]

Running throughout Ch'en's text is the assumption that "*shih* and *tz'u* have the same form and different functions"; this in fact, as he con-

---

which may have been his fondness for the song lyrics of Wen T'ing-yün, whom Chang Hui-yen also esteemed—in the appendix to *Pai-yü-chai tz'u-hua tsu-pen chiao-chu*, pp. 896–97.

82. *Tsu-pen chiao-chu*, 2:561; *Tz'u-hua ts'ung-pien*, vol. 5/18a.
83. *Tsu-pen chiao-chu*, 2:576; *Tz'u-hua ts'ung-pien*, vol. 5/19b.
84. *Tsu-pen chiao-chu*, 2:538–39; *Tz'u-hua ts'ung-pien*, vol. 5/12b–13a.
85. "Yü Yüan Chiu shu," in *Po Chü-i hsüan-chi*, ed. Wang Ju-pi (Shanghai: Shang-hai ku-chi ch'u-pan-she, 1980), p. 359.

tinues in this passage, links them more closely than *tz'u* and *ch'ü*, which "have different functions, and forms that are also slightly different. This cannot fail to be discriminated."[86] Ultimately, however, there is a recognizable priority assigned to *shih*, and on several grounds. The diction of the *shih*, for example, is inviolable: "Within a *shih* one cannot write in the language of *tz'u*, but within a *tz'u* there is no prohibition against the language of *shih*."[87] The mastery of one must also precede that of the other: "*Shih* and *tz'u* have one principle; nevertheless, someone who is not skilled at *tz'u* can be skilled at *shih*, but someone who is not skilled at *shih* decidedly cannot be skilled at *tz'u*. Therefore, in studying *tz'u* it is important first to master *shih*. If in writing *shih* one has not yet planted one's feet firmly anywhere and yet rushes off to study *tz'u*—I've never seen anyone manage both."[88] And finally, there is the intractable fact of temporal precedence: "*Shih* has its own realm, and *tz'u* has its own realm: the two share one principle. There are realms that have been opened up by *shih* poets, however, that *tz'u* poets have not yet seen, owing to the fact that one came before the other in time." Ch'en goes on to single out various *shih* poets whose "realms" have in fact been explored by counterparts in the *tz'u* tradition, but he insists that none has matched the achievements of T'ao Ch'ien and Tu Fu; that possibility, however, may certainly yet be fulfilled.[89]

CONCLUSION

The discussions that take place in these anthologies encapsulate the conflicts endemic to discourse on the song lyric up through the Ch'ing dynasty. On the one hand, the *tz'u* could be located squarely within, indeed at the very heart of, the lyric tradition and legitimated through treatment analogous to that accorded to texts by *shih* poets and through the appropriation of terms borrowed from the *shih* tradition. On the other, however, critics were on the whole neither able nor inclined to deny the special roots of the *tz'u* in a history of performance and song that would not necessarily wish to lay claim to the political and moral seriousness of other written forms. We have seen how persistent was the effort to eradicate, as much as possible, the questionable elements of

86. *Tsu-pen chiao-chu*, 2:778; *Tz'u-hua ts'ung-pien*, vol. 8/11a.

87. *Tsu-pen chiao-chu*, 2:573; *Tz'u-hua ts'ung-pien*, vol. 5/20b. This position runs directly counter to the dominant opinion, mentioned above, against importing the diction and methods of *shih* into *tz'u*.

88. *Tsu-pen chiao-chu*, 2:673; *Tz'u-hua ts'ung-pien*, vol. 7/1a.

89. *Tsu-pen chiao-chu*, 2:781–82; *Tz'u-hua ts'ung-pien*, vol. 8/11b–12a.

the history of *tz'u* and establish—though not without considerable disagreement—a canon within its own tradition. But much as contemporary critiques of dominant traditions have discovered the fineness of the line between difference and marginalization, so the emphasis on the distinctive aesthetics of *tz'u* ran the risk of consigning it to the privacy— and the isolation—of a room of its own. That the process of legitimation eventually explored more accommodating paths as well may account for what, by the end of the Ch'ing, could be recognized as its success. Early in the twentieth century, May Fourth rewritings of Chinese literary history that discovered and valorized what could be seen as popular genres within the written tradition consolidated this rehabilitation. What should be kept firmly in mind, finally, is the recognition of this entire history as a discursive process, one that does not necessarily reflect the actual dimensions of the interest in and composition of *tz'u*. And in the end, what may have appealed most powerfully was precisely what resisted appropriation and could never be acknowledged: the song lyric's claim on a private space of the affections within which to speak that which could not be spoken in the *shih*, whose canons of discourse were inexorably framed by public and political values.

TWO

Man's Voice / Woman's Voice:
Questions of Gender

Engendering the Lyric:
Her Image and Voice in Song

Grace S. Fong

In the song lyric genre, a conceptual "feminine" occupies a paradoxical position of centrality and alterity. There has always been within its poetics a nexus of the "feminine" around which complex issues of voice, representation, stylistics, and critical debate have revolved. Yet the song lyric as literary discourse was fashioned almost exclusively by male poets and critics. If this nexus of the "feminine" is a male construction, a reflector of male values and preferences, and if women had almost no active part in shaping the genre, it would be germane to begin by examining this "feminine" nexus in the song lyric, to articulate its origin and components in the poetics and critical discourse of the song lyric, and to ask what this poetic "feminine" has meant for women poets writing in the genre.

Since an important aspect of the "feminine" in the song lyric—perhaps the originating force of its theoretical and critical importance—is the representation or re-presentation of the image of woman, the implications for women poets attempting self-representation in the song lyric are especially significant. I wish to begin this study, therefore, by approaching the gendered aesthetics and poetics of the song lyric, part of which involves contextualizing the representation of women in relation to the history of the gaze in Chinese poetry, before proceeding to discuss if and how women poets re-created themselves in the feminized space of the song lyric.

YIN/YANG

Gender as a conceptual category of difference has always been implicated on some level in the poetics and critical perception of the song

107

lyric. In praxis, gender was often made into a prominent trope, deployed in rhetoric and affecting stylistic patterns, lyrical voice, and persona. When the song lyric became established as a distinct literary form, it was primarily associated with the boudoir theme, with images of women and love, and, therefore, with the "feminine" in language and sentiment. Evidence of this association is legion in the anthology *Hua-chien chi* (preface dated 940), the founding monument of the song lyric as a genre.

The perception of the "feminine" as an aesthetic and thematic value in song lyric poetics did not occlude the binary subdivision that took place. Gender-marked oppositional poetics appeared: alongside the female persona and feminine style commonly found in early song lyrics, a male voice and a masculine style developed.[1] But in the hierarchy of gender-marked styles evolved in the genealogy of *tz'u* poetics, the male-voiced, masculine (*hao-fang*) style was generally held as derivative or unorthodox. In mainstream criticism, the *wan-yüeh* style, coded as "feminine," came to be privileged as orthodox; thus, some aesthetic notion of femininity was regarded as a defining characteristic of the genre. Though certain critics championed the "masculine" style, the orthodox view, with its roots in the late Sung, came into currency during the Ming, and informed discourse on the song lyric during the Ch'ing.[2] "The song lyric in its essence excels by charm; it valorizes a feminine and pliant [*yin-jou*] kind of beauty."[3] This statement on the aesthetics of the song lyric made by the distinguished scholar Miao Yüeh several decades ago represents the crystallization of a long-standing view. More recently (1982), in an essay on the characteristics of the song lyric, Miao refers to the lyrics of the late T'ang and the Later Shu, that is, of the *Hua-chien chi*, as "having a delicate and refined style" that suited the thematic content and performance context of contemporary song lyrics,

---

1. The male voice is already evident in song lyrics by literati of the late T'ang, Five Dynasties, and early Northern Sung. But the masculine style, with its dramatic change in theme and diction, is introduced in a large number of song lyrics by Su Shih.

2. In the Southern Sung, the term *hao-fang*, "heroic-flamboyant," was already used to refer to song lyrics in the masculine style. The masculine style was apparently problematic for the music, that is, for singing. See Shen I-fu, *Yüeh-fu chih-mi*, in *Tz'u-hua ts'ung-pien*, ed. T'ang Kuei-chang (Peking: Chung-hua shu-chü, 1986), 1:282. The term *wan-yüeh*, in opposition to *hao-fang*, was first used in the Ming. See Kao Chien-chung, "Wan-yüeh, hao-fang yü cheng-pien," *Tz'u-hsüeh* 2 (1983):150–53. In the late Southern Sung–early Yüan, however, Chang Yen had already judged *tz'u* to be "more *wan* [graceful, feminine] than *shih* poetry when expressing feeling"; see his *Tz'u-yüan*, in *Tz'u-hua ts'ung-pien*, 1:263.

3. Miao Yüeh, *Shih tz'u san-lun* (rpt., Shanghai: Shang-hai ku-chi ch'u-pan-she, 1982), p. 68.

and as "having a kind of feminine beauty." He further glosses this
"feminine beauty" by Wang Kuo-wei's characterization of the song lyric
genre as "lovely and ornamented" (*yao-miao i-hsiu*).[4]

The very nature of the feminine style, however, problematized the
writing of song lyrics for some male poets. If the status and meaning of
poetry (*shih*) were changing within the intellectual and moral climate of
the Northern Sung, the status of the popular new genre of party songs
was questionable and unstable at best.[5] On a limited scale, Su Shih's
mocking remark to Ch'in Kuan that Ch'in had been learning to write in
Liu Yung's style aimed at devaluing precisely the sentimental, overly
feminized language of song lyrics.[6] More profoundly, the feminized song
lyric as the site for the expression of private, "unmanly" (and thus un-
seemly?) emotions, and of erotic love and passion in particular, seems to
have brought out deep unease and called for moralistic reaction and
self-censure in some male poets. As early as the Five Dynasties, Sun
Kuang-hsien (d. 968), a well-known song lyricist whose works are included in the *Hua-chien chi*, devoted an entry in the *Pei-meng so-yen* to his
contemporary Ho Ning (898–955), whose song lyrics are also included
in the *Hua-chien chi*. Sun noted that "the prime minister of Chin, Ho
Ning, was fond of composing song lyrics in his youth. His lyrics had

4. Miao Yüeh and Yeh Chia-ying, *Ling-hsi tz'u-shuo* (Shanghai: Shang-hai ku-chi
ch'u-pan-she, 1987), p. 30; quoting Wang Kuo-wei, *Jen-chien tz'u-hua*, in *Tz'u-hua ts'ung-pien*, ed. T'ang Kuei-chang, 5:4258. The phrase comes from the "Hsiang chün" of the
"Nine Songs," where it is used to describe the beautiful features of the goddess, "lady of
the lovely eyes and the winning smile"; tr. David Hawkes, *The Songs of the South: An
Ancient Chinese Anthology of Poems*, by Qu Yuan [Ch'ü Yüan] et al. (Harmondsworth: Penguin Books, 1985), p. 106.

5. The function of *shih* was questioned within the moral view of literature espoused
by the neo-Confucians (Tao-hsüeh school); a sure indicator of the changing status of
poetry composition relative to the body politic was its removal as a requirement for the
civil service examination. Literature—that is, *wen* (prose)—functioned as the vehicle for
the expression of the Tao, and *shih* lost the cosmic significance one senses, for example, in
the poetry of the great T'ang poets, Tu Fu in particular. It became a smaller tool for the
individual poet seeking self expression. Although the problem is more complex and requires further investigation, it is worth noting that the tension between the old conception of the *shih* genre and this new change in status, coming at a time when a young,
somewhat "frivolous" genre was drawing interest and creative energy, is related to the
evolution of a gender-based, inter-generic hierarchy of poetry in which the *shih* is the
marked term, the privileged genre. It is in this binary view of the two genres that the
organicism and dualism of Chinese cosmology found perhaps its most obvious and at
once insidious expression in literary history: the *yang* genre had located a *yin* counterpart,
and the song lyric became the "*shih*-surplus" (*shih-yü*), the Eve of Chinese poetry.

6. Quoted in Lung Yü-sheng, *T'ang Sung ming-chia tz'u-hsüan* (rpt., Hong Kong:
Shang-wu yin-shu-kuan, 1979), p. 142.

spread all over Lo-yang. When he assumed the post of prime minister, he expressly sent people to try to collect and burn them all without exception. To be minister of the state, however, means that one [must] be dignified and virtuous, so in the end he was disgraced by the erotic song lyrics [*yen-tz'u*] he had written."[7] In the sexuality of its language and subject matter, the genre was felt to have beauty to seduce and power to corrupt, like any temptress. Sexual analogy underlies much of the discourse.

FROM FEMALE VOICE TO MALE GAZE: MOLDING THE FEMININE IMAGE

The Chinese lyrical tradition has a history of female-voiced songs that are often anonymous and have folk or popular origins.[8] Examples can be found in the *Book of Songs* and *yüeh-fu* ballads of the Han, but it is in Southern Dynasties *yüeh-fu* folk songs that we find records of their flowering.[9] These lyrical female voices are fresh and direct in expressing emotion; they are often sensual when they sing of their love and desire. In the famous "Songs of Tzu-yeh" ("Tzu-yeh ko") cycle of the Wu region in the southeast, we hear the sinuous voice of a young woman in love:

> Long night, I cannot sleep,
> how brightly the moonbeams gleam.
> Thinking I hear a vague voice calling,
> vacantly I answer "Yes?" into the air.[10]

長夜不得眠
明月何灼灼
想聞散喚聲
虛應空中諾

7. Quoted in Shih I-tui, *Tz'u yü yin-yüeh kuan-hsi yen-chiu* (Peking: Chung-kuo she-hui k'o-hsüeh ch'u-pan-she, 1985), p. 159 n. 1. Other well-known examples of lyricists are Lu Yu, Wang Shih-chen, and Kung Tzu-chen. They all indulged in song lyric composition when they were young; some regretted it later and wisely stopped once they had grown mature and responsible, but some remained unfortunate addicts.

8. Cf. the useful discussion of female-voiced songs in John F. Plummer, ed., *Vox Feminae: Medieval Women's Lyrics* (Kalamazoo: Western Michigan University, 1981), p. v.

9. Since the *Book of Songs* (*Shih-ching*) occupied a special place in pre-Ch'in diplomacy, education, and culture and was canonized as a Confucian classic during the Han, it inspired schools of interpretation and exegesis that drew a veil across its contents' lyrical innocence, and the songs were consequently never quite read in a literal sense for their lyrical value.

10. Kuo Mao-ch'ien, ed., *Yüeh-fu shih-chi* (Peking: Chung-hua shu-chü, 1979), 2:643; hereafter referred to in the text as *YFSC*.

In this as in many other songs, we do not "see" the physical attributes of these women but simply "overhear" the musings of their hearts, the lyricism of their declarations of love. They sing openly of their excitement, joy, and grief, using the double entendres characteristic of the regional style.[11] The woman's voice in the following song, from the group preserved as "Western Melodies" ("Hsi-ch'ü ko") from western Hupei, is unabashed in the confession of physical desire:

> I've been waiting to see my lover for four or five years.
> It really has annoyed my heart.
> I wish we could find a place where no one's around,
> so I could turn around and let him hold me in his arms.

> 望歡四五年
> 實情將懊惱
> 願得無人處
> 回身與郎抱

> (*YFSC*, 3:715)

An interesting feature of these songs is that they are often strongly marked by the subject of utterance, not only in tone but actually with the first person *wo*, and more often with *nung* in the Wu dialect; and the lover, whether in evidence as the second-person addressee or absent from the lyrical present, is referred to with the characters *huan*, "pleasure," or *lang*, "young man," doubling as second- or third-person pronouns. Since these songs are anonymous, it is not sure whether they were authored by men or by women or, most likely, by both. But as women's songs, that is, love lyrics with a female speaker, they represent some of the strongest expressions of a female lyrical subject in the Chinese tradition.

Also found among these songs are those that are more descriptive, reproducing in words the physical image of the woman, or at least certain of her attributes. The voice in some of these descriptive songs tends to become ambiguous. While clearly female in some, with the female subject referring to her own physical appearance in the song, in others it becomes an impersonal singer/narrator who, assuming the male lover's proximity to the woman, views and describes her emotional and physical attitude:

> Presuming love, she seems on the point of entering;
> still shy, she's not quite willing to come forward.

11. See the list in Hsiao Ti-fei, *Han Wei Liu-ch'ao yüeh-fu wen-hsüeh-shih* (Peking: Jen-min wen-hsüeh ch'u-pan-she, 1984), pp. 208–10.

From carmine lips a sensuous song bursts forth,
while jade fingers play on seductive strings.

恃愛如欲進
含羞未肯前
朱口發艷歌
玉指弄嬌弦

(YFSC, 2:644)

Though the song above belongs to the "Songs of Tzu-yeh," the female
voice in it is silent, having been displaced by an image of singing. In
male vision, the female figure devolves into a sign of seductive surfaces
that can be played with and manipulated.

That the female-voiced popular love songs found an interested audience in the court and literati poets of the later Southern Dynasties, especially the Ch'i and Liang, is attested to by the imitations of these songs
produced by those poets. The preserved collections of southern folk
songs might even represent versions of the songs brought to the southern courts—an interesting intersection of genuine folk tradition and
elite (male) interests working on "native" (feminized) traditions. Significantly, these songs contributed to the formation of a sexual poetics in
the confluence of the court poets' interest in woman/surface/object and
the salon poetry of the period. In literary transformations of these songs
and in the extensive collection of love lyrics in the sixth-century anthology *Yü-t'ai hsin-yung* compiled at the Liang court, male poets also wrote
in a first-person female voice, but the tendency was to write a description of woman, to reproduce a female persona external to feminine subjectivity. Since to describe the physical appearance of a female persona
calls for discriminating taste rather than emotional empathy or identification, it would seem to be more easily and naturally accomplished
by male poets; moreover, the descriptive mode accommodated the
fashionable interest in playing with surfaces present in late Six Dynasties poetics. Thus, these songs indicate a shift from "hearing" the female
voice to "seeing" the female image:

Idly she goes to the pillow by the northern window,
the sun has not yet angled over the southern eaves.
The hook pulled, the gauze screen rolled down,
the plectrum put away, the lute is hung up.
Smiling as she dreams, lovely dimples appear;
sleeping on her chignon, crushed petals drop.
Patterns of the bamboo mat impressed on jade wrists,
fragrant perspiration soaks the red silk.
Her husband keeps her constant company,
so don't mistake her for a courtesan!

北窗聊就枕
南簷日未斜
攀鈎落綺障
插捩舉琵琶
夢笑開嬌靨
眠鬟壓落花
簟文生玉腕
香汗浸紅紗
夫婿恒相伴
莫誤是倡家

Liang Chien-wen-ti[12]

The male gaze is blatantly implicated in the poem above, and the
reader with it, as the movement of a voyeur's eyes leads to a visual
caressing of the female body. The female body/object lies there, eroticized
in its passivity and silence, and vulnerable to the transgressive gaze that
ravishes the fragile surfaces of skin and silk. The impropriety of the gaze
renders the female sign referentially ambiguous (is this a promiscuous
body?), and the clever, self-conscious closure slides the signified "wife"
underneath the signifier to contain the ambiguity. Even if the closure
were intended just as one of those ingenious devices to surprise and delight so prized in palace-style poetics, this gesture calls attention to and
thematizes the power of the gaze to contaminate and reinscribe the sign
with its own desire.

Whether in stasis or in motion—sleeping, sitting, dancing, waiting
for her lover, or putting on her makeup—in palace-style verse the
female figure is translated into an erotic object constituted by male gaze
and desire:

By the northern window she faces the mirror in the morning,
the brocade canopy has been hung aslant again.
So charming in her coyness—she will not come out,
she says still her toilet is not done.
Kohl patted on lengthens the contour of brows,
rouge of Yen highlights her cheeks.
When she is brought out in front of everyone,
she will certainly win the name of Loveworthy.

北窗向朝鏡
錦帳復斜縈
嬌羞不肯出
猶言粧未成
散黛隨眉廣

<hr>

12. Hsü Ling, comp., *Yü-t'ai hsin-yung* (rpt., Ch'eng-tu: Ch'eng-tu ku-chi shu-tien,
n.d.), p. 177; hereafter referred to in the text as *YTHY*.

燕脂逐臉生
試將持出眾
定得可憐名

Liang Chien-wen-ti (YTHY, p. 170)

In this poetry the female figure's surface is valorized while her interiority, when not left opaque, is colonized as the exclusive domain of love and longing. This moment of transformation has profound consequences for the representation of women in Chinese poetry: it constructs the poetic paradigm of a female image subordinated to the gaze and the play of desire.

ANOTHER BEGINNING:
THE FEMININE IN THE SONG LYRIC

In hindsight, the obsession with femininity in palace-style verse represents a powerful but momentary rupture of repressed sexuality and desire in elite literature. In the subsequent development of T'ang poetry, literary imitations of female-voiced *yüeh-fu* songs and poems representing women remain only a minor subgenre. *Shih* poetry in the T'ang, as in most periods of Chinese history, is a male discourse essentially founded on a poetics that is apparently non-gender-specific and "universal." Yet the "universal" poetics of *shih* poetry has all the underlying assumptions of male perspective and orientation. When literary ideology makes no allowance for the insertion of female subjectivity as such, in writing poetry women adopt the rhetoric and voice of subjectivity developed by male poets. This largely accounts for the usual lack of a distinct voice, poetics, or even sensibility that might be gender-based in most *shih* poems written by women. Women did not, in fact, have a language to write in.

If, as stated earlier, the feminine inscribes the language and sensibility of the song lyric, does the song lyric then offer a viable medium in which women can wrest their own voice from the two extremes of a silent female image constituted by the gaze and a lyrical voice that suppresses the complexity of gender? Traditional views on the subject would answer that it is not only possible but quite natural for women to express themselves, their feminine sensibilities, in the language of the song lyric, at least theoretically. I believe the forces at work are rather more complicated. The naturalness may simply mean the availability of a male-constructed female modality that women can internalize. If we recuperate some fragments and traces of women's voice in the history of the song lyric—and they are indeed but fragments and traces that have managed to break that vast silence in which women lived—we can attempt to explore their relation to image and self-expression. The account that follows is necessarily schematic, focusing as it does rather exclusively on issues of the "feminine" through a diachrony of materials.

In the anonymous popular and quasi-popular song lyrics of the eighth and ninth centuries preserved in the Tun-huang manuscripts there is evidence of the resurfacing or, depending on one's point of view, continuity of a vibrant female voice in the popular tradition.[13] Within the diverse body of Tun-huang songs, which encompass a wide range of themes and diction, subject matter, and typology of characters from both the secular and religious sectors of T'ang popular culture, the female-voiced songs and the songs descriptive of a female persona form a stable repertory.[14] Furthermore, this repertory of women's songs, as we might expect, takes on the themes of love and desire exclusively. These song lyrics incorporate an established convention that binds women to love, and the gaze is inscribed in the constitution of the female, even as speaking subject. In a culture and society where women are defined by their subordinate relationships to men, women's self-images become reflections of men's desired images of them. In literature as in life, women are accustomed to seeing themselves as they are seen in the eyes of men; in the love lyric, women value themselves according to the valuations they glimpse in the mirror of the male gaze, in which appearance is the figure of value. Consider the following anonymous song:

Hair bound in coils like clouds over the Hsiang River,
    in light makeup,
an early spring flower exudes fragrance next to her face.
Jade wrists slowly emerge from silken sleeves,
    offering a wine goblet.
Slender hands playing the *ling* melody blend with lithe green willows,
from her white throat songs issue forth and wind around the
    ornamented beams.
How can any young man keep himself from
    not losing his head?

---

13. The dating of these songs spreads over two to three centuries. For the text of the songs from Tun-huang, see Jen Pan-t'ang, *Tun-huang ko-tz'u tsung-pien* (Shanghai: Shanghai ku-chi ch'u-pan-she, 1987); hereafter referred to in the text as *THKT*.

14. All but one of the thirty-three song lyrics in the *Yün-yao chi* are women's love songs; see Jen Pan-t'ang, *Tun-huang ko-tz'u*, pp. 1–308. There are an additional forty or so love songs either written in the female voice or using the female persona.

髻綰湘雲淡淡妝
早春花向臉邊芳
玉腕慢從羅袖出
捧杯觴

纖手令行勻翠柳
素咽歌發繞雕梁
但是五陵爭忍得
不疏狂

Tune: "Huan hsi sha" (*THKT*, 1:185)

With the emphasis put on the surface allure of the woman, this song gives the impression of a promotional pitch for a singing girl—and that could well have been the case in this and several other songs. Even when calling attention to her musical skills, the description joins artistic talent to sensual appeal, if not subordinating it, as the syntactic ordering of images would suggest. As Jen Pan-t'ang notes, these love lyrics from the *Yün-yao chi* contain numerous references to various parts of the woman's body, her clothing, ornaments, deportment, and performance skills—references mostly to visual details.[15] Since women are supposed to adorn themselves to be seen, the poetic image of the female is constructed according to an assimilated male gaze.

Since the discovery of the Tun-huang manuscripts, there has been much discussion of the influence of the popular song tradition on the development of the literary song lyric.[16] It is especially relevant to the late T'ang, the earliest period from which a significant corpus of song lyrics by literati is extant. Influence no doubt flowed in both directions as the appeal of new song forms brought two social cultures, those of the literati and the artisans (musicians, singers, and courtesans), into points of interaction. The representation of the female image in song particularly formed an axis of mutual influence, it would seem. In the Tun-huang lyrics on the one hand, the language of description focusing on appearance and sensual appeal has partly incorporated aesthetic values derived from elite and literati connoisseurship of the feminine image. On the other hand, early song lyrics by literati preserved in the *Hua-chien chi* appear to be obsessed with the depiction of the female figure in the popular image of the singing girl.

Aside from the anonymous popular songs with a first-person female

15. Jen Pan-t'ang, *Tun-huang ko-tz'u*, p. 189.

16. See Kang-i Sun Chang, *The Evolution of Chinese Tz'u Poetry: From Late T'ang to Northern Sung* (Princeton: Princeton University Press, 1980), pp. 5–25; and Marsha L. Wagner, *The Lotus Boat: The Origins of Chinese Tz'u Poetry in T'ang Popular Culture* (New York: Columbia University Press, 1984).

voice, the gender of whose authorship is in any case uncertain, the evolution of the song lyric was largely shaped by the vision and practice of male poets—that is, until a gifted, assertive, and outspoken woman poet came along who registered her opinion in the discourse of the genre. Li Ch'ing-chao spared no man in her "Tz'u lun," a sweeping critique of her male predecessors in the song lyric genre: Liu Yung's song lyrics were vulgar, those by Chang Hsien and several others were fragmented, eminent scholars such as Ou-yang Hsiu and Su Shih simply wrote *shih* poems with irregular line-lengths, and Yen Chi-tao, Ho Chu, Ch'in Kuan, and Huang T'ing-chien's lyrics were all stylistically deficient in one manner or another. Worst of all, with few exceptions most of them did not seem able to distinguish the song lyric as a genre in praxis, that is, according to Li Ch'ing-chao, to recognize that one of its essential qualities was a precision in tonal decisions regarding the words that answered the demands of the music.[17]

What is interesting about Li Ch'ing-chao's critique from the perspective of this discussion is the tone of snobbish connoisseurship that she initiated into critical discourse on the song lyric. Criticizing with the voice of authority of an accomplished poet and connoisseur of the song lyric genre, Li was not concerned with the question of gender even though the objects of her criticism were all male poets and much of the genre's "distinctiveness" came from a privileging of feminine sensibility in the masculine/feminine antithesis of its poetics and from its playing the role of the feminine, the other, to *shih* poetry.[18] In her critical passage, she intimates an exclusive epistemological position for the true adept of the song lyric (Li Ch'ing-chao herself and a few select males?). Though she does not explicitly link her views and implied expertise to an implicit feminine praxis, male critics have been acutely conscious of the fact that she was a woman. If, as one modern scholar suggests, Li's unsparing criticism indeed represents her reaction as an accomplished *woman* poet to the condescending male attitude toward women's writing,[19] her attack implies the high esteem in which she held her own song lyrics but does not affirm women's song lyrics or writing. Neither can we expect such an affirmation from Li Ch'ing-chao, since in her

17. See Hu Tzu, *T'iao-hsi yü-yin ts'ung-hua—hou-chi* (rpt., Peking: Jen-min wen-hsüeh ch'u-pan-she, 1981), pp. 254–55, and Lin Shuen-fu's discussion of the essay elsewhere in this volume.

18. Though she also wrote *shih* poetry, it would seem quite inconceivable for Li Ch'ing-chao to have written a similar diatribe in the context of that genre.

19. See Chiang Chün-hsün, *Tz'u-hsüeh p'ing-lung shih-kao* (Hong Kong: Lung-men shu-tien, 1966), p. 38.

time women's writing did not form a recognizable tradition, nor were women recognized in the dominant tradition. The language of the song lyric does, however, have peculiarities with feminine connotations. How then do women poets negotiate the use of this language with its appropriation of the "feminine"?

WHEN WOMEN WRITE THEIR SONGS

In the formation of the "song lyric," a sort of *langue féminine* was introduced and promoted by popular practice. Whether as speaking voice or the more commonly figured persona, reproduction of the female role riveted the interest of literati poets in the late T'ang and early Sung. Elsewhere I have pursued the manipulation of the female persona and its implications for role-playing, masking, and self-revelation in song lyrics by male poets.[20] Here I wish to concentrate on the poetics of the feminine created by this trend and its implications for female poets.

For women poets attempting to write in the high tradition of the song lyric, in their own voice and as their own subjects, clearly the persona of the early song lyric, projected as either erotic object or lovelorn voice, though centered on the female, would not have been considered morally appropriate subject matter. Even for male poets, it was this erotic feminine center that was seductive and troubling. The popular tradition would have provided the context for an anonymous female voice to complain about her lover's absence and fickleness and then, desperate for his presence, to use her body as bargain and bait, as in the following Tun-huang song lyric:

Deep in my chamber,
empty and quiet.
How useless, guarding my body and heart, engendering loneliness.
Waiting for him to come,
I naturally pray to the gods.
Don't ever love a young man wild about flowers.

Light, my makeup,
seldom do I go around,
all because there's no sign of my young man, roaming afar.
The snow of my breasts
I'll let you bite,
so worried that you'll spend your gold on the smile of another.

---

20. "Persona and Mask in the Song Lyric," *Harvard Journal of Asiatic Studies* 50 (1990): 459–84.

洞房深
空悄悄
虛抱身心生寂寞
待來時
須祈禱
休戀狂花年少

淡勻粧
周旋少
只為五陵正渺渺
胸上雪
從君咬
恐犯千金買笑

Tune: "Yü-ko-tzu" (*THKT*, 1:276)

A post–May Fourth scholar of the song lyric might even appreciate the frank eroticism of this lyric as a facet of the genuine and direct voice found in popular songs. It may even be interpreted on some level of "realism" as depicting the life and predicaments of a singing girl. Had this song been found in the collection of Li Ch'ing-chao's lyrics, however, it would have scandalized the most liberal critic. To participate in writing, women were expected to internalize the stern moral attitude society held toward their gender. When Li Ch'ing-chao, or any woman of her time (and later times), learned to write song lyrics, she learned already established conventions of the representation of images and feelings, and she assimilated and reproduced a horizon of expectation (or we might say boundaries) defined not only by the genre, but also by her gender.

Li Ch'ing-chao was severely criticized by her contemporary Wang Cho (d. after 1149) in his treatise on the song lyric, the *Pi-chi man-chih*. The moralistic condemnation is worth noting for its *ad feminam* tone. Wang begins by duly recognizing Li Ch'ing-chao's incomparable literary talent among both her male and female contemporaries and noting that in her old age Li had remarried and sued for divorce. He then praises Li's consummate skill in writing song lyrics but condemns her for "using at will the dissolute language of vulgar neighborhoods [entertainment quarters]" and decries the fact that "there has never been a woman with literary talent from a good gentry family as unscrupulous as she was."[21] He goes on to quote examples of so-called dissolute, erotic lines of verse from other poets' *shih* and *tz'u*, emphasizing their mildness as a foil for the recklessness of this woman's style. Whether for reasons of propriety or because of the familiarity of Li's lyrics at

21. Wang Cho, *Pi-chi man-chih*, in *Tz'u-hua ts'ung-pien*, ed. T'ang Kuei-chang, 1:88.

that time, Wang does not provide a single example of her imprudent language. But a seemingly innocuous song lyric such as the following might well have offended the moral sensibilities of a Wang Cho:[22]

> From the flower vendor's load
> I bought a branch of spring about to blossom.
> Teardrops dye the light and even hue
> that still carries traces of rose clouds and morning dew.
>
> Afraid that my young man might look and say
> that my face is not as pretty as the flower's face,
> I pinned it aslant on my cloudlike hair,
> and just want to make him look and compare.

賣花擔上
買得一枝春欲放
淚染輕勻
猶帶彤霞曉露痕

怕郎猜道
奴面不如花面好
雲鬢斜簪
徒要教郎比並看

Tune: "Chien-tzu mu-lan-hua"[23]

The mirroring of her beauty in the flower does not suffice for the lyric persona's perception of herself. That beauty exists merely on the order of equivalence. In her self-confidence she introduces a third term, the lover's gaze, to disrupt this equivalence and institute herself as the winner. Despite the self-assertive and defiant tone in this lyric, the final constitution of the female image remains within the domain of the gaze. When the lyric persona is historicized, as Li Ch'ing-chao in this instance, the self-assertion and desire for the gaze produce a compromising image in the tradition: a sequestered woman of good family and a coquettish charmer displaying herself are images of the feminine at odds with each other. Thus, a female image that is an unmitigated reflection

22. There are problems of attribution regarding this and other song lyrics by Li Ch'ing-chao, and it is worth noting that the discussions of authenticity often have moral overtones. Chao Wan-li, the editor of a collection of Li Ch'ing-chao's song lyrics, the *Sou-yü tz'u*, has noted that "the idea in this song lyric is shallow and obvious; it indeed does not resemble her other lyrics." And Wang Chung-wen has expressed reservations about authenticating a lyric on the basis of its content and expression although he includes it among genuine lyrics by Li in *Li Ch'ing-chao chi chiao-chu* (Peking: Jen-min wen-hsüeh ch'u-pan-she, 1986), pp. 71–72.

23. Included in T'ang Kuei-chang, ed., *Ch'üan Sung tz'u* (Hong Kong: Chung-hua shu-chü, 1977), 2:932; hereafter referred to in the text as *CST*.

of the male gaze proves to be a dubious means of self-representation for women poets, as it has also proved to be a limited typology in the genre.[24]

Even as the song lyric was gradually shorn of the female surface in the image of a persona, a feminine diction and sensibility remained as its distinctive marks.[25] The following statement may be a gross simplification, but despite all the formal and rhetorical variables—in period styles, in the poetics of short or long melody patterns, degrees of simplicity or artfulness, generalized or personal tone—the ideal program of a song lyric of the mainstream feminine *wan-yüeh* style was to articulate subtle and elusive moods, perceptions, and states of feeling and emotion by means of feminized, "domesticated" imagery and diction.

The song lyric was identified with *ch'ing*, with the evocation of mood and the figuration of emotion; cultural stereotyping also equated woman with emotion. Through this common denominator the song lyric thus came to be seen in the poetic tradition as offering women a "natural" mode of expression. As mentioned earlier, since a condescending attitude was held toward the feminized song lyric among male poets, self-censure sometimes disrupted the writing of song lyrics; no such critical disapproval was expressed specifically toward women writing song lyrics. On the contrary, when a significant number of women began to take up the writing of song lyrics in the Ch'ing, prefaces to anthologies of *tz'u* by women often emphasized an affinity of sensibilities between the female gender and the feminine genre. It was considered "natural" for women to write song lyrics—within "clean" boundaries, to be sure.

VOICING EMOTION: "WHO WOULD LOOK UPON MY JOY AND HAPPINESS?"

When we examine *tz'u* by women, the emotional picture obtained often seems bleak indeed. On the one hand, this bleak picture collectively reflects women's empirical experience in traditional Chinese society, where they were circumscribed physically, emotionally, and intellectually: the confinement and isolation imposed on the lives of women pervade their lyrics. Melancholy, loneliness, depression, emptiness, and vague, unfulfilled longing are common themes in their songs. On the other hand, the morbidity is reinforced by and exaggerated in the normative emotional categories of the song lyric. The tension and

24. Grace Fong, "Persona and Mask in the Song Lyric," pp. 459–65, 484.

25. Li Ch'ing-chao's contribution to this perception of the song lyric by virtue of the conjunction of her practice and her gender is significant.

alienation wrought by social and emotional immurement at times have broken into song—into a smoldering, desperate voice of intense *ch'ing*, intense emotion. This section, then, presents a particularized women's "subculture"; it explores an emotional dimension that is associated with *tz'u* by gifted women who were extremely unfortunate in their life circumstances.

Springtime Resentment
Alone I walk, alone I sit,
alone I sing, alone I drink, and lie down again alone.
Standing long hurts my spirits,
but there's nothing I can do about this light chill that teases one.

This feeling—who will see it?
Tears have washed away the faded makeup, hardly any left on.
Sorrow and illness, one follows the other.
I have trimmed the entire wick of the cold lamp,
    still dreams have not taken shape.

獨行獨坐
獨倡獨酬還獨臥
佇立傷神
無奈輕寒著摸人

此情誰見
淚洗殘妝無一半
愁病相仍
剔盡寒燈夢不成

Chu Shu-chen, tune: "Chien-tzu mu-lan-hua" (*CST*, 2:1405)

The voice in this song lyric is well defined: it is a trapped voice. The insistent opening repetition ("Alone...alone...alone...alone... alone...") inscribes the rhetorical structure with an unrelieved psychological state that is later exacerbated by insomnia. The motif of the female persona confined in the boudoir and garden here is transformed into a living nightmare told by a female voice trapped in extreme isolation (the teasing touch of an anthropomorphized chill is the only physical contact she feels). All her movements are refractions of *ch'ing*—emotion, feeling—and the lyric captures a moment of imprisonment, without hope of communication or understanding: "This feeling—who will see it?" To whom can she sing of her melancholia? Who is the audience/perceiver? The song foregrounds the problematic relationship between being and being seen. The self-conscious positing of the male gaze, or, more correctly, of its absence, seems to efface the feminine identity—it washes away with the makeup.

By turning the emotional and psychological immurement of women inside out, this lyric thematizes radically the fate of talented women as outcasts in the tradition. While male poets participate in a tradition with role models from the literary and historical past, not to mention the friendships they enjoy with like-minded and understanding contemporaries (Tu Fu can admire a Li Po; Su Shih can look to a T'ao Ch'ien), women poets, while marginal at best in their relation to the male-dominated tradition, lack their own tradition and community.[26] Along with Pan Chao, Li Ch'ing-chao must be regarded as an extraordinary phenomenon in the conjunction of factors that allowed for her literary accomplishments. No other woman achieved the kind of literary identity and influence Li had in the elite, male-dominated tradition.

Women, therefore, if they were trained to write, wrote mostly undistinguished poetry as a light literary exercise, as many did in the late imperial period. But to some, such as Chu Shu-chen, high songstress of melancholia, writing poetry, especially the song lyric, would have provided a rare emotional outlet, a channel for the expression of feelings otherwise suppressed or ignored. Such poetry has its origin in the psychology of its practitioners. By focusing on her emotions (without an objective eye), a woman poet tends toward self-obsession in her poetry; she writes about herself over and over again.

On the Shadow

Low, the winding railing
locking in the secluded courtyard.
At night one tires of keeping smooth hair and attire.
In a vast, vast sea of regret,
I feel this body has already drowned.
How can one put up with this meddlesome lamp,
adding on one tiny shadow
when evening has only just arrived?

I really don't know what to do with you.
Even though I make it a point to care for you,
you don't know how to care for me.
Why are you again at the study window,
following me whether I walk or sit?
I guess it would be hard to drive you away,
but to avoid you should still be easy.
Hiding from your search, I pull open the bed-curtain and lie down.

---

26. There is more evidence of female friendships and literary circles in later periods; see the next section.

曲欄低
深院鎖
人晚倦梳裹
恨海茫茫
已覺此身墮
那堪多事青燈
黃昏才到
又添上影兒一箇

最無那
縱然著意憐卿
卿不解憐我
怎又書窗
依依伴行坐
算來驅去應難
避時尚易
索掩却、繡幃推卧

Wu Tsao, tune: "Chu Ying-t'ai chin"[27]

One cannot help being struck by the difference in tone and mood between this *tz'u* and Li Po's famous "Drinking Alone under the Moon" ("Yüeh-hsia tu cho"), which also personifies shadow. Perhaps animation is more appropriate in describing the male poet's relationship to his shadow: Li Po is the master puppeteer pulling the strings that bring the moon and shadow to life for his sole and supreme enjoyment. But here, in apostrophizing the shadow, Wu Tsao creates a problematic companion that is incapable of providing the loving companionship she craves. The lyric only foregrounds her state of loneliness and alienation. In contrast to the general exuberance and final invitation to transcendence in Li Po's poem—"Let us join in travels beyond human feelings / and plan to meet far in the river of stars"[28]—this lyric moves toward increasing confinement and isolation. The world closes in slowly from all sides: from an enclosed exterior space to a confined interior space, from daylight to engulfing darkness, from a self-consuming psychological space to a final symbolic interment in a bed of loneliness that obliterates light, consciousness, and symbolic companionship. The woman's voice extinguishes itself in monologue. Yet she sings of herself again, in another name:

27. Wu Hao, ed., *Kuei-hsiu pai-chia tz'u-hsüan* (1914, Sao-yeh shan-fang ed.), pp. 5b–6a.

28. Trans. by Stephen Owen, *The Great Age of Chinese Poetry* (New Haven: Yale University Press, 1981), p. 138.

In this world only deep feelings are hard to divulge.
Swallowed tears well up again.
Hands twist wilted flowers,
wordless, leaning against the screen.

I am shocked, seeing myself in the mirror,
a thin, straight form.
It's not a face of spring,
It's not a face of autumn:
can it be Shuang-ch'ing?

世間難吐只幽情
淚珠嗁盡還生
手撚殘花
無言倚屏

鏡裏相看自驚
瘦亭亭
春容不是
秋容不是
可是雙卿

Ho Shuang-ch'ing, tune: "Shih lo-i"[29]

As sometime readers of *tz'u*, we would agree that the lyric speaker in this song is a woman. Obvious feminine signs are deployed: teardrops, flowers, screen, mirror, and the gestures surrounding them. Something seems to disturb the conventional surface of the lyric, however, something held back, something threatening to subvert the sentiments and gestures. No languorous desire or longing seems to inhabit the words, only some deep, hidden emotion whose expression has been consigned to impossibility: "In this world only deep feelings are hard to divulge." The emotion is displaced in the subject's silent tears and her fidgeting with a faded flower. Speech is denied or lost; she is "wordless" both within and without the discourse. Taking the poetics of song lyrics that defines *her*, she writes within it and undoes it. Without it she would be "wordless," yet she sees herself outside the poetics and is "without words" of her own. Only the song form remains to tell an enigma, a paradox.

The mirror, a substitute for the gaze, usually reflects an image of feminine beauty or a woman's fear of losing that beauty. Here the male gaze is displaced; the woman sees herself through her own eyes. When

29. Shih Chen-lin, *Hsi-ch'ing san-chi* (hereafter referred to in the text as *HCSC*); in *Chung-kuo wen-hsüeh chen-pu ts'ung-shu*, ser. 1, vol. 5 (Shanghai: Shang-hai tsa-chih kung-ssu, 1935), p. 66; see also n. 33.

the subject looks into the mirror, she discards the metaphors that she has been transformed into—"a face of spring," "a face of autumn"—and sees an imaginary other/self with which she hesitates to identify herself. It is an image of ambiguity and dissociation. Yet through this doubling, ambiguity, and dissociation, a distinct voice is established. Paradoxically, the speaker inserts her identity by inscribing her name in a question of self-doubt: "Can it be Shuang-ch'ing?" But the paradox is only apparent. The rhetoric of negation, by discarding the gaze, creates the possibility of a female subject.

In the song lyrics of Ho Shuang-ch'ing, we find the lyric trope of self-reflexivity in the peculiarly feminine form already exhibited in Wu Tsao's song lyric on her shadow. That splitting or doubling of the self, which is projected onto an object in order to speak (of herself), recurs in Ho Shuang-ch'ing's lyrics:

> Fading Lamp
> Already dimming—I forget to blow on it:
> were it to shine brightly, who would trim it?
> In front of me, no flame that glows like fireflies.
> I listen to the cold rain on the earthen steps
> dripping through the third night-watch,
> alone by myself, sick and sleepless.
> Hard to extinguish—
> you too are excessive in feeling.
> The scented oil is finished,
> but your fragrant heart has not cooled;
> do keep company with Shuang-ch'ing for awhile.
>
> Star after star
> Fades gradually into motionlessness.
> But I hope you will suffer through
> and then blossom forth again.
> It will surpass those fishing lamps swaying
> in the chaotic wind on the wild pond.
> When autumn's hardworking moths scatter,
> I am already ill,
> and when has my illness ever diminished?
> Long we watch each other,
> vaguely sleep comes upon me. . . .
> In sleep I am frightened awake again.

已暗忘吹
欲明誰剔
向儂無焰如螢
聽土階寒雨

滴破三更
獨自慊慊耿耿
難斷處
也忝多情
香膏盡
芳心未冷
且伴雙卿

星星
漸微不動
還望你淹煎
有個花生
勝野塘風亂
搖曳漁燈
辛苦秋蛾散後
人已病
病減何曾
相看久
朦朧成睡
睡去還驚

Tune: "Feng-huang-t'ai shang i ch'ui-hsiao" (*HCSC*,
pp. 105–6)

A woman alone, at night, no longer waiting for or complaining about
her lover, a woman "without a mirror" talks to a dying lamp ardently,
with great feeling. It is so obvious in this song lyric that the personified
burning lamp is a figure of the self. The identification is drawn on the
basis of *ch'ing*, that intense, objectless, unnamable emotion that trans-
lates here into a will to live completely at odds with destiny: "Hard to
extinguish—/you too are excessive in feeling./The scented oil is
finished,/but your fragrant heart has not cooled." That single, self-
consuming flame of the lamp only illuminates the encroaching darkness:
it marks the site of struggle between the forces of destruction and survival. As she watches its slow dissipation, she sees an analogy for her
own life that is wasting away. She thus tries to console and encourage
the lamp as a way of encouraging herself. Yet ultimately there is no
escape from imminent destruction. We can guess only too easily at the
fate of the lamp as she starts up again from having drifted off to sleep.

Both in the ever-stressful wakefulness of the insomniac world of darkness and confinement, and in an apparently idyllic world of nature that
conceals dangers and deceptions, the self's doubles take on different
forms and shapes. It is often the survival of these object-doubles that
concerns Ho Shuang-ch'ing. About chrysanthemums she says, "I feel
gladdened that the flowers' stems have not grown thin:/incessant rain

they have endured past the Double Ninth/and fortunately survived to the time of Small Spring";[30] and she counsels the wild goose, "Do go along a sandy shore or half a stream/just to pass the fleeting years:/ with the rice grains recently used up,/the nets are just waiting in earnest."[31] These innocent creatures of nature—Ho Shuang-ch'ing's doubles, her scattered selves—are threatened by destructive forces that are not within their power to avert: even the enduring chrysanthemums finally "droop their heads" in the killing frost, and the companionless wild goose, "fatigued from flying, lodge by mistake in the fields" where the nets must lie hidden.

The impulse for an addressee/friend is so compelling in Ho Shuang-ch'ing's autobiographical discourse through song lyrics on objects that in a most telling example subtitled "Taking Food to Do Spring Ploughing" (tune: "Ch'un ts'ung t'ien-shang lai," *HCSC*, pp. 175–76), she transforms spring and springtime creatures into both agent and recipient of her emotions with whom she achieves a momentary sharing. Yet the duplicity of nature, in the ominous subtext of spring, disrupts that unitary vision. The first stanza begins in a narrative mode as she sets out on her farm chores in an idyllic setting:

Purpled paths bright in spring weather.
Slowly I tie a spring gauze scarf on my head
and eat by myself while spring ploughing.
The small plum tree is thin in spring,
fine blades of grass glisten in spring.
At each step along the fields spring springs to life.

紫陌春晴
慢額裹春紗
自餉春耕
小梅春瘦
細草春明
春田步步春生

At this point during her sprightly walk to the field, memory intrudes with a troubling subtext that punctures the glistening, innocent surface of spring:

I remember, that year in a fine spring
to a spring swallow
I blurted out spring feelings.
And now at this time,

30. To the tune "Erh-lang shen"; *HCSC*, p. 93.
31. To the tune "Hsi huang-hua man"; *HCSC*, p. 93.

I think spring letters and spring tears
have all melted with the spring ice.

記那年春好
向春燕
說破春情
到如今
想春箋春淚
都化春冰

The meaning of spring suddenly leaves its agrarian context and assumes the conventional poetic connotations of love and romance; the seasonal context has provoked a sudden remembrance of a failed love. It is a supremely vague, typological confession of the sentiment, *ch'ing*, that suits the connotative, subtle, "feminine" poetics of the song lyric; it is therefore immaterial whether that love in the past actually had a recipient or was simply the vague stirring of a young woman's heart that remained unfulfilled. The stanzaic structure of the song lyric also allows that ambiguity to be suspended, deferring its resolution.

The second stanza returns to a self-contained present with an anthropomorphized nature/spring as a companion with whom she shares the food she has brought:

I cherish spring, dote on spring—for how many springs?
By an expanse of spring mist
the spring oriole is locked in.
You present gifts to a springtime me,
and I offer presents to a springtime you:
am I, or are you, the spirit of spring?

憐春痛春春幾
被一片春煙
鎖住春鶯
贈與春儂
遞將春你
是儂是你春靈

Yet nature, to whom she turns and by whose office she seeks to lose her solitary state, is belied by its very duplicity and brings disenchantment, as she has intimated in her songs on the sad fates of its creatures. She seems to point to the delusory nature of the positive, innocent aspects of spring and finally slides back into a postlapsarian anguish, in which spring acquires a demonic mask:

You can count on the start and end of spring,
but in spring it'll be hard to count on my waking from a spring dream.

Why does the spring demon
make a whole spring of spring sickness?
Spring has misled Shuang-ch'ing.

算春頭春尾
也難算，春夢春醒
甚春魔
做一番春病
春誤雙卿

The late Ch'ing critic Ch'en T'ing-cho greatly admired Ho Shuang-
ch'ing's song lyrics; among his praise and comments on her song lyrics
in the *Pai-yü-chai tz'u-hua*, he notes that while they contain the characteristics of the "feminine" style, her diction does not resemble that of any
of the master orthodox poets such as Wen T'ing-yün and Wei Chuang
of the late T'ang, or Chou Pang-yen, Ch'in Kuan, Chiang K'uei, and
Shih Ta-tsu of the Sung. He concludes inconclusively: "So, is she an im-
mortal fairy or a ghost? I can't name her realm [*ching*]."[32]

Ho Shuang-ch'ing's song lyrics do indeed have a highly individual
and intense voice. The uncanny subjectivity and the overwhelming
psychological dimension of these songs sometimes make them appear
like the disturbed visions of an alienated woman. At the same time, her
lyrics are crafted pieces with a naturalness and flow that conceal the
artifice, in ways reminiscent of Li Ch'ing-chao's art. Certain poetic devices, such as effective use of reduplication and cumulative repetition of
words, are obvious emulations of Li Ch'ing-chao's famous style. In the
song lyric on spring ploughing quoted above, the character *ch'un*,
"spring," occurs in every line. Since spring is a double-edged metaphor,
its repetition is both apposite and central to the metamorphosis of
meaning. In another example (tune: "Feng-huang-t'ai shang i ch'ui-
hsiao" quoted below), reduplication is used unobtrusively in almost every line to produce a cumulative emotional force.

So far I have deliberately avoided giving any historical or biographical context for Ho Shuang-ch'ing's song lyrics, when in fact they would
frame an interesting set of questions regarding the "feminine" modality
of the song lyric, questions that lie outside the scope of this paper but
deserve to be explored. Briefly, Ho Shuang-ch'ing came from a peasant
family native to the rural regions of the southeast, and the way she
learned to read and write and compose poetry was quite by accident.
She had an uncle, a teacher in the village school, who, seeing that as a
child she was extremely intelligent and quick to learn, taught her how

---

32. In *Tz'u-hua ts'ung-pien*, ed. T'ang Kuei-chang, 4:3896; see also pp. 3895–97.

to read and write. When Ho Shuang-ch'ing grew up, her family, observing the class boundaries and social hierarchies of the time, married her off to a peasant. Her husband was not only illiterate, he was a perfect brute as well. Together with his mother, the proverbial evil mother-in-law, he abused Ho Shuang-ch'ing physically and emotionally. Suffering from malaria, she managed hard farm work and the household chores, although constantly berated and often beaten by her husband and his mother. Ho Shuang-ch'ing seems to have borne their abuses well, being the very model of a submissive and virtuous wife and daughter-in-law. She had the habit of writing poetry, especially song lyrics, which were much admired and sought after by the scholars and literati of the region. Not wanting her lyrics to be preserved, however, she often wrote them on leaves, using powder in place of ink, making them perhaps the most ephemeral compositions ever written. All in all, only about fifteen lyrics have been preserved. Most of these have appeared in anthologies of works by women poets of the last two hundred years, and they have all been acclaimed by some of the most astute critics and scholars of the song lyric in the late Ch'ing dynasty and the twentieth century.

Everything we know about Ho Shuang-ch'ing, including her extant poems, comes to us from a work called *Hsi-ch'ing san-chi* (Random notes from the western green) by Shih Chen-lin, a relatively unknown and unsuccessful literatus who lived in the eighteenth century.[33] Shih had traveled in the Hsiao-shan region where Ho Shuang-ch'ing lived. His work, which reads something like a diary, records his encounters with Ho Shuang-ch'ing, the tragic story of her life, her wasted talent. He tried, in short, to preserve her life and work for posterity. Some twentieth-century scholars, skeptical of the unverifiable source, have questioned Ho Shuang-ch'ing's identity, claiming that she is a fabrication of the author. Interestingly, the basic presumption of the non-fictionality of Chinese poetry has naturally led to a reading of her poems as records of the empirical experience of a historical person. And with their intense and passionate tone, her poems seem to stand out as records of emotion. Yet might not the author be exploiting precisely this empiricist assumption in the reading of poetry to create a fictional character with historical verisimilitude, and the genre's association with the "feminine" to construct the gender of this fictional character? Or, in a less convoluted manner, might he not have exploited the "feminine"

33. Ho Shuang-ch'ing is called simply Shuang-ch'ing in this work. It is not clear how or when she came to be referred to by the surname Ho. Lin Yutang has translated Shih Chen-lin's preface to the *Hsi-ch'ing san-chi* in *Translations from the Chinese (The Importance of Understanding)* (Cleveland: World Publishing Company, 1963), pp. 86–88.

mode to create some unique poems to attribute to a real woman whom he portrays as Ho Shuang-ch'ing? Or, simpler still, might he not have "edited" the poems as he recorded them, along with fragments of their author's life? The questions as they are phrased presume a complex set of motives and manipulative moves on the part of Shih Chen-lin, and an attempt to probe for answers would involve, to begin with, a careful reading and analysis of the content of *Hsi-ch'ing san-chi* and an examination of its textual strategies in a comparative context in relation to motives and modes of discourse in late Ch'ing China.

Here we have to conclude, like Ch'en T'ing-cho, with an inconclusive question: who wrote the following song lyric, Ho Shuang-ch'ing or Shih Chen-lin? According to Shih Chen-lin, Ho Shuang-ch'ing had a friend in a bright neighbor girl, a peasant who, though illiterate, had loved Ho Shuang-ch'ing's calligraphy and had asked her to copy out the *Heart Sutra* and to teach her to recite it. This girl was leaving the area soon to return to her new marital home after a visit at her parents'. Sick with a bout of malaria, Ho Shuang-ch'ing was unable to attend the farewell dinner, so her friend sent over some food she had wrapped up herself. On receiving it, Ho Shuang-ch'ing wrote two song lyrics, on leaves, lamenting the loss of the friendship.[34] The following song lyric is the second of the two:

> Inch on inch of scant clouds,
> ray after ray of fading light,
> being there and not there, flickering, will not vanish.
> Just at this moment, the brokenhearted soul is severed,
> reeling and swaying.
> I gaze and gaze at the hills and streams—
> the figure moves farther and farther away, indistinct.
> From now on,
> pain and plight
> will be only like tonight.

> The blue sky is remote.
> I ask heaven, it does not respond—
> look at tiny little Shuang-ch'ing,
> weak and frail and listless.
> Even worse, whom do I see and who sees me?
> Who would dote on the flower's charm?
> Who would look upon my joy and happiness
> and secretly sketch them in plain powder?
> Who would still care, age after age,
> night after night, day after day?

34. *Hsi-ch'ing san-chi*, pp. 127–28.

寸寸微雲
絲絲殘照
有無明滅難消
正斷魂魂斷
閃閃搖搖
望望山山水水
人去去隱隱迢迢
從今後
酸酸楚楚
只似今宵

青遙
問天不應
看小小雙卿
嫋嫋無聊
更見誰誰見
誰痛花嬌
誰望歡歡喜喜
偷素粉寫寫描描
誰還管生生世世
夜夜朝朝

Tune: "Feng-huang-t'ai shang i ch'ui-hsiao" (*HCSC*, p. 128)

In its "feminine" discourse, there is again that intense preoccupation with the relationship between being and being seen. The subject, in order to constitute its identity, needs an external perceiver. Though the perceiver would function as a reflector, thereby affirming the being of the woman perceived, it is not just the mirror, the male gaze, but that longed-for, absent *chih-yin*, the understanding and caring friend who can break through the boundaries of loneliness and alienation to touch the heartstrings of the self. *Ch'ing*, emotion, desires its fulfillment in the other. Who is the feminine subject of the song?

TOWARD A DREAM: WHEN LITERARY WOMEN FOUND EACH OTHER

During the late imperial period of the Ming and Ch'ing dynasties, the freedom and movement of women, and of those women belonging to the gentry and upper classes in particular, seemed more restricted than ever with the by then entrenched practice of foot-binding and more repressive social and legal codes enforcing virtuous conduct in women.[35] Even

35. The account provided here of the social and literary circumstances of women during the Ming and Ch'ing is skeletal. For a more detailed and complex picture, see, among a number of studies available, the excellent articles by Ellen Widmer, "The Epistolary World of Female Talent in Seventeenth-Century China," *Late Imperial China* 10,

so, and perhaps because of the increasing oppression of women, there
also arose male advocates for liberalization of the measures and norms
governing women's lives. They called for increasing the availability of
education to women; it would take the cataclysmic changes of the twentieth century, however, before Chinese women could actively take up
their own cause alongside their male sympathizers. In Ming and Ch'ing
China, the patriarchal social system made women passive recipients of
fates and destinies defined for them by the male world. Even those more
liberal-minded scholars and literati who championed education for
women did so within the accepted boundaries of gender ideologies.
Women should be taught to read and write, not so that they could function in society and certainly not so that they could compete with men,
but in order that they might further cultivate their womanly virtues.
Special books on feminine conduct, family instruction, and biographies
of exemplary virtuous women constituted their textbooks. Since poetry
had always been held to have an edifying, didactic, as well as artistic function, it was not excluded from the education of women. The
eighteenth-century poet Yüan Mei even accepted a number of female
students and disciples whom he taught to write poetry and whose work
he edited and had printed in collections.

As more and more women wrote verse, they began to compile anthologies of contemporary women's poetry; Ming and Ch'ing collections of
verse written by women and edited by women are still extant today.
Women of gentry and elite families also began to form their own literary
circles patterned on the male literati models. One exemplary member of
such circles was the woman poet Ku Ch'un (also known by her *tzu* T'ai-
ch'ing [1799–1870s]), who was a prolific writer of both *shih* and *tz'u* but
was much better known for the latter. Ku came from an educated, aristocratic, and probably Manchu family. Talented in the arts of poetry,
painting, and calligraphy, she was happily matched in marriage (as a
concubine) to I-hui, a prince of the Manchu imperial clan. Until I-hui's
relatively early death (he died in his forties), husband and wife had an
enviable conjugal relationship, actively sharing their many interests in
the arts. Ku's poetry is shaped by her experiences as a woman living in
an elite social and cultural milieu. From the themes running through
her poetry and the informational prefaces she wrote to her verse, we get
some understanding of the broad spectrum of her social and artistic
activities and the circle of women friends she moved in. These women

---

no. 2 (December 1989): 1–43; and Paul Ropp, "The Seeds of Change: Reflections on the
Condition of Women in the Early and Mid Ch'ing," *Signs* 2 (1976): 5–23.

were usually from the southeast, members of families accompanying high officials who had been posted to the capital. Much in the manner of male literati poets, these women often made excursions together and celebrated the occasions in verse, or they would write parting poems to friends leaving the capital and epistolary or commemorative verse to friends far away or departed from this life. Poetry for women of this class, then, was a genteel pastime and a cultivated art, with an actual audience and readership among its practitioners—a situation quite different from that of earlier women poets who wrote in isolation.

The collection of Ku Ch'un's *shih* poems and *tz'u* reads like a record of her daily life because of the detailed prefaces she provided for the individual pieces.[36] The prefaces to her song lyrics often indicate the date and occasion of the composition, whether the lyric was an inscription on a painting, an epigraph to a collection of poetry by a woman friend, a lyric written to match the rhymes of another lyric by her husband, a piece composed during a visit to a temple with a party of women, a farewell poem to a parting friend, or an epistolary poem sent to a distant one. The range of occasions is amazingly broad. This practice of writing occasional song lyrics in social settings with accompanying prefaces finds its model in the literati tradition of the song lyric initiated by Su Shih. Except when writing generic "exercise" pieces matching rhymes or imitating styles in the song lyric canon, Ku Ch'un puts the song lyric to social or occasional and self-expressive functions —functions conceived in the elite male tradition but situated within a female literary and social context.

Indicative of her education and learning, and therefore reflective of the literati model, Ku's song lyrics contain a measure of allusive language and contemplative themes. Both are less common in song lyrics by women and deserve attention as examples of a female poet's attempt, in self-definition, to insert her self (her image and her voice) into a male role. The following lyric, prefaced "Composed at Random," for instance, clearly adopts the detached attitude of the Taoist sage:

> Human life is an endless struggle—
> the post-horse and ploughing ox.

---

36. Her collected *shih* poetry, *T'ien-yu-ko chi*, is included in the *Feng-yü-lou ts'ung-shu*. The only complete manuscript of her collected *tz'u*, the *Tung-hai yü-ko* in six *chüan* (hereafter referred to as *THYK* in the text), was formerly in the private collection of the Japanese sinologist Naitō Konan and is now in the rare books collection of the Kyo-u sho-oku in Osaka. A three-*chüan* edition consisting of *chüan* 1, 3, and 4 was printed by the Hsi-ling yin-she in 1913; *chüan* 2 was published in *Tz'u-hsüeh chi-k'an* 1, no. 2 (Aug. 1933): 152–66 (hereafter referred to as *THCK* in the text).

On the brows of the Taoist sadness never sets:
in leisure holding the Book of Immortality,
sitting by the window, what is there to seek besides this?

Bright scenes in time depart far, far away,
impossible to detain the months and years.
In a hundred years everyone becomes a pat of mud,
so arrange for a peaceful and steady place in the
self's mind.
And move the boat with the flow of the stream.

人生競無休
驛馬耕牛
道人眉上不生愁
閒把丹書窗下坐
此外何求

光景去悠悠
歲月難留
百年同作土饅頭
打疊身心安穩處
順水行舟

Tune: "Lang t'ao sha" (*THYK*, 1.7b–8a)

This song lyric could easily pass for one of Su Shih's. It is indeed intended to be read in that tradition: the philosophical message overwrites any feminine signs. The term Taoist, *tao-jen*, is male-gendered. Yet in this song lyric it is a thin disguise, a persona for the poet—a woman, sitting by the window and, rather than embroidering, engaging in the unusual activity of reading a Taoist classic and contemplating the meaning of life, contemplation that can take an objective turn to observation or comment on the false and misleading drama of life. In Ku's often-anthologized piece on puppets, the satiric force of the description and rhetoric promote a metaphorical reading of the puppet theater:

Puppets on the stage, they behave most brashly:
passing on false stories, they beguile foolish children.
The founding tales of the T'ang and Sung are all spurious;
their magic lies in the clever transformations of devils and demons.

Riding red leopards,
attended by striped foxes,
with their fetching caps and gowns they put on a mighty pose.
Once they come down the stage and hang up high, what is their use then?
Carved wood and pulled strings—just this one moment.

傀儡當場任所為
訛傳故事惑癡兒

李唐趙宋皆無考
妙在妖魔變化奇
駕赤豹
從文貍
衣冠楚楚假威儀
下場高掛成何用
刻木牽絲此一時

Tune: "Che-ku t'ien" (*THCK*, pp. 152–53)

In one song lyric Ku Ch'un actually makes reference to the image of
the feminine in what is in fact a gesture toward difference: "You know
that I don't share in the fashions of the world, / so why bother to ask,
'Are you painting your eyebrows dark or light?'" ("Pu Ch'an-kung,"
THCK, 1.2 [1933], p. 163). The literary arts certainly seem to have
offered her a form of fulfillment, but they also brought disappointment:

Sitting at Night

I laugh at myself trying to work up some verses in those years—
those old traces are hard to find even in dreams.
How many scrolls of poems?
How many sheets of sketches?
How much time has been . . . ?

The jug broken from tapping, I scratch my head often,
wearing out my old aspirations.
And now all I've succeeded in getting is
a thousand strands of tears
and one sorrowful heart.

自笑當年費苦吟
陳跡夢難尋
幾卷詩篇
幾張畫稿
幾許光陰

唾壺擊碎頻搔首
磨滅舊胸襟
而今贏得
千絲眼淚
一個愁心

"Ch'iu-po mei" (*THYK*, 5.n.p.)

While poetry might have become a nice social art for women and a
form of exchange or support among them, it did not connect to any
"larger" purpose, since it was still confined within their world—and
there women were still outsiders to the male-dominant world of recognition, achievement, and fame. Until women could be integrated into

society, the desire for broader experience and participation could only remain a frustrated dream, even, to a large extent, for the most talented and enterprising:

Recording a Dream

Haze envelops the cold water, moonlight envelops the sand.
Floating on a magic raft,
I visit the immortals' home.
A clear stream all along the way,
the two oars row, breaking the mist.
Just after the little bridge the scenery changed:
under the bright moon,
I saw blossoming plum trees.

Shadows of myriad trees of plum blossoms intertwined.
To the edge of the hills,
to the edge of the waters.
Reflections fall into the heaven in the lake,
their beauty certainly worthy of praise.
I wanted to travel all over the sea of fragrant snow—
startled awake from the dream,
I blame the cawing crow.

烟籠寒水月籠沙
泛靈槎
訪仙家
一路清溪
雙槳破烟划
才過小橋風景變
明月下
見梅花

梅花萬樹影交加
山之涯
水之涯
影落湖天
韶秀總堪誇
我欲徧遊香雪海
驚夢醒
怨啼鴉

Ku Ch'un, tune: "Chiang-ch'eng tzu" (*THYK* 1.28b)

CODA: THE HEROIC FEMININE

In this filthy, grimy world,
how many brave and noble souls are there among men?
Only in the detachment of fair women
do we sometimes hear of an outstanding hero.

舣髒塵寰
問幾個男兒英哲
算只有蛾眉隊裏
時聞傑出

Ch'iu Chin, tune: "Man chiang hung"[37]

The values and import of *his* world are articulated in the dominant writing practices. In the song lyric, however, where gender constructs in language and representation were at first predominantly feminine and the genre was coded as "feminine"—an alterity in relation to *shih*—thematic values of the public, male world were largely excluded. Ironically, this strongly feminized poetics generated an intensely masculine mode of discourse in the song lyric. In order to embody the values and ideals of poetry as conceived in the high tradition—in other words, to speak of a public and private world outside the symbolic space of the boudoir and garden—a strongly marked male image and voice unadulterated by feminine coding had to be constructed. In forceful formulations, the *hao-fang*, or "heroic," mode is self-consciously masculine. The "masculine" quality is constructed chiefly through the choice of theme and diction within particular registers of "male" emotion, and the lyrics are written to appropriate tune patterns considered vigorous and virile in sound. By effacing the feminine, the song lyric participates in the dominant poetic tradition.[38] Man speaks:

Hair bristling with anger, bursting from its cap,
at the railing where I lean the beating rain has come to a stop.
I raise my eyes, gazing up, and howl long at heaven,
A stout heart fiercely rent.
At thirty my deeds and name are merely dust and dirt,
an eight-thousand-*li* route under moon and clouds.
Don't idle around—
when youthful head has turned to grey,
we will mourn in vain.

The Ching-k'ang reign's disgrace has not yet been wiped out.
The anguish of officers—when will it be dispelled?
Driving the war chariot, I will trample
the pass at Mount Ho-lan.
Manly ambition will feast hungrily on barbarian flesh,

37. *Ch'iu Chin chi* (Peking: Chung-hua shu-chü, 1960), p. 106; hereafter referred to as *CCC* in the text.

38. Later on in the reading tradition, the same aim was attempted by allegorizing the feminine. See Yeh Chia-ying, "The Ch'ang-chou School of *Tz'u* Criticism," *Harvard Journal of Asiatic Studies* 35 (1975): 101–31; and my "Contextualization and Generic Codes in the Allegorical Reading of *Tz'u* Poetry," *Tamkang Review* 19 (1988–89): 663–79.

amidst talk and laughter we will quench our thirst with Tartars' blood.
Let us begin again by recovering our former land
and paying our respects to the court.

怒髮衝冠
憑欄處
瀟瀟雨歇
擡望眼
仰天長嘯
壯懷激烈
三十功名塵與土
八千里路雲和月
莫等閒
白了少年頭
空悲切

靖康恥
猶未雪
臣子恨
何時滅
駕長車踏破
賀蘭山缺
壯士飢餐胡虜肉
笑談渴飲匈奴血
待從頭
收拾舊山河
朝天闕

Yüeh Fei, tune: "Man chiang hung" (*CST*, 2:1246)

There are many variations of the heroic song lyric (including the
antiheroic), but this paradigmatic version, attributed to the Southern
Sung general Yüeh Fei (1103–41), maintains a degree of celebrity probably equalled only by Su Shih's "Nien-nu chiao," subtitled "Recalling the Past at Red Cliff" (*CST*, 1:282). It made "Man chiang hung"
the most popular tune pattern for *hao-fang* lyrics, particularly those expressing loyalist or patriotic sentiments. The sustained drive, the barely
contained anger and frustration, and the persistent intent (here, re-
vanchism) are sentiments traditionally perceived as typically masculine.
Although the passionate tone and violent language in which they are expressed, especially in the lines speaking of cannibalism, cannot but
violate a generic sense of decorum, at the same time the radically masculine poetics declaims its difference and deviation from its "feminine"
counterpart, without which it would not appear so marked.

Predictably, the heroic mode, being the very antithesis of the feminine mode established in the song lyric, was not much adopted by

women poets—and here gender poetics delimits and complicates boundaries within the genre. While the reproduction of a female persona across the distance of the feminine interior was accepted practice for male (and female) poets, the reverse does not hold in the tradition. The male persona, when it is self-consciously gender-marked as the heroic persona is, cannot be reproduced from a point outside the male interior; it can only be represented by its own (male) voice. There are instances, however, of women poets who sought heroic models of their own gender as subjects for their song lyrics. Ku Ch'un, for example, wrote a series of allusive song lyrics on martial heroines figuring in *ch'uan-ch'i* tales of the T'ang, using a tune pattern with *hao-fang* associations, "Chin-lü ch'ü."[39] When writing reflectively on historical themes, women poets would also adopt an erudite, allusive language—a language without feminine associations—that was more appropriate to such themes. In "Crossing the Yangtze River," the woman poet Shen Shan-pao (a literary friend of Ku Ch'un's) combined contemplation of history with meditation on the fate of women. Note that she employs the tune "Man chiang hung" (and follows Yüeh Fei's rhyme):

Rolling on and on, the silvery waves
cannot write out all of that hot blood in my heart.
I ask about that year with those battle drums at Gold Mountain—
it was the achievement of a woman.
On my elbow Su Ch'in's seals of office will not be hung,
and in my bag there remains only Chiang Yen's brush.
Since ancient times, how many heroes can we count among women?
Too grieved to speak.

I look toward Mount Pei-ku in green autumn haze,
point to Mount Fu-yü, where the autumn sun rises.
I've been leaning by the boat's window,
beating time until the jar breaks.
Rain and tears soak into the wanderer's robes,
while frost alights on my parents' thinning hair.
I ask heaven on high, in giving me life, what did you want me to do?
Just to suffer ordeals?

滾滾銀濤
寫不盡
心頭熱血
問當年

39. See *Tung-hai yü-ko, chüan* 2, in *Tz'u-hsüeh chi-k'an*, pp. 155–56. The heroines are Hung-fu, Hung-hsien, and Hung-hsiao; all either had martial qualities or dedicated themselves to heroic men and their goals.

金山戰鼓
紅顏勳業
肘後難懸蘇季印
囊中剩有江淹筆
算古來
巾幗幾英雄
愁難說

望北固
秋煙碧
指浮玉
秋陽出
把篷窗倚遍
唾壺敲缺
游子征衫攙淚雨
高堂短鬢飛霜雪
問蒼蒼
生我欲何為
生磨折

Tune: "Man chiang hung"[40]

While crossing the Yangtze on boat, one woman recalls another woman in history: Shen Shan-pao thinks of Liang Hung-yü, the heroic wife of the Southern Sung general Han Shih-chung, who helped her husband's army to stay the Chin soldiers from crossing the river with her vigorous drumming.[41] Shen's admiration for the heroic achievements of an exceptional woman, however, leads her to lament the general restrictions placed on women's lives. While writing does provide a means of demonstrating their talent, women have no hope for advancement in the public world. In the end, she questions the purposelessness of her life and her suffering as a woman; she shakes her fist at heaven, even though she is powerless. Shen negotiates the masculine model of poetics to voice her frustration at the limitations imposed on women's lives.

A much more forceful attempt to appropriate the masculine image and voice for self-assertion can be read in the life and poetry of the late Ch'ing revolutionary martyr Ch'iu Chin (1879–1907).[42] Dedicating her life to the salvation of China, Ch'iu Chin left the feminine functions of

40. Yeh Kung-ch'o, comp. *Ch'üan Ch'ing tz'u ch'ao* (Hong Kong: Chung-hua shu-chü, 1975), 2:1730.

41. See Han Shih-chung's biography in the *Sung shih* 364.11361.

42. An excellent biographical study is provided in Mary Backus Rankin, "The Emergence of Women at the End of the Ch'ing: The Case of Ch'iu Chin," in *Women in Chinese Society*, ed. Margery Wolf and Roxane Witke (Stanford: Stanford University Press, 1975), pp. 39–66.

wife and mother to join the male ranks of revolutionaries. The male characteristics she assumed are largely derived from the traditional image of the hero. In addition to her prodigious ability to drink, her horseback riding, swordsmanship, and other legendary masculine traits, she is also known to have cross-dressed. By appropriating the male surface, cross-dressing became a signal gesture toward denying and deconstructing the male-constructed, often eroticized image of the feminine. The masculine *hao-fang* mode offers literary cross-dressing as a means to reject the conventional poetic "feminine." The following song lyric is also written to the same heroic tune:

> Short sojourn in the capital,
> so once again it is the fine festival of midautumn.
> There beneath the hedge, the yellow flowers are all in bloom,
> their autumn looks seem cleansed.
> As songs lingered on the four sides, Ch'u was finally penetrated;
> after eight years, vainly I long for the local flavors of Che.
> How unkind to have sent me by force to be a woman—
> surely there has been no caring.
>
> My body cannot get into the ranks of men,
> but my heart burns more fiercely than men's.
> Let me say that in my life my mettle has often been roused to fury
>   for others.
> What vulgar man would have a mind to know me?
> For the hero, there would be ordeal at the end of the road.
> In this ill-bred world of red dust,
> where can I seek an understanding friend?
> My green robe is tear-soaked.

小住京華
早又是
中秋佳節
為籬下
黃花開遍
秋容如拭
四面歌殘終破楚
八年風味徒思浙
苦將儂
強派作蛾眉
殊未屑

身不得
男兒列
心却比
男兒烈
算平生肝膽

因人常熱
俗子胸襟誰識我
英雄末路當磨折
莽紅塵
何處覓知音
青衫濕

       Tune: "Man chiang hung" (*CCC*, p. 97)

The voice we hear is at first "neutral" in gender, speaking of the season, the Midautumn Festival, and the conventional longing the two arouse for one's native region. But at the end of the stanza, this voice emerges as a female voice, resentful of having been born, without choice, a woman. In the second stanza, while still speaking as woman, this female voice adopts what is clearly masculine rhetoric. If the poet has been trapped in the physical and social constraints of her gender, she now inserts her voice into a masculine poetic form to call those constraints into question. In another lyric to the tune "Man chiang hung" Ch'iu Chin declares that "three inches of bow-shaped shoes are just too absurd, / they should be changed" (*CCC*, p. 10).

Because Ch'iu Chin valorizes heroic emotion, men become vulgar and worthless when they fail to live up to the heroic ideal. She believes that she is more "heroic" than most men, and her ideological distance from traditional typologies of gender roles makes her feel alone and friendless. By complicating voice and image in relation to gender, she conveys in the song lyric the social and emotional difficulties experienced by a woman who has rejected her traditional domestic and sexual roles for a greater purpose in life. It is not that women such as Shen Shan-pao and Ch'iu Chin did not write conventional song lyrics in the "feminine" style. On the contrary, most of their song lyrics are rather generic pieces in the *wan-yüeh* style. But when voicing their discontents as women, when trying to break the shackles of gender in literature, women had to reject the image and poetics of the feminine constructed in the dominant tradition. In trying to find a new voice and language to represent this consciousness in themselves, women realized in the song lyric a way to accomplish this by pressing into service the gendered poetics so clearly constituted in the genre. They tried to assert a "new" feminine, in contradistinction to the old, by appropriating the masculine.

The Poetry of Li Ch'ing-chao:
A Woman Author and Women's Authorship

John Timothy Wixted

The poetry of Li Ch'ing-chao (b. 1084)[1]—both her *tz'u* and *shih*—prompts fundamental questions when viewed from various twentieth-century Western perspectives, especially feminist ones. Is there a separate women's literary tradition in China? If so, what is her place in it? Has her corpus of writings been viewed as being specifically female, and has it been viewed differently by men and by women? Is there a distinct female consciousness operative in her writing as well as that of other women writers? In what sense, if any, might she be viewed as being a feminist? And finally, what light might analysis of her work shed on current Western theoretical debate about women's writing, which is often couched in universalist terms?

As for the question of whether there is a separate female literary tradition in China, this can be only partially addressed here. It is clear

---

1. Li Ch'ing-chao's date of birth follows Chiang Liang-fu, *Li-tai jen-wu nien-li t'ung-p'u* (1937; rpt., Taipei: Shih-chieh shu-chü, 1974), p. 284, which is confirmed by Hsia Ch'eng-tao, *T'ang Sung tz'u lun-ts'ung* (Shanghai: Ku tien shu-chü, 1956), pp. 190ff. The text followed in this article is Chung-hua shu-chü Shang-hai pien-chi-so, ed., *Li Ch'ing-chao chi* (Shanghai: Chung-hua shu-chü, 1962).

Song lyrics (*tz'u*) by Li Ch'ing-chao are numbered sequentially as found in that text; page numbers follow, referring first to this 1962 edition, and then to vol. 1 of the *Ch'üan Sung tz'u*, ed. T'ang Kuei-chang (Peking: Chung-hua shu-chü, 1965) (hereafter cited as *CST*): e.g., "song lyric #1 (1962, p. 1; *CST*, p. 927)." Note that song lyrics numbered #45 and above are identified by the editors of the 1962 edition as being of doubtful attribution to Li Ch'ing-chao.

Shih poems by Li Ch'ing-chao are also numbered consecutively (#S-1 through #S-17) as they appear in the 1962 edition, page references being to the same work: e.g., "#S-1, p. 62." *Shih* fragments (#F-1 through #F-7) are similarly cited: e.g., "#F-1, p. 68."

that Li Ch'ing-chao, the granddaughter of a first-place examination candidate and the daughter of a literate mother as well as father, does not reveal in the extant writing reliably attributed to her any special awareness of works by earlier women writers:[2] Pan chieh-yü (48?–after 6 B.C.),[3] Pan Chao (45–ca. 117), Ts'ai Yen (fl. 200), Tso Fen (fl. 275), Hsieh Tao-yün (fl. 376), Li Yeh (fl. 756), Hsüeh T'ao (770–832), Yü Hsüan-chi (ca. 844–68), and Hua-jui fu-jen (10th cent.).[4]

It is true that one or two of Li Ch'ing-chao's poems are surprisingly similar to those of her Sung predecessor, Wei fu-jen (ca. 1040–1103);[5] but these similarities may only be coincidence, made all the more possible in a genre like *tz'u* where theme and language are so subject to convention.

If Li Ch'ing-chao did not look to earlier female writers as models, one might legitimately ask to what extent did Li Ch'ing-chao herself, along with her near contemporary Chu Shu-chen, become the *terminus a quo*,[6] if

2. "Conditions under which the writings of early medieval gentry women may to some extent have circulated, been collected, or anthologized but subsequently lost remain unclear. In the bibliographical sections of the T'ang and Sung dynastic histories, and in independent Sung bibliographies, at least seven collections of women's writings (all but one titled simply *Fu-jen chi*, "Collection of Writings by Women") are listed: two from the southern Sung [Six Dynasties], two each from the Liang and Sui, one from the later Wei, and one from T'ang. These collections have not survived." Maureen Robertson, "Voicing the Feminine: Construction of the Female Subject in the Lyric Poetry of Medieval and Late Imperial China," paper prepared for the Colloquium on Poetry and Women's Culture in Late Imperial China, University of California, Los Angeles, October 20, 1990, p. 17.

3. The titles *chieh-yü, chü-shih, fei, fu-jen,* and *tao-jen* are retained (unitalicized and lower-case) when citing names.

4. It is true that Li Ch'ing-chao's residence outside Chi-nan in Shantung was named after Hsieh Tao-yün, which reflects conscious association with the earlier writer (see the poem by Tung I cited below). Song lyric #53 (1962, p. 46; not in *CST*) also includes an allusion to Hsieh Tao-yün, but the poem is of doubtful attribution.

5. There is the use of the crab apple (*hai-t'ang*) in Wei fu-jen's song lyrics #2 and #13 (as numbered sequentially in *CST; CST*, pp. 268 and 269), later celebrated in Li Ch'ing-chao's song lyric #2 (1962, p. 1; *CST*, p. 927). Note the reduplication in Wei fu-jen's song lyric #1 (*CST*, p. 268)—*T'ing-yüan shen-shen shen chi-hsü*—found also in Li Ch'ing-chao's song lyrics #26 and #27 (1962, pp. 18 and 19; *CST*, pp. 929 and 933), as well as in a famous line by Ou-yang Hsiu (1007–72).

The dates of Wei fu-jen (and for Sun Tao-hsüan, cited below) follow Jen Jih-kao, *Sung-tai nü-tz'u-jen p'ing-shu* (Taipei: Shang-wu yin-shu-kuan, 1984), p. 33 (and p. 36). For Wei fu-jen, see also n. 54 below.

6. The dates for Chu Shu-chen are problematic. Jen Jih-kao has "ca. 1040–1103"; *Sung-tai nü-tz'u-jen p'ing-shu*, p. 32. T'an Cheng-pi has "fl. 1131"; *Chung-kuo wen-hsüeh-chia ta-tz'u-tien* (Taipei: Hsiang-kang Shang-hai yin-shu-kuan, 1961), p. 675. And C. Bradford Langley states that "the most reliable evidence . . . places her in the Northern Sung

not for a tradition of separate female writing in China, at least for a tradition of female *tz'u* writing. My own reading of the poems by the fifty-nine writers in the *Ch'üan Sung tz'u* easily identified as being by women (fifty of whom postdate Li Ch'ing-chao),[7] as well as the five women writers included in the *Ch'üan Chin Yüan tz'u*, does not reveal any special awareness or actual emulation of Li Ch'ing-chao's *tz'u* by later women writers. Nor have I found any use of language by this group of writers that could be termed distinctively female.[8]

There is little critical reference to Li Ch'ing-chao being used as a model by women.[9] Chang Yen (fl. 1526) states that Chu Shu-chen modeled herself on (*tsu*) a specific poetic line by Li Ch'ing-chao.[10] In more general terms, Ch'en T'ing (fl. 1515) states, "Women *tz'u* writers of the past like Li Ch'ing-chao and Sun fu-jen [Sun Tao-hsüan (fl. 1131)] all had their collected writings circulate in the world. As Chu Shu-chen followed in their footsteps, it can be said that every generation has its worthies."[11] Ch'en Wei-sung (1625–82) says of the woman writer Hsü Ts'an (fl. 1653), "In her *tz'u* she looked upon Chu Shu-chen as a younger sister, and she was nurtured by Li Ch'ing-chao as one might be by an aunt."[12] And Yeh Shen-hsiang (Ch'ing dynasty) says in refer-

---

rather than the Southern"; "Chu Shu-chen," in *The Indiana Companion to Traditional Chinese Literature*, ed. and comp. William H. Nienhauser, Jr. (Bloomington: Indiana University Press, 1986), p. 334.

The dating is important, as some critics place Li Ch'ing-chao before Chu Shu-chen and would have her influencing Chu (e.g., Ch'en T'ing, cited immediately below), and others have it the other way around.

7. Or at least are listed in the *Ch'üan Sung tz'u* as postdating Li Ch'ing-chao. Note that Jen Jih-kao finds a total of ninety-six women *tz'u* writers in the Sung, not all of whose work is extant or included in *CST; Sung-tai nü-tz'u-jen p'ing-shu*, pp. 32–78.

8. Note that in their introduction the editors of the volume resulting from the 1982 conference Women and Literature in China state: "Considering that even in texts written by women in our own language we are hardly able to pinpoint traces of a women's language, our failure to tackle this issue may be more easily understood." Anna Gerstlacher et al., eds., *Women and Literature in China* (Bochum: Studienverlag Gerstlacher, 1985), p. ii.

9. Of course, this begs two complementary questions: whether Li Ch'ing-chao was used as a conscious or unconconscious model by women, without critics' or poets' stating she was being used; and whether or not a statement that someone has used Li Ch'ing-chao as a model is necessarily the case.

10. Ch'u Pin-chieh, Sun Ch'ung-en, and Jung Hsien-pin, eds., *Li Ch'ing-chao tzu-liao hui-pien* (Peking: Chung-hua shu-chü, 1984), p. 40 (hereafter cited as *LCC tzu-liao hui-pien*).

11. Ibid., p. 38.

12. Ibid., p. 72.

ence to another woman writer, "Chu Hsi-chen [dates uncertain] wished to succeed on the same level as [*chi-mei*] Li Ch'ing-chao."[13] Such statements are all couched in fairly general terms. There is virtually no discussion of any specific language of Li Ch'ing-chao's being used by later women writers, as there occasionally is about its use by men writers.

Li Ch'ing-chao is linked retrospectively with women writers who precede her. For example, Tung Fu-heng (fl. 1607) states, "Her expressions and strains outreverberate others' of her age, making her one with the group of Pan chieh-yü, Tso Fen, and Ts'ai Yen."[14] In a poem by Tung I (Ch'ing dynasty) she is yoked implicitly with Hsieh Tao-yün:

> In her postface she recalled past happiness,
> And growing old following military ships, crossed the Yangtze in hardship.
> Her fragrant chamber is wrongly compared with that of Ming fei—[15]
> Li Ch'ing-chao of Willow Catkins Spring.[16]

And in a context referring to her remarriage, Li Ch'ing-chao is compared unfavorably by Lang Ying (b. 1487) with another earlier woman writer: "Alas! How removed from Ts'ai Yen she is!"[17]

It is clear that Li Ch'ing-chao becomes the standard by which virtually all later women writers are measured. Of Wu Shu-chi (Northern Sung dynasty) it is stated:

> At her best, she is not inferior to Li Ch'ing-chao.[18]
>
>   Huang Sheng (Sung Dynasty)

> People say she is not inferior to Li Ch'ing-chao, but in fact she does not measure up to Li Ch'ing-chao in warmth and classical elegance [*wen-ya*].[19]
>
>   Lu Ch'ang (Ch'ing Dynasty)

---

13. Ibid., p. 100.

14. Ibid., p. 51.

15. Ming fei, i.e., Wang Chao-chün (a palace lady during the reign of Emperor Yüan of the Han [r. 49–33 B.C.]).

16. *LCC tzu-liao hui-pien*, p. 123. Willow Catkins Spring was Li Ch'ing-chao's home in Shantung. The name has associations with Hsieh Tao-yün, who was called a "willow catkins talent."

17. Ibid., p. 32. The circumstances of the remarriages of the two were different. Ts'ai Yen, who had been forced into her first marriage with a Hsiung-nu leader after being captured by "barbarians," married a Han Chinese after being released and returning to China.

18. Ibid., p. 20. Note the variation by Yeh Shen-hsiang (ibid., p. 99): "At her best, she does not surrender place to [i.e., is not in any way inferior to] Li Ch'ing-chao."

19. Ibid., p. 104.

At her best, she is a match for Li Ch'ing-chao. Regrettably, no one knows about her.[20]

Yüeh-lang tao-jen (Ch'ing dynasty)

Chou Ming (Ch'ing dynasty) compares Hsü Ts'an quite favorably with Li Ch'ing-chao:

> Hsü Ts'an is good at writing and well versed in both calligraphy and painting. In her *tz'u* she has succeeded in achieving a Northern Sung style, absolutely rejecting the habits of delicate complicatedness and frivolousness. Where she is stately, Li Ch'ing-chao should concede her position. Hsü Ts'an is the top-ranked one [female], and not only for this dynasty.[21]

And Li Ch'ing-chao is compared with both women and men *tz'u* writers by Ho Shang (fl. 1681):

> In *tz'u* writing, that which is difficult and beautiful is deemed well crafted, but in truth it does not approach the marvelousness of language of fundamental color [i.e., that which is true, basic, unadulterated, *pen-se*]. [One line each of the following five *tz'u* poets is then cited by way of example: Hsiao Shu-lan (dates uncertain), Wei fu-jen, Sun Kuang-hsien (d. 968), and Yen Jen (fl. 1200); the line cited for Li Ch'ing-chao is the third one in song lyric #46 (1962, p. 42; *CST*, p. 934), one of the poems whose attribution to her is doubtful.][22]

There is little premodern criticism by women regarding Li Ch'ing-chao, the following poem by Chang Hsien-ch'ing (late Ming dynasty) being exceptional:

On Reading Li Ch'ing-chao's Shu-yü chi

What talented woman has there been to compare with her?
Polished jade and strung pearls—vessels well laden.
As for "One more gracile than chrysanthemums,"[23]
She is like a chrysanthemum at the end of autumn.[24]

Reference to a separate tradition of women's writing, one involving Li Ch'ing-chao, can perhaps be read into the following two statements, the first by Li P'an-lung (1514–70): "In terms of writing in a woman's voice [*hsieh ch'u fu-jen sheng-k'ou*], Li Ch'ing-chao, together with Chu

---

20. Ibid., p. 107.
21. Ibid., p. 90.
22. Ibid., p. 82. Note that the same lines are cited by T'ien T'ung-chih (Ch'ing dynasty), except that Wei fu-jen is omitted; ibid., p. 95.
23. Song lyric #18 (1962, p. 11; *CST*, p. 929).
24. *LCC tzu-liao hui-pien*, p. 64.

Shu-chen, dominates *tz'u* [literally, "dominates the flower of *tz'u*," *tz'u-hua*]."[25] And Chang Yen, who (as earlier noted) spoke of Chu Shu-chen's modeling herself on a line by Li Ch'ing-chao, added to that comment, "Could it be that there is a special secret [*hsin-fa*] that women pass on to each other?"[26] Li P'an-lung's comment can be taken to be a figure of speech, however, and Chang Yen's to be a rhetorical expression of praise. They do not constitute recognition of a separate tradition.

Criticism of women writers was generally not benign, as exemplified by the following comments of Tung Ku (fl. 1522):

> From the Han on, women capable of writing poetry and prose, like T'ang-shan fu-jen [a favorite concubine of Emperor Kao of the Han (r. 202–195 B.C.)] and Pan Chao, set down words to serve as moral instruction; their style being ancient and their learning correct, they were not easy to follow. Ts'ai Yen and Li Ch'ing-chao can be censured for having violated chastity [by having remarried].[27] Prostitutes like Hsüeh T'ao are not worthy of mention. Since Chu Shu-chen suffers from excess of sadness and disaffection, she too was not a good woman. And the wife of Tou T'ao [Chin dynasty] gave over to her emotions. Apart from these, there are not many to note.[28]

Ch'en Chi-ju (1558–1639) cites a woman who makes a statement that is construed as being a general criticism of a failing common to women *tz'u* writers:

> Meng Shu-ch'ing [fl. 1476] of Ts'ai-chou, the daughter of Assistant Instructor Meng Ch'eng, was skilled at writing poetry [*shih*]; her courtesy name was Ching-shan chü-shih. She once wrote a poem discussing Chu Shu-chen:
>
>> In writing poetry one must evolve from the embryo and transform one's temperament,[29]
>> Only when Buddhist priests' poetry is without the whiff of incense is its informing spirit [*ch'i*] fine.

By the same token, it [Chu Shu-chen's writing, and that of women writers in general] should not have a powdered look to it. Chu Shu-chen did in-

---

25. Ibid., p. 38.
26. Ibid., p. 40.
27. Cf. the remarks of Lang Ying cited above.
28. *LCC tzu-liao hui-pien*, p. 40.
29. For discussion of the Huang T'ing-chien (1045–1105) expression, which this line is a variation of, see Adele Austin Rickett, "Method and Intuition: The Poetic Theories of Huang T'ing-chien," in *Chinese Approaches to Literature from Confucius to Liang Ch'i-ch'ao*, ed. idem (Princeton: Princeton University Press, 1978), pp. 109–15.

deed suffer from the malady of commonness [vulgarity, *su*]. Li Ch'ing-chao could also be mentioned in this regard.[30]

More fundamentally critical is the following view expressed by a woman, one doubtless reflective of a more general societal attitude; it is related by Lu Yu (1125–1210): "When Sun fu-jen [Sun Tao-hsüan] was young, since she was quite bright, the wife of Chao Ming-ch'eng of Chien-k'ang, surnamed Li, who was famous for her writing [i.e., Li Ch'ing-chao], wished to instruct her. At the time the girl was only in her teens. But she declined, saying, 'Literature is not a proper pursuit for a woman.'"[31] Finally, a different critical standard operative for women is suggested by Hsü Ang-hsiao (Ch'ing dynasty): "In crafting this *tz'u* [i.e., song lyric #40; 1962, p. 31; *CST*, p. 932], Li Ch'ing-chao is original and graceful; but whereas each line is fine, a broader unity is lacking. Could it be that people of the past did not chastise her for it, excusing her because she was a woman?"[32]

Yet Li Ch'ing-chao is generally compared favorably not only with female authors but also with male ones. Yang Shen puts her on a par with Ch'in Kuan (1049–1100) and Huang T'ing-chien.[33] Wang Shyh-chen (1634–1711),[34] as well, speaks of Li Ch'ing-chao and Ch'in Kuan as being equally outstanding;[35] and he places her, together with Yen Shu (991–1055) (and/or Yen Chi-tao [11th cent.]), Ou-yang Hsiu, and Ch'in Kuan, as an exemplary author in his broader category of "literati *tz'u*" (*wen-jen chih tz'u*).[36] The *Ssu-k'u ch'üan-shu* editors pair her with different male authors: "Even though Li Ch'ing-chao was a woman, her poetic framework [*ko*] is lofty and refined.[37] She can justly be matched

30. *LCC tzu-liao hui-pien*, pp. 45–46. Note that the editors of this volume punctuate the text so as to make the final part of the citation all part of Meng Shu-ch'ing's poem, which does not work prosodically. Moreover, the final line could also be read, "Li Ch'ing-chao ought to have brought it up with her."

31. Ibid., p. 10. Compare the case of Han Yü-fu (12th cent.), a woman said by Lu Ch'ang to have studied with Li Ch'ing-chao; ibid., p. 104.

32. Ibid., p. 120.

33. Ibid., p. 35.

34. The romanization Wang Shyh-chen is used for the Ch'ing dynasty critic, and Wang Shih-chen for the Ming dynasty one (whose names would normally be romanized the same).

35. *LCC tzu-liao hui-pien*, p. 78.

36. Ibid.

37. Note the definition of the term *ko* made by Yoshikawa Kōjirō when explicating Kao Ch'i's (1336–74) use of it in his criticism: "*Ko* is the rhythmic feeling that derives from a poem's sound and meaning." *Five Hundred Years of Chinese Poetry, 1150–1650: The Chin, Yuan, and Ming Dynasties*, trans. John Timothy Wixted (Princeton: Princeton University Press, 1989), p. 113.

with Chou Pang-yen [1056–1121] and Liu Yung [987–1053]."³⁸ She
is paired with Li Yü (937–78), albeit along clear gender lines, by
Shen Ch'ien (1620–70): "Among males, Li Yü, and among females,
Li Ch'ing-chao, are those who have ultimately captured the fundamental color [*pen-se*]."³⁹ Indeed, Li Ch'ing-chao is sometimes specifically spoken of as being superior to male authors:

> Among young ladies of the Sung, Li Ch'ing-chao stands out as a writer in
> her own right, one not inferior to Ch'in Kuan and Huang T'ing-chien.
> Not a single *tz'u* composition by her is poorly crafted. Where her writing
> is well tempered, she may wrest position from Wu Wen-ying [ca. 1200–
> ca. 1260], and regarding beauty of language she deserves to be classed
> with Lü T'ien-ju [Ming dynasty]. Not only does she look out over
> womankind, she also overwhelms the male world.⁴⁰

Li Ch'ing-chao also influenced later men writers, Hsin Ch'i-chi
(1140–1207) most obviously, but also Chu Tun-ju (1080/81–ca. 1175)
and others.⁴¹ However, her work simply becomes part of the ocean of
material that later writers draw on.⁴² Its language is not marked as
female language. The male authors Li Ch'ing-chao is compared with

38. *LCC tzu-liao hui-pien*, p. 98.

39. Ibid., p. 69. For explication of the "fundamental color," see the Ho Shang citation above.

40. Ibid., p. 97; Li T'iao-yüan (fl. 1778). Yang Shen (1488–1559) finds a poem of
hers better than one by Chou Pang-yen to the same tune; ibid., p. 33. (Yang Shen's
attribution is wrong; the poem is in fact by Ch'in Kuan and not Chou Pang-yen. But his
intended comparison of the two poets still holds.)

41. See the comments by Yang Shen and Hsü Shih-chün (fl. 1636) in ibid., pp. 35
and 61. For a poem by Hsin Ch'i-chi written "In Imitation of the Style of Li Ch'ing-
chao," see ibid., p. 13. Hsin Ch'i-chi's use of Li Ch'ing-chao as a model seems to have
created some anxiety in his admirers; Hu Ying-lin (1551–1602) felt prompted to write in
Hsin's defense: "Hsin Ch'i-chi and Li Ch'ing-chao both took part in the general move
south, the one not long after the other. Besides, both of them were crafters of *tz'u*. How
can one say that Hsin robbed from [*p'iao*] Li?" (ibid., p. 43). (For pre-Sung passages criticizing plagiarism, including one by Han Yü [768–824] in which *p'iao* is used, see John
Timothy Wixted, *Poems on Poetry: Literary Criticism by Yuan Hao-wen [1190–1257]* [Calligra-
phy by Eugenia Y. Tu], Münchener ostasiatische Studien, no. 33 [Wiesbaden: Franz
Steiner Verlag, 1982], pp. 302–3.)

Note also that Sung Lo (1634–1713) is quoted by Hsü Ch'iu (1636–1708) as saying
that a *tz'u* to the tune "I-chien mei" by Tung I-ning (fl. 1666) is "extremely similar to
[*k'u-ssu*]" Li Ch'ing-chao's song lyric #25 (1962, p. 16; *CST*, p. 928); *LCC tzu-liao hui-
pien*, p. 88.

42. The only exception to this I have noted concerns Shen Ch'ien (1620–70), who
says that when young, he did not dare to write a poem following Li Ch'ing-chao's
"Sheng-sheng man" (song lyric #40; 1962, p. 31; *CST*, p. 932) "for fear of being laughed
at by women"; *LCC tzu-liao hui-pien*, p. 69.

(or whom she is said to influence) are all *tz'u* writers; this is understandable, since it was her *tz'u* poetry that was exceptional. Still, inasmuch as the song lyric as a genre remained suspect, it is less surprising that a woman became viewed as one of its great practitioners.

In sum, Li Ch'ing-chao's poetry draws little on the writings of earlier women; nor do later women writers especially emulate her actual writing, even though many of the female authors who pre- and postdate her (regardless of the genre they were writing in) are retrospectively grouped together with her by later critics in the implicit class of "woman writer," for which Li Ch'ing-chao becomes the standard. From the material that is extant, there seems little evidence for a separate female literary tradition in China until the late imperial period, in terms of either lineation or language. Female authors are looked upon negatively by some critics; but Li Ch'ing-chao is compared favorably by other critics with the greatest *tz'u* poets, her work being acknowledged as having served as a model for male authors.

The preponderance of criticism concerning Li Ch'ing-chao's writing has been positive. It is instructive, however, to look at the comments that are negative to see to what extent her being a female is injected into the discussion.[43] The earliest such comments come from Wang Cho (fl. 1162):

> Li Ch'ing-chao wrote "long and short lines" (*tz'u*), molding them so intricately to suit her will. They are light, skillful, sharp and original, with infinite moods and postures. The fantastically vulgar expressions of the back alleys and streets, whatever suited her mood, she would write down in her poetry. Since time immemorial among the lettered women of cultured families there had never been one so completely defiant of convention as Li Ch'ing-chao.[44]

Wei Chung-kung (Sung dynasty), commenting on Hua-jui fu-jen and Li Ch'ing-chao, states, "It has been said, the writing of exquisite lines definitely is not for women. Hua-jui fu-jen of Shu and Li Ch'ing-chao of recent times are especially famous. Each has *tz'u* and *yüeh-fu* that circulate in the world. But those that everyone likes and knows number only

43. Negative comments by Tung Ku and Hsü Ang-hsiao have been noted above.

44. *LCC tzu-liao hui-pien*, pp. 4–5. Translation by Hsu Kai-yu, "The Poems of Li Ch'ing-chao (1084–1141)," *PMLA* 77 (1962):525. Cf. the translation of the latter part of the passage by Chung Ling: "She uses openly the lewd language of the streets. Since ancient times I have never known a woman writer from the gentry who was as shameless as she is." "Li Qingzhao: The Moulding of Her Spirit and Personality," in *Women and Literature in China*, ed. Anna Gerstlacher et al., p. 150.

one or two. They are not all fine."[45] Yang Wei-chen (1296–1370) makes
a group out of Pan Chao, Li Ch'ing-chao, and Chu Shu-chen. They
each may have a single poem or a single letter that moves people, he
says; "But since they issue from a limited view and constricted intelligence, and are hampered by lowness of spirit and habit [i.e., are not
cultivated], they do not accord with what is correct in individual temperament and feeling."[46] The remarks of P'ei Ch'ang (Ch'ing dynasty)
are the most critical ones in *ad hominem* terms: "Li Ch'ing-chao, being
very self-assured about her talent, looked down on everything. Her
poetry is scarcely worth preserving. However, that a woman should be
so outspoken [hyper-literally, 'should open such a big mouth,' *neng k'ai
tz'u ta-k'ou*]—this is presumptuousness that need not be questioned and
folly that is unequaled."[47] Finally, Chou Chih-ch'i (1782–1862), citing
two earlier critics who praised Li Ch'ing-chao for her "Sheng-sheng
man" poem (song lyric #40; 1962, p. 31; *CST*, p. 932), states, "Only
Hsü Kao-lu [dates uncertain] of Hai-yen notes that she displays a considerable amount of vulgarity [*ts'ang-ch'i*] [in the piece]. He can be
called a discerning critic."[48] Although there is a fair amount of additional negative comment about song lyric #40,[49] most criticism about
the "lowness" or "vulgarity" of her writing seems to have been prompted
by lines in only three of Li Ch'ing-chao's poems,[50] all of which are of
questionable attribution. As some of the above quotations illustrate,
not all of the negative comments about Li Ch'ing-chao make reference
to her being a woman.

Many of the male writers and critics who comment on Li Ch'ing-
chao's writing evince surprise that such good writing could come from a
woman. They comment on how difficult it was for a woman to manage
such an achievement:

Such expression is hard for a woman to accomplish.[51]
    Hu Tzu (fl. 1147), in reference to song lyric #18 (1962,
                    p. 11; *CST*, p. 929)

To think that a woman can be as originally creative as this![52]
    Lo Ta-ching (fl. 1224), in reference to song lyric #40
                    (1962, p. 31; *CST*, p. 932)

45. *LCC tzu-liao hui-pien*, p. 17.
46. Ibid., p. 26.
47. Ibid., p. 87.
48. Ibid., p. 101.
49. E.g., by Hsü Ang-hsiao, as cited in ibid., p. 121.
50. Song lyrics #45, #46, and #48 (1962, pp. 42, 42, and 43; not in *CST*).
51. *LCC tzu-liao hui-pien*, p. 6.
52. Ibid., p. 21.

That such creativity could come from a woman—how exceptional![53]
> Shen Chi-fei (Ming dynasty), in reference to the phrase
> cited in the next quotation

Who would have expected that these four words, "[the] green [is] fat, [the] red thin," are those of a woman?
> Yüeh-lang tao-jen, in reference to song lyric #2 (1962, p. 1; *CST*, p. 927)

Such comments are not limited to Li Ch'ing-chao's *tz'u*. Indeed, it is in reference to the following *shih* poem by Li Ch'ing-chao, which had contemporary political implications, that Chu Hsi (1130–1200) writes in a combination of surprise and admiration, "Such expressions—how could they be written by a woman!"[54]

On History
The two Hans succeeded one another as one dynasty;
The new House [of Wang Mang (r. A.D. 9–27)] was like an excrescence.
It is for this reason that Hsi K'ang
Until his death denigrated the Yin and Chou.[55]

Good *shih* poems by women on political topics, if anything, evince greater surprise and admiration than do *tz'u* poems. As one scholar has noted: "If we consider the aesthetic function of literature written by Chinese women and that of literature written by Chinese men, we see that the former was not meant to have a wider sphere of impact than was [*sic*] the environment of its origin (family soro[r]ities, courtesans' circles and their friends), while the aesthetic function of the latter was intended to have a wide field of activity, to affect, if possible, the entire intellectual sphere of Chinese society."[56] Hsü Po-ling (late Ming dy-

53. Ibid., p. 46.
54. Ibid., p. 12. Chu Hsi (ibid.) also spoke of Li Ch'ing-chao as "one of only two literate [*neng-wen*] women of the dynasty," the other being Wei fu-jen, the wife of the prime minister Tseng Pu (1035–1107). This latter statement by Chu Hsi is a reformulation of the words by Chung Hung (469–518) in the *Shih-p'in*: "Li Ling [d. 74 B.C.] and Pan chich-yü together spanned roughly a century; but discounting the woman, there was only one poet for the period." Ch'en Yen-chieh, *Shih-p'in chu* (1927 rpt., Taipei: K'ai-ming shu-chü, 1960), p. 2.
55. #S-10, p. 66. The precarious situation of the Sung vis-à-vis the Chin is said to be similar to the one Hsi K'ang (223–62) found himself in regarding the possible founding of a new dynasty; he criticized even the Yin and Chou for displacing, respectively, the Hsia and Yin dynasties.
     Note additional translations of the poem by Liang Paitchin, *Oeuvres poétiques complètes de Li Qingzhao* (Paris: Gallimard, 1977), p. 110; and Kenneth Rexroth and Chung Ling, *Li Ch'ing-chao: Complete Poems* (New York: New Directions, 1979), p. 66.
56. Marián Gálik, "On the Literature Written by Chinese Women prior to 1917," *Asian and African Studies* (Bratislava) 15 (1979): 70.

nasty), speaking of the above poem, also states in befuddled admiration, "A woman could not write this!"[57] Two other *shih* poems by Li Ch'ing-chao written to match the rhymes of a composition by Chang Lei (1054–1114) elicit similar comments:[58] "That a woman should be placed among these authors [i.e., contemporary Sung poets who wrote *shih* on the same topic]—unless a person [i.e., Li Ch'ing-chao] has really profound thought, would that be at all possible" (from the *Ch'ing-po tsa-chih*, as cited by Wang Shyh-chen);[59] also, "Although the two poems are not fine pieces, it was no simple matter that they issued from a woman's hand; need one mention her truly exceptional works [i.e., her *tz'u* pieces]? Therefore, I have recorded them" (Wang Shyh-chen).[60]

As citations in the above sections suggest, Li Ch'ing-chao is seldom spoken of in premodern times in the way that most modern critics favor, as being quintessentially expressive of female sensitivity.[61] Yet one might legitimately ask about any corpus of material by a woman author: if read without authorial attribution by a reader versed in the tradition of the genre (something of an oxymoron), would the text be identified as being by a woman?[62] (And conversely, in how many instances would the writings of male authors, if read without attribution by such a reader, be taken to be written by women and to be expressive of a separate female consciousness?) Regardless of whether such a consciousness or sensitivity exists (and if it exists, whether it is limited to

57. *LCC tzu-liao hui-pien*, p. 63.

58. #S-4, p. 63, and #S-5, p. 63. They were prompted by the recent discovery of an eighth-century monument celebrating the restoration of the T'ang court after the An Lu-shan Rebellion.

59. *LCC tzu-liao hui-pien*, p. 78.

60. Ibid., p. 76. Note the similar comments by Ch'en Hsi-lu (Ch'ing dynasty) about the *shih* fragment by Li Ch'ing-chao (#F-4, p. 69); *LCC tzu-liao hui-pien*, p. 92. The same sort of comment can be found in reference to her famous postface to the *Chin-shih lu*: "In this piece, the expression of feeling is fine and exquisite; it does not at all seem to be expression emitting from a woman. The writing is truly delightful!" Chu Ta-shao (Ming dynasty), as cited in *LCC tzu-liao hui-pien*, p. 42.

61. The examples among present-day writing on the poet, including Western-language discussion, are legion. For example, in a footnote appended to his translation of song lyric #56 (1962, p. 49; not in *CST*), James J. Y. Liu states: "This poem has also been attributed to Chou Pang-yen, but I am inclined to assign it to the poetess Li Ch'ing-chao, as the sentiments and sensibility seem particularly feminine." *The Art of Chinese Poetry* (London: Routledge & Kegan Paul, 1962), p. 51 n. 1.

62. Cf. the comment by Chung Ling concerning Li Ch'ing-chao's *shih* poetry: "In other words, a reader, versed in classical poetry, would have taken her *shi[h]* poems to have been written by a man, unless he was aware of the authorship." "Li Qingzhao: The Moulding," p. 159.

women, or whether all women necessarily have it), one item is clear: historically, most readers' expectations of Li Ch'ing-chao's work have been different precisely because it is identified as being by a woman.

Many *tz'u* by male authors have been praised for the understanding they are said to reveal of female psychology. Most such *tz'u*, as feminist critics would probably point out, tell us not of how women think or feel, but of how such male authors perceive women: how they think, or fancy, or would have it, that women think and feel.

The problem here is partly one of the genre and its conventional themes concerning women. What makes Li Ch'ing-chao different is that, as a woman, her writing is taken to be autobiographical in a more direct way than *tz'u* by male authors, specifically those written in the personas of women, possibly can be. In a word, Li Ch'ing-chao's *tz'u* are, in large measure, read as if they were *shih*: that is, as being revelatory of an experienced world. With only one exception I have noted so far, none of Li Ch'ing-chao's commentators even considers the possibility that the persona in any of her poems is fictive. That one exception, the critic Wang Fan, has written perceptively about many of Li Ch'ing-chao's *tz'u*, pointing out, for example, the two types of woman found, respectively, in song lyrics #3 (1962, p. 2; *CST*, p. 932) and #45 (1962, p. 42), both to the tune "Tien chiang ch'un":[63] the former represents the more helpless, listless sort of woman found in many *Hua-chien chi* poems; the latter presents a more spirited, playful, and seductive type of woman.[64] (There is nothing, of course, to preclude the autobiographical critic from finding different aspects of the poet's personality reflected in such different verses.)[65] The question highlights the porousness of the boundary between *shih* and *tz'u*, the latter having genre conventions that must have made authors, female as well as male, write in fictive guises. There has, of course, always been a thrust to read male authors' biographies into their *tz'u* poems as well: consider, for example, the supposed addressee of Wei Chuang's (836–910) "Yeh-chin men" *tz'u*,[66] the political (and other) circumstances read back into Li Yü's poems,[67] and

63. Wang Fan, *Li Ch'ing-chao yen-chiu ts'ung-kao* (Huhehot: Nei-Meng-ku jen-min ch'u-pan-she, 1987), pp. 119–24.

64. There is the question of the reliability of the attribution of the latter poem to Li Ch'ing-chao.

65. And this is precisely what Wang Fan does in the majority of cases.

66. Song lyrics #23 and #24 (as numbered in John Timothy Wixted, *The Song-Poetry of Wei Chuang [836–910 A.D.]* [Calligraphy by Eugenia Y. Tu], Occasional Paper no. 12 [Tempe: Center for Asian Studies, Arizona State University, 1979], pp. 64–67). She was said to be the poet's concubine, later appropriated by the ruler Wang Chien (r. 907–25).

67. Note Daniel Bryant's fun parody of the circularity inherent in this kind of ex-

the question of which female entertainers in Liu Yung's life are said to have inspired which poems.[68]

The received view concerning Li Ch'ing-chao's domestic life is that she and her husband were ideally suited to each other, sharing antiquarian interests. The earliest instance I find of their being portrayed as the ideal conjugal couple—in the comments of Lang Ying—however, dates from nearly four centuries after the two lived.[69] And the source for the view, Li Ch'ing-chao's postface to the *Chin-shih lu,* was written in 1134, five years after her husband had died and thirty years after the idyllic incidents it describes; also, the piece itself contains a strong countercurrent of suppressed discontent with the marriage as it evolved, reflected in the way Li Ch'ing-chao tells of her husband's developing mania for

---

plication; with slight modification it could well describe how Li Ch'ing-chao's poems are categorized and treated as biographical data.

Li Yü's lyrics can be divided into three (sometimes it is two, or even four) groups on the basis of their content, and these groups correspond to the major divisions of his life. That is, there are, to begin with, the carefree and exuberant poems of his youth, before he came to the throne, in which he celebrates the luxurious and unrestrained life that he enjoyed as a pampered prince. Then, there are the sadder poems of his middle period, when he was beset by the cares of state and afflicted by the successive deaths of his son, wife, and mother. Finally, there are the great lyrics of his last years in captivity, in which he pours out his homesickness and remorse. Of course we know that he was happy in his youth, for example, because we have those carefree and exuberant poems that he must have written then because that was when he was so carefree and exuberant, as the poems show . . . *Lyric Poets of the Southern T'ang: Feng Yen-ssu, 903–960, and Li Yü, 937–978* (Vancouver: University of British Columbia Press, 1982), p. xxviii.

68. As James R. Hightower notes:

There is little excuse for reading most of his songs as autobiographical, but no need to deny their author's familiarity with the milieu that is their setting. . . . It can be assumed that his songs were written to be sung by professional entertainers, and after them by their hearers, as were most *tz'u* before Su Shih; they were not primarily a vehicle for the expression of the poet's private feelings. This means that it is more appropriate to deal with this corpus of song words directly, without continually appealing back to the person of the poet and his presumed circumstances. "The Songwriter Liu Yung," pt. 1, *Harvard Journal of Asiatic Studies* 41 (1981): 340–41.

69. Note also the reference to their happy marriage by Fu Chao-lun (Ch'ing dynasty); *LCC tzu-liao hui-pien,* p. 142. Ting Shao-i (Ch'ing dynasty), however, looks at five marriages involving literary women and finds only one of them (not Li Ch'ing-chao's) ideal: "Good marriages like this [between Chao Te-lin and Wang fu-jen]—why is heaven so stingy about them?"; ibid., p. 129.

collecting artifacts.[70] If an autobiographical reading of her poems is maintained, she was clearly also unhappy when married.[71] One might also ask, if she and Chao Ming-ch'eng were such the loving couple, why was he so insensitive to her feelings of loss when he went away for extended periods to collect rubbings (a loss taken to be expressed in the poems she is said to have written at such times)? Furthermore, there is the story about song lyric #18 (1962, p. 11; *CST*, p. 929), the one with the famous lines: "How undeniably heartrending! / When the west wind stirs the blinds— / One more gracile than chrysanthemums." Chao Ming-ch'eng is said to have shut himself away to write fifty poems trying to match hers; when he presented his work mixed with hers to a friend to read, he was told that only three lines were exceptional: the ones by her, quoted above. If there is any basis to the story, one might find reflected in the incident additional pressures in their marriage.[72] Finally, reference to the difficulties members of her family are said to have had because she was their relative cannot be ascribed wholly to misogyny; Yeh Sheng (1420–74) says, "Wen-shu [her father] had the misfortune to have her as a daughter, and Te-fu [her husband] had the misfortune to have her as a wife."[73]

It is noteworthy that there is no reference in the poet's writing to the fact that she and her husband had no children. It is even more remarkable that none of her critics or commentators draws any conclusions from it: none criticizes her for it, in the few cases where it is noted,[74] in relation either to her marriage in general or to her roles of wife and potential mother.

The supposed remarriage of the poet is a different matter. Much ink has been spilled trying to deny that this apparently disastrous union took place.[75] Presumably, the remarriage of a widow carried little

70. Stephen Owen has written perceptively on this point; "The Sources of Memory," chapter 5 of *Remembrances: The Experience of the Past in Classical Chinese Poetry* (Cambridge: Harvard University Press, 1986), pp. 80–98.

71. The modern critics Ch'eng Ch'ien-fan and Hsü Yu-fu note that even though she was most compatible with Chao Ming-ch'eng, there must have been a void in her life that she needed to fill; *Li Ch'ing-chao* (Kiangsu: Chiang-su jen-min ch'u-pan-she, 1982), p. 10.

72. The incident is recounted by I Shih-chen (early Ming dynasty), as cited in *LCC tzu-liao hui-pien*, p. 28.

73. Ibid., p. 31. The comment is dismissed by Chang Yen (Ming dynasty) as being unworthy of mention; ibid., p. 40.

74. E.g., Chai Ch'i-nien (Southern Sung dynasty), as cited in ibid., p. 25.

75. There is an entire volume of reprinted essays devoted to the topic: Chu Ch'uan-yü, ed., *Li Ch'ing-chao kai-chia wen-t'i* (Taipei: T'ien-i ch'u-pan-she, 1982).

stigma at the time;[76] it is later critics who, applying their contemporary standards, were scandalized at the possibility that such a famous figure (by definition a good woman who could not have done such a thing) not only remarried but also divorced,[77] and they took pains to deny it.

As for the question in what sense if any might Li Ch'ing-chao be viewed, albeit anachronistically, as being a feminist, it is to the circumstances of her life and to both her *shih* poetry and prose writing that one must turn, not to her *tz'u*. She is famous for the lines addressed to her father-in-law, the New Laws–faction prime minister, requesting that her father, a conservative critic, be spared the current purge of anti–New Laws officials:

> Under the burning hand of authority, the heart turns cold;
> How much greater, the feelings of a daughter for her father.[78]

Although Li Ch'ing-chao's appeal proved of no avail, her lines do reveal an independence of spirit and a willingness to challenge authority both within the family circle and beyond it. Although only seventeen *shih* poems by her are extant,[79] many can be read to have direct political significance. It is through them that we know her hawkish views encouraging non-appeasement of the Chin. A couplet from one of these poems is revealing about the poet as woman, as a woman in society, and as a woman of affairs. It appears in one of two poems dedicated to important officials, old family acquaintances who are about to set off north as legates to sue for peace with the Chin:

> What do I, a widow living in humble circumstances, know?
> But it is with a missive written in an oath of blood that I beseech you.[80]

76. Ann Waltner, citing a 1980 unpublished paper by Patricia Ebrey, "Widows and the Structure of Society during the Sung," summarizes its findings as follows: "While remarriage was not seen as the preferred course of action for widows during the Sung, neither was it discouraged very strongly." "Widows and Remarriage in Ming and Early Qing China," in *Women in China: Current Directions in Historical Scholarship*, ed. Richard W. Guisso and Stanley Johannesen (Youngstown, N.Y.: Philo Press, 1981), p. 129 n. 3.

77. Note the comments by Lang Ying and Tung Ku above.

78. These lines are poetic fragments (#F-1, p. 68, and #F-2, p. 68), taken by some critics to be from the same poem. The first is always cited in the context noted.

79. Nineteen by the count of some scholars, who split #S-7, p. 65, and #S-14, p. 67, into two; e.g., Wang Yen-t'i, *Shu-yü-chi chu* (Shantung: Shan-tung wen-i ch'u-pan-she, 1984), pp. 71–97.

80. #S-7, p. 65. "I beseech you" is a tentative rendering. The poem is translated by Liang Paitchin, *Oeuvres poétiques*, pp. 127–30; and by Rexroth and Chung, *Li Ch'ing-chao*, pp. 62–65.

The poet as woman is inscribed in the text. Is she here literally abasing herself as a woman? (Doubtful.) Is Li Ch'ing-chao simply employing a variation of the self-deprecatory language one might find in any such poem of political comment and implied exhortation? (Yes; but women would have an additional pool of such terms to draw on, to fit the expectations of potential readers and the more immediate male addressees of the poems.) There is the further possibility that, as with all such language of self-effacement, the expression is really an inverted expression of pride (of the sort, "I'm just a Hoosier, but . . ."), which can serve to gull those foolish enough to think less of the speaker because of the role being donned. (This is surely also the case here, given the forcefulness of the rest of the poem.) In view of the political advice offered later in the poem, the writer is also laying the rhetorical groundwork for that self-assertion.

Other non-*tz'u* writings by Li Ch'ing-chao also reveal her to be a strong-willed person. As a critic, she expresses independent judgment, presuming to point out the shortcomings of many famous male predecessors in the genre, including Liu Yung, Su Shih (1037–1101), Ch'in Kuan, and Huang T'ing-chien.[81] Additionally, her rhymeprose "Ta-ma fu" is more than a piece describing a gambling game; as Liang Paitchin notes, "Dans ce long poème, l'amour du jeu se fond avec celui de la patrie en péril. Personnages, événements, batailles: tout est évoqué pour faire sentir un coeur palpitant de révolte et d'indignation; tout est soutenu et animé par une pensée impérieuse dont l'inspiration est profonde, et la marche, rapide."[82] Even Li Ch'ing-chao's postface to the *Chin-shih lu* inspires praise for its presumed no-nonsense approach.[83]

81. As summarized by one modern scholar: "She was a keen literary critic, expressing appreciation of the contribution of Liu Yung to rhyme and rhythm but disapproving of his vulgarity, admiring the genius of Su Shih while noting the erratic strain in his compositions. She remarked that Ch'in Kuan stressed affectivity at the expense of daily realities of life, while Huang T'ing-chien emphasised these realities but made mistakes of composition." Julia Ching, "Li Ch'ing-chao," *Sung Biographies*, ed. Herbert Franke, Münchener ostasiatische Studien, no. 16 (Wiesbaden: Franz Steiner Verlag, 1976), 2:538.

82. Liang Paitchin, *Oeuvres poétiques*, p. 35; the *fu* is translated in ibid., pp. 143–48, as "Le Jeu de petits chevaux." In English translation, the quotation reads: "In this long poem, love of the game is found together with that of the fatherland in peril. Personages, events, battles: all is evoked to make felt a heart beating in revolt and indignation; all is sustained and animated by an imperious thought, the inspiration for which is profound, the pace rapid."

83. Mao Chin (1599–1659) (as cited in *LCC tzu-liao hui-pien*, p. 59) argues: "At the end [of the *Shu-yü chi*] there is the postface to the *Chin-shih lu*, where one can glimpse the marvelousness of her prose. She was not only more stalwart than other gifted young

In sum, without the material available to us from these other sources, we would be hard-pressed to make out from Li Ch'ing-chao's *tz'u* alone the substantial figure she must have been.

The questions addressed above that most intersect with current issues in Western feminist literary theory concern whether there is a separate female literary tradition in China and whether there is a separate and universal female consciousness that is manifested in women's writing.[84]

Western feminist critics are divided on the latter question. Some argue for "an identifiable, homogeneous, 'essential' female consciousness, literary tradition, or style."[85] Others argue against a distinct female sensitivity, biology, or realm.[86] (The problem with both approaches is that they start with *a priori* notions that, more often than not, fit the arguer's agenda for what is deemed desirable social change in the world of today. Seldom is either more than an assertion.) There is little in premodern Chinese writing by women to argue a case for a universal separate female consciousness.

As for the question of whether there is a separate female literary tradition in China, generalizations about the early *shih* tradition are difficult to make.[87] Nonetheless, as noted earlier, one would be hard-

---

women of her generation, she also straightforwardly wiped clean the stench of assorted Confucianists after the general move south; she returned upstream to the Wei and Chin."

84. Quite useful for their summaries of recent Western scholarship on feminist literary theory are Vincent B. Leitch, *American Literary Criticism from the Thirties to the Eighties* (New York: Columbia University Press, 1988); and K. K. Ruthven, *Feminist Literary Studies: An Introduction* (Cambridge: Cambridge University Press, 1984).

85. Leitch, *American Literary Criticism*, p. 312 (referring to Patricia Meyer Spacks and others); see also p. 314. The image of the madwoman comes under this category. Found by Sandra Gilbert and Susan Grubar to be embodied in numerous nineteenth-century fictional characters, the figure "is usually in some sense the *author's* double, an image of her own" (*The Madwoman in the Attic: The Woman Writer and the Nineteenth-Century Literary Imagination* [New Haven: Yale University Press, 1979], p. 78). The madwoman figure, especially in its "angel" manifestations, must be viewed as being culture-bound to the West. The madwoman is simply a variation (albeit a pernicious one) of the demonic image in the West of the poet as the maker, the one breathed into by gods (or muses), the possessed, and above all, the creator or demigod. There is no such tradition in premodern China, where all writing is viewed as being a patterning reflective and revelatory of a self-generating cosmos.

86. See Leitch, *American Literary Criticism*, pp. 312–13 and 324.

87. "The lack of adequate archival sources for medieval women's writings raises a serious doubt about our ability to generalize concerning women's literary culture in earlier China. Even the works of prominent and prolific women associated with the imperial

pressed to argue for a separate women's literary style in China, certainly in reference to the *tz'u* of Li Ch'ing-chao and other Sung female writers in the genre. Nor does there seem to be a tradition of sororal emulation of Li Ch'ing-chao among *tz'u* writers who postdate her.[88]

This is not to deny, as noted earlier, that women's writing has often been labeled and read by many male Chinese readers and critics as being different. Given the "alterity" that this labeling effects in women's writing, what is surprising in the Chinese tradition is how seriously the work of a Li Ch'ing-chao has been taken over the centuries. Apart from the likelihood that the very excellence of her writings compelled their being appreciated, two paradigms may be operative here other than the one of male versus female. One has already been mentioned: *tz'u* poetry itself is represented in the Chinese literary tradition as being something of the "distaff side" of *shih* poetry.[89] It may have been more acceptable to find a woman supreme in this "other" (and, on the whole, lesser) realm than in the world of *shih*. In this regard, however, it is striking to find Li Ch'ing-chao portrayed as the "great patriarch" of the genre. Beginning at the end of the Ming dynasty, the poet seems virtually to have been brought under the category of male author by many critics, given some of the more global labels attached to her. Thus, Wang Shih-chen (1526–90) calls her the "true [correct, standard] patriarch [*cheng-tsung*] of *tz'u*." (The same term is also applied to her by Hsü Shih-chün, who makes Hsin Ch'i-chi the "auxiliary patriarch" [*p'ang-tsung*] of the genre: "Besides these two, no one else occupies these positions.") Li Ch'ing-

---

court have been lost, except for a handful of pieces in a few instances. The tiny amount of extant poetry by gentry women that survives makes the study of their literary culture and the affinities of their poetry with both the Six Dynasties models and T'ang literati poetry particularly difficult, while the slightly better preservation of the works of courtesans, entertainers, and Taoist women may create a misleading profile for this period." Maureen Robertson, "Voicing the Feminine," p. 18.

88. One scholar has noted that women in seventeenth-century Kiangnan "formed a loose literary network, exchanged correspondence and encouraged one another's endeavors." Ellen Widmer, "The Epistolary World of Female Talent in Seventeenth-Century China," *Late Imperial China* 10, no. 2 (Dec. 1989): 2. Note also the discussions in this volume by Kang-i Sun Chang on Liu Shih (1618–64) and by Grace S. Fong on Ku T'ai-ch'ing (1799–1870s).

Compare the categorical assertion by Paul W. Kroll: "There *was* no discernible Chinese tradition of literature written either by or for women" (emphasis in original); " . . . Fair and Yet Not Fond," a review article of *Brocade River Poems: Selected Works of the Tang Dynasty Courtesan Xue Tao*, ed. and trans. Jeanne Larsen (Princeton: Princeton University Press, 1987), *Journal of the American Oriental Society* 108 (1988): 623.

89. Note the references to this in the chapters by Grace Fong and Pauline Yu in this volume.

chao is "the great patriarch [*ta-tsung*]" of *tz'u* both in the *Chi-nan fu-chih* and in the writings of Chou Lo (Ch'ing dynasty), and she is "a great patriarch" (*i ta-tsung*) of the genre for editors of the *Ssu-k'u ch'üan-shu chien-ming mu-lu*, as well as for Wu Ch'ung-yao (1810–63). Feng Chin-po (Ch'ing dynasty) makes Ch'in Kuan and Li Ch'ing-chao the "patriarchs" (*tsung*) of *tz'u*. And Liang Shao-jen (b. 1792) even makes her the "patriarch of Northern Sung *tz'u*."⁹⁰ Granted, the term *tsung* in such usage is largely metaphorical. It is nonetheless ironic, given the strongly pejorative tone with which the term "patriarchy" has been used in current Western feminist discourse.

Another paradigm probably operative is that of the culture and society of Han Chinese versus anything that does not approach the society wholly in its own dominant culturalist terms. The acceptance of writings by sinicized authors of non-Chinese origins—Yeh-lü Ch'u-ts'ai (1189–1243), Kuan Yün-shih (1286–1324), and Na-lan Hsing-te (1655–85)—may provide a parallel typology. The writing of each of these "foreigners" has always been marked as being by an "other." But as long as that "other" fully accepts dominant Han Chinese cultural values, he or she can to a greater or lesser degree become an "inside outsider." Put in feminist terms, Li Ch'ing-chao for the most part accepts (or at least does not question in a threatening way) the dominant societal values of her time;⁹¹ and this probably helped allow for the

---

90. *LCC tzu-liao hui-pien*, pp. 41, 60, 132, 133, 98, 137, 124, and 122. An image strikingly exceptional to those just cited is the one employed by Sung Ssu-ching (Ch'ing dynasty). In his preface to *Li-tai ming-yüan shih-tz'u* (An anthology of poetry by famous ladies through the dynasties), he refers to three earlier female writers, characterizing them in masculine terms, and then adds to the list "Li Ch'ing-chao, the high priestess [*ta-wu*] of the Chao-ruled Sung" (*LCC tzu-liao hui-pien*, p. 104).

91. In one of her *shih* poems, Li Ch'ing-chao does express the view, "May the Empress have many, many *sons* [*nan*]!" (#S-15, p. 68; cf. the translations by Liang Paitchin, *Oeuvres poétiques*, p. 113; and Rexroth and Chung, *Li Ch'ing-chao*, p. 68). This could be interpreted as a conventional wish, but one arguably also reflective of the poet's "victimization" by current societal values. (The role and status of the empress, however, may make for something of a special case here. Also, the verse was part of a group of poems that Li Ch'ing-chao wrote on behalf of a relative.)

Julia Kristeva (after citing a passage in the "Ta-ma fu," using the Liang Paitchin translation) summarizes her thoughts on Li Ch'ing-chao:

An identification with men, an insistence on the values of the *literati*, a fascination with power and success: So be it. But there is also in Li Qingzhao a reminder of the political power of the (astonishingly accurate) written word, a defence of personal initiative against all orders. And all this in a musical, precise, and economical language that no translation can hope to reproduce. Li Qingzhao is the perfect example of the kind of excellence a woman can achieve on the condition that she

possibility that she be accepted as the superb practitioner of *tz'u* that she both was and, for the most part, was appreciated as being. She is still a "woman poet" for many, just as Na-lan Hsing-te is a "Manchu" one.[92]

---

cease to live as a woman. *About Chinese Women*, trans. Anita Barrows (New York: Urizen Books, 1977), p. 93.

In looking for female feminist writers in China, it is useful to note the quasi-parallel provided by British women novelists writing from 1840 to the present. Elaine Showalter in her study of such authors, *A Literature of Their Own: British Women Novelists from Brontë to Lessing* (Princeton: Princeton University Press, 1977), posits three periods—as summarized by Leitch, *American Literary Criticism*, pp. 312–13:

> The initial "Feminine phase," from 1840 to 1880, involved imitation by women novelists of the dominant tradition and internalization of its literary and social standards. The second "Feminist phase," from 1880 to 1920, entailed protest against prevailing modes and advocacy of minority values and rights. The final "Female phase," from 1920 onward, evidenced a turning inward in search of identity and a relaxation of dependency on opposition.

We may see some analogy in the work of Li Ch'ing-chao and other premodern women poets who imbue themselves with the dominant tradition and internalize its literary and social standards. Apart from exceptional comments such as the one by Yü Hsüan-chi regretting that, not being a male, she cannot take the civil service examinations,* protest by women writers does not occur until the late imperial period, becoming more pronounced in modern times with the introduction of Ibsen's Nora onto the scene (see Vera Schwarcz, "Ibsen's Nora: The Promise and the Trap," *Bulletin of Concerned Asian Scholars* 7.1 [Jan.–Mar. 1975]: 3–5). Showalter's third "Female phase" probably also then starts almost simultaneously, all three phases being in evidence at the same time in the twentieth century.

Ch'üan T'ang shih (Peking: Chung-hua shu-chü, 1960), 804.9050; as translated by Jan Wilson Walls, "The Poetry of Yü Hsüan-chi: A Translation, Annotation, Commentary and Critique" (Ph.D. diss., Indiana University, 1972), p. 174:

> I resent the silken gown
>   that subdues my poetry
> as I look up and envy in vain
>   the names on the Honor Roll.

Yü Hsüan-chi is also famous for her lament, "A priceless treasure is easy to seek / but a man with a heart is hard to find." *Ch'üan T'ang shih*, 804.9047; translation by Walls, "The Poetry of Yü Hsüan-chi," p. 87.

Note also that in the *Fan-hua meng* by the woman writer Wang Yün (dates uncertain), "[t]he author precedes the play with a *tz'u* poem in which she clearly expresses her regret that unlike men, she cannot have a good career of her own." Sharon Shih-jiuan Hou, "Women's Literature," in *The Indiana Companion to Traditional Chinese Literature*, ed. William H. Nienhauser, Jr., p. 192. (This article must be used with care. Note the many corrections provided by David R. Knechtges and Chang Taiping, "Notes on a Recent Handbook for Chinese Literature," *Journal of the American Oriental Society* 107 [1987]: 296–97.)

92. Along the same lines, it is no accident that Ch'ien Ch'ien-i's (1582–1664) mam-

The work in contemporary Western criticism perhaps most useful for examining *tz'u* in general, even more than the specific writings of Li Ch'ing-chao, is Lawrence Lipking's *Abandoned Women and Poetic Tradition.* One can argue that the figure of the abandoned woman (so central for Lipking), which in *shih* poetry can be traced back to the famous poem attributed to Pan chieh-yü about her fan (a symbol of her rejection), is *the* major topos of early *tz'u*. Much of the *Hua-chien chi* is simply a variation on the theme.[93] Although the topic is never *not* to be found in the corpus of any major *tz'u* writer, much of the development of the genre in Sung times can be traced in terms of its becoming only one of several topoi employed. *Tz'u* by Li Ch'ing-chao and Chu Shu-chen have traditionally had a special impact on readers because the authors, being women, are presumed to have been writing directly from their own experiences as "abandoned women."[94] Poems on the theme of the abandoned or jilted male—found especially in *tz'u* by Liu Yung, but also ambiguously present in many other *tz'u*, for example in those by Wei Chuang—although expressed with considerable feeling, do not engender the empathy that the writings by these women do, nor even the affect of poems written by men about abandoned women (other than the more conventional ones). There is, of course, an implied social dimension to all such readings. As the settings make clear, the women in such poems are literally cooped up or otherwise socially constrained; the men, even when heartbroken, are still free to move about in society. The accoutrements of the bedchamber become emblematic of a female condition; and even young female entertainers, as Liu Yung sardonically notes, have to make a living. So even if only two strata of female society are explicitly referred to in *tz'u*, their condition, by extrapolation, might be taken to stand for women in general.

   Lawrence Lipking writes with considerable insight and sensitivity of the pervasiveness of the "abandoned woman" theme in Western writings by both men and women, and of the implications to its being embodied in the personas of Ariadne, Sappho, Sybil, and his own creation, Aristotle's Sister. The theme, he finds, can be understood in the

moth anthology of Ming dynasty *shih* poetry, *Lieh-ch'ao shih-chi*, has as its final catchall section the assembled poems of Buddhist priests, Taoist adepts, women, eunuchs, foreigners, and so on. They are all marginalized.

   93. Interestingly, Li Ch'ing-chao is seldom mentioned together with Pan chieh-yü in the Chinese critical tradition. Both are mentioned by Yeh Shen-hsiang among a series of writers said to have been moved by personal circumstances to write; *LCC tzu-liao hui-pien*, p. 99.

   94. The term is here applied in the broad sense used by Lipking.

following ways, which (to widely varying degrees) are potentially relevant to its Chinese manifestations. The abandoned woman can be read

as a record of the oppression of women (in the terms noted in the preceding paragraph),

as an emblem of all oppressed people (possible only through a forced reading of Chinese examples),

as the instrument of religious love and yearning (although not applicable in the sense described by Lipking, the theme of personal rejection is linked with that of religious search or fulfillment in the poetry of Yü Hsüan-chi),[95]

as the voice of repressed psychological fears (operative in many *tz'u* by women, to the extent one adopts a psychobiographical approach), and

as the writing of the archetypal poet and figure of poetry (suggested, albeit in an attenuated way, by Li Ch'ing-chao's reference to her own writing in her *shih*).[96]

There has been a good deal of criticism of Lipking, part of it in reaction to the idea that the abandoned woman might serve as the archetype of the woman poet, part of it in reaction to the critic's being male. His work is invaluable for making an apparently limited theme far richer in implication than might otherwise be appreciated.

---

95. *Ch'üan T'ang shih*, 804.9049, 9050, and 9050–51; as translated by Walls, "The Poetry of Yü Hsüan-chi":

Disjoined, but not for long,
 in the end I have found fulfillment;
I see the emptiness of rise and fall,
 the meaning of True Mind. (p. 146)

> We've been living on the same lane
> but through the year we've [I've] had no call,
> . . . .
> The Taoist nature is colder than snow;
> The Zen mind scoffs at gorgeous silks.
> My steps have risen to the ends of the sky
> where no roads reach down to the misty waves. (p. 151)

I set free my feelings,
 cease resenting my heartless mate;
I nourish true nature,
 toss off the waves of the bitter sea. (p. 179)

96. #S-1, p. 62; cf. the translations by Liang Paitchin, *Oeuvres poétiques*, p. 120 ("Moi, je m'isole, faisant des poèmes derrière la porte close"); and Rexroth and Chung, *Li Ch'ing-chao*, p. 55.

Early viewed as being an outstanding writer or woman writer, Li Ch'ing-chao became the standard by which virtually all female Chinese writers, and many male writers of song lyrics, were compared. Yet her writing did not greatly influence actual writing by later women, nor is there much evidence to argue for a separate tradition of *tz'u* writing by women in the Sung-Yüan period, in the sense of women consciously modeling themselves on earlier women as part of a separate stream of writing. The reception of Li Ch'ing-chao's work, however, provides important data for the study of images of women and views of female writing in China. Premodern critics in their comments often lump together various women authors, sometimes quite disparate ones, in a way that emphasizes their shared "otherness." At the same time, many critics seem to treat Li Ch'ing-chao as an exception—in effect, as a (female) male among males, even as a "patriarch" in the ("other") world of *tz'u*.

Liu Shih and Hsü Ts'an:
Feminine or Feminist?

Kang-i Sun Chang

INTRODUCTION

Liu Shih (1618–64) and Hsü Ts'an (ca. 1610–after 1677) are two outstanding and representative women *tz'u* poets of the Ming-Ch'ing transition. They came from strikingly different backgrounds and apparently received educations of different sorts, but they were equals in terms of literary distinction. In many ways, they provided the basis for two new models for women engaged in literary careers—models that contrast somewhat with those of earlier periods, for the Ming-Ch'ing transition is marked by a differentiation of women poets into the courtesan tradition, represented by Liu Shih, and the gentry-woman tradition, represented by Hsü Ts'an.

The fact that these two distinguished women poets appeared at this particular time in the history of *tz'u* deserves our special attention, especially because by the early seventeenth century the song lyric had already been viewed as a "dying genre" for more than three centuries. It was Liu Shih, the courtesan-poet, who helped her lover Ch'en Tzu-lung (1608–47) establish the important Yün-chien school of *tz'u* revival.[1] Interestingly, while a number of male Ming authors seem to

I would like to thank Haun Saussy, Ron Egan, Yu-kung Kao, Anthony Yu, and two anonymous reviewers for offering helpful comments and suggestions. To Shih Chih-ts'un (Shi Zhi Cun) of Shanghai I owe a special debt of gratitude for all the important materials and information he has given me. I am also indebted to my students in the Ming-Ch'ing Women Poets seminar, and especially to Cheng-hua Wang, who provided me with valuable sources on Hsü Ts'an.

1. For details about Ch'en Tzu-lung's role in the Yün-chien school of *tz'u* revival, see chapter 4 of my book *The Late-Ming Poet Ch'en Tzu-lung: Crises of Love and Loyalism* (New

have been largely unaffected by the revival movement, *tz'u* suddenly became the main expressive vehicle for many late Ming women, notably
Hsü Ts'an, who is known primarily as a *tz'u* poet (rather than a writer of
shih) and has been praised by many scholars as the best of the women
tz'u poets of late imperial China, perhaps "even superior to the Sung
poet Li Ch'ing-chao."[2] Clearly, Liu Shih and Hsü Ts'an were exemplary women writers who lent color to seventeenth-century China and
considerable stature to the *tz'u* genre.

To understand the role of women in the revival of *tz'u*, we must first
ask why there were such unprecedented numbers of women poets in
the late Ming. (In the *tz'u* genre alone, there are more than eighty
late Ming women poets whose works have been recorded in modern
anthologies.)[3] One obvious reason is the rise in female literacy from the
sixteenth century onward, which no doubt provided women with the
skills and made viable the aspirations that were necessary for literary
creativity.[4] As they grew in number and confidence, these women began
to write in a great variety of poetic genres and eventually found their
way into print—hence the proliferation of collections and anthologies of
poetry by women at that time.[5] But a more important reason, I think,
has to do with the effort of many contemporary "male feminists," who
not only served as the editorial brains behind most of the anthologies of
women poets, but also actively tried to "canonize" women's writings by
associating them with the classical canons, the *Shih-ching* and "Li-sao."[6]

Haven: Yale University Press, 1991). See also Yeh Chia-ying, "Yu tz'u chih t'e-chih lun
ling-tz'u chih ch'ien-neng yü Ch'en Tzu-lung tz'u chih ch'eng-chiu," *Chung-wai wen-hsüeh*
19, no.1 (June 1990): 4–38.

2. See Hsü Nai-ch'ang's foreword to Hsü Ts'an's *Cho-cheng-yüan shih-yü*, in his *Hsiao-
t'an-luan shih kuei-hsiu tz'u* (1896), ser. 2. (Further references to this volume will be
abbreviated as *CCYSY* in the text.) Note that more than one hundred *tz'u* by Hsü Ts'an
have survived, while only three of her *shih* poems are extant.

3. See, for example, I Po-yin, ed., *Li-tai nü shih tz'u hsüan* (Taipei: Tang-tai t'u-shu
ch'u-pan-she, 1972), pp. 133–61, 215–16. Henceforth abbreviated as *LTNST*.

4. Joanna F. Handlin, "Lü K'un's New Audience: The Influence of Women's Liter-
acy on Sixteenth-Century Thought," in *Women in Chinese Society*, ed. Margery Wolf and
Roxane Witke (Stanford: Stanford University Press, 1975), pp. 13–38. See also Paul S.
Ropp, "Love, Literacy, and Laments: Themes of Women Writers in Late Imperial
China," *Women's History Review* 2.1 (1993): 107–41.

5. See Hu Wen-k'ai, *Li-tai fu-nü chu-tso k'ao*, rev. ed. (Shanghai: Shang-hai ku-chi
ch'u-pan-she, 1985). See also Chung Hui-ling, "Ch'ing-tai nü shih-jen yen-chiu" (Ph.D.
diss., National Cheng-chih University, 1981), pp. 92–135.

6. See my "Canon-Formation in Chinese Poetry: Problems of Gender and Genre,"
presented at the ICANAS Panel on the Concept of the Classic and Canon-Formation in

Many of these male editors—chief among them Chao Shih-chieh and Tsou I—argued that since the female substance was composed of the "purest cosmic essences" (*ling-hsiu chih ch'i*), women's writings were superior to men's.[7] In fact, one scholar even suggested that poetry by women, created out of the spirit of such purity and hence devoid of any political affiliations or biases, could be used as an ideal remedy for the confusing array of literary positions and schools in the Ming.[8] Perhaps because of this faith in the corrective function of women's poetry, most Ming (and later, Ch'ing) anthologists insisted on including *contemporary* women's works, which was indeed a departure from the traditional model of the anthology as containing works that were often different from, and even ran counter to, the prevailing taste of the present.[9] Chou Chih-piao, for instance, selected works of fourteen late Ming women poets for his two anthologies. The titles of both of these anthologies contain the phrase *nü-chung ch'i ts'ai-tzu* (seven female talents)[10]—a phrase apparently implying a comparison of contemporary women poets to the famous "Former Seven Masters" and "Latter Seven Masters" who so dominated the configurations of the Ming literary scene.

All this demonstrates that Chinese women poets like Liu Shih and Hsü Ts'an were fortunate in at least one respect: unlike many English-speaking women poets,[11] their poetic vocation did not arouse resistance on the part of male scholars and critics. In fact, late Ming women such as Liu Shih and Wang Tuan-shu were encouraged to become editors of poetry anthologies and were free to express critical views on individual

---

East Asia (Toronto, August 21, 1990). For the relationship between canon-formation and anthology making in ancient China, see Pauline Yu, "Poems in Their Place: Collections and Canons in Early Chinese Literature," *Harvard Journal of Asiatic Studies* 50(1990): 163–96.

7. Chao Shih-chieh, *Ku-chin nü-shih* (1628); Tsou I, *Hung-chiao chi* (printed early Ch'ing). See Hu Wen-k'ai, *Li-tai fu-nü*, pp. 889, 897.

8. Chung Hsing, ed., *Ming-yüan shih kuei* (ca. 1600). See Hu Wen-k'ai, *Li-tai fu-nü*, p. 883. Some Ch'ing scholars, among them Wang Shih-chen, seriously questioned the editorship of this anthology. But even if Chung Hsing did not edit the volume, someone else in his time must have done it.

9. This traditional view of the true canon has been summed up by Pauline Yu in her "Poems in Their Place," pp. 188–94.

10. Hu Wen-k'ai, *Li-tai fu-nü*, p. 844.

11. For the dichotomy of poetry and femininity in the English tradition, see Sandra M. Gilbert and Susan Gubar, *The Madwoman in the Attic: The Woman Writer and the Nineteenth-Century Literary Imagination* (New Haven: Yale University Press, 1979), pp. 540, 546.

authors[12]—which they did with a self-assurance that they seem to have
inherited from the Sung poet and woman of letters Li Ch'ing-chao, the
first literary critic of either sex to write so confidently about *tz'u* poetry.
What Lawrence Lipking has said about the sexist tendencies in Western
criticism—that "historically men have shown no interest at all in a
woman's poetics"[13]—does not seem to apply to the Chinese poetic
tradition. Various sources have proven that Ming-Ch'ing men were
truly interested in writings by women. As Ellen Widmer has observed,
"contemporary women writers strove to be included in women's poeti-
cal anthologies, and such books were read and admired by contemporaries, male and female."[14]

LIU SHIH AND THE COURTESAN TRADITION

Underlying the male enthusiasm and support for women's works is the
traditional respect for "talent" (*ts'ai*). Chinese women, however suppressed and mistreated socially, were taken seriously for the literature
(especially poetry) they produced. Since the T'ang, the concept of
"talented women" (*ts'ai-nü*) has represented the literati poets' attempt
to create a special image of women. The courtesan was the prototype of
the "talented woman," whose singing and verse writing, along with her
beauty, gave men the comforting illusion of meeting a goddess in a
fairyland—and courtesans hence were called "goddesses" (*shen-nü*) from
the T'ang dynasty forward. Po Chü-i and Yüan Chen captured the mys-
tique of the alluring courtesans in their *shih* poems,[15] while the courte-

12. Hu Wen-k'ai, *Li-tai fu-nü*, pp. 433–34, 894. Liu Shih's anthology of women
poets, included in Ch'ien Ch'ien-i's *Lieh-ch'ao shih-chi*, has become a standard text of poetry by women. Her *Ku-chin ming-yüan shih tz'u hsüan*, bringing together both *shih* and *tz'u*
poems by female authors, was perhaps the earliest anthology in the late Ming period to
have included so many representative *tz'u* works (totaling four hundred or more) by
women. Wang Tuan-shu said that her *Ming-yüan shih-wei* (preface dated 1661), an anthology of women poets in all major genres, was meant to compete with the classical *Shih-
ching*, a claim that the male scholar Ch'ien Ch'ien-i (who wrote the preface to the collection) apparently endorsed.
    13. Lawrence Lipking, "Aristotle's Sister: A Poetics of Abandonment," in *Canons*, ed.
Robert von Hallberg (Chicago: University of Chicago Press, 1984), p. 87. Also in Lawrence Lipking, *Abandoned Women and Poetic Tradition* (Chicago: University of Chicago
Press, 1988), p. 211.
    14. Ellen Widmer, "The Epistolary World of Female Talent in Seventeenth-Century
China," *Late Imperial China* 10, no. 2 (Dec. 1989): 22.
    15. K'ang Cheng-kuo, *Feng-sao yü yen-ch'ing* (Honan: Jen-min ch'u-pan-she, 1988), pp.
216–19.

san Hsüeh T'ao herself became a real *shih* poet, not a symbol.[16] In the late T'ang and the Sung, poets composed *tz'u* for courtesans to sing, weaving tender emotion and sensual love into the song lyric genre. In the seventeenth century the reputation of courtesans accelerated decisively, largely because many of them had become true artists specializing in poetry, calligraphy, painting, or the dramatic arts. These courtesans were respectable "women of learning," and their works were published privately or included in contemporary anthologies.[17] They were able to enter into the cultural elite of the Chiang-nan cities, and they often concluded romantic marriages with literati and scholar-poets. At the same time, these courtesans became identified with a role so familiar in contemporary fiction and drama, that of the talented woman who marries a gifted man (*ts'ai-tzu*)—though in reality they often ended up being merely the concubines of these men.[18]

In many ways, Liu Shih fit into the popular image of the talented woman. She became an accomplished poet-painter and calligrapher in her teens, and many literati in the Chiang-nan area came to admire her literary learning. She published her first collection of poems, *Wu-yin ts'ao* (1638), at the age of twenty and enjoyed a reputation as a courtesan of superb talent and beauty. Her intense love relationship with the young poet Ch'en Tzu-lung, and her later marriage to the literary giant Ch'ien Ch'ien-i, made her a legendary figure in the field of literature. Most important, her numerous love poems to Ch'en Tzu-lung (and for that matter, Ch'en's to her) engendered a whole new interest in *tz'u*, a genre characterized by intensity of emotion. Since traditionally proficiency in song lyrics was closely associated with the courtesan culture, we might expect that Liu Shih greatly influenced the *tz'u* revival—not only by her writings but also by serving as a "symbol."

It was no accident that Liu and Ch'en's *tz'u* revival took place at a time when the late Ming notion of *ch'ing* (love) encouraged a cultural reevaluation of human feeling. In late Ming fiction and drama, the "talented man" and "gifted woman" (*ts'ai-tzu chia-jen*) who exchange

16. Of course, as Jeanne Larsen points out, men at first were ambivalent about these liberal-minded women poets, as may be seen in the many scandalous stories they created about Hsüeh and other T'ang courtesans. See Jeanne Larsen's introduction to her *Brocade River Poems: Selected Works of the Tang Dynasty Courtesan Xue Tao* (Princeton: Princeton University Press, 1987), p. xiv.

17. For example, in Chou Chih-piao's *Nü-chung ch'i ts'ai-tzu lan-k'o chi* and Mao Yü-ch'ang's *Ch'in Huai ssu-chi shih* (The four courtesans of Ch'in Huai). See Hu Wen-k'ai, *Li-tai fu-nü*, p. 844.

18. See chapter 2 of my book *The Late-Ming Poet Ch'en Tzu-lung*, pp. 9–18.

poems are portrayed as lovers nearly consumed by passion but eventually saved by their unchanging devotion to each other. Love has the supreme power to defeat time and death (as in *Mu-tan t'ing*); and it bestows virtue upon the lovers (as in *Tzu-ch'ai chi*). The late Ming literati were the first to make the shift in values from allegorical love to real love based on reciprocity between male and female. The dramatist T'ang Hsien-tsu opens his play *Tzu-ch'ai chi* with the following words that affirm this new idea of *ch'ing*: "In this world, where can one find examples of love's longings? / Just see how people like ourselves are devoted to love."[19]

Liu Shih and Ch'en Tzu-lung's *tz'u* poetics was clearly patterned on the late Ming notion of reciprocal love. Liu's numerous poetic exchanges with Ch'en—in some cases, her poems are more elaborate in scope and length than Ch'en's—are framed as personal letters, telling the secret of a passion felt by two equally talented poets. Liu was no longer a mere singer like the Sung courtesans whose prime duty was to perform song lyrics for men. As a talented poet herself, she acquired a personal voice breathing the very spirit of purity, all the while addressing her lover as an equal. In her perhaps most brilliant song-series, "Meng Chiang-nan" (subtitled "Thinking of Someone," in twenty poems), she tells the moving story of her relationship with Ch'en, recounting her struggles with love's agonizing passion and describing the dreamlike nature of being in love. In the last song of the series she openly admits her love:

Where was he?
He was by my pillow side.
Nothing but endless tears at the quilt edge—
wiping them off secretly, but only inducing more,
for good or ill I want his love.[20]

人何在
人在枕函邊
只有被頭無限淚
一時偷拭又須牽
好否要他憐

Elsewhere, again in plain and sensuous language, Liu Shih analyzes her condition as if she were a heroine in a romantic play—for self-

19. T'ang Hsien-tsu, *T'ang Hsien-tsu chi*, ed. Ch'ien Nan-yang (Shanghai: Jen-min ch'u-pan-she, 1973), 3:1587.
20. The translation is taken from my book *The Late-Ming Poet Ch'en Tzu-lung*, p. 126, with modifications.

expression and self-dramatization are both at the heart of her *tz'u* poetics. In her *"Chin-ming ch'ih*: On the Cold Willow," she describes her dreams of love by evoking the images of the plum and moonlight borrowed from T'ang Hsien-tsu's romantic play *Tzu-ch'ai chi*:

> How I wish to invite the plum spirit in:
> at evening, by the dim moonlight,
> we could quietly speak of deep longing and love.[21]
>
> 待約箇梅魂
> 黃昏月淡
> 與伊深憐低語
>
> (lines 26–28)

Such a candid and emotional poem demands, as always, a response from the beloved, her "male counterpart" who suffers from the pain of love and pining. Indeed, in his "Chiang ch'eng tzu" for Liu Shih, subtitled "Getting up Ill When the Spring Is Over," Ch'en Tzu-lung confesses to being overcome by symptoms of lovesickness.[22] Clearly, Liu Shih and Ch'en Tzu-lung, by working through an original but stylized use of the literary convention from contemporary lyrical drama, have assumed the roles of hero and heroine exchanging love poems in *tz'u*. This is a bold revision of the song lyric tradition; but at the same time Liu and Ch'en were rescuing the genre from prolonged neglect, and in time their Yün-chien school was to set the models for imitation.

I think late Ming courtesan-poets like Liu Shih are the ultimate symbol of *tz'u* poetry, for human emotion defines itself in the song lyric. To the courtesan-poets, love is power; personal meaning is determined by the intimate male-female relationship. Thus, the courtesans Wang Wei (Hsiu Wei) and Cheng T'o (Ju-ying) dwell on images of consuming passion, vowing undying love and perpetual longing. Yang Wan creates unmistakable fantasy, dreaming about the pleasures of "holding hands" with her beloved. Ma Shou-chen broods over the beautiful lyrics given her by her departed lover and continues to love in mournful solitude. And Chao Ts'ai-chi in her "Everlasting Longing" ("Ch'ang hsiang-ssu") emphasizes her sufferings as a lover, using words such as *hsiang-ssu* (longing) and *ch'ing* (love) to dramatize feelings of tenderness, fidelity, and devotion.[23]

---

21. Ch'en Yin-k'o, ed., *Liu Ju-shih pieh-chuan* (Shanghai: Shang-hai ku-chi ch'u-pan-she, 1980), 1:336–37.

22. Ch'en Tzu-lung, *Ch'en Tzu-lung shih-chi*, ed. Shih Chih-ts'un and Ma Tsu-hsi (Shanghai: Shang-hai ku-chi ch'u-pan-she, 1983), 2:616.

23. For the poems referred to above, see *LTNST*, pp. 153–54, 153, 150, and 152, re-

The connection between song lyrics and love, or other emotions, is no doubt what makes the *tz'u* genre "feminine." But femininity is not the same as femaleness.[24] Femininity in Chinese poetry is an aesthetic quality, the cultivation of refined elegance and tender feeling—a quality akin to the "delicate restraint" (*wan-yüeh*) typical of the majority of Sung *tz'u* written by men. Women poets did not invent femininity in *tz'u*; male poets did. Even if the song lyric was long thought to be a "feminine" genre, most major *tz'u* poets before the Ming were male, with the notable exception of Li Ch'ing-chao and Chu Shu-chen. But male scholars of the seventeenth century, in their enthusiastic attempt to promote women poets, began to argue that women, being "female," were able to produce better song lyrics.[25] This common confusion (or convergence) between femaleness and femininity no doubt encouraged many Ming-Ch'ing women to engage in *tz'u* writing, inadvertently bringing about a reflowering of the genre.

Most women *tz'u* poets of the seventeenth century, however, understood that "femininity" was only a generic trait of the song lyric. Thus, although their *tz'u* songs were generally characterized by refined imagery and eloquence of emotion, their *shih* poems were filled with references to Confucian morality, social injustice, political crises, and historical events.[26] In Liu Shih's poetry in particular, we find a clear sense of generic discrimination: whereas her *tz'u* are written in the language of emotional realism and passionate love, her *shih* often evoke an aura of sublimity and philosophical reflection, and were occasionally praised for a "heroic" tone generally associated with the works of male writers.[27] Such a sense of genre falls perfectly within the tradition of early *tz'u* criticism. The Sung scholar Shen I-fu says in his *Yüeh-fu chih-mi*: "Writing *tz'u* is different from writing *shih*. Even in writing about flowers, a *tz'u*

---

spectively. Works by Cheng T'o, Ma Shou-chen, and Chao Ts'ai-chi were brought together in the seventeenth-century anthology *Ch'in Huai ssu-chi shih*. See Hu Wen-k'ai, *Li-tai fu-nü*, p. 844.

24. Camille Paglia makes an important distinction between "femininity" and "femaleness" in her recent book *Sexual Personae: Art and Decadence from Nefertiti to Emily Dickinson* (New Haven: Yale University Press, 1990), pp. 56–60.

25. For example, Yu T'ung, in his preface to *Lin-hsia tz'u-hsüan* (an anthology of *tz'u* by women, printed sometime after 1662), made such an argument by drawing examples from many female Ming poets. See Hu Wen-k'ai, *Li-tai fu-nü*, p. 895.

26. See, e.g., *LTNST*, pp. 129–31, 165–206.

27. See my *Late-Ming Poet Ch'en Tzu-lung*, p. 80. Also Ch'en Yin-k'o, *Liu Ju-shih pieh-chuan*, 1:112.

poem must evoke love and feeling [*ch'ing-i*] or touch on matters concerning the inner chamber."[28]

HSÜ TS'AN AND THE GENTRY-WOMAN TRADITION

The theme of the "inner chamber" is another element central to the song lyric. The term I have translated as "gentry-women poets" literally means "poets of the inner chamber" (*kuei-ko shih-jen*). Unlike the courtesans who usually saw themselves with reference to their gentleman friends, the gentry-women poets of the late Ming often considered women as a group, in a spirit of female-bonding.[29] These women regularly formed poetry clubs in intimate, domestic settings to promote their literary interests and expertise, and those invited were usually limited to female relatives and friends—in sharp contrast to the courtesans who usually belonged to male literary societies like the Fu-she and Chi-she and moved about more actively. In the gentry women's societies, members served as teachers and pupils to one another and often exchanged poems set to the same rhyme patterns. Hsü Ts'an was known as one of the "Five Talented Poets" (*wu-tzu*) in the most prestigious female poetry club in Chekiang, the Banana Garden Club (Chiao-yüan shih-she).[30]

There seems to have been some fragmentation or split among contemporary male scholars over the issue of publication with regard to gentry-women poets. On the one hand, an unprecedentedly large number of collections and anthologies of works by women in the late Ming convinces us that gentry women were encouraged by their male relatives or friends to publish their poems—a classic example being Yeh Shao-yüan (1589–1649), who published works of his wife, Shen I-hsiu (1590–1635), along with poems by his three talented daughters, Yeh Wan-wan (1610–32), Yeh Hsiao-wan, and Yeh Hsiao-luan (1616–32).[31]

28. T'ang Kuei-chang, ed., *Tz'u-hua ts'ung-pien* (Peking: Chung-hua shu-chü, 1986), 1:281.

29. Ellen Widmer observes that relationships between gentry women "show the importance of solidarity among women themselves, rather than associations centered on men, in developing female talent." See Widmer, "The Epistolary World of Female Talent," p. 3.

30. According to one source, the other four "talented poets" were Ch'ai Ching-i, Chu Jou-tse, Lin I-ning, and Ch'ien Yün-i; see Chung Hui-ling, "Ch'ing-tai nü shih-jen," p. 126.

31. Yeh Shao-yüan, *Wu-meng t'ang ch'üan-chi*, in *Chung-kuo wen-hsüeh chen-pen ts'ung-shu*, ser. 1, vol. 49 (Shanghai: Pei-yeh shan-fang, 1936). I have benefited from reading

But on the other hand, there were men who did not wish to see their own daughters, wives, or mothers becoming excessively intellectual—though it seems to have been acceptable to them that courtesans attain literary renown.[32] Moreover, there had been a tradition—somewhat out of fashion by the late Ming—of gentry women burning their own poems for fear of exposing their poetic talents to the outside world. In any case, compared to their courtesan contemporaries, gentry women were more restricted in their educations, it seems: they studied prescribed classics like the Nü Ssu-shu (Four books for women) and were taught "improvements in morals" and "household management."[33] Perhaps for this reason, the famous gentry woman poet Hsü Yüan (incidentally, a great aunt of Hsü Ts'an's) had been accused of "fishing for fame but lacking in learning" (hao-ming wu-hsüeh). It is interesting to observe that the well-rounded and unusually learned courtesan Liu Shih agreed that there might be some justification for such severe criticism, though she was also trying to speak in defense of Hsü Yüan.[34]

By all accounts, Hsü Ts'an, a favorite of her father, was extremely privileged in her education from early childhood on. She grew up in Soochow, a cultural center in the late Ming, and became well versed in poetry and art at a young age. Well born, well educated, and well married (her husband, Ch'en Chih-lin, of the prominent Ch'en family of Hai-ning, later became a chief minister), Hsü Ts'an should have been the envy of many contemporary women. But unfortunately, Hsü Ts'an had to endure a fate that had haunted Chinese gentry women since times of old: sometime in the early 1640s her husband acquired a concubine, who apparently lived with him in the capital at Peking while Hsü Ts'an remained at home in the south.

A Chinese woman in such circumstances was expected to exercise the virtues of a supportive wife. In the late Ming we can find many instances of such exemplary wives. The wife of Mao Hsiang (one of the "Four Aristocratic Youths") may be most well known to modern readers. Mao Hsiang wrote in his Ying-mei-an i-yü that his virtuous wife even went out of her way to bring Tung Pai (the famous courtesan who was

---

Chung-lan Wang's "The Tz'u Poetry of Shen I-hsiu, Yeh Wan-wan, and Yeh Hsiao-luan" (Term paper, 1990).

32. Widmer, "The Epistolary World of Female Talent," pp. 29–30.

33. Jonathan Spence, The Search for Modern China (New York: Norton, 1990), p. 9.

34. See Liu Shih's section on women poets, in Ch'ien Ch'ien-i, Lieh-ch'ao shih-chi hsiao-chuan (Shanghai: Shang-hai ku-chi ch'u-pan-she, 1983), 2:752. According to Hu Wen-k'ai, Liu Shih was responsible for the extensive annotations on women poets anthologized in Ch'ien Ch'ien-i's Lieh-ch'ao shih-chi. See Hu Wen-k'ai, Li-tai fu-nü, p. 433.

Mao Hsiang's lover and later his concubine) to their house so that the two lovers could be formally united.[35] Unlike Mao Hsiang's wife, Hsü Ts'an refused to accept her fate in silence. She expressed her feelings of resentment in many song lyrics, with a candor and directness rarely encountered in a literary tradition where women's emotions were expected to be moderated. Hsü Ts'an viewed herself as an "abandoned wife," suffering the mental torments of jealousy, disappointment, and helpless resignation—a situation that reaches back to the "Nineteen Old Poems." In a *tz'u* addressed to her husband, "I Ch'in-o," subtitled "Spring Feelings," Hsü Ts'an complains that she has suddenly been "abandoned" (*p'ao-p'ieh*):

> My heart aches as if crying,
> as if crying,
> old love gone, when new love found.

> 悽悽似痛還如咽
> 還如咽
> 舊恩新寵

(CCYSY, 1.9a–b)

Ironically, in his preface to his wife's collection of song lyrics, *Cho-cheng-yüan shih-yü*, Ch'en Chih-lin praises Hsü Ts'an for her expression of *wen-jou tun-hou* (meekness and gentleness), a phrase coined in reference to the *Shih-ching*, the foremost of canonical sources. *Wen-jou tun-hou* is the quality of emotional restraint, long celebrated in traditional Chinese literary criticism. Obviously, like all conventional Chinese literati, Ch'en Chih-lin was perhaps a bit too anxious to find "sorrow without anger" (*ai erh pu-yüan*) in all "abandoned wife" poems, including those by his own wife. He was perhaps reading into Hsü Ts'an's lyric the ideal virtue of the queen in the first poem of the *Shih-ching* ("Kuan-chü"), who was lauded for her conscientious efforts to find her husband a suitable young concubine (as some Confucian commentators would read it). Indeed, it is most interesting that Ch'en seems to have missed completely the tone of protest and defiance in Hsü Ts'an's song lyrics.

Generally, in evaluating a poem with the theme of the "abandoned wife," we must first ask whether the language is personal and original or conventional and formulaic. This is an especially crucial question because since the times of Ch'ü Yüan (d. 315 B.C.?) and Ts'ao Chih (192–232), the Chinese poet, when demoted or exiled, had been accustomed to speak through the female voice of the "abandoned wife" (*ch'i-fu*), in-

---

35. Pan Tze-yen, trans., *The Reminiscences of Tung Hsiao-wan*, by Mao P'i-chiang [Mao Hsiang] (Shanghai: Commercial Press, 1931), p. 38.

tending the words to be read as political allegory. In fact, the whole
theme of the "abandoned wife" in Chinese poetry can be said to have
been made popular by male poets. But what happened when women
poets finally began writing poetry?

To a large extent, women poets since Pao Ling-hui (5th cent.) had
been trying to model their works on those of male authors (naturally
enough, given that the female poetic tradition was yet to be shaped).[36]
But the "abandoned wife" poems of women guided by personal experience and female sensitivity added a new dimension to Chinese poetry—
they are concrete, confessional, and often filled with realistic detail.
Most important, they speak in a language of their own, a true, rather
than an allegorical, voice. In *tz'u* poetry in particular, we find women
poets like Li Ch'ing-chao writing out their lives, creating a wonderful
poetic fusion of convention and originality, of the female and male traditions. And that is what Hsü Ts'an and other Ming-Ch'ing women poets
set out to do in their song lyrics—to find some way to incorporate the
male tradition in the expression of their own pure, personal, unmediated feelings as women.

In sharp contrast to contemporary courtesan-poets like Liu Shih who
took romantic love as the main theme in their *tz'u*, Hsü Ts'an and other
gentry-women poets focused on self-pity or on their complaints as
"abandoned wives."[37] Courtesans were, of course, often—if not more
often—abandoned by men too, but in their song lyrics they tended to
dwell on the power of passion and the vivid memories of love. Gentry
women, on the other hand, emphasized the passivity of their situations
and their feelings of abandonment (even when they were not actually
abandoned, only separated from their husbands). There is a basis in
real life for this sharp distinction between poetic styles: unlike the courtesans, gentry women who were married were not free to write overtly
passionate love songs lest they be accused of extramarital liaisons.
(Even unmarried women were concerned about guarding their reputations.) The unwritten rule since ancient times was that when husbands
were away, it was inappropriate for chaste wives to dress up or adorn
themselves.[38] Of course, women also tended to neglect personal appear-

36. For Pao Ling-hui's poems modeled on the "Nineteen Old Poems," see Anne Birrell, trans., *New Songs from a Jade Terrace* (New York: Penguin, 1986), pp. 122–24.
37. Lawrence Lipking would call both kinds of women "abandoned women," as they
both experience similar kinds of "passive suffering." See his *Abandoned Women and Poetic
Tradition*, p. 3. But in the context of *tz'u*, I feel it is useful to make the distinction, however fine, between the lover and the abandoned wife.
38. K'ang Cheng-kuo, *Feng-sao yü yen-ch'ing*, pp. 42–43.

ance when feeling "abandoned."[39] This explains why one pervasive
theme in "abandoned wife" *tz'u* is a woman's self-evaluation of her fad-
ing beauty (which she notices when looking into the mirror)[40] and her
reluctance to comb her hair (a theme that is also prevalent in Li Ch'ing-
chao's song lyrics)—all so she can demonstrate her husband's mistreat-
ment of her and her own adherence to the rules.

In response to the social pressure and poetic decorum imposed upon
traditional wives, Ming-Ch'ing gentry-women poets seem to have found
another, new outlet for their repressed emotional lives by expressing
their friendship with other women as though it were romantic love. In
tz'u addressed specifically to female friends, they often used such words
as *hsiang-ssu* (love's longings), *tuan-hun* (heartbroken), and *lien* (love),[41]
and even made references to courtship poems of the *Shih-ching* that could
be literally interpreted as alluding to a lover's frustration at being separated from a loved one.[42] Indeed, the language used in these song lyrics
is often so full of erotic overtones that many of these poems could easily
be interpreted by modern readers as expressions of lesbian love.[43]

Hsü Ts'an, however, used a different channel for expressing her feelings of "lovesickness," converting personal love into political loyalty:

My old country, far away,
how can a boat take me there?
The setting sun flows with the river, gone . . .

故國茫茫
扁舟何許
夕陽一片江流去…

                              (*CCYSY*, 1.11)

39. Anne Birrell calls this the "neglect syndrome." See her "Dusty Mirror: Courtly
Portraits of Woman in Southern Dynasties Love Poetry," in *Expressions of Self in Chinese
Literature*, ed. Robert E. Hegel and Richard C. Hessney (New York: Columbia University
Press, 1985), p. 59.

40. Mary E. Kivlen, "Beyond 'the Mirror of Time': Reflections on Mirror Imagery in
Ming-Ch'ing Women's Verse" (Term paper, 1990).

41. See, for example, *LTNST*, pp. 135–36.

42. A good example may be found in Wu Shan, a female artist known for her painting and calligraphy. See Ruth Rogaski, "A Woman Named Mountain: The Life and
Poetry of Wu Shan" (Term paper, 1990), p. 12.

43. Apparently lesbian love was rather common among traditional Chinese women
(see Ch'en Tung-yüan, *Chung-kuo fu-nü sheng-huo shih*, [1937; rpt., Taipei: Shang-wu yin-
shu-kuan, 1977], pp. 212, 300). It was not, however, generally considered a poetic subject, though it appears frequently in prose fiction and memoirs from the seventeenth century on. The nineteenth-century woman poet Wu Tsao broke taboos in the tradition of
poetry by women by celebrating lesbian love and introducing sexual frankness into the
song lyric, perhaps most explicitly in her *tz'u* addressed to a certain courtesan named

These lines remind us of Li Yü's *tz'u* mourning the fall of his kingdom of Southern T'ang. But far more interesting for us here may be those song lyrics in which Hsü Ts'an juxtaposes two kinds of emotion—personal loss and loyalist passion—for it just so happened that the fall of the Ming dynasty coincided almost exactly with Ch'en Chih-lin's acquisition of a concubine. The woman poet suffered two losses, endured two forms of "mourning"—but one kind of abandonment, abandonment by both her country and her husband. In her song lyric to "Shao-nien yu" subtitled "A Kind of Feeling," Hsü Ts'an expresses her longings for the "past dynasty" in the first stanza, while in the second stanza she subtly laments her fate as an abandoned wife. In her more elaborate *tz'u* set to the tune "Man chiang hung," she uses a similar procedure by first describing how the "rivers and mountains" remind her of the fallen Ming and then complaining about her husband's "breaking his vow."[44]

And it was not just a personal vow that Hsü Ts'an's husband was breaking: Ch'en Chih-lin had surrendered to the Ch'ing, and in 1645 he began to serve the Manchu government in Peking—an act of betrayal that his wife apparently condemned. In her song lyric to "Ch'ing-yü-an," Hsü Ts'an writes:[45]

> The misty water knew nothing about the wrongs of human affairs;
> warships extending tens of thousands of miles
> all lowered their sails to surrender.
> Do not blame my slow lotus steps.

> 煙水不知人事錯
> 戈舩千里
> 降帆一片
> 莫怨蓮花步

(CCYSY, 2.4a)

These lines suggest that the boundaries of Hsü Ts'an's *tz'u* stretched far beyond the limits of the inner chamber. Few readers of song lyrics by women had met her likeness before, for Hsü Ts'an, in her loyalist *tz'u*, incorporated into her basically feminine style the strong voice of "masculinity" typical of the "heroic" (*hao-fang*) school of *tz'u*. The Sung

---

Ch'ing-lin. See Wu Tsao, *Wu Tsao tz'u*, Tz'u-hsüeh hsiao ts'ung-shu, no. 9 (Shanghai: Chiao-yü shu-tien, 1949), pp. 41–42; and Judy Liu, "World of Words: Wu Tsao and the Conversion of Life into Art" (Term paper, 1990), pp. 21–22. See also Kenneth Rexroth and Ling Chung, trans. and eds., *Women Poets of China*, rev. ed. (New York: New Directions, 1982), p. 135, where Rexroth and Chung call Wu Tsao "one of the greatest lesbian poets of all time."

44. For the lyrics cited above, see *CCYSY*, 1.7a and 3.4a, respectively.

45. Cheng-hua Wang, "On Hsü Ts'an's Poetry" (Term paper, 1989), pp. 12–13.

poet Li Ch'ing-chao had of course explored patriotic concerns in her *shih*, but never in her *tz'u* (being a purist in genre properties). And Liu Shih, though involving herself in all sorts of loyalist resistance movements after the fall of the Ming and though known as a woman of courage and chivalry, did not at all develop the topic of loyalism in her song lyrics.[46] In sharp contrast to all these female poets, Hsü Ts'an adopted a special and rather unusual poetic strategy in *tz'u* in order to bridge what was thought to be an infinite gap between gentle femininity and heroic masculinity, and ultimately to cross generic and sexual boundaries in poetry. Just as femininity in *tz'u* is not necessarily female, Hsü Ts'an seems to argue, masculinity as expressed in the *hao-fang* mode is only an artistic strategy and is therefore not necessarily male. In a way, women poets like Hsü Ts'an may be called feminist in their *tz'u*,[47] while Liu Shih and other courtesans were primarily feminine in theirs—although in their life roles they seem to have been exactly the opposite.

For her loyalist lyrics, Hsü Ts'an deliberately chose tunes that were traditionally associated with patriotism, such as "Man chiang hung" (made famous by the Sung hero Yüeh Fei) and the well-known "Yung-yü-lo" (recognized as typical of the Hsin Ch'i-chi style). In all of her experiments with the theme, Hsü worked toward a balance between masculinity and femininity, so that the impression created is femaleness made more heroic, femaleness realized by being freer and more concrete. Thus, in one of her song lyrics to "Man chiang hung," Hsü describes both "heroic deeds" (*ying-hsiung yeh*) and "heartbroken steles" (*tuan-ch'ang pei*), mixing extremely masculine images with refined words of feminine sentiment—no doubt in an attempt to identify femaleness with creative self-liberation.[48] Generally Hsü Ts'an uses the style of "heroic abandon" in the first stanza of her loyalist poems but reserves the second stanza for a more "delicate and restrained" expression of private feelings. A case in point is her "Yung-yü lo," subtitled "Thinking of the Past While on a Boat," where she writes in the first stanza:

46. See my *Late-Ming Poet Ch'en Tzu-lung*, p. 17.

47. Some modern critics may argue that Hsü's adoption of the *hao-fang* style, a mere male convention, is not enough to make her a feminist, because feminism (as we understand it today) seems to imply some challenge to the male order, not simply a willingness to participate in it. Viewed *historically*, however, there is no doubt that for seventeenth-century female *tz'u* writers Hsü Ts'an's new poetics represented a true liberation of women. Hers was indeed "an outlook that transcended the accepted value systems of the time," which is, of course, one aspect of feminism. See Cheris Kramarae and Paula A. Treichler, "Feminism," in their *Feminist Dictionary* (London: Pandora Press, 1985), p. 158.

48. *CCYSY*, 3.4a–b.

The dragon is gone, the swords disappeared—
how many heroes' tears and blood?
Sorrows of a thousand ages—
rivers and mountains, how many still remain?

龍歸劍杳
多少英雄淚血
千古恨
河山如許

But in the second stanza she dwells on smaller and more refined images:

Human affairs are as fleeting clouds,
this life is like floating catkins—
Enough to make the heartbroken apes grieve and cry.

世事流雲
人生飛絮
都付斷猨悲咽

(CCYSY, 3.6b)

Hsü Ts'an's song lyrics seem completely to have escaped the attention of Ch'en Tzu-lung, the leader of the Yün-chien revival for whom the *wan-yüeh*, rather than the *hao-fang*, style was suited to *tz'u* writing. For Ch'en, even loyalist song lyrics were to be written as love poems from beginning to end, encoding passionate longings in refined, even sensual, images.[49] But it was perhaps because of Hsü Ts'an's ability to transcend the purely *wan-yüeh* style of the "inner chamber" *tz'u* that Ch'en Wei-sung, a poet known for his style of "heroic abandon," later came to praise Hsü so highly, regarding her as "the greatest gentry woman poet since the Southern Sung."[50] Hsü Ts'an's husband, Ch'en Chih-lin, also argued that what distinguished her from Hsü Yüan, her great aunt and an eminent *tz'u* poet, was Hsü Ts'an's experience of suffering as a Ming loyalist and her ability to record that experience vividly in song lyrics.[51] In this regard, Hsü Ts'an seems to have set an example for other contemporary gentry-women poets to follow—Wu Shan, for example, called herself a "female loyalist" (*nü i-min*) and expressed loyalist sentiments in her *tz'u*.[52] Interestingly, it was the "masculine" side of these seventeenth-century song lyrics by women that later came to influence

49. See my *Late-Ming Poet Ch'en Tzu-lung*, pp. 83–101.
50. See Ch'en Wei-sung, *Fu-jen chi* (*Chao-tai ts'ung-shu* ed.), 36.3b–4a.
51. See Ch'en Chih-lin's preface to Hsü's *Cho-cheng-yüan shih-yü*, 1b–2a.
52. Rogaski, "A Woman Named Mountain," p. 16.

the works of patriotic female poets like Ch'iu Chin at the end of the Ch'ing dynasty.

CONCLUSION

Can we then make the assumption that there was an absolute distinction between the courtesan tradition and the gentry-woman tradition in seventeenth-century *tz'u*? The problem with such an assumption is that some Ming-Ch'ing women did change their marital status and social affiliations in the course of their lives. For example, Liu Shih became a gentry woman after marrying Ch'ien Ch'ien-i in 1643, and came to be actively associated with other gentry women (like Huang Yüan-chieh) as well as distinguished courtesans (like Lin Hsüeh). The same is true of Ku Mei, the well-known courtesan and artist of Chin-huai, after her marriage to Kung Ting-tzu. As Ellen Widmer has pointed out, for courtesans, literary and artistic achievements often led in the "desirable direction of marriage with gentry men."[53] However, we can certainly argue for a relative distinction between the courtesan and gentry-woman traditions *purely* in terms of poetic style and rhetoric, as I have attempted to do in this chapter. For these two styles, the feminine and the feminist, two different kinds of literary construct found in seventeenth-century *tz'u*, remained the crucial elements in song lyrics written by women. One of the surprises encountered in studying these two poetic traditions was learning that the courtesan-poets are, generically and thematically, more timid than the gentry-women poets.

One final point that needs to be considered is the fact that while courtesan-poets of the seventeenth century enjoyed a position of equal importance with the gentry-women poets, by the eighteenth century courtesans were virtually excluded from the literary world and their poems were generally rejected from respectable anthologies of poetry by women. This marks a sharp contrast indeed with late Ming times, when male anthologists like Chou Chih-piao were eager to preserve writings by courtesans and even referred to these women poets with the respectable title *nü ts'ai-tzu* (female talents).[54] The suppression of courtesans' writings during the Ch'ing dynasty was greatly influenced by the views of some Confucian moralists, for most editors then considered it immoral to print works by those "undisciplined" women. Not surprisingly, some male scholars began to criticize late Ming anthologists like

53. Widmer, "The Epistolary World of Female Talent," p. 30.
54. Hu Wen-k'ai, *Li-tai fu-nü*, p. 844.

Ch'en Wei-sung for collecting poems by "morally indecent courtesans" and for discussing poetics with such women.[55]

Even more poignant is the fact that women themselves began to adopt the same moralistic view. (This of course may seem to have been inevitable, in view of the fact that most women poets were wives of men who would have been attracted to the courtesans—no gender solidarity here.) A case in point is the female scholar Yün Chu, editor of the prestigious anthology *Kuo-ch'ao kuei-hsiu cheng-shih chi* (1836), who boasted of having excluded all courtesans' poems from her collection (which represents works by close to one thousand gentry-women poets) *solely* on moral grounds.[56] Another woman, the wife of Hsü Shih-fu, threatened to burn her two-hundred-some poems for fear of being included in the same anthology as courtesans.[57]

It is no surprise, then, that Liu Shih, who enjoyed the privilege of being the foremost courtesan-poet of the seventeenth century, was now excluded from most later poetry anthologies. But it is ironic that although Liu Shih the person was rejected by the eighteenth-century moralists, poems of hers collected in privately printed volumes became secret models for poetically talented gentry women. One female poet called Yeh Hung-hsiang, for example, modeled her "Wang Chiang-nan" lyrics after Liu Shih's "Wang Chiang-nan" song-series, using almost identical sentence structures and images.[58] The truth is that the courtesan tradition in *tz'u* had not died; it was simply being absorbed into the gentry-woman tradition.

In the meantime, several factors made the eighteenth-century gentry women the legitimate successors to the late Ming courtesans. First, under the influence of people like Yüan Mei, many gentry women began to meet outside their homes and mingle socially with male literati, a kind of freedom formerly restricted to courtesans or, to a certain extent, Taoist nuns. Second, it had become possible for gentry women, whether widows or estranged wives, to support themselves by selling their paintings and poetry[59]—in an earlier age many of these talented and self-supporting women would have had no alternative but to become courtesans. Third, increasingly common were marriages that reflected the

55. Ibid., p. 915.
56. See Yao P'in-wen, "Ch'ing-tai fu-nü shih-ko ti fan-jung yü li-hsüeh ti kuan-hsi," in *Chiang-hsi shih-fan ta-hsüeh hsüeh-pao* 1985, no. 1:57. See also Hu Wen-k'ai, *Li-tai fu-nü*, p. 918.
57. K'ang Cheng-kuo, *Feng-sao yü yen-ch'ing*, p. 326.
58. *LTNST*, p. 223.
59. Widmer, "The Epistolary World of Female Talent," p. 33.

ideal match between "talented husband and gifted wife" who exchanged poems regularly and had mutual access to each other's intellectual and emotional lives[60]—a relationship that reminds us of the popular literatus-courtesan model of the late Ming. Indeed, this was an age when gentry women had the confidence to claim both sides of the female poetic tradition for their own, both to preserve the late Ming legacy and to value their own innovations.

It was this same pluralism that eventually promoted the position of female *tz'u* poets from the marginal to the legitimate. The increasingly large number of collections of *tz'u* written by women and anthologized by women was undoubtedly instrumental in this process. In fact, only a few years after Liu Shih's and Hsü Ts'an's deaths, four respectable women poets of the Ch'ing published an ambitious anthology of *tz'u* called *Ku-chin ming-yüan pai-hua shih-yü* (1685), in which works of women poets from the Sung to the Ch'ing were arranged according to the sequence of the four seasons, a symbolic device associating the women with the hundreds of flowers (*pai-hua*) that bloom in the spring, summer, autumn, and winter.[61] Thus, being female, the four editors (Kuei Shu-fen, Shen Li, Sun Hui-yüan, and Shen Chen-yung) also symbolized certain qualities of *tz'u*—*kao-ya* (lofty and elegant), *ch'ing-hua* (pure and flowery), and so on—qualities that make *tz'u* the quintessential vehicle for women's self-expression, for "the song lyric is nothing less than the expression of personal qualities" (*tz'u-yün erh jen-yün che yeh*).[62] In retrospect, Liu Shih and Hsü Ts'an, apparently so dissimilar, are equally important female personas of the complex, rich, and inexhaustible resources of the song lyric.

60. K'ang Cheng-kuo, *Feng-sao yü yen-ch'ing*, p. 341. During the Ming, such an ideal match as Shang Ching-lan's marriage to Ch'i Piao-chia (who never took a concubine) must have been considered an exception.

61. Hu Wen-k'ai, *Li-tai fu-nü*, pp. 899–900.

62. Ibid., p. 900.

THREE

From Voice to Text:
Questions of Genealogy

The Problem of the Repute of *Tz'u* During the Northern Sung

Ronald C. Egan

Despite the increased attention that has been given in recent years to Sung dynasty *shih* poetry, the impression persists in many quarters that *tz'u* was the real focus of poetic interest and excitement during the dynasty. This is an impression that owes as much to the many valuable studies of *tz'u* that have appeared in the past decade, which have elucidated the achievements of the Sung *tz'u* writers, as it does to the old formulation about the genres (*T'ang shih Sung tz'u*), which has had remarkable staying power. We are apt, therefore, to think of *tz'u* as the form that was fresh, vital, and unexplored upon the establishment of the Sung. Once we accept this image of *tz'u*, which certainly has some validity, it is natural then to want to delve more deeply still into the accomplishments of particular writers, to study both their individual traits and the dynamics of the development of the genre through the dynasty. No doubt the linguistic difficulties *tz'u* presents, because of its colloquial and specialized diction, have contributed to the aura that surrounds it as a challenging object for scholarly study. However, as the subject becomes ever more firmly established as a field of inquiry, and as our attention is focused ever more intently upon the distinctive, if subtle, marks of each writer's corpus, we are apt to overlook certain aspects of early appraisals or criticism of the genre, especially anything that runs counter to our perception of *tz'u* as a pillar of Sung literature. This paper concerns one such issue in the history of Sung *tz'u*: its disrepute among large numbers of the lettered elite and its struggle for acceptance, especially during the Northern Sung. This, then, is primarily a study of early perceptions and criticism of *tz'u*, rather than of *tz'u* stylistics. But I shall also argue that *tz'u*'s struggle to gain acceptance sometimes significantly affected the way it was written.

So long as we confine our attention to collections of *tz'u*, it is easy to work under the assumption, whether we are conscious of it or not, that this was a universally accepted poetic form during the Sung. After all, a great amount of it was produced, and many of the writers were eminent figures in Sung letters and public life. But as soon as we look outside of the *tz'u* collections for confirmation of our assumption, we are apt to be dismayed. The first and lasting impression given by Northern Sung sources is one of silence. It is almost as if *tz'u* never existed, for it goes unmentioned in the channels normally used to confer and sustain literary prestige. Two areas of silence or absence are particularly significant: literary collections (*wen-chi*) and prefaces. It was the rule throughout the Northern Sung to exclude *tz'u* from literary collections. In none of the earliest recensions of the literary collections of the major writers (Yen Shu, Fan Chung-yen, Ou-yang Hsiu, Chang Hsien, Su Shih, Huang T'ing-chien, Ch'in Kuan, Ch'ao Pu-chih, Ho Chu, and Ch'en Shih-tao) were *tz'u* included alongside the prose and *shih* poetry. We know that in many if not all cases the writers themselves edited their literary collections, so that the exclusion of *tz'u* was their own decision. Simply put, what that decision shows is that *tz'u* were not considered to be sufficiently *wen*, "literary," for inclusion in a *wen-chi*. These same men regularly excluded other of their more unpolished writings (for example, *shu-chien* or *ch'ih-tu*, notes or informal letters, as opposed to the more literary letter, *shu*) for apparently the same reason. It was only in later centuries, when a writer's "complete works" were compiled, that *tz'u* began to make their appearance together with other forms. Before that time, and in many cases after it as well, a writer's *tz'u* circulated independently, in what must have been small and, to judge from the record of lost works, ephemeral editions. From the mid–Southern Sung on, of course, there were *tz'u* anthologies as well.

The lack of prefaces for *tz'u* collections is equally striking. In Sung literati culture, prefaces were a major vehicle through which writings were legitimated and standards of taste proclaimed. The leading writers wrote dozens of prefaces for the poetry and prose collections of their acquaintances. But among the surviving works only two *tz'u* prefaces can be found.[1] This nearly complete lack of introductory state-

---

1. See the prefaces by Chang Lei (1054–1104) and Huang T'ing-chien (1045–1105), discussed at the end of this paper. In addition, the somewhat earlier Northern Sung writer Chang Hsien is said to have written a preface for Yen Shu's collection of *tz'u*, but this piece does not survive. See Jao Tsung-i, *Tz'u-chi k'ao* (Hong Kong: Hsiang-kang ta-hsüeh ch'u-pan-she, 1963), p. 36.

ments suggests that *tz'u* were generally not even considered worthy of a defense.

As we would expect, *tz'u* are hardly ever mentioned in another sort of document, the colophon (*t'i-pa*). The important colophon writers of the Northern Sung left hundreds of notices on all sorts of literary texts, calligraphy, paintings, and scholarly paraphernalia (inkstones, musical instruments, etc.). But they refrained almost entirely from making reference to *tz'u*.[2] It is only in the anecdotal record that one finds substantial mention of *tz'u*. There are plenty of stories that somehow involve a contemporary *tz'u*. It is significant, though, that these stories were transmitted by lesser figures—men who are remembered primarily as compilers of anecdotes. They and their compilations are located a rung or two down from the highest levels of literati culture. Their writings amount at times to little more than gossip about the really prestigious persons of their age. The other qualification that should be stated is that the Sung anecdotal record is so rich that our ability to find mention of *tz'u* in it is hardly surprising. For every reference to *tz'u*, there must be ten to *shih* poetry.

The situation is an odd one: to judge from the songs themselves, the eleventh century was a heyday of *tz'u* writing, a lively and creative period that saw the development of an impressive range of unprecedented individual styles. Obviously, the authors relished their *tz'u* writing, but they also avoided calling attention to their activity. The Southern Sung critic Hu Yin observed that nearly all the scholars of the day expressed themselves in *tz'u*, but then they "immediately covered their tracks" and explained, if noticed, that they were just playing around.[3] Why was there this ambivalence, which is certainly much more pronounced with *tz'u* than with *shih* poetry? It is unlikely that the relative newness of *tz'u* accounts for these scholars' reticence to adver-

2. Huang T'ing-chien, who left several hundred colophons, has but a single notice on *tz'u*—it is on one of Su Shih's compositions; see *Yü-chang Huang hsien-sheng wen-chi* (*SPTK* ed.), 26.7a. For Su Shih's lone colophon on earlier *tz'u*, see below. See also his single colophons on the *tz'u* of Huang and Ch'in Hsuan, *Su Shih wen-chi*, ed. K'ung Fan-li (Peking: Chung-hua shu-chü, 1986), 68.2157 and 68.2161.

Although it consists mostly of post–Northern Sung materials, a recent compilation of prefaces and colophons on T'ang and Sung *tz'u* conveniently gathers together most of the Northern Sung writings on *tz'u* that survive (except for passing references to *tz'u* in letters, etc.). See Chin Ch'i-hua et al., *T'ang Sung tz'u-chi hsü-pa hui-pien* (Kiangsu: Chiang-su chiao-yü ch'u-pan-she, 1990). The compilation happens also to illustrate the point made here about the scarcity of such materials from the Northern Sung period.

3. Hu Yin (1098–1156), preface to *Chiu-pien tz'u*, by Hsiang Tzu-yin, in *Sung liu-shih ming-chia tz'u*, ed. Mao Chin (*Kuo-hsüeh chi-pen ts'ung-shu* ed.), p. i.

tise their involvement with it. After all, there were ample instances of *tz'u* writing from well over a hundred years earlier that could have been adduced. Moreover, in other areas of cultural endeavor (e.g., in painting) the leading Sung scholars were hardly reluctant to discuss their unprecedented involvement.

TZ'U, *TZ'U* WRITERS, SINGING GIRLS

Surely the close association between *tz'u* and professional female entertainers must bear on any answer to the question. To remind the reader of how extensive that association was, I shall begin here by reviewing and discussing some representative passages in anecdotal writings that depict it. I will concentrate on sources that concern two men of letters, Ch'in Kuan and Huang T'ing-chien. Both men were prolific *tz'u* writers, but unlike, say, a man such as Liu Yung, who was known for little else than his dissipations in the pleasure quarters, Ch'in Kuan and Huang T'ing-chien were also serious *shih* poets and, more importantly, holders of prestigious literary posts in the capital (e.g., court historian, drafter of decrees, erudite at the imperial academy). We would be wrong to think that it was only men of low or little stature, like Liu Yung, who were depicted in contemporary sources as being in close and intimate contact with professional entertainers.

An early twelfth-century collection of anecdotes about *tz'u*, Yang T'i's *Ku-chin tz'u-hua*, contains the following story about one of Ch'in Kuan's compositions:

> When Ch'in Shao-yu was staying in the capital, a high official once invited him to a feast, during which he brought out Emerald Peach, one of his favorite concubines, to encourage the guests to drink. She did it, however, listlessly. Shao-yu understood what was on her mind, and he, in turn, raised a cup and urged Emerald Peach to drink. The high official said, "Emerald Peach has never been much of a drinker," not wanting Shao-yu to impose on her. But she said, "Today, on this academician's behalf, I'll get dead drunk!" She grabbed a large winecup and took a long drink. On the spot, Shao-yu then composed this song to the tune "Lady Yü":
>
> > An emerald peach in heaven grows amid sweet dew,
> > not an ordinary flower.
> > Deep in jumbled hills, where the river winds,
> > how touching! A single branch like a painting,
> > for whom does it blossom?
> >
> > Light chill and fine rain—boundless feelings!
> > No one knew spring would be so hard to control.

Why shouldn't I get drunk for you?
My only worry is that once I'm sober,
a heart will break.

碧桃天上栽和露
不是凡花數
亂山深處水縈回
可惜一枝如畫
為誰開

輕寒細雨情何限
不道春難管
為君沉醉又何妨
只怕酒醒時候
斷人腸

Everyone regretted what had happened. The high official said, "Don't ever let this concubine appear at one of our feasts again!" With that, the guests all laughed.[4]

There are many such anecdotes that purport to describe the circumstances under which a *tz'u* was written. A substantial proportion of them are quite unconvincing. Often the connection between the song and the story is tenuous, or the particulars may even be contradictory.[5] This story, however, actually helps to make sense out of the song, which is indeed found in Ch'in Kuan's collection of *tz'u*.[6] Of course, even without the story we would realize that "Emerald Peach" (Pi-t'ao) must be the name of a girl. But the second stanza, whose language is more vague than the translation suggests, would otherwise be rather unclear, especially the third line, where it would be uncertain who was getting drunk for whom. The story clarifies these lines by giving a sensible account of the dynamics between three persons: the bored singing girl, the attractive Ch'in Kuan, and the jealous and protective host. Ch'in's song, with its frank and aloof depiction of the girl's unenviable situation, has the effect of deflating the spirits of the revelers. The host then pretends to be

4. Yang T'i (early 12th cent.), *Ku-chin tz'u-hua* (in *Chiao-chi Sung Chin Yüan jen tz'u*, ed. Chao Wan-li (Taipei: Chung-yang yen-chiu-yüan, li-shih yü-yen yen-chiu-so, 1972), p. 10b. For the text of the *tz'u* I have adopted the textual variants in the *Ch'üan Sung tz'u* version of the piece (see n. 6 below).

5. See, for example, the anecdote about one of Chou Pang-yen's *tz'u* discussed by James R. Hightower, "The Songs of Chou Pang-yen," *Harvard Journal of Asiatic Studies* 37 (1977): 237–38, as well as that referred to in my study, *The Literary Works of Ou-yang Hsiu (1007–72)* (Cambridge: Cambridge University Press, 1984), pp. 136–37.

6. The piece is "Yü mei-jen," no. 2. See T'ang Kuei-chang, ed., *Ch'üan Sung tz'u* (Hong Kong: Chung-hua shu-chü, 1977), 1:467; hereafter abbreviated *CST*.

outraged, trying to relax the tension and put everyone back at ease. The story is a plausible account of how the song might have been written, whether or not it is historically accurate.

Ch'in Kuan evidently had a reputation as something of a gallant, an image that must have been founded largely on the widespread popularity of the romantic songs he wrote. Several anecdotes tell of singing girls or courtesans who fell in love with him. The most elaborate story (whose reliability certainly *is* open to question) has him traveling through the undistinguished city of Ch'ang-sha, on his way into exile, when he meets a singing girl who possesses, to Ch'in's amazement, a manuscript copy of his *tz'u*. Without revealing his identity, Ch'in speaks with the girl and learns that she could sing all of his songs but had no interest in those by other writers. "Have you ever met this Academician Ch'in?" he asks her. "I live here in a remote and uncultured area. He is a high-placed gentleman of the capital. Why would he ever come here? And even if he did, why would he look at me?" Ch'in persists: "You say you are in love with Academician Ch'in, but it's just his songs you like. If you saw his face, you might feel differently." "No," she replies, "If I could ever meet him and somehow become his slave, I would die with no regrets." Ch'in finally reveals his identity, and the girl withdraws respectfully from the room. Shortly she reappears, dressed in formal attire, and bows to Ch'in from the doorway. A feast is prepared by the girl's mother, and when Ch'in is seated the place beside him is left vacant in deference to him. The girl performs her entire repertoire of his songs. At the end of the evening, the girl welcomes Ch'in to her bed. Ch'in stays on a few days with her, and when he finally resumes his journey, the girl vows to wait for him until he is pardoned. Ch'in goes off to exile, where he eventually dies. The girl receives news of his death in a dream, whereupon she sets out to mourn him. When she arrives beside his coffin, she walks around it, cries out, and expires.[7]

In its present form this story is surely romanticized fiction, but the bulk of it, without the ending, may well have its roots in a popular image of Ch'in as a man whose songs could win for him the hearts of singing girls. Unfortunately, the girl in this story is unnamed. Other of the girls Ch'in is said to have favored are supposed to have their names coded into songs he wrote for them. More than one source reports that when Ch'in Kuan was serving in Ts'ai-chou he had an affair with a singing girl named Lou Wan, whose polite name was Tung-yü. He is

7. Hung Mai (1123–1202), *I-chien chih* (Peking: Chung-hua shu-chü, 1981), "pu" section 2.1559–61.

said to have written a *tz'u* for her, one that is likewise found in his collection,[8] whose opening line reads: *hsiao-lou lien-yüan heng-k'ung*, "The small storied house with a garden blocks the sky." The opening line of the second stanza is: *yü-p'ei ting-tung pieh-hou*, "His jade pendant chimes after he departs." The first line encodes the girl's formal name (*hsiao-lou* for Lou, and *yüan* is a pun on Wan), and the second her polite name.[9] Ch'in is supposed to have gone a step further in a song he wrote for another girl, T'ao Hsin-erh. The closing line reads: *t'ien-wai i-kou ts'an-yüeh tai san-hsing*, "Beyond the sky, a hook of a moon with three stars attached"—a clever way of describing the written character *hsin* (heart), the girl's name.[10] Both of these songs are quite conventional portraits of longing and separation, and neither of them has a preface or any other indication that they were written for a particular woman. But the assertions that they were deserve to be taken seriously because they help to explain what otherwise strike the reader as oddities in these two songs: the phrase *lien-yüan* (literally, "with a garden") seems slightly odd in its line (thus, some texts have *lien-yüan*, "stretching afar," instead),[11] and the detail about the moon and three stars seems gratuitous without some reason for its presence.

If Ch'in Kuan was the romantic poet whom the singing girls were apt to fall for, a rather different image of Huang T'ing-chien emerges from his *tz'u* and the anecdotes surrounding them. Huang T'ing-chien is primarily known, of course, as a *shih* poet, and one whose highly allusive and bookish style seems at first sight quite unpromising for any involvement with *tz'u*. It is interesting, then, to learn that not only was Huang also a prolific *tz'u* writer, he was one who used extremely colloquial language in his *tz'u*—so colloquial that the meaning of some of his songs now escapes us. But it is not only the diction of Huang's *tz'u* that makes them singular: a sizable portion of them present a particular voice that is not often encountered in other *tz'u* of the time. It is the voice of an aging official who is infatuated with one or another singing girl but gener-

8. "Shui lung yin," *CST*, 1:455.

9. The sources are Tseng Tsao's (d. ca. 1155) *Kao-chai shih-hua* (Hu Tzu [1082–1143], *T'iao-hsi yü-yin ts'ung-hua—ch'ien-chi* [Peking: Jen-min wen-hsüeh ch'u-pan-she, 1981], 50.338), and Tseng Chi-li's (late 12th cent.) *T'ing-chai shih-hua*, in *Li-tai shih-hua hsü-pien*, ed. Ting Fu-pao (Peking: Chung-hua shu-chü, 1983), 1:309 (Lung Mu-hsün, ed., *Su-men ssu-hsüeh-shih tz'u* [Peking: Chung-hua shu-chü, 1957], vol. 1, *Huai-hai chü-shih ch'ang-tuan chü*, p. 81).

10. The *tz'u* is "Nan ko-tzu," no. 1, *CST*, 1:468. The source for this reading of the *tz'u* is Tseng Tsao, *Kao-chai shih-hua* (Hu Tzu, *T'iao-hsi—ch'ien-chi*, 50.338).

11. This is what is found in *CST*, 1:455, but the *shih-hua* texts cited above have *yüan*, "garden," instead.

ally cannot attain the object of his desires. Huang apparently wrote *tz'u*
that cultivate this voice all through his life. Several of them, in which
the speaker identifies himself as an old man, were written in the last
years of Huang's life, during his southwestern exiles to Ch'ien-chou,
Jung-chou, and I-chou.

What is really striking about these *tz'u* of Huang's is how many spe-
cifics they contain that encourage us to read them autobiographically.
These are not vague expressions of male love and longing. Thanks to
details found both in the songs themselves and in their subtitles or prefaces, these compositions appear firmly rooted in Huang's life. We
know, for example, that as an old man Huang wrote three songs for a
very young singing girl named Ch'en Hsiang ("just over thirteen, spring
not yet complete"), whom he met in Heng-yang while on his way into
exile in 1104. The songs allude to a brief romance followed by the songwriter's forced departure, and dwell on the speaker's worry that by the
time he is able to return the girl will have chosen another man. Huang
continued to write for Ch'en Hsiang after his departure. It seems that
she took up calligraphy and wrote to Huang (the master calligrapher!)
asking for a sample of his characters in small regular style. The sample
he sent back to her was yet another *tz'u*, which describes her and refers
to her progress at her new avocation.[12]

One relies heavily upon the subtitles to Huang's songs for such information, and it should be acknowledged here that those subtitles
might conceivably have been added by some later editor who, working
on the presumption that the songs were autobiographical, did his best
to identify their original settings. On balance, however, the chance of
this is slight. Several of the subtitles are indisputably written in the first
person. As for those subtitles whose point of view is ambiguous and
might either be read as first-person or third-person statements (a problem commonly encountered in literary Chinese), the very specificity of
their information argues against the possibility that they are from an
editor's hand. Su Shih had, of course, established a convention of writing such identifying tags to one's own *tz'u*, and it is preferable to think
that Huang simply followed his example.

The song translated below is less explicit than some, but the information it does contain makes it easy to reconstruct a setting grounded in
Huang's biography:

---

12. This information is gleaned from three of Huang's songs and their subtitles: "Mo-
shan hsi," *CST*, 1:388; "Mo-shan hsi," no. 2, *CST*, 1:402; and "Juan lang kuei," no. 1,
CST, 1:402.

To the tune "Swaying Courtyard Bamboo"[13]
Written outside the Chi-chou city wall,
while serving as magistrate of T'ai-ho

Soughing winds at the south hall blow plum blossoms,
ravens cry, startled in treetop nests.
Our meeting in a dream did not last long,
across the city wall tonight you understand.
I sit up late, the water turns emerald pointlessly.
The glow of the mountain moon sinks in the west.

I bought a place to lodge you in,
but stubbornly you wouldn't come.
Today Heaven glares at you,[14]
you'll go among fowl forever, abused by them.
Useless now is my pity for you![15]
Wind and sun will injure the branch of blossoms.

撼庭竹
　　宰太和日吉州城外作
嗚咽南樓吹落梅
聞鴉樹驚棲
夢中相見不多時
隔城今夜也應知
坐久水空碧
山月影沈西

買箇宅兒住著伊
剛不肯相隨
如今果被天瞋作
永落雞羣被雞欺
空恁可憐伊
風日損花枝

Huang served as magistrate of T'ai-ho hsien from 1081 to 1083. T'ai-ho was part of Chi-chou prefecture (modern Chi-an, Kiangsi), and Huang must have made periodic visits to the prefectural seat. This song was evidently written as Huang was leaving Chi-chou to return to his post in T'ai-ho. The song, together with its subtitle, suggests that Huang had met a singing girl during his stay in the city and tried to convince her to go back to the outlying T'ai-ho with him, assuring her that he would set her up in her own house. She refused, and Huang, frustrated

13. "Han t'ing chu," *CST*, 1:390.
14. Adopting the variant *ni* for *tso* (Lung Mu-hsün, *Su-men*, vol. 2, *Yü-chang Huang hsien-sheng tz'u*, p. 22) since the word must rhyme.
15. Adopting the variant *o-lien* "intense love" for *k'o-lien* (Lung Mu-hsün, *Su-men*, vol. 2, *Yü-chang Huang hsien-sheng tz'u*, p. 22).

and bitter, wrote this song (and possibly even sent it to her) on the first
night of his journey home. To "go among fowl" must mean to stay with
the other girls Huang had found her among. Another of Huang's *tz'u*
singles out a girl as a "kingfisher among the fowl."[16]

In his later years, it was more common for Huang to represent the
girl as willing but his own circumstances as unfavorable. An anecdote in
Wu Tseng's *Neng-kai chai man-lu* (1157) confirms the information given
in the song's subtitle, which dates it to Huang's fifty-eighth year:[17]

> *To the tune "A Happy Event Draws Near"*[18]
> *In T'ai-p'ing prefecture a little singing girl, Yang Chu, played the zither and
> presented wine*

Once she touches those heart-awakening strings,
her feelings show on two slanted hills.
When she plays the part where men of old sorrowed,
pearls hang on her eyelashes.

This governor does not choose to come or go,
don't let tears mark your red cheeks.
What a pity that in old age I dislike wine
and disappoint the brimming plantain leaf.[19]

好事近
　太平州小妓楊姝彈琴送酒
一弄醒心弦
情在兩山斜疊
彈到古人愁處
有真珠承睫

使君來去本無心
休淚界紅顏
自恨老來憎酒
負十分蕉葉

The reader of Huang's songs soon becomes accustomed to taking the
term *shih-chün*, "governor," as a reference to Huang himself, especially
in the context of forced travel. (In fact, nine days after arriving at his
post as governor of T'ai-p'ing, Huang was demoted and ordered to
leave.) The situation implied here is that the girl loves the songwriter
deeply and is brokenhearted over his imminent departure. As soon as
she begins to play, her sorrow is evident in the music and on her face

---

16. "Mu-lan hua ling," no. 46, *CST*, 1:393.

17. Wu Tseng (late 12th cent.), *Neng-kai chai man-lu* (*TSCC* ed.), 17.487.

18. "Hao-shih chin," no. 2, *CST*, 1:411.

19. Adopting the textual variant *chiao*, "plantain," for *chin*; see Lung Mu-hsün, *Su-men*, vol. 2, *Yü-chang Huang hsien-sheng tz'u*, p. 66.

(the "slanting hills" are her eyebrows). The governor, meanwhile, is so old and infirm that he cannot even find solace in wine.

It turns out that Huang wrote a *shih* poem about the same singing girl, as Wu Tseng points out. The contrast between the two pieces is revealing:

Written in T'ai-p'ing Prefecture (no. 2) [20]

Timeless emotions are conveyed by her fingertips,
Yang Chu in misty moonlight, year after year.
To whom does her own heart fly?
She plays "Pine Wind" so fervently, she nearly
    breaks a string.

太平州作
千古人心指下傳
楊姝煙月過年年
不知心向誰邊切
彈盡松風欲斷弦

It is precisely the personal involvement of the author with the girl that is absent from the *shih* poem.

THE DISREPUTE OF *TZ'U*

My purpose in reviewing these particular *tz'u* and anecdotes here is to describe the nexus of associations that prevailed between the literati, the *tz'u* they composed, and the female singers who performed them. In the Northern Sung, there was not yet such a phenomenon as the literary *tz'u*, divorced from music and the female entertainer. On the contrary, *tz'u* then could almost be viewed as a kind of dialogue between literatus and singing girl (there are, in fact, records of lively exchanges between male poets and female singers, each extemporizing new songs' lyrics). [21] But while the contact between *tz'u* writers and singing girls was extensive and featured the appearance, at the very least, of romantic liaisons, it was not approved of in all quarters. The silence, noted earlier, maintained by the *tz'u* writers concerning their compositions must be due in large part to an awareness that their works were looked on unfavorably

20. Huang T'ing-chien, "T'ai-p'ing chou tso," no. 2, *Shan-ku shih chi* (*Kuo-hsüeh chi-pen ts'ung-shu* ed.), "wai-chi" 17.400.

21. For a protracted exchange of songs between Huang T'ing-chien and the singer Hsi-hsi, see Yang T'i, *Ku-chin tz'u-hua*, 10a–b. On this sort of contact and exchange in the earlier history of the genre, see Marsha L. Wagner, *The Lotus Boat: The Origins of Chinese Tz'u Poetry in T'ang Popular Culture* (New York: Columbia University Press, 1984), pp. 81–91 and 101–2.

by many members of the educated elite. The literati continued to set words to song anyway—it was far too pleasurable to stop—but they kept quiet in the more acceptable forms of written expression about what they were doing.

What is the evidence of the disrepute of *tz'u*, aside from the authors' own silence? It survives in various forms, ranging from outright denunciations and scandal to covert attempts to de-emphasize the social setting of the songs, thus making them more acceptable. To begin with the denunciations, one that is recorded in several sources is that addressed by the monk Fa-hsiu to his friend, Huang T'ing-chien:

> Fa-yün-hsiu, a native of Kuan-hsi, had a face of iron and was stern and cold. He was good at using reason to best other men in argument. After Lu-chih [Huang T'ing-chien] had become famous throughout the empire, whenever he wrote a new *shih* or *tz'u* people would rush to circulate it. One day the dharma master [Fa-hsiu] said to Lu-chih, "There's no harm in writing as many *shih* as you like, but you should stop composing erotic songs and little *tz'u*." Lu-chih laughed, "They are just words in the air. I'm not killing anyone, and I'm not stealing. Surely I won't be sentenced to one of the evil destinies for writing these songs." The dharma master replied, "If you use wicked words to arouse lust in men's hearts, causing them to ignore propriety and violate the law, then your words will be a source of crime and wrong, and I'm afraid you will not merely be punished with evil destinies." Lu-Chih nodded and subsequently stopped writing songs.[22]

In Huang's own version of this exchange Fa-hsiu is more forthcoming about the punishment that awaits him if he does not desist: he will be reborn in the Hell of Slit Tongues, a place reserved for those who used offensive words in life.[23]

These stories emphasize Fa-hsiu's skill in argument, so naturally they conclude with Huang heeding Fa-hsiu's advice. In fact, all the evidence suggests that Huang's *tz'u* writing was not the least affected by Fa-hsiu's reproof and, if anything, seems to have become more abundant in his later years. The Southern Sung scholar Hu Tzu noted, with marked disappointment, this discrepancy between the conclusion of the anecdote and Huang's later record.[24]

Hu Tzu's attitude indicates that we should not dismiss Fa-hsiu's criticism out-of-hand as a kind of puritanism found only among Buddhist monks. Disapproval of *tz'u* was not limited to any single group in Sung society. When reference was made once, in the presence of Lü Hui-

22. Hui-hung (1071–1128), *Leng-chai yeh-hua* (*Yin-li tsai ssu t'ang ts'ung-shu* ed.), 10.3a.
23. See p. 222 below, and cf. Hu Tzu, *T'iao-hsi—ch'ien-chi*, 57.390.
24. Hu Tzu, *T'iao-hsi—ch'ien-chi*, 57.390.

ch'ing (Wang An-shih's assistant grand councilor), to the fact that Yen
Shu, an earlier grand councilor, had been fond of composing *tz'u*, Lü
Hui-ch'ing remarked impatiently, "Anyone who governs the realm is
supposed to start by 'banishing the tunes of Cheng.' How could he himself compose more of them!"[25] Lü's outburst equates *tz'u* with the
"licentious" songs of the ancient states of Cheng (and Wei), which Confucius, whom Lü quotes, had condemned.[26] Yen Shu's son, Yen Chi-
tao, once found himself the object of a similar sort of moral indignation.
In the 1080s, while he was serving as a lowly garrison supervisor, Yen
sent copies of his writings to the governor of his prefecture, Han Wei, in
an apparent attempt to impress the superior official. This was a common enough practice, but in this case Yen Chi-tao had misjudged his
recipient badly. Yen had sent copies of his *tz'u*, and Han Wei, who was
a distinguished scholar but not a literary man (and would later be
appointed tutor to the heir apparent), was neither impressed nor
amused. Han Wei sent an admonishing letter in reply, observing that
Yen had "more than enough" talent, but that his moral cultivation was
inadequate. He urged Yen to look to this deficiency.[27]

With such denunciations in mind, it will surprise no one to learn that
Ch'eng I, the Northern Sung Confucian philosopher whose low opinion
of belles lettres is well known, also registered his disapproval of certain lines found in well-known *tz'u*. What is particularly interesting
about the following passage is the way Ch'eng I's criticism is taken
up and elaborated upon by the Southern Sung scholar Ch'en Ku, who
recorded it:

> I-ch'uan [Ch'eng I] once read Ch'in Shao-yu's *tz'u* with the lines, "If
> Heaven only knew, / Heaven too would grow thin!"[28] and remarked,
> "The Lord of Heaven lives in exaltation high above us. How can this man
> be so disrespectful toward him?" I-ch'uan also saw Yen Chi-tao's *tz'u*,
> which reads, "My dreaming soul is unaccustomed to any constraints. / It
> treads on willow catkins, crossing Hsieh Bridge,"[29] and said, "These are
> the words of a ghost!" Actually, Shao-yu's lines are derived from Li

25. Wei T'ai (d. 1110), *Tung-hsüan pi-lu* (Peking: Chung-hua shu-chü, 1983), 5.52
(Hsia Ch'eng-t'ao, *T'ang Sung tz'u jen nien-p'u* [Shanghai: Shang-hai ku-chi ch'u-pan-she,
1979], p. 240).

26. *Lun-yü* 15/11.

27. Shao Po (d. 1158), *Shao-shih wen-chien hou-lu* (*Hsüeh-chin t'ao-yüan* ed.), 19.151–52
(Hsia Ch'eng-t'ao, *T'ang Sung tz'u-jen nien-p'u*, pp. 258–59).

28. From Ch'in's "Shui lung yin," no. 6, *CST*, 1:455–56.

29. From Yen's "Che-ku t'ien," no. 33, *CST*, 1:226–27. Hsieh Bridge must be a place
where the speaker, a male, used to meet his lover. Cf. the meaning of "Miss Hsieh"
(*Hsieh-niang* or *Hsieh-nü*) in other *tz'u*, as explained by Wen Kuang-i, *T'ang Sung tz'u
ch'ang-yung yü shih li* (Huhehot: Nei-Meng-ku ch'u-pan-she, 1978), pp. 167–68.

Ch'ang-chi's [Li Ho's], "If Heaven had feelings, / Heaven too would grow old,"[30] which are similarly disrespectful. Shao-yu eventually died in exile and Shu-yuan [Yen Chi-tao] likewise did not live to an old age. Although it is said that there is such a thing as fate, their deaths were caused as well by their error of using words to encourage promiscuity.[31]

Ch'en Ku's attitude, clearly, is a reformulation of Fa-hsiu's opinion that *tz'u* are so immoral and harmful to society that the writers are apt to be punished for the misdeed of "encouraging promiscuity" (*ch'üan yin*). But whereas Fa-hsiu referred to unfavorable rebirth, Ch'en Ku alludes to the Confucian notion of early death. Without Ch'en Ku's remarks, it would be easy to interpret Ch'eng I's criticisms as nothing more than the sort of fussy intolerance that literal-minded scholars often show for poetic language. But a case can be made for finding more in Ch'eng I's comments than just this, and the case is supported by Ch'en Ku's expansion of the criticism. What precisely, we might ask, is so objectionable to Ch'eng I about the reference to Heaven in Ch'in Kuan's *tz'u*? Those lines are, of course, part of a description of a lonely woman who is pining away for her lover who has deserted her. The *tz'u* is a portrait of lovesickness, and the lines in question assert that the illness is so powerful that it could overcome even Heaven (if Heaven only understood what was happening). There is, after all, a sense in which one of the functions of Sung *tz'u* was to document and legitimate emotions that contemporary society barely gave notice to, much less sanctioned. Love and its associated longings may be so strong, Ch'in Kuan implies, that they become the central fact about a life. They take control of the person and of her health, and they would do the same for Heaven if Heaven could experience them. These are assertions, even if not explicitly made, that seemed preposterous, or even worse, to men of other persuasions like Ch'eng I. One could trace a similar objection to Yen Chi-tao's lines about the dreamer: it may have been a commonplace in love songs to speak of a soul emerging from the body during sleep and visiting a distant lover, but unromantic minds, once again, were unwilling to attribute such powers to love. They knew that the *hun* soul could only leave the body at death, which is why Ch'eng I says what he does.

The fate of Ou-yang Hsiu and his *tz'u* provides evidence of another kind of the uncertain status of this genre during the Sung. As famous as

30. Li Ho, "Chin-t'ung hsien-jen tz'u Han ko," *Ch'üan T'ang shih* (Peking: Chung-hua shu-chü, 1960), 391.4403.

31. Ch'en Ku (early 13th cent.), *Hsi t'ang chi ch'i-chiu hsü-wen* (*Chih-pu-tsu chai ts'ung-shu* ed.), 8.6a.

he was during his lifetime as a statesman, scholar, and poet, Ou-yang also lived through more than the usual share of controversy. Unlike many other prominent Sung officials who were charged from time to time with abuses of power or disloyalty to the throne, Ou-yang Hsiu was charged with immoral conduct in his personal life. In his middle age Ou-yang was accused of having had an illicit affair with a niece (the girl herself brought the charge), and years later he was denounced for having committed incest with a daughter-in-law. Both times a formal investigation was held, Ou-yang adamantly maintaining his innocence, and both times the charges were eventually dropped (though damage was done in each case to Ou-yang's reputation and career).[32]

We certainly do not have enough information to pass judgment on Ou-yang's culpability in these cases. It is clear that the charges against Ou-yang were seized upon by his political enemies, if they did not plant them in the first place, and used in an attempt to topple him from power. Of course, there might have been some combination of wrong-doing on Ou-yang's part and opportunism on the part of his rivals. We do not know. It is likely that Ou-yang's reputation as a man who "enjoyed life" and had a weakness for young girls made him seem particularly vulnerable, in the eyes of his enemies, to this sort of scandal. If so, we can say that Ou-yang's fame as a *tz'u* writer, which was considerable, helped to make him vulnerable, for his *tz'u* projected that image of him. At the least, we can say that Ou-yang's activities as a *tz'u* writer figured in these scandals. It is virtually certain that during the first case, and perhaps the second as well, *tz'u* that dwelled on infatuation with a young girl were composed by Ou-yang's accusers and falsely circulated under Ou-yang's name. Thus did his enemies seek to defame and incriminate him.

This sheds new light on the reasons Northern Sung scholars had for keeping *tz'u* out of their literary collections. But if *tz'u* could be this damaging, why weren't other *tz'u* writers similarly implicated in scandal? Why were Ou-yang's problems unique? The answer, I believe, is that Ou-yang's circumstances lent themselves uniquely to his trouble. Prominence was, of course, one of the necessary conditions. Through the entire Northern Sung, aside from Ou-yang there were really only two other prolific *tz'u* writers who were politically powerful: Yen Shu, just older than Ou-yang, and Su Shih, a generation younger. Yen Shu held the highest offices in the empire and although, as mentioned above,

32. For a fuller discussion of the issues raised in this and the following paragraphs, see my *Ou-yang Hsiu*, pp. 5–11 and 133–95.

he was eventually subjected to some criticism for combining this emi-
nence with *tz'u* writing,[33] his career as such seems to have been remarkably free of controversy. He was not the leader of a major movement or
faction, and no one was determined to topple him. Ou-yang, by contrast, was repeatedly at the center of factional strife. He was a major
spokesman for the reform movement led by Fan Chung-yen in the
1040s, whose defeat coincided with Ou-yang's Niece Chang case, and
he was also embroiled in the bitter rituals controversy of the late 1060s,
when the second charge of sexual offense against him surfaced. Su Shih
was even more regularly involved in political struggle than Ou-yang, his
mentor, had been. But Su Shih's enemies did not need to resort to in-
nuendo about incontinence. Incautious remonstrator that he was, Su's
criticisms of court policy gave his adversaries plenty of material to use
against him. It was, after all, more efficient to question a man's loyalty
to the emperor than his sexual conduct. Another consideration is that
neither Yen Shu nor Su Shih wrote such racy *tz'u*—colloquial in their
diction and relatively explicit in their references to lovemaking—as Ou-
yang did. Yen Shu was known for his elegantly restrained and "aristocratic" *tz'u* style. Su Shih of course pioneered a new approach to *tz'u*,
avoiding the old preoccupation with romance and adopting instead the
broad range of subjects of the *shih* poet. (Here was a man who wrote a
famous *tz'u* on his deceased wife—hardly the stuff of scandal.) There
may be one other factor: Ou-yang Hsiu had something of the stuffy
moralist in him. He is one who set himself up as a champion of neglected Confucian virtues and encouraged a comparison between himself and the great Han Yü. For the enemies of such a man there is, naturally, nothing so satisfying as seeing him dogged by questions about
moral probity in his personal life.

The later textual history of Ou-yang Hsiu's *tz'u* reveals, in its own
way, the stigma attached to some songs. By the time that literary critics
and anthologists addressed themselves to Ou-yang's *tz'u* in the Southern
Sung, so august was Ou-yang's reputation as a statesman and writer
that it had simply become, for several of the critics, incompatible with
the more colloquial and explicit of his *tz'u*. Tseng Tsao, the compiler of
the anthology *Yüeh-fu ya-tz'u*, wrote in his preface: "Mr. Ou-yang was
the most venerable Confucian of his day. He also prided himself on his
ability to enjoy life. He wrote songs that are graceful and charming, a

33. Wang An-shih himself, in addition to Lü Hui-ch'ing, expressed misgivings over
Yen Shu's being both grand councilor and *tz'u* writer; see Wei T'ai, *Tung-hsüan pi-lu*,
5.52.

style that all the world came to emulate. However, during his lifetime certain scoundrels composed erotic songs and falsely attributed them to him. I have excluded all such songs from my anthology."[34] These Southern Sung scholars took advantage of the stories of forged, slanderous *tz'u* to disassociate a substantial proportion of Ou-yang's pieces from his name, retaining only the most *ya*, "elegant," of his compositions. In the late twelfth century, Lo Mi edited a new "complete" collection of Ou-yang's *tz'u*. Working, so far as I can tell, with nothing more authoritative than his own notions about the limits of Ou-yang's good taste, he went through an earlier collection of Ou-yang's *tz'u* and excised dozens of pieces that struck him as improbably vulgar. His "editing" caused the confusion over Ou-yang's corpus and identity as a *tz'u* writer that has lasted down to this day.

SU SHIH

The attitudes we have been examining acquire additional interest when it is understood that not only did they affect the ways *tz'u* were talked about and transmitted, they could influence as well the way *tz'u* were written. It was not just that certain moralists looked down upon *tz'u* as improper, while *tz'u* writers, gaily oblivious of this disapproval, went on producing new compositions. Literati themselves were apt to be ambivalent about *tz'u*, and this ambivalence spurred some of them on to explore new ways of writing. The argument can be made, at the least, that what everyone recognizes as a major eleventh-century innovation in *tz'u* writing—that undertaken by Su Shih—was directly linked to the shadow of disrepute the genre lived under. Su Shih's development of the new "bold and unrestrained" *tz'u* style, or his novel decision to "use the methods of *shih* to compose *tz'u*," is partly explained, according to this view, as an effort to rid the genre of its disreputable elements and to make it more acceptable. No doubt Su had other motives as well. I will present the argument for this one in the following pages, citing the more important supporting sources, since if it is valid it is one of the more significant ramifications of the points discussed above.

We are accustomed to thinking of Su Shih as one of the major *tz'u* writers not only of the Sung but of all of Chinese history. Several of the songs he wrote are among the most famous of all *tz'u*. These individual successes are complemented by his prodigious output: with over three hundred pieces to his credit, Su Shih is the most prolific of all Northern

34. Tseng Tsao, *Yüeh-fu ya-tz'u* (*TSCC* ed.), p. i.

Sung *tz'u* writers. Despite his credentials in the *tz'u* field, however, it is evident that Su Shih too partook on occasion of the biases we have been examining. Below is a colophon Su Shih wrote on the *shih* collection of Chang Hsien:

> Chang Tzu-yeh's *shih* poetry and prose are mature and masterful. His *tz'u* are nothing more than an ancillary skill. For example, his [*shih* poem] "West Creek at Hu-chou" contains the lines "At breaks in the floating duckweed you see the mountain's reflection, / as the light skiff starts home you hear the river grasses," and his poem written to rhyme with mine has the couplet "As sad as the *kuan* fish that knows the night is long, / as tired as the butterfly during busy spring." These and other of his lines are every bit the equal of those written by ancient poets. However, the world only knows to praise his *tz'u*. Formerly, the portraits painted by Chou Fang were all in the "inspired" rank [*shen p'in*], but the world paid attention only to his portraits of aristocratic ladies. Is this not a case of "never having seen a man who loved morality as much as he loves feminine beauty"?[35]

To the extent that Su Shih is here attempting to enhance the stature of Chang Hsien's *shih*, we may say that he fails completely. By the end of the Sung, Chang Hsien's *shih* collection had been lost. Chang has been remembered subsequently, as he was evidently known in his day, solely for his *tz'u*.

Knowing that Chang's fame is based on his *tz'u*, Su Shih begins with an attempt to rectify the world's understanding: Chang's gift for *tz'u* is merely an ancillary skill. His real talent is in the more profound forms, prose and *shih* poetry. Subsequently, Su reveals the reason for the low evaluation he presents here of Chang's *tz'u*. Su likens them to the T'ang painter Chou Fang's famous portraits of high-placed women. Both describe feminine beauty. Both promote sensuousness and appeal to the base instincts and appetites of men. Su concludes by quoting Confucius on the lamentable popularity of such appeal.[36] Surprisingly, here we find Su Shih, the great *tz'u* writer, delivering an opinion on the genre that is not far removed from the condemnation expressed by contemporary Buddhist and Confucian moralists. This does not mean, of course, that Su Shih had no appreciation of Chang Hsien's *tz'u*. Actually, Su Shih seems to have begun writing *tz'u* largely under Chang Hsien's tutelage in Hang-chou in the early 1070s.[37] When the occasion was a

35. Su Shih, "T'i Chang Tzu-yeh shih-chi hou," *Su Shih wen-chi*, 68.2146.
36. *Lun-yü* 9/18.
37. Nishi Noriaki, "Tōba no shoki no sōbetsu-shi," *Chūgoku chūsei bungaku kenkyū* 7 (1968): 67–71.

formal one, however, Su Shih would reiterate the hierarchy of literary genres that was conventional.[38]

In Su Shih's day, and well on into the Southern Sung, one of the methods used by those who wrote and appreciated *tz'u* to enhance their stature was to draw a distinction between two types or schools of *tz'u*, the "elegant" and the "vulgar" (*ya* and *su*), and then to heap scorn upon the latter. Once the "vulgar" *tz'u* were separated out and identified as a distinct (and degenerate) subgenre, it was easier to accept what remained as a legitimate part of the high poetic tradition. We have seen one manifestation of this process in the textual history of Ou-yang Hsiu's *tz'u*. But the premier example of this prejudice is the Sung treatment of Liu Yung and his *tz'u*. No Sung *tz'u* writer comes in for so much abuse as Liu Yung. His character and morals are regularly impugned, and his compositions dismissed. (Li Ch'ing-chao, for example, calls his language "low as dirt.")[39] Liu Yung's uniqueness in the historical and critical record must stem from the fact that no other writer produced a corpus of *tz'u* that is so consistently colloquial in its diction or so convincing in its descriptions of love—and its frustrations—between literati and singing girls. (There is good reason to think, moreover, that no other writer's compositions were as popular with the singers and their audiences as Liu Yung's, which may help to account for the virulence of his detractors.) There are stories about the emperor intervening to fail Liu Yung on the civil service examinations because of his reputation as a dissolute songwriter, and stories about him having to change his name to escape his disrepute.[40] The story that best represents the attempt to distinguish his style of *tz'u* from the more respectable kind is the well-known anecdote that describes a meeting of Liu and Yen Shu, who was then grand councilor:

> After Liu San-pien [Yung] had offended Jen-tsung with a song, the Board of Personnel would not give him a new appointment, and San-pien could

38. Wu Hsiung-ho suggests a different interpretation of Su Shih's colophon, linking Su's opening comment about Chang's *tz'u* with the term widely used to designate *tz'u* in the Southern Sung: *shih-yü* (Su wrote that Chang's *tz'u* was his *yü-chih*). Wu attempts to establish that the phrase *shih-yü* was not pejorative. That is really a separate issue, and a complex one. In any case, Su Shih did not use the term *shih-yü* to designate *tz'u*. Moreover, Wu quotes Su's colophon out of context and distorts the gist of his remark. See Wu's *T'ang Sung tz'u t'ung-lun* (Hangchow: Che-chiang ku-chi ch'u-pan-she, 1985), pp. 289–90.

39. Hu Tzu, *T'iao-hsi—hou-chi*, 33.254.

40. See James R. Hightower, "The Songwriter Liu Yung," pt. 1, *Harvard Journal of Asiatic Studies* 41 (1981): 325–29.

not stand it. He went to the government office, where His Excellency Yen [Shu] said, "Do you, sir, write songs?"

"Even as Your Excellency, I too write songs."

"I may write songs, but I never wrote anything like 'Tired of her needle work, she nestles close to him.'" Whereupon Liu withdrew.[41]

In this anecdote, as in literary history, Yen Shu epitomizes the "elegant" *tz'u* tradition. That is why Liu Yung's attempt to defuse the censure implicit in Yen's opening question backfires. It is true that I write *tz'u*, Yen Shu replies, but I do not write *your* sort of *tz'u*, which treat so openly of flirtation and love. In his *tz'u*, as this anecdote suggests, Yen Shu did indeed remain true to the *Hua-chien chi* tradition of more restrained and evocative treatments of love, in which the poignant loneliness of separated lovers is more prominent than scenes of trysting.

Su Shih's views on Liu Yung are, predictably enough, mixed. Su is on record as having expressed admiration for certain of Liu Yung's lines.[42] There is little doubt, however, that Su's appraisal of the bold depiction of love found in Liu Yung's works was unfavorable.[43] Nevertheless, the really interesting aspect of Su's remarks about Liu Yung is that they are not in neat agreement with the *ya/su* dichotomy as normally conceived. Su's comments reveal, first, an awareness that there is no absolute division between the two, which is certainly true, and, second, that he is not entirely satisfied or comfortable even with the *ya* or "elegant" tradition because of its preoccupation with love, however evocatively described.

More than once Su Shih teased his protégé Ch'in Kuan about the affinities Ch'in's songs had with Liu Yung's. These are gentle reproofs, to be sure, and uttered partly in jest. But there is a serious point behind the humor: it is not right for a man of Ch'in's education and stature to imitate the man who was the darling of the singing girls. That Su would even recognize and acknowledge this similarity between Ch'in's and Liu's songs is unexpected. In fact, Ch'in Kuan's songs generally con-

41. Chang Shun-min (d. ca. 1110), *Hua-man lu* (*Pai-hai* ed.), 1.30b; trans. Hightower, "Liu Yung," pt. 1, p. 332.

42. Chao Ling-chih (1061–1134), *Hou cheng lu* (*Chih-pu-tsu chai ts'ung-shu* ed.), 7.11a, quoted by Chu Ching-hua, "Su Shih 'i shih wei tz'u' ts'u-ch'eng tz'u-t'i ko-ming," in *Tung-p'o tz'u lun-ts'ung*, ed. Su Shih yen-chiu hsüeh-hui (Ch'eng-tu: Ssu-ch'uan jen-min wen-hsüeh ch'u-pan-she, 1982), p. 9. Chu argues that Su Shih's opinion of Liu Yung's *tz'u* was not as negative as usually thought.

43. This point is made by Yeh Chia-ying, "Lun Su Shih tz'u," in Yeh Chia-ying and Miao Yüeh, *Ling-hsi tz'u-shuo* (Shanghai: Shang-hai ku-chi ch'u-pan-she, 1987), pp. 201–2.

tinue the *Hua-chien* tradition and would have been termed "elegant" by most critics. Although Su disapproves of the "vulgar" style, his remarks betray an awareness of how easily elements of it could find their way into the songs of literati poets—in other words, of how murky the distinction between the two "styles" was:

> When Shao-yu [Ch'in Kuan] returned to the capital from K'uai-chi and saw Tung-p'o, Tung-p'o said to him, "I never thought that after we parted you would write *tz'u* in the manner of Liu Ch'i [Yung]."
> "Although I have no learning," Shao-yu replied, "I would not stoop to that."
> "'My soul wastes away, facing this scene': are these not lines like Liu Ch'i's?"[44]

The lines Su Shih quotes here are from one of Ch'in Kuan's best-known *tz'u*, one that is written in a male voice and describes the man's sorrow as he parts from his lover, a professional entertainer.[45] A contemporary source asserts that Ch'in Kuan wrote the song for a singing girl he was in love with and had to leave.[46]

Su Shih's uneasiness over Ch'in Kuan's *tz'u* surfaces again in the following passage, found in Yeh Meng-te's *Pi-shu lu-hua*. Su Shih refers once again to the same Ch'in Kuan song, this time by its opening lines: "Mountains brush wisps of clouds, / the sky sticks against withering grasses":

> Among the four scholars who were his followers, Su Tzu-chan had the highest regard for Shao-yu. Tzu-chan always had words of praise for all of Shao-yu's writings, not just his *tz'u*. However, Su felt that the style [of Shao-yu's *tz'u*] was flawed. He used to tease Shao-yu, saying, "Academician Ch'in, whose 'mountains brush wisps of clouds,' / State Farms Administrator Liu, whose 'dewy blossoms cast shadows.'"[47]

It cannot be Ch'in's line about mountains and clouds that Su Shih objects to. Su uses the line as a tag to call to mind Ch'in's song, and Su is surely thinking as well of the many other songs like it that Ch'in wrote. Ch'in Kuan's status as an academician and erudite at the imperial academy is implicitly at odds with such songs, and Su Shih juxtaposes his official title here with the song words to emphasize the incongruity. The criticism is developed further by the matching line about Liu Yung,

44. Tseng Tsao, *Kao-chai shih-hua* (Lung Mu-hsün, *Su-men*, vol. 1, *Huai-hai chü-shih*, p. 82, quoting *Yü-hsüan li-tai shih-yü*).
45. "Man t'ing fang," no. 1, *CST*, 1:458.
46. Yen Yu-i (mid-12th cent.), *I-yüan tz'u-huang* (Hu Tzu, *T'iao-hsi—hou-chi*, 33.248).
47. Yeh Meng-te (1077–1148), *Pi-shu lu-hua* (*Hsüeh-chin t'ao-yüan* ed.), B.2b.

whose disrepute was well established and whose highest office, assistant administrator of state farms, was a far cry from the prestige of academician.

Su Shih does not cling to the *ya/su* distinction as his contemporaries did, using it to claim respectability for a certain style of *tz'u*. Instead of disassociating the more literary from the more colloquial tradition, Su's comments have the effect of drawing the two together, even if only so that he can express disapproval of both. Another remark Su makes about Liu Yung shows that Su was eager to develop an entirely new sort of alternative to Liu's type of songs and, indeed, that Su thought of Liu's compositions as typical of *tz'u* generally. The remark is made in a personal letter to a friend in which Su talks about his own *tz'u*:

> Recently I have written several little *tz'u*. They may not have the flavor of Mr. Liu Ch'i's [Yung's] compositions, but they too represent a style of their own. Ha-ha! A few days ago I went hunting in the countryside and caught quite a few animals. I wrote this song about it. If you have a brawny northeasterner sing it, clapping his hands and stamping his feet, and have pipes and drums play along in accompaniment, it makes for quite a manly sight! I have copied it out to amuse you.[48]

The song this letter accompanies is a *tz'u* describing a hunt and thus departs, both in its diction and tone, from virtually everything that readers normally associated with *tz'u*.[49] It marks, in other words, as much of a break with the *Hua-chien* tradition as it does with that exemplified by Liu Yung. This piece constitutes an early and radical attempt by Su Shih to put *tz'u* to a new use, having it sung by brawny northeasterners rather than female entertainers. Su Shih did not continue in this particular vein, which we might term "martial *tz'u*," and was soon to find another way to produce *tz'u* that might be called "manly" (*chuang*). Nevertheless, I take Su's reference to Liu Yung here, followed by his guffaw, as a disparagement of *tz'u* generally, and a sign of his discomfort with its unmanliness.

Among earlier *tz'u* writers literary history reserves a special place for Li Yü, the last ruler of the Southern T'ang, who saw his kingdom destroyed and lived his final years as a captive in the Sung capital. Li Yü had already produced a corpus of *tz'u* that sounded intensely personal and departed from the preoccupation with beautiful ladies and the

---

48. *Su Shih wen-chi*, 53.1560. Kang-i Sun Chang also quotes form this letter in her discussion of Su Shih's innovations; see *The Evolution of* Tz'u *Poetry from Late T'ang to Northern Sung* (Princeton: Princeton University Press, 1980), p. 160.

49. "Chiang shen-tzu," no. 4, *CST*, 1:299.

adoption of feminine personas of the *Hua-chien chi* anthology. However, in his only comment on this leading Five Dynasties *tz'u* writer, Su Shih seizes upon the feminine element in one of Li Yü's songs and rails against it. The *tz'u* in question, one of many in which Li Yü laments the loss of his realm, ends with the lines, "Worst of all was the day I bid a hurried farewell to my court: / the royal musicians played parting songs, / I wept before my palace women." The man had brought his state to ruin, Su Shih observes impatiently, "He should have wailed aloud at the ancestral shrine of the royal clan and admitted his guilt publicly to his people before leaving. What was he doing shedding tears in front of his palace women and listening to musicians play parting songs?"[50] Su Shih finds Li Yü's lines offensive rather than poignant. Standing as Su's sole remark on Li Yü, the comment suggests that Su Shih was as dissatisfied with the deposed king's *tz'u* as he was with Liu Yung's, and for much the same reason, as dissimilar as the two men and their songs might seem to us.

Here again, as with Chang Hsien above, we encounter the issue of multiple modes of response to an earlier writer's compositions. As a reader and listener, Su Shih may have been fond of Li Yü's *tz'u*. As a *tz'u* writer, Su Shih may have been influenced by Li Yü's compositions. But in the more formal role of written commentator (i.e., in a colophon), Su Shih's aversion to the unmanliness of *tz'u* eclipses whatever literary appreciation he may have had for Li Yü's works.

Su Shih may not have always been so disapproving of *tz'u*, but once one takes note of remarks such as those above, one begins to hear echoes elsewhere in Su Shih, even where they are muted, of this same uneasiness with the feminine and romantic elements traditionally found in *tz'u*. Huang T'ing-chien had written the following *tz'u* about a fisherman:

To the tune "Sands of the Washing Stream"[51]

Over Bride Jetty painted eyebrows are sad,
by Maiden Pool watery eyes have the look of autumn.
A startled fish mistakes the hook of the sinking moon.

A cap of green leaves, and countless cares
beneath a verdant reed jacket are forgotten.
Slanting winds blow the drizzle, turning the bow of the boat.

---

50. "Shu Li chu tz'u," *Su Shih wen-chi*, 68.2151–52. Li Yü's *tz'u* is "P'o chen-tzu," *Ch'üan T'ang Wu-tai tz'u*, ed. Chang Chang and Huang Yü (Taipei: Wen-shih-che, 1980), 1:231–32; translated and discussed by Chang, *Evolution of* Tz'u, pp. 85–86.
51. "Huan hsi sha," *CST*, 1:398–99.

浣溪沙
新婦灘頭眉黛愁
女兒浦口眼波秋
驚魚錯認月沈鉤

青箬笠前無限事
綠簑衣底一時休
斜風吹雨轉船頭

Su Shih wrote a colophon on this *tz'u*, in which he reports that when Huang himself was asked what he liked best about his composition he referred to the opening two lines, which use images of a woman's face metaphorically to describe the dark hills and autumnal river. Su Shih appends this comment: "However, as soon as he leaves 'Bride Jetty,' he enters 'Maiden Pool.' Isn't this fisherman too much of a philanderer [*t'ai lan-lang*]?"[52] It must be Su Shih's lingering dissatisfaction with the romantic sentimentality so typical of *tz'u* that makes him unable to resist making such comments, even when they are uttered, as here, in jest.

Su Shih also figures in one of the stories that survive about a Hang-chou singing girl named Ch'in-ts'ao, "Zither Melody." Ch'in was known for her quick wit, and especially her ability to extemporize *tz'u* or change the rhyme of an extant composition. This particular story, however, highlights Su Shih's wit as she addresses questions to him (aping the manner of a Buddhist novice toward his spiritual teacher). Su's answers are all couplets quoted from earlier poetic works:

> Once when Tung-p'o was at West Lake, he said playfully to Ch'in, "Come, I'll be your master. You ask me questions."
>
> Ch'in asked him, "What is a lake scene?"
>
> Su replied, "'Autumn waters and distant skies are one color, / sunset clouds and a lone duck fly off together.'"[53]
>
> "What is the person like in the scene?"
>
> "'Her skirt displays six panels of Hsiao-hsiang River, / her hairdo suspends a patch of Wu Mountain clouds.'"[54]
>
> "What is on her mind?"
>
> "'She loves that Scholar Yang / and nearly kills Adjutant Pao with jealousy.'"
>
> "How did it all end?"

52. "Pa Ch'ien-an chü-shih 'Yü fu tz'u,'" *Su Shih wen-chi*, 68.2157. Also recorded in Wu Tseng, *Neng-kai chai man-lu*, 16.473; and Hu Tzu, *T'iao-hsi—ch'ien-chi*, 48.330.

53. Wang Po (648–75), "T'eng-wang-ko hsü," *Ch'üan T'ang wen* (1814 ed.), 181.19a.

54. Li Ch'ün-yü (mid-9th cent.), "T'ung Cheng Hsiang ping ko-chi hsiao-yin hsi tseng," *Ch'üan T'ang shih*, 569.6602.

"'Her gateway is deserted, horse and carriage rarely pass. / In old age she becomes a traveling merchant's wife.'"[55]

Hearing this, Ch'in suddenly became enlightened. She shaved her head and became a nun.[56]

Su Shih's final couplet is taken from the description in Po Chü-i's "Lute Song" of the sad later years of a former entertainer. Although we might first suppose that there is nothing special about Su Shih's appearance in this story, and that almost any literatus might equally well have been Ch'in's questioner, my argument is that Su Shih does have some degree of special appropriateness in such an anecdote. Whether or not the anecdote has any basis in historical fact, Su Shih's role here befits his habit of questioning the fascination shown conventionally in *tz'u* with the courtesan and her romantic liaisons.

There is an obvious objection to the argument presented here, which is that Su Shih's own corpus of *tz'u* is filled with songs that are addressed to or describe singing girls.[57] It is certainly not true, despite how often it is claimed or implied, that Su Shih rejected the conventional methods of *tz'u* writing outright and poured all his energies into developing his famed "heroic and unrestrained" alternative. But if Su produced numerous *tz'u* that are faithful to the *Hua-chien* tradition and its alluring portraits of female entertainers, what are we to make of his remarks discussed above?

My answer is that if we read Su Shih's *tz'u* chronologically, the apparent contradiction loses much of its urgency.[58] It is well known that Su Shih did not begin to produce *tz'u* in any quantity until surprisingly late, during his first assignment to Hang-chou (when he was already in his late thirties). It is likely that this late start itself reflects some early ambivalence he felt toward the genre. When he did begin he stayed, naturally enough, within boundaries that were well established. Some scholars, it is true, have detected even in Su Shih's early *tz'u*, especially those written as farewells to friends, signs of the breakthrough that was later to come.[59] But it is questionable whether those signs are really sig-

55. Po Chü-i (772–846), "P'i-p'a hsing," *Ch'üan T'ang shih*, 435.4822.

56. Wu Tseng, *Neng-kai chai man-lu*, 16.483.

57. Support for this point can be found in the recent article by Ch'eng Shan-k'ai on images of singing girls in Su Shih's *tz'u*, "Tung-p'o yüeh-fu chung ko-chi ti mei-hsüeh i-i," in *T'ung-p'o tz'u lun-ts'ung*, pp. 90–106.

58. The most complete chronological arrangement of Su Shih's *tz'u* is Ts'ao Shu-ming's *Tung-p'o tz'u* (Hong Kong: Hsiang-kang Shang-hai yin-shu-kuan, 1968), which supersedes in its dating of the pieces, though not in its annotations, Lung Mu-hsün's *Tung-p'o yüeh-fu chien* (Shanghai: Shang-wu yin-shu-kuan, 1936).

59. See Nishi Noriaki, "Tōba no shoki no sōbetsu-shi," pp. 64–73.

nificant except in retrospect. It must be said that during his first decade as a *tz'u* writer, the 1070s, while he served in Hang-chou, Mi-chou, and Hsü-chou, Su Shih produced a large number of quite conventional compositions. However, what the reader of his corpus for these years finds is that every now and then, on rare occasions, Su Shih departed from conventional methods. He undertook then to write intensely autobiographical *tz'u*, and it is precisely these that became famous (e.g., his hunting piece, his dream of his late wife, his autumn moon-festival song for Tzu-yu, his historical reflections at Yen-tzu-lou, and his P'ing-shan Hall lament for Ou-yang Hsiu).[60] These pieces are linked by their common repudiation, for that is what it amounts to, of the world of romanticized courtesans, and their adoption instead of many of the conventions of occasional *shih* poetry. This, I would suggest, is a more useful way of describing Su's innovation than vaguely to characterize it as "heroic and unrestrained." Read against the other *tz'u* Su Shih wrote during these years, these pieces fairly jump off the page, so distinctive are they in subject and tone. In these few pieces Su Shih had already found an approach to *tz'u* that flourished during his subsequent Huang-chou exile (when the political trouble his *shih* writing had brought him encouraged him to experiment with "little *tz'u*" instead).[61] Huang-chou and the years after comprise the period of Su's greatness as a *tz'u* writer, when he demonstrated how powerful was this new coupling of *shih* poetry conventions with the lyricism, informality, and spontaneity of *tz'u*. Su himself wrote in Huang-chou to a friend, "Recently I have composed many new musical verses, and each one is extraordinary."[62]

The Southern Sung scholar Hu Yin said of Su Shih's *tz'u* that they "washed away in one stroke all the colored silks and perfumed oils" of earlier compositions.[63] Hu Yin was thinking, of course, of Su Shih's innovative *tz'u* when he wrote this. As a characterization of those *tz'u* Hu Yin's statement is accurate enough, but it is problematic if applied to

---

60. "Chiang shen-tzu," no. 9, *CST*, 1:300 (no. 54); "Chiang shen-tzu," no. 4, *CST*, 1:299 (no. 56); "Shui-tiao ko t'ou," no. 3, *CST*, 1:280 (no. 65); "Yung yü lo," no. 2, *CST*, 1:302 (no. 86); and "Hsi chiang yüeh," no. 12, *CST*, 1:285 (no. 93). (The numbers in parentheses are those assigned in Ts'ao Shu-ming's edition.)

61. See Su's remarks to this effect in his letter "Yü Ch'en Ta-fu," no. 3, *Su Shih wen-chi*, 56.1698.

62. "Yü Ch'en Chi-ch'ang," no. 9, *Su Shih wen-chi*, 53.1567. It is evident that Wang Shui-chao also takes this comment (and the crucial term *ch'üeh*) to refer to Su's *tz'u*; see his "Lun Su Shih ch'uang-tso ti fa-chan chieh-tuan," *She-hui k'o-hsüeh chan-hsien* 1984, no. 1:264.

63. Hu Yin (1098–1156), preface to *Chiu-pien tz'u*, p. i.

Su Shih's corpus as a whole, simply because it took Su some years to effect his break with the *tz'u* tradition, and occasionally he even lapsed back into that tradition—which should hardly surprise us—after his new style was established.

OTHER DEFENSES

Su Shih's innovation, as important as it was, did not transform everyone's idea of how *tz'u* should be written. There were scholars, even within Su's own "circle," who continued to compose *tz'u* that stayed well within the *Hua-chien* style. To conclude this discussion, I would like to return to this more traditional style of *tz'u* and to consider some of the statements that were made in defense of it. Topics already discussed above, including the recourse taken to distinguishing "elegant" from "vulgar" *tz'u* and Su Shih's new approach, constitute what were probably the most significant and well-known reactions to the problem of *tz'u*'s low stature. But other solutions or defenses were raised as well, even if they were offered more tentatively and did not gain any great prominence.

We might begin with an amusing if not serious defense, one that shows, through its contorted argument, how great the pressure could be to find legitimation for *tz'u*. In a conversation with a P'u Ch'uan-cheng, Yen Chi-tao once broached the subject of his father's (Yen Shu's) *tz'u* writing. Chi-tao begins:

"My father may have written a great many little *tz'u*, but he never wrote women's words."

Ch'uan-cheng said, "'Green willows, fragrant grasses by the post-station road, / the young man [*nien-shao*] abandons me, leaving carelessly.'[64] What are these if not women's words?"

Yen asked, "What do you think *nien-shao* means?"

Ch'uan-cheng replied, "It refers to her lover, doesn't it?"

Yen said, "If we use your interpretation, then how are we to understand Lo-t'ien's [Po Chü-i's] lines, 'I wanted to detain my youth [*nien-shao*] to await wealth and honor, / but wealth and honor did not come and youth left me'?"[65]

Ch'uan-cheng laughed and saw the point.[66]

64. The quotation is from Yen Shu's "Yü-lou ch'un," *CST*, 1:108–9.
65. From Po's poem "Hao-ko hsing," *Ch'üan T'ang shih*, 435.4810–11.
66. Hu Tzu, *T'iao-hsi—ch'ien-chi*, 26.178.

Yen Chi-tao is trying to exonerate his father, admitting that he wrote *tz'u* but claiming that he did not go so far as to write in the persona of a woman, especially a lovesick woman. Yen sounds eager here to promote an image of his father as a philosophical or autobiographical *tz'u* poet. Ch'uan-cheng immediately challenges Yen's claim with a quote from one of Yen Shu's better-known compositions.

The song in question is filled with topoi that are commonly found in *tz'u* on parting, loneliness, and separation. In addition to the willow and the post-station of the opening line, there is reference to an interrupted dream, parting sorrow (*li-ch'ing*), a tangled heart, and endless romantic longing (*hsiang-ssu*). Given the conventional associations of such language, the most natural reading of the *tz'u* is that Ch'uan-cheng first adopts (reflected also in several modern commentaries on the piece):[67] the song is written in the persona of a woman whose young lover (*nien-shao*, interchangeable in this sense with *shao-nien*) has lightly abandoned her. The verb used in line two (*p'ao*) normally refers to just such abandonment or rejection in love (especially a man's rejecting a woman). But this *tz'u*, like many whose theme is loneliness, need not be read exclusively as a jilted woman's complaint. The language is vague enough to permit interpreting the piece as a nonspecific expression of grief over partings. We need not even identify the speaking voice with either sex. The second line might refer to a parted friend (or friends) rather than a particular lover, or it might even be read as a generalized statement: "In youth we abandon others (i.e., friends, lovers) too lightly."[68]

However, that is not what Yen Chi-tao is saying. He is insisting that the phrase *nien-shao* be taken as "my youthful years" (rather than "the young man") and that it is here personified, so that the speaker talks of its going off and deserting him. This is indeed the way the phrase *nien-shao* is used in the Po Chü-i poem Yen cites, a poem about aging. This is, however, a most unlikely meaning for *nien-shao* in this particular *tz'u*, with all of its subsequent language that must refer to real, not metaphorical, parting. Yen Chi-tao is forcing a very peculiar reading on his father's *tz'u*, and he is doing so to try to make it more respectable. Ch'uan-cheng is said to be persuaded, but we need not be so gullible. Yen Chi-tao began with a claim that was specious (as the *Ssu-k'u ch'üan*

67. See Ch'en Yung-cheng, *Yen Shu Yen Chi-tao tz'u hsüan* (Hong Kong: San-lien shu-tien, 1984), p. 73, Ch'en Hung-chih, *T'ang Sung tz'u ming-tso hsi-p'ing* (Taipei: Wen-chin ch'u-pan-she, 1976), pp. 102–3, and Chiang Shang-hsien, *T'ang Sung ming-chia tz'u hsin-hsüan* (Taipei: Published by the author, 1963), pp. 103–5.

68. This is the reading suggested by Han Ch'iu-pai in Ho Hsin-hui, *Sung tz'u chien-shang tz'u'u-tien* (Peking: Yen-shan ch'u-pan-she, 1987), pp. 112–13.

shu editors have pointed out) and was forced into a further distortion to back it up.[69]

Earlier we passed over a remark that deserves to be closely examined, for it brings up a potentially more serious defense. When Fa-hsiu first criticized Huang T'ing-chien for writing "erotic songs and little *tz'u*," Huang tried to deny any wrongdoing, saying, "They are just words in the air [*k'ung-chung yü erh*]. I'm not killing anyone, and I'm not stealing. Surely I won't be sentenced to one of the evil destinies for writing these songs." This response brings up a number of issues. It is not immediately clear what Huang means by "words in the air." The phrase might conceivably refer to the fictionality of these literary works, or even to the distinction between the "voice" or persona of the songs and the author. In either case, Huang would be saying, in effect, that it is unfair for any listener to connect Huang personally with the emotions or liaisons described in his songs. (Thus, the voice of an older man infatuated with young girls, so common in Huang's songs, is not to be identified with Huang himself.) Huang would be shielding himself from criticism by appealing to the fictional world of the songs and the right a writer has to create such a world without being personally implicated in it.

Such distinctions are, of course, familiar to us and are regularly employed in our own reading of *tz'u*. In light of the rest of Huang's comment, however, it seems that the distinction he has in mind might more accurately be described as one of words versus deeds rather than that of persona versus author (if he is not simply thinking of the orality of the words "in the air" as they are sung for the listeners' enjoyment). These two vary in their focus: the former focuses on the author and the difference between what he says and what he does, while the latter focuses on the literary work and the question of whose voice it presents. There is, at the same time, another point or argument implicit in Huang's remarks: whatever culpability may be assigned to him, it is certainly of a minor sort and far less serious than that which results in murder or theft. Neither argument carries any weight with the Buddhist Fa-hsiu, who counters that insofar as Huang's erotic songs incite other men to immoral behavior, Huang's culpability is heavy indeed. Huang seems to have no response to this charge about the effects his songs may have upon male listeners.

Chang Lei wrote one of the two surviving Northern Sung prefaces for *tz'u*, one for the works of Ho Chu.[70] The preface is a concise apology for

69. See *Ho-yin Ssu-k'u ch'üan-shu tsung-mu t'i-yao chi Ssu-k'u wei-shou shu-mu chin-hui shu-mu* (Taipei: Shang-wu yin-shu-kuan, 1978), 5:4419.

70. *Chang Yu-shih wen-chi* (*SPTK* ed.), 51.15b–16a.

Ho's compositions and is fraught with the sense that some sort of defense is necessary. Essentially, Chang seeks to exonerate Ho by arguing,
first, that he could not help himself and, second, that he certainly did
not put any effort or thought into his compositions. Chang's statement
is particularly noteworthy for its squeamishness over the sentiment in
Ho Chu's *tz'u*. Chang points out that even Liu Pang and Hsiang Yü,
rival claimants to the throne after the fall of the Ch'in dynasty, had
their sentimental moments. And yet how could they, of all men, be considered "girlish"? Chang even attempts to separate the author somewhat from the emotion found in the lines he wrote: the author merely
uses the songs to "lodge his intent" (not "his emotion").

The last defense of *tz'u* that will be considered here may be the best-
known one from the Northern Sung. It is the preface Huang T'ing-chien
wrote for Yen Chi-tao's *tz'u*. The piece is not dated, but it must have
been written toward the end of the eleventh century.[71] Huang T'ing-
chien died in 1105, and Yen Chi-tao died at roughly the same time. The
preface reads as if it is intended to console Yen Chi-tao in his final
years.

As the seventh and last son of Grand Councilor Yen Shu, Yen Chi-tao
had a remarkably undistinguished career. We know that he sometimes
held the assignment of vice prefect and that he once served as supervisor of Hsü-t'ien Garrison.[72] These were hardly eminent positions for a
man who had spent his boyhood in the environs of the imperial palace
(and is reported to have once impressed Jen-tsung at a banquet with his
poetic ability).[73] It is also recorded that Yen Chi-tao was once imprisoned for his connections with Cheng Hsia, a man who protested Wang
An-shih's reforms too vigorously in the 1070s, and that Yen removed
himself from government service well before the normal retirement age,
after which he went on living privately in the capital.[74] All in all, Yen
Chi-tao can hardly be said to have lived up to what might fairly have
been expected of him, given his advantages.

For his literary friends and would-be eulogizers, Yen Chi-tao's life
presented yet another problem. He seems to have written *tz'u* almost ex-

71. Hsia Ch'eng-t'ao (*T'ang Sung tz'u-jen nien-p'u*, p. 261) estimates that Yen Chi-tao
compiled his collection of *tz'u* in approximately 1101. This matches my speculation about
the date of the collection's preface.

72. My source for Yen Chi-tao's biography is Hsia Ch'eng-t'ao's *nien-p'u* in his *T'ang
Sung tz'u-jen nien-p'u*. See also Yang Chi-hsiu, *Hsiao-shan tz'u yen-chiu* (Taipei: Li-ming
wen-hua shu-chü, 1985), pp. 5–10.

73. Huang Sheng (mid-13th cent.), *T'ang Sung chu-hsien chüeh-miao tz'u-hsüan* (*SPTK*
ed.), 3.12a–b.

74. Wang Cho (early 12th cent.), *Pi-chi man-chih* (*THTP* ed.), 2.6a.

clusively. He did not leave a collection of *shih* poetry or other writings (the first important Northern Sung *tz'u* writer to fail to do so). Thus, compensation for his lackluster official career could not be found in his literary work, or at least it could not be found in the conventional ways. We do not know whether Yen Chi-tao asked Huang T'ing-chien to write this preface or if Huang volunteered to do so out of fondness for Yen. Although Yen was not one of Huang's close friends, Huang was kindly disposed toward him (as shown by his attempt to introduce Yen to Su Shih). In any case, the task Huang undertook was not an easy one. He responded by pursuing various lines of defense and justification:

> Yen Shu-yüan is the youngest son of the lord of Lin-tzu [Yen Shu]. He is a large man with an imposing manner and is a stranger to inhibition. In writing and calligraphy he makes his own rules. He is fond of evaluating other men but has no use for the world's judgment of him. Although the gentlemen of the age praise and love him, they consider him lacking in self-restraint. So it is that he has always been confined to low positions. All his life he hid his mind in the six arts and delighted in the philosophers. The opinions he held were lofty, but he never sought to peddle them in the world. Puzzled over this, once I asked him about it. "Even as I crawl meekly along," he answered, "I am the object of other men's ill will. Were I to get angry and express my feelings, I would be spitting in people's faces." Therefore, he simply amused himself with the vestiges of *yüeh-fu* [i.e., *tz'u*], using the techniques of *shih* poets to write them. His compositions are fresh, vigorous, and forceful, so that they move any listener's heart. Gentlemen and officials circulate them, saying only that they capture the style of Lin-tzu's compositions. Few men are really able to appreciate their flavor.
>
> I have said this of Shu-yüan: he is definitely an outstanding man, but his foolishness is also exceptional. Those who love Shu-yüan were annoyed and asked me for the particulars. I said, "He has always been hobbled in his career and yet has never once stood outside the gate of powerful officials—this is one foolishness. He writes prose essays in his own style and refuses ever to adopt the language of recent *chin-shih* recipients—this is another foolishness. He spends cash by the million until his family members go cold and hungry, and yet his face maintains the expression of a little child—this is another foolishness. People are untrue to him but he bears no grudge, and once he trusts someone he cannot dream that the man will ever deceive him—this is another foolishness." My listeners allowed that it was all true.
>
> Despite everything, his *yüeh-fu* could be called the "Greater Odes" of the entertainment quarters, the ceremonial music of men of high standing. The best of them are in the tradition of the "Kao-t'ang" and "Lo Goddess" rhapsodies, and even the lesser ones are not inferior to the

"Peach Leaf" and "Round Fan" songs.[75] As a young man I myself used to write *yüeh-fu* occasionally, to accompany drinking and other amusements. The monk Fa-hsiu alone found fault with me, accusing me of using brush and ink to encourage promiscuity, and saying that according to the dharma I should be imprisoned in the Hell of Slit Tongues. But had he never seen Shu-yüan's songs? Regardless, in all comfortable households of the wealthy and powerful, where there are clever girls with pretty faces, if the master appreciates good writing, he will spend a thousand cash in the market to get a fine copy of Shu-yüan's lyrics, saying to anyone who criticizes him, "Aren't you also a man of Shu-yüan's era?" Handsome gentlemen in their prime who have recently come to know the enjoyments of women and wine, as well as undernourished scholars who have suffered for their principles and discover only late in life the attractions of flowing skirts—to cause both sorts of men to have these songs played and danced to while they poison themselves with feasting and pleasure and have no regret, this is the extent of Shu-yüan's crime![76]

There are three main points or arguments in this preface. Huang devotes the bulk of his preface to his theme of Yen Chi-tao as an eccentric and "foolish" man. From the very opening, with its reference to Yen as a "stranger to inhibition," on through the second paragraph, we are told to think of Yen as a maverick who has no thought for the world's opinion of him. The foolishnesses that are enumerated in the second paragraph are, of course, intended to sound endearing and even to be seen as marks of Yen's high moral standards. The implication is that Yen's *tz'u* themselves are another of these foolishnesses and that, as such, we are wrong to dismiss them as frivolous.

Huang is anxious to establish the point that the true intent or meaning of Yen Chi-tao's works is of a quite different and more profound order than their subject matter—women and wine. But why did Yen choose those subjects? His decision, Huang would have us believe, was rooted in his peculiar personality. The world failed to appreciate Yen, and Yen, of course, refused to alter his ways to win the world's esteem. Yen even refused to explain himself or vent his frustrations in the sort of literature (*shih* poetry) normally used for such purposes. (This would be "spitting in people's faces.") And so he turned instead to *tz'u*. Yen writes *tz'u* effectively, and those who hear them cannot but be moved by his words. But Huang, we gather, is moved by something else: when-

75. For these Chin dynasty love songs, see Kuo Mao-ch'ien (late 11th cent.), ed., *Yüeh-fu shih-chi* (Peking: Chung-hua shu-chü, 1979), 45.660 and 45.664–65.
76. Huang T'ing-chien, *Yü-chang Huang hsien-sheng wen-chi* (*SPTK* ed.), 16.24a–25a.

ever he hears Yen's *tz'u* he thinks of how misunderstood the author is and how he refuses to write seriously about being misunderstood. That is the true "flavor" of Yen's *tz'u* as they reverberate in Huang's ears. This is a twist upon the tactic, common in prefaces to *shih* collections, of pointing to a man's literary works as evidence of his *ts'ai*, "ability," that went unused by the world. Huang appreciates Yen's *tz'u* for what they do not say. This too is a recourse to a moralistic reading or defense of literature. In this case, the peculiarity of the reasoning has its roots in Yen's odd habit of writing nothing but *tz'u*.

Huang's second argument, broached just briefly at the start of his concluding paragraph, is that *tz'u* are, after all, just one more genre in a long and respectable line of song forms. He refers first to the ancient court and ceremonial music, and later to well-known early rhapsodies on goddesses and to pre-T'ang love songs. This defense was to become commonplace in the Southern Sung and can be found in the writings of many *tz'u* anthologists and critics, where it becomes a virtually obligatory opening statement. It is really quite unpersuasive, because it ignores the considerable differences in subject, tone, social role, and quantity between *tz'u* and earlier song forms. There was nothing in earlier literary history that very much resembled *tz'u*—certainly not the ceremonial odes in the *Book of Songs* or the goddess rhapsodies, whose origins must be in shamanistic incantations—and assertions to the contrary are transparent attempts to lay claim to a lineage that does not exist.

The third point Huang makes is more interesting. He confronts head-on the real problem with *tz'u*: the pervasive links that were perceived between these songs, female entertainers, and men of letters (who were interested in both). Huang gets around to his point by recalling, first, Fa-hsiu's criticism of Huang's own *tz'u*. It is almost as if Huang wants another chance, years later, to respond to the monk. Huang implies that Yen Chi-tao's songs are in even "worse taste" than his own and have greater potential for encouraging immoral conduct. Immediately, however, Huang falls back upon the songs' popularity: how, Huang wonders, can anything so widely accepted really be that bad? In his closing lines Huang's tone becomes ironic as he describes Yen's "crime" in terms calculated to make it sound utterly innocuous. This is a bold stroke: to face the charge of wrongdoing, admit guilt, and then laugh off the incrimination. No other Northern Sung defender of *tz'u* so openly confronts and brazenly dismisses, even if he does not really refute, the views of *tz'u*'s detractors.

Huang T'ing-chien's preface, coming as it does near the end of the Northern Sung, makes an apt terminus of this survey of attitudes toward *tz'u* in that period. The era came to a close before the "problem" of *tz'u* was really resolved. But partial justifications were being formulated, and some authors (e.g., Su Shih) even altered the way they wrote *tz'u* by way of response. Strictly speaking, it is illogical to suggest that the advances evident in Huang T'ing-chien's thinking about *tz'u* may have been connected or indebted to the innovations Su Shih made in practice. Huang T'ing-chien should have been thinking about the traditional subjects and tone of *tz'u*, not Su Shih's new style, when he wrote his preface for Yen Chi-tao. As is often pointed out, Huang and other of Su Shih's "followers" did not follow their mentor's lead in their own writing of *tz'u*.

Illogical as it may be, I suspect that there is some connection between Su Shih's new approach to *tz'u* writing and the new boldness his colleague shows in defending the genre. The effort Su Shih put into writing sober and highly personal *tz'u* from the mid-1070s onward cannot have gone unnoticed by his literary friends and must have had an impact on how the genre was perceived. There is something very public about Su Shih's involvement with *tz'u*. We know that many of his pieces were composed at parties amid gatherings of friends. As for the writers of the preceding generation (Yen Shu, Ou-yang Hsiu), we may speculate that their *tz'u* often had similar origins. But Su Shih tells us explicitly in prefaces and other notes when and why he wrote his songs. He calls attention to his engagement with the genre in a way that no writer had previously done. It is difficult to imagine Huang T'ing-chien broaching, in his preface to Yen Chi-tao's *tz'u*, such subjects as a seriousness underlying apparently frivolous pieces or the harmlessness of listening to songs if the prestigious Su Shih had not, through the openness of his involvement with songs, lent to the form a new respectability. Huang even appropriates the phrase that was commonly used to characterize Su Shih's innovation: writing *tz'u* using the techniques of *shih* poetry.

The stature of *tz'u* seems to have been enhanced somewhat by the end of the eleventh century. When Liu Yung died decades before, leaving nothing but an enormously popular collection of songs, no literatus saw fit to legitimate it with a preface. Likewise, Yen Shu and Ou-yang Hsiu remained remarkably silent about their own *tz'u* and kept them out of their literary collections. When these men died, no one mentioned *tz'u* in the various funerary and eulogistic pieces that commemorated their lives. But with Chang Hsien, who died in 1078, we begin to detect a change. In his preface to Chang's *shih* collection, Su Shih could still complain that the world appreciated Chang's *tz'u* but neglected his important literary work, his *shih*. This is a vestige of the old attitudes. But in another place, a formal panegyric for Chang Hsien, Su Shih actually mentions Chang's *tz'u* and suggests that they developed out of his *shih*.[77] Then, by the end of the century, we meet the novel case of Yen Chi-tao, the son of a grand councilor who was content to write nothing but *tz'u*, and we also encounter Huang T'ing-chien, who tried valiantly to defend him. At just about the same time Chang Lei took it upon himself to defend Ho Chu's *tz'u* writing.

If this change is accepted, it is tempting to go a step further and link it to a growing acceptance of various sorts of aesthetic endeavors, a proliferation of artistic legitimacies, that is evident in the exact same period. The causes of these changes outside the field of *tz'u* are too complex to explore here. But it can be said that in the last two decades of the century new claims are made for the seriousness of *shih* poetry, for calligraphy, and for scholarly painting. Su Shih and his friends had evidently become intrigued by the idea that a person must throw his energies into some activity to attain insight into the underlying principles of the world.[78] Virtually any activity would do (even tea connoisseurship),[79] anything that brought the person out of vacuous introspection and put him in intimate contact with some aspect of "the world" (*wu*). *Tz'u* is not specifically cited as one of the acceptable pursuits, and so any link between the small but discernible rise in its stature and this current of thought will have to remain speculative. The whole thrust of this new idea, however, is to lend legitimacy to activities formerly looked upon by many as less than profound. It is likely that the increasing acceptance of *tz'u* was peripherally connected with this idea and that in some complex way men like Yen Chi-tao are related, perhaps both as cause and consequence, to the new seriousness accorded to a broad array of cultural pursuits.

77. "Chi Chang Tzu-yeh wen," *Su Shih wen-chi*, 63.1943.

78. The clearest statement of this notion is contained in Su Shih's farewell to the monk Ssu-ts'ung, "Sung Ch'ien-t'ang seng Ssu-ts'ung kuei Ku-shan hsü," *Su Shih wen-chi*, 10.325–26.

79. See Su's "Shu Huang Tao-fu *P'in ch'a yao-lu* hou," *Su Shih wen-chi*, 66.2067.

Contexts of the Song Lyric in Sung Times:
Communication Technology, Social Change, Morality

Stuart H. Sargent

The song lyric embodies in its very form the experiencing of emotion, its prosody creating a morphology of feeling unprecedented in Chinese poetry (see the chapter by Stephen Owen in this volume). This characteristic prosody reminds us of the genre's musical origins and of the fact that it was once preeminently performance literature. Yet from the beginning the song lyric also existed in handwritten texts. Moreover, it soon passed into print and, far from being ephemeral, was seen by posterity as the most important Sung contribution to Chinese poetry.

The following essay addresses the significance of the various means by which lyrics were preserved in writing. I shall give special attention along the way to the printing of song lyrics in Chiang-nan West Circuit and the ideological affiliations and changing geographical distribution of the song lyric composers there. Finally, I shall touch upon possible implications of the parallel flourishing of song lyrics and printing in China up into the thirteenth century, with regard to both the genre's evolution and its acceptance as an art form open to morally serious persons.

PERFORMANCE AND TEXT: INKED AND ENGRAVED INSCRIPTIONS

The song lyric, though it may occasionally share themes and imagery with poems (*shih*), differs from poetry in that its characteristic phrasing

This study would not have been possible without a semester's leave funded by the Office of Graduate Studies and Research, University of Maryland, College Park Campus.

suggests very strongly its origins in oral performance, a musical performance in which pauses, turns, and variations in rhythm could mimic the experiencing of emotions. Yet this genre was stored in writing from the beginning and composed in writing centuries after its music was lost. To understand the genre, we cannot ignore the ways song lyrics functioned in written, and later printed, texts and the circumstances under which they became part of the print culture of the Sung dynasty.

It is because song lyrics were often written down that we know in remarkable detail the range of songs performed during the T'ang and Five Dynasties: many of the earliest examples were preserved in the dry air of cave 17 at Tun-huang. Included in the song lyrics recorded in blank spaces on the various Tun-huang documents is performance poetry of all types, from refined compositions to the popular song lyrics that we might have expected to have died with their oral culture.

We do not know who recorded these lyrics or why they did so. While the vast majority of the Chinese must have been illiterate until well into modern times, in absolute terms the number of merchants, government clerks, monks, and professional entertainers whose occupations required some degree of literacy was also quite high. Tun-huang, remote from the centers of agrarian Chinese civilization but an important stopping place on the trade routes through Central Asia, was a locus of activity for all these categories of people, and it must be their tastes that are reflected in the songs preserved there, whether the song texts were written down at Tun-huang or imported from other parts of China.

It is sometimes said that song lyrics found on the margins or backs of various documents were simply texts used for writing practice. But many of the words in the lyrics must have been of no immediate practical use for the novice accountant, monk, or clerk. I suggest that these notations represent rather the simple storage of favorite songs as an aid to memorization or a backup to recollection: once the song lyric was fixed in the mind or successfully performed, the written text had discharged its function.

Such notations contrast with cases in which chirographic song lyric texts were treated with more reverence, evidently preserved and treasured for their own sake. P. 3994, a four-page booklet datable to the first half of the ninth century, is an extant example of such a text. It contains six song lyrics: four of these are clearly elite compositions (three are attributed elsewhere to known literati), and two are rough and unrefined. Marsha Wagner observes:

> The neat calligraphy of booklet P. 3994 suggests that this handbook was not the exercise of a schoolboy. It was perhaps copied out by an educated

man as a memento of a visit, perhaps to a Chiang-nan entertainment center. Or it may have been intended as an art object for trade. Whatever its purpose, it includes a wide stylistic range, from an abstract and evocative elite poem to a concrete and flat popular verse, with several intermediate gradations between these two extremes.[1]

One of the "Palace Lyrics" by Lady Androecia (Hua-jui fu-jen) of the Later Shu court may help explain how P. 3994 came into being. It tells of the text of a new song lyric being bestowed on courtiers by their ruler in booklet (*pen*) form, then copied avidly in (commercial?) scriptoria (*shu-chia*).[2]

We do not know whether such a booklet would have been read silently or used simply as an aid to a performer's memory. But in format and in its relation to performance, P. 3994 may be usefully compared with certain little printed pamphlets of sixteenth-century Germany: these contained one to four sets of lyrics (usually hymns, sometimes political propaganda), and on their title pages were designated the old tunes to which the new lyrics were to be sung.[3] In both the Chinese and the German cases, the music to which the lyrics were to be sung must have been so familiar that the owner of such a booklet could have sung them as he or she read them, either mentally or aloud. (Of course, in terms of content, the Chinese booklets and the German pamphlets are very different; while the motivation for copying the former would appear to have been aesthetic, the latter were clearly printed as propaganda. But this distinction may be too crude. Those who sang the German songs may have found it musically pleasurable to do so; and those who obtained copies of the songs bestowed on the court by the king of Later Shu surely would have treasured them for social reasons as well as aesthetic ones.)

Xylographic or Wood-block printing would seem to be the next step in song lyric preservation, but two other kinds of publication that were common in Sung China—inked inscriptions and stone engravings—raise several interesting issues.

1. Marsha L. Wagner, *The Lotus Boat: The Origins of Chinese* Tz'u *Poetry in T'ang Popular Culture* (New York: Columbia University Press, 1984), pp. 46–47.

2. *Ch'üan T'ang shih* (Peking: Chung-hua shu-chü, 1960), 798.8979; hereafter cited as *CTS*. Dr. Shih I-tui notes that this reveals the value which the elite and popular cultures alike placed on such texts. See his *Tz'u yü yin-yüeh kuan-hsi yen-chiu* (Peking: Chung-kuo she-hui k'o-hsüeh ch'u-pan she, 1989), p. 39.

3. See Kyle C. Sessions, "Song Pamphlets: Media Changeover in Sixteenth-Century Publicization," in *Print and Culture in the Renaissance*, ed. Gerald P. Tyson and Sylvia S. Wagenheim (Newark: University of Delaware Press, 1986), pp. 110–19.

The inked inscription written on a wall or other fixed surface resembles a manuscript text insofar as it must be copied manually to reach a wide audience. But it differs in that this form of publication was commonly done by the song lyricist himself as a personal statement. For example, Su Shih once went on a spring evening excursion that included a stop at a wineshop. When he awoke the following morning next to a bridge, he took out brush and ink and inscribed a song lyric to the *tiao*, or tune, "Hsi chiang yüeh" on a pier of the bridge.[4] In such a case, we may ask, who was the intended audience? Su Shih's composition utilizes an allusive wit that would not have been immediately accessible to the casual tourist, I think—if there were any "casual tourists" in Huang prefecture, where he was in exile at the time (1080–85). It is arguable that Su Shih wrote his new work on the pier because he lacked paper and needed to write either in the process of composition or as a memorandum of what he had orally composed (a crucial distinction, but one inaccessible to us nine centuries after the fact). But in addition, he surely knew his song lyric would be circulated by others, as were so many of his jottings. Even if the inscription had been made for his own purposes, it spoke to a larger audience he would never see, and he knew from experience that it would reach that audience in spite of the apparent inefficiency and transiency of his medium.

The process by which a song lyric inscription would be circulated is seen in the story of the lovely song lyric Hsieh I (d. 1113) left on the wall of a rest station in Apricot Village in the same prefecture. It is said that the keeper of the station got so tired of people asking to borrow writing brushes to copy it that he smeared it over with mud![5] Again, the lyricist must have known that his inscription would find a larger audience. In fact, Hsieh I's works were quite popular in his day, and we might suspect him of writing the inscription as a conscious means of feeding that popularity.

There are also stories of women who came to tragic ends in times of national crisis and left song lyric inscriptions clearly intended as testimonies for others to read. Abducted by soldiers, the women somehow

---

4.   He evidently made a copy for himself at some point, adding a preface to detail the circumstances of the lyric's composition. See T'ang Kuei-chang, ed., *Ch'üan Sung tz'u* (Hong Kong: Chung-hua shu-chü, 1977), 1:284–85; hereafter cited as *CST*. For helpful notes, see Wang Shui-chao, *Su Shih hsüan-chi* (Shanghai: Shang-hai ku-chi ch'u-pan-she, 1984), pp. 285–86.

5.   Hsüeh Li-jo, *Sung tz'u t'ung-lun* (Hong Kong: Chung-liu ch'u-pan-she, 1974), p. 155; "Chiang shen tzu," no. 2 (*CST*, 2:650) appears to be the song lyric, although Hsüeh identifies it as "Chiang ch'eng tzu."

escaped supervision long enough to pen their song lyrics on a wall and (usually) commit suicide.

Wei Chü-an (1268 *chin-shih*) relates two such incidents, though the eventual fates of the song-lyricist subjects are not mentioned. One involves a very young woman whose father died in the Chin attack that toppled the Northern Sung dynasty and who was subsequently taken north as a prisoner. When the convoy reached Hsiung-chou (approximately a hundred kilometers west of modern Tientsin), she wrote the details of her plight on the wall of a way station there and added a short song lyric (forty-four syllables to the tune "Chien tzu mu-lan-hua").[6] The other incident took place in 1277, in the last days of the Southern Sung. Passing troops kidnapped a woman. When they passed through Ch'ang-hsing, on the western side of Lake T'ai, she paused to inscribe a long and bitter lament in the form of "Ch'in-yüan ch'un" on the front of a wine storehouse, signing it "Liu of Yen-feng." Her work strikes me as a rather artless piece, but perhaps all the more pathetic for that very quality.[7]

We may wonder whether anyone could have had the discipline or composure to write song lyrics under such difficult conditions, and suspect that some stories might have been made up to frame or explain song lyrics whose actual provenance was unknown. If the stories ring true, of course, the song lyrics themselves still might have been touched up or refined in the process of copying and recopying as they entered the written record. But Liu's song lyric was probably not, to judge by its style, refined in the course of its transmission. Her story also establishes that a woman of the late thirteenth century could indeed have known at least some song lyric meters quite well, for if this were not the case, Wei Chü-an's anecdote would have had little credibility. Liu must have been confident that others could make sense of her text, either because they, too, knew the music that determined its prosody, or because they were accustomed to reading song lyrics as purely written texts.[8] Perhaps both are true.

6. *CST*, 2:988; *Mei-chien shih-hua* (*TSCC* 2572), C.39.
7. *CST*, 5:3420; *Mei-chien shih-hua*, C.39.
8. *Reading* a lyric, it seems to me, would be somewhat analogous to reading texts in premodern Malay, whose orthography was based on Arabic script and did not represent many of the vowels. The reciter had to comprehend large chunks of text at once to remove the ambiguities in the orthography of the individual words. The fact that literature in the Malay world was largely an aural experience made this less problematic than it would have been in a print culture; the texts were full of the formulas and repetitions which met the expectations of the audience and also provided the large units of meaning

The song lyric is functioning here in a stereotypical situation that probably reflects both real patterns of feminine resistance and paradigms of loyalty idealized by the survivors who did not martyr themselves. T'ao Tsung-i, who lived into the Ming dynasty, leaves among his jottings (concerning everything from Yüan dynasty bureaucracy to a castrated male dog's giving birth to puppies) a cluster of similar anecdotes about women who maintained their integrity after the fall of the Sung and invariably left behind poems or song lyrics as testimony. One such woman, captured in 1266 when Hang-chou fell, left a song lyric to the *tiao* "Man chiang hung" on a way station wall, lamenting the end of her life as a palace lady. (After resettling in the north, she became a Taoist nun.) Another, the wife of a man of Yüeh-chou, on the eastern shore of Lake Tung-t'ing, was taken east to Hang-chou. On the way she used her wits to avoid rape and her beauty to avoid execution; but when it became clear that her captor in the fallen capital was going to have his way with her, she asked for a few private moments to pray to her late husband, used the time allotted to write a song lyric to "Man t'ing fang" on a wall, and drowned herself in a pond. Her song lyric is a medium-length lament for the fallen dynasty. There are similar anecdotes involving other forms of literature.[9]

These women captured T'ao's imagination. Their plights symbolized the helplessness of the whole society, and their refusal to yield to their captors was a model for male resistance. The symbolism is not perfect, to be sure: these women have the power to thwart the foe's invasion of their bodies by committing suicide; to prevent the invasion of one's homeland requires a collective sacrifice on the part of many individual defenders over an extended period of time. But resistance on either scale calls for resoluteness, and that is what the anecdotes are about. The song lyric, too, plays a crucial role in the stories: without these inscriptions to initiate the publication of the women's "fine reputations," their suicides would have been forgotten gestures.

---

needed by the reciter. See Amin Sweeney, *A Full Hearing: Orality and Literacy in the Malay World* (Berkeley: University of California Press, 1987), pp. 85, 89–90. The absence of punctuation or line breaks in premodern Chinese orthography creates an ambiguity corresponding somewhat to the paucity of vowels in old Malay manuscripts. In the Chinese case, the individual morphemes are clearer, but the reader may hesitate in deciding the boundaries of words, phrases, and rhythmic units. Therefore, storage and transmission of lyrics in written form presupposes enough acquaintance on the part of the reader with the underlying music to make the meter intelligible.

9. *Ch'o-keng lu* (*TSCC* 0218), 3.57–59. *CST*, 5:3420, has the lyric from the second anecdote mentioned above, with only one variant character, citing a *Tung-yüan k'o-t'an*.

Another kind of song lyric publication is the engraving of texts on stone. Here we are no longer dealing with the lyricist's own motives and his or her expectations as to who the audience might be, but with the motives of those who caused the engravings to be made. Perhaps, engraved in fine calligraphy and placed in scenic spots, such song lyrics served to enhance the landscape. But engravings might also have been executed for the purpose of making rubbings that could circulate in greater quantity and more efficiently than handwritten copies from a scriptorium.[10]

For example, ten song lyrics by P'an Lang (d. 1009) on the various charms of Hang-chou and its West Lake were engraved on stone at a government office in Hsü-chou; later, a minor official employed in Hang-chou obtained the text and, thinking it appropriate to have the lyrics engraved at West Lake, did so in 1108.[11] We would expect the text engraved at Hsü-chou, far from West Lake, to have been destined for distribution in the form of rubbings; the West Lake inscription might have been intended for either display or mass reproduction.

When lyrics are engraved for display, the question arises as to how intelligible they were to the nonspecialist public; it is likely that people from many walks of life would have seen the engraved text, like the inked inscription, whether they understood it or not. An intriguing variation in the rhyme schemes of the ten song lyrics by P'an Lang must have given pause to the casual reader. The first one rhymes *abb, aacc*, but in the other nine song lyrics the first line rhymes with no other line. Moreover, the second through seventh song lyrics establish an *alternating* pattern of three rhymes—*xaa, bbcc*—(nos. 2, 4, 6) and two rhymes—*xaa, bbaa* (nos. 3, 5, 7). The last three song lyrics revert to the three-rhyme scheme *xaa, bbcc*. Ideally, this cycle should have been performed, so the elements of repetition and surprise could have been highlighted by singer and musicians to give shape and pleasure to what would otherwise have been merely a challenging puzzle. But I doubt

10. Almost all of Su Shih's letters were engraved on stone and circulated as rubbings. See Chu Ch'uan-yü, *Sung-tai hsin-wen shih* (Taipei: Shang-wu yin-shu-kuan, 1967), introduction.

11. Jao Tsung-i, *Tz'u-chi k'ao* (Hong Kong: Hsiang-kang ta-hsüeh ch'u-pan-she, 1963), 2.34–35. The minor official was named Huang Ching; he became a *chin-shih* only in 1112; see Ch'ang Pi-te et al., eds., *Sung-jen chuan-chi tzu-liao so-yin* (Taipei: Ting-wen shu-chü, 1974–75), 4:2875. Individual lyrics from this cycle had attracted attention long before Huang Ching's time; see Chao Wan-li, ed., *Chiao-chi Sung Chin Yüan jen tz'u* (Peiping: Kuo-li chung-yang yen-chiu yüan, li-shih yü-yen yen-chiu-so, 1931), p. 2a. Only one lyric besides the decade on Hangchow is attributed to P'an Lang; see *CST*, 1:5–6, for the lot.

that many people in 1108 could sing them readily, for they are in an anomalous form of a *tiao* that is itself rare in the written record.[12] It is likely, therefore, that those who caused P'an Lang's ten song lyrics to be inscribed at Hsü-chou and Hang-chou published them either for the specialist or for readers who would treasure them simply as mementos of West Lake (or of a song lyric performance heard there), regardless of their own ability to recreate them fully as musical or literary experiences.

Hu Tzu (1082–1143) records two conflicting stories about the discovery of an old inscription that I believe must have been made for the production of rubbings. Known to us as "Fish Sport in the Spring Waters" ("Yü yu ch'un-shui"),[13] the song lyric is perhaps pre-Sung in origin. According to one account, it was discovered in Yüeh-chou (modern Shao-hsing, Chekiang) during the Cheng-ho period (1111–18), on the back of an old stele. Such a "recycled" stone would not have served for display purposes, but it would have provided a ready-made surface for engraving a text for rubbings. According to the other source, the song lyric was found on a stone uncovered near K'ai-feng in the course of excavations undertaken for flood control. It had no name and, in the words of the former account, "no *p'u*," no designation for music. In both accounts, the song lyric was presented to the emperor, Hui-tsung, who gave it its title and had it set to music.[14] Now, if this song lyric, whose theme is the separation of a couple during spring, was in fact engraved without the name of its *tiao*, this could mean that the song was so popular originally that no such information was necessary. But in the twelfth century, music being extremely ephemeral in the absence of sophisticated notational techniques, Hui-tsung had to command his experts to provide new music to make it performable again: this suggests that a song lyric still could not be properly enjoyed without being performed musically, although it could be argued that Hui-tsung would have

12. Of all the other lyricists represented in *CST* and born before 1108, only four use *tiao* by the same name, but in every case the last line of each stanza has two fewer syllables, there is a single rhyme, and the second line of the second stanza never rhymes. Yen Shu (991–1055) wrote two (*CST*, 1:95); Ch'ao Pu-chih (1053–1101), one (1:555); Wang Cho, one (2:1035); and Ts'ao Hsün (1098–1162), five, four of which are unique in rhyming the fourth syllable—like the first lyric in P'an Lang's series (2:1229 and 1231).

13. *CST*, 5:3651.

14. See Hu Tzu's *T'iao-hsi yü-yin ts'ung-hua—hou-chi* (1167), in *Pi-chi hsiao-shuo ta-kuan* (Taipei: Hsin-hsing shu-chü, 1983), vol. 35, 39.325. One account cited by Hu, in the *Fu-chai man-lu*, quotes the lyric; it is 89 syllables in length. The other, in *Ku-chin tz'u-hua* (cf. the *Chiao-chi Sung Chin Yüan jen tz'u* ed., pp. 18–19), quotes the lyric in 89 syllables but states that it has 94 syllables.

demanded the court performance of this old text in any case in order to endow its recovery with a significance auspicious for his reign.

Despite what I have just said, it should be noted that certain *tiao* could be performed without complex musical accompaniment. Some examples are found among the song lyrics that frequently served the proselytical purposes of Buddhism. In form, these songs were evidently thought to be derived from fishermen's songs; their melodies are variously identified as "Fisherman's Pride" ("Yü-chia ao"), "Oar Thrust" ("Po cho-tzu"), or "Fisherman's Song" ("Yü ko-tzu"). The early Sung *Shih-shih yao-lan* attests to contemporary "Ch'an masters in the south" using "Fisherman" and "Oar-Thrusting" song lyrics for preaching; the author of the *Shih-shih yao-lan*, a Hang-chou monk named Tao-ch'eng, traces this practice back to the Indian beginnings of Buddhism, citing a musician in Rajagrha who made songs to inspire believers.[15]

Several anecdotes suggest that such songs required little more than the human voice for performance. In one case, a monk named Tsung-kao (also known as Ta-hui, 1089–1163) goes boating with a friend named Li P'eng. Beating time with an oar, Tsung-kao sings "The Fisherman" ("Yü-fu"), then challenges Li to write hymns of praise for the various masters in the lineage of his first teacher, which he will then sing to the same tune. Li P'eng produces ten such song lyrics "in jest" before their outing is finished.[16] This episode tells us that these songs were sung with no musical accompaniment other than a percussion beat; we know also that Ou-yang Hsiu (1007–72) used the *tiao* "Yü-chia ao" to write a set of song lyrics on the twelve months for performance with a small drum (although there is some confusion as to which of two such sets is properly attributable to him).[17] Perhaps the beat was often marked even more simply, by clapping the hands or striking two sticks together. Wang An-shih (1021–86) used to go walking in the hills with the sometime monk Yü-ch'an, who sang for him the "Yü-chia ao" he composed;[18] presumably, there was no elaborate musical accompani-

15. T.2127.305a. See also Wu Tseng's *Neng-kai chai man-lu* (1157) (TSCC ed.), 2.33; in *Pi-chi hsiao-shuo ta-kuan* (Yangchow: Chiang-su Kuang-ling ku-chi k'o-yin-she, 1984), vol. 4; it appears at 1.20a. Wu appears to copy Tao-ch'eng, but mentions the Indian precedent last, rather than first.

16. Hsiao-ying, *Kan-shan yün-wo chi-t'an*, quoted by Kanda Kiichirō, *Nihon ni okeru Chūgoku bungaku*, vol. 1, *Nihon tenshi shiwa* (Tokyo: Nigensha, 1965), p. 40.

17. *CST*, 1:136–38.

18. Wei Ch'ing-chih (13th cent.), *Shih-jen yü-hsieh*, 2d ed. (Shanghai: Shang-hai ku-chi ch'u-pan-she, 1978), 2:404.

ment for these *al fresco* performances. (We do not know the content of
Yü-ch'an's songs, but the pair of "Yü-chia ao" lyrics in Wang's own
collected works describe simple country scenes and quiet thoughts such
as might have been experienced on such outings.)[19] The fact that every
line in this *tiao* rhymes, with no change in rhyme throughout, creates an
insistent, recurrent element that suggests a strong percussive beat.[20]

To sum up what we know so far: chirographic preservation of song
lyrics served as an aid to memorization, but handsome texts could be
treasured as souvenirs; inscriptions that were written on walls or engraved on stone were more likely to achieve successful "publication" of
song lyrics, and suggest the existence of a fairly sizable public that could
decipher or sing metrically complex texts.

PRINTING AND THE SONG LYRIC: THE SOCIAL DIMENSION

Printed books containing song lyrics often tell us something about the
motivations of their publishers, but do not necessarily tell us any more
about how the printed song lyrics were used by the owners of the books
than do the forms of publication discussed so far. Sample data from
Chiang-nan West Circuit, where eighteen localities are known to have
published books during the Sung,[21] will acquaint us with the types of
projects that resulted in song lyrics' being stored in print as well as the
changing social context of their composition and preservation.

Twenty-five song lyricists from Chiang-nan West Circuit are represented in the *Ch'üan Sung tz'u* by twenty or more song lyrics. Of these
twenty-five lyricists, twelve were published in one or more series put out
by commercial publishers outside the circuit around the beginning of
the thirteenth century. These are Yen Shu (991–1055), Ou-yang Hsiu,
Yen Chi-tao, Huang T'ing-chien, Hsieh I, Wang T'ing-kuei (1080–
1172), Yang Wu-chiu (1097–1171), Yüan Ch'ü-hua (1145 *chin-shih*),
Ching T'ang (1138–1200), Shih Hsiao-yu (1166 *chin-shih*), Chao Shih-

19. *Lin-ch'uan hsien-sheng ch'üan-chi* (Hong Kong: Chung-hua shu-chü, 1971), 37.400.

20. As Ch'en Pang-yen pointed out in his paper for this conference, however, the nature of a given song lyric depends as much on its theme and the style of the poet as on
the *tiao* selected. It should be noted that "Yü-chia ao" is the *tiao* most frequently used (14
times) in the song lyrics of Yen Shu (991–1055), who is known for his soft and romantic
style. See Wu Hsiung-ho, *T'ang Sung tz'u t'ung-lun*, 2d ed. (Shanghai: Shang-hai ku-chi
ch'u-pan she, 1978), p. 134.

21. See Chang Hsiu-min, "Nan Sung (1127–1279) k'o-shu ti-yü k'ao," *T'u-shu kuan*
1961, no. 3: 53, for a chart of all 173 localities with known publication activity in the
Southern Sung.

hsia (1175 *chin-shih*), and Yang Yen-cheng (1145–?). I shall discuss these commercial editions in more detail later.

Within the circuit, perhaps the earliest printing of a native son's works that included song lyrics was the 1196 publication of Ou-yang Hsiu's collected works in Lu-ling, the administrative seat of Chi prefecture. Chi was not only home to the major kilns of Sung and Yüan times, but also one of the richest rice-growing areas in the country. Already fifth in production of *chin-shih* in the first century of the Northern Sung, the prefecture supported a large literati population.[22] In fact, the entire Kan River basin from Chi prefecture north to Nan-ch'ang was as prosperous in terms of its agricultural yield as it was in terms of its examination graduates.

Ou-yang Hsiu was not born in the prefecture, but his family was registered in Lu-ling, and it is natural that a major compilation of the works of such an illustrious "native" should be undertaken and printed there. As early as 1122, a version of his works had been published by the Envoy Storehouse (*kung-shih k'u*) in Lu-ling. Established to serve the needs of visiting capital envoys, such units had opportunities to siphon off funds for publication projects as well as for private favors.[23] The 1196 edition of Ou-yang's works, more complete, was reprinted at least twice soon afterwards in other parts of the circuit.[24] There is no evidence that this 1196 project was either a commercial or government-sponsored endeavor; it was probably a private effort by the local elite. One Lo Mi was responsible for editing the portion devoted to Ou-yang's song lyrics.[25]

Chou Pi-ta (1126–1204), who was directing the Ou-yang Hsiu project, at about the same time also had a hand in printing the works of Wang T'ing-kuei from An-fu, about fifty-five kilometers to the north-

22. John W. Chaffee, *The Thorny Gates of Learning in Sung China: A Social History of Examinations* (Cambridge: Cambridge University Press, 1985), pp. 111, 149.

23. See Li Chih-chung, "Sung-tai k'o-shu shu-lüeh," *Wen-shih* 14 (July 1982): 157. The title of the 1122 edition of Ou-yang's works is given there as *Liu-i chü-shih chi*, in fifty *chüan* with another fifty-*chüan* continuation. There is no mention of lyrics. Li also notes that an Envoy Storehouse at O-chou in Ching-hu North Circuit (near modern Wu-han) published the *Hua-chien chi* in 1187. On the establishment of the Envoy Storehouses at the beginning of the dynasty and the danger of storehouse funds' being misused, see Liu Ts'en (1087–1167), as quoted in Wang Ming-ch'ing, *Hui-chu hou-lu* (1194) (*TSCC* ed.), 1.208–9.

24. Abe Ryūichi, "Tenri toshokan zō Sō Kin Gan hambon kō," *Biblia* 75 (October 1980): 407. One of these later editions must be the 1198 version mentioned by Li Chih-chung, "Sung-tai k'o-shu," p. 159.

25. Ronald C. Egan, *The Literary Works of Ou-yang Hsiu (1007–72)* (Cambridge: Cambridge University Press, 1984), pp. 2, 10.

west of Lu-ling but still in Chi prefecture. This edition apparently did
not include Wang's song lyrics. (Most of his forty-two surviving lyrics
are minor works celebrating plum blossoms, social outings, and the
like.) The work was edited by a protégé and carried prefaces by such
prominent locals as Hu Ch'üan (1102–80) and Yang Wan-li (1127–
1206), both of whom, with Chou Pi-ta, were outspoken critics of the
weak, despotic, and corrupt central government.

Wang T'ing-kuei was respected locally as a literary figure just as Ou-
yang Hsiu was throughout the empire, and yet the publication of their
literary works could be seen as a political act. If we look more closely at
the prefaces to Wang T'ing-kuei's works and the identities of their authors, we find that Hu Ch'üan was one of a number of hostile opponents
of Ch'in Kuei's policy of negotiation with the Chin state in 1138. It was
because of a farewell poem Wang presented to Hu when the latter
was on his way to exile—the result of petitioning for Ch'in Kuei's
execution[26]—that Wang T'ing-kuei himself was exiled to a remote post
in Ching-hu North Circuit in 1148 (some sources say 1143 or 1149). In
Ou-yang Hsiu's case, Lo Mi's decision to exclude song lyrics he felt unworthy of his image underscores the fact that the scholarly urge to preserve was at least matched by the urge to uphold certain moral ideals.[27]

Lu-ling song lyricists Yang Yen-cheng (a cousin of Yang Wan-li) and
Liu Kuo (1154–1206) were both associated with Hsin Ch'i-chi (1140–
1207), and their styles show evidence of his influence. The works of Liu
Kuo as edited by his younger brother included his song lyrics; they were
printed in the mid-1230s, but the nature and the place of publication
are obscure.

We do know that the song lyrics of Liu Hsien-lun (fl. late 12th cent.)
were published in Lu-ling: a Chi prefecture edition is mentioned by
Huang Sheng in the mid-thirteenth century.[28] Among the thirty-one
song lyrics ascribed to Liu in the *Ch'üan Sung tz'u* are song lyrics composed for birthdays and banquets, but there are also a few compositions
voicing vaguely heroic frustrations, leading the modern scholar Hsüeh
Li-jo to place Liu Hsien-lun, with Yang Yen-cheng, in a line of "indig-
nant" song lyricists who shared the ethos of Hsin Ch'i-chi.[29]

The publications by Chou Pi-ta that came out of Chi prefecture were
presumably printed at private facilities. The expense need not have

---

26. See Jao Tsung-i, *Tz'u-chi k'ao*, 4.130; and Teraji Jun's superb *Nan Sō shoki seijishi
kenkyū* (Hiroshima: Keisuisha, 1988), pp. 172 and 471.

27. See Egan, *Ou-yang Hsiu*, p. 194, for a summary of Lo Mi's decisions.

28. Huang faults it for being incomplete; see Jao Tsung-i, *Tz'u-chi k'ao*, 4.170.

29. Hsüeh Li-jo, *Sung tz'u t'ung-lun*, p. 235.

been great; xylography in China required far less capital investment and technological expertise than printing with movable type.[30] Song lyrics were also printed at facilities one would normally suppose to have been publicly funded. We have already noted an 1122 Envoy Store-house edition of Ou-yang Hsiu's works. Likewise, schools affiliated with various local administrative units could be mobilized to publish the works of an individual. It was in the school of his native Nan-ch'ang, the administrative seat of Hung prefecture in Chiang-nan West Circuit, that the works of Ching T'ang were printed in 1199, one year before his death.[31]

Because xylography was relatively inexpensive, local government academies found publishing a lucrative way of raising funds.[32] But the man who undertook the Ching T'ang project in Nan-ch'ang, Huang Ju-chia, may have had other motives: Huang considered himself a protégé of Ching, who at that time held high office in the Han T'o-chou adminis-tration. Huang's private publication in the same year of Lü Pen-chung's (1084–1145) works, possibly including song lyrics, is therefore some-what puzzling at first glance.[33] Lü (who was not a native of Chiang-nan West Circuit but had moved south to Hang-chou from Huai-nan West) took his intellectual direction from the major neo-Confucian thinker Yang Shih (1053–1135), which would seem to place him in the tradition of the "false learning" whose proponents were persecuted by the Han T'o-chou administration from 1195 through 1200. But Lü was also one of a number of scholars allied with Chao Ting (1085–1147), who, while he had influence at court from 1134 to 1138, had advocated a strong but cautious strategy against the Chin state.[34] Ching T'ang held similar

30. See Evelyn S. Rawski, "Economic and Social Foundations of Late Imperial Cul-ture," in *Popular Culture in Late Imperial China*, ed. David Johnson, Andrew J. Nathan, and Evelyn S. Rawski (Berkeley and Los Angeles: University of California Press, 1985), pp. 17–22.

31. Jao Tsung-i, *Tz'u-chi k'ao*, 4.165. The lyrics included were largely composed as re-sponses to other people's lyrics or in connection with seasonal outings Ching took while serving in Szechuan. See *CST*, 3:1841.

32. Ming-sun Poon, "Books and Printing in Sung China (960–1279)" (Ph. D. diss., University of Chicago, 1979), pp. 95–97.

33. Li Chih-chung, "Sung-tai k'o-shu," p. 159, is my source for the date and pub-lisher of this edition. The *wai-chi* in three *chüan*, which is mentioned by Li but not by Jao (*Tz'u-chi k'ao*, 3.95), would have been the place to look for lyrics, if they were included.

34. Chao advocated concentration of military power, which was decentralized and somewhat uncontrollable at the time, under the emperor; he urged Kao-tsung to per-sonally lead a punitive expedition against the puppet state of Ch'i, as long as it could be done without directly engaging Ch'i's Chin backers. See Teraji Jun, *Nan Sō seijishi*, pp. 111–36.

views in his generation, and Huang must have been confident in 1199 that his mentor and Lü Pen-chung shared like minds and, perhaps, moral fiber as members of administrations committed to aggressive but responsible foreign policies. At the time Huang undertook publication of their works, Han T'o-chou's reckless northern campaign was still several years in the future.

The son or protégé of a man had an understandable interest in preserving that man's works, but print technology preserves *in surplus*, ensuring that the works will be part of the acknowledged body of literature not only for the contemporary generation but for posterity as well. The power imparted by this multiplication could enhance ideological solidarity or regional pride, justifying investment of the resources of the local elite or their educational institutions in the publication of a native son's collected works, even if no blood relation or master-disciple relationship was involved. These motivations can be inferred in the publication of Wang T'ing-kuei, Ou-yang Hsiu, and possibly Liu Hsien-lun in Lu-ling, and of Ching T'ang in Nan-ch'ang.

A growing regionalism is suggested by changes in the career patterns and geographical distribution of song lyricists in Chiang-nan West Circuit. Table 1 is based on one by John Chaffee,[35] with the addition of known song lyricists for the circuit who meet the criterion of a corpus of twenty or more extant song lyrics. It shows that the number of song lyricists rises dramatically along with the number of *chin-shih* in four of the five more populous core prefectures, but falls just as strikingly in Fu prefecture. One way to explain this anomaly would be to say that the disappearance of song lyricists from Lin-ch'uan was compensated for by the appearance of three Southern Sung song lyricists in Nan-feng, a mere hundred kilometers upriver in Chien-ch'ang military prefecture. The fact that the prose master Tseng Kung (1019–83), a native of Nan-feng, had founded a charitable estate in Lin-ch'uan suggests that the two towns could be considered part of the same subregion though they belonged to different prefectures. In this connection, the printing in Lin-ch'uan of the collected works of Ch'en Shih-tao (1053–1101), including his song lyrics, may be significant.[36] Ch'en was not a native son; and I would speculate that this project may have been supported by

35. Chaffee, *Thorny Gates of Learning*, Appendix 3, p. 197.

36. Knowledge of this edition comes by way of the thirteenth-century book collector Ch'en Chen-sun, who says it was published by a Liu Hsia-wei. See Chan Chih, ed., *Huang T'ing-chien ho Chiang-hsi shih-p'ai chüan* (Peking: Chung-hua shu-chü, 1978), 2:507–8. Liu entered the bureaucracy under the *yin* privilege but advanced to prominent national offices.

TABLE 1.   Song Lyricists of Chiang-nan West Circuit

Northern Sung		Southern Sung
	Chi Prefecture	
266 *chin-shih*		643 *chin-shih*
	An-fu	
		Wang T'ing-kuei (1080–1172)
	Lu-ling	
Ou-yang Hsiu (1007–72)		Yang Yen-cheng (1145–?)
		Liu Kuo (1154–1206)
		Liu Hsien-lun (fl. late 12th cent.)
		Liu Ch'en-weng (1232–97)
		P'eng Yüan-sun
		Chao Wen (1239–1315)
		Liu Chiang-sun (1257–?)
	Chiang Prefecture	
54 *chin-shih*		38 *chin-shih*
	Chien-ch'ang Military Prefecture	
195 *chin-shih*		452 *chin-shih*
	Nan-feng	
		Chao Ch'ang-ch'ing
		Chao Ch'ung-po (1198–1256)
		Liu Hsün (1240–1319)
	Ch'ien Prefecture	
76 *chin-shih*		87 *chin-shih*
	Fu Prefecture	
179 *chin-shih*		445 *chin-shih*
	Lin-ch'uan	
Yen Shu (991–1055)		
Wang An-shih (1021–86)		
Yen Chi-tao		
Hsieh I (d. 1113)		
	Hsing-kuo Military Prefecture	
22 *chin-shih*		52 *chin-shih*
	Yung-hsing	
Wu Tse-li (d. 1121)		

TABLE 1. (cont.)

Northern Sung		Southern Sung
	Hung Prefecture (Lung-hsing *fu*)	
174 *chin-shih*		375 *chin-shih*
	Fen-ning	
Huang T'ing-chien (1045–1105)	Feng-hsin	
		Yüan Ch'ü-hua (1145 *chin-shih*)
	Nan-ch'ang	
		Ching T'ang (1138–1200) Chao Shan-kua Shih Hsiao-yu (1166 *chin-shih*)
	Lin-chiang Military Prefecture	
156 *chin-shih*		234 *chin-shih*
	Ch'ing-chiang	Yang Wu-chiu (1097–1171)
	Hsin-kan	
		Chao Shih-hsia (1175 *chin-shih*)
	Nan-an Military Prefecture	
13 *chin-shih*		50 *chin-shih*
	Yüan Prefecture	
57 *chin-shih*		66 *chin-shih*
	Yün Prefecture	
33 *chin-shih*		114 *chin-shih*
	Kao-an	
Hui-hung (1071–1128)		

NOTE: Wang T'ing-kuei's life spanned both Northern and Southern Sung, but I have counted him among the Chi song lyricists of the Southern Sung; Ou-yang Hsiu is thus the sole representative of that prefecture in the Northern Sung, although he never lived there.

Tseng Kung's charitable estate because Ch'en had considered himself a student of the prose master in the 1070s.[37]

But we are dealing with more than a geographical shift. The four Lin-ch'uan song lyricists, like Huang T'ing-chien of Hung prefecture and Hui-hung of Yün, left Chiang-nan West and became widely known figures with few ties to their home regions. Their interests were probably more closely linked to their status as members of the bureaucracy than to the local economy. The three Nan-feng song lyricists, on the other hand, were not prominent outside their home region. Chao Ch'ang-ch'ing, an imperial agnate who left behind a considerable number of song lyrics, does not seem to have had a significant political career. Like several other lyricists from the circuit, he had some connection with Chang Hsiao-hsiang (1132–70), a native of Li-yang in Huai-nan East Circuit who played a distinguished role in the early part of the third Sung-Chin war (1161), which toppled the vestiges of the Ch'in Kuei regime. Chang was a serious song lyricist who measured himself against Su Shih.[38]

Chao Ch'ung-po, another imperial descendant in Nan-feng, similarly did not figure importantly in politics, though it must be noted that he often spoke out against various abuses during his career.[39] Liu Hsün was a Sung loyalist who composed poems on the martyrs and patriots of the fallen dynasty and served as instructor in a Confucian School in Fu-chien[40] during the Yüan dynasty. His thirty surviving song lyrics sing of eremitism and nostalgia.[41]

37. The estate was still supporting Tseng agnates in 1333, when a shrine hall was erected in Lin-ch'uan to further focus their sense of history and unity. See the commemorative essay by Yü Chi (1272–1348) in his *Tao-yüan hsüeh-ku lu* (*SPTK* ed.), 35.304a–b. See also Robert Hymes, *Statesmen and Gentlemen: The Elite of Fu-chou, Chiang-hsi, in Northern and Southern Sung* (Cambridge: Cambridge University Press, 1986), pp. 106–9.

38. Jao Tsung-i, *Tz'u-chi k'ao*, 3.119–20. Jao wonders if the editor of Chao Ch'ang-ch'ing's lyrics, Liu Tse, has any connection with the Liu bookshop and publishing business in Changsha; I wonder whether he has any connection with the Liu Hsiao-wei who published Ch'en Shih-tao's works in nearby Lin-ch'uan. Jao dates the lyric connected with Chang Hsiao-hsiang (*CST*, 3:1785) to 1264. On Chang, see Teraji Jun, *Nan Sō sei-jishi*, pp. 426–32, 470–72; and Wu Hsiung-ho, *T'ang Sung tz'u*, pp. 247–48.

39. See, for example, Chou Mi's *Ch'i-tung yeh-yü*, 2.83–84 (*TSCC* ed.), relating Chao's support for an attack on corruption when he was an assistant minister in the Chief Office of Imperial Clan Affairs. Only twenty of his lyrics survive.

40. Yves Hervouet, ed., *A Sung Bibliography* (Hong Kong: The Chinese University Press, 1978), p. 445 (where his name is romanized as Hsüan); Ch'ang Pi-te, *Sung-jen chuan-chi tzu-liao so-yin*, 5:3907. Hymes, *Statesmen*, p. 127, lists him as one of several Southern Sung "local advocates" in Fu prefecture who made appeals to the court for specific local relief—a pattern not seen in Northern Sung.

41. *CST*, 5:3331.

Other studies have suggested that the national government was losing importance through the Southern Sung and into the Yüan both as a promising arena in which to compete for power and position, and as an effective arbiter of local affairs.[42] During the effective reign of Ch'in Kuei, that is, 1142–55, most levels of government were monopolized by people who had personal ties to Ch'in or to the emperor; others were shifted from post to post so rapidly that their offices ceased to have any effective function. At the county level, fully one-third of the magistrate positions in the empire were vacant when Ch'in Kuei died, revealing both a remarkable failure to organize the 2,741 examination graduates of his regime[43] into a working bureaucracy and a strong local sentiment against participation in or cooperation with the government. Even in the 122 counties of the Liang-che circuits and Chiang-nan East, where the urgent need to establish Southern Sung sovereignty insured that most county-level posts were filled, almost no appointees can be demonstrated to have belonged to Ch'in Kuei's faction, and many of those who would become influential in the dismantling of his administration after 1155 rose from those ranks.[44]

This is not to say that the elite of Chiang-nan West Circuit cut themselves off from national politics; they did not. But the fact that the song lyricists cluster increasingly along the primary commercial routes through Nan-ch'ang, Feng-ch'eng, Lin-chiang military prefecture, Hsin-kan, and Lu-ling suggests that their fortunes were tied more to the local economies than to imperial largesse. This change is apparent when one looks at the distribution of song lyricists within each prefecture, summarized in table 1.

In Hung prefecture, Huang T'ing-chien was from the northwest hinterland, but as soon as we enter the Southern Sung, we are confined to the Kan River. Yüan Ch'ü-hua's native Feng-hsin is upstream from Nan-ch'ang. Like Chao Ch'ang-ch'ing of Nan-feng, Yüan Ch'ü-hua is the author of a song lyric that can be connected with Chang Hsiao-hsiang: Chang, a noted calligrapher as well as a strategist, had so liked Yüan's song lyric on a terrace in Ch'ang-sha that he wrote it out in his own hand.[45] This and similar song lyrics by Yüan are said to display

42. See Robert P. Hymes, "Marriage, Descent Groups, and the Localist Strategy in Sung and Yüan Fu-chou," in *Kinship Organization in Late Imperial China, 1000–1940*, ed. Patricia Buckley Ebrey and James L. Watson (Berkeley and Los Angeles: University of California Press, 1986), pp. 95–136; and Hymes, *Statesmen, passim*.

43. Teraji Jun, *Nan Sō seijishi*, p. 506 n. 132.

44. Ibid., pp. 323–91.

45. Jao Tsung-i, *Tz'u-chi k'ao*, 4.137. Jao ascribes this to sometime between 1165 and 1174, when Chang was administrator in Changsha.

the heroic qualities of Hsin Ch'i-chi's *tz'u*.[46] For Nan-ch'ang itself, we have Ching T'ang, exceptional as a prominent figure abroad as well as locally. Chao Shan-kua was an imperial agnate registered in Nan-ch'ang.[47] Among his song lyrics are one following the rhymes of a lyric Hsin Ch'i-chi wrote in 1179 at O prefecture in Ching-hu North Circuit—Chao was administrator there in that year—and two following the rhymes of a lyric Hsin wrote in 1181 at a new home in Hsin-chou, 150 kilometers east of Nan-ch'ang in Chiang-nan East Circuit.[48] Shih Hsiao-yu of Nan-ch'ang is known more for his song lyrics than anything else.[49] His admiration for Chang Hsiao-hsiang was expressed in a song lyric written sometime between the time Chang was made a drafter in the Secretariat and his death in 1170.

Moving south up the river, we find that the two song lyricists from Lin-chiang military prefecture are both men of the Southern Sung and both from locales on the Kan River itself. Yang Wu-chiu, who refused to serve under the first Southern Sung emperor, exchanged many song lyrics with Hsiang Tzu-yin, a member of a prominent old K'ai-feng family who fled to Lin-chiang and invested large sums in a school and a charitable estate for Hsiang's family. (In 1138, Hsiang played an important role in the Chao Ting government as an advocate of using rewards and punishments to bring order to the Sung armies, but he also contributed to a split in his faction by siding with Ch'in Kuei and against his own friends in advocating a peace treaty with the Chin.)[50] Chao Shih-hsia, an imperial agnate, lived upriver in Hsin-kan, eight kilometers south of Lin-chiang, although he was born before the fall of the Northern Sung and identifies himself in a postface (1187) to the *Tung-ching meng-hua lu* as a native of K'ai-feng.[51] Much of his career was spent in Chiang-nan West Circuit (1172–74, 1179–86) and Ching-hu South (1167, 1188–89, 1197). His literary and political affiliations are unclear; his song lyrics are occasional in theme.

In Chi prefecture, all song lyricists after Wang T'ing-kuei are from Lu-ling on the Kan River. We have already mentioned Yang Yen-cheng and Liu Kuo, both affiliated with Hsin Ch'i-chi, and Liu Hsien-lun, who was also vaguely in the same camp. After a brief hiatus, another

46. Hsüeh Li-jo, *Sung tz'u t'ung-lun*, pp. 232–33.
47. *CST*, 3:1980.
48. See *CST*, 3:1983 and 1981; and Hsin Ch'i-chi, *Chia-hsüan tz'u pien-nien chien-chu* (Taipei: Chung-hua shu-chü, 1970), 1.55 and 1.76.
49. *CST*, 3:2031.
50. Teraji Jun, *Nan Sō seijishi*, pp. 121, 143, 156–57.
51. Jao Tsung-i, *Tz'u-chi k'ao*, 4.162.

generation of Lu-ling song lyricists appears in the middle of the thirteenth century, taking us beyond the Sung. Liu Ch'en-weng (1232–97),
P'eng Yüan-sun, Chao Wen (1239–1315), and Liu Chiang-sun (1257–?)
are all Lu-ling song lyricists who survived into the Yüan. I have no information on the publication of their song lyrics as independent collections, but Liu Ch'en-weng, fearless critic of Chia Ssu-tao, and Chao
Wen, protégé of Wen T'ien-hsiang, both possess the Lu-ling spirit of
moral integrity. Liu Ch'en-weng and Liu Chiang-sun were both heads
of academies (*shu-yüan*).

Unlike the Northern Sung song lyricists from the peripheral areas of
the circuit, the Kan basin lyricists are generally not themselves pivotal
figures, either in literature or in administration. They appear generally
to have avoided association with the more venal regimes of the age; instead, we often find them using song lyrics to establish or commemorate
relationships with such figures as Hsin Ch'i-chi and Chang Hsiao-
hsiang.

PRINTING AND THE SONG LYRIC:
THE COMMERCIAL DIMENSION

In Ch'ang-sha in Ching-hu South Circuit (modern Hunan), a remarkable project was undertaken by a bookstore in the first decade of the
thirteenth century to publish the song lyrics of "a hundred poets" in
series. Ninety-seven poets are known to have been covered, in 128 *chüan*.
Nearly half of them have fewer than twenty song lyrics extant today; the
major criticism leveled at this project was that the publisher became
less and less selective in the quality and importance of the poets he
included as he filled out the series.[52]

Interestingly, only two song lyricists with twenty or more extant
lyrics were native to the prefecture of which Ch'ang-sha was the administrative seat, and neither of them native to Ch'ang-sha itself: Wang I-
ning, who relieved the siege of T'ai-yüan in 1126 and held various posts
outside the circuit into the 1140s,[53] and Liao Hsing-chih (1137–89),
whose career never took him outside the region.[54] To be sure, a number
of important song lyricists, many of whom were also important political
figures, passed through Ch'ang-sha's prefecture: Huang T'ing-chien, in
1104; Li Kang (1083–1140), in 1126 and 1132; Chao Shih-hsia, in 1167

52. See Wu Hsiung-ho, *T'ang Sung tz'u*, pp. 320–25, for the dating and contents of the
series.
53. *CST*, 2:1062.
54. *CST*, 3:1834.

and 1197; Hsin Ch'i-chi in 1180; and Liu Sheng-chi in 1181. Neverthe-less, in a region that was home to so few significant song lyricists, the bookstore must have pinned its hopes of turning a profit on a general audience of officials and merchants who would purchase song lyrics in print.

A second multivolume commercial series was the *Ch'in-ch'ü wai-pien* series published in Fu-chien. The scope and contents of the original are unknown; at present we are able to determine the names of only nine of the song lyricists published in the series. Starting with Ou-yang Hsiu and ending with Chen Te-hsiu (1178–1235), all are literary figures well known in their times, giving the impression that this publisher was more selective than the Ch'ang-sha bookseller.[55]

Devoting one volume to each poet, these series were designed to appeal to the buyer who read song lyrics as literature or as the literary product of a certain admirable personality. Anthologies produced in the Southern Sung are similarly arranged by poet, indicating that they functioned in the same way. To be sure, the arrangement of a text is not an infallible indication of its intended use. The *Hua-chien chi* of 940 was originally compiled, according to its preface, to provide high-quality songs for *performance*,[56] and the title of the *Tsun-ch'ien chi* (In front of the winecups), an anthology of thirty-six Five Dynasties song lyricists compiled sometime in the second or third quarter of the eleventh cen-tury, signals a similar function—even though both anthologies are in fact arranged by poet, not by *tiao* or theme. Nevertheless, prefaces to some surviving printed editions of the *Hua-chien chi*, published in 1148, 1184, 1185, and around 1205, indicate that the anthology had come to serve the purposes of literary history: the preservation of the old and the skillful, or the recording of an age's best literary efforts at a time when other genres were supposedly in decline.[57] Wu Ch'ang-shou is probably correct in his observation that most anthologies from Tseng Tsao's 1148 *Yüeh-fu ya-tz'u* on were compiled not for the sake of performance but for the sake of the texts themselves.[58]

55. See Wu Hsiung-ho, *T'ang Sung tz'u*, pp. 326–27. Wu identifies only eight titles in the series, neglecting to mention Chao Yen-tuan (1121–75); see Jao Tsung-i, *Tz'u-chi k'ao*, 4.136–37. Jao, on the other hand, does not include Chen Te-hsiu in his study, pos-sibly because all but one of his lyrics (*CST*, 4:2423) are lost.

56. See Kang-i Sun Chang, *The Evolution of Chinese Tz'u Poetry: From Late T'ang to Northern Sung* (Princeton: Princeton University Press, 1980), pp. 15–16.

57. See the 1148 preface by Ch'ao Ch'ien-chih and the 1205 postface by Lu Yu, quoted in Wu Hsiung-ho, *T'ang Sung tz'u*, pp. 331–32.

58. Quoted by Wu Hsiung-ho, *T'ang Sung tz'u*, pp. 328–29.

In Tseng Tsao's case, simple preservation of the materials collected by his family over the years was the expressed purpose.[59] Besides the works of thirty-four mainstream song lyricists, he includes over a hundred acclaimed song lyrics of unknown authorship and suites of songs designed for concert performance with dance—a type of song lyric most Sung poets were neither trained nor required to produce, and therefore consigned to the margins of the canon.

THE EFFECT OF PRINT CULTURE ON THE SONG LYRIC

We have discussed motivations for preserving song lyrics in print: a strong interest in literary history seems to have been basic to these motivations, although this interest could have derived from aesthetic, antiquarian, or political and social concerns, depending on the individual case. It is important to keep these motivations in mind. But what, if any, influence did these motivations for preserving the genre in print have on the form or content of the song lyric itself? Attempting to answer this question involves us in broader issues crossing cultural and temporal boundaries.

Scholars (and others) have commonly divided humanity into the literate and the illiterate, with fundamental differences between the two in thought patterns, transmission of knowledge, and literary expression. The work of Ruth Finnegan and others has shown, however, that oral and written modes of communication take such a variety of forms and stand in so many relationships to each other in different societies that it is questionable whether this division is meaningful or even useful.[60] Perhaps a transformation more fundamental than the move from orality to literacy in a given culture, then, is the leap to print. Print communication interacts with oral and written communication in complex and variable ways, but it stands in opposition to both chirographic and oral systems in that it permits the reproduction and storage of information in quantities far beyond the capacity of either.

We have seen that as the Sung progressed, more and more song lyrics passed into print in great volume. This was part of a wider cultural transformation. One of the first priorities in the use of the new technology of printing was the fixing and disseminating of vast seas of

59. See his preface in Wu Hsiung-ho, *T'ang Sung tz'u*, pp. 338–39, or in the *SPTK* edition of *Yüeh-fu ya-tz'u*.

60. Ruth Finnegan, *Literacy and Orality: Studies in the Technology of Communication* (Oxford: Basil Blackwell, 1988).

knowledge, surely because the standardization and preservation of information was one means of unifying a new empire, indoctrinating its bureaucrats, and defining the canons of powerful religions. The first Sung government printing project produced China's first printed code of laws, in 963. Eight years later, the first of six Sung printings of the Buddhist Tripitaka was undertaken. Classics, histories, medical treatises, and the like were also printed by the government. The state often rewarded officials for using the presses of local government units to print books (which the officials sometimes gave away as gifts or sold for private gain).

The unprecedented power of print could not be monopolized by the government, however. As early as the ninth century, print usurped one of the sacred functions of the court when privately printed family calendars went into circulation even before the government versions were approved.[61] In the Northern Sung, the texts of court debates on foreign policy were leaked, printed, sold, and quickly found their way across borders and into the hands of the foreigners who were the subjects of those debates.[62] The works of dissident officials became even more dangerous when they were picked up and disseminated by commercial publishers, Su Shih's works again being the prime example. If a text were proscribed, or had a limited market, the printing blocks could simply be stored away until conditions favored a renewed printing at some later date—a major advantage over movable type.

Most students who entered schools with hopes of embarking on official careers would encounter government-printed editions of the classics. Many of these students would never join the bureaucracy, and hundreds of private academy students would study with no intention of seeking government posts, but most of these literate men would participate in the economic life of the society at some point, whether as merchants or merely as managers of their patrimonies. They would have the means to purchase a variety of printed materials—including song lyrics.

These men would always be aware that a vast amount of knowledge and thought was safely fixed in print somewhere, and they knew it was often organized by chapter and verse for easy retrieval. The European experience tells us that printing was first harnessed to do what writing and memorization had always done badly and with great effort: to re-

61. Tsien Tsuen-hsuin, *Paper and Printing*, part 1 of Joseph Needham, ed., *Science and Civilisation in China*, vol. 5, *Chemistry and Chemical Technology* (Cambridge: Cambridge University Press, 1985), p. 151.

62. Poon, "Books and Printing," pp. 48–50, 55–63.

claim the knowledge of the ancients and support the oral, rhetorical tradition with encyclopedic compendia of formulas and tropes. Gradually, with knowledge stored in books, the function of writing changed from the retention of essential verities and the rehearsal of the rational to the exploration of the new, the unique, and the mysterious. Reports of voyages across the planet could be published and compared against the ancient texts; poets could safely scorn the commonplaces of rhetoric and pursue originality.[63] In China, of course, print technology developed under vastly different linguistic, social, and material conditions; both the timing and the specific contours of the cultural and social results of the shift were bound to be different.[64] But the Western evidence alerts us to the possibility that print might shape the literature that flourished in its environment.

It is striking how closely the rise and spread of print coincide with the development of the song lyric. To be sure, imported music, economic prosperity, relative domestic peace, and the large numbers of women supporting themselves as professional entertainers in the growing cities all helped to foster the new genre; the development of print culture cannot be given all the credit. Nevertheless, I would like to posit three theses for inquiry.

The first thesis is that when those members of a society who care about the preservation of knowledge are confident that it has indeed become securely preserved, their writings will place less emphasis on the shared tradition and more on individual feeling. Walter Ong has argued that this is what eventually brought about the "preoccupation with otherness, with what is different, remote, mysterious, inaccessible, exotic, even bizarre"—what we call Romanticism—after print had transformed Europe.[65] The rise of the song lyric in the tenth and eleventh centuries certainly bespeaks an increasing interest on the part of the literate elite of China in exploring nuances of emotion through a new poetic form uniquely suited to evoking the process of feeling and inner reflection.

63. See Walter J. Ong, *Rhetoric, Romance, and Technology: Studies in the Interaction of Expression and Culture* (Ithaca: Cornell University Press, 1971); and Elizabeth Eisenstein, *The Printing Press as an Agent of Change: Communications and Cultural Transformations in Early-Modern Europe* (Cambridge: Cambridge University Press, 1979).

64. In China for example, the invention of inexpensive paper preceded the invention of printing by centuries. The availability of paper quickly encouraged scholarly breadth, although more complete organization and preservation of knowledge awaited the arrival of printing. See Shimizu Shigeru, "Kami no hatsumei to Gokan no gakufū," *Tōhō gaku* 79 (Jan. 1990): 1–13.

65. Ong, *Rhetoric, Romance, and Technology*, p. 255.

It is clear that print did have an effect on the way Sung people read and wrote. The unprecedented flood of writing in Sung times, often in the form of collections of trivia, appears to reflect both the lure of publication in print and the new, casual function writing could assume when freed from weightier tasks.[66] It is significant that "books which classify, itemize, or summarize so as to facilitate easy reference" were a major part of the book trade.[67] The availability of such reference works, and indeed the abundance of books in general, clearly facilitated scholarship, but it was also said to devalue the individual text and encourage "lazy" perusal.[68] In a manuscript culture, "lazy" perusal is a threat to society's store of knowledge and an insult to those who try to keep it intact. If print opened the gates of knowledge to less scholarly readers, this does not mean, however, that serious readers disappeared. Examination candidates expended great energy mastering canonical texts, and scholars sometimes devoted a good portion of their lives to a given classic. Yet print enabled these tasks to be supported by, or even to center on, the collocation of considerable amounts of knowledge—a task very different from the fundamental ones of preservation and transmission in a manuscript culture.

More study is needed on how print culture encourages new kinds of scholarship and aesthetic expression: the rise of the song lyric may not be comparable to Western Romanticism as a quest for the "exotic" and "bizarre," but perhaps the song lyric's adoption by the elite and scholarly class does signal a new attitude toward the function of literature in a new medium.

My second thesis is that the popularity of song lyrics in Sung times is an effect of printing, one closely related to the flourishing of prose writing at the same time: because both forms of literature are more difficult to memorize than pentasyllabic or heptasyllabic poems, they depend on print to enable them to compete with *shih* poetry in terms of dissemination.

It has been observed that in T'ang times the literature that circulated most widely was *shih* poetry because it was most easily memorized and orally disseminated.[69] If song lyrics are a genre of performance literature, that does not necessarily mean they were easily memorized or disseminated: the musical talent their performance required limited their

66. Poon, "Books and Printing," pp. 68–70.
67. Ibid., p. 102, quoting Yüeh K'o (1183–1240), *K'uei t'an lu* (ca. 1214) (*TSCC* ed.), p. 78.
68. Poon, "Books and Printing," pp. 79–80.
69. Ibid., pp. 68–70.

reproduction as oral texts to specialists, though their audiences might have been extensive. Without print, the genre would have been more ephemeral and less likely to have developed in the direction of longer and more literary compositions.

This brings us to the third thesis: that print encouraged the development of increasingly refined, linguistically complex song lyrics in the thirteenth century, particularly as seen in the works of Chiang K'uei (ca. 1155–ca. 1221) and Wu Wen-ying (ca. 1200–ca. 1260), different as these two leading song lyricists are.

Through the late eleventh century, simple distinctions of level and deflected tones were generally sufficient to make a song lyric's sound structure fit the music, though there were places in some *tiao* where only more precisely designated tones would serve. Chou Pang-yen was the first to rigorously govern the tones of his syllables according to the music, but he still allowed a degree of variation. During his time, performance of the song lyric was usually accompanied by stringed instruments, which apparently permitted a looser fit between the music and the singer's voice. In the Southern Sung, wind instruments came to dominate, encouraging finer distinctions in the quality of each sung syllable. Perhaps it was the greater musical subtlety required of them that made it possible for Southern Sung experts to recognize Chou's achievements, if belatedly (Chou's contemporary song lyricists had scarcely seemed aware of his existence). Song lyricists such as Fang Ch'ien-li, Yang Tse-min, and Ch'en Yün-p'ing admired Chou so much that they wrote compositions following the rhymes of most of his song lyrics.[70] That much was no great novelty, but they also followed the tonal patterns of his song lyrics in each syllable. Wu Wen-ying did the same in the over sixty *tiao* he took from Chou.

This obsession with perfecting the sound pattern of the words of a song is in one sense a sign of the lyric's separation from living musical practice, for it was a pattern abstracted from the words of a poet long dead that was directing the music, not the evolving music that was controlling the production of new texts. It was a remarkable event in the thirteenth century to find someone who could actually sing Chou Pang-yen's song lyrics. Even a new song by Wu Wen-ying himself, without a broad-based musical culture to sustain it, was likely to have been unsingable a mere decade or two after it was written.[71]

---

70. *CST*, 4:2488–504, 4:2999–3016, and 5:3113–34, respectively.

71. See the preface by Chang Yen (1248–1320) to his "Hsi tzu chiang man," *CST*, 5:3475.

In the same age, however, the older musician–song lyricist Chiang K'uei was using a flute to determine the sound quality of each syllable of a song and writing his own music (sometimes before, sometimes after he wrote the words);[72] the relationship between music and song lyric in such a case was tighter than before. But like composition by model rather than by musical sense, this tight relationship is also the product of an elite art. Great specialization is required to create, perform, and appreciate song lyrics under such conditions. Chiang K'uei's song lyrics neither came from nor spread among popular entertainers. This stands in striking contrast to the earlier case of Liu Yung, who adopted and re-vised so much non-elite music:[73] the variability of Liu's tone patterns indicates that it was in performance, not in abstract planning, that word and note were harmonized.

The song lyric was not yet a fossil, of course. We have noted stories of women abducted by hostile troops using their final moments to com-pose song lyrics. The *tiao* they employed must have been in common use, even though the details of performance would have been different from earlier decades. Both "Ch'in-yüan ch'un" and "Man t'ing fang," two of the *tiao* used by thirteenth-century women in the stories re-counted above, are examples of patterns that remained relatively loosely defined by level/deflected tone distinctions alone.[74]

But those elite Southern Sung song lyricists who, as we have seen, structured their tonal patterns after those of Chou Pang-yen were clearly estranged from the song lyric as oral performance. Chou himself, and Chiang K'uei even more, both consummate musical minds, would appear to have reversed that estrangement, but in fact their verbal pat-terns, so tightly bound to their music, *have all the fixity of print*. In per-formance they must have been exquisite, but they had been worked out beforehand through a sophisticated matching of word and music that reveals an established confidence in the authority and stability of the written or printed text.

If this seems paradoxical, we should remember that it was by *writing* (and rewriting) his text that Isocrates, the first Greek to write for (oral) publication by others, perfected the sounds and rhythms of an *oral* style.[75] Similarly, we may say that the innovative and dense diction of

72. On the above several points, see Wu Hsiung-ho, *T'ang Sung tz'u*, pp. 69, 70, 75, 139, 219, and 222; and Shih I-tui, *Tz'u yü yin-yüeh*, pp. 121–26.

73. Shih I-tui, *Tz'u yü yin-yüeh*, p. 125.

74. Wu Hsiung-ho, *T'ang Sung tz'u*, p. 69.

75. Tony M. Lentz, *Orality and Literacy in Hellenic Greece* (Carbondale and Edwards-ville: Southern Illinois University Press, 1989), pp. 122–35.

Wu Wen-ying was possible in the song lyric only after the genre had become as much a written as an oral one, if not more.

Although there are in some oral cultures literary compositions of great verbal richness and subtlety,[76] the predictability and schematic patterning that generally support aural comprehension and oral composition become liabilities as members of a culture begin to compose in writing for a reading audience. We have noted that after the accumulation of knowledge in print had undermined the rationale for residual orality in Europe, the "commonplace" in writing became not a vital structuring device but a blemish. In the Malay world, study of the language of illiterate and literate storytellers (in our age of print) reveals that the latter give more weight to individual word choice and seek, almost unconsciously, variations in phrasing.[77] Thus, I would suggest that there is a connection between Su Shih's innovative production of highly "literate" song lyrics and his awareness that his works were being circulated as printed texts.[78] We should recognize, too, Wu Wen-ying's "poetics of density," which sharply limited the appreciation of his lyrics in performance,[79] as the product of a mature print culture.

PRINT AND MORAL DISTANCING: A CAUTIOUS PROPOSAL

When I began to research the contexts of the song lyric in Sung times, I wanted to understand two paradoxes: that the song lyric should have been a significant mode of expression for certain morally serious men; and that a genre of performance literature should circulate in print. I now think there is a relationship between these two phenomena. For reasons of space, I have had to reserve an extensive discussion of the writing of song lyrics by Buddhist monks for publication elsewhere. Let me simply state that some monks did write song lyrics in Sung times, as did generals and statesmen, despite the genre's association with love and the more personal emotions. Might the new print culture have fostered the consciousness that made it possible for such people to use a

76. Finnegan, *Literacy and Orality*, pp. 69–77.

77. Sweeney, *Full Hearing*, pp. 241–66.

78. When Su Shih was tried in late 1079 on the charge of slandering the emperor, his accusers noted that his "satirical writings" had been printed and sold in the marketplace, and they produced four volumes of his printed works. See Murakami Tetsumi, "So Tōba shokan no denrai to Tōbashu shohon no keifu ni tsuite," *Chūgoku bungaku hō* 27 (1977): 51–87.

79. Grace S. Fong, *Wu Wenying and the Art of Southern Song Ci Poetry* (Princeton: Princeton University Press, 1987), esp. pp. 63–64.

genre that simulated the experiencing of emotion, but to use it without seeming to be trapped by emotion?

Such an attitude of detachment from one's morally suspect actions, "lodging" emotions and thoughts without being "detained" by them, was a stated philosophical ideal in the times;[80] it might also have been a personality trait of some individuals. But detachment or distancing is sometimes said to be characteristic of a literate, analytical culture. Although the universality of such a rule is questionable, we must ask whether it wasn't the intensification of just such a culture through the flourishing of print in Sung China that enabled monks and morally serious men to believe they could "lodge" in the song lyric without being "detained" by it. The commonly presumed association of literacy and writing with abstract thought, logical argument, and distancing between performer and performance would seem to validate this theory.[81]

It is certainly reasonable to postulate that the simultaneous rise of a new genre of literature and a new type of information technology points to some kind of cause-and-effect relationship between the literature and the technology, although it must always be stressed that this relationship is not necessarily unidirectional and that other factors— aesthetic, social, economic—play an important part in it. Since some kind of mechanism of moral distancing seems to have come into play at the same time as the rise of print culture to enable the song lyric to gain acceptance among statesmen and certain monks, print could be singled out as a factor in this distancing. I believe this is a useful line of inquiry that may throw new light on Chinese culture from Sung times on. But it raises at least two kinds of questions.

First, print was not the only new force in Sung society that can be associated with distancing. Money has a definite distancing effect, as reflected in the contrasting functions of money and food offerings in ritual contexts in China.[82] It is well known that a money economy began to flourish in the Sung dynasty; would that not have had an effect on the culture at least as great as the effect of print? The song lyric was part of the new money economy, for the women entertainers among whom the genre developed in the growing commercial metropolises performed for money; and my discussion of the publication of lyrics has

---

80. For some relevant texts, see Ronald Egan, "Ou-yang Hsiu and Su Shih on Calligraphy," *Harvard Journal of Asiatic Studies* 49 (1989): 402–12.

81. To cite just two works in which these associations are articulated: see Sweeney, *Full Hearing*, p. 97; and Lentz, *Hellenic Greece*, pp. 3–6 and 177–81.

82. See John McCreery, "Why Don't We See Some Real Money Here? Offerings in Chinese Religion," *Journal of Chinese Religions* 18 (1990):1–24.

touched on many ways in which books, whether published commercially or by government schools, were printed for the same purpose. So an analysis of the relationship between exchange mechanisms and culture may be a fruitful path for future research.

Second, we find that it is very difficult to generalize about the influence of communication technology on consciousness. In the Chinese case, the common attribution to literacy of such virtues as analytical thinking, separation of performer and performance, and logic may be valid, since these are all features of Chinese thought in classical times, when literacy was becoming widespread among record keepers and rhetoricians who served the feudal courts and produced philosophical and historical texts. If there was linkage between print and the new kind of moral distancing that permitted the writing of song lyrics among the elite and the religious in Sung times, we must wrestle with the question of whether print culture is simply an intensification of literate culture or represents a leap to a new stage of culture. I have already noted that in terms of the efficiency of knowledge storage and retrieval, the fundamental dividing line in human cultures is not between oral and literate but between print on one side and the oral or chirographic on the other. We have also seen discernible effects of print on the kind of information that was stored and the manner of its use in the period under study. It would seem, then, that we must do more work to define the differences between the consciousness characteristic of print culture and that ascribable to mere literacy. The fact that much of the scholarship in this area does not distinguish between chirographic and print cultures when making comparisons with oral cultures complicates our work. The issues go far beyond the study of a single genre of poetry; they must be addressed diachronically and across several disciplines.

Indeed, the very assumption that aesthetic or moral distancing depends on either literacy or print should not go unquestioned; at the least, the terms used and the scope of their application must be carefully defined. For there are in fact many devices that produce aesthetic distancing in oral cultures (masks, for example, animal parables, evocation of ancestors as authority, etc.). Similarly, certain cultural environments have been known to foster a sophisticated awareness of language and linguistic questioning in peoples without any writing system.[83] That is to say, literacy and/or print may not be necessary conditions for detachment from performance, even if they have apparently been sufficient conditions in some cultures. If the linkage I have suggested is

83. Finnegan, *Literacy and Orality*, pp. 66 and 47–50.

valid for the song lyric in the print culture of Sung China, we still cannot easily extrapolate from it a general rule for the causes of "distancing."

A comparative approach has helped us understand some relationships between the song lyric and its social and material context; but
this approach has also alerted us to the need to reexamine the simplistic
dichotomies and supposed universals that underlie much of the existing
scholarship. I believe that the hypotheses I have posited concerning the
song lyric and the culture in which it developed can be accepted heuris-
tically and will stimulate fresh approaches to Sung literature and culture. The wider theoretical implications this research on the song lyric
seems to indicate should also be pursued, but only with the greatest
care.

Wang Kuo-wei's Song Lyrics in the Light of His Own Theories

Yeh Chia-ying

Over the past few years 1 have come to a new understanding of Wang Kuo-wei's (1827–1927) profound and often cryptic pronouncements about what makes the song lyric (*tz'u*) such a distinctive form of poetry in China. In this essay I propose to apply his critical insights to the songs he himself wrote. I will begin by stating briefly the results of two papers I have previously published on the subject[1] and will then proceed with a detailed analysis of four song lyrics.

THE THREE LEVELS OF *CHING-CHIEH*

In his *Jen-chien tz'u-hua* Wang Kuo-wei uses the crucial term *ching-chieh* in three distinct ways: as a term referring to the "setting" or "content" of a poem, as a critical term applicable to poetry generally, and as a critical term applying uniquely to *tz'u*. In its first and most obvious use, the phrase refers to the setting presented in the poem, as when Wang writes, "There is the scene [*ching-chieh*] as perceived by the poet, and then there is the scene perceived by the ordinary man";[2] as an example

I wish to acknowledge here the help of Professor James R. Hightower in preparing the English-language version of this essay. I should also like to express my gratitude to the Social Sciences and Humanities Research Council of Canada for giving me a grant to go to Cambridge to conduct my work on it.

1. Yeh Chia-ying, *Chung-kuo tz'u-hsüeh ti hsien-tai kuan* (Taipei: Ta-an ch'u-pan-she, 1988), pp. 21–32.

2. Hsü T'iao-fu, *Chiao-chu Jen-chien tz'u-hua* (Shanghai: K'ai-ming shu-tien, 1943), p. 80; hereafter cited as *JCTH*.

of a scene borrowed from an earlier poet for incorporation into one's
own poem, he then cites a couplet by Chia Tao (793–865),

> The autumn wind blows across the Wei River,
> falling leaves fill Ch'ang-an,[3]
> 秋風吹渭水
> 落葉滿長安

and comments that by adapting this passage in their songs, Chou
Pang-yen (1056–1121) and Pai P'u (1226–?) had "borrowed the setting
[*ching-chieh*] from an older poet and made it their own."[4] Chou Pang-
yen's song reads:

> Over the Wei River, the west wind,
> in Ch'ang-an, flying leaves—
> in vain I remember.[5]
> 渭水西風
> 長安落葉
> 空憶詩情宛轉

And Pai P'u wrote:

> I hear the falling leaves in the west wind over the Wei River.[6]
> 聽落葉西風渭水

And again in an aria:

> Desolate for my native land—
> the west wind on the Wei River,
> the setting sun over Ch'ang-an.[7]
> 傷心故園
> 西風渭水
> 落日長安

The autumnal scene, the same in all these verses, is what the later poets
borrowed: the Wei River, Ch'ang-an, and the west wind.

On the next level Wang expands the meaning of *ching-chieh* as "scene"
to include the feeling the scene conveys, its emotional coloration—and
thereby injects a value judgment into its use, making of it a critical

---

3. Chia Tao, "I chiang-shang Wu Ch'u-shih," in *Ch'üan T'ang shih* (Peking: Chung-
hua shu-chü, 1960), p. 6647.

4. *JCTH*, p. 48.

5. Chou Pang-yen, *P'ien-yü chi chi-chu* (Yangchow: Ku-chi shu-tien, 1980), 5.30.

6. *Yang-ch'un pai-hsüeh pu-chi*, in *San-ch'ü ts'ung-k'an*, ed. Jen Chung-min (Shanghai:
Chung-hua shu-chü, 1931), A2.1b.

7. *Wu-t'ung yü*, in *Yüan-jen tsa-chü hsüan-chu* (Taipei: Shih-chieh shu-chü, 1959), p. 95.

term: it is no longer a neutral but a particular kind of scene that is deserving of the label *ching-chieh*. He writes: "*Ching-chieh* refers not only to external scenes; the emotions—joy, anger, grief, pleasure—are also a *ching-chieh* of the human heart. So it can be said of someone who can portray true scenes and true feelings that he achieves *ching-chieh*."[8] The condition demanded here, that the scenes be true scenes and the feelings true feelings, makes the achievement of *ching-chieh* the prerogative of the poet; simply borrowing another poet's scene is not enough: "If you don't have *ching-chieh* yourself, the old poets will be of no use to you."[9] Nor, furthermore, can the mere scenes of the external world—birdsong, running water, the blossoming of flowers, the movement of the clouds— of themselves be termed *ching-chieh* before they have been encompassed by the poet's sensitivity or capacity for feeling.[10]

Wang Kuo-wei applied *ching-chieh* in this sense of a particular, desirable quality of scene in judging *shih* poetry as well as *tz'u*. He writes, "There are settings [*ching-chieh*] on differing scales, but the scale of a setting does not determine its value,"[11] and provides some examples:

> With fine rain the little fish appear,
> swallows dip in the gentle breeze.[12]
> 細雨魚兒出
> 微風燕子斜

This is in no way inferior to

> The setting sun lights up the great banner,
> horses neigh in the soughing wind.[13]
> 落日照大旗
> 馬鳴風蕭蕭

Or

> The costly curtain hangs limp from the little silver hook.[14]
> 寶簾閒掛小銀鉤

8. *JCTH*, p. 3.

9. Ibid., p. 48.

10. See my discussion of this in *Chia-ling lun tz'u ts'ung-kao* (Shanghai: Shang-hai ku-chi ch'u-pan-she, 1980), p. 277.

11. *JCTH*, p. 4.

12. Tu Fu (712–70), "Shui-chien ch'ien hsin," in *Tu-shih hsiang-chu*, ed. Ch'iu Chao-ao (Shanghai: Shang-hai ku-chi ch'u-pan-she, 1964), 10.9.

13. Tu Fu, "Hou ch'u sai," no. 2, in Ch'iu Chao-ao, *Tu-shih hsiang-chu*, 4.18.

14. Ch'in Kuan (1049–1100), *Huai-hai chü-shih ch'ang-tuan-chü* (Taipei: Shih-chieh shu-chü, 1959), p. 20.

And it is just as good as

> Mist hides the storied tower,
> In the moonlight we fail to find the ferry.[15]

霧失樓臺
月迷津渡

Since Wang uses lines of *shih* poetry by Tu Fu and verses from Ch'in Kuan's songs, it follows that *ching-chieh* as setting can apply equally to *shih* and *tz'u*, as well as functioning as a criterion for a value judgment.

Furthermore, among possible scenes he also distinguishes "invented scene" (*tsao-ching*) from "described scene" (*hsieh-ching*); scenes involving the poet (*yu wo*) and scenes from which the poet remains detached (*wu wo*); "ideal scenes" (*li-hsiang*) and "real scenes" (*hsieh-shih*). "Described scenes" and "invented scenes" refer to the provenance of the poet's material. Scenes "involving the poet" or "from which he remains detached" refer to the relation of the poet's persona to the episode in the poem. "Ideal scene" and "real scene" are simply refinements of invented scene and described scene. Although what a described scene portrays belongs to an actual situation, once written in a poem it is no longer subject to the limitations of reality; and although an invented scene is not an actual situation, still its structure and the materials of which it is put together must accord with reality.[16] Thus, Wang could write in the context of his use of those terms, "The scenes created by a great poet are all in accord with the natural, and the scenes he describes also approach the ideal."[17]

A third level of *ching-chieh* that is even more vital to a deeper understanding of his art is discussed in the following statements from Wang's *Jen-chien tz'u-hua*:

> The essence of *tz'u* is in a subtle and refined beauty [*yao-miao i-hsiu*] that makes it possible to say what cannot be said in *shih* and yet keeps *tz'u* from being able to say everything *shih* can say. The realm of *shih* is wide; the language of *tz'u* is far-reaching.[18]

> Whether *tz'u* is refined or vulgar depends on the spirit, not what appears on the surface. The songs of Ou-yang Hsiu and Ch'in Kuan may contain erotic language, but they remain decent.[19]

15. Ibid., p. 16.
16. This idea was much influenced by Schopenhauer; see Yeh Chia-ying, *Wang Kuo-wei chi ch'i wen-hsüeh p'i-p'ing* (Hong Kong: Chung-hua shu-chü, 1978), p. 230.
17. *JCTH*, p. 1.
18. Ibid., p. 48.
19. Ibid., p. 19.

The contrast between "refined" (*ya*) and "vulgar" (*Cheng*) refers to Confucius' characterization of a section of the *Shih-ching* (Book of songs)—"The songs of Cheng . . . are licentious"—and means that qualification of a love song as "refined" depends on whether it can be read as something more than what it seems to be. This third level moves from emphasis on a standard of genuine feeling and scene to the profoundly subtle and refined beauty achieved through suggestion and association beyond the surface of the things and feelings directly portrayed. This evocative beauty is a special characteristic of the song lyric.[20]

In its three aspects, then, Wang Kuo-wei's *ching-chieh* applies to the feelings aroused by the song lyric, but it cannot be said that these are deliberately or even consciously invoked by the poet; rather, they are a product of the rich suggestive power created in the poem. Most of the erotic songs of the Five Dynasties lack this power, and these Wang Kuo-wei simply disregards. It is precisely this quality of latent suggestive power, I believe, that he is referring to when he writes, "The best songs have *ching-chieh*. A song with *ching-chieh* automatically belongs to the highest category and will have memorable lines as a matter of course."[21]

THE THREE CATEGORIES OF THE SONG LYRIC

Tz'u possessing the refined and subtle beauty of *ching-chieh* can be found in any of the three general categories of the song lyric. The first category is composed of real song words, written by poets as words for tunes, with no intention of expressing their own feelings. Sometimes, however, these short songs (*hsiao-ling*) written for amusement will inadvertently reveal the essential nature of the poet's mind as shaped by his personality and experience, resulting in that refined, subtle beauty Wang Kuo-wei found in such songs.

The second category contains those song lyrics no longer written to be sung, being rather poems in song form. These, poets were consciously using as vehicles for self-expression, but they too could achieve a refined, subtle beauty through the depth and complexity of their poetic inspiration (*ch'ing-chih*) and the suggestiveness or ramifications of their procedure (*fang-shih*); even though written as self-expression, the subtle beauty is still present.

The third category consists of those *tz'u* that have taken on the manner of rhapsody (*fu*), where the poet is deliberately working toward an

20. See my *Chung-kuo tz'u-hsüeh*, pp. 5–19.
21. *JCTH*, p. 1.

elaborate structure, an architectonic design. And in these enigmatic and expository compositions there can also be a subtle, refined beauty.

These three categories are distinguished by the attitude of the poet toward his composition.[22] From the point of view of the critic we need to know what to look for to determine whether the poet has achieved this beauty. Chang Hui-yen (1761–1802) can be taken as representative of one method, which looks for code words (*yü-ma*) and associated events to construct moralizing interpretations about the author's intentions and the theme of the poem. Wang Kuo-wei is representative of the other kind of critic, for he relies chiefly on the nature of the feeling conveyed by the poem, and from what that suggests he provides a sort of virtuoso elaboration. His method is most successful when applied to songs of the first category, and Chang Hui-yen's method works best on the third category.[23]

BIOGRAPHICAL CONSIDERATIONS

In considering the content of Wang Kuo-wei's songs we must draw upon what we know of his emotional nature and, like Chang Hui-yen, look for code words and items of personal history. This requires a glance at the chronology of Wang's poems, to relate them to the events of his life and to the development of his character and ideas. Only 115 of his songs are extant, twenty-three of them published in 1917,[24] and the remainder in posthumous collections of his works.[25] However, most of them were written between 1905 and 1909, the period during which he was preoccupied with *tz'u* composition; very few were written after that time.[26]

22. See my *Chung-kuo tz'u-hsüeh*, pp. 5–19.

23. Ibid.

24. In his *Kuan-t'ang chi-lin*; see *Wang Kuan-t'ang hsien-sheng ch'üan-chi* (hereafter cited as *WKTCC*) (Taipei: Wen-hua ch'u-pan kung-ssu, 1968), 3:1200–206.

25. *T'iao-hua tz'u, WKTCC*, 4:1505–37.

26. Wang's own note appended to the *tz'u* in *Kuan-t'ang chi-lin* states that they were written between the years 1905 and 1909; Fan Chih-hou's preface to the *Jen-chien tz'u i-chi* is dated 1907. See Wang Te-i, "Kuan-t'ang hsien-sheng chu-shu k'ao," in idem., *Wang Kuo-wei nien-p'u*, pp. 413–22 (Taipei: Shang-wu yin-shu-kuan, 1967). After this brief period of song writing, Wang Kuo-wei's interests turned to historical and philological research. The last four *tz'u* in the *Vine Flowers* collection (*T'iao-hua chi*) include a date of composition from 1918 to 1920. Very possibly these were added by Lo Chen-yü when he edited Wang's literary remains. These four *tz'u* are quite different in character from his earlier songs and deviate considerably from the standards he set in his critical writings. I am excluding them from my discussion. I have discussed the circumstances and reasons for Wang's abandonment of poetry and literary studies generally in my book.

Wang Kuo-wei was by nature both intellectual and passionate, a combination that enabled him to excel in scholarship, but which also made him vulnerable in the practical world to a conflict between intellect and feeling from which he could not extricate himself. He thus occupied himself with *tz'u*, hoping to find in poetry comfort for the pain this conflict caused him. This conflict in temperament and this motive for writing song lyrics is the first thing we should look for in considering the content of Wang's songs.

The second is his naturally pessimistic temperament. He said of himself: "Physically weak, by nature melancholy—I am continually confronted with the problem of human existence."[27] Not surprisingly, therefore, when first encountering Western thought, he was strongly attracted to the pessimistic philosophy of Schopenhauer. Inspired by Schopenhauer's theory of genius and melancholy, he wrote in his essay "Schopenhauer and Nietzche" ("Shu-pen-hua yü Ni-ts'ai"):

> Genius is begrudged by Heaven and a disaster to the individual. Ignorant people eat when they are hungry and drink when thirsty. They grow old and raise their sons to carry on their wishes, and that is all. . . . The man of genius has the same disabilities as others, but is alone in being able to perceive wherein those disabilities lie. He and ignorant people are alike alive, but he is alone in questioning the reason for life.[28]

And in his "Essay on the *Dream of Red Mansions*" ("*Hung-lou meng* p'ing-lun"), where he discusses expectations and disappointments in human life, he observed:

> What is the nature of life? It is simply desire. It is the nature of desire to be insatiable. It arises in a lack, and the state of lack is pain. Fulfill a desire, and that desire is done, but only that one desire has been satisfied, with tens and hundreds of others left unsatisfied. One desire has been fulfilled and all the others are there to follow, so no final satisfaction is possible.[29]

It was in this melancholic, pessimistic state of mind that Wang Kuo-wei wrote his "Essay on Human Nature" ("Lun hsing"), "An Interpretation of Reason" ("Shih li"), and "Essay on Destiny" ("Yüan ming"),[30] seeking for an answer to the riddle of human life and human nature. And what answers did he come up with? He concluded that there is a constant struggle between good and evil in human nature, that reason is of

27. "Tzu hsü," in *Ching-an wen-chi hsü-pien, WKTCC*, 5:1825.
28. *Ching-an wen-chi, WKTCC*, 5:1690.
29. Ibid., p. 1630.
30. Ibid., pp. 1549, 1570; and *Ching-an wen-chi hsü-pien, WKTCC*, 5:1787.

no use in propelling human nature toward good, nor does it provide a criterion for conduct. In the essay on destiny he concluded that wealth and longevity are determined by fate; likewise, that fate decides whether a man is good or evil, worthy or unworthy. Looking at the human world in such terms, Wang Kuo-wei found no hope for salvation from evil and pain. It is this pessimism and melancholy that we will find embodied in Wang's songs.

A third distinctive trait of character is his tenacity in the pursuit of an ideal. Throughout his life he had only contempt for profit and despised the pursuit of worldly success, again influenced by Schopenhauer's account of the man of genius. On the contrast between the common man and the man of genius Wang wrote, "The true value of the highest form of intelligence lies not in the practical but in the theoretical, in the subjective, not in the objective: it concentrates all its strength on seeking out the truth and making it manifest. He will sacrifice his whole life's happiness and die for his objective goal, unable to deviate in the least degree, however much he might wish to."[31] Such tenacity in the pursuit of the ideal would naturally also manifest itself in his songs.

We should also take into account the events of his personal life during the short period when he was writing his songs. First, his father died in the seventh month of 1906, when Wang had gone to Peking to work in the Department of Education (*hsüeh-pu*) with Lo Chen-yü. He immediately returned to his hometown for the funeral. The next summer his wife fell gravely ill, and he again returned home, arriving only ten days before her death. One can imagine his shock and grief at losing both his father and wife in such a short time. And only half a year later, in January 1908, his foster mother died after a month's illness; again he hastened back home for the funeral.[32] This series of deaths in the family naturally cast a shadow over his poetry and contributed yet another element to their emotional background that we cannot ignore.

SIMPLE DESCRIPTIVE SCENES IN SONG LYRICS

I will begin with examples of straightforward description of nature, where direct observation underlies the scene presented. Wang Kuo-wei wrote few poems of pure description, and these are the weakest of his lyrics. For example, one to the tune "Paint the Lips Red" ("Tien chiang ch'un"):

31. "Shu-pen-hua yü Ni-ts'ai," in *Ching-an wen-chi, WKTCC*, 5:1680–81.
32. Wang Te-i, *Wang Kuo-wei nien-p'u.*

Waves chase the flowing clouds,
the boatman's song recedes across the waves.
The notes blend with the oars
and enter the reed-grown bank.

The setting sun strikes the flowing water.
A few dots of idle sea gulls
flying low
into the innumerable reeds and rushes
whisper in the breeze.[33]

波逐流雲
棹歌裊裊凌波去
數聲和櫓
遠入兼葭浦

落日中流
幾點閒鷗鷺
低飛處
抵蒲無數
瑟瑟風前語

To the tune "Sands of the Washing Stream" ("Huan hsi sha"):

The boat follows the clear stream, turn after turn.
Drooping willows open up for a sight of green hills—
cascading green locks covering the misty hairknot.[34]

舟逐清溪彎復彎
垂楊開處見青山
氄氄綠髮覆煙鬟

To the same tune:

The road twists, the peaks turn as you leave Painted Pond.
A whole mountain of maple leaves reflects the dying sun.
As you look, it's not at all like an autumn scene.[35]

路轉峯迴出畫塘
一山楓葉背殘陽
看來渾不似秋光

All these verses effectively portray the beauty of a natural scene and qualify as examples of Wang's "described scenery." There are other examples of scenes that are actual but have nothing to do with natural

33. T'ien Chih-tou, ed., *Wang Kuo-wei tz'u chu* (Hong Kong: San-lien shu-tien, 1985), p. 72; hereafter cited as *WKWTC*.
34. Ibid., p. 160.
35. Ibid., p. 82.

scenery, being concerned rather with real-life situations. This lyric to the tune "Bodhisattva Barbarian" ("P'u-sa-man"), for instance, portrays a dinner at which the waitress prepares and serves grilled mutton:

> On a jade platter tender onion shoots cut up,
> a serving of thin-sliced shoulder of mutton—
> I would not want to refuse it as too strong
> since you prepared it with your own hands.
>
> The glowing grill reddens your white face.
> Drunk, I loosen my fur coat.
> I'm still a bit wild on the way home,
> treading night frost on the capital boulevard.[36]

玉盤寸斷葱芽嫩
彎刀細割羊肩進
不敢厭腥臊
緣君親手調

紅爐幀素面
醉把貂裘緩
歸路有餘狂
天街宵踏霜

Another such lyric is written to the tune "Sands of the Washing Stream":

> The thin silk like water does not hold in the fragrance,
> the golden waves just now engulf the little winding corridors:
> thick clumps of chrysanthemums already deep yellow.
>
> Away with the painted lamp, welcome the unadorned moon
> to bring out the flower radiance in her face.
> Where in our world is there any harsh frost?[37]

似水輕紗不隔香
金波初轉小廻廊
離離叢菊已深黃

盡撤華燈招素月
更緣人面發花光
人間何處有嚴霜

These songs all contain lively, vivid description, but none of them carries any deeper meaning. They belong to the category of described (i.e., not invented) scenes treated realistically and with genuine feeling without, however, revealing anything of their author's character or

36. Ibid., p. 58.
37. Ibid., p. 48.

philosophy. If all he had written were like the songs just quoted above, he certainly would not have the place alongside his predecessors to which he laid claim, and we must go beyond these to discover songs in which he actually did surpass the ancients.

POEM NO. 1: SYMBOLIC DIMENSIONS OF THE NATURAL SCENE

It is in their intellectual content and the way that content is presented, the interaction between content and form, that the essential character of Wang Kuo-wei's songs appears. In all of his best songs, whether descriptive or narrative or purely lyrical, there is always hidden a subtle idea, characteristic of the third level of his *ching-chieh* theory. This can be demonstrated in the following example, to the tune "Sands of the Washing Stream":

In the moonlight I saw the perched crows as leaves.
When I opened the window, they fell fluttering from the branches.
The frosty sky was high, the wind still, as alone I leaned on the rail.

Trying for a line, a gut feeling is still there.
I close the book and weep fruitless tears.
For whom, alas, does my belt grow loose?[38]

月底棲鴉當葉看
推窗跕跕墮枝間
霜高風定獨憑欄

覓句心肝終復在
掩書涕淚苦無端
可憐衣帶為誰寬

In the first four words of the first line Wang is describing a perfectly ordinary scene that could be there in front of him, but as soon as he adds "I perceived them as leaves," it takes on the tone of a symbolical or imagined scene. This comes from the implication that the tree outside his window has already lost its leaves, and the crows have taken refuge there in the cold, moonlit winter night—a scene of chill and solitude. But the poet has at first perversely wanted to take these roosting crows, appropriate to a winter scene, as leaves on a green tree, belonging to a different season. This one line shows the poet making an effort to seek some consolation in the midst of disappointment and despair. But then reality reasserts itself. Whatever the poet's feelings and how-

38. Collected in *T'iao-hua tz'u*, WKTCC, 5:1515.

ever great his hope and fantasies, stubborn reality in the end shatters them all. So when the poet opens the window that cuts him off, seeking to come a bit closer to the fantasized scene, it is to discover that those branches are not only bare, but those roosting crows he was casting in the role of leaves have already taken flight, every last one of them.

The phrase "fell fluttering down" comes from Ma Yüan's *Hou-Han shu* biography, from a passage describing the southern expedition to Indochina's encounter with a climate so hot, an atmosphere so miasmic, that even flying birds could not survive, and as the general and his men watched, "kites fell fluttering into the water."[39] Wang Kuo-wei makes excellent use of the allusion. Like all such allusions, it brings a touch of classic elegance to his song. More to the point, the phrase was used of a kind of bird, and so it is appropriate as applied to crows. Of course, in terms of the actual scene, the crows should have flown away on being startled when the window was opened, instead of dropping fluttering to the ground like the kites in Ma Yüan's biography. But having begun by perceiving the crows as leaves growing on the tree, the poet, when they suddenly vanish, can only imagine the leaves falling to the ground a second time. And this second shedding of leaves provides a repetition of what he has already experienced this year, summer's beauties destroyed by the onset of winter. So the fantasy of crows as leaves is in the end only the occasion for another leaf fall, and the lovely scene conjured up in the poet's imagination is shattered, gone without a trace. This three-word allusion, *tieh-tieh to*, has taken on a metaphoric function transcending realism.

There is even more to it than that. In its original context, the birds dropped out of the sky because the environment was so hostile, and there remains a suggestion that the same might apply to the poet's world. These first two lines leave the poet, his illusion shattered, desolate and cold, without shelter or the consolation of beauty.

These lines are followed by "The frosty sky was high, the wind still, as alone I leaned on the rail." Literally it reads, "The frost is high," *shuang kao*—the words make one feel that the cold enveloping the whole world reaches up to the sky. "The wind is still," *feng ting*—some might think it would have been more effective to say that the wind was strong (*chin*), but I find "still" superior, both for its impact and for its suggestiveness. "Strong" leaves one with only the feeling that the wind continues to blow hard, its force not yet slackened. But "the wind is still" suggests that even after the destructive force of the wind has passed,

39. "Ma Yüan chuan," *Hou-Han shu* (Peking: Chung-hua shu-chü, 1965), 24.838.

there is no undoing the damage already done. It's the idea expressed in Li Shang-yin's (813?–58) line, "When the lotus flower is withered, autumn sorrow is complete,"[40] or the song in the *Dream of Red Mansions*,

> It's as though the food is no sooner gone than the birds have fled to
>   the woods.
> The whole bare desolate earth is quite clean,[41]

好一似食盡鳥投林
落了片白茫茫大地真乾淨

where all beauty has quickly dwindled into barren waste. The poet, faced with such a scene, leans on the railing, alone, and with what feelings? All his sorrows, his disappointments, his feelings of loneliness and isolation, come together at once, but he writes with deliberate restraint, "alone I leaned on the rail." Truly this is a scene worthy of Wang Kuo-wei's best songs. This first stanza has concentrated on the external scene, but by infusing it with a complex emotional tone he has transformed a scene merely described into a created scene with allegorical implications and an effective amalgamation of imagery and allegory.

The second stanza dispenses with description and allegory, presenting the poet's feelings directly. There are two versions of this stanza; as first published, it read:

> Making new songs has cost me all my hair.[42]
> The tragedy I chance to see brings fruitless tears.
> For whom alas does my belt grow loose?[43]

為制新詞髭盡斷
偶聽悲劇淚無端
可憐衣帶為誰寬

I prefer the later version. In it, to express the difficulty of writing a song, he adapted the line "To find one word for your poem, you rub off several whiskers."[44] The play he sees makes him weep because of his own pent-up feelings, and that's the sum of it. The revised version is considerably richer in the layers of feeling it brings out, and the effects come from the appositeness and strength of the words used. In "Trying for a line, a gut feeling is still there," he is also concerned with the effort

40. "Mu ch'iu tu yu Ch'ü-chiang," in *Li I-shan shih-chi* (*SPTK* ed.), 6:59.
41. Ts'ao Hsüeh-ch'in and Kao O, *Hung-lou meng* (Peking: Jen-min wen-hsüeh ch'u-pan-she, 1982), p. 89.
42. Lit., "whiskers," from rubbing the chin in perplexity.
43. *WKWTC*, p. 109.
44. Lu Yen-jang, "K'u yin," in *Ch'üan T'ang shih* (Peking: Chung-hua shu-chü, 1979), 715.8212.

of song writing, but it carries a potential for suggestion lacking in the
earlier draft. First the verb "trying for" (*mi*), literally "looking for," suggests from the start the effort of a search. The next phrase, "a gut feeling" (*hsin-kan*), literally "heart and liver," derives its meaning from the
particular internal organs considered to be the seat of the emotions.
"Heart and liver" won't do in English, nor would "heart and bowels,"
in spite of the Biblical "bowels of compassion." English and Chinese
both agree that the "heart" has to do with the feelings; in Chinese it
carries special literary overtones, starting with the classical definition of
poetry: "Poetry is where the intentions/feelings take us; emotions are
stirred inside and given form in words."[45] So the heart as imaginary
construct becomes the source for the emotions that lead to the creation
of poetry.

For ordinary purposes Wang Kuo-wei could have written "The feelings [*hsin ch'ing* or *hsin huai*] come as I look for a line." Instead, however,
he chose an expression that also carries down-to-earth associations with
real organs. On first reading, it is a bit disconcerting, and yet its impact
is profound. Both in wording and effect, it resembles the line in Ts'ai
Yen's (b. ca. 178) "Song of Sorrow" where she expresses her despair—
"Sorrow corrodes liver and lungs"[46]—and of Tu Fu's expression of his
feelings—"I sigh, my bowels inside burn."[47] It seems to me that Wang
Kuo-wei's use of *hsin-kan* conveys yet a further association deriving from
the figurative use of the term in common speech—when someone who
acts out of wholly selfish interests and has no social conscience is described as "completely lacking in heart and liver" (*ch'üan wu hsin-kan*).
Wang Kuo-wei turns this around: "heart and liver still present after
all," implying that he is still capable of becoming emotionally involved
in this cold and unfeeling human world.

The words "in the end is still there," *chung fu tsai*, remind one of the
obsessive attachment that knows no end or respite in Li Shang-yin's

Ch'ang-o grinds simples and is never done,
Jade Lady plays tosspot and never rests.[48]

姮娥擣藥無時已
玉女投壺未肯休

45. "Great Preface," *Mao shih chu-shu*, in *Shih-san-ching chu-shu* (Taipei: Wen-hua t'u-
shu kung-ssu, 1970), 1:270.

46. Ts'ai Yen, "Pei fen shih," *Ch'üan Han shih*, 4.14a; in Ting Fu-pao, comp., *Ch'üan
Han San-kuo Chin Nan-pei-ch'ao shih* (rpt., Taipei: I-wen yin-shu-kuan, n.d.). Dynastic collections in Ting Fu-pao's anthology hereafter cited by individual title (e.g., *Ch'üan Han
shih*).

47. "Fu Feng-hsien hsien yung huai," in Ch'iu Chao-ao, *Tu shih hsiang-chu*, 4.7.

48. "Chi yüan," in Chu Ho-ling, ed., *Li I-shan shih chi* (*SPTK*), 6.61.

Wang Kuo-wei saw clearly the misery and evil of the human world, and a deep-seated compassion for the suffering in the world prevented him from being indifferent.[49] When he left his home in Hai-ning as a young man to study in Shanghai and then went abroad to study in Japan, it was with the determination to be of use to the world and make it a better place. Even when he experienced repeated disappointments and was composing song lyrics to distract himself, he was also writing a number of prose essays on education and reform: "Reflections on Education" ("Chiao-yü ou-kan"), "On Popular Education" ("Lun p'ing-fan chih chiao-yü chu-i"), "Goals of Education" ("Lun chiao-yü chih tsung-chih"), "Basis for Success in Education" ("Chiao-yü p'u-chi chih ken-pen pan-fa"), "Studies in People's Tastes" ("Jen-chien shih-hao chih yen-chiu"), "Do Away with Opium" ("Ch'u tu p'ien")[50]—all of which reveal his deep commitment to human affairs. When he wrote "Trying for a line, a gut feeling is still there," it was precisely this commitment that he was referring to, and the diction conveys the intensity of this deeply ingrained feeling.

The next line is also superior to the variant, where the tears shed are clearly precipitated by the play he has seen, though he says the tears were "fruitless" (*wu tuan*). By giving a reason for his feeling, he has imposed a limit that also restricts the impact of the line on its reader. The line in the version I have chosen, "I weep fruitless tears," includes the word *k'u*, "alas," which reinforces the "pointless, fruitless," implying that he has looked for a reason for the tears and regrets his failure to find it. It makes his grief not so much pointless as something outside his conscious control: "No one did it but it happened, no one brought it but it's there." It is a grief that is a part of his very being, and the grief he writes about becomes limitless, not restricted to a particular circumstance.

The line begins with "I close the book." On the surface this can be taken as the cause for shedding tears, but in fact closing a book is in itself a simple act with no emotional overtones. If you connect that act with what follows, however, and read it in the context of Wang Kuo-wei's own concerns, the significance to him of such an act brings up all sorts of associations. Reading was his greatest passion; as he wrote, "Books have been my lifelong companions, and they have been for me what I most loved and was most reluctant to lay aside."[51] The main

49. I have discussed this elsewhere, in *Wang Kuo-wei chi ch'i wen-hsüeh p'i-p'ing*, p. 21.
50. See *Ching-an wen-chi*, *WKTCC*, 5:1753, 1762, 1767; and *Ching-an wen-chi hsü-pien*, *WKTCC*, 5:1795, 1870, 1902.
51. See Chao Wan-li, "Wang Ching-an hsien-sheng shou chiao shou p'i shu mu," *Kuo-hsüeh lun-ts'ung* 1, no. 3 (n.d.):147.

reasons for his addiction to reading, it seems to me, were two: he hoped
to find in books the answer to the problem of human life, and he sought
a formula for saving the world. It was for the former reason that he read
philosophy,[52] and for the latter, history.[53] But Wang Kuo-wei's study of
philosophy provided him with no final answer to the problem of human
existence, and his study of history offered no support to his idealistic
hope of saving the world. Given such expectations and such disappointment, it is easy to imagine that this was the reason for shedding futile
tears on closing a book.

Wang Kuo-wei also read with the hope of finding consolation and an
escape from himself. He wrote, "Recently my taste has shifted from philosophy to literature, where I hope to find immediate consolation,"[54]
and remarked in a poem, "Trying to Fly" ("P'in fei"),

> If I don't write a poem about sorrow,
> how can I even for a moment escape sorrow?[55]

> 不有言愁詩句在
> 閑愁那得暫時消

Again, the outcome of his search for consolation and escape from himself led only to greater melancholy and isolation. In another song he
wrote,

> I close my book—all my life long a hundred cares,
> fed up with worries, I've turned stupid and dull.
> I just heard the cuckoo lamenting spring's passing.
> I came to feel there was nothing to get me through the days,
> and I might as well go on collating old texts.
> No place for idle sorrow, let alone happiness.[56]

> 掩卷平生有百端
> 飽更憂患轉冥頑
> 偶聽啼鴂怨春殘
> 坐覺無何消白日
> 更緣隨例弄丹鉛
> 閑愁無分況清歡

Whether he sought consolation in literary studies and creative writing,
or tried to escape into scholarly research, in the end he "closed his

---

52. "Tzu hsü," in *Ching-an wen-chi hsü-pien*, *WKTCC*, vol. 5:1825.
53. "*Kuo-hsüeh ts'ung-k'an hsü*," in *Kuan-t'ang pieh-chi*, *WKTCC*, 4:1409.
54. "Tzu hsü, erh," in *Ching-an wen-chi hsü-pien*, *WKTCC*, 5:1827.
55. *Ching-an shih-kao*, *WKTCC*, 5:1778.
56. *WKWTC*, p. 46.

book" and was left with his lifelong cares, the same old sorrows. This song becomes a commentary on the same act and justifies reading into it a gesture of despair: we can understand that the fruitless tears he sheds are for those lifelong cares, but who is there to know about the pain he feels, his anguish over human suffering? So he concludes with "For whom, alas, does my belt grow loose?" This line reminds us of the lines from Liu Yung's (fl. 1034) song to the tune "Phoenix in the Phoenix Tree" ("Feng ch'i wu"),

> I never regretted my belt grown loose—
> He's worth wasting away for,[57]
>
> 衣帶漸寬終不悔
> 為伊消得人憔悴

which Wang used to illustrate a remark in *Jen-chien tz'u-hua*, "Whoever accomplishes a great undertaking or a great study must pass through three stages," commenting, "This is precisely the second stage." This can serve as a commentary on the significance for Wang of the "belt grown loose." It suggests the pleasure taken in the pursuit of a remote ideal and the resolve not to regret what that pursuit has cost. But where the protagonist in Liu Yung's song was suffering "for him," Wang must ask "for whom?"

In this song Wang Kuo-wei has begun by describing a real scene that he has made the vehicle for deep feeling and philosophical thought. There are many such songs in his collection that begin with a present scene and then develop it into a multilayered symbol with manifold implications; for example,

> Bitter the waters of the Ch'ien-t'ang Bore,
> every day flowing west,
> every day racing east to the sea.[58]
>
> 辛苦錢塘江上水
> 日日西流
> 日日東趨海

> I rise at night and lean out the upper story.
> Over a corner the Jade String hangs low.[59]
>
> 夜起倚危樓
> 樓角玉繩低亞

57. *Ch'üan Sung tz'u* (Peking: Chung-hua shu-chü, 1965), 1:25.
58. *WKWTC*, p. 171.
59. Ibid., p. 89.

West Garden flowers fall deep enough to sweep.
Before my eyes the spring scene too quickly gone.[60]
西園花落深堪掃
過眼韶華真草草

In all these songs, beyond the scene described in the opening lines there
are subtle and far-reaching suggestions that the attentive reader can
observe for himself.

POEM NO. 2: SYMBOLISM OF THE HUMAN FIGURE

After this example of a poem describing a natural scene that at the same
time carries a wealth of subtle nuance, I would like to consider one that
presents a situation involving a human figure that also invites an inter-
pretative reading.

To the tune "Butterfly Loves Flowers" ("Tieh lien hua")

Lovely, modest girl of Yen, fifteen years old,
trailing her usual long skirt—
no mincing gait for her.
When she casts a glance, smiling, in the crowd,
the sirens of the world are like dirt.

A single tree in early bloom—
no other term fits,
except the words "as Heaven made it."
The girl there from Wu who boasts of her dancing skill—
too bad the supple waist misleads.[61]
窈窕燕姬年十五
慣曳長裙
不作纖纖步
衆裡嫣然通一顧
人間顏色如塵土

一樹亭亭花乍吐
除却天然
欲贈渾無語
當面吳娘誇善舞
可憐總被腰肢誤

I long considered this song to be an example of a lyric constructed
around an invented episode, since it has that nuanced quality with a
flavor of symbolism that provokes rich associations, and especially be-

60. Ibid., p. 170.
61. Ibid., p. 168.

cause the symbolic figure is consonant with both Wang Kuo-wei's own
character and also with the critical ideas he advocated for song writing.
I therefore believed that in writing this song Wang Kuo-wei was probably symbolizing himself. In an annotated edition of his songs by Hsiao
Ai, however, I recently came across mention of an episode that might
underlie the making of this poem. Hsiao Ai writes that he learned from
Professor Liu Hui-sun that Wang Kuo-wei composed this song about "a
Manchu girl wine-seller";[62] further, that several of the lines were written by his father, Liu Chi-ying, who asked Wang to complete the poem.
Liu Hui-sun learned this information from a conversation he overheard
between his father and his uncle Lo Chün-mei. Since the sons of Liu
Chi-ying and Wang Kuo-wei were married to daughters of Lo Chen-yü,
it is quite possible that Liu could have asked Wang to finish a poem he
had begun. So this song could also be considered as an example of one
written around an actual experience. Wang Kuo-wei himself remarked
on the difficulty of distinguishing between a real and an imagined scene:
"There is the invented scene and the described scene; it is what distinguishes the idealist and realist schools. But the two are rather difficult
to distinguish, for the scene imagined by a great poet is consistent with
the natural, and the described scene with the ideal." The song to the
tune "Sands of the Washing Stream" dealt with earlier illustrates Wang
Kuo-wei's point: there the "perched crows," "pushing open a window,"
"leaning on the railing," and especially "trying for a line" and "closing
the book," are all part of a scene or episode that is taking place and
naturally describe something that happened. But when we consider
the implications and the subtle suggestions generated, Wang's claim
that the scenes described by a great poet also belong to the ideal is
confirmed.

Another example, from a song to the same tune,

> Striving to ascend the highest peak for a close look at the white moon,
> I chanced to open a celestial eye and look down to the red dust:
> my own self alas there among those I see,[63]

> 試上高峯窺皓月
> 偶開天眼覷紅塵
> 可憐身是眼中人

presents a scene unmistakably drawn from the imagination, but the
opening lines of the song could easily belong to the world of experience:

---

62. Hsiao Ai, *Wang Kuo-wei shih-tz'u chien-chiao* (Hunan: Jen-min ch'u-pan-she, 1984),
pp. 123–24.

63. *WKWTC*, p. 124.

The mountain temple indistinct in the setting sun,
before birds in flight arrive, half the mountain is dark.
山寺微茫背夕曛
鳥飛不到半山昏

These images lack only the immediacy of someone pushing open a window or leaning on a railing, and are worth citing as illustrations of Wang's claim that invented scenes accord with nature.[64]

The song we are presently concerned with can of course be classed with others that simply describe a scene or recount an episode, if we accept Hsiao Ai's account of its origin, but it carries a rich suggestiveness that raises it to the level of an idealized, imagined scene. This can be demonstrated by a line-by-line examination of its imagery and method of presentation. In the first line one can see the dual possibility of a real event or an idealized, imagined one: "Lovely, modest girl of Yen, fifteen years old." In light of Mr. Hsiao's story, this could easily be a Manchu girl wine-seller in Peking (Yen), lovely, modest, and just of that age. While each item lends itself to such a circumstantial reading, there remains oddly enough a flavor of something more, something not simply observed.

First, the narrative voice is impersonal, removing this lovely, modest girl of Yen from the everyday world of human relations and making her an independent aesthetic object. Next, the vocabulary of the song makes use of code words that call up associations with a rich cultural heritage. The expression *yao-t'iao* (here translated "lovely and modest"), for example, originally appeared in the first poem of the *Book of Songs*, from which it already carries an aura of antique elegance and the familiarity of long use. At the same time this term has acquired from its heritage several layers of meaning: "good," "lovely," "secluded"; it can apply to beauty of character or of face. The multiple meanings of this first word of Wang Kuo-wei's song incline one already to a symbolical reading of the whole poem. If one were to substitute the unambiguous word *mei-li* (beautiful), the immediate sense would be the same, the meter would be unchanged, but the effect would be so commonplace and obvious that all trace of symbolism would vanish. So it is clear that the word *yao-t'iao* was used to generate a symbolic character for this song.

The "girl of Yen" also has long been used in Chinese poetry to stand for a pretty girl, and so is an indefinite term, not applying to a girl from a specific place. The twelfth of the "Nineteen Old Poems" includes the

64. See my *Chia-ling lun tz'u ts'ung-kao*, pp. 251–57.

line "In Yen and Chao are many lovely ladies";[65] a poem by Fu Hsüan
(217–78) notes that "The women of Yen are lovely, / the girls of Chao
are pretty";[66] and in a poem by Liu Hsiao-ch'o (481–539), "In Yen and
Chao are many beauties."[67] Obviously "girls from Yen" and "women
from Chao" are only general designations that can be applied to beautiful women anywhere. Such expressions go beyond pointing to a specific
referent and take on the possibility of a symbolic use.

"Fifteen years old" sounds definite enough to be the factually reported age of the "girl of Yen." But this too is a code word with a long
history in Chinese culture. Fifteen is the age at which a girl reaches
maturity and can be given in marriage—the time her hair is symbolically pinned up (*chi fan*), corresponding to the boy's capping ceremony
(*chia kuan*).[68] Poets have traditionally used the age fifteen for girls as a
symbolical counterpart to the capping age, when a boy becomes a man
old enough to take office; thus, Li Shang-yin's "Untitled Poem" begins,
"At eight years she stole a look in the mirror,"[69] and follows her preparation for her expected role in life from that moment, when she starts to
paint her eyebrows, through learning to dress attractively, until at fourteen she is kept out of sight at home, waiting for a proposal, and then,
still not engaged at fifteen, she stands by the garden swing, weeping in
the spring wind. Here the disappointed girl is a symbol for the young
man who, conscious of his endowments, finds himself unappreciated
and passed over among the candidates for public office. So "age fifteen"
is a code word with a weight of historical background that lends it symbolical value.

The next couplet also has a dual reading and the potential for multiple meanings:

Trailing her usual long skirt—
no mincing gait for her.

Hsiao Ai explains this as an objective description: these lines tell us that
she was wearing a Manchu dress and that she walked naturally, something that could be said of Manchu girls, for they did not have bound
feet. This of course fits the reported origin of the poem. But the value of
this song lies not in the veracity of the episode it uses but in how effectively it makes use of it, and here again the excellence of these two lines

65. *Wen hsüan* (Taipei: Wen-hua t'u-shu kung-ssu, 1975), 29.403.
66. Fu Hsüan, "Wu Ch'u ko," in Ting Fu-pao, *Ch'üan Chin shih*, 2.12b.
67. Liu Hsiao-ch'o, "Ku i," in Ting Fu-pao, *Ch'üan Liang shih*, 10.20a.
68. See the "Nei tse" chapter of *Li chi*, in *Shih-san-ching chu-shu*, 5:538–39.
69. "Wu t'i," in *Li I-shan shih chi* (*SPTK*), 1.5.

comes from associations in the mind of the reader. This is achieved, I think, through the obvious contrast between the dissimilar attitudes conveyed by the two phrases "trailing a long skirt" and "a mincing gait." One associates with the former an aristocrat moving easily and with dignity in a long gown, while the latter suggests a delicate, pretty figure. The former belongs to a dignified, self-confident person, the latter to someone anxious to please. This contrast provides the possibility of symbolism, particularly when the first phrase is qualified with the word "usual" or "customary" and the second is negated, "not for her," implying "not like those others," so that in addition to the contrast in attitudes there is also the contrast between what one does and what one does not do, bringing with it an implication of moral character and steadfastness.

In the following lines, "When she casts a glance, smiling, in the crowd, / the sirens of the world are like dirt," the word "smiling" (*yen-jan*) occurs in the Sung Yü rhapsody "Lechery of Master Teng-t'u," where it is applied to the charms of the neighbor girl whose single smile was enough to bewilder the whole city.[70] The phrase *yen-se ju ch'en-t'u* recalls Po Chü-i's (772–846) "Song of Everlasting Sorrow" ("Ch'ang hen ko"), where the palace ladies lose their looks (*wu yen-se*) when Yang Kuei-fei turns her head and with a single smile reveals her manifold charms,[71] and Ch'en Hung's "Story of the Song of Everlasting Sorrow" ("Ch'ang-hen chuan"), which adds that "their beauty was like dirt" (*fen-se ju t'u*).[72] Such associations take us beyond the simple description of the beauty of the Manchu wine-seller of the anecdote.

In Chinese literary history there has long been a tradition of using a beautiful woman as the symbol for a man of virtue or for oneself so considered, beginning with Ch'ü Yüan's "Li-sao." The words "cast a glance" (*t'ung i ku*) in this song earlier appeared in a poem, "Fang-ko hsing," by the poet Ch'en Shih-tao (1052–1102):

> The spring breeze on Everlasting Lane where the beauty, confined,
> has long brought undeserved fame to the green houses.
> She might raise the curtain to cast a glance outside
> but fears that he would not get a good look.[73]

70. "Teng-t'u-tzu hao se fu," in *Wen hsüan*, 25.253.

71. Chou Shu-jen [Lu Hsün], ed., *T'ang Sung ch'uan-ch'i chi* (Peking: Wen-hsüeh ku-chi k'an-hsing-she, 1956), p. 115.

72. Ibid., p. 111. Ch'en Hung was a contemporary of Po Chü-i; he served as a *chu-k'o lang-chung* (Director of the Bureau of Receptions) during the reign of Emperor Te-tsung (780–804).

73. *Hou-shan shih ch'ao*, in Lü Liu-liang, Wu Chih-chen, and Wu Tzu-mu, eds., *Sung shih ch'ao* (Taipei: Shih-chieh shu-chü, 1962), 1.31a. "Everlasting Lane" was where palace ladies in disgrace were confined.

春風永巷閉娉婷
長使青樓誤得名
不惜捲簾通一顧
怕君著眼未分明

That Ch'en Shih-tao was using the neglected palace lady allegorically was noted by his contemporary and mentor Huang T'ing-chien (1045– 1105), who is quoted as having remarked disparagingly of this poem, "Lingering over his own reflection, he is too much of a show-off."[74] If we are reminded of Ch'en Shih-tao's poem as we read Wang Kuo-wei's, the potential for an allegorical meaning naturally increases, particularly so when the phrase "casts a glance" comes after "in the crowd," first setting the lovely girl in contrast to all others, and then in the next line placing her far above all the other beauties in the world and translating her into the highest imaginable realm.

Given the strong possibility of such a reading, there remains the question of how the symbol of a beautiful woman is to be taken. She could stand for the poet himself. I have already suggested a reason for such an interpretation: the poem begins by taking the figure of the woman impersonally, as an aesthetic object, like the girl in the Li Shang-yin poem, and here too she could be a symbol for the poet himself. Likewise, in Ch'en Shih-tao's allegory, a palace lady failed to get the favor of her lord; now that she lives shut up in Everlasting Lane, her beauty hidden out of sight, ordinary women's looks gain an undeserved praise. And even though this beauty does not regret her loss of position and, rolling up the curtain, shows her face, it is to be feared that no one will recognize or appreciate her outstanding beauty. In this poem the beautiful woman certainly stands for the poet himself.

Finally, in some of Wang Kuo-wei's own songs lovely ladies do symbolize the poet,[75] so such a reading here is in line with his tastes and practice. Thus, there are many reasons for believing that Wang Kuo-wei was presenting his own situation through the figure of the woman.

Interestingly enough, however, the suggestion implicit in these lines could also apply to something other than the poet. In the first place, the lovely girl presented as an aesthetic object could easily stand for any ideal of beauty in the poet's mind. And if we take Wang Kuo-wei's phrase "casts a glance" without reference to Ch'en Shih-tao's poem, the phrase could just as well apply to an observer, one who was a part of the crowd but who perceives the extraordinary beauty of the girl: just

74. *Wang Chih-fang shih-hua*, in Kuo Shao-yü, ed., *Sung shih-hua chi-i, Yen-ching hsüeh-pao chuan-hao*, 14 (Peiping: Harvard Yenching Institute, 1937), 1.57.
75. "Yü mei-jen," in *WKWTC*, p. 30; and "Tieh lien hua," in *WKWTC*, p. 178.

when she looked, smiling, she caught his eye, and from this momentary exchange of glances, all other women of the world were as dust to him. Such an occurrence could symbolize some precious and exalted ideal in the mind.

Furthermore, Wang Kuo-wei often expressed such ideas in his other songs, where a sudden moment of philosophical insight comes unawares. For example, "the solitary chime from up above" and "climbing the high peak for a glimpse of the white moon"[76] and "the nearby fairy mountains with the towers and pavilions visible from afar"[77]—these all belong to a kind of exalted, imagined realm of which one catches only a glimpse. So it is clear that taking something other than the poet as the thing symbolized yields a reading compatible with the spiritual goal Wang Kuo-wei was preoccupied with.

So much for the possibilities of interpretation offered by the first stanza. The second offers fewer ambiguities.

> A single tree in early bloom—
> no other term fits,
> except the words "as Heaven made it."

These lines are a paean to natural beauty. Read in terms of the anecdote, they would apply to the unadorned beauty of the Manchu wineseller, but even such straightforward verses have in fact the potential for symbolism. One comes to this stanza with expectations developed in the first stanza with its aura of symbolism and finds in the burgeoning tree bursting with flowers an obvious symbol for beauty, one that need not be restricted to a woman's good looks, and indeed there is here no direct mention of a person. What is praised is natural, unadorned beauty, something Wang Kuo-wei repeatedly found occasion to commend as a characteristic of the songs he admired. Even Hsiao Ai, to whom we owe the anecdotal reference, remarks, "Through this song we can catch a glimpse of Ching-an's [Wang Kuo-wei's] aesthetic views. When he writes about song lyrics, he strongly praises the natural and genuine, and in discussing the good qualities of Yüan opera he also writes, 'To sum it up in a word, natural is all,' and, 'Lack of makeup and careless dress still cannot hide an outstanding beauty.' 'Heaven-given' says it all." And T'ien Chih-tou in his commentary on Wang Kuo-wei's songs also says of this song, "This healthy, beautiful girl of the north made a deep impression on the poet. 'Heaven-given' is the aesthetic standard for Wang. 'The lotus emerging from clear water, Heaven-given, dis-

76. "Huan hsi sha," in *WKWTC*, p. 124.
77. "Tieh lien hua," in *WKWTC*, p. 36.

penses with ornament'—this is the natural excellence given highest
praise in his song lyric criticism. . . . This song could be read as a piece
of *tz'u* criticism."[78]

While noticing the possibility of an allegorical reading of these lines,
both Hsiao and T'ien believe that it is primarily the description of the
girl of the anecdote, and that Wang Kuo-wei merely associated his concept of beauty in the song lyric with the girl's beauty. I think it is not
only the quality of "Heaven-given" that is common to the beauty of the
girl and what he advocated as an ideal for the lyric; rather, every line of
the song is a part of the symbolism. These three lines praise Heaven-
given beauty, but we must take them in the context of the following
lines: "The girl there from Wu who boasts of her dancing skill—/ too
bad the supple waist misleads," and notice the implied invidious contrast between the "girl from Wu" and the girl of Yen who embodies that
beauty. Taken together, it becomes apparent that "Heaven-given" and
"dancing skill" represent yet another contrast in character, besides the
one already noticed in the first stanza, between "trailing a long skirt"
and "mincing gait." There Wang Kuo-wei was already comparing two
kinds of beauty, and using them symbolically. In this case the contrast
becomes stronger when we recall the sort of associations one has with
dancing skill as it comes up in traditional Chinese poetry, where it suggests obsequious behavior—as in Hsin Ch'i-chi's (1140–1207) song to
the tune "The Boy Tickles the Fish" ("Mo yü erh"):

Don't dance—
don't you see,
Yü-huan and Fei-yen are both turned to dust?[79]
君莫舞
君不見
玉環飛燕皆塵土

Wang Kuo-wei's "too bad the supple waist misleads" makes his negative view of dancing skill even more obvious.

The Heaven-given beauty that Wang praises is not only consonant
with his ideal of beauty in song lyrics, it also symbolizes his ideal of human character and conduct. If we look back at the whole poem, we will
see that the entire text of this song not only lends itself to a symbolical
interpretation, the meaning and structure of the symbol, too, are completely consistent with this dual interpretation.

78. *WKWTC*, p. 168.
79. Hsin Ch'i-chi, *Chia-hsüan tz'u pien-nien chien-chu* (Shanghai: Ku-tien wen-hsüeh
ch'u-pan-she, 1968), 1.52.

I am not of course denying the possibility of a straightforward reading of the text in terms of the reported anecdote, but it is worth emphasizing that even those song lyrics of Wang's that are presented as descriptive of real events frequently contain the suggestion of a deeper, subtler reading, resulting in what is essentially a created scene. As Wang Kuo-wei himself said in the statement cited earlier, "The scenes [a great poet] describes also approach the ideal," and "whether *tz'u* is refined or vulgar comes from the spirit, not what appears on the surface." This song can be taken as an illustration of these poetic principles.

POEM NO. 3: INVENTED SCENES, ALLUSION, AND ALLEGORY

To the tune "Partridge in the Sky" ("Che-ku t'ien")

Over the covered gallery wind flaps a fifty-foot banner,
the storied structure thrusts up level with the clouds.
All that remains, alas: full moons lined up like coins
that do not illumine the red flowers hanging from the ceiling.

Repeatedly I grope, again I scramble,
a thousand gates, a myriad doors—is it real or not?
Everything in the world is open to doubt,
only this doubt is not to be doubted.[80]

閣道風飄五丈旗
層樓突兀與雲齊
空餘明月連錢列
不照紅葩倒并披

頻摸索, 且攀躋
千門萬戶是耶非
人間總是堪疑處
唯有茲疑不可疑

Whatever the status of the preceding lyrics as presenting a real or imagined scene, there can be no doubt about this one: the scene is bizarre enough not to be taken for something actually observed. But what about Wang Kuo-wei's insistence that even the imagined scene be compatible with nature? There should be some reasonable basis for the poet's invention. Readers generally have found this particular song obscure or unintelligible, even in its general purport. It becomes clearer if we look

---

80. *WKWTC*, p. 134.

for the sources of Wang Kuo-wei's imagined scene and consider the
song in the light of his basic intellectual attitudes.

Take the first two lines: "Over the covered gallery wind flaps a fifty-
foot banner, / the storied structure thrusts up level with the clouds."
There is a power in the imagined scene to move and involve the reader,
not only in its grandeur but also in its lifting, soaring quality. From line
5 ("Repeatedly I grope, again I scramble") we can infer that this scene
which the reader finds so moving is also the object of the poet's search,
and from Wang Kuo-wei's own practice, a scene that is the goal of a
search is always something in the imagination, not in the real world.
For example, the search for the Fairy Mountain in the sea (in the
song to the tune "The Butterfly Loves Flowers") and the effort to ascend
the mountain peak to view the white moon ("Sands of the Washing
Stream")[81] are typical of the symbolical use of an imagined scene as
the goal of a search for the ideal.

But the Fairy Mountain is a reference to the familiar legend of the
Three Fairy Mountains in the Po Sea.[82] Since the "mountain temple"
and the "highest peak" in the "Sands of the Washing Stream" song are
not part of an allusion, some readers are led to assume that what is
involved there is a real scene; but when the second stanza concludes
with the purely philosophical "I chanced to open a celestial eye to look
down to the red dust: / my own self alas there among those I see," it
seems obvious that this scene is also an imagined one. Anyhow, these
imagined scenes are good illustrations of Wang's claim that the scenes
imagined by a great poet will always accord with the natural, their
elements always be found in nature, and their structure always reflect
the natural.

In this poem, however, the covered gallery and fifty-foot banner present definite problems. They are not an obvious allusion like the Fairy
Mountains, nor are they a part of a natural scene like the mountain
temple. In using an unfamiliar scene to represent the sought-for goal,
this song, it seems to me, is more deliberately symbolical than the above
two examples. The scene presented in the first line derives from the description of the O-pang Palace in the "Annals of the First Emperor" in
Ssu-ma Ch'ien's *Historical Records*: "The palace in front is O-p'ang, ex-
tending east to west five hundred paces and north to south five hundred

81. Ibid., pp. 36, 124.
82. "Chiao ssu chih," *Han shu* (Peking: Chung-hua shu-chü, 1962), 25.1204; also
Wang Tzu-nien, "Shih-i ming shan chi," in *Chiu hsiao-shuo*, ed. Wu Tseng-chi (Shanghai:
Shang-wu yin-shu-kuan, 1944), 1:65–67.

paces. A myriad of men could be seated above, and below is place for a
fifty-foot banner."[83] It must have been one of the largest palaces ever
built in China, and when Wang Kuo-wei was looking for the most
magnificent and imposing structure as the symbol for the object he pursued in his imagination, he chose to base it on the *Shih-chi* description of
the O-p'ang Palace.

We can see, of course, that the palace's primary function as a symbol
in his song derives from its grandeur, but that is not its only purpose:
there is also the detail of the covered gallery (*ko-tao*) in the opening
line. The *Shih-chi* description of the O-p'ang Palace continues: "Running
around it was a covered way [*ko-tao*] leading down from the palace to
connect with [Chung-nan] Mountain, marking the highest point of the
mountain with a gate tower. A corridor was made from O-p'ang crossing the Wei [River] and connecting with Hsien-yang." The symbolism of
this structure is clearly stated: "[The palace] represents the [constella-
tion] Zenith [*t'ien-chi*], where the Covered Gallery cuts across the Milky
Way to reach the constellation Ying-shih."[84] It is obvious that this
structure was planned with an astronomical counterpart. As far as the
O-p'ang Palace is concerned, the covered gallery simply connects the
palace with the capital Hsien-yang across the Wei River. But it also has
a symbolical function connected with astronomy: the whole structure
was built to symbolize the seat of the Lord of Heaven, so that the palace
itself is the constellation Zenith, the highest point in the heavens.
Covered Gallery is also the name of a constellation. In the "Essay on
Astronomy" we read, "The last six stars of the Purple Palace [*tzu-kung*]
that cross the Milky Way and reach the Ying-shih [constellation] are
called the Covered Gallery."[85] Chang Shou-chieh's commentary on this
passage states that "the seven stars of the constellation Ying-shih are
the palace of the Son of Heaven [*t'ien-tzu*]."[86] From this it is clear that
the covered gallery of O-p'ang Palace was constructed to symbolize the
Purple Palace of the Zenith. Its crossing the Wei River to connect with
the palaces in Hsien-yang coincides with the trajectory of the six last
stars of the Purple Palace as they cross the Milky Way and connect
with the palace of the Son of Heaven, that is, the abode of the Lord of
Heaven.

83. "Ch'in Shih-huang pen-chi," *Shih-chi* (Peking: Chung-hua shu-chü, 1962),
6.256. Commentators gloss the name of the palace as meaning "near the capital" and
read it therefore as *o-p'ang* (rather than *a-fang*).

84. Ibid.

85. "T'ien-kuan shu," *Shih-chi*, 27.1290.

86. Ibid., 27.1291.

The choice of the setting of a fifty-foot banner waving over a covered gallery as a symbol for the goal of his pursuit enriches the poem with another set of associations. Had Wang Kuo-wei merely used a lofty, remote setting like the mountain temple or the high cliff, his symbol would have conveyed nothing more than that—something beyond easy reach. But by using terms that have a specific reference, he has greatly increased the resonance of his symbol. Since the Covered Gallery in the *Shih-chi* was meant symbolically as a passage to the seat of the Lord of Heaven, there is the implication that it was the goal he was groping and scrambling toward. In terms of Wang Kuo-wei's lifelong and passionate preoccupation with the problem, it could well symbolize his striving for an understanding of human life.

This kind of symbolic interpretation also accords with Wang Kuo-wei's own critical practice, and in his songs this passionate pursuit of a final answer to the problem is repeatedly expressed through the metaphor of a spiritual intercourse with Heaven. For example,

On the topmost peak are no clouds,
last night it rained—
I come to listen to Heaven's voice
絕頂無雲
昨宵有雨
我來此地聞天語

and

How can I bear last night's dream in the west house,
when I walked with sleeves full of plucked stars?[87]
更堪此夜西樓夢
摘得星辰滿袖行

There are many such lines showing Wang Kuo-wei's frequent use of an imagined lofty and remote setting that not only symbolizes a high ideal but also suggests a desire to ascend to heaven to seek the answers to the fundamental problem of human existence. But this image as used in these other songs is both conventional and natural, while in the present song it appears unusual and anything but natural; it also carries an extra layer of implication from its original context in the *Historical Records*. And so from this first line we can conclude that this song, compared with the others, is one in which the poet deliberately was creating a setting with an allegorical dimension.

87. "T'a so hsing" and "Che-ku t'ien," in *WKWTC*, pp. 106, 102, respectively.

Since it begins with an allegorical setting, it must continue in the same mode. The images used in this imagined setting are derived from books that Wang Kuo-wei had read, some of them familiar and some not likely to be known to every reader. First, the line "The storied structure thrusts up level with the clouds" probably derives from a couplet in the fifth of the "Nineteen Old Poems":

> In the northwest is a lofty tower
> rising up level with the floating clouds,[88]
> 西北有高樓
> 上與浮雲齊

lines surely familiar to every reader. Wang Kuo-wei has introduced a couple of changes: "storied" (*ts'eng*) in place of "lofty" (*kao*) ("structure," "tower" is the same Chinese word *lou*), and "thrusts up" (*t'u wu*) for "rises" (*shang*). Changes like this in lines taken from classical texts are dealt with in a remark in Wang Kuo-wei's critical writing,[89] where such borrowing is approved on principle, so long as it contributes to setting. The changes he has introduced here adapt the line to the setting he was creating, which is not that of the original poem. The original adjective "lofty" conveys no suggestion of anything beyond "height," while "storied" adds a more complicated feeling: along with the idea of "high" is the suggestion of a structure elaborated, substantially constructed, and imposing. Add the words "thrusts up," and it achieves an almost dizzying force. In the context of a covered gallery that stretches from a mountain top across a river and into the city, it adds scale and motion to the image, especially when enlivened by the enormous banner flapping in the wind above it. This resurrects in the imagination the grandeur and magnificence of the First Ch'in Emperor's O-p'ang Palace and brings it before our eyes, much as Tu Fu could imagine "Han Wu-ti's banners before my eyes" as he remembered the K'un-ming Lake, constructed a thousand years earlier.[90]

The next couplet imposes a discordant atmosphere on this magnificent image:

> All that remains, alas: full moons lined up like coins
> that do not illumine the red flowers hanging from the ceiling.

The source for these lines also lies in Wang Kuo-wei's reading, transformed through his imagination. Pan Ku's (32–92) "Rhapsody on the

---

88. *Wen hsüan*, 29.402.
89. *JCTH*, p. 489.
90. "Ch'iu hsing," in Ch'iu Chao-ao, *Tu shih hsiang chu*, 17:69.

Western Capital" provides the full moons lined up like coins. He was describing the Chao-yang Palace: "Lord Sui's full moons everywhere in between, / jade discs clasped in gold, like rows of coins."[91] Lord Sui's "full moon" alludes to the night-shining pearl (*ming-yüeh chu*) given Lord Sui by the grateful snake he treated, according to Li Shan's commentary.[92] The "jade disks clasped in gold" provide a more immediately intelligible basis for the image "making a row of coins" (*shih wei lieh-ch'ien*) than do the pearls, which are all Wang Kuo-wei's line mentions, and perhaps they should be appropriated as part of the allusion. Since the song began with the covered gallery that symbolically leads to the abode of the Lord of Heaven, the night-shining pearls and associated jade discs are part of the resplendent ornamentation of his palace.

The mysterious pink flowers hanging from the ceiling come from Chang Heng's (78–139) "Rhapsody on the Western Capital," where he describes the Lung-shou Hall in front of the Wei-yang Palace with "lotus stems upside down on the painted ceiling."[93] Tso Ssu (ca. 253– ca. 307) describes a similar palace ceiling in his "Rhapsody on the Capital of Wei,"[94] but Wang Kuo-wei no doubt had in mind the Chang Heng passage, since it involves a palace in the Western Capital, closer to the site of O-p'ang Palace. In sum, the song has described the magnificence and beauty of a palace, enriched by borrowings from the two rhapsodies to suggest an idealized conception of the seat of the Lord of Heaven.

So much for a surface reading. Notable are the qualifying introductory phrases: "All that remains, alas" (*k'ung yü*) and "that do not illumine" (*pu chao*). Their function is an important one. The first refers to the ruin of the imagined palace and expresses regret that it is no longer intact, and the next line continues with a lament of disappointment at the loss of the hoped-for spectacle.

I have already mentioned Wang Kuo-wei's dedication to the search for an ideal and elsewhere have cited a number of his own writings to show that he always disregarded material advantage in his pursuit of an ideal goal, concluding that his willingness to sacrifice himself in striving for an ideal was part of his genius and beyond his control to change.[95] There was no way ever to bring this search to fruition, and in many

---

91. Pan Ku, "Hsi-tu fu," in *Wen hsüan*, 1.5.
92. Ibid.
93. Chang Heng, "Hsi-ching fu," in *Wen hsüan*, 2.19.
94. Tso Ssu, "Wei tu fu," in *Wen hsüan*, 6.81.
95. See my *Wang Kuo-wei chi ch'i wen-hsüeh p'i-p'ing*, p. 17.

of his songs there is a lament for a search that ends in failure and disappointment.[96] However, some force kept him from ever giving up this pursuit of the ideal; the light of idealism was always preserved in the poet's heart. So, in our song the rows of night-shining pearls still seem to emit a glimmer of light, even though it is not enough to illuminate the pink blossoms hanging down from the painted ceiling. It is a situation comparable to that in Juan Chi's (210–63) "Song of Sorrow," no. 19: "There's a lovely lady to the west," where the poet sees a beautiful woman who is "floating indistinct"[97] but appears to let her eyes fall on him. In the end he is unable to make contact with her, and the result is

> Attractive she was, but we never came together;
> seeing her has made me sad.
> 悅懌未交接
> 晤言用感傷

Thus, in the first stanza of Wang Kuo-wei's song, the search for an ideal realm in an imagined setting—and its failure—are expressed in terms of symbols based on allusions to ancient texts. It combines clarity with elegance, radiance with obscurity, in a vision of soaring majesty— a truly notable example of an imagined setting. The second stanza begins with a direct statement of the frustration of his efforts: "Repeatedly I grope, again I scramble." The words "repeatedly" (*p'in*) and "again" (*ch'ieh*) emphasize the difficulty of abandoning the search and its futility. The "thousand gates" and "myriad doors" take us back to the image of the palace (the phrase comes from the *Historical Records*, "Annals of Wu-ti," where it describes the Chien-chang Palace)[98] and symbolize the confusion and wrong turns connected with the search. The words "is it real . . . ," describing something indistinctly glimpsed and then lost sight of, are adapted from an old text, Han Wu-ti's song about the apparition of the Lady Li:

> Is it real, is it not?
> Indistinctly seen from afar.
> Wavering, how slowly she comes![99]

---

96. See, for example, "Tieh lien hua," *WKWTC*, p. 36, and "Huan hsi sha," *WKWTC*, p. 124.

97. "Yung huai," in Juan Chi, *Juan Pu-ping yung huai shih chu* (Hong Kong: Shang-wu yin-shu-kuan, 1961), pp. 25–26.

98. "Hsiao-wu pen-chi," *Shih-chi*, 12.482.

99. Han Wu-ti, "Li fu-jen ko," in Ting Fu-pao, *Ch'üan Han shih*, 1.2a.

是耶非耶
立而望之
翩何姍姍其來遲

They bring to the groping search for a lost palace the association of a beautiful woman. Though such a suggestion was not necessarily in Wang Kuo-wei's conscious mind, given the associations attached to the source of the words, the potential effect is there. Furthermore, the analogy between expecting a meeting with a beautiful woman and the pursuit of an ideal links them together, and so such a reading is unquestionably a factor in creating resonances that enrich our appreciation of this poem. The concluding couplet, "Everything in the world is open to doubt, / only this doubt is not to be doubted," marks the ultimate futility of the search. He has given a slight twist to Descartes's famous dictum that everything is subject to doubt except the fact of doubting. For Wang Kuo-wei it is precisely *this* doubt—the uncertainty of his search, of its very goal—that is not in doubt, transforming a logical, philosophical concept into a cry of despair. Since the object of his search is unobtainable, there can be no solution to his uncertainties; this is a conviction that repeatedly appears in his writing, and this song is representative of those that create an imagined setting to reveal his fundamental "pattern of consciousness," to borrow a term from the "Criticism of Consciousness" school.

The setting projected in the song is so fanciful, so bizarre, that readers have often completely failed to understand its meaning,[100] and so I have taken it as one of my examples, hoping to show that beneath the fanciful imagery and obscure allusions is an intelligible and moving poem.

POEM NO. 4: WRITING ABOUT WRITING

To the tune "Sands of the Washing Stream"
The new song—is it a real love affair?
The tender words are too vague.
For whom are you writing with such pain in the lamplight?

---

100. Joey Bonner, for example, in her book, *Wang Kuo-wei, an Intellectual Biography* (Cambridge: Harvard University Press, 1986), p. 115, misled by the common meaning of the word *ching*, explains the pink flowers hanging from the ceiling as referring to the drowning of the palace lady Chen Fei in a well.

I lean on the desk for a glimpse of your new poem
and then turn away from the lamp to reflect on the good times we've had—
it matches none of the things I recall.[101]

本事新詞定有無
這般綺語太胡盧
燈前腸斷為誰書

隱几窺君新製作
背燈數妾舊歡娛
區區情事總難符

Before discussing this song, I should explain why I have chosen it as
one of my four examples, when so many of his better-known song lyrics
present an imagined episode.[102] There are too many, certainly, to deal
with adequately here. My choice was in part determined by the very
unfamiliarity of this song—no need to explain one that everyone
already appreciates. This one has the further attraction of not obviously
belonging to my category of invented episodes, for on the surface it
appears to be the realistic presentation of an intimate scene, while
actually it conveys a subtle and involved allegorical meaning that is
worth elucidating. Finally, all the other songs I might have used deal
with themes that recur repeatedly in Wang Kuo-wei's works: the man
who maintains his integrity in a hostile world,[103] the disappointing
contrast between dream and reality,[104] the devotion that asks no
recompense,[105] the realization that one cannot detach oneself from the
common lot of humanity[106]—all those ethical and philosophical ideas
dear to his heart.

The song I have chosen has the unusual theme of poetic composition,
something not only unusual in the short song (hsiao-ling) form, but extremely difficult to achieve through an ostensibly realistic love song.
That Wang Kuo-wei did it successfully is my real reason for using
this as an example of a song that describes an invented episode.

To begin with the surface level of meaning: the scene is of a couple in
a room. The voice is a woman's; the man has been writing a song,

101. *WKWTC*, p. 54.

102. For example, those to the tunes "Yü mei-jen"(*WKWTC*, p. 30) and "The Butterfly Loves Flowers" (*WKWTC*, pp. 178, 157, 98, 28, 32) are all extremely effective and
complex poems.

103. "Yü mei-jen," *WKWTC*, p. 30; "Tieh lien hua," *WKWTC*, p. 178.

104. "Tieh lien hua," *WKWTC*, p. 157; "Su-mu-che," *WKWTC*, p. 60.

105. "Tieh lien hua," *WKWTC*, p. 28; "Ch'ing-p'ing yüeh," *WKWTC*, p. 75.

106. "Tieh lien hua," *WKWTC*, p. 32; "Huan hsi sha," *WKWTC*, p. 124.

which she has been reading over his shoulder. The first line—"The new song—is it a real affair?"—is the woman's reaction on reading it: "The love affair you are writing about, is it something that really happened?" The setting makes this the obvious first meaning of the word *pen-shih*, "affair," which can of course be completely non-committal as to what sort of "affair" is meant. The word "really" (*ting*) reflects her compulsion to know the truth: did it really exist or not (*ting yu wu*)? The next line, "The tender words are too vague," gives the reasons for her uncertainty—the tender words and their effect. It's the "tender words" (*ch'i yü*) that lead the woman to believe that the affair is a love affair; but they are too ambiguous, so vague and obscure that it is hard to decide to whom they apply.[107] These first two lines provide the causes of the woman's puzzled suspicion.

There is another reason for her doubt: "For whom are you writing with such pain in the lamplight?" The distress (*ch'ang tuan*) showing in the face of the man writing the song must be connected with the person about whom he is writing those tender words. The lamplight defines a setting (inside a room, at night) appropriate to pensive reflection. Accompanied by signs of strong emotion, it gives further support to the supposition that he is writing about a love affair. But since the tender words are vague, it is hard to know who the object of his feeling might be.

The first stanza is devoted to the doubts roused in the woman's mind as she reads a song the man has been writing. The second stanza continues as she ponders over what she has just read. Having looked surreptitiously (*k'uei*) over his shoulder to see what he was writing, she turns away to consider whether it might possibly be about her:

> I lean on the desk for a glimpse of your new poem
> and then turn away from the lamp to reflect on the good times we've had—

Vague though the song's tender words may have been, none of it matches anything that she can remember of their relation. So in the end her doubts remain unresolved: is the song about a real love affair or not?

So much for a reading of this song as a simple love poem. The vocabulary common to such songs ("affair," "tender words," "heartbroken in the lamplight," "leaning on the desk," "turning away from the lamp,"

---

107. There is another version of this line in *Kuan-t'ang chi lin*: "Slanting lines of cursive script are obscure," i.e., the writing is hard to read. It has no direct connection with the preceding line, and I follow the text given in Ch'en Nai-wen's *Ching-an tz'u* as the better reading.

"the good times") and the convincingly implied narrative put in the
woman's voice make it sound like an episode in a love affair. I am
convinced, however, that it is an invented allegory. In the first place,
although the tone is lively and realistic, it lacks any real expression of
feeling, whether love, jealousy, grief, or joy, as compared with Wang's
101 other love poems, such as the one celebrating a reunion with
his wife,[108] or the lament on seeing her on her deathbed after a
separation[109]—events in his life that can be verified. Too, the feelings in
those songs are conveyed through a subjective, personal voice that is
unmistakable and contrasts strongly with the voice of the female persona adopted in this one, objectivized as the narrator. Thus, the affair
implied in the song becomes a symbol providing the possibility of an
allegorical reading.

Furthermore, it can hardly be a coincidence that every line of the
poem suggests an experience connected with artistic creation; the allegory must be deliberate. I will give my interpretation of the poem read
in such terms. To begin with the first line again: "The new song—is it
a real affair?" The word *pen-shih* in traditional Chinese poetry and song
has two possible meanings. In the wide sense, as applied to a poem's
content, it can be any episode, real or imagined. *Pen-shih* in the narrow
sense means "a love affair," and so it appears in the first reading of our
song. Now any mention of love in a poem is calculated to rouse the
reader's interest—he wants to know more about it. But in the eyes of
traditional Confucian moralists a love affair is a most improper business, and this attitude produces two results: where the reader of such
poetry has his interest strongly roused, the writer's response to the reader's curiosity is to refuse to explain. The matter is further complicated
by the long-standing Chinese tradition of love poetry as allegory, so that
any love poem provides the reader with a potentially double understanding, first for the emotion directly expressed and then a possible
allegorical dimension. A poem about a love affair easily raises the doubt
in the interested reader's mind as to whether the poem might be allegorical or just a love poem and, if the latter, whether the event is a real episode in the poet's life. This uncertainty has always been a problem for
readers of Chinese poetry, and Wang Kuo-wei's song begins by asking
the question, "The new song—is it about a real affair?" thus devoting
the strategic place in the poem to a problem prominent in understanding Chinese poetry. To compress so much in a short line and to do it so
vividly is a remarkable achievement.

108. *WKWTC*, p. 130.
109. Ibid., p. 117.

Wang Kuo-wei, however, is not just posing a general literary problem. It is a problem associated with a particular genre, and the words
"new song" (*hsin tz'u*) in the first line are followed in the second by
"The tender words are too vague," which in addition to its surface
meaning is also descriptive of a special characteristic of the literary
art of the song lyric. For most songs are love songs: their currency is
"tender words." This recalls, again, Wang's statement in the *Jen-chien
tz'u-hua* cited earlier that "the essence of *tz'u* is in a subtle and refined
beauty" [*yao-miao i-hsiu*];[110] it should avoid the obvious, preferring the
vague and suggestive to the definite and specific. And, moreover,
whereas the range of the song lyric is limited—largely to the subject of
love—by the very imprecision of its language, *tz'u* is more suggestive
than *shih* and carries the reader beyond the surface meaning of the
words, leading to doubt about its true meaning or the poet's intention
in writing. This simultaneous characteristic and limitation are described dramatically in the line "The tender words are too vague."

So far we have been considering only the features peculiar to the song
lyric that distinguish it from *shih* poetry. If we look at it from the point
of view of the poet who is writing the one or the other, we can see a difference in the way each is composed. When writing a *shih* poem, the
poet is self-consciously expressing his own feelings, so that the poem
always has a theme clearly discernible by the reader. The songwriter,
however, is primarily providing words for a tune, filling in a pattern,
and though the song lyrics by later poets were not really intended for
singers to perform, the poet was chiefly concerned with providing a text
for parting sorrow or the passing of spring rather than directly giving
vent to his own feelings, with the result that, like the reader, he too is
uncertain about the precise meaning of the romantic words he puts
down in the song pattern. But though the poet may not be deliberately
expressing his own feelings, still, in the course of writing, the secret
thoughts and feelings in the depths of his unconscious can be inadvertently revealed in his poem. And when his deepest feelings are touched,
the process of composition can be accompanied by great anguish. But in
terms of the poet's own consciousness, it is by no means certain that he
can make himself logically aware of what forces have been at work. This
is a difficulty admirably and appropriately conveyed by the line "For
whom are you writing with such pain in the lamplight?" which can
apply to the pain caused by the poet's reflection on the feelings stirred
within him by the song lyric he is writing.

110. *JCTH*, p. 48.

The second stanza clearly identifies the writer of the song as a man (*chün*) and the reader as a woman (*ch'ieh*), two separate individuals. But it is easy to identify both with the poet himself, as two aspects of his being. As I have previously suggested, Wang Kuo-wei used the terms "observing the object outside" (*kuan wu*) and "observing one's own feeling" (*kuan wo*) to refer, in the former, to the description of an object or event and, in the latter, to the poet's own feelings as the object of description. But of course it is the poet who observes and who describes, and he not only observes his own feelings and ideas, he can also adopt a stance of viewing himself writing. Hence the two protagonists both coincide with the poet himself, the man who writes the poem and the woman who reads it and turns away from the lamp to reflect on the good times.

All poets in the process of composition have a component within themselves that observes and criticizes, and the result of this critical observation is frequently the realization that what one has written is an inadequate expression of what one has been feeling. As Lu Chi (261–303) expressed it in his "Rhapsody on Literature": "Whenever I write, I am more and more aware of what is involved: I always worry lest my ideas are not equal to my subject, and that my writing fails to convey my ideas."[111] This has precisely the meaning of "it matches none of the things I recall."

Given the limitations of the *hsiao-ling* lyric form, vague and obscure in comparison with all other verse forms, the difficulty faced by the poet in bringing his subtle feelings into congruence with his words is even greater than what Lu Chi was describing. Lu Chi's rhapsody is universally praised for using a verse form to write literary criticism, but Wang Kuo-wei has used the short song for the same purpose, and his allegory on *tz'u* criticism is a unique achievement in the annals of Chinese song writing.

CONCLUSION

In considering Wang Kuo-wei's place as a song lyricist in a Chinese tradition of such poetry that goes back a good thousand years, it is worth noting that there is a discrepancy between his practice of song writing and his critical theory. He strove to approximate the ideal of the first category of true song words, and superficially his short songs and especially certain of his love poems come close as far as content is con-

---

111. Lu Chi, "Wen fu," in *Wen hsüan*, 17.224.

cerned, but their real character tends rather toward the third type. This calls for elaboration.

The basic reason for this discrepancy between practice and theory comes from his not being able to make his composition a purely spontaneous act. This in turn has its causes. First of all, Wang Kuo-wei was writing at the end of the nineteenth century, a period wholly unlike the Five Dynasties and Northern Sung. Then *tz'u* were simply songs for entertainment, while by Wang's time they were a literary form, used like *shih* poetry for self-expression, so he could hardly avoid being self-conscious in writing them. Furthermore, in those earlier times poets writing words for musical settings were not constrained by any body of theory or criticism relating to their art—they could be spontaneous in a way denied later writers, especially a scholar like Wang Kuo-wei, who had been actively concerned with criticism and studies of the genre at the time he was writing songs. Accordingly, when he was himself occupied with creative writing, he could not help deliberately striving for the sort of special beauty and evocative power that he admired, but this deliberate effort was basically antagonistic to the goal he sought. The result was that the songs he wrote were at variance with the models he advocated.

Moreover, Wang was a scholar and a philosopher who, as noted earlier, had gradually moved from philosophy to literature, looking for some immediate consolation. And of his philosophical studies he said, "The problem of human existence is always before my eyes."[112] So everywhere in his songs we find reflected his philosophical concerns and ideas, with the result that his own *tz'u* deviated even more from those of his preferred first category, true song words. The quality he detected and valued in earlier songwriters was something achieved spontaneously, and to deliberately set about achieving it was bound to result in songs more like those of the third, expository type that Wang disapproved of. However, whereas Sung dynasty poets who wrote songs of this third category were exercising their self-conscious art on long songs (*man-tz'u*), Wang wrote short songs in the unmannered, intimate style of the earlier Five Dynasties and Northern Sung. A poet writing a long song concentrated his effort on the technique of composition on a verbal level, whereas in the *hsiao-ling* Wang could focus on devising a situation or episode sufficiently concentrated or ambiguous to convey the complexity of his thought, producing a natural difference in style. The subject matter also differed, since writers of expository songs typically

112. "Tzu hsü," in *Ching-an wen-chi hsü-pien, WKTCC*, 5:1825.

applied their skills to political topics or love affairs in the real world, whereas Wang devoted his effort to giving symbolic expression to his in- most philosophical ideas through specific episodes or scenes. While he has a self-conscious artistry in common with those earlier writers of *tz'u* of the third category and shares an ideal of the form with the poets of the first, his own song lyrics are different from both.

What about the second category, the song lyrics written for the same reason as *shih* poetry, intentionally to express the poet's feelings? The commonest failing of such songs is that they lose the subtle depth that is the special beauty of *tz'u*. To succeed as song lyrics, they must come from a poet whose feelings have a deeply ambiguous cast, one who can successfully reconcile those complex feelings with the formal prosodic demands of the song form and, while giving his feelings clear expres- sion, can still preserve the qualities peculiar to song. Two poets who satisfied these conditions were Su Shih (1036–1101) and Hsin Ch'i-chi. When we compare the few songs Wang Kuo-wei wrote where it is clear that he was deliberately expressing feelings that normally would have been written in *shih* form, we discover some resemblance to those poets, but also considerable difference. Su Shih and Hsin Ch'i-chi employed shifting perspectives to present a wide range of concerns both personal and public, and they could usually achieve subtle depth even in writing songs deliberately expressing their feelings. When Wang tried it, he could not avoid an impression of monotony and obviousness. On the other hand, his philosophical ideas were something lacking in the songs of Su and Hsin. On the technical side, their use of allusion, their diction and overall organization seem to have been achieved with a natural ease that eluded Wang, who relied on deliberately constructed allegory, making one feel that he was working too hard.

After this comparison of Wang Kuo-wei's songs with those of his pre- decessors over a period of a thousand years, it should not be hard to establish his place in the company of China's preeminent writers of *tz'u*. He is an important poet who draws upon the past and blends tradition with innovative and original elements of his own. Wang's song lyrics combine many of the features of traditional *tz'u* without ever fitting wholly into any of the traditional categories. His distinctive incorpora- tion of philosophical ideas and reflection of his own critical ideas in the very song lyrics he wrote represent a significant development in the realm of *tz'u* content and practice. Wang was aware of his accomplish- ment, and in his preface he ventured to claim: "Though I have not yet written as many as a hundred songs, there are only one or two poets since Southern Sung times who can match me—of this I am always confident. In comparison to the great *tz'u* writers of the Five Dynasties and Northern Sung, I must confess that in some ways I am not their equal, but in some respects these same poets are not as good as I am."[113] By means of a multifaceted approach incorporating both traditional critical methods and modern analytical techniques, I have endeavored to indicate the breadth of his many achievements.

113. "Tzu hsü, erh," in *Ching-an wen-chi hsü-pien*, *WKTCC*, 5:1828.

Messages of Uncertain Origin:
The Textual Tradition of the *Nan-T'ang erh-chu tz'u*

Daniel Bryant

Writing almost ten years ago, in the preface to my book, *Lyric Poets of the Southern T'ang: Feng Yen-ssu, 903–960, and Li Yü, 937–978*, I tried to excuse my failure to provide any discussion of textual questions by promising to produce in due course a separate study dealing specifically with such questions. This chapter is both more and less than the promised study. Less than promised because it does not discuss the works of Feng Yen-ssu, it is also something more than I envisioned at the time, for it leads to questions about the nature of textual history that surely have implications for all who work with traditional Chinese texts.

This study owes a good deal to other people. Some parts of it go back many years to work done as a student at the University of British Columbia, and I am grateful to my teachers there, E. G. Pulleyblank, Florence C. Y. Chao (Yeh Chia-ying), and Jan W. Walls, for all the advice and encouragement they offered then or have since. The portions of the study that involve the use of a computer were made possible by a series of grants from the President's Committee on Faculty Travel and Research, University of Victoria. I am particularly grateful to Professor Vinton A. Dearing of the University of California at Los Angeles, author of the programs used, and to Mr. Martin Milner and Ms. Laura Proctor, formerly consultants for Computing Services at the University of Victoria, for the extensive help they rendered me in this portion of the project, as well as for their patience with my questions and mistakes. Needless to say, all the errors, omissions, oversights, and misjudgments are mine.

Abbreviations used in Notes and Bibliography

PP Pai-pu ts'ung-shu chi-ch'eng reprint. Citations are given in the form *PP* x/y, where x is the series number and y the number of the case (*t'ao*) within the series. Pagination is the same for the original *ts'ung-shu* edition and the reprint.

SPTK Ssu-pu ts'ung-k'an reprint. Page numbers are given both for the original and (in parentheses) the consecutive pagination of the reprint.

Getting to the implications will, however, require that we traverse a good deal of terrain, much of it heavily thicketed in prickly detail. Our journey comprises five distinct stages, as follows. 1) Because the nature and authenticity of the *Tsun-ch'ien chi* bear crucially on issues to be taken up in later sections, we shall begin by reviewing the problems and evidence surrounding this anthology. 2) On taking up the textual tradition with which we are chiefly concerned, the *Nan-T'ang erh-chu tz'u*, we shall first examine the compilation process that formed the text. The discussion is long and in many ways inconclusive, but it serves both to set the stage and to suggest the need for the section that follows. 3) Having examined aspects of the *Nan-T'ang erh-chu tz'u* from a bibliographic standpoint, we shall turn next to an analysis of the genealogy of the extant editions, employing a computer-assisted methodology that has not, so far as I know, previously been brought to bear on a Chinese textual tradition. The process aims first to construct a "directionless diagram" representing the relationships among the different editions ("states" of the tradition), and second to locate within this diagram an archetype, transforming the diagram into a genealogical "tree" and allowing us— or so we will argue—to resolve many cases of variant readings in the tradition. 4) From the discussion of the process for locating an archetype for the *Nan-T'ang erh-chu tz'u* it becomes evident that some further advance in our understanding of a particular problem in the text of the *Tsun-ch'ien chi* may be possible. We shall return to that collection briefly in order to explore this problem and strengthen the claim of the *Tsun-ch'ien chi* to textual authority. 5) Finally, we shall consider some of the implications of our findings, both as they apply to a particular poem (one also discussed by Stephen Owen in another chapter) and as they reflect on the methodology employed. Readers rendered faint of heart by the prospect of so long and arduous a trek may wish to consult this final section first before deciding to saddle up.

THE AUTHENTICITY OF THE *TSUN-CH'IEN CHI*

The overriding problem raised by the *Tsun-ch'ien chi* is that of authenticity. There are actually two different questions at issue. The first, with which students of the collection have been chiefly concerned hitherto, has to do with the date and authenticity of the collection itself, the second with the reliability of its attributions of the poems that it contains, regardless of when or how they came to be gathered into it.

The second question can be dealt with quite simply. Although the *Tsun-ch'ien chi*'s attributions of individual poems to particular poets

clearly cannot be relied upon in every case, in general, and with one important exception, the *Tsun-ch'ien chi* is clearly a collection of poems that
are genuine products of the periods to which they are assigned. The exception referred to is of course the selection of poems attributed to Li
Po, which have been shown elsewhere to be works of the tenth century.[1]
The period authenticity of the other poems is supported by a comparison of their rhyming categories with those of contemporary *shih* and *tz'u*
poems known from other sources.[2]

The problems associated with deciding on the authenticity of the
anthology itself are more complex. Much of the doubt that has tended
to cling to the *Tsun-ch'ien chi* derives from the preface to it written in
1582 by one Ku Wu-fang, who published an edition that is a direct or
indirect ancestor of several of those currently extant.[3] Ku's preface is a
frustratingly ambiguous document. After an introductory passage comparing the *tz'u* to older forms of poetry, he continues,

> As for Hsüan-tsung's "Hao shih kuang," Li Po's "P'u-sa-man," Chang
> Chih-ho's "Yü-fu," and Wei Ying-wu's "San-t'ai," the grace of their tones
> is of far-reaching import and their wonders surpass those of a thousand
> ages. Others, such as Wang [Chien], Tu [Mu], Liu [Yü-hsi], and Po
> [Chü-i] towered aloft as great masters. After them came the group of
> worthy officials at the end of T'ang.[4] Linking their creations to form two
> *chüan*, first and second, [the collection] has been titled *Tsun-ch'ien chi* and
> carved on blocks to be passed on to fellow aficionados.
>
> Earlier, there were the *Hua-chien chi* from T'ang and the *Ts'ao-t'ang shih-
> yü* from Sung, which were current, while few had heard of the *Tsun-ch'ien
> chi.*

Ku goes on to lament the contamination of China by "despicable
northern tastes" consequent on the Chin and Yüan occupations of the
"central districts," having particularly in mind the supplanting of the
tz'u by the *ch'ü*, which he regards as completing an unhappy development begun by the evolution of the *tz'u* itself in the direction of longer

1. See Daniel Bryant, "On the Authenticity of the *Tz'u* Attributed to Li Po," *T'ang
Studies* 7 (1989): 105–36.
2. See Daniel Bryant, "The Rhyming Categories of Tenth Century Chinese Poetry,"
Monumenta Serica 34 (1979–80): 319–47.
3. Ku Wu-fang (*hao* Ts'un-i chü-shih) is not otherwise known. Chao Tsun-yüeh identified him with Ku Ch'i-feng ("Tz'u-chi t'i-yao," *Tz'u-hsüeh chi-k'an* 3, no. 3 [Sept. 1936]:
65–71), but he gave no evidence, and the *Dictionary of Ming Biography*, ed. L. Carrington
Goodrich (New York: Columbia University Press, 1976), p. 736, lists Ch'i-feng as a
younger brother of Ku Ch'i-yüan (1565–1628), which means that he was no more than a
teenager, if that, in 1582, the date of Wu-fang's preface.
4. This listing of poets and poems is consistent with the contents of the *Tsun-ch'ien chi.*

melodies. He continues: "I am simply more fond of the *Hua-chien chi* than of the *Ts'ao-t'ang shih-yü* and wish to disseminate it and pass it on. Some years ago, [I] was staying in Wu-hsing. Mr. Mao had also been 'attaching and supplementing,' and what I had compiled and put in order was of a similar kind [*Mao shih chien yu fu pu erh yü ssu pien ti yu lei yen*]."

Now the first passage, with its reference to "linking" (*lien*) and publication, along with the assigning of a title, emerges quite suddenly, with no prior mention of Ku's personal interest, and one might take this passage in isolation as descriptive of the formation of the text in the remote past, especially since it is followed by an account of the vicissitudes of the *tz'u* tradition after Sung. The second translated passage must be understood as referring to the *hsiao-ling* (short song) tradition by way of the *Hua-chien chi* and to an effort, similar to his own, by "Mr. Mao" to supplement that text by collecting other short *tz'u* from the T'ang and Five Dynasties period. In light of this passage, we might understand the extended complaint about the eclipse of this tradition as serving to link the reference to compilation and publication to the appearance of Mr. Mao and his similar production.

But all this succeeds better in raising questions than in resolving them. What exactly is Ku claiming to have done? Is this preface attached to his own compilation, to Mao's, to some conflation of the two, or to a preexisting work that he is only claiming to have compiled? If to his own work, did its publication precede or follow his acquaintance with Mr. Mao and that gentleman's work? Was the "attaching and supplementing" done to an existing *Tsun-ch'ien chi* or are we to understand that the *Tsun-ch'ien chi* was compiled as an attachment and supplement to the *Hua-chien chi*?

The latter interpretation was evidently adopted by the celebrated seventeenth-century publisher Mao Chin, who reprinted Ku's edition as part of his *Tz'u-yüan ying-hua* collection and asserted in his colophon to it that Ku had simply gathered a variety of early *tz'u* poems together into a new anthology and published it under the old title. Mao's skepticism was soon challenged. Chu I-tsun (1629–1709), in a colophon dated 1671, recorded that he had compared a copy of Ku Wu-fang's edition with an old manuscript text in the hand of Wu K'uan (1436–1504) and found their contents to be substantially the same. Later, the great bibliophile Ting Ping (1832–99) described a Ming dynasty manuscript edition lacking Ku's preface but bearing the seal of the noted scholar, dramatist, and publisher Mei Ting-tso (1549–1618). Ting's conclusion was that the collection was genuine, for if it had not been, Mei Ting-tso would not have treasured his manuscript version of it, since he was close enough in time—a contemporary, almost—to Ku Wu-fang to be able to judge its authenticity.[5]

Indeed, it now seems possible to be reasonably certain that the presently extant *Tsun-ch'ien chi* is a genuine compilation of Northern Sung date, put together sometime during the eleventh century, but perhaps slightly altered or supplemented in the course of transmission. We shall not try to narrow down the date of compilation of the *Tsun-ch'ien chi* here, being chiefly concerned with showing it to be a Sung collection rather than one compiled in the Ming. Wang Chung-wen has argued that it cannot be later than the Yüan-feng period (1078–86), since it is mentioned in a colophon to Feng Yen-ssu's collected *tz'u*, the *Yang-ch'un chi*, which is dated to that time. Nor can it, Wang adds, be earlier than the reign of Jen-tsung (r. 1023–64), since it misattributes a poem by Li Kuan, active in Jen-tsung's time, to Li Yü.[6] The latter argument, of course, is valid only if one agrees that Li Kuan wrote the poem in question. In any event, something like 1040–80 seems a reasonable approximate date for the *Tsun-ch'ien chi*. The *Ssu-k'u* editors were troubled by the lack of any listing of it in the Sung bibliography *Chih-chai shu-lu chieh-t'i*, but a number of Sung references to the title were later discovered and discussed by Wu Ch'ang-shou, Wang Kuo-wei, and subsequent writers. These references match, in general, the text as it stands today. Shizukuishi Kōichi has since displayed remarkable resourcefulness in further demonstrating the Sung provenance of the current text, showing that it was used in the compilation of the supplement (*wai-chi*) to the works of Liu Yü-hsi and that the "mode" (*tiao*) names used in it correspond to those current in the time of Chang Hsien (990–1078).[7]

The only recent scholar strongly skeptical of the authenticity of the *Tsun-ch'ien chi* is Ch'i Huai-mei, who points out that the "Wu K'uan" manuscript that Chu I-tsun saw could well have been a forgery, that the agreements between Ku Wu-fang's text and scattered Sung extracts could simply be the result of Ku's having copied the latter, and that Ting Ping was perhaps not justified in assuming that Mei Ting-tso was convinced of the authenticity of the *Tsun-ch'ien chi* just because his seal is found on a copy of it.[8] There is, of course, something to be said for all of

5. *Shan-pen Shu-shih ts'ang-shu chih* (rpt., Taipei: Kuang-wen shu-chü, 1967) 40.30a–b (pp. 2087–88). Ting gives Ku's name as Wan-fang.

6. Wang Chung-wen, ed., *Nan-T'ang erh-chu tz'u chiao-ting* (Peking: Jen-min wen-hsüeh ch'u-pan-she, 1957), p. 20.

7. Shizukuishi Kōichi, "*Sonzenshū zakkō*," *Kangakkai zasshi* 9 (1941): 97–106.

8. Ch'i Huai-mei, "*Hua-chien chi* chih yen-chiu," *Tai-wan sheng-li Shih-fan ta-hsüeh yen-chiu chi-k'an* 4 (1960): 507–604.

these objections, but they really do no more than remind us how far from "proof" in any legal or scientific sense so much of our reasoning about early Chinese bibliography really is. The surest way of dealing with these problems is by the full and imaginative use of internal evidence, the method adopted by Shizukuishi Kōichi, reference to whose work might have saved Ch'i from error. With respect to Ch'i's last point, though, it might be added that Mao Kuang-sheng too discounts Ting Ping's testimony. Mao is inclined to adopt a suggestion originally made only tentatively by Wang Kuo-wei, that the *Tsun-ch'ien chi* goes back to a collection made by a man of the T'ang period named Lü P'eng.[9] As Wang himself admitted, there is only the slimmest evidence for this attribution, and since nothing whatever is known of Lü P'eng, not much more can be said of it. Since many of the *tz'u* in the *Tsun-ch'ien chi* are of post-T'ang date, the collection would have to have been extensively supplemented some time between the time of Lü P'eng and that of Wu K'uan.

More recently, the printing of another old edition of the *Tsun-ch'ien chi* has tended to confirm the authenticity of Ku Wu-fang's text, although it raises new questions about his role in editing it. This copy is part of the *T'ang Sung ming-hsien pai-chia tz'u*, a collection put together by Wu Na (1372–1457), but not printed until 1940. This text, provided that it is genuine—and there appears to be no reason to doubt this—antedates Ku Wu-fang's preface by more than a century, but it is nearly identical to his edition in its contents and arrangement.[10]

The available early editions now number three: Wu Na's collection, the edition published by Mao Chin in the *Tz'u-yüan ying-hua*, which he copied from Ku Wu-fang's text, and the edition published by Chu Tsu-mou in the *Chiang-ts'un ts'ung-shu*. Chu Tsu-mou says in his colophon (dated 1914/15) that he followed the manuscript that had been in Mei Ting-tso's possession as his copy-text but emended it where necessary on the basis of Mao Chin's text. There is also a manuscript copy in the collection of the Tōyō Bunko in Tokyo, with a colophon by Wang Kuo-wei. Wang records that he copied the first *chüan* from Chu I-tsun's copy of the text printed by Ku Wu-fang and then added the second *chüan*

9. Mao Kuang-sheng, "*Tsun-ch'ien chi* chiao-chi," pts. 1, 2, *T'ung-sheng yüeh-k'an* 2, no. 6 (June 1942): 73–78; 2, no. 9 (Sept. 1942): 82–94.

10. One possibility is that the manuscript that Mei Ting-tso and Ting Ping saw was Wu Na's. I tend to doubt this, since Wu Na's edition was part of a much larger collection. As we shall see later, in discussing the edition of the *Nan-T'ang erh-chu tz'u* included in Wu's compendium, the typeset edition introduced many "corrections" into the text, but there is no reason to suppose that these extended so far as to invalidate the significance of Wu Na's text for our argument here.

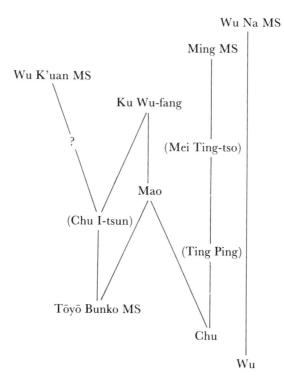

Figure 1. *Nan-T'ang erh-chu tz'u:* tentative filiation of the known texts. Names in parentheses refer to persons who describe the text, not to separate exemplars.

from Mao. The arrangement of the text is the same as that of Mao, wherever this differs from Chu and Wu. The three chief exemplars will be referred to henceforth as Wu, Mao, and Chu. On the basis of the external evidence discussed so far—and it is not proposed to go much further, in the present study, into the relationship between the different editions of the *Tsun-ch'ien chi*—we can construct a tentative filiation of the known texts (Fig. 1).[11]

11. Shao I-ch'en's bibliography of editions, the *Ssu-k'u chien-ming mu-lu piao-chu* (rpt., Taipei: Shih-chieh shu-chü, 1967), pp. 955–56, as supplemented by Shao Ch'ang, lists eight exemplars. In addition to Mao and Chu, these are Ku Wu-fang's printed edition, Chu I-tsun's manuscript, a copy printed in the tenth year of Wan-li (1582—Ku Wu-fang's?), a Sung manuscript, an early Ming reproduction of a Sung edition, and a Ming manuscript. I have not seen any of these additional exemplars. There are, of course, several other recent printed editions, such as that included in Shih-chieh shu-chü's Kuo-hsüeh ming-chu series, but these are all clearly based on one of the old editions.

The importance to us of this diagram does not lie in its claim to represent the recent history of the textual tradition of the *Tsun-ch'ien chi* so
much as in what it suggests about the form in which we find the text.
That is, first, since there is virtually no difference in the contents of the
three extant editions, and since at least one of them (Wu) and quite
possibly a second (Chu) can be traced back to a time earlier than Ku
Wu-fang, it follows that Ku's role as "editor" was limited to deciding
what readings to follow when his copy-text was unclear in some way
and that he was not responsible for actually collecting any poems at all,
even as a supplement. Second, the nature of the slight differences that
do exist suggests that the Wu Na manuscript and the one owned by Mei
Ting-tso may have been more closely related to each other than either
was to the ancestor of Ku Wu-fang's.

The differences are two. First, Wu and Chu are in one *chüan*, while
Mao is in two. The location of the division is quite arbitrary, occurring
in the midst of a group of related poets, and may have been added by
Ku Wu-fang.[12] The second difference concerns the location of a poem
by Li Yü. In the Chu and Wu editions it is found by itself, following a
group of seven lyrics by Feng Yen-ssu that in turn follow eight others by
Li Yü.[13] In the Mao text, this poem comes directly after these latter
eight and before those by Feng Yen-ssu, with a note to the effect that in
"another edition" it occurs separately. In all three editions the heading
to the larger group reads "Eight Poems." The confusion may be related
to uncertainty as to whether the melody "Wang Chiang-nan," which begins the group of eight poems, should be counted as two single-stanza
poems, as in Chu and Wu, or as one poem of two stanzas, as in Mao.
We shall return to consider this question in more detail below. For the
moment, we need only point out that both of the differences were
apparently introduced by Ku Wu-fang or Mao Chin—which suggests
that the ancestors of Ku Wu-fang's edition were essentially similar

12. Juan T'ing-cho has called attention to Shao I-ch'en's listing of a Sung manu
script in two *chüan*; see Juan, "Chi-ku-ko pen *Tsun-ch'ien chi* pa," in *Ch'ing-chu Jui-an Lin
Ching-i hsien-sheng liu-chih tan-ch'en lun-wen-chi*, ed. Ch'ing-chu Jui-an Lin Ching-i hsien-
sheng liu-chih tan-ch'en lun-wen-chi pien-chi wei-yüan-hui (Taipei: Kuo-li Cheng-chih
ta-hsüeh kuo-wen yen-chiu-so, 1969), pp. 2389–90 (also published in *Ta-lu tsa-chih* 40
[1970]: 376). Provided that Shao judged its age correctly, this would substantiate the
existence of editions in two *chüan* much earlier than Ku Wu-fang's. Ku's rather awk-
ward division may simply reflect an attempt to restore an earlier state of the text that he
did not know at first hand, rather than corresponding to the division in the original.
13. Actually, six by Li Yü, one by his father Li Ching, and one by Wen T'ing-yün—
but all are attributed here to "Prince Li" (Li-wang).

to Wu Na's edition and the Ming manuscript ancestral to Chu Tsu-mou's.

Actually, it is the location of some of the poems by Li Yü and Feng Yen-ssu that raises the most difficult questions about the arrangement of the text. To discuss this, however, it will first be necessary to digress somewhat by summarizing the contents of the *Tsun-ch'ien chi* and taking up a few other related points. Although no grouping of the poets is explicit in the text, they do fall neatly into the following clusters:

> T'ang emperors (3 poets; 7 poems) and "Prince Li" (5 poems)
> Poets of the T'ang and Southern T'ang (13 poets, including Li Po, Liu Yü-hsi, and Feng Yen-ssu; 131 poems)
> Poets of the Hua-chien school (12 poets, from Wen T'ing-yün to Li Hsün, in the same sequence employed in the *Hua-chien chi*; 120 poems)[14]
> "Prince Li" (8 poems; 9 in the Mao text)
> Feng Yen-ssu (7 poems, followed in Chu and Wu by one by "Prince Li")
> Miscellaneous (7 poets not included earlier, including two from the Hua-chien school; 10 poems)

Both the identical ordering of the Hua-chien poets in the *Tsun-ch'ien chi* and *Hua-chien chi* and the near absence of overlap between the contents of the two anthologies suggest, as Ku's preface implies and Shizukuishi was again apparently the first to notice, that the former was compiled with the conscious intent of supplementing the latter. Shizukuishi (p. 103) tabulates the eight poems duplicated in the two. Three of these are poems by Wen T'ing-yün to the melody "Keng-lou-tzu" that are attributed to Li Yü (one in each group of his poems) and Feng Yen-ssu in the *Tsun-ch'ien chi*. Then there are four to the melody "P'u-sa-man" by Wen T'ing-yün and one to "Hsi-ch'i-tzu" by Li Hsün attributed to the same poets in both anthologies. Evidently unaware of Shizukuishi's work, Ch'i Huai-mei and Li Hsin-lung both consider the question of poems duplicated in the two collections, and here each has something new to add. Ch'i, while missing three of the duplications that Shizukuishi noticed, caught another, although she does not make its nature clear. This is the first of the "P'u-sa-man" poems attributed to Li Po in the *Tsun-ch'ien chi*, which is in fact made up entirely of lines selected from two separate lyrics to this melody attributed, and no doubt cor-

---

14. The Mao text claims 33 lyrics by Sun Kuang-hsien in both of its tables of contents, as well as in the heading to the poems proper, but in fact only 23 poems are included, just as in the Wu and Chu editions.

rectly, to Wei Chuang in the *Hua-chien chi*. Li Hsin-lung makes more clearly and thoroughly a point that Ch'i had only mentioned in passing (Ch'i was, after all, chiefly concerned with the *Hua-chien chi*), that the location of the duplicated poems suggests that they may be evidence of textual supplementation in the editing of one of the anthologies. That is, the four "P'u-sa-man" poems by Wen T'ing-yün not only occur in the same order in both anthologies, but also come at the end of Wen's "P'u-sa-man" poems in both, as if they had been "tacked on" at the end, as it were. Li's hunch is that in this case it may actually have been the *Tsun-ch'ien chi* that was being used to "restore" a damaged *Hua-chien chi*.[15] If this is what happened, it must have taken place quite early, for an early Southern Sung printed edition of the *Hua-chien chi* is extant in which these poems are already included. Presumably it was the well-defined length of the *Hua-chien chi* (exactly five hundred poems) that invited the attempt at restoration.

Even more evident than any relationship between the two anthologies is the appearance the *Tsun-ch'ien chi* gives of having been supplemented after its initial compilation by the addition of more poems by "Prince Li," Feng Yen-ssu, and the miscellaneous group at the end. When did this happen and who was responsible for it? All we can say at this point is that it was not the work of Ku Wu-fang.[16] This question is one we shall be returning to more than once in what follows.

THE COMPILATION OF THE *NAN-T'ANG ERH-CHU TZ'U*

It is curious that the *Nan-T'ang erh-chu tz'u*, which is without doubt more often read than the *Tsun-ch'ien chi*, and about whose principal poet, Li Yü, there has grown up an extensive (if generally lightweight) body of secondary literature, has attracted the attention of fewer textual scholars than has the latter anthology. There are, however, two excellent brief discussions of it, and we are, as a result, in a position to date the text at least roughly.

It was Wang Kuo-wei who, in his colophon (dated 1909) to the edition of the *Nan-T'ang erh-chu tz'u* printed in the *Ch'en-feng ko ts'ung-shu*, made the first serious attempt to date it and describe its compilation.

---

15. Li Hsin-lung, "*Tsun-ch'ien chi* yen-chiu," in *Ch'ing-chu Jui-an Lin Ching-i hsien-sheng*, pp. 2261–388.

16. Wang Chao-yung's hypothesis that the supplementing of the text was evidence of Ku Wu-fang's careful editing is thus no longer tenable, reasonable, indeed acute, as it was at the time he advanced it; "Chi-ku-ko pen *Tsun-ch'ien chi* shu-hou," *Tz'u-hsüeh chi-k'an* 3, no. 2 (June 1936): 161–62.

Relying on the names and official titles of several persons mentioned in the notes to the original, particularly Ts'ao Hsün, he proposed that the *Nan-T'ang erh-chu tz'u* was put together early in the Southern Sung, during the Shao-hsing period (1131–63).

In his comments on this colophon, which he reprints as part of an appendix to his *Nan-T'ang erh-chu tz'u chiao-ting*, Wang Chung-wen makes several additional points (pp. 103–4). In the first place, he notes that all of the extracts from *tz'u-hua* writings and the like that are included in the original text can be found in the compendium *T'iao-hsi yü-yin ts'ung-hua* of Hu Tzu, which was presumably the source from which they were taken. Thus, Wang reasons, the *Nan-T'ang erh-chu tz'u* can only have been compiled after the completion of Hu's work, that is, after 1167. The *terminus ante quem* cannot, he continues, be fixed much earlier than the death of Ts'ao Hsün (1174), who is referred to in the text as *chieh-tu* (military governor), a title that he received in 1150. This would not have been used after his elevation to grand protector (*t'ai-wei*), which took place sometime during the reign of Emperor Hsiao-tsung (r. 1163–90). Second, Wang points out that the *Nan-T'ang erh-chu tz'u*, unlike most other Sung *tz'u* collections, is not arranged according to melody name, chronology, musical mode, or seasonal reference, nor does it follow any other apparent principle of order. He suggests, therefore, that it was compiled in a bookshop, specifically for publication as a commercial venture, as was at least one other well-known early *tz'u* anthology, the *Ts'ao-t'ang shih-yü*. Wang's conclusions are very persuasive, although it does seem possible that the consultation of the *T'iao-hsi yü-yin ts'ung-hua* could have taken place quite late in the process of compiling the *Nan-T'ang erh-chu tz'u*, the larger part of which may have occurred before 1167. In any case, the present compilation must have been printed by 1208, since it heads a series of *tz'u* collections published by the Liu clan's Changsha bookstore and recorded in the *Chih-chai shu-lu chieh-t'i*. The series was titled *Pai-chia tz'u*, and was evidently the ancestor of Wu Na's compendium. The latter, however, included the *Tsun-ch'ien chi*, which is not included in the *Chih-chai* list.[17]

Lacking a compiler's name or an original preface, even an anonymous one, we cannot tell just who was responsible for putting the collection together or how it was done. The one source of information that we do have is the various notes appended to the poems or to their titles. These clearly formed part of the original text, and they are found with

17. See Jao Tsung-i, *Tz'u-chi k'ao* (Hong Kong: Hsiang-kang ta-hsüeh ch'u-pan-she, 1963), pp. 28–31. The *Chih-chai* description of the *Nan-T'ang erh-chu tz'u* will be taken up below.

only minor variants in all extant exemplars of it.[18] They report on the
sources from which the poems were taken, raise questions of attribution,
and recount anecdotes associated with the poems. Since much of the
discussion to follow will refer to particular poems or the notes attached
to them, it will prove convenient if all thirty-seven poems in the *Nan-
T'ang erh-chu tz'u* are listed here. For each poem, the following table sup-
plies a serial position in the collection, the melody title, and the opening
phrase. (These phrases are transcribed as given in Wang Chung-wen's
text, without prejudice as to arguments that may be advanced later concerning the readings.) In addition, the editorial notes are translated or
summarized as they occur:

1. "Ying t'ien ch'ang" *i kou ch'u yüeh lin chuang ching*
   Headnote: "Hou-chu's inscription reads, 'Lyrics composed
   by the late emperor.' The manuscript belongs to the household of Ch'ao Kung-liu."[19]
2. "Wang yüan hsing" *pi ch'i hua kuang chin hsiu ming*
3. "Huan hsi sha" *shou chüan chen chu shang yü kou*
   Appended note: Quotes the *Man-sou shih-hua*, discussing a
   tasteless emendation of the poem.[20]
4. "Huan hsi sha" *han t'an hsiang hsiao ts'ui yeh ts'an*
   First appended note: Anecdote involving a witty exchange
   between Li Ching and Feng Yen-ssu in which this poem is
   quoted; no source is given in the note.
   Second appended note: Anecdote relating a conversation
   about *tz'u* between Wang An-shih and Huang T'ing-chien in
   which this poem is cited; no source is given in the note.
5. "Yü mei-jen" *ch'un hua ch'iu yüeh ho shih liao*
   Headnote: "In the *Tsun-ch'ien chi* there are eight poems in all,
   lyrics by the last ruler, Ch'ung-kuang [Li Yü]."
6. "Wu yeh t'i" *tso yeh feng chien yü*
7. "I hu chu" *hsiao chuang ch'u kuo*

18. While the notes that refer to published works might conceivably have been added
later, those that identify manuscript sources can scarcely be from any hand but that of
the original compiler. As we shall see in the next section, the textual evidence provided
by these notes is important in the establishment of a genealogy of the extant editions.
That it contributes to a consistent interpretation shows that, at the very least, the notes
were part of a common ancestor of all the extant editions.

19. Ch'ao Kung-liu is unidentified, but he must have been related to Ch'ao Yüeh-
chih, who is said elsewhere to have added an inscription to the manuscript. See below.

20. The *Man-sou shih-hua* is extant only in fragments. See Kuo Shao-yü, *Sung shih-hua
chi-i* (1937; rpt., Taipei: Wen-ch'üan ko, 1972), A.429–51.

8. "Tzu-yeh ko" *jen sheng ch'ou hen ho neng mien*
9. "Keng-lou-tzu" *chin ch'üeh ch'ai*
10. "Lin chiang hsien" *ying t'ao lo chin ch'un kuei ch'ü*
    Appended note: Quotes an anecdote from the *Hsi-ch'ing shih-hua* that purports to explain the unfinished state of this poem as it is found in the *Nan-T'ang erh-chu tz'u*; a continuation comments on the anecdote.[21]
11. "Wang Chiang-nan" *to shao hen*
12. "Ch'ing-p'ing yüeh" *pieh lai ch'un pan*
13. "Ts'ai sang-tzu" *t'ing ch'ien ch'un chu hung ying chin*
14. "Hsi ch'ien ying" *hsiao yüeh chui*
15. "Tieh lien hua" *yao yeh t'ing kao hsien hsin pu*
    Headnote: "Found in the *Tsun-ch'ien chi*; the *Pen-shih ch'ü* treats it as a work by Li Kuan of Shantung."[22]
16. "Wu yeh t'i" *lin hua hsieh liao ch'un hung*
17. "Ch'ang hsiang-ssu" *yün i kua*
    Headnote: "When Tseng Tuan-po collected the [*Yüeh-fu*] *ya-tz'u*, he treated this as a work by Sun Hsiao-chih; this is incorrect."[23]

---

21. The *Hsi-ch'ing shih-hua* too is extant only in fragmentary form; see Kuo, *Sung shih-hua*, A.317–70. This poem and the anecdotes related to it are discussed in considerable detail in Daniel Bryant, "The 'Hsieh Hsin En' Fragments of Li Yü and His Lyric to the Melody 'Lin Chiang Hsien,'" *Chinese Literature: Essays, Articles, Reviews* 7 (1985): 37–66.

22. On the *Pen-shih ch'ü*, see Liang Ch'i-ch'ao, "Chi *Shih-hsien Pen-shih ch'ü-tzu chi*," *Pei-p'ing Pei-hai t'u-shu-kuan yüeh-k'an* 2 (1929): 1–3, and She Chih, "Li-tai tz'u-hsüan-chi hsü-lu," pt. 2, *Tz'u-hsüeh* 2 (1983): 238–39. According to Liang, this collection was a large and relatively early collection of *tz'u* and anecdotes related to them. She Chih, on the other hand, doubts that it was all that large. It appears to have been lost by the end of the Yüan dynasty, and the only surviving references to it are in notes such as this one in the *Nan-T'ang erh-chu tz'u*. The compiler of the *Pen-shih ch'ü* was one Yang Hui (1027–88), a political opponent of Wang An-shih. Li Kuan failed to pass the *chin-shih* examination, but did hold minor local office. Little else is known of him.

23. Tseng Tuan-po is Tseng Tsao (d. 1185), compiler of several books of various sorts. For his *Yüeh-fu ya-tz'u*, see Chao Tsun-yüeh, "Tz'u-chi t'i-yao," *Tz'u-hsüeh chi-k'an* 6, no. 2 (n.d.): 14; Li Ting-fang, "Sung-jen hsüan-pien ti Sung tz'u tsung-chi," *Wen-hsüeh i-ch'an* 1980, no. 3: 148; She Chih, "Li-tai tz'u hsüan-chi hsü-lu," pt. 1, *Tz'u-hsüeh* 1 (1981): 284–86; and Wu Hsiung-ho, *T'ang Sung tz'u t'ung-lun* (Hangchow: Che-chiang ku-chi ch'u-pan-she, 1985), pp. 338–40. The *Yüeh-fu ya-tz'u* was transmitted in manuscript form for a long period before it was printed, and consequently has suffered textual loss and corruption, although it remains a valuable source. Sun Hsiao-chih is Sun T'an, a virtual cipher. The *Ch'üan Sung tz'u*, ed. T'ang Kuei-chang (Peking: Chung-hua shu-chü, 1965), p. 1037, prints two poems under his name, the authenticity of both being in dispute.

18. "Tao lien-tzu ling" *shen yüan ching*
    Headnote: "Comes from the *Lan-wan ch'ü-hui*."[24]
19. "Huan hsi sha" *hung jih i kao san chang t'ou*
    Headnote: "This *tz'u* is found in the *Hsi-ch'ing shih-hua*."
20. "P'u-sa-man" *hua ming yüeh an lung ch'ing wu*
    Headnote: "Found in the *Tsun-ch'ien chi*; the *Tu Shou-yü tz'u*
    also includes this poem, with some variants in the text."[25]
21. "Wang Chiang mei" *hsien meng yüan*
22. "P'u-sa-man" *p'eng lai yüan pi t'ien t'ai nü*
23. "P'u-sa-man" *t'ung huang yün ts'ui ch'iang han chu*
24. "Juan lang kuei" *tung feng ch'ui shui jih hsien shan*
    Headnote: "Presented to the prince of Cheng, my twelfth
    brother."[26]
    Additional note: "Followed by the seal of the Heir Appar-
    ent's Library in clerical script."
25. "Lang t'ao sha" *wang shih chih k'an ai*
    Headnote: "Comes from the Hsia family at Ch'ih-chou."[27]
26. "Ts'ai sang-tzu" *lu lu chin ching wu t'ung wan*
    Headnote: "The autograph of these two *tz'u* is in the house-
    hold of Examiner Wang Chi-kung."[28]
27. "Yü mei-jen" *feng hui hsiao yüan t'ing wu lü*
28. "Yü-lou ch'un" *wan chuang ch'u liao ming chi hsüeh*
    Headnote: "The following two *tz'u* come from the household
    of Governor Ts'ao Kung-hsien; it is said that the autograph
    used to be in the quarters of an old gentleman living in re-
    tirement in the Prince Li Monastery outside the Liang Gate

---

24. For the *Lan-wan ch'ü-hui*, see Liang Ch'i-ch'ao, "Chi *Lan-wan chi*," *Pei-p'ing Pei-hai t'u-shu-kuan yüeh-k'an* 2 (1929): 5–6; Chao Tsun-yüeh, "Tz'u-chi t'i-yao," *Tz'u-hsüeh chi-k'an* 3, no. 3 (Sept. 1936): 53–54; She Chih, "Tz'u-hsüan-chi," pt. 2, pp. 236–37; and Wu Hsiung-ho, *T'ang Sung tz'u*, pp. 335–36. Liang points out that the *Lan-wan chi* must be earlier than 1196, since it is cited in a book of that date. It was compiled by K'ung I, a friend of Yang Hui, and so was probably contemporaneous with Yang's *Pen-shih ch'u*. Chao Tsun-yüeh cites references to the *Lan-wan chi* in notes to the *Yang-ch'un chi* and con-cludes that it must predate the latter collection (1057) . This point seems to conflict with its having been compiled by K'ung I, who did not pass the *chin-shih* examination until the period 1086–94. The text of the *Lan-wan chi* has long been lost.
25. The *Tu Shou-yü tz'u* is the collected *tz'u* of Tu An-shih, about whom little is known.
26. The prince of Cheng was Ts'ung-shan, who was later held prisoner in the north by the Sung court.
27. Ch'ih-chou is in modern Kuei-ch'ih, in Anhwei.
28. I have been unable to identify this person.

of the capital, and that as a consequence it is in poor condition and hard to read."[29]

29. "Tzu-yeh ko" *hsün ch'un hsü shih hsien ch'un tsao*
30. "Hsieh hsin en" *chin ch'uang li k'un ch'i huan yung*
    Headnote: "The autograph of the following six poems is in
    the household of Prince Meng."[30]
31. "Hsieh hsin en" *ch'in lou pu chien ch'ui hsiao nü*
32. "Hsieh hsin en" *ying hua lo chin chieh ch'ien yüeh*
33. "Hsieh hsin en" *t'ing k'ung k'o san jen kuei hou*
34. "Hsieh hsin en" *ying hua lo chin ch'un chiang k'un*
35. "Hsieh hsin en" *jan jan ch'iu kuang liu pu chu*
36. "P'o chen-tzu" *ssu shih nien lai chia kuo*
    Appended note: Quotes [Su] Tung-p'o's description of Li
    Yü's departure from his conquered state, to which the poem
    apparently refers.
37. "Lang t'ao sha ling" *lien wai yü ch'an ch'an*
    Appended note: Quotes the *Hsi-ch'ing shih-hua* on Li Yü's
    homesickness in captivity.

Wang Chung-wen has already wrung from these notes what little information they can be made to yield on the subjects of the dating and
authenticity of the poems. It remains to be seen if further examination
of them can advance us to a better understanding of how the book was
compiled. Once again, a table will be the clearest way of summarizing
the material. For each poem, one or more sources is given, unless none
is known. Sources explicitly referred to in the notes summarized and
translated above are given without parentheses; sources given here in
parentheses are those known to have been in existence by the time of
the compilation of the *Nan-T'ang erh-chu tz'u* but not mentioned in its
notes. The three groups of poems assigned to "Prince Li" in the *Tsun-
ch'ien chi* are designated by the letters A, B, and C, and the poems are
numbered according to their position in each group. For example, "TCC
A-4" means "the fourth poem in the first group of 'Prince Li' poems in
the *Tsun-ch'ien chi*."[31]

29. Ts'ao Kung-hsien is Ts'ao Hsün; see above. The temple would have been in
Kaifeng, the Northern Sung capital where Li Yü died while in captivity.
30. Prince Meng is Meng Chung-hou (d. 1157), the elder brother of the empress of
Emperor Che-tsung (r. 1086–1101). He held a number of official posts under both Northern and Southern Sung. He was created prince of Hsin-an prefecture in 1137. For a full
discussion of the textual problems in the poems from this autograph, see Bryant, "The
'Hsieh Hsin En' Fragments."
31. TCC B-3 is a poem by Wen T'ing-yün not included in the *Nan-T'ang erh-chu tz'u*;
see below. TCC C-1 appears under the melody title "Tzu-yeh t'i" in the *Tsun-ch'ien chi*, but
under "P'u-sa-man" in the *Nan-T'ang erh-chu tz'u*.

1–4. manuscript from Ch'ao Kung-liu (3 is TCC A-4; 4 is TCC B-8)
   5. TCC A-5 (headnote says that there were eight poems in TCC)
   6. (no other source is known for this poem before the Ming dynasty)
   7. (TCC A-1)
   8. (TCC A-2)
   9. (TCC A-3; *Hua-chien chi* attributes it to Wen T'ing-yün)
   10. *Hsi-ch'ing shih-hua*; (*T'iao-hsi yü-yin ts'ung-hua*)
   11. (TCC B-1,2)
   12. (TCC B-5)
   13. (TCC B-6)
   14. (TCC B-7)
   15. TCC B-4; *Pen-shih ch'ü* attributes it to Li Kuan; (*Yüeh-fu ya-tz'u* attributes it to Ou-yang Hsiu)
   16. (*Yüeh-fu ya-tz'u*, anonymous)
   17. *Yüeh-fu ya-tz'u*, anonymous
   18. *Lan-wan ch'ü-hui*; (TCC attributes it to Feng Yen-ssu)
   19. *Hsi-ch'ing shih-hua*
   20. TCC C-1; *Shou-yü tz'u* attributes it to Tu An-shih
   21–23. (no other source is known for these poems before the Ming dynasty)
   24. manuscript from the Heir Apparent's Library; (*Yüeh-fu ya-tz'u* attributes it to Ou-yang Hsiu; *Yang-ch'un chi* attributes it to Feng Yen-ssu, with an editorial note in some editions reading, "Misattributed to Yen Shu in the *Lan-wan chi*")
   25. manuscript from the Hsia family in Ch'ih-chou
   26–27. manuscript from the household of Wang Chi-kung
   28–29. manuscript from the household of Ts'ao Hsün
   30–35. manuscript from the household of Meng Chung-hou
   36. *Tung-p'o chih-lin*; (*T'iao-hsi yü-yin ts'ung-hua*)
   37. *Hsi-ch'ing shih-hua*; (*T'iao-hsi yü-yin ts'ung-hua*)

Now, there is a certain amount of order to be found here. The poems by Li Ching, all from the same manuscript source, are placed at the beginning; all other poems from manuscripts (24–35) are grouped together, the last being the fragmentary set of poems on the unique pattern "Hsieh hsin en." Three of the four poems found in the *Yüeh-fu ya-tz'u* are grouped together, as are three of the four poems known from no other pre-Ming source. The poems taken from (or at least appearing in) the *Tsun-ch'ien chi* are found in the same three groups as in that collection and appear at first glance to have been treated with considerable care. The two poems by Li Ching are transferred to his works, and one by Wen T'ing-yün is silently excluded (B-3). In two cases (15, 20) involving poems whose attribution to Li Yü in the *Tsun-ch'ien chi* is contested by another source, the discrepancy is mentioned in the headnotes.

In view of all this, it seems all the more curious that the following questions arise: Why is the division of the poems into three groups followed? Why is another poem by Wen T'ing-yün (9, TCC A-3), whose spurious character is just as evident as that of the one excluded (B-3), included here without comment? Why is poem 18 included on the basis of the *Lan-wan ch'ü-hui* without any mention of its attribution to Feng Yen-ssu in the *Tsun-ch'ien chi*? Why does the headnote to poem 5 simply and specifically say that the latter collection includes eight poems by Li Yü, when there are fourteen poems attributed to "Prince Li" there, and from nine to twelve (depending upon whether one counts poems 11 and 21 as two or four poems, whether one includes poem 18, and so on) from the *Tsun-ch'ien chi* appearing in the *Nan-T'ang erh-chu tz'u*?

In addressing these questions, we shall, in the interest of clarity of presentation, examine the poems in the following groups: 1–4, poems by Li Ching from the Ch'ao manuscript; 5–14, poems from the *Tsun-ch'ien chi*, with interpolations and deletions; 15–23, poems from other published or unknown sources; 24–35, poems from manuscript sources; 36–37, poems apparently added from the *T'iao-hsi yü-yin ts'ung-hua*.

If it were not for the manuscript from which poems 1–4 were entered into the *Nan-T'ang erh-chu tz'u*, it is unlikely that we would know them to be the work of Li Ching, for the *Tsun-ch'ien chi* makes no distinction between Ching and his son Yü, suggesting that the collection's editor did not know that Ching was a poet.[32] There seems to be no good reason, however, for doubting the authenticity of the manuscript, which is described in more detail in the *Chih-chai shu-lu chieh-t'i*. Moreover, some of the poems are cited in anecdotes concerning Li Ching that are recorded in historical sources, in particular the *Nan-T'ang shu* of Ma Ling. The compiler of the *Chih-chai shu-lu chieh-t'i*, Ch'en Chen-sun (fl. 1230–50), offered the following comment:

> The *Nan-T'ang erh-chu tz'u*, in one *chüan*, by the second ruler, Li Ching, and the third ruler, Li Yü. The four poems at the beginning, to "Ying t'ien ch'ang," "Wang yüan hsing" (one each), and two to "Huan hsi sha," are by the second ruler. Ch'ung-kuang [Li Yü] wrote them out, the autograph being with the Ch'ao clan in Hsü-chiang. The inscription reads, "Lyrics composed by the late emperor." I have seen it. It is on *mai-kuang*

---

32. Ch'i Huai-mei takes this as evidence that the *Tsun-ch'ien chi* cannot have been compiled very early in the Northern Sung.

paper, in the *po-teng* style of script, with an inscription by Ch'ao Ching-yü. I do not know where it is now. The rest of the poems are by Ch'ung-kuang.[33]

Taking this manuscript as authority, the compiler of the *Nan-T'ang erh-chu tz'u* evidently began the collection with these four poems on the assumption that the father's work ought to precede that of the son, even if there were fewer of the father's poems.

Poems 5–14 are somewhat more difficult to account for. It seems clear that the compiler's next step was essentially to transcribe the poems that were found in the *Tsun-ch'ien chi*. But it is just as clear that this was not done in a mechanical way, at least not from a *Tsun-ch'ien chi* identical to the texts now current. A straight listing of the poems in the *Tsun-ch'ien chi* according to their sequence in the *Nan-T'ang erh-chu tz'u* gives the following order: Group A: 7, 8, 9, 3, 5; Group B: 11a, 11b, (Wen T'ing-yün poem not included), 15, 12, 13, 14, 4; Group C: 20. It is not impossible to see what was done instead. Poems 3 and 4, of course, were omitted, since they had already been included on the basis of the Ch'ao manuscript; 11a and 11b were treated as one, the Wen T'ing-yün poem was simply dropped as spurious, poems 15 and 20 were set aside temporarily because of questions concerning their authenticity, and—and this is simply conjecture—poem 5 was shifted to the head of the group just because it is one of Li Yü's most beautiful and best-known creations and seemed to deserve pride of place.[34] Such a procedure would give the sequence 5, 7, 8, 9, 11, 12, 13, 14, and these are

33. Ch'en Chen-sun, *Chih-chai shu-lu chieh-t'i* (*Chü-chen pan ts'ung-shu* ed.) (*PP* 27/35), 21.1b. *Mai-kuang* was a special type of paper made from hemp fibers. Li Yü was an acknowledged master of the *po-teng* or "light in the stirrups" style of calligraphy. Ch'ao Ching-yü is Ch'ao Yüeh-chih, an important literary figure of the Northern Sung. The Ch'ao clan was prominent during the entire Northern Sung and followed the common Chinese practice of having all members of a single generation share one character of their personal names. Thus, the personal names of Ch'ao Yüeh-chih's brother and cousins all end with *chih* (it). The character shared by members of the next generation was *kung*, as in Kung-liu, the owner of the manuscript. Some members of the Ch'ao clan settled in Hsü-chiang, in Kiangsi, at the beginning of the Southern Sung. It is possible that Kung-liu was the son, or at least a nephew, of one of them. Presumably they carried the Li Ching manuscript south, and it seems likely, if it was in their possession, that they were brothers or close cousins of Yüeh-chih.

34. The placement of this poem and of another great "late" poem, "Lang t'ao sha ling," which comes at the very end of the collection, has a striking analogue in the placement of *The Tempest* and *The Winter's Tale* at the beginning and end of the canon of Shakespeare's comedies. In that case, as in this, there appears to be insufficient evidence for anything more than speculation.

presumably the eight poems referred to in the headnote, which must have been added at this time.

The questions that remain are two. First, why was poem 9 not omitted at the same time as the other one by Wen T'ing-yün? And second, where did poems 6 and 10 come from, and when were they added? The omitted poem is the first of the "Keng-lou-tzu" lyrics by Wen T'ing-yün in the *Hua-chien chi*, while poem 9 is the third. One might suppose that the first poem's position called attention to it, while the other one was missed because it was not quite so "visible," though it is only a few lines away in the text. At any event, the oversight probably originated within the textual tradition of the *Tsun-ch'ien chi*, rather than in that of the *Nan-T'ang erh-chu tz'u*. In the former, both poems have a headnote specifying the mode to which the lyric was to be sung, but this is augmented in the Wu and Mao editions by a reference to Wen T'ing-yün's possible authorship of the poem not found in the *Nan-T'ang erh-chu tz'u*. Since in general the Wu and Chu editions agree *against* Mao, Wang Chung-wen's suggestion (p. 65) that the additional note was omitted in the manuscript belonging to Mei Ting-tso, from which Chu was printed, is probably correct. If the additional note goes back so far in the textual tradition of the *Tsun-ch'ien chi* that it is shared by the Mao and Wu editions, then it may have been present in the original, or at least added to the text by the time of the compilation of the *Nan-T'ang erh-chu tz'u*, whose compiler would have been sufficiently reassured by it that he would not have troubled to check poem 9 against the *Hua-chien chi* (or Wen T'ing-yün's collected *tz'u*, to which the *Tsun-ch'ien chi* note refers) himself, assuming that this had already been done. This hypothesis is consistent with what we can deduce of the care that went into the compilation of the two texts. The *Tsun-ch'ien chi*, valuable as it is, is prone to misattributions and careless errors, while the *Nan-T'ang erh-chu tz'u* seems to be the product of an editor who, if not infallible, was remarkably careful and thorough in his work.

Unfortunately, he was not quite so thorough as to tell us where he got poems 6 and 10, or why he entered them where he did. It seems very likely that 10 came either directly from the *Hsi-ch'ing shih-hua*, with the additional comments added later from the *T'iao-hsi yü-yin ts'ung-hua*, or else, with both comments, directly from the latter, which quotes the *Hsi-ch'ing shih-hua*. The question then is not so much where the poem came from, but rather why it was inserted where it was.[35] The same

35. Wang Kuo-wei's hypothesis, offered in his colophon to the *Tsun-ch'ien chi*, that the latter originally included poem 10 but that Ku Wu-fang dropped it because it was incomplete, is rendered implausible by the arguments presented here.

question can be asked about poem 6, except that here there is an added element of uncertainty, since *no* other source for this poem earlier than the Ming dynasty is known. We shall return to this problem after other questions of a simpler nature have been dealt with.

If understanding how the compiler of the *Nan-T'ang erh-chu tz'u* incorporated the poems taken from the *Tsun-ch'ien chi* has required a measure of ingenuity and left behind a residue of unresolved doubts, the measure and the residue that are required and left behind in dealing with the next group of poems are considerably greater. In fact, the rationale for treating poems 15–23 as a group lies only in their being distinct from poems 5–14 before them and from 24–35 after. One can divide them into a number of subgroups. Poem 15, taken from the *Tsun-ch'ien chi* (B-4), seems to have been shifted here simply to separate it from the eight poems in that source that required no additional discussion. There seems to be no good reason why poem 20 could not have been treated in the same way and placed immediately before or, more consistently, after 15, but this was not done. The poems found in the *Yüeh-fu ya-tz'u* present a particular problem due to the present state of the text of that work. It has clearly suffered a good deal of corruption, particularly as regards the names of the authors of the poems that it includes. The compiler of the *Nan-T'ang erh-chu tz'u* seems to have supposed that poems without an author's name attached were by the writer of the preceding poem, and this may even have been true, in general, of the edition at hand. But it led to the assumption that poem 17 was attributed to Sun T'an in the *Yüeh-fu ya-tz'u*, although it is not so attributed in the current text, only the poem that precedes it. The more puzzling questions about the four poems found in both the *Yüeh-fu ya-tz'u* and the *Nan-T'ang erh-chu tz'u* are these: Why is poem 24 separated from the other three? And why, since the headnote to poem 17 cites the *Yüeh-fu ya-tz'u* only to disagree with it, are the other poems from the same collection (15, 16, 24) not credited to it in separate headnotes? The first question is not too hard to answer. It seems clear that poem 24 was entered on the basis of the old manuscript that had once been in the Heir Apparent's Library—the heir, of course, was Li Yü himself. That it was also to be found attributed to Ou-yang Hsiu in the *Yüeh-fu ya-tz'u* and to Feng Yen-ssu in the *Yang-ch'un chi* was apparently overlooked by the compiler; or perhaps, having the autograph in hand, he did not think the discrepancy worth discussing.

It is possible that poems 16 and 17 were entered not from the *Yüeh-fu ya-tz'u*, but from some other source, specified in a headnote to poem 16 that has since disappeared from the text, as Wang Chung-wen suggests

(p. 28).[36] Clearly there must have been *some* other source for poem 17, for otherwise there would have been nothing to contradict the supposed attribution to Sun T'an. No other extant Sung source includes either poem, however, so we cannot suggest what the alternative source may have been.

The source for poem 18 is not a problem in itself, since it is specified in the headnote. The poem is, however, also found in the *Tsun-ch'ien chi*, where it is attributed to Feng Yen-ssu. It was not included in the *Yang-ch'un chi*, Feng's collected *tz'u*, and this suggests that the attribution to Feng in the *Tsun-ch'ien chi* may be erroneous.

The problem with poem 19 is not so much its source, which is specified in the note, as its location. That is, one poem from the *Hsi-ch'ing shih-hua*, 10, is entered earlier, and one, 37, later. To complicate matters, it is very possible that the direct source for 10 and 37 was in fact not the *Hsi-ch'ing shih-hua* itself, but rather the *T'iao-hsi yü-yin ts'ung-hua*, which quotes it. But the latter collection also includes this poem, the source cited there being not the *Hsi-ch'ing shih-hua*, but another, no longer extant book of Northern Sung date, the *Chih-i* of Liu Fu.[37] Why the *Chih-i* is not mentioned in the note to this poem is hard to say. It is possible that Ts'ai T'ao, the compiler of the *Hsi-ch'ing shih-hua*, took the poem from the *Chih-i* without acknowledging this, and that the compiler of the *Nan-T'ang erh-chu tz'u* got it from the *Hsi-ch'ing shih-hua*, while Hu Tzu cited the original source. The poem is also cited in another Sung dynasty source, the *Men-shih hsin-hua* of Ch'en Shan, where it is treated as a *shih* poem.[38]

Reference has already been made to the puzzling separation of poems 15 and 20, which one would have expected to be grouped together. Poem 20 is also cited in Ma Ling's *Nan-T'ang shu*, but this text is not explicitly referred to in the *Nan-T'ang erh-chu tz'u*. The separation is probably not related to poem 20's uncertain placement in the *Tsun-ch'ien chi*, which placement is, as already noted, most readily explained as the result of an unrelated event in the textual history of that collection.

Poems 21–23 are also something of a puzzle, since they, like poem 6, are known from no other source earlier than the Ming dynasty. Had they come from a manuscript, its origin would presumably have been cited, and they probably would have been placed after the poem taken from the autograph with Li Yü's own seal on it.

---

36. Both poems are found in the *shih-i* (supplement) section of the *Yüeh-fu ya-tz'u*, which consists of poems probably set apart because their authors were unknown.

37. Almost nothing is known of Liu Fu.

38. Ch'en Shan, *Men-shih hsin-hua* (*Ju-hsüeh ching-wu* ed.) (*PP* 1/1), A.2.8b (33.8b).

The poems from manuscript sources (24–35) are the easiest to deal with, since, except for poem 24, there are no disputed attributions and no questions about the ordering of the poems. Some of them are textually corrupt or incomplete, but that is a different sort of problem.

The last two poems too are quite straightforward, so far as their source, the *T'iao-hsi yü-yin ts'ung-hua*, is concerned. The authenticity of poem 36 has been questioned on the grounds that it comes from a book of doubtful authenticity, the *Tung-p'o chih-lin*. As has been pointed out elsewhere, the challenge rests on very shaky logic and is best ignored.[39]

Now, what sort of general conclusions can we draw about the compilation of the *Nan-T'ang erh-chu tz'u* on the basis of the specific observations above? Perhaps the most important one is that a remarkable amount of care went into it, at least in the earlier stages of the process. Both the searching of numerous published works and the gathering of copies from scattered manuscript sources suggest that every effort was taken to make the collection as complete and accurate as possible. Only four poems are still extant that are likely to have been Li Yü's work but not included in the *Nan-T'ang erh-chu tz'u*. Two of these are written to the melody "Yü-fu." They were inscribed on a painting and then copied into an eleventh-century history of Five Dynasties painting, the *Wu-tai ming-hua pu-i* of Liu Tao-ch'un.[40] One, to the melody "Liu-chih," is cited as a *shih* poem in several Northern Sung works; only much later is it treated as a *tz'u*.[41] The "Yü-fu" melody too is close to a *shih* in structure, and it is possible that some or all of these poems were known to the compiler of the *Nan-T'ang erh-chu tz'u*, who excluded them as not being true *tz'u*. The other omitted poem, to the melody "Wu yeh t'i," was attributed to Meng Ch'ang in an early Southern Sung work, the *Ku-chin tz'u-hua* of Yang Shih, and to Li Yü only—among extant works —in the later, but generally more reliable anthology *T'ang Sung chu-hsien chüeh-miao tz'u-hsüan*, compiled by Huang Sheng.[42] It is quite possible, then, that the compiler of the *Nan-T'ang erh-chu tz'u* knew this poem too but did not have sufficient reason to attribute it to Li Yü.

If a good deal of care and effort went into gathering and evaluating the materials that went into the collection, the apparently haphazard

39. See the introduction to Daniel Bryant, *Lyric Poets of the Southern T'ang: Feng Yen-ssu, 903–960, and Li Yü, 937–978* (Vancouver: University of British Columbia Press, 1982), and the article cited there, K'ung Ying-te, "Li Hou-chu wang-kuo shih-tz'u pien-cheng," *Li-hsüeh* 2 (1934): 91–97.

40. Liu Tao-ch'un, *Wu-tai ming-hua pu-i, Ssu-k'u ch'üan-shu chen-pen*, ser. 5 ed., p. 11b.

41. See, for example, Shao Po, *Shao-shih wen-chien hou-lu* (*Hsüeh-chin t'ao-yüan* ed.) (*PP* 46/24), 17.4a; and Chang Pang-chi, *Mo-chuang man-lu* (*Pai-hai* ed.) (*PP* 14/3), 2.7b.

42. Huang Sheng, *T'ang Sung chu-hsien chüeh-miao tz'u-hsüan* (*SPTK* ed.), 1.22b (p. 15).

arrangement of the whole calls for some explanation, even if it is only conjecture. The work of collecting materials must have been done by someone with access to high social circles, possibly a member of the educated class himself, for the manuscript sources were presumably in collections that would not have been readily accessible. The materials gathered would have been transcribed on separate sheets of paper as they were located, with an identifying note attached to each. The sheets may have been loosely bound in a fixed order, or they may simply have been left sorted but unassembled. Eventually, however, they would have been recopied in order, in preparation for printing. It is possible that the preparation of this transcribed "final" copy, and perhaps some tasks of the later stages of collecting as well, were not the work of the original compiler, that someone else undertook to publish the collection and in so doing either mixed up a few of the sheets or perhaps simply added newly found material on blank parts of sheets that had not been completely filled. If poem 5, for example, had been copied separately by the original compiler with the intention of setting it at the beginning of Li Yü's *tz'u* (i.e., out of order with respect to its source, the *Tsun-ch'ien chi*), there might well have been room for poem 6 to have been added on the rest of the sheet later, perhaps by a different hand. Poem 10 might similarly have been added at the end of what was originally the A group of poems from the *Tsun-ch'ien chi*, and so forth. Of course, it is possible to imagine various other ways in which the text as it presently exists might have taken shape. Our concern should be not so much to determine the indeterminable as to delimit and reduce—eliminate, if possible—the inexplicable, and some variant of the "careful compiler + conscientious but less meticulous publisher" formula seems to offer the most reasonable way of doing this. The collection of most, if not all, of the materials, the addition of the editorial headnotes, and at least a rough ordering of the contents would have been the work of the former. Preparation of the final copy, perhaps with the addition of some poems or of the anecdotes from the *T'iao-hsi yü-yin ts'ung-hua*, very probably with a certain amount of rearrangement of the material and perhaps the accidental omission of one or more editorial notes, that of the latter.

Our curiosity is naturally aroused by the question of the original compiler's identity. There is no reason to suppose that we shall ever know who was responsible for assembling the book, but we can deduce a good deal about what sort of person it could have been: a careful scholar, perhaps, well-connected socially, interested in *tz'u* poetry, and present in Hangchow during some part of the period 1150–70 or so. The lack of a compiler's name attached to the text itself could be due to any of a variety of circumstances, from political disgrace to accidental loss of the editor's preface from the original text. One doubts, in any case, that identifying the actual compiler of the *Nan-T'ang erh-chu tz'u* will ever become as popular a pastime as proving that someone else wrote the plays of Shakespeare.

THE TEXTUAL GENEALOGY OF THE *NAN-T'ANG ERH-CHU TZ'U*

In the preceding section, we have been concerned only with the compilation of the *Nan-T'ang erh-chu tz'u* as a bibliographic problem. That is, we have not been directly concerned with such problems as choosing between variant readings or determining which of the extant editions of the text is closest to the original compilation or, at an even more remote level, the intentions of the poets themselves. These problems are at once more difficult and more important to solve, for the purpose of bibliography is surely to provide us with better texts. But in the case of these poems, the difficulties are very formidable. In the first place, the standard collection of them was not, as we have seen, assembled until two centuries after the poems were written, and then on the basis of materials of widely varying reliability. Some of the poems had already been included in anthologies or cited in historical or literary works, and such inclusion and citation has continued until the present day. In working with the poems, whether as a critic and interpreter, a translator, or simply an active reader, one faces uncertainties in virtually every line that only a detailed textual study can really resolve: Which edition of the *Nan-T'ang erh-chu tz'u* is to be preferred? Is the *Tsun-ch'ien chi*, as an earlier compilation, to be followed where it differs from the *Nan-T'ang erh-chu tz'u*? In isolated cases one may avoid facing these larger questions by simply rejecting a clearly erroneous reading on its own demerits, so to speak, by sticking to one copy-text, such as one of the early editions of the *Nan-T'ang erh-chu tz'u*, except when it is manifestly wrong, or by simply choosing a preferred reading on impressionistic grounds.[43] But the questions remain, and perhaps the time has come to face them squarely.

To say this is not to suggest that earlier students of the text have been negligent in not undertaking the job before now. The human labor

---

43. Among the many merits of Wang Chung-wen's edition is his clear statement of his practice, which is to follow the "Mo-hua chai" edition of Lü Yüan (see below) in general, emending on occasion by adopting a reading from one of the other states of the text and making the fact of emendation explicit in each case.

required to construct a logically consistent textual genealogy of the sort referred to, one that takes into account all of the testimony from the several dozen different witnesses whose readings are incorporated into Wang Chung-wen's magisterial apparatus, would be immense, probably beyond the capacity of a single scholar with only one lifetime to devote to the task. The only practicable way of carrying out such a project is with the help of a computer, and it is with such help that much of what follows was accomplished.[44]

44. I have provided a full account of the methods adopted in my "Computer-Assisted Determination of Textual Genealogy in Chinese Literature" (unpublished manuscript), in which two smaller texts are used as examples. The program employed, PRELIMDI, was developed by Professor Vinton Dearing of the University of California at Los Angeles, whose *Principles and Practice of Textual Analysis* (Berkeley and Los Angeles: University of California Press, 1974) describes the theory on which it is based and the mechanics of its application.

In essence, there are two stages to the process of arriving at a preliminary diagram (one that shows how the states are related to one another, without suggesting descent). First, all inconsistencies in the variations are identified (a "variation" is a single instance of disagreement among the states). For example, given four states labeled A, B, C, and D, the variations A,B/C,D (A agrees with B against C and D, which agree between themselves) and A,C/B,D are inconsistent because they imply a genealogical "ring," a relationship in which each state has two potential ancestors and within which no reasoning about descent is possible (Fig. 2).

In the second stage, all the rings so discovered are broken by rewriting at least one variation. For example, one might break the ring above by rewriting the first variation as A,B/C/D, disregarding the agreement of C and D as in some way exceptional (i.e., as the result of contamination or independent emendation). Doing so replaces the ring with the diagram C—A—B—D, within which, provided an archetype can be located, one may draw conclusions about which states are descended from which.

It must be borne in mind that these two stages are separate. The identification of inconsistencies is a "descriptive" operation whose results are objectively implied by the data. The process of resolving the inconsistencies involves choices that have implications for our interpretation of the texts from which that data is derived. Dearing's program proceeds by choosing a group to divide (e.g., C,D), and hence a variation to rewrite, on the basis of a comparison of the number of times each state agrees with each other state in the entire corpus of variations. Other criteria might be applied instead (e.g., dividing the group that would resolve the largest number of remaining inconsistencies), but in all

Figure 2. A genealogical "ring."

The question we shall investigate here is that of the relationships between the five extant independent editions of the *Nan-T'ang erh-chu tz'u*. These are the only sources to include all the poems, but no other works. The five editions (in each case preceded by the siglum to be used in subsequent discussion) are the following:[45]

CHEN: The *Ch'en-feng ko ts'ung-shu* edition. This *ts'ung-shu* was published by Shen Tsung-chi in 1909, but the editing of the *Nan-T'ang erh-chu tz'u* was the work of Wang Kuo-wei (the edition was subsequently included in Wang's collected works). The base text was a "Nan-tz'u" edition now held in the Peking Library.[46]

HOU: The *Shih ming-chia tz'u* edition. This *ts'ung-shu* was compiled by Hou Wen-ts'an in the third year of the K'ang-hsi reign (1689) and reissued in 1887 by Chin Wu-hsiang as part of his *Su-hsiang shih ts'ung-shu*.

HSIAO: This is a manuscript edition prepared by Hsiao Chiang-sheng during the K'ang-hsi period. Our analysis relies on Wang Chung-wen's report of this edition, also in the collection of the Peking Library.[47]

LU: This edition was published by one Lü Yüan in the *keng-shen* year of the Wan-li reign (1620). The copy consulted is in the library of the Jimbun Kagaku Kenkyūjo at Kyoto University. It has a note by Yü P'ing-po attached. The collation of the text was carried out by one T'an Erh-chin.

WU: This is the *T'ang Sung ming-hsien pai-chia tz'u* edition compiled by Wu Na during the Ming (see the discussion of the *Tsun-ch'ien chi* above). The analysis here is based on Wang Chung-wen's apparatus, which reports on the original manuscript edition. A typeset

cases the essential principle is that of parsimony; the goal is to keep to a minimum the number of rewritten variations whose existence can only be explained as the result of some exceptional event not characteristic of the history of the textual tradition as a whole (e.g., contamination of C by D, or vice versa). I would stress here my conviction, based on experience, that the use of computers for this kind of research not only leads to much more satisfactory results, but also, far from challenging the need for sound traditional philology, relentlessly and mercilessly exposes any failure to master it.

45. The numbering of the variations is based on Wang Chung-wen's apparatus, which I follow throughout this analysis. In most cases, I was able to check it against the original sources he cites. I found only one error in his collation. In come cases, Wang includes several variations in one note; these I have divided.

46. Pei-ching t'u-shu-kuan shan-pen-pu, ed., *Pei-ching t'u-shu-kuan shan-pen shu-mu* (Peking: Chung-hua shu-chü, 1959), 8.61a. The catalogue number is 10972. It is not clear why this edition was not collated by Wang Chung-wen.

47. Ibid., 8.67b, number 7175. The date is given as K'ang-hsi 54 (1715/16).

edition edited by Lin Ta-ch'un was produced in Shanghai in 1940 by the Commercial Press.[48]

There are 142 variations to be considered, places in the text where these five states of the text are not in agreement. Nine of these variations are identified by the computer's sorting process as inconsistent with the simplest logical interpretation of the relationships between the five editions.

(1) 1.2b: This is a variation in the headnote to the first poem in the collection.[49] HOU and LU omit the phrase "imperially composed song text" (*yü-chih ko-tz'u*), which is found in CHEN, HSIAO, and WU. The computer process divides CHEN, HSIAO, and WU here. The bibliographic implication of this is that two of these states, or an intermediary between two of them, restored the phrase, either by reference to the other or on the basis of the familiar passage in the *Chih-chai shu-lu chieh-t'i*—which T'an Erh-chin, the editor of the LU text, cites in his preface. That WU records the words in a different place, following the book title rather than the melody title, a feature recorded in variation 1.2c, supports this interpretation. The alternative possibility is that the omissions in HOU and LU are independent. We shall test this possibility as well, but in any case variation 1.2b and its formal duplicates 34.1 and 34.3 (see below) are inconsistent with fifteen of the other variations, including nine that would have to be rewritten if 1.2b, 34.1, and 34.3 were not (the other six are themselves rewritten by the computer).

(2) 4.5: This variation occurs in the third line of the second of Li Ching's poems to the melody "Huan hsi sha." The reading *yüan* (distant) is shared by HSIAO, LU, and WU, against *huan* (return), which is found not only in CHEN and HOU, but also in all other texts that include these poems.[50] The computer separates CHEN

48. There is a recent study of Wu Na's collection: Ch'in Hui-min, "*T'ang Sung ming-hsien pai-chia tz'u-chi pan-pen k'ao-pien*," *Tz'u-hsüeh* 3 (1985): 146–60. Ch'in notes that Lin Ta-ch'un did some silent "correcting" of the text while preparing it for publication. In fact, it is clear that he did a great deal, making Lin's edition virtually useless as evidence for the readings of Wu Na's text. See also Wu Hsiung-ho, *T'ang Sung tz'u*, pp. 320–25.

49. Since the various editorial notes were part of the original collection, we take them into account. They are "authorial" in the sense that they were present in the archetype of the *collection*, even though they were not the work of the authors, Li Ching and Li Yü, whose work the poems are said to be.

50. LU includes a textual note saying that the reading of the *Hua-chien chi* was *huan*.

and HOU. It may be that either, or both, of them was contaminated by the rest of the tradition, or that CHEN took its reading from HOU (or even that HOU took its reading from an ancestor of CHEN).[51] Whatever the cause of this variation, it is inconsistent with thirty-four others, thirty-one of them not rewritten by the computer.

(3) 6.5: In the sixth line of the poem "Wu yeh t'i," where CHEN and HOU read *meng-li* (in dream), WU reads only *meng*, with no space for a missing character,[52] and HSIAO and LU (along with all other texts that include this poem) read *i meng* (a single dream). Here again the computer divides CHEN and HOU. Variation 6.5 and its formal duplicate 27.4 are inconsistent with thirty-five other variations, thirty-one of which are not rewritten by the computer program.

(4) 14.4: In the third phrase of "Hsi ch'ien ying," CHEN, HOU, and WU read *p'ing* (rely), while HSIAO and LU (along with the *Tsun-ch'ien chi* and all but one of the later anthologies to include the poem) read *p'in* (frequent). The computer divides HSIAO and LU. Here again the implication is independent agreement. This possibility is supported to some extent by a note added to the poem in the *Su-hsiang shih ts'ung-shu* reissue of HOU, which says that *p'ing* should perhaps be *p'in* instead. Here it is twenty-four variations, twenty of them not rewritten, that conflict with the one chosen by the computer for division.

(5) 27.4: In the penultimate line of "Yü mei-jen," HSIAO and LU read *t'ang* (hall); WU reads *ko* (song), which Wang Chung-wen char-

---

There are, of course, no poems attributed to Li Ching or Li Yü in the *Hua-chien chi*, nor does this line occur in any poem presently contained in that collection. It is probable that T'an Erh-chin had in mind the *Hua-chien chi pu*, as Wang Chung-wen suggests (*Nan-T'ang erh-chu*, p. 4, discussing variation 2.7). Because this note is clearly an editorial addition to LU, we do not include a variation recording it in the data files submitted to the computer. The same holds for analogous notes to 2.7 and 4.13. Note that the glosses for text variants supplied in parentheses are intended only as mnemonics to help mitigate the absence of characters in the text of the paper.

51. We know that Wang Kuo-wei consulted HOU while preparing CHEN. He reports that the "Nan-tz'u" edition lacked poem 24 and that he made up the omission by taking his text for this poem from HOU. Wang Chung-wen (*Nan-T'ang erh-chu*, pp. 35–36) concludes that the omission of poem 24 was a peculiarity of the "Nan-tz'u" edition rather than a characteristic of the original *Nan-T'ang erh-chu tz'u*. The results of our analysis support Wang's conclusion; see below.

52. *Li* is supplied in the typeset edition of WU. In variation 34.1 (discussed below), the typeset edition agrees with HOU and LU.

acterizes as an error; CHEN and HOU, along with all but one of the other texts to include the poem, have *lou* (tower). Here again the computer divides CHEN and HOU, and contamination seems the likely explanation.

(6) 29.6: This variation is a formal duplicate of 14.4, occurring in the penultimate line of "Tzu-yeh ko." HSIAO and LU agree in reading *p'ing* (critique), while CHEN, HOU, and WU have a homophone meaning "level." The former is clearly the better reading. That the computer divides the two states that have it, HSIAO and LU, is consistent with our interpretation that one or both emended the received text.

(7) 30.2: In the headnote to the shortest of the "Hsieh hsin en" fragments, CHEN, HOU, and HSIAO read *chen* (true), while LU and WU read *mo* (ink) (the *Su-hsiang shih* reedition of HOU reads *mo*).[53] The computer divides HOU from CHEN and HSIAO. Both readings are plausible, and it is hard to see why the variation would occur. It is inconsistent with fourteen others, nine of them not rewritten.

(8) 34.1: This variation, which occurs in the first line of the penultimate poem in the "Hsieh hsin en" group, is a formal duplicate of 1.2b, and so the computer treats it in the same way, dividing WU from CHEN and HSIAO. These states read *ying-hua* (cherry blossom) while HOU and LU read *ying-t'ao* (bush cherry). This variation was probably affected by the reading *ying-hua* in the corresponding position in poem 32. The implication is that either WU or an intermediary between CHEN and HSIAO was emended on the basis of the parallel passage.

(9) 34.3: This variation is the occasion of the only error to have been discovered in Wang Chung-wen's apparatus. Wang notes that the word *an* (dark) is missing in HOU. In fact, it is also missing in LU, which makes the variation a formal duplicate of 1.2b and 34.1. In this case, however, the form of the note makes it unlikely that WU and an intermediary between CHEN and HSIAO could have come to their agreement independently, so we intervene to divide HOU and LU in this variation.[54]

---

53. The reading of HOU is to be found in Wang's account of variation 30.3.

54. A test of the consequences of dividing HOU and LU in variations 1.2b and 34.1 as well produces the same preliminary diagram as the unaltered process but divides two variations differently, 14.4 and 29.6, in both of which, given a prior division of HOU and LU in 1.2b and 34.1, the computer divides CHEN from HOU and WU. This division (of states having the less satisfactory readings) is clearly less plausible on bibliographic grounds than the computer's original sorting process.

Figure 3. Relationships among the five states in *Nan-T'ang erh-chu tz'u*. The points numbered 1–3 are inferential intermediaries.

There are two points to be made about these variations before we proceed.

The first is that they are strikingly few in number. The *Nan-T'ang erh-chu tz'u* is a very short text, to be sure, less than two thousand characters, even including the original editorial notes. All the same, and especially considering the relatively large number of variations that occur, that only nine of them are inconsistent with the genealogical diagram implied by all the rest calls attention to the relative isolation within which the textual tradition of the collection appears to have evolved.

The second point is perhaps incidental, but still worth making. It is that the "automatic" process has produced results that are entirely plausible when set against the text itself (the computer process, of course, works only with the abstract relations among sigla as reported in variations). Where the computer has rewritten variations, they have, with the one exception of 34.3, been ones in which either emendation of an evidently less satisfactory reading or contamination from other texts can be seen as providing explanatory occasions.

The computer program concludes this stage of the process by constructing a directionless preliminary diagram that shows the relationships among the five states without implying the location of an archetype (Fig. 3).

The next problem is the location of the archetype. It should be recognized at the outset that any archetype that may be reconstructed for the *Nan-T'ang erh-chu tz'u* can be claimed to be significant only for the collection as it was assembled in twelfth-century Hangchow (if that was indeed where the compilation took place). If we are to comment at all on the earlier history of the tradition of these poems, we shall have to take other materials into account.

The formal archetype may be located at any of fifteen points on the preliminary diagram—that is, at one of the five states examined, at one of the three inferential intermediaries, or at a point on one of the seven lines connecting these. The search for the formal archetype is essentially a process of elimination.[55] One looks for clearly directional variations and eliminates the states or intermediaries with the descendant readings. It must be emphasized that the identification of clearly directional variations is not the same as simply identifying variations in which one reading is obviously better than another.

The reason for this is clear if we consider the relation between the manuscript state WU, as reported in Wang Chung-wen's apparatus, and the typeset edition produced from it by Lin Ta-ch'un. No other type of variation is as common in the tradition of the *Nan-T'ang erh-chu tz'u* as those that divide WU off from all the other states (twenty-four examples), and the readings unique to WU are often manifestly inferior, as Wang Chung-wen unceasingly points out. It is precisely this manifest inferiority that makes the variations poor candidates for recognition as clearly directional. The more obviously wrong a reading is, the more likely it is to be corrected, and this is what we see in the typeset edition of WU, in which time after time the errors of the manuscript are replaced by readings found elsewhere in the tradition.

The significance of this is of course that it presents us with an example, though perhaps an exaggerated one, of what may have happened in the past as the textual tradition of the *Nan-T'ang erh-chu tz'u* was being transmitted. The lesson for the textual analyst is that great caution is required in the selection of clearly directional variations. This is perhaps particularly important in *tz'u* poetry, in view of both the highly determined metrical structures and the tendency to conventionalized diction characteristic of the *tz'u*. It is often easy to see what is "wrong" with a *tz'u* text, and not much less easy to replace it with something "right." What we shall look for are readings that are not so obviously wrong as to provoke an editor's or copyist's instinct to emend or conflate, while, on the other hand, they can be seen as clearly descended from better readings. The following variations in the *Nan-T'ang erh-chu tz'u* seem to be possible candidates for the status of clearly directional:

> (1) 1.1: The omission of *shu* (written) in CHEN, HSIAO, and 1 slightly weakens the clarity of the note but hardly suggests a need for emendation. It is important to bear in mind that the notes of the original compiler are as much a part of the text of the *Nan-*

55. For more detailed comments on the process of locating an archetype, see Bryant, "Computer-Assisted Determination." Dearing's comments on clearly directional variations are particularly illuminating; see *Principles and Practice*, pp. 42–56. Dearing has developed a program for locating an archetype as well, but this problem is sufficiently simple to allow its solution by hand.

T'ang erh-chu tz'u as the poems. Indeed, because they are not subject to the thematic and structural conventions of the poems, they are potentially of particular importance to the textual analyst. Note also that variation 1.2b cannot be treated as clearly directional since the group with the apparently "authorial" reading has been divided by the computer and the evidence of the variations alone cannot tell us which of the resulting subgroups is authorial and which the result of emendation or conflation.

(2) 2.10: Liao-yang is clearly preferable here, being parallel to Mo-ling in the next phrase. The reading found in CHEN, *ts'an* (remnant), is both a possible misreading of a cursive *liao* and, combined with the *yüeh* (moon) that follows, a convincing example of *tz'u* diction. WU leaves a blank here, also non-authorial.

(3) 5.3: The omission of the headnote in HOU is evidently non-authorial.

(4) 7.7: The editorial note that a character is lacking is typical of the textual notes found in the original and is thus probably authorial in the states including it, HOU and WU.

(5) 17.3: We know from other sources that the *tz'u* of Sun T'an was Hsiao-chih, written with *hsiao* (disperse), as found in HOU and LU. The homophone meaning "sleet" found in CHEN and HSIAO is thus probably a mistake, but we cannot say for certain that it was not the reading of the original compilation. The reading in WU, on the other hand, *chih* (substance), is both wrong and readily understood as a misreading of "disperse" arising after Sun T'an's brief period as a current poet was past.

(6) 18.2: The misplacement of the note in CHEN is non-authorial. As Wang Chung-wen points out, the note actually belongs with the next poem.

(7) 20.3a: The lack of much of the headnote to this poem in HOU is non-authorial.

(8) 25.4: The reading *so* (lock) in LU and WU (and hence in 2 and 3) is, we should argue, ancestral both to the homophonic *so* (tiny) in CHEN and HSIAO and to the *chien* (sword) in HOU. The latter looks, at first sight, like the best reading, given the phrase *chuang-ch'i* (valiant manner) in the next line, and this is why, once introduced into the textual tradition, it was not corrected. (Indeed, it is common in the anthologies, in which it even gives rise to a variant of its own.) But the whole poem, in fact, is an evocation of the deserted palace, within which "lock" is surely the authorial reading.

(9) 29.4: All states but HSIAO indicate two missing characters, with an editorial note reporting that the manuscript source from which the poem was copied into the *Nan-T'ang erh-chu tz'u* was damaged and illegible but that the characters were perhaps *ho fang* (what obstacle). HSIAO simply inserts *ho fang* into the text proper and drops the note, which makes its reading non-authorial. (Variation 29.4a records a difference in the note. CHEN and LU have *mo-mieh* [worn away], while HOU and WU have *man-mieh* [smudged].)

(10) 31.1: The note in CHEN is different in nature from all the rest and thus probably non-authorial.

(11) 31.6: It appears that the "authorial" text had a blank space followed by *liu* (remain), as in CHEN and HSIAO. LU and WU have the single character *ti* (flute), while HOU reads *ko* (item). The latter is hardly intelligible in the context, so it cannot be considered non-authorial on its own. "Flute," on the other hand, makes sense of a sort: "In a jasper window, dreams of a flute in the last of day." But comparison with the adjacent poems makes it clear that this line should have seven syllables, and in fact an argument can be made for filling the lacuna in CHEN and HSIAO with *tuan* (broken).[56] The *ko* in HOU can plausibly be seen as a variation on *ti* by an editor or copyist who could no longer "see" the lacuna and had to work with the text as he found it.

When we combine the evidence of these eleven variations, we find that all but one of them agree on a location for the archetype. That is, it is clear, to begin with, that four of the five extant states are excluded: CHEN, by 2.10, 18.2, and 31.1; HOU, by 5.3 and 20.3a; HSIAO, by 29.4; and WU, by 2.10 and 17.3. Inferential intermediary 1 (and hence CHEN and HSIAO) is excluded by 1.1 and 25.4, while 3 (along with LU, 2, HOU, and WU), is ruled out by 31.6. The one point that will satisfy all ten variations is located between inferential intermediaries 1 and 3. The exceptional variation is 7.7, the textual note in HOU and WU, which requires that the archetype be located either at 2 or at a point between 2 and 3. The argument that this note is authorial because it is similar in kind to others that are is not of course ironclad. The note itself is puzzling in that it seems clear that no character is in fact missing at this point. Therefore, it seems reasonable to adopt, at least provisionally, the location of the archetype implied by the other ten variations.

Now that the archetype has been located, we have a "tree" that

56. See Bryant, "The 'Hsieh Hsin En' Fragments," p. 44.

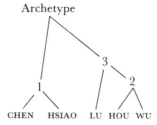

Figure 4. *Nan-T'ang erh-chu tz'u:* the derivation of the five extant states from the logical archetype.

shows the derivation of the five extant states from the logical archetype (Fig. 4). Such a diagram allows us to determine by inspection the archetypal reading in all variations except those in which the inferential intermediaries 1 and 3 do not agree. In addition, it is now possible to comment collectively on the variations occurring at each link of the tree and hence to characterize the processes involved in the production of each of the states. Although this discussion of the variations is in one sense the goal of the entire procedure (it amounts, in effect, to the critical apparatus for a variorum edition), it is here treated as a by-product of our exploration of the history of the textual tradition and is placed in an appendix below.

THE *NAN-T'ANG ERH-CHU TZ'U* AND THE *TSUN-CH'IEN CHI*

We now return one last time to the *Tsun-ch'ien chi.* That we have been able to construct a plausible genealogy for the textual tradition of the *Nan-T'ang erh-chu tz'u* naturally suggests the possibility of applying the same methodology to the *Tsun-ch'ien chi.* We shall not attempt to do this for the entire text of the latter collection, but we shall take up the particularly interesting question of the two (or three) separate groups of poems in it by "Prince Li."

What we should like to know, of course, is if these groups have a consistent common genealogy, which would suggest that they were all included in the earlier editions of the text. If, on the other hand, their genealogies differ, this would suggest that at least one group was added to the text later than the other (or others). We shall not argue that our findings here are conclusive, but rather that they are undeniably suggestive.

In cases such as this one, the advantages of working with a computer

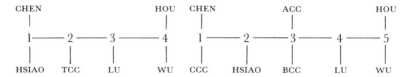

Figure 5. Alternative assumptions about the history of the *Tsun-ch'ien chi*.

become even more apparent, in that it allows us to test alternative hypotheses quickly and consistently. In the present case, we can not only add the *Tsun-ch'ien chi* to our *Nan-T'ang erh-chu tz'u* problem to see how the two anthologies are related, we can also embody in our tests different assumptions about the history of the *Tsun-ch'ien chi*. We do this by preparing two different data files. In one of these, all readings from the *Tsun-ch'ien chi* are treated as though they came from one homogeneous source, represented by the siglum TCC. In the second file, the readings are treated as though they came from three different sources, ACC, BCC, and CCC. The resulting diagrams are shown in Figure 5.

There are at least three interesting points to notice about these diagrams (we shall consider shortly the variations rewritten in the tests). The first is that the position of ACC and BCC in the right-hand diagram supports the hypothesis that these two groups of poems share a common history at least as far back in the tradition of the *Tsun-ch'ien chi* as we can see. We cannot prove, of course, that these poems were not added in two stages of compilation, but we can suggest with some confidence that the addition, if it took place at all, did so early in the history of the text.

The second concerns the point at which ACC and BCC are joined to the diagram: it is just where we located the archetype for the textual tradition of the *Nan-T'ang erh-chu tz'u*. This again does not constitute proof, but it surely adds support to the argument in favor of that location of the archetype.

The third concerns CCC, which is joined to the diagram not at the "archetype" point, but "out on a limb," as it were. CCC consists of poem 20 alone and is, moreover, a separate group in only two of the three editions of the *Tsun-ch'ien chi*. We shall consider this point in more detail at the end of our examination of the variations rewritten in these two tests.[57]

57. Testing for each of the three editions separately, in both TCC and ACC/BCC/CCC forms (ACC/BCC in the case of Mao Chin's edition), produces results entirely consistent with these two tests. We shall not pursue further here the question of how the three

(1) 3.6: This variation is rewritten only in the TCC problem, where it is found inconsistent with 5.1 (see below). In the second line of the poem, virtually all states of the text read *ch'ung-lou* (storeyed pavilion). The exceptions are the Wu and Chu editions of TCC, which read *mei-t'ou* (eyebrow). The program divides the Mao edition of TCC from the other states. The bibliographic interpretation is probable emendation by contamination in TCC (Mao).

(2) 4.5: See the discussion of the *Nan-T'ang erh-chu tz'u* problem in the preceding section for this variation. The computer divides as follows in this problem: /CHEN/HOU/TCC/.

(3) 5.1: This variation is rewritten only in the ACC/BCC/CCC problem. The same inconsistency between it and 3.6 is discovered, but ACC includes fewer variations than TCC (of which it is only a section), and this shifts the way in which the inconsistency is resolved. The variation consists of ACC (Wu) and ACC (Mao) giving the melody of poem 5 as "Yü mei-jen ying," while ACC (Chu) agrees with all editions of the *Nan-T'ang erh-chu tz'u* in lacking the *ying* (image). The bibliographic explanation is analogous to that in 3.6: emendation of ACC (Chu) by contamination from the tradition of the *Nan-T'ang erh-chu tz'u*.

(4) 7.14: In the penultimate line, all states but LU and the Wu edition of TCC read *jung* (gauze); the contrasting reading is a homophone meaning "tangled." Since other variations do not suggest any pattern of contamination between LU and TCC (Wu), the likelihood is that the convergence is the result of independent emendation or error conditioned by homophony. The two characters are occasionally used interchangeably.

(5) 14.4: For this variation, see the discussion of the *Nan-T'ang erh-chu tz'u* above (TCC agrees with LU and HSIAO). In this case, however, the program divides CHEN from HOU and WU. As this division is also consistent with the tree constructed for the *Nan-T'ang erh-chu tz'u* editions taken alone, we do not intervene.

(6) 20.7: In the second line, where all editions of the *Nan-T'ang erh-chu tz'u* except CHEN read *chao* (morning), CHEN and TCC (followed by many later anthologies and compendia) read *hsiao* (night). The latter is the *lectio facilior*, and we are thus inclined to accept the program's division of CHEN from TCC and explain it in bib-

---

editions of the *Tsun-ch'ien chi* are related to one another, as this could only be done by analyzing the variations found in the entire text.

liographic terms as emendation by contamination in CHEN.[58] This
variation occurs only in the TCC problem. In the ACC/BCC/
CCC version, there is no inconsistency because CCC is entirely distinct from ACC and BCC. Instead, this variation, not rewritten,
"pulls" CCC to its position adjacent to CHEN. That there is a ready
bibliographic explanation for the inconsistency of course weakens
the need to treat CCC independently at all.

CONCLUDING REFLECTIONS

We shall conclude with reflections that are theoretical, or at least meth-
odological, in nature. Before inflicting these on a reader perhaps already
weary of technicalities, we might well ask what bearing our findings
have on the reader who is not interested in textual problems per se. The
simplest way to respond to such a question is to look at an actual case.

We shall consider, for this purpose, the fifth poem in the *Nan-T'ang
erh-chu tz'u*, Li Yü's famous song lyric to the melody "Yü mei-jen." The
following text is that of Wang Chung-wen's edition; the translation is
Stephen Owen's, as it appears in his chapter in this volume. We shall be
suggesting one emendation in the course of the discussion that follows.

Spring flowers, autumn moonlight—when will they end?
How much of what is past can we know?
In the small building last night, spring wind once again.
To my homeland I dare not turn my head in the bright moonlight.

Carved balustrades and stairs of jade—I'm sure they are still there,
it's only the color of a young man's face that changes.
I ask you, how much sorrow can there be?—
it's just like a riverful of spring water flowing to the east.

春花秋月何時了
往事知多少
小樓昨夜又東風
故國不堪回首月明中

雕欄玉砌依然在
只是朱顏改
問君都有幾多愁
恰似一江春水向東流

Professor Owen discusses this poem in his essay, recognizing the
existence of textual variants and commenting on one of them. Wang
Chung-wen's apparatus numbers sixteen variations associated with this

---

58. The Wu edition of TCC has a homophone meaning "sleet," an independent error.

poem. Subtracting the five in the headnote and two that involve only very late and rarely consulted texts, and lumping together several that are best treated in clusters, we are left with six significant variations in the text of the poem proper, some of them variations that have already appeared in our discussion. We will take them up one by one:

5.7: This variation is found in a famous line and presents a real quandary. Should we read "autumn moon" (*ch'iu yüeh*) or "autumn leaves" (*ch'iu yeh*)? CHEN and HSIAO, together with the only other texts of Sung date to include the poem, prefer "leaves"; HOU, LU, and WU, together with all post-Sung texts, choose "moon." We might best approach the problem by asking two separate questions: First, how might the variation have arisen? Second, which reading is to be preferred?

A likely answer to the first question seems obvious enough, at least to the reader who "hears" these poems in Mandarin. *Yeh* and *yüeh* are, after all, close to being homophones in modern Mandarin, sharing even the same tone. That the matter is not necessarily so simple is clear as soon as we consider their pronunciation in Li Yü's place and time, *yiap* and *ngüat*.[59] Although these differences might have been lost by the end of the thirteenth century in northern China, perhaps even around Nanking, they persist to this day in the Hangchow area, where the *Nan-T'ang erh-chu tz'u* was probably compiled. Nonetheless, the variation is surely more likely to have arisen from a confusion of the two sounds than from a confusion of the two characters. Hence, it is likely to have arisen after the time of the compilation of the *Nan-T'ang erh-chu tz'u*, and among speakers of an early form of Mandarin rather than among "true southerners."

In order to consider which reading is better, we have to decide first what we mean by "better." Highly qualified contemporary readers differ on the question of which is the more satisfactory version. Some argue, in favor of the less familiar *yeh*, that the repetition of words in *tz'u* is uncommon except occasionally in parallel positions (*yüeh* appears also in the fourth line), that the poem must be "placed" in one of the two seasons, that the third and the final lines argue for spring (though Professor Owen might object that the latter is a "quoted" season), and that two "vegetable" images make the more appropriate pair to balance the two seasons. Readers who favor *yüeh* have the familiarity of the reading on their side—only specialists are likely to be aware of the alternative—and can respond to the opposing arguments in the Olympian idiom of Arthur Waley, "If the poem were by P'an Lang, we should entirely

59. For an account of the transcription system used, see Bryant, *Lyric Poets*, pp. xlvii–li.

agree."[60] In short, if our question is which reading is aesthetically superior, the evidence is indecisive and the best judges are split.

We might, on the other hand, ask which reading is more likely to have been the original. Bearing in mind both that the occasion of the derived reading's first occurrence is likely to have been northern and late, and that the three texts whose traditions go back the farthest, the *Nan-T'ang erh-chu tz'u*, the *Tsun-ch'ien chi*, and the *T'ang Sung chu-hsien chüeh-miao tz'u-hsüan* all include the poem and all read *yeh* (to be sure, only one of the two limbs leading from the archetype of the *Nan-T'ang erh-chu tz'u* does), it seems clear that the evidence favors *yeh* as the archetypal, and indeed the authorial, reading. "Favors," of course, is not the same as "proves," but it shifts the burden of proof in the direction of those who favor the *yüeh* reading. They must explain how, if *yeh* did not enter the tradition until the thirteenth century or later, it is to be found in, and only in, the three textual traditions that go most reliably back to earlier times, traditions that were, moreover, relatively "inert"—little known and rarely reproduced until comparatively recent times.

At the same time, we might usefully wonder when the *yüeh* reading, if not archetypal, entered the tradition and why it has become commonly accepted. What follows is speculative, but perhaps not too remote from actuality. The earliest textual tradition to show the *yüeh* reading is that of the *Ts'ao-t'ang shih-yü*, an "active" tradition (as opposed to the "inert" variety characterized above). This text was originally compiled in the Sung dynasty, but was extensively and repeatedly reedited in Ming and Ch'ing times, during which it was *the* classic anthology of Sung *tz'u*.[61] It seems reasonable to suppose that *yüeh* appeared, by phonetic confusion, in this text first and then spread because of its popularity.

One might pursue this speculative history of *yeh* and *yüeh* one step farther by asking why contemporary scholars and editors continue to

---

60. In a review of Ivan Morris, *The World of the Shining Prince*, which contains an appendix setting out a series of cogent arguments for believing that the *Genji monogatari* is unfinished, Waley quotes his own translation of the ending of the received text, pronounces himself entirely satisfied by this, and dismisses all of Morris's arguments with, "If the novel were by Willkie Collins, I should entirely agree." See Ivan Morris, ed., *Madly Singing in the Mountains: An Appreciation and Anthology of Arthur Waley* (1970; rpt., New York: Harper and Row, 1972), pp. 375–78.

61. This work has had, in part because of its recognized importance, a complex history. See Li Ting-fang, "Sung-jen tsung-chi"; T'ang Kuei-chang, "Tu tz'u hsü-chi," *Wen-hsüeh i-ch'an* 1981, no. 2:88, where T'ang argues, on the basis of materials supplied by Shimizu Shigeru of Kyoto University, that the original compiler of the work was one Ho Shih-hsin; She Chih, "Tz'u hsüan-chi," pt. 2, pp. 226–28; Wu Hsiung-ho, *T'ang Sung tz'u*, pp. 340–42; and Ch'in Huan-ming, "Kuan-yü *Ts'ao-t'ang shih-yü* ti liu-ch'uan yen-pien," *Wen shih* 29 (1988): 413–19.

prefer *yüeh* over *yeh*, assuming either that the textual evidence supports it or that such evidence is hopelessly inconclusive and that judgment can be made only on aesthetic grounds. Whether one of the readings is preferable on such grounds is, as we have seen, not a question that can be answered here. What can be ventured is an account of how the reading of the whole poem is affected by the variation. If the poem begins "Spring flowers, autumn leaves," it has a particular "location," a garden in which the alternation of spring and autumn is seen from a single vantage point located in the physical world, whether this is the tiny pavilion in Pien-ching of the first stanza or the carved railings in Chien-k'ang of the second. If, on the other hand, we begin with "Spring flowers, autumn moon," the "location" of the poem is shifted from the garden to the poet's mind; the angle of vision moves from the outward gaze in which the aspect of a single plant can be seen to alternate with the cycle of the seasons to an inward reflection in the mind that perceives flowers in springtime and the moon in autumn as parallel elements in its inner experience of the universe "outside." This kind of difference is perhaps particularly significant in this poem, which is built around the alternation between those lines, the first in each rhymed pair, that register perceptions of something outside, and those, the answering second lines, that respond. (In the last two lines, it is an imagined interlocutor who asks, and the poetic persona who aligns his sorrow with the image of the river.) To read *yüeh* in the first line does not change this larger pattern, but it blurs the focus, as though the "jadeite stairs" of the fifth line were to be replaced with "bright mirrors." That this blurring was either not noticed or was thought an improvement seems symptomatic of the rise of sentiment (*ch'ing*) in the Ming and Ch'ing periods, when a *tz'u* could be read as though it were framed within some imagined drama. In such a context, the sooner the inner locus for the poetic event is established, the better, and "leaves" is less significantly loaded for this purpose than "moon."

The remaining variations can be dealt with much more briefly, since the evidence concerning them is much less complex and its import more readily grasped.

5.8, 5.9, 5.10: Ma Ling's *Nan-T'ang shu* quotes the third and fourth lines of this poem as an example of Li Yü's poetry reflecting his homesickness in captivity. There are no fewer than three variant readings, none of which is found in any other text: "Last night to my small *garden* [*yüan*] the *west* [*hsi*] wind came again; I could not bear to *raise* [*ch'iao*] my head to my old kingdom shining beneath the moon."[62] Now, Ma

62. Ma Ling, *Nan-T'ang shu* (*SPTK hsü-pien* ed.), 5.10b; also *Mo-hai chin-hu* ed. (*PP* 47/3), 5.9a.

Ling quotes all or part of five different poems found in the *Nan-T'ang
erh-chu tz'u* in his history, which was compiled around 1100. Variant
readings found in Ma Ling's text are found nowhere else in the tradition
except in later works that cite it explicitly. The nature of these variants
suggests neither the graphic confusion that arises in the copying of
documents nor the phonetic confusion (e.g., *yüeh* for *yeh*) that occurs
when a text is misheard or misremembered. They are instead substitutions involving words of parallel function, as in the three variants in this
poem, a sort of variation that tends to occur when a text is being quoted
not for its own sake, but as a "token" signifying some attitude or event
connected with a character in a historical narrative. Nonetheless, these
three variants are not to be dismissed simply because their absence elsewhere in the tradition makes them unfamiliar. There is something to be
said in favor of each of them. Reference to a garden would take up more
naturally from the images of the first line, especially if they were flowers
and leaves rather than flowers and the moon, as we have suggested. A
"west" wind would avoid the repetition in the final line. It would also,
of course, suggest autumn rather than spring, and this does not resonate
well with the poem's final line. As for *ch'iao*, it is the more natural
motion of someone looking at the moon, and also not the commonplace
reading that "look back" is, considered as a piece of poetic diction. We
shall not argue that any of these readings is authorial, but they are all
early, perhaps earlier than the *Tsun-ch'ien chi*, and they call attention to
the instability of textual traditions in their early history.

  5.11: Stephen Owen calls attention to this variation in his essay. This
is a case in which there is no doubt about the archetypal reading of the
Nan-T'ang erh-chu tz'u, but room for discussion, at least, of what the authorial reading might have been. *I-jan* (just the same) is the reading of
all editions both of the *Nan-T'ang erh-chu tz'u* and the *Tsun-ch'ien chi*, *ying
yu* (must still) that of all other texts. This is not a case in which the
arguments made in favor of the "leaves" reading in 5.7 can be persuasive. Although the pronunciation of both phrases has evolved, along
with the rest of the language, between the Nanking of Li Yü's day and
the Peking of ours, the changes are not striking and certainly do not
allow us to argue that confusion would have occurred more readily at
one time than at another. This variation does not appear to be the
result of phonetic confusion in any case, but rather a matter of "substitution in context," rather like the three in Ma Ling's history. Moreover,
both variants were known in Sung times, *ying yu* being found both in the
T'ang Sung chu-hsien chüeh-miao tz'u-hsüan and, as Wang Chung-wen points
out, in Ch'en Yüan-lung's notes (which appear first in an edition dated

1211–12) to the song lyrics of Chou Pang-yen. These are later texts than the *Nan-T'ang erh-chu tz'u* and the *Tsun-ch'ien chi*, but not so much so as to render their readings necessarily less probable. The likeliest ground for choice, aside from the early agreement of the *Nan-T'ang erh-chu tz'u* and *Tsun-ch'ien chi*, may be one raised by Stephen Owen: that *ying yu* would be the less likely reading in T'ang poetic forms that are functionally, if not formally, antecedent to the song lyric. Neither form appears in the *Hua-chien chi*, nor does any phrase similar to *ying yu*; but *i-chiu* (just as of old) is found there seven times.[63]

5.12, 5.16: These two variations are not adjacent, but parallel, so it will be convenient to treat them together. In place of the phrases *wen chün* (I ask you) and *ch'ia ssu* (exactly resembles), which open the last two lines of the poem, the *Tsun-ch'ien chi*, followed by only a few later texts, reads *pu chih* (do not know) and *ch'ia shih* (exactly is). Here again, substitution of functionally equivalent "lead-in" phrases seems to lie behind the variation. It is worth pointing out that this kind of variant is particularly likely to arise in the case of performance literature, such as these lyrics for singing. A performer may not remember the right words, but something must be sung, and something that makes sense in the context. It needs to be recognized that one argument adduced in favor of reading *i-jan* in 5.11 above pulls the other way here: *pu chih* is common in the *Hua-chien chi*, while *wen chün* is not found. Which is the more satisfying pair of readings depends a good deal on how one reads the rest of the poem. The consistent alternation of outer and inner within each pair of lines, discussed above, is hardly possible with *pu chih*. On the other hand, the sort of reversal, on which Professor Owen remarks, of the "things, then feelings" pattern (and breaking a pattern is, after all, a common strategy in final couplets) is unaffected by the alternation between *wen chün* and *pu chih*, while his reading of the final line as embodying a quasi-quotation is, if anything, strengthened by reading *ch'ia shih* rather than *ch'ia ssu*. This, however, only contributes to a preference for *ch'ia ssu* (and hence *wen chün*), for his reading of the poem as a self-conscious combination of frames and clichés inspires its own Waleyesque response (in light of Kang-i Sun Chang's discussion in another essay), "If the poem were by Ch'en Tzu-lung, we should entirely agree."

5.13: The last two variations to be discussed come as an anticlimax; they are both more complicated and essentially trivial. We shall be brief

---

63. Aoyama Hiroshi, comp., *Kakanshū sakuin*, Tōyōgaku Bunken Sentā sōkan, no. 21 (Tokyo: Tōkyō daigaku, 1974), p. 247.

in consequence. All editions of the *Nan-T'ang erh-chu tz'u* except CHEN have, in the penultimate line, *tou yu* (in all have), the alternative reading being *neng yu* (possibly have). There are, in fact, three other possibilities recorded by Wang Chung-wen, including *huan yu* (still have) in the *T'ang Sung chu-hsien chüeh-miao tz'u-hsüan* and other texts. *Neng yu* is found in Sung texts, but only in a fragment of the poem quoted in an anecdote. Such readings do not usually influence the textual tradition of the whole text, but this one apparently did, for it is found in several of the most commonly consulted late compendia, including the *Ch'üan T'ang shih*. It was apparently one of these late texts that contaminated CHEN.

5.14: This variation is discussed in the Appendix. Either reading makes sense. In fact, given the line's function as a rhetorical question, both make about the same sense. Since the *Tsun-ch'ien chi* and *T'ang Sung chu-hsien chüeh-miao tz'u-hsüan* both agree with HOU, LU, and WU against CHEN and HSIAO, to read *chi* would perhaps show good judgment, while to avoid spending a great deal of energy on the decision would surely be wisdom itself.

Finally, it may be worthwhile to return to the simple tree constructed for the *Nan-T'ang erh-chu tz'u* and to look more reflectively at the four sorts of elements that compose it—the extant states, the inferential intermediaries, the archetype, and the links among the other three. They are elements in a logical genealogy of states; what are their possible relationships with records, with the actual printing blocks and paper and ink, the voices and memories and inspirations by which these poems have been conveyed across a millennium from the poets' minds to ours?

Let us begin with the states. What is LU, for example? Is it Lü Yüan's edition, as printed? Is it the photocopy, taken from an exemplar of that edition now in the collection of the Jimbun Kagaku Kenkyūjo at Kyoto University, used in checking? Is it the sum of the readings in some other copy of the edition, as reported in Wang Chung-wen's apparatus? Is it the result of the check of the Kyoto photocopy against Wang Chung-wen (recall that this check turned up Wang's only error)? In fact, it is none of these, though if our work has been done well and if the Kyoto text really is a copy of the Lü Yüan edition, it will be a duplicate of all of them except the third (because we differ with Wang at that one point). What it really is, of course, is the account, found in the data file prepared for the computer, of the evidence for the readings in Lü's edition. If Wang's apparatus has been misinterpreted or if additional errors in it have been missed, LU will be a fifth "version" of Lü Yüan's edition and one clearly of less value than the others. If, on the other hand, LU succeeds in incorporating a true account of Lü Yüan's text, then it is, for the purpose of textual analysis, a duplicate of it.

In the simplest case, each of the inferential intermediaries represents an actual, distinct edition that has not been collated but whose existence can be inferred on the basis of the readings of the collated states. Like most "simplest cases," this one rarely occurs. What an inferential intermediary really is, is a collection of readings whose existence is necessary to explain the relationship between the collated states. For example, the intermediary labelled 1 accounts for the agreements of CHEN and HSIAO against LU, HOU, and WU; it certainly does not amount to an assertion that there was exactly one version of the text intermediate between the archetype and CHEN or HSIAO. In many cases, inspection of the variations and of the external bibliographic evidence suggests that the number of actual intermediaries may have been either greater or less than that proposed by the program, whose operations observe the principle of parsimony. It is inherently unlikely, though not demonstrably impossible, that the textual tradition has been transmitted directly from the archetype of ca. 1160 to CHEN, dated 1909, with only one intervening edition, but the program can only infer intermediaries that have at least two independent descendants.[64] That the number of actual intermediaries might be greater is more immediately apparent than that it might be less. It is possible for a single edition to appear in more than one place in the diagram. We see no likely case of this in the *Nan-T'ang erh-chu tz'u* problem, but it does occur in other textual traditions.[65] Suppose an exemplar of edition A, from which a descendant B derives, is subsequently damaged. If the damaged exemplar and the descendant, but no undamaged examplar, are collated, they will be found to be joined by an inferential intermediary. This latter is, of course, in bibliographic terms the same artifact as its damaged "descendant," but the textual analyst treats them as separate states because the readings they provide are no longer identical.

In other words, both the inferential intermediaries and the collated states are treated by the program as collections of readings, rather than as physical objects, and the value of the process lies above all in its consistent handling of the evidence provided by these readings, which are, after all, by far the most concrete, detailed, and reliable evidence available. The links between elements in the diagram are thus not necessarily lines of descent from one edition to another (although they often are), but rather the loci of textual variation. This is why it is important to

64. For example, Wang Kuo-wei's report that the copy-text he used in preparing CHEN, the "Nan-tz'u" edition, lacked poem 24 tells us that there must have been at least one intermediary between CHEN and 1, which the evidence of HSIAO shows must have included the poem.

65. See Bryant, "Computer-Assisted Determination."

examine the variations occurring at each link, for doing so often reveals patterns that can be useful in the process of relating the diagram to bibliographic evidence.

The archetype remains to be considered. As we have seen, the archetype reconstructed for the *Nan-T'ang erh-chu tz'u* can be considered valid only for the collection as compiled in the twelfth century. In order to approximate any more closely the authorial states of the poems, we must take into consideration the sources of the collection, as in our discussion of "Yü mei-jen." Even when this has been done, the relationship between an "archetype," as reconstructed by the process followed here, and the textual analyst's presumed final goal, the recovery of the author's last and best intentions concerning the text of his work remains problematic. It should be obvious that even under the most favorable conditions the analyst can never be certain of having entirely attained this goal, and in most cases failure to have done so must be assumed.

Faced with such uncertainty, we can only reiterate the need to acknowledge the difficulties and to devise means of overcoming them to the greatest possible extent. Crucial to such means is the application of the sort of consistent testing mechanism that the computer programs used here represent. We may not find answers to all our questions, but we must be sure that we have asked all the questions possible and sought answers to them in a logical and consistent way. By so doing we can expect not only to have greater confidence in the answers we do arrive at, but also to have a more precise understanding of what the unanswerable questions really are and why they cannot be answered.[66]

APPENDIX: COMMENTARY ON THE VARIATIONS

The following commentary is organized according to the links in the tree diagram on p. 331, moving from left to right. For each link, defined by the two states (extant or inferential) that it joins, a list of variations is given, followed by the commentary.

1-CHEN: 2.8, 2.10, 4.6, 5.13, 5.14a, 12.2, 13.3, 13.7, 14.2, 16.3, 16.4, 18.1a, 18.2, 20.2, 20.7, 20.23, 21.2, 25.6, 26.11, 28.2, 28.17, 28.18, 28.19,

---

66. One may reasonably ask how much effect such an examination of the textual tradition can have. As an instance, I offer my book, *Lyric Poets*, in which I generally followed Wang Chung-wen's already very carefully edited text. I now see five places where I would emend my text as a result of the analysis presented here, one of them being "leaves" in place of "moon" in "Yü mei-jen." Perhaps equally important are all the variations in which I would not emend, the crucial gain in both cases being a more confident sense of just how much interpretive weight the text can bear at any particular point.

29.3, 31.1, 31.5, 32.1, 35.1, 37.3, 37.9; plus the rewritten variations 4.5, 6.5, and 27.4. Of these, 2.8, 5.14a, 12.2, 13.3, 13.7, 14.2, 18.1a, 18.2, 20.2, 21.2, 28.2, 28.18, 29.3, 31.1, 32.1, and 35.1 are singleton readings; that is, they are unique to CHEN, being found in no other source. In all the other variations, CHEN agrees with from one to twenty-one other texts, though not with any other state of the *Nan-T'ang erh-chu tz'u*. It is too early in the analysis to offer an explanation of this phenomenon (as we shall see, it stands in considerable contrast to the case of the other four states of the *Nan-T'ang erh-chu tz'u*). In eight of the fourteen variations, there is at least one Sung text in agreement with CHEN, but in all cases there is at least one late text so agreeing, including the *Li-tai shih-yü* in all but two cases. These agreements suggest that CHEN was more "present" in the transmission of the tradition of *tz'u* poetry than were some of the other states of the *Nan-T'ang erh-chu tz'u*, but at this stage we cannot say whether this was a matter of CHEN's being contaminated by other texts or of its being more readily available as a source for later works. In any case, this tendency of CHEN to agree with texts outside the tradition of the *Nan-T'ang erh-chu tz'u* is consistent with the pattern of the rewritten variations 4.5, 6.5, and 27.4, in each of which CHEN and HOU shared a common reading with such other texts.

1-HSIAO: 3.9, 4.6, 5.14a, 7.16, 10.21, 13.4, 17.7, 17.17, 17.18, 19.7, 21.1, 21.3, 26.11, 29.4, 29.4a, 30.1, 30.4, 31.5, 33.3a, 33.4a, 33.5, 35.2, 35.3, 36.5, and 36.7; plus the rewritten variations 14.4 and 29.6. The contrast with CHEN is striking here. In all but four of the non-rewritten variations (3.9, 17.18, 21.3, and 29.4) HSIAO has a singleton reading, and only one text agrees with HSIAO more than once among these four (the *Ch'üan T'ang shih*, in 3.9 and 21.3). In most cases, the readings unique to HSIAO are plainly careless errors. In the two rewritten variations, however, the reading common to HSIAO and LU is the better one. If it were characteristic of HSIAO to "improve" its text in general, we should feel more comfortable with assuming independent emendation in HSIAO and LU in these two cases. On the other hand, in 29.6, no other texts agree with CHEN, HOU, and WU, so this variation is unlike those rewritten by dividing CHEN from HOU (4.5, 6.5, and 27.4). In the latter cases, CHEN and HOU share their reading with other texts, which suggests the possibility of contamination.

1-3: 1.1, 2.1, 2.5, 3.2, 4.6, 4.11, 4.13, 5.7, 5.14 (5.14a), 6.3, 9.6, 15.4, 17.3, 22.2, 23.4, 25.3, 25.4, 26.11, 28.3, 28.12, 31.3, 31.5, 31.6, 34.4, 37.4; plus the rewritten variations 1.2b, 30.2, and 34.1. This is the link within which the archetype is located, which means that in none of these variations can we identify an archetypal reading simply by reference to the tree. Four of them (1.1, 17.3, 25.4, and 31.6) are among the "clearly directional variations" used in locating the archetype. The rest can only be dealt with individually and provisionally. We shall discuss them in four groups.

(a) Variations dividing only states of the *Nan-T'ang erh-chu tz'u*:

28.3: In the note to this poem to the melody "Yü-lou ch'un," 1 read *ni* (nun), while 3 read *chü-shih* (recluse). It is easy to see how the confusion could arise from the shapes of the characters, difficult to be sure which reading is preferable.

34.4: In a textual note to another of the "Hsieh hsin en" poems, 1 had *shih* (is), while 3 read *jih* (sun). *Shih* appears to be the better reading, and Wang Chung-wen adopts it. In the *Ch'üan T'ang Wu-tai tz'u* of Chang Chang and Huang Yü (rpt., Taipei: Wen-shih-che, 1986), p. 485, the reading in HOU is reported to be *yüeh* (says). I have not seen HOU since the appearance of the *Ch'üan T'ang Wu-tai tz'u*, but the *Su-hsiang shih* reprint of it reads *jih*. Chang and Huang are probably right in supposing that either form would be evidence of an ancestral *shih* either miscopied or derived from a damaged ancestor.

(b) Variations in which other texts agree only with 1:

4.13: While 1 and all other texts read *i* (lean), 3 evidently read *chi* (send). The former reading is clearly better, and its being found in all other Sung texts that include this passage tends to confirm that it was the reading of the archetype. It is significant that Wang Chung-wen, who generally follows LU as his copy-text, reads *i* here. Indeed, he follows 1 in all five variations in this group.

15.4: The reading of 3 (found in HOU, LU, and WU), *tao* (reverse) for *hsin* (trust), is unintelligible, as Wang Chung-wen argues. The other texts that include this passage, five of them of Sung date, all read *hsin*.

26.11: The reading of 3 was a lacuna, while CHEN reads *ch'ü* (bends) and HSIAO, *yüeh* (moon). One of the latter is probably the archetypal reading. Both make sense in the context, but *ch'ü* makes more and better sense. It is also the reading of all other texts that include this poem, and this tends to support its claim to be the reading of the archetype.

28.12: The lacuna in 3, in place of *chien* (interval) or *hsien* (leisure), cannot be authorial. The typeset edition of WU and the *Su-hsiang shih* reedition of HOU both restore the text.

31.5: This variation is most conveniently discussed here, although it is not entirely analogous to the others in the group. The reading of 3 was *chin* (suffer), which does not make sense in the context. HSIAO reads *chih* (branch). The reading of CHEN, *chin* (band), is a homophone of that in 3 and is also written with a similar character. Although the latter two readings both make good sense, the similarity of those in CHEN and 3 suggests that one of them was the reading in 1, and we are naturally inclined to suppose that it was that of CHEN, which is also found in the only other text, a late anthology, to include the poem. On the other hand, if 1 already had an intelligible reading, the chances of variation occurring between it and HSIAO would naturally be reduced. In short, we propose "band" with greater confidence as the authorial reading for the poem than we do as the reading of the archetype of the *Nan-T'ang erh-chu tz'u*.

(c) Variations in which other texts agree only with 3:

2.1: The reading of 1 was *yü* (jadeite). WU leaves a space here, and 3 read *pi* (emerald). Neither reading is clearly preferable, but it may be significant that the *T'ang Sung chu-hsien chüeh-miao tz'u-hsüan*, the only other Sung text to include the poem, agrees with 3.

3.2: That 1 read *erh shou* (two poems) after the title of this poem while 3 did not is not a dilemma that reference to other texts can resolve; nor is it one of much importance.

4.11: Both the *ho* (what) of 3 and the *wu* (without) of 1 are satisfactory readings in the context. That the *Tsun-ch'ien chi* and the *T'ang Sung chu-hsien chüeh-miao tz'u-hsüan* both read *ho* increases the plausibility of accepting it as the authorial reading.

9.6: This variation resembles the preceding. Both *shan* ("hill," i.e., "high") in 3 and its homophone meaning "coral" in 1 are acceptable readings. That both the *Tsun-ch'ien chi*, which attributes the poem to "Prince Li," and the *Hua-chien chi*, in which it is included as the work of Wen T'ing-yün, read "hill" similarly tends to support it as the authorial reading.

22.2: The two homophones in this variation, both read *so* ("tiny" in 1, and "lock" in 3), occur as substitutions for one another fairly frequently, meaning "chain" or "link." Here the other texts are few in number and late, so they do not help much in resolving this variation, which is of little significance in any case. We are inclined to adopt the "lock" form to be consistent with the clearly directional variation 25.4 (see above), which involves the same pair of homophones. That the elements of the pair take the same positions on either side of the archetype in both variations naturally suggests that we may be dealing with a case of "scribal style."

25.3: Two late texts agree with 3 in reading *hang* (row), which makes easier sense than *jen* (allow), the reading of 1. Other late texts have other readings still. While *hang* is the easier reading, *jen* remains possible ("One allows the beaded curtains to hang idly unrolled *all the time*, [since] all day long no one visits").

31.3: The variation between *chin* (gold) in 3 and *han* (enclose) in 1 is clearly the result of graphic confusion. "Gold" is probably the better reading, as it matches the *fen* (pink) earlier in the line.

d) Variations in which other texts agree with both 1 and 3:

2.5: The reading of 1 was *yeh* (night), while that of 3 was *yü* (remnant) (WU leaves a blank here). The *T'ang Sung chu-hsien chüeh-miao tz'u-hsüan* agrees with 3, while a late compendium, the *Hua-ts'ao ts'ui-pien*, agrees with 1. "Night" is the easier reading, perhaps, but it is not decisively better.

4.6: The reading of 3 here was *jung* (countenance), with which several Sung collections of anecdotes that cite the poem, as well as a number of later texts, agree. CHEN has *shao* (beautiful), with which the *Tsun-ch'ien chi*, the *T'ang Sung chu-hsien chüeh-miao tz'u-hsüan*, and most later texts agree. HSIAO reads *han* (cold). The latter looks like an error derived from the reading of 3, which suggests that 1 also may have read *jung*, in which case the error in HSIAO would be independent of the reading in CHEN, which might be the result of contamination. Alternatively, the reading of 1 (and perhaps even of the archetype) may have been *han*. Choice of an archetypal reading here is not possible on formal grounds. All three make good sense in the context. That *han* is found only as a singleton in HSIAO greatly reduces the likelihood of its being archetypal, but the division of even the Sung sources between *jung* and *shao* is equivocal.

5.7: See the concluding section of the essay for a full discussion of this variation, in which the reading of 1 was *yeh* (leaves), while that of 3 was *yüeh* (moon). We argue there that *yeh* has the better chance of being the reading of the archetype.

5.14: This variation might well have been classed with group 3 above, as only one late text agrees with 1 in reading *hsü* (quite), while all others, including seven of Sung date, read *chi* (how much). This suggests that *chi* is more likely to have been the reading of the archetype.

6.3: This is a more complex case than most, in that the reading of 3 cannot be determined on formal grounds. The reading of 1, with which several late texts agree, is *ti* (drip). LU and one late text read *tuan* (broken). The lacuna in 2, in place of *tuan* or *ti*, is non-authorial (the typeset edition of WU fills it with *tuan*). The difficulty is, of course, that the reading of 3 cannot be determined when 2 and LU disagree, and this is particularly important since the reading of the archetype was probably that of 3.

23.4: This poem is not included in any Sung texts other than the *Nan-T'ang erh-chu tz'u*, so it is not so significant (at least not for our attempt to determine the reading of the archetype) that only one late text agrees with 1 in reading *hun* (soul), while many agree with 3 in reading *meng* (dream).

37.4: Most of the Sung texts that include this poem agree with 3 in reading *nuan* (warm), while the *Lei shuo* and a few minor texts read *nai*[1] or *nai*[2] (help, fend off) with 1. The latter reading makes the whole line one sentence ("Gossamer covers do not fend off the fifth-watch chill"), while the former makes it two independent clauses ("Gossamer covers are not warm; the fifth watch is chilly").

In short, whenever the archetype is located on a link in the diagram, rather than at a particular state or inferential intermediary, variations occurring across that link can be resolved only by such nonce methods as the authority of other texts or the judgment of an editor.

3-LU: 6.2, 6.3, 7.14, 8.1, 13.4, 19.7, 20.10, 21.3, 23.5, 23.5a, 26.10, 28.16, 37.1, 37.11; plus the rewritten variations 14.4, 29.6, and 34.3. The first point to note about these variations is that they are relatively few in number, fewer than those occurring across any other link leading to an extant state. Only four of them (7.14, 8.1, 23.5a, and 37.1) are not singleton variations, and even in these four the agreements with other texts are not of great significance. Although only in the case of the complex variation 6.3 (see above) can we argue that LU's reading is possibly archetypal, the relatively small number of variations arising at this link suggests that LU is generally the most reliable of the extant states. The result of our formal analysis of the variations thus agrees with Wang Chung-wen's judgment, when he chose LU as the copy-text for his edition.

3-2: 6.3, 7.7, 8.4, 16.4, 19.1, 19.9, 20.5, 29.3, 29.4a, 34.5. These variations too are strikingly few in number. In the most common case, the reading of 2 was a lacuna. In only one of these variations, 20.5, do other texts share the reading of 2. The two Sung texts to include the poem, the *Tsun-ch'ien chi* and the *T'ang Sung chu-hsien chüeh-miao tz'u-hsüan* (the latter attributes it to Tu An-shih), both agree with 3 (and hence with the archetypal reading of the *Nan-T'ang erh-chu tz'u*) in reading *lung* (cage), and many later texts agree. This seems a much more interesting reading in the context than the *fei* (fly) of 2 and a number of later texts.

2-HOU: 1.2a, 1.6, 1.13, 5.3, 8.2, 9.7, 14.1, 15.1, 17.4, 18.1b, 19.2, 20.3, 20.3a, 20.16, 25.1, 25.4, 26.2, 28.4, 30.3, 31.6, 31.7, 35.4; plus the rewritten variations 4.5, 6.5, 27.4, 30.2, and 34.3. Here again, virtually all the variations consist of singleton readings unique to HOU. The three exceptions, 1.6, 20.16, and 25.4 (see above), are all cases of a *lectio* if not *facilior*, then at least *facilis*, and it is possible that independent error is responsible for one or more of them. Most of the other variants in HOU are clearly erroneous readings or slight variations in the placement of the notes.

2-WU: 1.2c, 1.15, 2.1, 2.3, 2.5, 2.9, 2.10, 3.1, 4.10, 5.2, 6.4, 6.5, 10.4, 13.8, 15.3, 16.2, 16.5, 17.2, 17.3, 24.7, 26.9, 26.10, 27.4, 27.5, 29.2, 29.5, 29.7, 31.2, 31.7, 32.2, 34.2, 37.6; plus the rewritten variations 1.2b and 34.1. In all but one of these numerous variations (the exception is trivial), WU has a singleton reading, and one that is in the majority of cases manifestly inferior, as Wang Chung-wen frequently points out in his apparatus. Many of these errors are "corrected" in the typeset edition.

CONTRIBUTORS

DANIEL BRYANT is Associate Professor of Chinese at the University of Victoria. A student of Yeh Chia-ying and E. G. Pulleyblank, he received his doctorate in Chinese from the University of British Columbia in 1978 with a dissertation on the High T'ang poet Meng Hao-jan. He has since published a book on the song lyric poets of the Southern T'ang and a variety of articles and reviews concerning Chinese literature of the T'ang, Sung, and Ming periods, as well as translations of premodern poetry and contemporary fiction. His current project is a book on the Ming poet Ho Ching-ming (1483–1521).

KANG-I SUN CHANG is Professor and Chair, Department of East Asian Languages and Literatures at Yale University. Her publications include *The Evolution of Chinese* Tz'u *Poetry* (1980), *Six Dynasties Poetry* (1986), *The Late-Ming Poet Ch'en Tzu-lung* (1991), and many articles in both English and Chinese addressing issues in the fields of Chinese poetry and literary criticism. She is also editor of *An Anthology of Chinese Women Poets* (forthcoming from Yale).

RONALD C. EGAN is Professor of Chinese at the University of California, Santa Barbara. He is the author of *The Literary Works of Ou-yang Hsiu (1007–72)* (1984) and specializes in Sung dynasty literati culture. His biographical and literary study of Su Shih is forthcoming from Harvard.

GRACE S. FONG is Associate Professor of Chinese Literature at McGill University and Associate Director of its Centre for East Asian Studies. She is the author of *Wu Wenying and the Art of Southern Song* Ci *Poetry* (1987), and her recent publications include "Persona and Mask in the

Song Lyric" in the *Harvard Journal of Asiatic Studies*. Her current research focuses on gender issues in Chinese literature, and she is writing a book on aesthetics and the feminine in Chinese poetry.

SHUEN-FU LIN received his Ph.D. from Princeton University and is Professor of Chinese Language and Literature at the University of Michigan, Ann Arbor. He is the author of *The Transformation of the Chinese Lyrical Tradition: Chiang K'uei and Southern Sung Tz'u Poetry* (1978) and a number of articles on Chinese aesthetics, fiction, philosophical prose, and poetry. He is also cotranslator of *The Tower of Myriad Mirrors: A Supplement to Journey to the West* [by Tung Yüeh] (1978, 1988) and coeditor of *The Vitality of the Lyric Voice: Shih Poetry from the Late Han to the T'ang* (1986).

STEPHEN OWEN received his Ph.D. from Yale University and is currently Professor of Chinese and Comparative Literature at Harvard University. He is the author of various books on Chinese poetry, literary criticism, and comparative literature, the most recent being *Remembrances: The Experience of the Past in Classical Chinese Poetry* (1986); *Mi-lou: Poetry and the Labyrinth of Desire* (1989); and *Readings in Chinese Literary Thought* (1992).

STUART H. SARGENT is Associate Professor of Chinese at the University of Maryland, College Park, where he has taught since 1979. His research centers on the poets of the late Northern Sung period, especially Su Shih, Huang T'ing-chien, Ch'en Shih-tao, and Ho Chu. Director of a project to produce a computer-generated Chinese character concordance to the poems of Su Shih, he also oversees the Maryland Summer Institute for Teachers of Chinese.

JOHN TIMOTHY WIXTED (B.A., Toronto; M.A., Stanford; D.Phil., Oxford) is Professor of Asian Languages at Arizona State University, where he teaches Chinese and Japanese language and literature. He is the author of two books on traditional Chinese poetry, *The Song-Poetry of Wei Chuang (836–910 A.D.)* (1979) and *Poems on Poetry: Literary Criticism by Yuan Hao-wen (1190–1257)* (1982). He is the translator of a third volume: Yoshikawa Kōjirō, *Five Hundred Years of Chinese Poetry, 1150–1650: The Chin, Yuan, and Ming Dynasties* (1989). And he is the compiler of a fourth work: *Japanese Scholars of China: A Bibliographical Handbook* (1992).

YEH CHIA-YING is Professor Emerita of Chinese Literature at the University of British Columbia. She has published widely in both English and Chinese on Chinese poetry and poetics and has served, most recently, as Visiting Professor at Tsing Hua University in Taiwan (1990–91) and as Director of the Institute for the Comparative Study of Chinese Literature at Nankai University in the People's Republic (1991–).

PAULINE YU is Professor of Chinese Literature and Chair of the Department of East Asian Languages and Literatures at the University of California, Irvine. She is the author of *The Poetry of Wang Wei: New Translations and Commentary* (1980), *The Reading of Imagery in the Chinese Poetic Tradition* (1987), and numerous articles on Chinese and comparative poetry and literary theory.

GLOSSARY

ai erh pu-yüan 哀而不怨

ai-p'in 愛品

an 暗

An-fu 安福

Cha Wei-jen 查為仁

Chai Ch'i-nien 翟耆年

Ch'ai Ching-i 柴靜儀

Chang Chi 張輯

Chang Chih-ho 張志和

Chang Chu 張翥

Chang Heng 張衡

Chang Hsiao-hsiang 張孝祥

Chang Hsien (Tzu-yeh) 張先（子野）

Chang Hsien-ch'ing 張嫻婧

Chang Hui-yen 張惠言

Chang Shou-chieh 張守節

Chang Tuan-i 張端義

Chang Yen (Ming) 張綖

Chang Yen (Sung) 張炎

Ch'ang-an 長安

Ch'ang-chou 常州

"Ch'ang-hen chuan" 長恨傳

"Ch'ang hen ko" 長恨歌

"Ch'ang hsiang-ssu" 長相思

Ch'ang-hsing 長興

ch'ang-tiao 長調

ch'ang-tuan-chü 長短句

Chao (family name) 趙

chao ("morning") 朝

Chao Ch'ang-ch'ing 趙長卿

Chao Ch'ung-po 趙崇燔

Chao Ch'ung-tso 趙崇祚

Chao I-fu 趙以夫

Chao Ming-ch'eng 趙明誠

Chao Shan-kua 趙善括

Chao Shih-chieh 趙世杰

Chao Shih-hsia 趙師俠

Chao Te-lin 趙德麟

Chao Ting 趙鼎

Chao Ts'ai-chi (Chin-yen) 趙彩姬 （今燕）

Chao Wen 趙文

Chao Wen-li 趙聞禮

Ch'ao Ch'ien-chih 晁謙之

Ch'ao Ching-yü 晁景迂

Ch'ao I-tao 晁以道

Ch'ao Kung-liu 晁公留

Ch'ao Pu-chih 晁補之

Ch'ao Tz'u-ying 晁次膺

Ch'ao Yüeh-chih 晁說之

che 這

"Che-ku t'ien" 鷓鴣天

che tz'u-ti 這次第

chen 真

Chen Fei 珍妃

Chen Te-hsiu 真德秀

Ch'en Chi-ch'ang 陳季常

Ch'en Chi-ju 陳繼儒

Ch'en Chih-lin 陳之遴

Ch'en-feng-ko ts'ung-shu 晨風閣叢書

Ch'en Hsi-lu 陳錫露

Ch'en Hsiang 陳湘

Ch'en Hung 陳鴻

Ch'en Nai-wen 陳乃文

Ch'en Pang-yen 陳邦炎

Ch'en Shih-tao 陳師道

Ch'en T'ing 陳霆

Ch'en T'ing-cho 陳廷焯

Ch'en Tzu-lung 陳子龍

Ch'en Wei-sung 陳維崧

Ch'en Yüan-lung 陳元龍

Ch'en Yün-heng 陳允衡

Ch'en Yün-p'ing 陳允平

cheng ("orthodox") 正

Cheng (place-name) 鄭

Cheng-ho 政和

Cheng Hsia 鄭俠

Cheng T'o (Ju-ying) 鄭妥(如英)

cheng-tsung 正宗

Cheng Wei chih sheng 鄭衛之聲

Cheng Wei chih yin 鄭衛之音

Ch'eng I (I-ch'uan) 程頤(伊川)

Ch'eng-tu 成都

chi ("how much") 幾

chi ("send") 寄

Chi-an 吉安

"Chi Chang Tzu-yeh wen" 祭張子野文

Chi-chou 吉州

chi fan 及笄

chi-mei 繼美

Chi-nan fu-chih 濟南府志

Chi-she 幾社

chi yüan 寄遠

ch'i 氣

ch'i-ch'i ts'an-ts'an ch'i-ch'i 悽悽慘慘戚戚

ch'i-fu 棄婦

Ch'i Piao-chia 祁彪佳

Ch'i-tung yeh-yu 齊東野語

Ch'i-yen 齊言

ch'i yü 綺語

chia kuan 加冠

Chia Ssu-tao 賈似道

Chia Tao 賈島

ch'ia shih 恰是

ch'ia ssu 恰似

"Chiang-ch'eng tzu" 江城子

Chiang Chieh 蔣捷

Chiang-chou 江舟

Chiang-hsi shih-p'ai 江西詩派

Chiang K'uei (Yao-chang)
姜夔(堯章)

Chiang-nan　江南

"Chiang shen-tzu"　江神子

Chiang-ts'un ts'ung-shu　彊村叢書

Chiang Yen　江淹

chiao　蕉

chiao-fang　教坊

Chiao-fang chi　教坊記

"Chiao ssu chih"　郊祀志

"Chiao-yü ou-kan"　教育偶感

"Chiao-yü p'u-chi chih ken-pen pan-
　fa"　教育普及之根本辦法

Chiao-yüan shih-she　蕉園詩社

ch'iao　翹

chieh-yü　婕妤

ch'ieh ("concubine")　妾

ch'ieh ("intense")　切

ch'ieh ("just")　且

chien ("interval")　間

chien ("sword")　劍

Chien-ch'ang-chün　建昌軍

Chien-k'ang　建康

"Chien tzu mu-lan-hua"　減字木蘭花

Ch'ien Ch'ien-i　錢謙益

Ch'ien-chou　黔州

Ch'ien Liang-yu　錢良祐

Ch'ien Wei-yen　錢惟演

Ch'ien Yüeh　錢岳

Ch'ien Yün-i　錢雲儀

chih ("branch")　植

chih ("it")　之

chih ("substance")　質

chih-ch'ih　咫尺

Chih-i　摭遺

chih-shih　質實

chih-tao　知道

chih-yin　知音

Ch'ih-chou　池州

ch'ih-tu　尺牘

chin ("band")　衿

chin ("gold," name of dynasty)　金

chin ("strength")　勁

chin ("suffer")　矜

Chin-ch'üan chi　金荃集

chin ch'uang li k'un ch'i huan yung
　金窗力困起還慵

chin ch'üeh ch'ai　金雀釵

Chin-ling　金陵

"Chin-lü ch'ü"　金縷曲

"Chin-ming ch'ih"　金明池

chin-shih　進士

Chin-shih lu　金石錄

chin-t'i shih　近體詩

"Chin-t'ung hsien-jen tz'u Han ko"
　金銅仙人辭漢歌

Chin Wu-hsiang　金武祥

Ch'in-ch'ü wai-pien　琴趣外編

Ch'in Huai ssu-chi shih　秦淮四姬詩

Ch'in Huan-ming　秦寰明

Ch'in Hui-min　秦惠民

Ch'in Kuan (Shao-yu)　秦觀(少游)

Ch'in Kuei (or Ch'in Hui)　秦檜

ch'in lou pu chien ch'ui hsiao nü　秦樓不
　見吹簫女

"Ch'in Shih-huang pen-chi"　秦始皇
　本紀

Ch'in-ts'ao　琴操

"Ch'in-yüan ch'un"　沁園春

ching　境

Ching-an　靜安

Ching-an tz'u　靜安詞

Ching-an wen-chi　靜安文集

Ching-an wen-chi hsü-pien　靜安文集續編

ching-chieh　境界

Ching-hu　荆湖

Ching-shan chü-shih　荆山居士

Ching T'ang　京鐙

ch'ing ("light")　輕

ch'ing ("love," "emotion")　情

Ch'ing-chiang　清江

ch'ing-ch'iao　輕巧

ch'ing-chih　情致

ch'ing-ch'ing　清清

ch'ing-hua　清華

ch'ing-i　情意

ch'ing-k'ung　清空

Ch'ing-lin　青林

"Ch'ing-p'ing yüeh"　清平樂

Ch'ing-po tsa-chih　清波雜志

"Ch'ing-yü-an"　青玉案

ch'ing-yüeh　清樂

Chiu hsiao-shuo　舊小說

Ch'iu Chin　秋瑾

Ch'iu hsing　秋興

"Ch'iu-po mei"　秋波媚

ch'iu yeh　秋葉

"Ch'iu-yeh yüeh"　秋夜月

ch'iu yüeh　秋月

Ch'o-keng lu　輟耕錄

Chou　紂

Chou Chi　周濟

Chou Chih-ch'i　周之琦

Chou Chih-piao　周之標

Chou Fang　周昉

Chou Lo　周樂

Chou Mi (Ts'ao-ch'uang)　周密(草窗)

Chou Ming　周銘

Chou Pang-yen　周邦彥

Chou Pi-ta　周必大

"Ch'ou Chang shao-fu"　酬張少府

Chu Ho-ling　朱鶴齡

Chu Hsi　朱熹

Chu Hsi-chen　朱希真

Chu I-tsun　朱彝尊

Chu Jou-tse　朱柔則

Chu Pien　朱弁

Chu Shu-chen　朱淑真

Chu Ta-shao　朱大韶

Chu Tsu-mou　朱祖謀

Chu Tun-ju　朱敦儒

"Chu Ying-t'ai chin"　祝英臺近

Chu Yün-ming　祝允明

ch'u-shih　處士

Ch'u-tz'u　楚辭

chü-shih　居士

ch'ü ("departing")　去

ch'ü ("song")　曲

"Ch'ü tu p'ien"　去毒篇

ch'ü-tzu-tz'u　曲子詞

Ch'ü Yu　瞿佑

Ch'ü Yüan　屈原

ch'uan-jen　傳人

chüan　卷

ch'üan wu hsin-kan　全無心肝

ch'üan-yin　勸淫

chuang　壯

chuang-ch'i　壯氣

Chuang-tzu 莊子

chüeh 角

chüeh-chü 絕句

Chüeh-miao hao-tz'u 絕妙好詞

ch'üeh 闋

ch'üeh-shih chiu-shih hsiang-shih
却是舊時相識

"Ch'üeh t'a chih" 鵲踏枝

Ch'ui-chien lu 吹劍錄

Ch'un-ch'iu 春秋

ch'un hua ch'iu yüeh ho shih liao
春花秋月何時了

"Ch'un ts'ung t'ien-shang lai"
春從天上來

chün 君

Ch'ün-ya tz'u-chi 羣雅詞集

chung 重

chung fu tsai 終復在

Chung-hsiang chi 衆香集

Chung Hsing 鍾惺

Chung-hsing i-lai chüeh-miao tz'u-hsüan
中興以來絕妙詞選

Chung Hung (Chung Jung) 鍾嶸

Chung-nan 終南

chung-tiao 中調

Ch'ung-kuang 重光

ch'ung-lou 重樓

erh shou 二首

Fa-hsiu 法秀

Fa-yün-hsiu 法雲秀

Fan Chih-hou 樊志厚

Fan Chung-yen 范仲淹

Fan-hua meng 繁華夢

Fang Ch'ien-li 方千里

fang-ko 放歌

"Fang ko hsing" 放歌行

fang-shih 方式

fei ("fly") 飛

fei ("consort") 妃

fen 粉

Fen-ning 分寧

fen-se ju t'u 粉色如土

Feng-ch'eng 豐城

"Feng ch'i wu" 鳳棲梧

Feng Chin-po 馮金伯

Feng-hsin 奉新

"Feng-huang-t'ai shang i ch'ui-hsiao"
鳳凰臺上憶吹簫

feng hui hsiao yüan t'ing wu lü 風回
小院庭蕪綠

feng ting 風定

Feng Yen-ssu 馮延巳

fu ("exposition") 賦

fu ("float") 浮

Fu-chai man-lu 復齋漫錄

Fu Chao-lun 符兆綸

Fu-chou 撫州

"Fu Feng-hsien hsien yung huai"
赴奉先縣詠懷

Fu Hsieh-t'ung 傅爕詗

Fu Hsüan 傅玄

fu-jen 夫人

Fu-jen chi 夫人集

fu-jen yü 婦人語

Fu-she 復社

Fu-ya ko-tz'u 復雅歌詞

Hai-ning 海寧

hai-t'ang 海棠

han ("cold") 寒

han ("enclose")　含

Han Ch'iu-pai　韓秋白

han pu-chin chih i　含不盡之意

Han Shih-chung　韓世忠

Han shu　漢書

han tan hsiang hsiao ts'ui yeh ts'an
　菡萏香銷翠葉殘

Han T'o-chou　韓侂冑

Han Wei　漢魏

Han Wu-ti　漢武帝

Han Yü　韓愈

Han Yü-fu　韓玉父

hang　行

hao-fang　豪放

"Hao ko hsing"　浩歌行

hao-ming wu-hsüeh　好名無學

"Hao shih kuang"　好時光

"Hen fu"　恨賦

Heng-yang　衡陽

ho　何

Ho Ching-ming　何景明

Ho Chu　賀鑄

ho fang　何妨

Ho Ning　和凝

Ho Shang　賀裳

Ho Shih-hsin　何士信

Ho Shuang-ch'ing　賀雙卿

Hou Chih　侯寘

"Hou ch'u sai"　後出塞

Hou-Han shu　後漢書

Hou-shan shih ch'ao　後山詩鈔

Hou-shan shih-hua　後山詩話

Hou Wen-ts'an　侯文燦

hsi　西

"Hsi-ch'i-tzu"　西溪子

"Hsi chiang yüeh"　西江月

"Hsi ch'ien ying"　喜遷鶯

"Hsi-ching fu"　西京賦

Hsi-ch'ing san-chi　西青散記

Hsi-ch'ing shih-hua　西清詩話

"Hsi-ch'ü ko"　西曲歌

Hsi-hsi　盼盼

Hsi K'ang　嵇康

"Hsi-pei yu kao-lou"　西北有高樓

"Hsi-tu fu"　西都賦

Hsi-tz'u chuan　繫辭傳

hsia ("below")　下

hsia ("narrow")　狹

"Hsiang-chien huan"　相見歡

hsiang-ssu　相思

Hsiang Tzu-yin　向子諲

Hsiang-yang　襄陽

Hsiang Yü　項羽

hsiao ("disperse")　肖

hsiao ("night")　宵

hsiao ("sleet")　霄

Hsiao Chiang-sheng　蕭江聲

hsiao chuang ch'u kuo　曉妝初過

hsiao ko-tz'u　小歌辭

hsiao-ling　小令

hsiao-lou lien-yüan heng-k'ung　小樓連
　苑橫空

Hsiao-shan　綃山

Hsiao Shu-lan　蕭淑蘭

hsiao tao　小道

hsiao-tz'u　小詞

"Hsiao-wu pen-chi"　孝武本紀

Hsiao-ying　曉瑩

hsiao yüeh chui　曉月墜

hsieh-ching　寫境

hsieh ch'u fu-jen sheng-k'ou 寫出
婦人聲口

"Hsieh hsin en" 謝新恩

Hsieh I 謝逸

Hsieh-niang 謝娘

Hsieh-nü 謝女

hsieh-shih 寫實

Hsieh Tao-yün 謝道韞

hsien 閒

hsien-ch'ing 閒情

hsien meng yüan 閒夢遠

Hsien-yang 咸陽

Hsien-yu-shan tao-shih 仙游山道士

hsin ("heart") 心

hsin ("trust") 信

Hsin Ch'i-chi (Chia-hsüan)
辛棄疾(稼軒)

hsin ch'ing 心情

Hsin-chou 信州

hsin-fa 心法

hsin huai 心懷

Hsin-kan 新淦

hsin tz'u 新詞

Hsing-kuo chün 興國軍

Hsiung-chou 雄州

Hsiung-nu 匈奴

hsü ("empty") 虛

hsü ("quite") 許

Hsü Ang-hsiao 許昂霄

Hsü-chiang 盱江

Hsü Ch'iu 徐釚

Hsü-chou 徐州

Hsü Kao-lu 許蒿廬

Hsü Ling 徐陵

Hsü Po-ling 徐伯齡

Hsü Shih-chün 徐士俊

Hsü Shih-fu 許世溥

Hsü Shih-tseng 徐師曾

Hsü-t'ien 許田

Hsü Ts'an 徐燦

Hsü T'ung-tien 續通典

hsü-tzu 虛字

Hsü Yuan 徐媛

Hsüan-tsung 玄宗

hsüeh-pu 學部

Hsüeh T'ao 薛濤

hsüh ch'un hsü shih hsien ch'un tsao
尋春須是先春早

hsün-hsün mi-mi 尋尋覓覓

Hu-chou 湖州

Hu Ch'üan 胡銓

Hu Te-fang 胡德方

Hu Tzu 胡仔

Hu Yin 胡寅

Hu Ying-lin 胡應麟

Hua-an tz'u-hsüan 花庵詞選

Hua-chien chi 花間集

Hua-chien chi pu 花間集補

Hua-jui fu-jen 花蕊夫人

hua ming yüeh an lung ch'ing wu
花明月暗籠輕霧

Hua-ts'ao meng-shih 花草蒙拾

Hua-ts'ao ts'ui-pien 花草粹編

Huai-nan 淮南

huan ("happy") 歡

huan ("return") 還

"Huan hsi sha" 浣溪紗

huan-t'ou 換頭

huan yu 還有

Huang Ching 黃靜

Huang-chou　黃州

Huang-fu Sung　皇甫松

Huang Ju-chia　黃汝嘉

Huang Sheng (Hua-an, Shu-yang, Yü-lin)　黃昇(花庵, 叔暘, 玉林)

Huang Ta-yü (Tsai-wan)　黃大輿 (載萬)

Huang T'ing-chien (Lu-chih, Shan-ku)　黃庭堅(魯直, 山谷)

Huang Yüan-chieh　黃媛介

Hui-chu hou-lu　揮麈後錄

Hui-chu lu　揮麈錄

Hui-feng tz'u-hua　蕙風詞話

Hui-hung　惠洪

Hui-tsung　徽宗

hun　魂

Hung-chiao chi　紅蕉集

Hung-chou　洪州

Hung-fu　紅拂

Hung-hsiao　紅綃

Hung-hsien　紅線

hung jih i kao san chang t'ou　紅日已高三丈透

Hung lou meng　紅樓夢

"*Hung-lou meng* p'ing-lun"　紅樓夢評論

i ("ease")　逸

i ("meaning")　意

"I chiang-shang Wu Ch'u-shih"　憶江上吳處士

"I-chien mei"　一剪梅

"I Ch'in-o"　憶秦娥

i-chiu　依舊

I-chou　伊州

"I hu chu"　一斛珠

I-hui　奕繪

i-jan　依然

i-ko ch'ou tzu　一箇愁字

i kou ch'u yüeh lin chuang ching　一鉤初月臨妝鏡

i-meng　一夢

i nei yen wai　意內言外

i-sheng t'ien-tz'u　倚聲填詞

I Shih-chen　伊世珍

i shih wei tz'u　以詩為詞

i ta-tsung　一大宗

i yen ch'iung li . . . liang tzu ch'iung hsing　一言窮理...兩字窮形

I-yüan tz'u-huang　藝苑雌黃

i-yüeh　夷樂

jan jan ch'iu kuang liu pu chu　冉冉秋光留不住

jen　任

"Jen-chien shih-hao chih yen-chiu"　人間嗜好之研究

Jen-chien tz'u i-chi　人間詞乙集

jen-nao　人腦

jen sheng ch'ou hen ho neng mien　人生愁恨何能免

Jen-tsung　仁宗

jih　日

ju　入

Juan Chi　阮籍

"Juan lang kuei"　阮郎歸

jung ("countenance")　容

jung ("gauze")　絨

jung ("tangled")　茸

Jung-chou　戎州

k'ai-tsung　開宗

kan ("feel")　感

Kan (river)　贛

Kan-shan yün-wo chi-t'an　感山雲臥紀談

"Kan ts'ao tzu"　甘草子

k'an wei chen　看未真

K'ang-hsi　康熙

kao　高

Kao-an　高安

Kao-chai shih-hua　高齋詩話

Kao Ch'i　高啓

Kao Kuan-kuo　高觀國

Kao Ping　高棅

Kao Shih-ch'i　高士奇

Kao-t'ang　高唐

kao-ya　高雅

keng-chien　更兼

"Keng-lou-tzu"　更漏子

keng-shen　庚申

ko ("item")　箇

ko ("song")　歌

ko-hsing　歌行

"Ko lien t'ing"　隔簾聽

ko-tao　閣道

k'o-lien　可憐

Ku Ch'i-feng　顧起鳳

Ku Ch'i-yüan　顧起元

Ku-chin ming-yüan pai-hua shih-yü　古今名媛百花詩餘

Ku-chin ming-yüan shih tz'u hsüan　古今名媛詩詞選

Ku-chin nü-shih　古今女史

Ku-chin tz'u-hua　古今詞話

Ku Ch'un (T'ai-ch'ing)　顧春(太清)

"Ku i"　古意

Ku-liang chuan　穀梁傳

Ku Mei　顧媚

ku-shih　古詩

"Ku-shih shih-chiu shou"　古詩十九首

Ku Ts'ai　顧彩

Ku Ts'ung-ching　顧從敬

ku-wen　古文

Ku Wu-fang　顧梧芳

k'u　苦

k'u-ssu　酷似

"K'u yin"　苦吟

K'uai-chi　會稽

kuan　鰥

"Kuan-chü"　關雎

Kuan-hsi　關西

kuan wo　觀我

kuan wu　觀物

Kuan Yün-shih　貫雲石

K'uang Chou-i　況周頤

Kuei-erh chi　貴耳集

"Kuei-chih hsiang"　桂枝香

Kuei-ch'ih　貴池

kuei-ch'ing　閨情

kuei-ko shih-jen　閨閣詩人

Kuei Shu-fen　歸淑芬

Kuei-t'ien lu　歸田錄

k'uei　窺

K'uei t'an lu　傀郯錄

K'un-ming　昆明

kung　宮

kung-shih k'u　公使庫

kung-t'i shih　宮體詩

Kung Ting-tzu　龔鼎孳

Kung-yang chuan　公羊傳

Kung Ying-te　弓英德

k'ung-chung yü erh　空中語耳

K'ung I　孔夷

k'ung yü　空餘

Kuo-ch'ao kuei-hsiu cheng-shih chi　國朝閨秀正始集

Kuo-hsüeh lun-ts'ung　國學論叢

Kuo Mao-ch'ien　郭茂倩

Kuo Shao-yü　郭紹虞

Kuo-yü　國語

Lan-wan ch'ü-hui　蘭畹曲會

lang　郎

"Lang t'ao sha"　浪淘沙

"Lang t'ao sha ling"　浪淘沙令

Lang Ying　郎瑛

Lei-pien ts'ao-t'ang shih-yü　類編草堂詩餘

Lei shuo　類說

leng-leng　冷冷

li ("beautiful")　麗

li ("pattern")　理

Li Chih-i　李之儀

Li Ching　李璟

li-ch'ing　離情

Li Ch'ing-chao　李清照

li-ch'ou chien pu tuan　離愁剪不斷

Li Ch'ün-yu　李群玉

Li fu-jen ko　李夫人歌

Li Ho (Ch'ang-chi)　李賀(長吉)

li-hsiang　理想

Li Hsün　李珣

Li I-shan shih chi　李義山詩集

Li Kang　李綱

Li Kuan　李冠

Li Ling　李陵

Li O　厲鶚

Li Pa-lang　李八郎

Li P'an-lung　李攀龍

Li P'eng　李彭

Li Po　李白

"Li-sao"　離騷

Li Shan　李善

Li Shang-yin　李商隱

Li-tai ming-yüan shih-tz'u　歷代名媛詩詞

Li-tai shih-yü　歷代詩餘

Li-tai shih-yü tz'u-hua　歷代詩餘詞話

Li T'iao-yüan　李調元

Li-yang　歷陽

Li Yeh　李冶

Li Yü　李煜

Liang-che　兩浙

Liang Chien-wen-ti　梁簡文帝

Liang Hung-yü　梁紅玉

Liang Shao-jen　梁紹壬

Liao　遼

Liao Hsing-chih　廖行之

liao-te　了得

Liao-yang　遼陽

Lieh-ch'ao shih-chi　列朝詩集

lien　戀

lien-chang　聯章

lien wai yü ch'an ch'an　簾外雨潺潺

lien-yüan ("stretching afar")　連遠

lien-yüan ("with a garden")　連苑

Lin-chiang-chün　臨江軍

"Lin chiang hsien"　臨江仙

Lin-ch'uan　臨川

Lin-hsia tz'u-hsüan　林下詞選

Lin Hsüeh　林雪

lin hua hsieh liao ch'un hung　林花謝
了春紅

Lin I-ning　林以寧

Lin-tzu　臨淄

ling-chü tzu　領句字

ling-hsiu chih ch'i　靈秀之氣

liu　留

Liu Ch'en-weng　劉長翁

Liu Chi-ying　劉季英

Liu Chiang-sun　劉將孫

"Liu-chih"　柳枝

Liu Fu　劉斧

Liu Hsiao-ch'o　劉孝綽

Liu Hsiao-wei　劉孝鷝

Liu Hsieh　劉勰

Liu Hsien-lun　劉仙倫

Liu Hsün　劉壎

Liu Hui-sun　劉蕙蓀

Liu-i chü-shih chi　六一居士集

Liu-i shih-hua　六一詩話

Liu Kuo (Kai-chih)　劉過(改之)

"Liu of Yen-feng"　雁峯劉氏

Liu Pang　劉邦

Liu Sheng-chi　劉勝己

Liu Shih　柳是

Liu Tao-ch'un　劉道醇

Liu Tse　劉澤

Liu Ts'en　劉岑

Liu Yü-hsi　劉禹錫

Liu Yung (Ch'i, San-pien)　柳永
(七, 三變)

Lo Chen-yü　羅振玉

Lo Chün-mei　羅君美

"Lo Goddess"　洛神

Lo Mi　羅泌

Lo Ta-ching　羅大經

lou　樓

Lou Wan　樓婉

Lu Ch'ang　陸昶

Lu Chi　陸機

"Lu Chüeh chuan"　陸厥傳

Lu-ling　廬陵

lu lu chin ching wu t'ung wan　轆轤金
井梧桐晚

Lu Yen-jang　盧延讓

Lu Yu　陸游

Lü Hui-ch'ing　呂惠卿

Lü Liu-liang　呂留良

Lü Pen-chung　呂本中

Lü P'eng　呂鵬

lü-shih　律詩

Lü T'ien-ju　律天如

Lü Yüan　呂遠

"Lun chiao-yü chih tsung-
chih"　論教育之宗旨

"Lun hsing"　論性

"Lun p'ing-fan chih chiao-yü chu-
i"　論平凡之教育主義

Lun-yü　論語

lung　籠

Lung-hsing fu　龍興府

Ma Ling　馬令

Ma Shou-chen　馬守貞

Ma Yuan　馬援

"Ma Yüan chuan"　馬援傳

mai-kuang　麥光

"Man chiang hung"　滿江紅

man-mieh　漫滅

Man-sou shih-hua　漫叟詩話

"Man t'ing fang"　滿庭芳

man-tz'u　慢詞

Mao Chin　毛晉

Mao Hsiang　冒襄

Mao shih chien yu fu pu erh yü ssu pien ti
　yu lei yen　茅氏兼有附補而余
　斯編第有類焉

Mao shih hsü　毛詩序

Mao Yü-ch'ang　冒愈昌

mei　媚

Mei-chien shih-hua　梅磵詩話

mei-li　美麗

Mei Ting-tso　梅鼎祚

mei-t'ou　眉頭

Mei yüan　梅苑

Men-shih hsin-hua　捫蝨新話

meng　夢

Meng Ch'ang　孟昶

Meng Ch'eng　孟澄

"Meng Chiang-nan"　夢江南

Meng Chung-hou　孟忠厚

Meng Hao-jan　孟浩然

meng-li　夢裏

Meng Shu-ch'ing　孟淑卿

Meng Yen-lin tz'u　孟彥林詞

mi　覓

Mi-chou　密州

mi-mi　覓覓

mi-mi chih yüeh　靡靡之樂

Ming fei　明妃

Ming-hung yü-yin　鳴鶴餘音

Ming-yüan shih kuei　名媛詩歸

Ming-yüan shih-wei　名媛詩緯

ming-yüeh chu　明月珠

mo　墨

Mo-chuang man-lu　墨莊漫錄

Mo-hua chai　墨華齋

Mo-ling　秣陵

mo-mieh　磨滅

"Mo-shan hsi"　驀山溪

"Mo yü erh"　摸魚兒

"Mu ch'iu tu yu Ch'ü-chiang"
　暮秋獨遊曲江

"Mu-lan hua ling"　木蘭花令

Mu-tan t'ing　牡丹亭

Na-lan Hsing-te　納蘭性德

nai[1] ("help," "fend off")　耐

nai[2] ("help," "fend off")　奈

Naitō Konan　內藤湖南

nan　男

Nan-an chün　南安郡

Nan-ch'ang　南昌

Nan-feng　南豐

"Nan ko-tz'u"　南歌子

nan-kuo ch'an-chüan　南國嬋娟

Nan-T'ang shu　南唐書

"Nan-tz'u"　南詞

nei　內

nei-tsai yin-yüeh　內在音樂

"Nei tse"　內則

Neng-kai chai man-lu　能改齋漫錄

neng k'ai tz'u ta-k'ou　能開此大口

neng wen　能文

neng yu　能有

ni ("nun")　尼

ni ("you")　你

"Nien-nu chiao"　念奴嬌

nien-shao　年少

nien-yü　念語

Niu Hsi-chi　牛希濟

Nü-chung ch'i ts'ai-tzu lan-k'o chi
　女中七才子蘭咳集

nü i-min　女遺民

Nü Ssu-shu　女四書

nü ts'ai-tzu　女才子

nuan　暖

nung　儂

O-chou　鄂州

o-lien　惡憐

O-p'ang　阿房

Ou-yang Chiung　歐陽烱

Ou-yang Hsiu (Liu-i)　歐陽修(六一)

pa-ku-wen　八股文

Pa Wu Ssu-tao hsiao-tz'u　跋吳思道小詞

Pai-chia tz'u　百家詞

Pai P'u　白樸

Pai-yü-chai tz'u-hua　白雨齋詞話

"Pai-yün yao"　白雲謠

p'ai　派

Pan Chao　班昭

Pan chieh-yü　班婕妤

Pan Ku　班固

P'an Lang　潘閬

p'ang-tsung　旁宗

Pao Ling-hui　鮑令暉

p'ao　拋

"Pei Ch'ing pan"　悲青坂

"Pei fen shih"　悲憤詩

Pei-meng so-yen　北夢瑣言

P'ei Ch'ang　裴暢

pen　本

pen-se　本色

pen-shih　本事

Pen-shih ch'ü　本事曲

Pen-shih shih　本事詩

P'eng Chih-chung　彭致中

p'eng lai yüan pi t'ien t'ai nü　蓬萊院
　閉天台女

P'eng Yüan-hsün　彭元遜

pi ("brush")　筆

pi ("emerald")　碧

Pi-chi hsiao-shuo ta-kuan　筆記小說大觀

Pi-chi man-chih　碧雞漫志

pi ch'i hua kuang chin hsiu ming
　碧砌花光錦繡明

pi-hsing　比興

Pi-t'ao　碧桃

"P'i-p'a hsing"　琵琶行

p'iao　飄

pieh lai ch'un pan　別來春半

pieh-shih　別是

pieh-tiao　別調

pien　變

pien-ko　便歌

p'in　頻

"P'in fei"　拼飛

p'ing ("critique")　評

p'ing ("level")　平

p'ing ("rely")　憑

P'ing pen-ch'ao yüeh-chang　評本朝樂章

P'ing-shan Hall　平山堂

"Po cho-tzu"　撥棹子

Po Chü-i (Lo-t'ien)　白居易(樂天)

po-teng 撥鐙

"P'o chen-tzu" 破陣子

"Pu Ch'an-kung" 步蟾宮

pu chih 不知

pu k'an 不堪

p'u 譜

P'u Ch'uan-cheng 蒲傳正

p'u-hsü 鋪叙

"P'u-sa-man" 菩薩蠻

San-ch'ü ts'ung-k'an 散曲叢刊

"San-t'ai" 三臺

shan ("coral") 珊

shan ("hill") 山

"Shan-chung wen-ta" 山中問答

shan-ko 山歌

shang ("commerce") 商

shang ("rising") 上

Shang Ching-lan 商景蘭

Shang-shu 尚書

shao 韶

Shao Chang 邵章

shao-nien 少年

"Shao-nien yu" 少年遊

Shao Po 邵博

Shao-shih wen-chien hou-lu 邵氏聞見後錄

shen 深

Shen Chen-yung 沈貞永

Shen Chi-fei 沈際飛

Shen Ch'ien 沈謙

Shen I-fu 沈義父

Shen I-hsiu 沈宜修

Shen Li 沈栗

shen-nü 神女

shen p'in 神品

Shen Shan-pao 沈善寶

Shen T'ang 沈唐

Shen Te-ch'ien 沈德潛

Shen Tsung-chi 沈宗畸

shen yüan ching 深院靜

Shen Yüeh 沈約

Sheng P'ei 盛配

"Sheng-sheng man" 聲聲慢

sheng-shih 聲詩

shih ("is") 是

shih ("poetry") 詩

Shih Chen-lin 史震林

Shih-chi 史記

Shih-ching 詩經

shih-chün 使君

Shih Hsiao-yu 石孝友

shih-hua 詩話

shih-i 拾遺

Shih-i ming shan chi 拾遺名山記

Shih-jen yü-hsieh 詩人玉屑

shih-ko yin-yüeh-hua 詩歌音樂化

shih-k'o ch'ü-tzu-tz'u 詩客曲子詞

"Shih-kuo" 十過

"Shih li" 釋理

"Shih lo-i" 濕羅衣

Shih ming-chia tz'u 十名家詞

Shih-p'in 詩品

Shih-shih yao-lan 釋氏要覽

Shih Ta-tsu 史達祖

shih wei lieh-ch'ien 是為列錢

Shih Yen 師延

shih yen chih 詩言志

shih-yü 詩餘

Shih-yü t'u-p'u　詩餘圖譜

shou-che　守著

shou chüan chen chu shang yü kou
　手捲真珠上玉鉤

shu　書

Shu　蜀

shu-chia　書家

shu-chien　書簡

"Shu Huang Tao-fu *P'in-ch'a yao-lu
hou*"　書黃道輔品茶要錄後

"*Shu-pen-hua yü Ni-ts'ai*"　叔本華
　與尼采

Shu-yü chi　漱玉集

shu-yüan　書院

shuang kao　霜高

Shui-chien ch'ien hsin　水檻遣心

"Shui lung yin"　水龍吟

"Shui-tiao ko t'ou"　水調歌頭

so ("lock")　鎖

so ("tiny")　瑣

Ssu-k'u ch'üan-shu chien-ming mu-lu
　四庫全書簡明目錄

Ssu-ma Ch'ien　司馬遷

ssu shih nien lai chia kuo　四十年
　來家國

Ssu-ts'ung　思聰

su　俗

"Su chung-ch'ing"　訴衷情

Su-hsiang shih ts'ung-shu　粟香室叢書

Su Shih (Tung-p'o, Tzu-chan)
　蘇軾（東坡，子瞻）

Sui　隋

Sun fu-jen　孫夫人

Sun Hui-yüan　孫惠媛

Sun Kuang-hsien　孫光憲

Sun T'an (Hsiao-chih)　孫忱（肖之）

Sun Tao-hsüan　孫道絢

Sung Ch'i　宋祁

"Sung Ch'ien-t'ang seng Ssu-ts'ung
kuei Ku-shan hsü"　送錢塘僧思
聰歸孤山敍

sung-hsi ho-ts'eng yu p'ing-chü　送喜
　何曾有憑據

Sung Hsiang　宋庠

Sung Hsiang-feng　宋翔鳳

Sung Lo　宋犖

Sung Ssu-ching　宋思敬

Sung Yü　宋玉

"Ta Ch'en Chi-ch'ang shu"　答陳
　季常書

ta-ch'ü　大曲

"Ta hsü"　大序

Ta-hui　大慧

"Ta-ma fu"　打馬賦

Ta-sheng-fu　大晟府

ta-tsung　大宗

ta-wu　大巫

"Ta ya"　大雅

"T'a so hsing"　踏莎行

T'ai-ho　太和

T'ai-hu　太湖

t'ai lan-lang　太瀾浪

T'ai-p'ing　太平

T'ai-yïan　太原

T'an Erh-chin　譚爾進

tang hang-chia yü　當行家語

t'ang　堂

T'ang Ming-huang　唐明皇

T'ang-shan fu-jen　唐山夫人

T'ang shih p'in-hui　唐詩品彙

T'ang shih Sung tz'u　唐詩宋詞

T'ang shu   唐書

tao   倒

Tao-ch'eng   道誠

tao-jen   道人

"Tao lien-tzu ling"   搗練子令

Tao-yüan hsüeh-ku lu   道園學古錄

t'ao   套

T'ao Ch'ien   陶潛

T'ao Hsin-erh   陶心兒

T'ao Tsung-i   陶宗儀

Teng-t'u   登徒

"Teng-t'u-tzu hao se fu"   登徒子好色賦

"T'eng-wang-ko hsü"   滕王閣序

ti ("drip")   滴

ti ("flute")   笛

"T'i Chang Tzu-yeh shih-chi hou"   題張子野詩集後

t'i-pa   題跋

tiao   調

T'iao-hsi yü-yin ts'ung-hua   苕溪漁隱叢話

T'iao-hua tz'u   苕華詞

"Tieh lien hua"   蝶戀花

"Tieh-tieh to"   跕跕墮

tieh-tzu   疊字

"Tien chiang ch'un"   點絳唇

tien-chung   典重

tien-nao   電腦

tien-tien ti-ti   點點滴滴

tien-ya   典雅

t'ien-chi   天極

T'ien Chih-tou   田志豆

"T'ien-kuan shu"   天官書

T'ien T'ung-chih   田同之

t'ien-tzu   天子

t'ien-wai i-kou ts'an-yüeh tai san-hsing   天外一鉤殘月帶三星

ting   定

Ting Shao-i   丁紹儀

ting yu wu   定有無

t'ing ch'ien ch'un chu hung ying chin   亭前春逐紅英盡

T'ing-ch'iu-sheng-kuan tz'u-hua   聽秋聲館詞話

t'ing k'ung k'o san jen kuei hou   庭空客散人歸後

t'ing-yüan shen-shen shen chi-hsü   庭院深深深幾許

to shao hen   多少恨

t'o-kao   脫稿

Tou T'ao   竇滔

tou yu   都有

tsa-t'i   雜體

tsa-yen   雜言

ts'ai   才

Ts'ai-chou   蔡州

ts'ai-nü   才女

"Ts'ai sang-tzu"   采桑子

Ts'ai T'ao   蔡條

ts'ai-tzu   才子

ts'ai-tzu chia-jen   才子佳人

Ts'ai Yen   蔡琰

"Ts'ai-yün kuei"   彩雲歸

ts'an   殘

ts'ang-ch'i   傖氣

Ts'ang-lang shih-hua   滄浪詩話

tsao-ching   造境

Ts'ao An   曹安

Ts'ao Chih   曹植

Ts'ao Hsün 曹勛

Ts'ao Kung-hsien 曹功顯

Ts'ao-t'ang shih-yü 草堂詩餘

Ts'ao-t'ang ssu-hsiang 草堂嗣響

tse 仄

tsen i-ko "i" tzu liao-te 怎一箇意字了得

tsen sheng te 怎生得

tsen-ti 怎敵

Tseng-hsiu chien-chu miao-hsüan ch'ün-ying ts'ao-t'ang shih-yü 增修箋注妙選群英草堂詩餘

Tseng Kung 曾鞏

Tseng Pu 曾布

Tseng Tsao (Tuan-po) 曾慥(端伯)

tso 作

Tso-chuan 左傳

Tso Fen 左芬

Tso Ssu 左思

tso-yeh 昨夜

tso yeh feng chien yü 昨夜風兼雨

Tsou Hsü-shih (Chih-mo) 鄒訏士(祇謨)

Tsou I 鄒漪

tsu 祖

"Tsui kung-tzu" 醉公子

Ts'ui Kung-tu 崔公度

Ts'ui Ling-ch'in 崔令欽

Tsun-ch'ien chi 尊前集

tsun-t'i 尊體

Ts'un-i chü-shih 存一居士

tsung 宗

Tsung-kao 宗杲

Ts'ung-shan 從善

ts'ung-shu 叢書

Tu An-shih 杜安世

Tu Fu 杜甫

Tu Mu 杜牧

Tu Shou-yü tz'u 杜壽域詞

Tu Yu 杜佑

t'u wu 突兀

tuan 斷

tuan-ch'ang pei 斷腸碑

tuan-hun 斷魂

Tui Ch'u-wang wen 對楚王問

Tun-huang 敦煌

Tung-ching meng-hua lu 東京夢華錄

tung feng ch'ui shui jih hsien shan 東風吹水日銜山

Tung Fu-heng 董復亨

Tung-hai yü-ko 東海漁歌

Tung I 董藝

Tung I-ning 董以寧

Tung Ku 董穀

Tung Pai 董白

Tung-p'o chih-lin 東坡志林

Tung-t'ing 洞庭

Tung-yü 東玉

Tung-yüan k'o-t'an 東園客談

"T'ung Cheng Hsiang ping ko-chi hsiao-yin hsi tseng" 同鄭相并歌姬小飲戲贈

t'ung huang yün ts'ui ch'iang han chu 銅簧韻脆鏘寒竹

t'ung i ku 通一顧

T'ung-pien 通變

T'ung-tien 通典

T'ung-yang chü-shih 銅陽居士

tzu 字

Tzu-ch'ai chi 紫釵記

"Tzu hsü" 自序

"Tzu hsü, erh" 自序二

tzu-jan wu-ju 自然悟入

tzu-kung 紫宮

"Tzu-yeh ko" 子夜歌

"Tzu-yeh t'i" 子夜啼

Tzu-yu 子由

tz'u 詞

tz'u-hua 詞華

Tz'u-kou ch'u-p'ien 詞觏初篇

Tz'u-kuei 詞軌

Tz'u-lin wan-hsüan 詞林萬選

"Tz'u lun" 詞論

tz'u pieh shih i-chia 詞別是一家

Tz'u-pien 詞辨

Tz'u-t'an ts'ung-hua 詞壇叢話

tz'u-ti 次第

Tz'u-tiao ting-lü 詞調訂律

Tz'u-tse 詞則

Tz'u tsung 詞綜

tz'u yen ch'ing 詞言情

Tz'u-yüan 詞源

Tz'u-yüan ying-hua 詞苑英華

tz'u-yün erh jen-yün che yeh 詞韻而人韻者也

wai 外

wai-chi 外集

wai-tsai yin-yüeh 外在音樂

wan 婉

wan chuang ch'u liao ming chi hsüeh 晚妝初了明肌雪

Wan-fang 玩芳

Wan-li 萬曆

wan-yüeh 婉約

Wang An-shih 王安石

Wang Chao-chün 王昭君

Wang Chao-yung 汪兆鏞

Wang Chi-kung 王季宮

"Wang Chiang mei" 望江梅

"Wang Chiang-nan" 望江南

Wang Chien 王建

Wang Chih-fang shih hua 王直方詩話

Wang Cho 王灼

Wang fu-jen 王夫人

Wang I-ning 王以寧

Wang I-sun 王沂孫

Wang Kuo-wei 王國維

Wang Mang 王莽

Wang Ming-ch'ing 王明清

Wang Po 王勃

Wang Sen 汪森

Wang Shih-chen (1526–90) 王世禎

Wang Shih-chen (1634–1711) 王士禎

wang shih chih k'an ai 往事只堪哀

Wang Shyh-chen 王士禎

Wang Te-i 王德毅

Wang T'ing-kuei 王庭珪

Wang Tuan-shu 王端淑

Wang Tzu-nien 王子年

Wang Wei (Hsiu Wei) 王微(修微)

Wang Yü-ch'eng 王禹偁

"Wang yüan hsing" 望遠行

Wang Yün 王筠

wei 緯

Wei Ch'ing-chih 魏慶之

Wei Chü-an 韋居安

wei-ch'ü chin-ch'ing 委曲盡情

Wei Chuang 韋莊

Wei Chung-kung 魏仲恭

Wei fu-jen 魏夫人

Wei River 渭水

"Wei tu fu" 魏都賦

Wei Ying-wu 韋應物

wen 文

wen-chi 文集

wen chün 問君

"Wen fu" 文賦

Wen-hsien t'ung-k'ao 文獻通考

Wen hsüan 文選

wen-jen chih tz'u 文人之詞

wen-jou tun-hou 溫柔敦厚

Wen-shih 文史

Wen T'ien-hsiang 文天祥

Wen T'ing-yün 溫庭筠

wen-ya 溫雅

wo 我

wu ("the world") 物

wu ("without") 無

Wu Ch'ang-shou 吳昌綬

"Wu Ch'u ko" 吳楚歌

Wu Ch'ung-yao 伍崇曜

wu-i-pu-k'o-ju 無意不可入

Wu K'uan 吳寬

Wu Na 吳訥

"Wu se" 物色

Wu Shan 吳山

wu-shih-pu-k'o-yen 無事不可言

Wu Shu-chi 吳淑姬

Wu-tai ming-hua pu-i 五代名畫補遺

wu t'i 無題

Wu Tsao 吳藻

Wu Tse-li 吳則禮

Wu Tseng 吳曾

wu tuan 無端

wu-tzu 五子

Wu Wen-ying 吳文英

wu wo 無我

"Wu yeh t'i" 烏夜啼

wu yen-se 無顏色

ya 雅

ya-yüeh 雅樂

Yang-ch'un chi 陽春集

Yang-ch'un pai-hsüeh chi 陽春白雪集

Yang-ch'un pai-hsüeh pu-chi 陽春白雪補集

Yang Hsi-min 楊希閔

Yang Hui 楊繪

Yang Kuei-fei 楊貴妃

Yang Shen 楊慎

Yang Shih 楊時

Yang Tse-min 楊澤民

Yang Wan 楊宛

Yang Wan-li 楊萬里

Yang Wei-chen 楊維楨

Yang Wu-chiu 楊無咎

Yang Yen-cheng 楊炎正

yao-miao i-hsiu 要眇宜修

yao-t'iao 窈窕

yao-yao 杳杳

yao yeh t'ing kao hsien hsin pu 遙夜庭皋閒信步

yeh ("leaves") 葉

yeh ("night") 夜

"Yeh-chin men" 謁金門

Yeh Hsiao-luan 葉小鸞

Yeh Hsiao-wan 葉小紈

Yeh Hung-hsiang　葉宏湘

Yeh-lü Ch'u-ts'ai　耶律楚材

Yeh Shen-hsiang　葉申薌

Yeh Sheng　葉盛

Yeh Wan-wan　葉紈紈

yen　艷

Yen Chi-tao (Shu-yüan)　晏幾道
　（叔原）

yen chih　言志

yen-ch'ing　艷情

Yen-feng　雁峰

yen-jan　嫣然

Yen Jen　嚴仁

yen kuo yeh, / cheng shang hsin　雁風也，
　正傷心

yen pu chin i　言不盡意

yen-se ju ch'en-t'u　顏色如塵土

Yen Shu　晏殊

Yen-tzu-lou　燕子樓

yen-tz'u　艷詞

Yen Yu-i　嚴有翼

yen-yü　艷語

Yen Yü　嚴羽

yen-yüeh　燕樂

yin-jou　陰柔

yin-sheng　淫聲

ying　影

"Ying-chun yüeh"　迎春樂

Ying-hsiung yeh　英雄業

ying-hua　櫻花

ying hua lo chin chieh ch'ien yüeh
　櫻花落盡階前月

ying hua lo chin ch'un chiang k'un
　櫻花落盡春將困

Ying-mei-an i-yü　影梅庵憶語

Ying-shih　營室

ying-t'ao　櫻桃

*ying t'ao lo chin ch'un kuei
　ch'ü*　櫻桃落盡春歸去

ying-te　贏得

"Ying t'ien ch'ang"　應天長

ying yu tsai　應猶在

Yu T'ung　尤侗

yu wo　有我

yü ("feather")　羽

yü ("jadeite")　玉

yü ("remnant")　餘

Yü-ch'an　俞澹

"Yü Ch'en Chi-ch'ang"　與陳季常

"Yü Ch'en Ta-fu"　與陳大夫

Yü Chi　虞集

"Yü-chia ao"　漁家傲

yü-chih　餘枝

yü-chih ko-tz'u　御製歌詞

"Yü-ch'ih pei"　尉遲杯

"Yü-chung hua"　雨中花

"Yü-fu"　漁父

"Yü Hsien-yü Tzu-chün shu"
　與鮮于子駿書

Yü Hsüan-chi　魚玄機

Yü-hsuan li-tai shih-yü　御選歷代詩餘

"Yü ko-tzu"　漁歌子

"Yü-lou ch'un"　玉樓春

yü-ma　語碼

"Yü mei-jen"　虞美人

"Yü mei-jen ying"　虞美人影

yü-p'ei ting-tung pieh-hou　玉佩丁東別後

Yü-t'ai hsin-yung　玉臺新詠

yü-tz'u　語辭

Yü Wen-pao　俞文豹

"Yü yu ch'un-shui" 魚游春水

"Yü Yüan Chiu shu" 與元九書

yüan ("distant") 遠

yüan ("garden") 園

Yüan Chen 元稹

Yüan Chiang 元絳

yüan ch'ing erh ch'i-mi 緣情而綺靡

Yüan-chou 袁州

Yüan Ch'ü-hua 袁去華

Yüan-feng 元豐

Yüan Mei 袁枚

"Yüan ming" 原命

yüeh ("moon") 月

yüeh ("says") 曰

Yüeh-chou (Hunan) 岳州

Yüeh-chou (Chekiang) 越州

Yüeh Fei 岳飛

yüeh-fu 樂府

Yüeh-fu chih mi 樂府指迷

"Yüeh-hsia tu cho" 月下獨酌

Yüeh K'o 岳珂

Yüeh-lang tao-jen 月朗道人

Yün-chien 雲間

Yün-chou 筠州

Yün Chu 惲珠

yün i kua 雲一緺

Yün-shao chi 雲韶集

Yün-yao chi 雲謠集

Yung-hsing 永興

Yung huai 詠懷

"Yung-yü lo" 永遇樂

BIBLIOGRAPHY

ABBREVIATIONS USED

PP   *Pai-pu ts'ung-shu* 百部叢書
SPTK   *Ssu-pu ts'ung-k'an* 四部叢刊
THTP   *Tz'u-hua ts'ung-pien* 詞話叢編
TSCC   *Ts'ung-shu chi-ch'eng* 叢書集成

Abe Ryūichi 阿部隆一. "Tenri toshokan zō Sō Kin Gan hambon kō" 天理圖書館藏宋金元版本考. *Biblia* 75 (October 1980): 389–410.

Aoyama Hiroshi 青山宏, comp. *Kakanshū sakuin* 花間集所引. Tōyōgaku Bunken Sentā sōkan 東洋学文献センター叢刊, no. 21. Tokyo: Tōkyō daigaku, 1974.

Bickford, Maggie. *Bones of Jade, Soul of Ice: The Flowering Plum in Chinese Art.* New Haven: Yale University Art Gallery, 1985.

Birrell, Anne, trans. *New Songs from a Jade Terrace.* New York: Penguin, 1986.

———. "The Dusty Mirror: Courtly Portraits of Women in Southern Dynasties Love Poetry." In *Expressions of Self in Chinese Literature*, ed. Robert E. Hegel and Richard C. Hessney, pp. 33–69. New York: Columbia University Press, 1985.

Bonner, Joey. *Wang Kuo-wei, an Intellectual Biography.* Cambridge: Harvard University Press, 1986.

Bryant, Daniel. "Computer-Assisted Determination of Textual Genealogy in Chinese Literature." Unpublished manuscript.

———. "The 'Hsieh Hsin En' 謝新恩 Fragments by Li Yü 李煜 and His Lyric to the Melody 'Lin Chiang Hsien' 臨江仙." *Chinese Literature: Essays, Articles, Reviews* 7 (1985): 37–66.

———. *Lyric Poets of the Southern Tang: Feng Yen-ssu, 903–960, and Li Yü, 937–978.* Vancouver: University of British Columbia Press, 1982.

———. "On the Authenticity of the *Tz'u* Attributed to Li Po," *Tang Studies* 7 (1989): 105–36.

————. "The Rhyming Categories of Tenth Century Chinese Poetry," *Monumenta Serica* 34 (1979–80): 319–47.

Buell, Lawrence. *New England Literary Culture.* Cambridge: Cambridge University Press, 1986.

Chaffee, John W. *The Thorny Gates of Learning in Sung China: A Social History of Examinations.* Cambridge: Cambridge University Press, 1985.

Chan Chih 湛之, ed. *Huang T'ing-chien ho Chiang-hsi shih-p'ai chüan* 黃庭堅和江西詩派卷. *Ku-tien wen-hsüeh yen-chiu tzu-liao hui-pien* 古典文學研究資料彙編. Peking: Chung-hua shu-chü, 1978.

Chang Chang 張章 and Huang Yü 黃畬, eds. *Ch'üan T'ang Wu-tai tz'u* 全唐五代詞. Rpt. Taipei: Wen-shih-che, 1986.

Chang Hsiu-min 張秀民. "Nan Sung (1127–1279) k'o-shu ti-yü k'ao" 南宋 (1127–1279) 刻書地域考. *T'u-shu-kuan* 1961, no. 3: 52–56.

Chang, Kang-i Sun. "Canon-Formation in Chinese Poetry: Problems of Gender and Genre." Paper presented at the ICANAS Panel on the Concept of the Classic and Canon-Formation in East Asia, Toronto, August 21, 1990.

————. *The Evolution of Chinese Tz'u Poetry: From Late T'ang to Northern Sung.* Princeton: Princeton University Press, 1980.

————. *The Late-Ming Poet Ch'en Tzu-lung: Crises of Love and Loyalism.* New Haven: Yale University Press, 1991.

Chang Lei 張耒. *Chang Yu-shih wen-chi* 張右史文集. *SPTK* ed.

Chang Pang-chi 張邦基. *Mo-chuang man-lu* 墨莊漫錄. *Pai-hai* 稗海 ed. (*PP* 14/3)

Chang Shun-min 張舜民. *Hua-man lu* 畫墁錄. *Pai-hai* 稗海 ed.

Chang Yen 張炎. *Tz'u-yüan* 詞源. *THTP* ed.

Ch'ang Pi-te 昌彼得 et al., eds. *Sung-jen chuan-chi tzu-liao so-yin* 宋人傳記資料索引. Taipei: Ting-wen shu-chü, 1974–75.

Chao, Chia-ying Yeh. [*See also* Yeh Chia-ying.] "The Ch'ang-chou School of Tz'u Criticism." In *Chinese Approaches to Literature from Confucius to Liang Ch'i-chao*, ed. Adele Austin Rickett, pp. 151–88. (Also published in *Harvard Journal of Asiatic Studies* 35 [1975]: 101–31.)

Chao Ling-chih 趙令畤. *Hou cheng lu* 侯鯖錄. *Chih-pu-tsu chai ts'ung-shu* 知不足齋叢書 ed.

Chao Tsun-yüeh 趙尊嶽. "Tz'u-chi t'i-yao" 詞集提要. Parts 1–6. *Tz'u-hsüeh chi-k'an* 詞學季刊 1, no. 1 (April 1933): 91–105; 1, no. 2 (August 1933): 81–85; 2, no. 3 (April 1935): 67–95; 3, no. 1 (March 1936): 41–45; 3, no. 3 (Sept. 1936) 53–71; 6, no. 2 (n.d.): 14.

Chao Wan-li 趙萬里, ed. *Chiao-chi Sung Chin Yüan jen tz'u* 校輯宋金元人詞. Peiping Kuo-li chung-yang yen-chiu yüan, li-shih yü-yen yen-chiu so, 1931.

————. "Wang Ching-an hsien-sheng shou chiao shou p'i shu mu" 王靜安先生手校手批書目. *Kuo-hsüeh lun-ts'ung* 國學論叢 1, no. 3 (n.d.): 145–79.

Ch'en Chen-sun 陳振孫. *Chih-chai shu-lu chieh-t'i* 直齋書錄解題. *Chü-chen pan ts'ung-shu* 聚珍版叢書 ed. (*PP* 27/35)

Ch'en Ch'i-yu 陳奇猷, ed. *Han Fei-tzu chi-shih* 韓非子集釋. Shanghai: Chung-hua shu-chü, 1958.

Ch'en Hung-chih 陳弘治. *T'ang Sung tz'u ming-tso hsi-p'ing* 唐宋詞名作析評. Taipei: Wen-chin ch'u-pan-she, 1976.

Ch'en Ku 陳鵠. *Hsi t'ang chi ch'i-chiu hsü-wen* 西塘集耆舊續聞. *Chih-pu-tsu chai ts'ung-shu* 知不足齋叢書 ed.

Ch'en Shan 陳善. *Men-shih hsin-hua* 捫蝨新話. *Ju-hsüeh ching-wu* 儒學警悟 ed. (*PP* 1/1)

Ch'en Tung-yüan 陳東原. *Chung-kuo fu-nü sheng-huo shih* 中國婦女生活史. 1937. Rpt. Taipei: Shang-wu yin-shu-kuan, 1977.

Ch'en Tzu-lung 陳子龍. *Ch'en Tzu-lung shih-chi* 陳子龍詩集. Ed. Shih Chih-ts'un 施蟄存 and Ma Tsu-hsi 馬祖熙. 2 vols. Shanghai: Shang-hai ku-chi ch'u-pan-she, 1983.

Ch'en Wei-sung 陳維崧. *Fu-jen chi* 婦人集. *Chao-tai ts'ung-shu* 昭代叢書 ed.

Ch'en Yen-chieh 陳延傑. *Shih-p'in chu* 詩品注. Rpt. Taipei: K'ai-ming shu-chü, 1960.

Ch'en Yin-k'o 陳寅恪. *Liu Ju-shih pieh-chuan* 柳如是別傳. 3 vols. Shanghai: Shang-hai ku-chi ch'u-pan-she, 1980.

Ch'en Yung-cheng 陳永正. *Yen Shu Yen Chi-tao tz'u hsüan* 晏殊晏幾道詞選. Hong Kong: San-lien shu-tien, 1984.

Ch'eng Ch'ien-fan 程千帆 and Hsü Yu-fu 徐有富. *Li Ch'ing-chao* 李清照. Kiangsu: Chiang-su jen-min ch'u-pan-she, 1982.

Ch'eng Shan-k'ai 成善楷. "Tung-p'o yüeh-fu chung ko-chi ti mei-hsüeh i-i" 東坡樂府中歌妓的美學意義. *Tung-p'o tz'u lun-ts'ung*, ed. Su Shih yen-chiu hsüeh-hui, pp. 90–106.

Chi Yün 紀昀. *Shen-shih ssu-sheng k'ao* 沈氏四聲考. Rpt. Changsha: Shang-wu yin-shu-kuan, 1941.

Ch'i Huai-mei 祁懷美. "*Hua-chien chi* chih yen-chiu" 花間集之研究. *T'ai-wan sheng-li shih-fan ta-hsüeh kuo-wen yen-chiu-so chi-k'an* 台灣省立師範大學國文研究所集刊 4 (1960): 507–604.

Chiang Jun-hsün 江潤勳. *Tz'u-hsüeh p'ing-lun shih-kao* 詞學評論史稿. Hong Kong: Lung-men shu-tien, 1966.

Chiang Liang-fu 姜亮夫. *Li-tai jen-wu nien-li t'ung-p'u* 歷代人物年里通譜. 1927. Rpt. Taipei: Shih-chieh shu-chü, 1974.

Chiang Shang-hsien 姜尚賢. *T'ang Sung ming-chia tz'u hsin-hsüan* 唐宋名家詞新選. Taipei: Published by the author, 1963.

Ch'ien Ch'ien-i 錢謙益, ed. *Lieh-ch'ao shih-chi* 列朝詩集. 1652(?) ed.

———. *Lieh-ch'ao shih-chi hsiao-chuan* 列朝詩集小傳. Shanghai: Shang-hai ku-chi ch'u-pan-she, 1983.

Chin Ch'i-hua 金啓華 et al., comps. *T'ang Sung tz'u-chi hsü-pa hui-pien* 唐宋詞集序跋匯編. Kiangsu: Chiang-su chiao-yü ch'u-pan-she, 1990.

Ch'in Huan-ming 秦寰明. "Kuan-yü *Ts'ao-t'ang shih-yü* ti liu-ch'uan yen-pien" 關於草堂詩餘的流傳演變. *Wen shih* 文史 29 (1988): 413–19.

Ch'in Hui-min 秦惠民. "*T'ang Sung ming-hsien pai-chia tz'u-chi* pan-pen k'ao-pien" 唐宋名賢百家詞集版本考辨. *Tz'u hsüeh* 詞學 3 (1985): 146–60.

Ch'in Kuan 秦觀. *Huai-hai chü-shih ch'ang-tuan-chü* 淮海居士長短句. Taipei: Shih-chieh shu-chü, 1959.

Ching, Julia. "Li Ch'ing-chao." In *Sung Biographies*, ed. Herbert Franke, 2:530–34. Münchener ostasiatische Studien, no. 16. Wiesbaden: Franz Steiner Verlag, 1976.

Ch'iu Chao-ao 仇兆鰲, ed. *Tu-shih hsiang-chu* 杜詩詳注. Shanghai: Shang-hai ku-chi ch'u-pan-she, 1964. Peking: Chung-hua shu-chü, 1979.

Ch'iu Chin 秋瑾. *Ch'iu Chin chi* 秋瑾集. Peking: Chung-hua shu-chü, 1960.

Chou Chen-fu 周振甫, ed. *Wen-hsin tiao-lung chu-shih* 文心雕龍注釋, by Liu Hsieh 劉勰. Peking: Jen-min wen-hsüeh ch'u-pan-she, 1981.

Chou Mi 周密. *Ch'i-tung yeh-yü* 齊東野語. *TSCC* ed. (2780).

———. *Chüeh-miao hao-tz'u chien* 絕妙好詞箋. Rpt. Shanghai: Shang-hai ku-chi ch'u-pan-she, 1983.

Chou Pang-yen 周邦彥. *P'ien-yü chi chi-chu* 片玉集集注. Yangchow: Ku-chi shu-tien, 1980.

Chou Sheng-wei 周聖偉. "Ts'ung shih yü yüeh ti hsiang-hu kuan-hsi k'an tz'u-t'i ti ch'i-yüan yü hsing-ch'eng" 從詩與樂的相互關係看詞體的起源與形成. In *Tz'u-hsüeh lun-kao* 詞學論稿, ed. Hua-tung shih-fan ta-hsüeh Chung-wen hsi Chung-kuo ku-tien wen-hsüeh yen-chiu-shih 華東師範大學中文系中國古典文學研究室, pp. 14–15. Shanghai: Hua-tung shih-fan ta-hsüeh ch'u-pan-she, 1986.

Chou Shu-jen 周樹人[Lu Hsün 魯迅]. *T'ang Sung ch'uan-ch'i chi* 唐宋傳奇集. Peking: Wen-hsüeh ku-chi k'an-hsing-she, 1956.

Chu Ching-hua 朱靖華. "Su Shih 'i shih wei tz'u' ts'u-ch'eng tz'u-t'i ko-ming" 蘇軾「以詩為詞」促成詞體革命. In *Tung-p'o tz'u lun-ts'ung*, ed. Su Shih yen-chiu hsüeh hui, pp. 1–16.

Chu Ch'uan-yü 朱傳譽. *Sung-tai hsin-wen shih* 宋代新聞史. Taipei: Shang-wu yin-shu-kuan, 1967.

———, ed. *Li Ch'ing-chao kai-chia wen-t'i* 李清照改嫁問題. Taipei: T'ien-i ch'u-pan-she, 1982.

Chu I-tsun 朱彝尊, ed. *Tz'u-tsung* 詞綜. Rpt. N.p.: Chung-hua shu-chü, 1973.

Chu, Madeline. "Interplay between Tradition and Innovation: The Seventeenth-Century Tz'u Revival." *Chinese Literature: Essays, Articles, Reviews* 9 (1987): 71–88.

Ch'u Pin-chieh 褚斌杰, Sun Ch'ung-en 孫崇恩, and Jung Hsien-pin 榮憲賓, eds. *Li Ch'ing-chao tzu-liao hui-pien* 李清照資料彙編. Peking: Chung-hua shu-chü, 1984.

Ch'ü Hsing-kuo 屈興國, ed. *Pai-yü-chai tz'u-hua tsu-pen chiao-chu* 白雨齋詞話足本校注, by Ch'en T'ing-cho 陳廷焯. 2 vols. Tsinan: Ch'i Lu shu-she, 1983.

Ch'üan T'ang shih 全唐詩. Peking: Chung-hua shu-chü, 1960.

Ch'üan T'ang wen 全唐文. 1814 ed.

Chung Hui-ling 鍾慧玲. "Ch'ing-tai nü shih-jen yen-chiu" 清代女詩人研究. Ph.D. diss., National Cheng-chih University, 1981.

Chung Ling. "Li Qingzhao: The Moulding of Her Spirit and Personality." In *Women and Literature in China*, ed. Anna Gerstlacher et al., pp. 141–64.

Dearing, Vinton. *Principles and Practice of Textual Analysis*. Berkeley and Los Angeles: University of California Press, 1974.

Egan, Ronald C. *The Literary Works of Ou-yang Hsiu (1007–72)*. Cambridge: Cambridge University Press, 1984.

———. "Ou-yang Hsiu and Su Shih on Calligraphy." *Harvard Journal of Asiatic Studies* 49 (1989): 365–419.

Eisenstein, Elizabeth. *The Printing Press as an Agent of Change: Communications and Cultural Transformations in Early-Modern Europe*. Cambridge: Cambridge University Press, 1979.

Fei Ping-hsün 費秉勛. "Li Ch'ing-chao 'Tz'u lun' hsin-t'an" 李清照詞論新探. In *Li Ch'ing-chao yen-chiu lun-wen hsüan* 李清照研究論文選, pp. 230–42. Shanghai: Shang-hai ku-chi ch'u-pan-she, 1986.

Feng Ch'i-yung 馮其庸. "Lun Pei-Sung ch'ien-ch'i liang-chung pu-t'ung ti tz'u-feng" 論北宋前期兩種不同的詞風. In *Tz'u-hsüeh yen-chiu lun-wen-chi (1949–1979 nien)*, ed. Hua-tung ta-hsüeh Chung-wen-hsi ku-tien wen-hsüeh yen-chiu-shih, pp. 186–208.

Finnegan, Ruth. *Literacy and Orality: Studies in the Technology of Communication*. Oxford: Basil Blackwell, 1988.

Fong, Grace S. "Contextualization and Generic Codes in the Allegorical Reading of *Tz'u* Poetry." *Tamkang Review* 19 (1988–89): 663–79.

———. "Persona and Mask in the Song Lyric," *Harvard Journal of Asiatic Studies* 50 (1990): 459–84.

———. *Wu Wenying and the Art of Southern Song Ci Poetry*. Princeton: Princeton University Press, 1987.

Foucault, Michel. *The Archaeology of Knowledge and the Discourse on Language*. Trans. A. M. Sheridan Smith. New York: Pantheon, 1972.

Fusek, Lois, tr. *Among the Flowers: The Hua-chien chi*. New York: Columbia University Press, 1982.

Galik, Marian. "On the Literature Written by Chinese Women prior to 1917." *Asian and African Studies* (Bratislava) 15 (1979): 65–99.

Gerstlacher, Anna, et al., eds. *Women and Literature in China*. Bochum: Studienverlag Gerstlacher, 1985.

Gilbert, Sandra M., and Susan Gubar. *The Madwoman in the Attic: The Woman Writer and the Nineteenth-Century Literary Imagination*. New Haven: Yale University Press, 1979.

Goodrich, L. Carrington, and Chaoying Fang, eds. *Dictionary of Ming Biography*. 2 vols. New York: Columbia University Press, 1976.

Guillory, John. "Canonical and Non-canonical: A Critique of the Current Debate." *ELH* 54 (1987): 483–527.

Han shu 漢書. Peking: Chung-hua shu-chü, 1962.

Handlin, Joanna F. "Lü K'un's New Audience: The Influence of Women's Literacy on Seventeenth-Century Thought." In *Women in Chinese Society*, ed. Margery Wolf and Roxane Witke, pp. 13–38. Stanford: Stanford University Press, 1975.

Hawkes, David, tr. and ed. *The Songs of the South: An Ancient Chinese Anthology of Poems*, by Qu Yuan et al. Harmondsworth: Penguin Books, 1985.

Hervouet, Yves, ed. *A Sung Bibliography*. Hong Kong: The Chinese University Press, 1978.

Hightower, James R. "The Songs of Chou Pang-yen." *Harvard Journal of Asiatic Studies* 37 (1977): 233–72.

———. "The Songwriter Liu Yung." Parts 1, 2. *Harvard Journal of Asiatic Studies* 41 (1981): 323–76; 42 (1982): 5–66.

Hirsch, E. D., Jr. *Validity in Interpretation.* New Haven: Yale University Press, 1967.

Ho Hsin-hui 賀新輝. *Sung tz'u chien-shang tz'u-tien* 宋詞鑒賞辭典. Peking: Yen-shan ch'u-pan-she, 1987.

Ho-yin Ssu-k'u ch'üan-shu tsung-mu t'i-yao chi Ssu-k'u wei-shou shu-mu chin-hui shu-mu 合印四庫全書總目提要及四庫未收書目禁燬書目. 5 vols. Taipei: Shang-wu yin-shu-kuan, 1978.

Hou-Han shu 後漢書. Peking: Chung-hua shu-chü, 1965.

Hou, Sharon Shih-jiuan. "Women's Literature." In *The Indiana Companion to Traditional Chinese Literature*, ed. and comp. William H. Nienhauser, Jr., pp. 175–94.

Hsia Ch'eng-t'ao 夏承燾. "*Ssu-k'u ch'üan-shu* tz'u-chi t'i-yao chiao-i" 四庫全書詞籍提要校議. In idem, *T'ang Sung tz'u lun-ts'ung* 唐宋詞論叢, pp. 240–87. Hong Kong: Chung-hua shu-chü, 1973.

———. "Ssu-sheng i-shuo" 四聲繹說. In idem, *Yüeh-lun-shan tz'u-lun chi* 月輪山詞論集, pp. 149–60. Peking: Chung-hua shu-chü, 1979.

———. *T'ang Sung tz'u-jen nien-p'u* 唐宋詞人年譜. Shanghai: Shang-hai ku-chi ch'u-pan-she, 1979.

———. *T'ang Sung tz'u lun-ts'ung* 唐宋詞論叢. Shanghai: Ku-tien shu-chü, 1956. Peking: Chung-hua shu-chü, 1962. Hong Kong: Chung-hua shu-chü, 1973.

———. "T'ang Sung tz'u tzu-sheng chih yen-pien" 唐宋詞字聲之演變. In idem, *T'ang Sung tz'u lun-ts'ung* 唐宋詞論叢, pp. 53–89. Peking: Chung-hua shu-chü, 1962.

———, ed. *Po-shih shih-tz'u chi* 白石詩詞集, by Chiang K'uei 姜夔. Peking: Jen-min wen-hsüeh ch'u-pan-she, 1959.

Hsia Ch'eng-t'ao 夏承燾 and Wu Hsiung-ho 吳熊和. *Tsen-yang tu T'ang Sung tz'u* 怎樣讀唐宋詞. Hangchow: Che-chiang jen-min ch'u-pan-she, 1958.

Hsiao Ai 蕭艾, ed. *Wang Kuo-wei shih tz'u chien-chiao* 王國維詩詞箋校. Changsha: Hu-nan jen-min ch'u-pan-she, 1984.

Hsiao Ti-fei 蕭滌非. *Han Wei Liu-ch'ao yüeh-fu wen-hsüeh-shih* 漢魏六朝樂府文學史. Peking: Jen-min wen-hsüeh ch'u-pan-she, 1984.

Hsin Ch'i-chi 辛棄疾. *Chia-hsüan tz'u pien-nien chien-chu* 稼軒詞編年箋注. Ed. Teng Kuang-ming 鄧廣銘. Shanghai: Ku-tien ch'u-pan-she, 1968. Rpt. Taipei: Chung-hua shu-chü, 1970.

Hsu Kai-yu. "The Poems of Li Ch'ing-chao (1084–1141)." *PMLA* 77 (1962): 521–28.

Hsü Ling 徐陵, comp. *Yü-t'ai hsin-yung* 玉臺新詠. Rpt. Ch'eng-tu: Ch'eng-tu ku-chi shu-tien, n.d.

Hsü T'iao-fu 徐調孚. *Chiao-chu Jen-chien tz'u-hua* 校注人間詞話. Shanghai: K'ai-ming shu-tien, 1943.

Hsü Ts'an 徐燦. *Cho-cheng-yüan shih-yü* 拙政園詩餘. In *Hsiao-t'an-luan shih kuei-hsiu tz'u* 小檀欒室閨秀詞, ed. Hsü Nai-ch'ang 徐乃昌, ser. 2. 1896.

Hsüeh Li-jo 薛礪若. *Sung tz'u t'ung-lun* 宋詞通論. Hong Kong: Chung-liu ch'u-pan-she, 1974.

Hu Tzu 胡仔, comp. *T'iao-hsi yü-yin ts'ung-hua* 苕溪漁隱叢話. Taipei: Shih-chieh shu-chü, 1966. Peking: Jen-min wen-hsüeh ch'u-pan-she, 1981. Also in *Pi-chi hsiao-shuo ta-kuan* 筆記小說大觀, vol. 35, Taipei: Hsin-sheng shu-chü, 1983.

Hu Wen-k'ai 胡文楷. *Li-tai fu-nü chu-tso k'ao* 歷代婦女著作考. Rev. ed. Shang-hai: Shang-hai ku-chi ch'u-pan-she, 1985.

Hu Yin 胡寅. Preface to *Chiu-pien tz'u* 酒邊詞, by Hsiang Tzu-yin 向子諲. In *Sung liu-shih ming-chia tz'u* 宋六十名家詞, ed. Mao Chin 毛晉. *Kuo-hsüeh chi-pen ts'ung-shu* 國學基本叢書 ed.

Hua Chung-yen 華鍾彥, ed. *Hua-chien chi chu* 花間集注. Honan: Chung-chou shu-hua-she, 1983.

Huang Mo-ku 黃墨谷. *Ch'ung-chi Li Ch'ing-chao chi* 重輯李清照集. Shantung: Ch'i Lu shu-she, 1981.

Huang Sheng 黃昇. *Hua-an tz'u-hsüan* 花庵詞選. Rpt. Hong Kong: Chung-hua shu-chü, 1973.

———. *T'ang Sung chu-hsien chüeh-miao tz'u-hsüan* 唐宋諸賢絕妙詞選. *SPTK* ed.

Huang T'ing-chien 黃庭堅. *Shan-ku shih chi* 山谷詩集. *Kuo-hsüeh chi-pen ts'ung-shu* 國學基本叢書 ed.

———. *Yü-chang Huang hsien-sheng wen-chi* 豫章黃先生文集. *SPTK* ed.

Hui-hung 惠洪. *Leng-chai yeh-hua* 冷齋夜話. *Yin-li tsai ssu t'ang ts'ung-shu* 殷禮在斯堂叢書 ed.

Hung Mai 洪邁. *I-chien chih* 夷堅志. Peking: Chung-hua shu-chü, 1981.

Hymes, Robert P. "Marriage, Descent Groups, and the Localist Strategy in Sung and Yuan Fu-chou." In *Kinship Organization in Late Imperial China, 1000–1940*, ed. Patricia Buckley Ebrey and James L. Watson, pp. 95–136. Berkeley and Los Angeles: University of California Press, 1986.

———. *Statesmen and Gentlemen: The Elite of Fu-chou, Chiang-hsi, in Northern and Southern Sung*. Cambridge: Cambridge University Press, 1986.

I Po-yin 裔柏蔭, ed. *Li-tai nü shih tz'u hsüan* 歷代女詩詞選. Taipei: Tang-tai t'u-shu ch'u-pan-she, 1972.

Indiana Companion to Traditional Chinese Literature. William H. Nienhauser, Jr., ed. and comp. Bloomington: Indiana University Press, 1986.

Iser, Wolfgang. *The Art of Reading—A Theory of Aesthetic Response*. Baltimore: Johns Hopkins University Press, 1984.

Jao Tsung-i 饒宗頤. *Tz'u-chi k'ao* 詞籍考. Hong Kong: Hsiang-kang ta-hsüeh ch'u-pan-she, 1963.

Jen Erh-pei 任二北 [Jen Na 任訥]. *Tun-huang ch'ü ch'u-t'an* 敦煌曲初探. Shanghai: Wen-i lien-ho ch'u-pan-she, 1954.

Jen Jih-kao 任日鎬. *Sung-tai nü-tz'u-jen p'ing-shu* 宋代女詞人評書. Taipei: Shang-wu yin-shu-kuan, 1984.

Jen Pan-t'ang 任半塘 [Jen Na 任訥]. *T'ang sheng-shih* 唐聲詩. Shanghai: Shang-hai ku-chi ch'u-pan-she, 1982.

———. *Tun-huang ko-tz'u tsung-pien* 敦煌歌詞總編. 3 vols. Shanghai: Shang-hai ku-chi ch'u-pan-she, 1987.

Juan Chi 阮籍. *Juan Pu-ping yung huai shih chu* 阮步兵詠懷詩注. Ed. Huang Chieh 黃節. Hong Kong: Shang-wu yin-shu-kuan, 1961.

Juan T'ing-cho 阮廷焯. "Chi-ku-ko pen *Tsun-ch'ien chi* pa" 汲古閣本尊前集跋. In *Ch'ing-chu Jui-an Lin Ching-i hsien-sheng liu-chih tan-ch'en lun-wen-chi* 慶祝瑞安林景伊先生六秩誕辰論文集, ed. Ch'ing-chu Jui-an Lin Ching-i hsien-sheng liu-chih tan-ch'en lun-wen-chi pien-chi wei-yüan-hui 慶祝瑞安林景伊先生六秩誕辰論文集編輯委員會, pp. 2389–90. Taipei: Kuo-li Cheng-chih ta-hsüeh kuo-wen yen-chiu-so, 1969. (Also published in *Ta-lu tsa-chih* 大陸雜誌 40 [1970]: 376.)

Kanda, Kiichirō 神田喜一郎. *Nihon ni okeru Chūgoku bungaku* 日本における中國文學. Vol. 1, *Nihon tenshi shiwa* 日本填詞史話. Tokyo: Nigensha, 1965.

K'ang Cheng-kuo 康正果. *Feng-sao yü yen-ch'ing* 風騷與艷情. Honan: Jen-min ch'u-pan-she, 1988.

Kao Chien-chung 高建中. "Shih-lun liang Sung wan-yüeh-tz'u ti li-shih ti-wei" 試論兩宋婉約詞的歷史地位. In *Chung-kuo ku-tien wen-hsüeh lun-ts'ung* 中國古典文學論叢, vol. 4, ed. Jen-min wen-hsüeh ch'u-pan-she ku-tien wen-hsüeh pien-chi-shih 人民文學出版社古典文學編輯室, pp. 124–54. Peking: Jen-min wen-hsüeh ch'u-pan-she, 1986.

———. "Wan-yüeh, hao-fang yü cheng-pien" 婉約豪放與正變. *Tz'u-hsueh* 詞學 2 (1983): 150–53.

Kao, Yu-kung. "The Aesthetics of Regulated Verse." In *The Vitality of the Lyric Voice*: Shih *Poetry from the Late Han to the T'ang*, ed. Shuen-fu Lin and Stephen Owen, pp. 332–85. Princeton: Princeton University Press, 1986.

Kivlen, Mary E. "Beyond 'the Mirror of Time': Reflections on Mirror Imagery in Ming-Ch'ing Women's Verse." Term paper, 1990.

Knechtges, David R., and Chang Taiping. "Notes on a Recent Handbook for Chinese Literature." Review article of *The Indiana Companion to Traditional Chinese Literature*, ed. and comp. William H. Nienhauser, Jr. *Journal of the American Oriental Society* 107 (1987): 293–304.

Kramarae, Cheris, and Paula A. Treichler. *A Feminist Dictionary*. London: Pandora Press, 1985.

Kristeva, Julia. *About Chinese Women*. Trans. Anita Barrows. New York: Urizen Books, 1977.

Kroll, Paul W. ". . . Fair and Yet Not Fond." Review article of *Brocade River Poems: Selected Works of the Tang Dynasty Courtesan Xue Tao*, ed. and trans. Jeanne Larsen. *JAOS* 108 (1988): 621–26.

Ku Ch'un 顧春 [Ku T'ai-ch'ing 太清]. *T'ien-yu-ko chi* 天游閣集. *Feng-yü-lou ts'ung-shu* 風雨樓叢書 ed.

———. *Tung-hai yü-ko* 東海漁歌. MS copy in six *chüan*, now housed in the rare books collection of the Kyo-u sho-oku, Osaka.

———. "*Tung-hai yü-ko*, erh" 東海漁歌二. *Tz'u-hsüeh chi-k'an* 詞學季刊 1, no. 2 (Aug. 1933):152–66.

K'uang Chou-i 況周頤. *Hui-feng tz'u-hua* 蕙風詞話. Ed. Wang Yao-an 王幼安. Peking: Jen-min wen-hsüeh ch'u-pan-she, 1982.

Kung Ying-te 弓英德. "Li Hou-chu wang-kuo shih-tz'u pien-cheng" 李後主亡國詩詞辨證. *Li-hsüeh* 勵學 2 (1934): 91–97.

Kuo Mao-ch'ien 郭茂倩, ed. *Yüeh-fu shih-chi* 樂府詩集. 4 vols. Peking: Chung-hua shu-chü, 1979.

Kuo Shao-yü 郭紹虞. *Sung shih-hua chi-i* 宋詩話輯佚. *Yen-ching hsüeh-pao chuan-hao* 燕京學報專號 14. Peiping: Harvard Yenching Institute, 1937. Rpt. Taipei: Wen-ch'üan ko, 1972.

Langer, Susanne K. *Philosophy in a New Key*. New York: New American Library, 1951.

Langley, C. Bradford. "Chu Shu-chen." In *The Indiana Companion to Traditional Chinese Literature*, ed. and comp. William H. Nienhauser, Jr., pp. 334–36.

Larsen, Jeanne, ed. and trans. *Brocade River Poems: Selected Works of the Tang Dynasty Courtesan Xue Tao*. Princeton: Princeton University Press, 1987.

Leitch, Vincent B. *American Literary Criticism from the Thirties to the Eighties*. New York: Columbia University Press, 1988.

Lentz, Tony M. *Orality and Literacy in Hellenic Greece*. Carbondale and Edwardsville: Southern Illinois University Press, 1989.

Li chi 禮記. Vol. 5 of *Shih-san-ching chu-shu* 十三經注疏. Taipei: Wen-hua t'u-shu kung-ssu, 1975.

Li Chih-chung 李致忠. "Sung-tai k'o-shu shu-lüeh." 宋代刻書述略. *Wen shih* 文史 14 (July 1982): 145–73.

Li Ch'ing-chao 李清照. *Li Ch'ing-chao chi* 李清照集. Ed. Chung-hua shu-chü Shang-hai pien-chi-so 中華書局上海編輯所. Shanghai: Chung-hua shu-chü, 1962.

Li Hsin-lung 李信隆. "*Tsun-ch'ien chi* yen-chiu" 尊前集研究. In *Ch'ing-chu Jui-an Lin Ching-i hsien-sheng liu-chih tan-ch'en lun-wen-chi* 慶祝瑞安林景伊先生六秩誕辰論文集, ed. Ch'ing-chu Jui-an Lin Ching-i hsien-sheng liu-chih tan-ch'en lun-wen-chi pien-chi wei-yüan-hui 慶祝瑞安林景伊先生六秩誕辰論文集編輯委員會, pp. 2261–388. Taipei: Kuo-li Cheng-chih ta-hsüeh kuo-wen yen-chiu-so, 1969.

Li I-mang 李一泯, ed. *Hua-chien chi chiao* 花間集校. 2d ed. Hong Kong: Shang-wu yin-shu-kuan, 1973.

Li Shang-yin 李商隱. *Li I-shan shih-chi* 李義山詩集. *SPTK* ed. Ed. Chu Ho-ling 朱鶴齡.

Li Ting-fang 李鼎芳. "Sung-jen hsüan-pien ti Sung tz'u tsung-chi" 宋人選編的宋詞總集. *Wen-hsüeh i-ch'an* 文學遺產 1980, no. 3: 118–50.

Liang Ch'i-ch'ao 梁啓超. "Chi *Lan-wan chi*" 記蘭畹集. *Pei-p'ing Pei-hai t'u-shu-kuan yüeh-k'an* 北平北海圖書館月刊 2 (1929): 5–6.

———. "Chi *Shih-hsien pen-shih ch'ü-tzu chi*" 記時賢本事曲子集. *Pei-p'ing Pei-hai t'u-shu-kuan yüeh-k'an* 北平北海圖書館月刊 2 (1929): 1–3.

Liang Ming-yüeh. "The *Tz'u* Music of Chiang K'uei: Its Style and Compositional Strategy." In *Song without Music*, ed. Stephen C. Soong, pp. 211–46.

Liang Paitchin. *Oeuvres poétiques complètes de Li Qingzhao*. Paris: Gallimard, 1977.

Lin Mei-i 林玫儀. "Lun Tun-huang ch'ü ti she-hui-hsing" 論敦煌曲的社會性.

In idem, *Tz'u-hsüeh k'ao-ch'üan* 詞學考詮, pp. 45–86. Taipei: Lien-ching ch'u-pan shih-yeh kung-ssu, 1987.

Lin, Shuen-fu. "Intrinsic Music in the Medieval Chinese Lyric." In *The Lyrical Arts: A Humanities Symposium*, a special issue of *Ars Lyrica*, ed. Erling B. Holtsmark and Judith Aikin, pp. 20–54. Guilford: Lyrica Society, 1988.

———. *The Transformation of the Chinese Lyrical Tradition: Chiang K'uei and Southern Sung Tz'u Poetry*. Princeton: Princeton University Press, 1978.

Lin Ta-ch'un 林大椿, ed. *T'ang Wu-tai tz'u* 唐五代詞. 1933. Rev. ed. Shanghai: Wen-hsüeh ku-chi k'an-hsing-she, 1956.

Lin Yutang 林語堂. *Translations from the Chinese (The Importance of Understanding)*. Cleveland: World Publishing Company, 1963.

Lipking, Lawrence. *Abandoned Women and Poetic Tradition*. Chicago: University of Chicago Press, 1988.

———. "Aristotle's Sister: A Poetics of Abandonment." In *Canons*, ed. Robert von Hallberg, pp. 85–105.

Liu Hsi-tsai 劉熙載. *I kai* 藝概. Shanghai: Shang-hai ku-chi ch'u-pan-she, 1978.

Liu, James J. Y. *The Art of Chinese Poetry*. London: Routledge & Kegan Paul, 1962.

———. *Major Lyricists of the Northern Sung*. Princeton: Princeton University Press, 1974.

Liu, Judy. "World of Words: Wu Tsao and the Conversion of Life into Art." Term paper, 1990.

Liu Shih 柳是. *Wu-yin ts'ao* 戊寅草. Preface by Ch'en Tzu-lung 陳子龍. 1638 ed. (Now in Chekiang Provincial Library.)

Liu Tao-ch'un 劉道醇. *Wu-tai ming-hua pu-i* 五代名畫補遺. *Ssu-k'u ch'üan-shu chen-pen* 四庫全書珍本, ser. 5, ed.

Liu Yao-min 劉堯民. *Tz'u yü yin-yüeh* 詞與音樂. Kunming: Yün-nan jen-min ch'u-pan-she, 1982.

Lo Ken-tse 羅根澤 and Yü Pei-shan 于北山, eds. *Wen-chang pien-t'i hsü-shuo* 文章辨體序說, by Wu Na 吳納, and *Wen-t'i ming-pien hsü-shuo* 文體明辨序說, by Hsü Shih-tseng 徐師曾. Peking: Jen-min wen-hsüeh ch'u-pan-she, 1962.

Lü Liu-liang 呂留良, Wu Chih-chen 吳之振, and Wu Tzu-mu 吳自牧, eds. *Sung shih ch'ao* 宋詩鈔. Taipei: Shih-chieh shu-chü, 1962.

Lung Ch'ien-an 龍潛菴. *Sung Yüan yü-yen tz'u-tien* 宋元語言詞典. Shanghai: Shang-hai tz'u-shu ch'u-pan-she, 1985.

Lung Mu-hsün 龍沐勛 [Lung Yü-sheng 龍榆生]. "Hsüan tz'u piao-chun lun" 選詞標準論. *Tz'u-hsüeh chi-k'an* 詞學季刊 1, no. 2 (August 1933): 1–28.

———, ed. *Su-men ssu-hsüeh-shih tz'u* 蘇門四學士詞. 4 vols. Peking: Chung-hua shu-chü, 1957.

———, ed. *T'ang Sung ming-chia tz'u-hsüan* 唐宋名家詞選. Rpt. Taipei: Ho-lo t'u-shu ch'u-pan-she, 1975. Hong Kong: Shang-wu yin-shu-kuan, 1979.

———. *Tung-p'o yüeh-fu chien* 東坡樂府淺. Shanghai: Shang-wu yin-shu-kuan, 1936.

Lynn, Richard John. "Orthodoxy and Enlightenment: Wang Shih-chen's Theory of Poetry and Its Antecedents." In *The Unfolding of Neo-Confucianism*, ed. W. T. de Bary, pp. 217–69. Studies in Oriental Culture, no. 10. New York: Columbia University Press, 1975.

Ma Ling 馬令. *Nan-T'ang shu* 南唐書. *SPTK hsü-pien* 續編 ed.; *Mo-hai chin-hu* 墨海金壺 ed. (*PP* 47/3)

Mao Kuang-sheng 冒廣生. "*Tsun-ch'ien chi* chiao-chi" 尊前集校記. Parts 1, 2. *T'ung-sheng yüeh-k'an* 同聲月刊 2, no. 6 (June 1942): 73–78; 2, no. 9 (Sept. 1942): 82–94.

Mao shih chu-shu 毛詩注疏. Vol. 2 of *Shih-san-ching chu-shu* 十三經注疏. Taipei: I-wen yin-shu-kuan, 1965. Also vol. 1 of *Shih-san-ching chu-shu*, Taipei: Wen-hua t'u-shu kung-ssu, 1970.

McCraw, David. *Chinese Lyricists of the Seventeenth Century*. Honolulu: University of Hawaii Press, 1990.

McCreery, John. "Why Don't We See Some Real Money Here? Offerings in Chinese Religion." *Journal of Chinese Religions* 18 (1990): 1–24.

Miao Yüeh 繆鉞. "Lun Li Ch'ing-chao tz'u" 論李清照詞. In Yeh Chia-ying and Miao Yüeh, *Ling-hsi tz'u-shuo*, pp. 331–49.

———. *Shih tz'u san-lun* 詩詞散論. Rpt. Shanghai: Shang-hai ku-chi ch'u-pan-she, 1982.

Miao Yüeh 繆鉞 and Yeh Chia-ying 葉嘉瑩. *Ling-hsi tz'u-shuo* 靈谿詞說. Shanghai: Shang-hai ku-chi ch'u-pan-she, 1987.

Morris, Ivan, ed. *Madly Singing in the Mountains: An Appreciation and Anthology of Arthur Waley*. 1970. Rpt. New York: Harper and Row, 1972.

Murakami Tetsumi 村上哲見. "So Tōba shokan no denrai to Tōbashu shohon no keifu ni tsuite" 蘇東坡書簡の伝來と東坡集諸本の系譜について. *Chūgoku bungaku hō* 中國文學報 27 (1977): 51–87.

Nishi Noriaki 西紀昭. "Tōba no shoki no sōbetsu-shi" 東坡の初期の送別詞. *Chūgoku chūsei bungaku kenkyū* 中國中世文學研究 7 (1968): 64–73.

———. "Su Shih ch'u-ch'i ti sung-pieh tz'u" 蘇軾初期的送別詞. Trans. Sun Kang-i 孫康宜. *Chung-wai wen-hsüeh* 中外文學 7, no. 5 (Oct. 1978): 64–77.

Ong, Walter J. *Rhetoric, Romance, and Technology: Studies in the Interaction of Expression and Culture*. Ithaca: Cornell University Press, 1971.

Owen, Stephen. *The Great Age of Chinese Poetry: The High T'ang*. New Haven: Yale University Press, 1981.

———. *Remembrances: The Experience of the Past in Classical Chinese Poetry*. Cambridge: Harvard University Press, 1986.

Paglia, Camille. *Sexual Personae: Art and Decadence from Nefertiti to Emily Dickinson*. New Haven: Yale University Press, 1990.

Pai P'u 白樸. *Wu-t'ung yü* 梧桐雨. In *Yüan-jen tsa-chü hsüan-chu* 元人雜劇選注, pp. 77–113. Taipei: Shih-chieh shu-chü, 1958.

Pan Tze-yen, trans. *The Reminiscences of Tung Hsiao-wan*, by Mao P'i-chiang [Mao Hsiang]. Shanghai: Commercial Press, 1931.

Pei-ching t'u-shu-kuan shan-pen-pu 北京圖書館善本部, ed. *Pei-ching t'u-shu-kuan shan-pen shu-mu* 北京圖書館善本書目. Peking: Chung-hua shu-chü, 1959.

Plummer, John F., ed. *Vox Feminae: Medieval Women's Lyrics*. Kalamazoo: Western Michigan University, 1981.

Poon, Ming-sun. "Books and Printing in Sung China (960–1279)." Ph.D. diss., University of Chicago, 1979.

Rankin, Mary Backus. "The Emergence of Women at the End of the Ch'ing: The Case of Ch'iu Chin." In *Women in Chinese Society*, ed. Margery Wolf and Roxane Witke, pp. 39–66. Stanford: Stanford University Press, 1975.

Rawski, Evelyn S. "Economic and Social Foundations of Late Imperial Culture." In *Popular Culture in Late Imperial China*, ed. David Johnson, Andrew J. Nathan, and Evelyn S. Rawski, pp. 3–33. Berkeley and Los Angeles: University of California Press, 1985.

Rexroth, Kenneth, and Chung Ling, trans. and eds. *Li Ch'ing-chao: Complete Poems*. New York: New Directions, 1979.

———. *Women Poets of China*. Rev. ed. New York: New Directions, 1982.

Rickett, Adele Austin. "Method and Intuition: The Poetic Theories of Huang T'ing-chien." In *Chinese Approaches to Literature from Confucius to Liang Ch'i-ch'ao*, ed. idem, pp. 97–119.

———, ed. *Chinese Approaches to Literature from Confucius to Liang Ch'i-ch'ao*. Princeton: Princeton University Press, 1978.

Robertson, Maureen. "Voicing the Feminine: Construction of the Female Subject in the Lyric Poetry of Medieval and Late Imperial China." Paper prepared for the Colloquium on Poetry and Women's Culture in Late Imperial China, University of California, Los Angeles, October 20, 1990.

Rodway, Allan. "Generic Criticism: The Approach through Type, Mode and Kind." In *Contemporary Criticism*, ed. Malcolm Bradbury and David Palmer, pp. 83–105. Stratford-Upon-Avon Studies, no. 12. London: Edward Arnold, 1970.

Rogaski, Ruth. "A Woman Named Mountain: The Life and Poetry of Wu Shan." Term paper, 1990.

Ropp, Paul S. "Love, Literacy, and Laments: Themes of Women Writers in Late Imperial China," *Women's History Review* 2.1 (1993): 107–41.

———. "The Seeds of Change: Reflections on the Condition of Women in the Early and Mid Ch'ing." *Signs* 2 (1976): 5–23.

Rouzer, Paul. "Watching the Voyeurs." *Chinese Literature: Essays, Articles, Reviews* 11 (1989): 13–34.

Ruthven, K. K. *Feminist Literary Studies: An Introduction*. Cambridge: Cambridge University Press, 1984.

Schwarcz, Vera. "Ibsen's Nora: The Promise and the Trap." *Bulletin of Concerned Asian Scholars* 7.1 (Jan.–Mar. 1975): 3–5.

Sessions, Kyle C. "Song Pamphlets: Media Changeover in Sixteenth-Century Publicization." In *Print and Culture in the Renaissance*, ed. Gerald P. Tyson and Sylvia S. Wagenheim, pp. 110–19. Newark: University of Delaware Press, 1986.

Shao I-ch'en 邵懿辰. *Ssu-k'u chien-ming mu-lu piao-chu* 四庫簡明目錄標注. Rpt. Taipei: Shih-chieh shu-chü, 1967.

Shao Po 邵博. *Shao-shih wen-chien hou-lu* 邵氏聞見後錄. *Hsüeh-chin t'ao yüan* 學津討原 ed. (*PP* 46/24)

She Chih 舍之 [Shih Chih-ts'un 施蟄存]. "Li-tai tz'u-hsüan-chi hsü-lu" 歷代詞選集叙錄. Parts 1–5. *Tz'u-hsüeh* 詞學 1 (1981): 276–87; 2 (1982): 226–40; 3 (1985): 273–80; 4 (1986): 242–55; 5 (1986): 255–67.

Shen I-fu 沈義父. *Tz'u yü yin-yüeh kuan-hsi yen-chiu* 詞與音樂關係研究. Peking: Chung-kuo she-hui k'o-hsüeh ch'u-pan-she, 1985.

Shen Te-ch'ien 沈德潛, ed. *Ku-shih yüan* 古詩源. Taipei: Hsin-lu shu-chü, 1967.

Shih Chen-lin 史震林. *Hsi-ch'ing san-chi* 西青散記. *Chung-kuo wen-hsüeh chen-pen ts'ung-shu* 中國文學珍本叢書, ser. 1, vol. 5. Shanghai: Shang-hai tsa-chih kung-ssu, 1935.

Shih chi 史記. Peking: Chung-hua shu-chü, 1962.

Shih Chih-ts'un 施蟄存. "T'ang nü shih-jen" 唐女詩人. In idem, *T'ang-shih pai-hua* 唐詩百話, pp. 720–29. Shanghai: Shang-hai ku-chi ch'u-pan-she, 1987.

Shih I-tui [Shi Yi-dui] 施議對. "Chien-kuo i-lai hsin-k'an tz'u-chi hui-p'ing" 建國以來新刊詞籍彙評. *Wen-hsueh i-ch'an* 文學遺產 1984, no. 3: 133–39.

———. "Chien-kuo i-lai tz'u-hsüeh yen-chiu shu-p'ing" 建國以來詞學研究述評. *Chung-kuo she-hui k'o-hsüeh* 中國社會科學 1984, no. 1: 157–74.

———. *Tz'u yü yin-yüeh kuan-hsi yen-chiu* 詞與音樂關係研究. Peking: Chung-kuo she-hui k'o-hsüeh ch'u-pan-she, 1985. Rpt. *Chung-kuo she-hui k'o-hsüeh po-shih lun-wen wen-k'u* 中國社會科興博士論文文庫, 1989.

Shimizu Shigeru 清水茂. "Kami no hatsumei to Gokan no gakufū" 紙の発明と後漢の學風. *Tōhōgaku* 東方學 79 (Jan. 1990): 1–13.

Shizukuishi Kōichi 雫石浩一. "Sonzenshū zakkō" 尊前集雜考. *Kangakkai zasshi* 漢學会雜誌 9 (1941): 97–106.

Showalter, Elaine. "Literary Criticism." *Signs* 1 (1975): 435–50.

———. *A Literature of Their Own: British Women Novelists from Brontë to Lessing.* Princeton: Princeton University Press, 1977.

Soong, Stephen C., ed. *Song Without Music: Chinese Tz'u Poetry.* Hong Kong: The Chinese University Press, 1980.

Spence, Jonathan. *The Search for Modern China.* New York: Norton, 1990.

Ssu-k'u ch'üan-shu tsung-mu t'i-yao 四庫全書總目提要. 5 vols. Rpt. Taipei: Shang-wu yin-shu-kuan, 1976.

Su Shih 蘇軾. *Su Shih wen-chi* 蘇軾文集. Ed. K'ung Fan-li 孔凡禮. Peking: Chung-hua shu-chü, 1986.

Sung shih 宋史. Peking: Chung-hua shu-chü, 1977.

Sweeney, Amin. *A Full Hearing: Orality and Literacy in the Malay World.* Berkeley and Los Angeles: University of California Press, 1987.

T'an Cheng-pi 譚正璧. *Chung-kuo wen-hsüeh-chia ta-tz'u-tien* 中國文學家大辭典. Taipei: Hsiang-kang Shang-hai yin-shu-kuan, 1961.

T'ang Hsien-tsu 湯顯祖. *T'ang Hsien-tsu chi* 湯顯祖集. Vols. 3–4, *Hsi-ch'ü chi* 戲曲集. Ed. Ch'ien Nan-yang 錢南揚. Shanghai: Jen-min ch'u-pan-she, 1973.

T'ang Kuei-chang 唐圭璋. "Tu tz'u hsü-chi" 讀詞續記. *Wen-hsüeh i-ch'an* 文學遺產 1981, no. 2: 81–90.

———, ed. *Ch'üan Sung tz'u* 全宋詞. 5 vols. Hong Kong: Chung-hua shu-chü, 1977.

————, ed. *Tz'u-hua ts'ung-pien* 詞話叢編. 1934 ed. Taipei: Kuang-wen shu-chü, 1969. Peking: Chung-hua shu-chü, 1986.

T'ang Kuei-chang 唐圭璋 and Chin Ch'i-hua 金啓華. "Li-tai tz'u-hsüeh yen-chiu shu-lüeh" 歷代詞學研究述略. *Tz'u-hsüeh* 詞學 1 (1981): 1–20.

T'ao Tsung-i 陶宗儀. *Ch'o-keng lu* 輟耕錄. *TSCC* ed. (0128).

Teraji Jun 寺地遵. *Nan Sō shoki seijishi kenkyū* 南宋初期政治史研究. Hiroshima: Keisuisha, 1988.

T'ien Chih-tou 田志豆, ed. *Wang Kuo-wei tz'u chu* 王國維詞注. Hong Kong: San-lien shu-tien, 1985.

Ting Fu-pao 丁福保, comp. *Ch'üan Han San-kuo Chin Nan-pei-ch'ao shih* 全漢三國晉南北朝詩. Rpt. Taipei: I-wen yin-shu-kuan, n.d.

Ting Ping 丁丙. *Shan-pen shu-shih ts'ang-shu chih* 善本書室藏書志. Rpt. Taipei: Kuang-wen shu-chü, 1967.

Ting Shao-i 丁紹儀. *Ch'ing tz'u-tsung pu* 清詞宗補. 3 vols. Rpt. Peking: Chung-hai yin-shu-kuan, 1968.

Ts'ao Hsüeh-ch'in 曹雪芹 and Kao O 高鶚. *Hung-lou meng* 紅樓夢. Peking: Jen-min wen-hsüeh ch'u-pan-she, 1982.

Ts'ao Shu-ming 曹樹銘. *Tung-p'o tz'u* 東坡詞. Hong Kong: Hsiang-kang Shang-hai yin-shu-kuan, 1968.

Tseng Chi-li 曾季貍. *T'ing-chai shih-hua* 艇齋詩話. In *Li-tai shih-hua hsü-pien* 歷代詩話續編, ed. Ting Fu-pao 丁福保, 1:282–326. 3 vols. Peking: Chung-hua shu-chü, 1983.

Tseng Tsao 曾慥. *Yüeh-fu ya-tz'u* 樂府雅詞. *TSCC* ed.

Tsien Tsuen-hsuin. *Paper and Printing.* Part 1 of Joseph Needham, ed., *Science and Civilisation in China*, vol. 5, *Chemistry and Chemical Technology.* Cambridge: Cambridge University Press, 1985.

Tung-p'o tz'u lun-ts'ung 東坡詞論叢. Ed. Su Shih yen-chiu hsüeh-hui 蘇軾研究學會. Ch'eng-tu: Ssu-ch'uan jen-min ch'u-pan-she, 1982.

Tz'u-hsüeh yen-chiu lun-wen-chi (1949–1979 nien) 詞學研究論文集 (1949–1979 年). Ed. Hua-tung ta-hsüeh Chung-wen-hsi ku-tien wen-hsüeh yen-chiu-shih 華東大學中文系古典文學研究室. Shanghai: Shang-hai ku-chi ch'u-pan-she, 1982.

von Hallberg, Robert, ed. *Canons.* Chicago: University of Chicago Press, 1984.

Wagner, Marsha L. *The Lotus Boat: The Origins of Chinese Tz'u Poetry in T'ang Popular Culture.* New York: Columbia University Press, 1984.

Walls, Jan Wilson. "The Poetry of Yü Hsüan-chi: A Translation, Annotation, Commentary and Critique." Ph.D. diss., Indiana University, 1972.

Waltner, Ann. "Widows and Remarriage in Ming and Early Qing China." In *Women in China: Current Directions in Historical Scholarship*, ed. Richard W. Guisso and Stanley Johannesen, pp. 129–46. Youngstown, N. Y.: Philo Press, 1981.

Wang An-shih 王安石. *Lin-ch'uan hsien-sheng ch'üan-chi* 臨川先生全集. Hong Kong: Chung-hua shu-chü, 1971.

Wang Chao-yung 汪兆鏞. "Chi-ku-ko pen *Tsun-ch'ien chi* shu-hou" 汲古閣本尊前集書後. *Tz'u-hsüeh chi-kan* 詞學季刊 3, no. 2 (June 1936): 161–62.

Wang Cheng-hua. "On Hsü Ts'an's Poetry." Term paper, 1989.

Wang Cho 王灼. *Pi-chi man-chih* 碧雞漫志. *THTP* ed.

Wang Chung-lan. "The *Tz'u* Poetry of Shen I-hsiu, Yeh Wan-wan, and Yeh Hsiao-luan." Term paper, 1990.

Wang Chung-min 王重民. *Tun-huang ch'ü-tzu-tz'u* 敦煌曲子詞. Shanghai: Shang-wu yin-shu-kuan, 1950.

Wang Chung-wen 王仲聞, ed. *Li Ch'ing-chao chi chiao-chu* 李清照集校注. Peking: Jen-min wen-hsüeh ch'u-pan-she, 1986.

———, ed. *Nan-T'ang erh-chu tz'u chiao-ting* 南唐二主詞校訂. Peking: Jen-min wen-hsüeh ch'u-pan-she, 1957.

Wang Fan 王璠. *Li Ch'ing-chao yen-chiu ts'ung-k'ao* 李清照研究叢考. Huhehot: Nei-Meng-ku jen-min ch'u-pan-she, 1987.

Wang Ju-pi 王如弼, ed. *Po Chü-i hsüan-chi* 白居易選集. Shanghai: Shang-hai ku-chi ch'u-pan-she, 1980.

Wang Kuo-wei 王國維. *Jen-chien tz'u-hua* 人間詞話. *THTP* ed.

———. *Wang Kuan-t'ang hsien-sheng ch'üan-chi* 王觀堂先生全集. 16 vols. Taipei: Wen-hua ch'u-pan kung-ssu, 1968.

Wang Ming-ch'ing 王明清. *Hui-chu hou-lu* 揮麈後錄. *TSCC* ed. (2770).

Wang Shui-chao 王水照. "Lun Su Shih ch'uang-tso ti fa-chan chieh-tuan" 論蘇軾創作的發展階段. *She-hui k'o-hsüeh chan-hsien* 社會科學戰線 1984, no. 1: 259–69.

———, ed. *Su Shih hsüan-chi* 蘇軾選集. Shanghai: Shang-hai ku-chi ch'u-pan-she, 1984.

Wang Te-i 王德毅. *Wang Kuo-wei nien-p'u* 王國維年譜. Taipei: Shang-wu yin-shu-kuan, 1967.

Wang Yen-t'i 王延梯, ed. *Shu-yü-chi chu* 漱玉集注. Shantung: Shan-tung wen-i ch'u-pan-she, 1984.

Watson, Burton. *Chinese Lyricism: Shih Poetry from the Second to the Twelfth Century.* New York: Columbia University Press, 1971.

Wei Ch'ing-chih 魏慶之. *Shih-jen yü-hsieh* 詩人玉屑. 2d ed. Shanghai: Shang-hai ku-chi ch'u-pan-she, 1978.

Wei T'ai 魏泰. *Tung-hsüan pi-lu* 東軒筆錄. Peking: Chung-hua shu-chü, 1983.

Wellek, Rene, and Austin Warren. *Theory of Literature.* 3d ed. New York: Harcourt, Brace & World, 1956.

Wen hsüan 文選. Taipei: Wen-hua t'u-shu kung-ssu, 1975.

Wen Kuang-i 溫廣義. *T'ang Sung tz'u ch'ang-yung yü shih-li* 唐宋詞常用語釋例. Huhehot: Nei-Meng-ku jen-min ch'u-pan-she, 1978.

Widmer, Ellen. "The Epistolary World of Female Talent in Seventeenth-Century China." *Late Imperial China* 10, no. 2 (Dec. 1989): 1–43.

Wixted, John Timothy. *Poems on Poetry: Literary Criticism by Yuan Hao-wen (1190–1257).* Calligraphy by Eugenia Y. Tu. Münchener ostasiatische Studien, no. 33. Wiesbaden: Franz Steiner Verlag, 1982.

―――. *The Song-Poetry of Wei Chuang (836–910 A.D.)*. Calligraphy by Eugenia Y. Tu. Occasional Paper no. 12. Tempe: Center for Asian Studies, Arizona State University, 1979. Rpt. 1991.

Wu Hao 吳灝, ed. *Kuei-hsiu pai-chia tz'u-hsüan* 閨秀百家詞選. Sao-yeh shan-fang, 1914, ed.

Wu Hsiung-ho 吳熊和. *Tang Sung tz'u t'ung-lun* 唐宋詞通論. Hangchow: Che-chiang ku-chi ch'u-pan-she, 1985.

Wu Tsao 吳藻. *Wu Tsao tz'u* 吳藻詞. *Tz'u-hsüeh hsiao ts'ung-shu* 詞學小叢書, no. 9. Shanghai: Chiao-yü shu-tien, 1949.

Wu Tseng 吳曾. *Neng-kai chai man-lu* 能改齋漫錄. *TSCC* ed. (0289).

Wu Tseng-ch'i 吳曾祺, ed. *Chiu hsiao-shuo* 舊小說. Shanghai: Shang-wu yin-shu-kuan, 1944.

Yang Chi-hsiu 楊繼修. *Hsiao-shan tz'u yen-chiu* 小山詞研究. Taipei: Li-ming wen-hua shu-chü, 1985.

Yang-ch'un pai-hsüeh pu-chi 陽春白雪補集. In *San-ch'ü ts'ung-k'an* 散曲叢刊. Ed. Jen Chung-min 任中敏. Shanghai: Chung-hua shu-chü, 1931, A2.1b.

Yang Hai-ming 楊海明. "Li Ch'ing-chao 'Tz'u lun' pu-t'i Chou Pang-yen ti liang-chung t'an-ts'e" 李清照詞論不提周邦彥的兩種探測. In idem, *T'ang Sung tz'u lun-kao* 唐宋詞論稿, pp. 304–10.

―――. *T'ang Sung tz'u feng-ko-lun* 唐宋詞風格論. Shanghai: She-hui-k'o-hsüeh-yüan ch'u-pan-she, 1986.

―――. *T'ang Sung tz'u lun-kao* 唐宋詞論稿. Hangchow: Che-chiang ku-chi ch'u-pan-she, 1988.

Yang T'i 楊偍. *Ku-chin tz'u-hua* 古今詞話. In *Chiao-chi Sung Chin Yüan jen tz'u* 校輯宋金元人詞, ed. Chao Wan-li 趙萬里.

Yao P'in-wen 姚品文. "Ch'ing-tai fu-nü shih-ko ti fan-jung yü li-hsüeh ti kuan-hsi" 清代婦女詩歌的繁榮與理學的關系. *Chiang-hsi shih-fan ta-hsüeh hsüeh-pao* 江西師範大學學報 1985, no. 1: 53–58.

Yeh Chia-ying 葉嘉瑩. [*See also* Chao, Chia-ying Yeh.] *Chia-ling lun tz'u ts'ung-kao* 迦陵論詞叢稿. Shanghai: Shang-hai ku-chi ch'u-pan-she, 1980.

―――. *Chung-kuo tz'u-hsüeh ti hsien-tai kuan* 中國詞學的現代觀. Taipei: Ta-an ch'u-pan-she, 1988.

―――. *Wang Kuo-wei chi ch'i wen-hsüeh p'i-p'ing* 王國維及其文學批評. Hong Kong: Chung-hua shu-chü, 1978.

―――. "Yu tz'u chih t'e-chih lun ling-tz'u chih ch'ien-neng yü Ch'en Tzu-lung tz'u chih ch'eng-chiu" 由詞之特質論令詞之潛能與陳子龍詞之成就. *Chung-wai wen-hsüeh* 中外文學 19, no. 1 (June 1990): 4–38.

Yeh Chia-ying 葉嘉瑩 and Miao Yüeh 繆鉞. *Ling-hsi tz'u-shuo* 靈溪詞說. Shang-hai: Shang-hai ku-chi ch'u-pan-she, 1987.

―――. *T'ang Sung ming-chia tz'u shang-hsi* 唐宋名家詞賞析. Vol. 1, *Wen T'ing-yün, Wei Chuang, Feng Yen-ssu, Li Yü* 溫庭筠, 韋莊, 馮延巳, 李煜. Taipei: Ta-an ch'u-pan-she, 1988.

Yeh Kung-chao 葉恭綽, comp. *Ch'üan Ch'ing tz'u ch'ao* 全清詞鈔. Hong Kong: Chung-hua shu-chü, 1975.

Yeh Meng-te 葉夢得. *Pi-shu lu-hua* 避暑錄話. *Hsüeh-chin t'ao-yüan* 學津討原 ed.

Yeh Shao-yüan 葉紹袁. *Wu-meng t'ang ch'üan-chi* 午夢堂全集. In *Chung-kuo wen-hsüeh chen-pen ts'ung-shu* 中國文學珍本叢書, ser. 1, vol. 49. Shanghai: Pei-yeh shan-fang, 1936.

Yen Yü 嚴羽. *Ts'ang-lang shih-hua chiao-shih* 滄浪詩話校釋. Ed. Kuo Shao-yü 郭紹虞. Peking: Jen-min wen-hsüeh ch'u-pan-she, 1962.

Yin Fan 殷璠. *Ho-yüeh ying-ling-chi* 河岳英靈集. In Yüan Chieh 元結 et al. *T'ang-jen hsüan T'ang-shih* 唐人選唐詩. Peking: Chung-hua shu-chü, 1958.

Yoshikawa Kōjirō. *Five Hundred Years of Chinese Poetry, 1150–1650: The Chin, Yuan, and Ming Dynasties.* Trans. John Timothy Wixted. Princeton: Princeton University Press, 1989.

Yu, Pauline. "Poems in Their Place: Collections and Canons in Early Chinese Literature." *Harvard Journal of Asiatic Studies* 50 (1990): 163–96.

———. *The Reading of Imagery in the Chinese Poetic Tradition.* Princeton: Princeton University Press, 1987.

Yü Chi 虞集. *Tao-yuan hsüeh-ku lu* 道園學古錄. *SPTK* ed.

Yü P'ing-po 俞平伯. "*T'ang Sung tz'u hsüan* ch'ien yen" 《唐宋詞選》前言. In *Tz'u-hsüeh yen-chiu lun-wen-chi (1949–1979 nien)*, ed. Hua-tung shih-fan ta-hsüeh Chung-wen-hsi ku-tien wen-hsüeh yen-chiu-shih, pp. 143–55.

Yüeh K'o 岳珂. *K'uei t'an lu* 傀郯錄. *TSCC* ed. (842).

INDEX

Abe Ryūichi, 236n.24
ai-p'in (favorite type), 33–34, 44
Aikin, Judith, 12n.30
An-fu, 236, 240
An Lu-shan Rebellion, 156n.58
ancient-style poetry, 23
Anhwei, 311n.27
Aoyama Hiroshi, 339n
Ariadne, 166
Aristotle, 166, 172n.13

Bakhtin, Mikhail, 95
Bernikow, Louise, 71
Birrell, Anne, 180n.36, 181n.39
Bonner, Jody, 289n.100
Book of Songs. See *Shih-ching*
bound-term, 51n.30
Bryant, Daniel, xiiin, xix, 65n.51, 80n.25,
    157n.67, 300nn.1, 2, 310n.21, 312n.30,
    319n.39, 328n, 330n, 335, 341n.65, 342,
    342n, 349
Buddhism, 202, 208, 214, 219, 234; Buddhist
    priest's poetry, 150, 166n.92, 253; Bud-
    dhist religious hymns, 15; Tripitaka of,
    248
Buell, Lawrence, 5n.7
Bureau of Grand Music. See *ta-sheng fu*

Cha Wei-jen, 86, 91n.53
Chaffee, John W., 236n.22, 239, 239n.35
Ch'ai Ch'i-nien, 159n.74
Ch'ai Ching-i, 177n.30

Chan Chih, 239n.36
Ch'an Buddhism, 92n.55, 95, 234
Chang Chang and Huang Yü, 213n.50, 344
Chang Chi, 94
Chang Chieh, 94
Chang Chih-ho, 300
Chang Chu, 94
Chang Heng, 287, 287n.93
Chang Hsiao-hsiang, 242, 242n.38, 243,
    243n.45, 244–45
Chang Hsien, 18–19, 19n.64, 20, 22, 27, 29,
    52n, 117, 192, 192n, 208, 209n.38, 224–
    25, 302
Chang Hsien-ch'ing, 149
Chang Hsiu-min, 235n.21
Chang Hui-yen, 95–96, 98–99, 99n.74, 100,
    101n.81, 262
Chang, Kang-i Sun, xiiin, xvii, xx, 5n.8,
    12nn.31, 32, 15n.44, 16nn.47, 48, 17n.53,
    19nn.63, 64, 21n.67, 22n.72, 23, 23nn.79,
    81, 24n.82, 44n.19, 116n.16, 163n.88,
    170n.6, 173n.18, 174n.20, 176n.27,
    183n.46, 183n.48, 186n.57, 212n.48,
    213n.50, 246n.56, 339, 349; *Evolution of
    Chinese Tz'u Poetry: From the Late T'ang to
    the Northern Sung, The*, xiiin, 5n.8, 12nn.31,
    32, 15n.44, 16, 16nn.47, 48, 17n.53,
    19nn.63, 64, 21n.67, 22n.72, 23nn.77, 79,
    81, 24n.82, 44n.19, 116n.16, 212n.48,
    213n.50, 246n.56, 349
Chang Lei, 156, 192n, 219-20, 225
Chang Pang-chi, 319

393

Compositor: Asco Trade Typesetting Ltd.
Printer: Thomson-Shore, Inc.
Binder: Thomson-Shore, Inc.
Text: 10/12 Baskerville
Display: Baskerville